# HENRI THEIL'S CONTRIBUTIONS TO ECONOMICS AND ECONOMETRICS

**Advanced Studies in Theoretical and Applied Econometrics**

**Volume 24**

---



*The titles published in this series are listed at the end of this volume.*

# Henri Theil's Contributions to Economics and Econometrics

Volume II:

## Consumer Demand Analysis and Information Theory

Edited by

Baldev Raj

*Wilfrid Laurier University, Waterloo, Ontario, Canada*

and

Johan Koerts

*Erasmus University, Rotterdam, The Netherlands*

SPRINGER SCIENCE+BUSINESS MEDIA, B.V.

Library of Congress Cataloging-in-Publication Data

(Revised for vol. 2)
Henri Theil's contribution to economics and econometrics / edited by
Baldev Raj, J. Koerts.
p. cm. - (Advanced studies in theoretical and applie'
econometrics: v. 23, 24)
Includes index.
Contents: v. 1. Econometric theory and methodology. - v. 2.
Consumer demand analysis and information theory.
ISBN 978-94-010-5062-3 ISBN 978-94-011-2408-9 (eBook)
DOI 10.1007/978-94-011-2408-9
1. Theil, Henri - Contributions to Econometrics. I. Theil, Henri.
II. Raj, Baldev, 1941- . III. Koerts, J. IV. Series.
HB139.H46 1991 330'01'5195 91-38183

ISBN 978-94-010-5062-3

*Printed on acid-free paper*

# DEDICATION

To

Eleonore Theil

Balbeer Raj

and

Maria Koerts

# CONTENTS OF THE COLLECTION

## VOLUME I

## VOLUME III

# PREFACE TO THE COLLECTION

## PREAMBLE

The editors are pleased to present a selection of Henri Theil's contributions to economics and econometrics in three volumes. In Volume I we have provided an overview of Theil's contributions, a brief biography, an annotated bibliography of his research, and a selection of published and unpublished articles and chapters in books dealing with topics in econometrics. Volume II contains Theil's contributions to demand analysis and information theory. Volume III includes Theil's contributions in economic policy and forecasting, and management science.

The selection of articles is intended to provide examples of Theil's many seminal and pathbreaking contributions to economics in such areas as econometrics, statistics, demand analysis, information theory, economic policy analysis, aggregation theory, forecasting, index numbers, management science, sociology, operations research, higher education and much more. The collection is also intended to serve as a tribute to him on the occasion of his 68th birthday.[1] These three volumes also highlight some of Theil's contributions and service to the profession as a leader, advisor, administrator, teacher, and researcher.

Theil's contributions, which encompass many disciplines, have been extensively cited both in scientific and professional journals. These citations often place Theil among the top 10 researchers (ranked according to number of times cited) in the world in various disciplines.

This collection is not intended to provide a normative assessment of his pioneering and influential contributions or serve as a definitive statement on his lifetime of contributions. Furthermore, no attempt is made to provide a documented history of Theil's contribution to the development of the theory and application of econometrics or other disciplines. The collection merely provides the basic building blocks for a more detailed historical inquiry into his influence on the development of these disciplines.

While we have made every attempt to include a significant number of his important contributions, some key contributions could not be included in the three volumes for a variety of reasons. Firstly, we were faced with budget constraints; secondly some of Theil's contributions are contained in books and reprinting them would have been impractical and expensive. The exclusion of some of these contributions is regrettable but could not be avoided.

[1] Theil's Fertschrift will also be published in 1991. It is entitled, *Contributions to Consumer Demand and Econometrics* and is jointly edited by R.F. Bewley and Tran Van Hoa (MacMillan Press).

## ACKNOWLEDGEMENTS

The collection has benefited from the insights and comments of a large number of individuals. In addition, a number of our colleagues and friends have provided helpful suggestions and encouragement which made the task of editing these volumes (which took about two years to complete) quite enjoyable. We extend special thanks to Anton P. Barten, Kenneth W. Clements, Denzil G. Fiebig, Arthur S. Goldberger, Esfandiar Maasoumi, and Roy Radner who shared with us background material on Theil or commented on our initial selection. Helpful comments from Professor Henri Theil and two anonymous referees on our initial proposal led to additions and deletions to the list of included contributions. Their help is also gratefully acknowledged.

We are also grateful to Peter Kennedy and Adolf Buse for their help in refereeing one of the unpublished articles and A.P. Barten and William E. Griffiths for supplying us with an English version of a paper from their personal libraries. In addition, it is a pleasure to thank all those who contributed in other ways to the completion of this project. This list includes Ronald Bewley, Jack Gould, John Kraft, Barry McPherson, Frank Millerd, Alex J. Murray, A.L. Nagar, Russell Muncaster, Tran Van Hoa, Alan Powell and John Weir.

The editors are grateful to the following societies, associations, publishers, and individuals for their permission to reprint articles and chapters from journals and books.

American Economic Association
American Political Science Association
American Statistical Association
Cambridge University Press
Econometric Society
De Economist
Elsevier Science Publishers and North Holland Publishers
Gordon and Breach Science Publishers, Inc.
H.E. Stenfert Kroese B.V.
International Economic Review
Institut de Statistique, Université de Paris
International Federation of Operational Research Societies
Institute for Scientific Information
Institute of Management Sciences
International Statistical Institute
JAI Press
Journal of Accounting Research
MacMillan Publishing Co.
Maandschrift Economie
Metroeconomica
Netherlands Organization for International Co-operation in Higher Education
Pergamon Press Ltd.
Sage Publications Inc.
Roy Radner
Royal Netherlands Academy of Arts and Science
Sloan Management Review Association

Henri Theil
Weltwirtschaftliches Archiv

**FINANCIAL SUPPORT**

This project was made possible by financial support or research assistance from a number of institutions which are listed below:

- Erasmus University (Faculty Development Fund)
- Wilfrid Laurier University (Academic Development Fund, Laurier Institute, and Research Office)
- McKethan-Matherly Chair of the University of Florida
- University of Chicago (Graduate School of Business)
- Inter-library Loans, Erasmus University and Wilfrid Laurier University Libraries
- Society of Management Accountants of Ontario

**RESEARCH ASSISTANCE**

The typing work was skilfully performed by the following individuals:

- Elli Hoek Van Dijke (Erasmus University)
- Elsie Grogan and Lori Kapshey (Word Processing Department, Wilfrid Laurier University)
- Andrew and Joan Zador (Science Scribe, Waterloo, Ontario)

In addition, Trudy Trudel helped us with the typing of a few papers. The professional copy-editing of the manuscript (to bring it to a uniform style) as well as proof-reading was performed by Dave Kroeker and Maura Brown. Margaret Forsyth, Tim Kuehn, Ildiko Tiszovszky, and Dr. C. Dubbelman provided competent research assistance including proofreading the retyped material. Gerry Anderson, Abby Brubacher and Chantel Thiel helped with library and secretarial tasks. The help of all these individuals is gratefully acknowledged.

The acquisitions editor, Marie M. Stratta and her assistant Lorraine Jordens from Kluwer Academic Publishers were very helpful throughout the project; it has been a pleasure to work with them. This project would not have been completed without the support of Professor Henri Theil and our spouses Balbeer Raj and Maria Koerts. We thank them sincerely for their moral support.

Baldev Raj,
Wilfrid Laurier University
Waterloo, Ontario, Canada

Johan Koerts,
Erasmus University,
Rotterdam, The Netherlands

# CONTENTS OF VOLUME II

# PART THREE:
# DEMAND ANALYSIS

## SECTION 3.1: THREE EARLY PAPERS

CHAPTER 34

# QUALITIES, PRICES AND BUDGET ENQUIRIES*

HENRI THEIL
*Economic Research Institute*
*University of Amsterdam*
*Amsterdam, The Netherlands*

## 1. Introduction

Most "commodities" distinguished in budget enquiries are heterogeneous; often they can be described as "aggregates" of more perfectly homogeneous "qualities." A consequence of this well-known fact is that an increase of the expenditures on a certain commodity brought about by (e.g.) an increase of income may be caused partly by an increase of the quantity bought (measured in physical units), partly by a transition to a better quality. It may even happen that the quantity is reduced and the increase is wholly caused by an ameliorization of the "quality," or vice versa. Hence it is clear that the "ordinary" income elasticities[1] for heterogeneous commodities derived from budget data will in general be different from the income elasticities for the quantities of these commodities, which are in many cases more interesting.[2]

Let us define a quality as a perfectly homogeneous good, at least as a good the heterogeneity of which may be neglected. Let us define a commodity as a set of qualities; the number of elements of such a set is, of course, to a certain extent arbitrary. The problem, how qualities may be grouped to commodities, will be indicated below.

As long as we deal with qualities the traditional theory of consumers' behavior may be regarded as fundamentally correct with respect to the problems considered above. However, the number of qualities is usually tremendous, so that the quantity bought of each of these qualities will often be quite small unless the period considered is very long.[3] Hence the difficult problem of indivisibility obtains its greatest importance just in the case when the commodity problem is reduced to a triviality. Moreover, a theory dealing with such a large number of goods (≡ qualities) cannot be said to be manageable with respect to the usual budget data.

* This article first appeared in *The Review of Economic Studies*, **19** (1952), 129-147. Reprinted with the permission of Elsevier Science Publishers B.V. (North-Holland).

[1] I.e., the income elasticities of the amounts spent.

[2] Compare R. Stone (1950) and H.S. Houthakker and S.J. Prais (1951).

[3] I.e. the consumer will in general buy a number of qualities of each commodity; it is not necessarily true that he buys one quality of a commodity only.

Therefore, we have some reason to investigate the possibilities of a theory of consumers' behavior that gives explicit attention to the problems of heterogeneity. To formulate such a theory is the first object of this paper. The second purpose is an empirical one: the last part of this paper gives some empirical results derived from the Amsterdam budget data of the years 1934-35.

## 2. A Sketch of a Theory

### 2.1 THE CASE OF ONE COMMODITY AND OF FIXED PRICES OF ALL QUALITIES

Let us suppose that a consumer has a fixed income, $y$, and that he spends it on the qualities of one single commodity; suppose further that these qualities have fixed prices. No doubt this case is a highly simplified one but sometimes it has a certain degree of reality, e.g., if a soldier decides to spend his "income" on cigarettes only; then he has the choice of buying a large quantity of cheap cigarettes or a smaller quantity of more expensive ones. Moreover, the case of one commodity can be discussed by means of simple diagrams, which has its advantages.

In this case the consumer is able to vary the quantity of the commodity and the qualities bought. Of course, these variations are not independent, if his outlays are equal to $y$, for a worse quality usually implies a lower price than a better quality (if it does not, we can rule out the worse quality altogether).[4]

In order to simplify the analysis we shall use the average price paid (defined as the ratio of the amount spent to the quantity bought[5]) as a "quality indicator" of the set of qualities bought. This procedure may be considered useful even if the consumer buys a number of different qualities in the same period (e.g., butter for Sunday and margarine for the other days), because then the average price paid is an indicator of the "average" quality bought; of course, certain difficulties arise if quality prices change, but this has been excluded here.

So we have two variables, viz.: the quantity bought ($x$) and the average price paid ($p$), which are the arguments of the utility function.[6] It may be added that the way in which $p$ enters into this function has no necessary relationship with the behavior of a consumer who reacts according to Veblen's description.[7] Such a consumer attaches value

---

[4] It will be clear that the terms "worse" and "better" have a subjective meaning with respect to the consumer considered.

[5] Alternatively: the average price paid is a weighted average of the constituent quality prices, the weights being the quantities bought of the individual qualities.

[6] We shall pay no attention to the problem how utility might be influenced by those changes in the quantities bought of the individual qualities which leave both $x$ and $p$ unchanged. We shall assume that for each pair $(x, p)$ the quantities of the qualities are chosen such that utility is maximized subject to the condition implied by this pair.

[7] Cf. T. Veblen (1924).

to some commodity *because* its price is high. In our case the average price paid is only a quality indicator such that, if a consumer prefers some cheap quality to a more expensive one (*ceteris paribus*), the latter quality is left out of consideration.

The utility function has to be maximized subject to the following side relation:

$$px = y \ ,$$

which is represented by a hyperbola in an $x$, $p$-diagram, contrary to the linear budget line of traditional consumption theory; see Diagram 1.

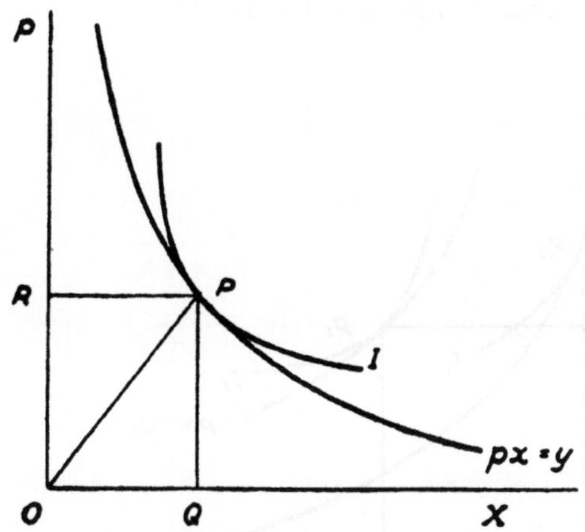


Diagram 1

$I$ represents an indifference curve, a locus of points $(x, p)$ which are considered as indifferent by our consumer. He will choose that point $P$ of his hyperbolic budget line that has the property that the indifference curve through $P$ touches the budget line in $P$.

Now there are two interesting questions. The first deals with the stability of equilibrium. It is clear that the ordinary convexity condition is not sufficient for equilibrium stability here. If the budget line were linear it would be sufficient that the radius of curvation of $I$ in $P$ is finite, no matter how large (the center of gravity lying above the budget line). But in this case of a curvilinear budget line the radius of curvation of $I$ in $P$ must not be larger than a certain finite number, in order that equilibrium is stable.[8] The same thing can be said in a slightly different way. If equilibrium is stable the second derivative of price with respect to quantity along the budget line must be larger (at least not smaller) than the same derivative along the budget line. The reader is

[8] Elementary considerations show that this number is equal to the cube of $OP$ divided by twice the area $OQPR$.

invited to verify that this implies that the rate of change of elasticity of substitution between $x$ and $p$ along the indifference curve must be non-negative:

$$\frac{d}{dx}\left(\frac{Ep}{Ex}\right) \geq 0.$$ [9]

The second interesting problem is: what will happen if income increases or decreases? One might think that an increase of income always causes the consumer to buy more expensive qualities. However, this proposition is incorrect, at least it cannot be deduced from the stability condition. A case in which an increase of income causes the average price paid to be reduced is given in Diagram 2.

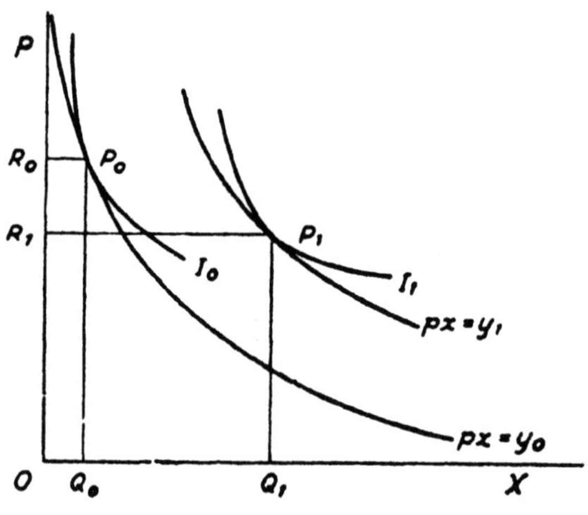


Diagram 2

In this case the average price paid is reduced from $P_0Q_0$ to $P_1Q_1$ in spite of an increase of income from $y_0$ to $y_1$.

Of course, in the case of one commodity it is impossible that quantity would be reduced as well, because then the product $px$ would decrease contrary to the assumption that $y$ (= $px$) increases. However, if there are two or more commodities, such an effect may take place. It is easy to give realistic examples, especially when a commodity has two (or more) alternative uses. Take, e.g, margarine; one may spread it on his bread or use it for cooking, etc. Let us assume that a consumer buys a more expensive quality for his bread. Now suppose that his income increases. Then it is possible that he will use butter (which is considered as a different commodity) for his bread and a slightly better quality of margarine for cooking, such as to reduce both the average price paid and the quantity

[9] For operations with elasticities see R.G.D. Allen (1938, pp. 252-254).

bought of margarine. Hence we may have "inferiority" effects for average prices paid as well.

Of course, such a result is highly dependent on the way in which qualities are grouped to commodities. If we had considered butter and margarine as one commodity instead of two, the average price paid would have increased. But precisely the same is true for quantities: one can always, except perhaps in pathological cases, define commodities in such a way that an increase of income causes the quantity bought of none of the commodities to be reduced.[10]

## 2.2 A MORE GENERAL APPROACH

In this section we shall give a brief discussion of the general case, in which there are $n$ commodities and the individual quality prices are allowed to change.

Let us suppose that the qualitative nature of a quantity $x_i$ of a commodity $i$ ($i = 1, \ldots, n$) can be completely described by means of a vector $e_i = [e_{i1}, \ldots, e_{im_i}]$. The elements of $e_i$ may be quantitative things like specific gravity, etc., or may be qualitative such as color, etc. Sometimes qualitative elements can be reduced to quantitative ones, e.g., the qualitative notion of color may be transformed to quantitative criteria by its position in the color triangle. Sometimes, however, such a transformation is impossible; then it is necessary to break up the functions to be considered below into separate functions and to apply the maximization process of this section to each of these functions.[11]

It will be clear that the average price paid for a unit of commodity $i$, $p_i$, depends on the vector $e_i$. Hence we have the following side relation:

$$\sum_{i=1}^{n} x_i p_i(e_i) - y = 0 ,$$

subject to which the utility function:

$$u(x_1, \ldots, x_n, e_1, \ldots, e_n)$$

has to be maximized. The following marginal conditions are easily obtained:

$$\frac{\partial u}{\partial x_i} - \lambda p_i = 0 \qquad (i = 1, \ldots, n ; h = 1, \ldots, m_i)$$

$$\frac{\partial u}{\partial e_{ih}} - \lambda x_i \frac{\partial p_i}{\partial e_{ih}} = 0 ,$$

[10] Compare the remark of R.G.D. Allen (1942, p. 190, fn. 2).

[11] Compare H. Brems (1951, pp. 26-28, 56-57).

in which $\lambda$ is a Lagrange multiplier. In words: the marginal utility of a quantity $x_i$ is proportional to its price $p_i$; the marginal utility of an element $e_{ih}$ of the vector $e_i$ is proportional to the corresponding quantity $x_i$ and the partial derivative of the price $p_i$ with respect to $e_{ih}$; in both cases the proportionality constant is the same.[12] The first of these marginal conditions is identical with Gossen's Law. The second, too, is quite simple; roughly speaking, it tells us that, if (in equilibrium) an increment of $e_{ih}$ has a large influence upon $p_i$ (i.e., if this qualitative improvement is expensive) and if the quantity bought $x_i$ is large, the marginal utility of $e_{ih}$ must (in equilibrium) also be large.

We shall not give the stability conditions for this general case. It is not difficult to derive them if all $e_{ih}$ can be presented by quantitative numbers, but if this is not true certain difficulties arise, especially when a transition from one qualitative value of an $e_{ih}$ to another enters into the picture. We, therefore, prefer first to give a brief discussion of commodity prices and of the relation between commodities and qualities.

## 2.3 COMMODITIES AND THEIR PRICES

In this approach commodity prices have a dual nature. On the one hand, the average prices can be chosen by the consumer, at least to a certain extent. On the other hand the prices of the individual qualities (the average commodity prices being simple functions of subsets of these prices) are data for him: they are fixed by other subjects, such as retailers, house-owners, the Government, etc. Now it is interesting to see what happens if these quality prices change. The general approach of section 2.2 gives—in principle, at least—the opportunity to analyze such changes, because variations in quality prices alter the way in which an element $e_{ih}$ of the vector $e_i$ influences the price $p_i$. Hence, by assuming some definite relation between each quality price and the way in which the corresponding $p_i$ is influenced by the $e_{ih}$ ($h = 1, \ldots, m_i$) one could analyze the influence of varying quality prices on the equilibrium values of $x_i$, $e_i$ ($i = 1, \cdots, n$).

However, even if we pay no attention to the difficulties arising from the fact that some of the $e_{ih}$ cannot be represented in a quantitative way, the results would be complicated. This is the reason why we prefer to make use of a degree of freedom which has been left unused so far, viz., the way in which qualities are grouped to commodities.

This grouping problem is usually solved in a linguistic manner. If the language one uses contains a substantive covering a set of qualities this fact alone is often responsible for the definition of such a set as a "commodity." It is clear that such a way of defining has no necessary advantages for economic analysis. Nevertheless, the qualities coming under a common substantive have often (but not always) a closely related significance for the satisfaction of the consumer's wants, so that in many cases at least the heterogeneity of such a commodity will not have so large a disturbing influence as to render further analysis useless. In spite of this a situation characterized by concepts that are based on linguistic considerations only cannot be called a highly satisfactory one.

---

[12] It is, of course, not necessary to assume the existence of a cardinal utility function.

Therefore, we shall proceed in quite another way. We think that it has great advantages if the definition of a commodity depends on the behavior of quality prices. So we shall define a set of qualities to be a commodity *only if* the prices of these qualities have a certain functional relationship to each other during the period considered. Such a relationship might be that these prices move proportionally; it might be that the increments and decrements of these prices are identical; it might be that these prices obey a cubic with the same parameters, which are fixed by retailers, etc.

We may add that, if a set of qualities happens to be such a commodity and it appears that there is another quality the price of which has the same functional relationship to the prices of the first-mentioned qualities as these prices have among each other, it is not necessary to include the latter quality into this commodity. E.g., if a set of tea brands is such a commodity and if a quality of peanuts obeys the above-mentioned condition, there may be sufficient reasons not to add this peanut quality to the set of tea brands. It will be clear that the above is in accordance with the words "only if" in the last paragraph.

It may be useful to give some further examples. Many empirical investigations show that the prices of butter and margarine are often highly correlated. If this is true, our definition of a commodity allows us to consider these goods as one single commodity.[13] This possibility has important advantages in time series analysis, because an accurate description of the consumption of butter and margarine separately in terms of both prices is usually impossible, if these prices are highly correlated. On the other hand, a commodity like foot-gear is quite heterogeneous, much more than the butter-margarine combination; dancing-shoes and waders are much less related in a consumer's preference system than butter and margarine. Moreover, one may assume that there exists no simple functional relationship between the prices of dancing-shoes and waders, so that according to our definition these goods do not belong to the same commodity. So we see that it is of importance to reject the linguistically based commodity of foot-gear in favor of another grouping of qualities.

To these remarks it may be added that the notion of a commodity so defined may be different in different places and different periods. In Holland, e.g., the Government policy with respect to white bread and wheaten bread has been quite different in the last few years. So we must consider both kinds of bread as two commodities in this period, contrary to previous periods, in which these prices were more closely related.

In section 2.4 we shall consider the case in which commodities are defined such that the prices of the constituent qualities move proportionally. This case (which can easily be generalized to the case of commodities defined by means of more complicated relationships) will appear to have an interesting resemblance to the case dealt with by traditional consumption theory, at least in certain respects.

---

[13] Even if the functional relationship used in this definition does not hold exactly but only approximately, it may be useful to admit small deviations from this relationship and to regard the resulting errors as random disturbances.

## 2.4 THE CASE OF PROPORTIONALLY MOVING PRICES OF THE QUALITIES WITHIN EACH COMMUNITY

2.4.1 *Equilibrium and stability conditions.* In this case the average price paid for commodity $i$ may be written as the product $\pi_i p_i$, in which $p_i$ is a *quality indicator* with the same meaning as the $p$ of section 2.1 and $\pi_i$ is a proportionality constant, which is a datum for the consumer. This constant, which is a decision variable of retailers, etc., will be called a *price coefficient.*

So we have the following utility function:

$$u = u(x_1, \ldots, x_n, p_1, \ldots, p_n) , \tag{1}$$

which the consumer will maximize subject to the side relation

$$\sum_{i=1}^{n} \pi_i p_i x_i - y = 0 . \tag{2}$$

It is seen that the function (1) is equivalent to the utility function of section 2.2, if we replace the vectors $e_i$ by the scalar quantity indicators $p_i$; (2) is equivalent with the side relation of section 2.2, if we replace the average prices $p_i(e_i)$ by the products $\pi_i p_i$.[14] Moreover, it appears that the $x$'s and the $p$'s enter into (1) and (2) in a symmetrical way; hence it is possible to prove a proposition for a $p_i$ such that the corresponding proposition for the $x_i$ does not hold, and vice versa. In particular it will appear that it is impossible to prove that an increase of income always causes a quality indicator to rise (cf. section 2.1).

When writing

$$\frac{\partial u}{\partial x_i} = u_i^x ; \quad \frac{\partial u}{\partial p_i} = u_i^p \qquad (i = 1, \ldots, n)$$

we have, if $\lambda$ is a Lagrange multiplier,

$$u_i^x - \lambda \pi_i p_i = 0 \qquad (i = 1, \ldots, n) \tag{3}$$

$$u_i^p - \lambda \pi_i x_i = 0 , \tag{4}$$

the marginal conditions. We write the second derivatives as follows:

[14] The partial derivative $\partial p_i / \partial e_{ih}$ of section 2.2 is here simply equal to $\pi_i$.

$$\frac{\partial^2 u}{\partial x_i \partial x_j} = u_{ij}^{xx} \; ; \; \frac{\partial^2 u}{\partial p_i \partial p_j} = u_{ij}^{pp} \qquad (i,j = 1, \ldots, n)$$

$$\frac{\partial^2 u}{\partial x_i \partial p_j} = \frac{\partial^2 u}{\partial p_j \partial x_i} = u_{ij}^{xp} = u_{ji}^{px}$$

and introduce the determinant:

$$U = \begin{vmatrix} 0 & u_j^x & u_j^p \\ u_i^x & v_{ij}^{xx} & v_{ij}^{xp}(\lambda) \\ u_i^p & v_{ij}^{px}(\lambda) & v_{ij}^{pp} \end{vmatrix}$$

in which $u_j^x$ and $u_j^p$ are the row vectors $(u_1^x, \cdots, u_n^x)$ and $(u_1^p, \ldots, u_n^p)$ respective; $u_i^x$ and $u_i^p$ are their transposes; $v_{ij}^{xx}$ is the $n \times n$ matrix $[u_{ij}^{xx}]$; $v_{ij}^{pp}$ is the $n \times n$ matrix $[u_{ij}^{pp}]$; $v_{ij}^{xp}(\lambda)$ is the $n \times n$ matrix $[u_{ij}^{xp}] - \lambda I$, $I$ being the $n \times n$ unit matrix; $v_{ij}^{px}(\lambda)$ is the $n \times n$ matrix $[u_{ij}^{px}] - \lambda I$.

We shall denote the co-factors in $U$ in the following way:

| *Elements* | | *Co-factors of these elements* |
|---|---|---|
| $u_i^x$ | $(i = 1, \ldots, n)$ | $U_i^x$ |
| $u_i^p$ | $(i = 1, \ldots, n)$ | $U_i^p$ |
| $u_{ij}^{xx}$ | $(i,j = 1, \ldots, n)$ | $U_{ij}^{xx}$ |
| $u_{ij}^{pp}$ | $(i,j = 1, \ldots, n)$ | $U_{ij}^{pp}$ |
| $u_{ij}^{xp}$ | $(i,j = 1, \ldots, n, i \neq j)$ | $U_{ij}^{xp}$ |
| $u_{ii}^{xp} - \lambda$ | $(i = 1, \ldots, n)$ | $U_{ii}^{xp}$ |
| $u_{ij}^{px}$ | $(i,j = 1, \ldots, n, i \neq j)$ | $U_{ij}^{px}$ |
| $u_{ii}^{px} - \lambda$ | $(i = 1, \ldots, n)$ | $U_{ii}^{px}$ |

By means of this notation one can easily give expressions for the stability conditions; we leave this to the interested reader.[15] The following particular consequences of these conditions will be used below:

[15] See, e.g., P.A. Samuelson (1948, pp. 362-365).

$$\lambda \frac{U_{ii}^{xx}}{U} < 0 \; ; \quad \lambda \frac{U_{ii}^{pp}}{U} < 0 \tag{5}$$

$$\frac{\lambda}{U}\left(p_i^2 U_{ii}^{xx} + p_i x_i U_{ii}^{xp} + p_i x_i U_{ii}^{px} + x_i^2 U_{ii}^{pp}\right) < 0 \tag{6}$$

Finally, we shall make use of the simple symmetry conditions:

$$U_{ij}^{xx} = U_{ji}^{xx} \; ; \quad U_{ij}^{xp} = U_{ji}^{px} \; ; \quad U_{ij}^{pp} = U_{ji}^{pp} \tag{7}$$

2.4.2 *The partial derivatives of $x_i$ and $p_i$.* We shall write for the ratios of the co-factors $U_i^x$, $U_i^p$, $U_{ij}^{xx}$, . . . , to $\lambda^{-1}U$: $K_i^x$, $K_i^p$, $K_{ij}^{xx}$, etc.[16] Then, after differentiating the equations (2), (3) and (4) with respect to income and price coefficients and solving, we obtain the following expressions for the partial derivatives of $x_i$, $p_i$ with respect to these parameters:

$$\frac{\partial x_i}{\partial y} = K_i^x \tag{8}$$

$$\frac{\partial p_i}{\partial y} = K_i^p \tag{9}$$

$$\frac{\partial x_i}{\partial \pi_j} = - p_j x_j K_i^x + p_j K_{ji}^{xx} + x_j K_{ij}^{px} \tag{10}$$

$$\frac{\partial p_i}{\partial \pi_j} = - p_j x_j K_i^p + p_j K_{ji}^{xp} + x_j K_{ji}^{pp} \; . \tag{11}$$

$$(i, j = 1 , \ldots , n) \; .$$

From these equations a number of interesting results can be derived. E.g., it follows from (7), (8), (9), (10) and (11) that:

$$\frac{\partial (p_i x_i)}{\partial \pi_j} + p_j x_j \frac{\partial (p_j x_i)}{\partial y} = \frac{\partial (p_j x_j)}{\partial \pi_i} + p_i x_i \frac{\partial (p_j x_j)}{\partial y} \; , \tag{12}$$

---

[16] It is easy to see that these $K$-terms are invariant against substitutions $\phi(u)$ of $u$, if only $\phi'(u)$ is positive; compare footnote 12 and J.R. Hicks (1946, pp. 306-307).

both sides being equal to:

$$p_i p_j K_{ij}^{xx} + p_i x_j K_{ij}^{xp} + p_j x_i K_{ji}^{xp} + x_i x_j K_{ij}^{pp} .$$

This result is closely related to a well-known equation of traditional consumption theory. When writing $k_i$ for the proportion of income spent on commodity $i$ we have in elasticities:

$$k_i \frac{E(p_i x_i)}{E\pi_j} + k_i k_j \frac{E(p_i x_i)}{Ey} = k_j \frac{E(p_j x_j)}{E\pi_i} + k_j k_i \frac{E(p_j x_j)}{Ey} \tag{13}$$

Furthermore, it follows from (6) that, if $i = j$, both sides of the equation (12) are negative:

$$\frac{\partial(p_i x_i)}{\partial\pi_i} + p_i x_i \frac{\partial(p_i x_i)}{\partial y} < 0 \tag{14}$$

or

$$\frac{E(p_i x_i)}{E\pi_i} + k_i \frac{E(p_i x_i)}{Ey} < 0 . \tag{15}$$

The relations (12) and (14) or (13) and (15) have a very close resemblance to the traditional theory of consumers' behavior in which all commodity prices are assumed to be data for the subject considered. We shall not proceed to give further analogies here; it is more interesting to look after relations that lack a counterpart in traditional theory.

Such a relation can be obtained by eliminating:

$$K_{ii}^{xp} = K_{ii}^{px}$$

in (10) and (11) for the case $i = j$:

$$\frac{\partial\left(\frac{p_i}{x_i}\right)}{\partial\pi_i} + p_i x_i \frac{\partial\left(\frac{p_i}{x_i}\right)}{\partial y} = K_{ii}^{pp} - \left(\frac{p_i}{x_i}\right)^2 K_{ii}^{xx} \tag{16}$$

or

$$\frac{E\left(\frac{p_i}{x_i}\right)}{E\pi_i} + k_i \frac{E\left(\frac{p_i}{x_i}\right)}{Ey} = k_i y \left(\frac{K_{ii}^{pp}}{p_i^2} - \frac{K_{ii}^{xx}}{x_i^2}\right). \tag{17}$$

The left-hand side of these equations represents the influence of an increase of a price indicator $\pi_i$ upon the fraction $p_i/x_i$, corrected for income effects. This fraction may be considered as "the ratio of quality to quantity." As the right-hand sides of (16) and (17) are equal to the difference of two negative quantities, one cannot be sure about the sign of the change in $p_i/x_i$ caused by an increase of $\pi_i$, as is to be expected. Nevertheless, it is interesting to see that the left-hand expressions of (16) and (17) are simple functions of the terms $K_{ii}^{xx}$ and $K_{ii}^{pp}$.

For the general case $i \lesseqgtr j$ we obtain in the same way:

$$x_j \frac{\partial p_j}{\partial \pi_i} - p_i \frac{\partial x_i}{\partial \pi_j} + p_i x_i^2 x_j \frac{\partial\left(\frac{p_j}{x_i}\right)}{\partial y} = x_i x_j K_{ij}^{pp} - p_i p_j K_{ij}^{xx} \tag{18}$$

or

$$k_j \frac{Ep_j}{E\pi_i} - k_i \frac{Ex_i}{E\pi_j} + k_i k_j \frac{E\left(\frac{p_j}{x_i}\right)}{Ey} = k_i k_j \left(\frac{K_{ij}^{pp}}{p_i p_j} - \frac{K_{ij}^{xx}}{x_i x_j}\right). \tag{19}$$

2.4.3 *Further discussion of the K-terms.* Consider the partial derivative $\partial x_i/\partial \pi_i$. Suppose that the change in $\pi_i$ is combined with such a change in $y$ as to compensate the change in "real" income caused by the change of this price coefficient. This yields the following expression:

$$\frac{\partial x_i}{\partial \pi_i} + p_i x_i \frac{\partial x_i}{\partial y} .$$

One cannot be sure about the sign of this term. In traditional consumption theory this sign would be a negative one[17]; here, however, such a statement has no general validity, because it is possible that, if $\pi_i$ increases (combined with a compensated increase of $y$), the consumer prefers a reduction in quality ($\equiv p_i$) to a reduction in quantity; and the empirical results of section 3.3.3 below suggests that this possibility must not be underestimated. The proposition that the above expression may be positive is in accordance with the equation (cf. (8) and (10)):

$$\frac{\partial x_i}{\partial \pi_i} + p_i x_i \frac{\partial x_i}{\partial y} = p_i K_{ii}^{xx} + x_i K_{ii}^{px} . \tag{20}$$

[17] It will be clear that the corresponding expression in traditional theory is slightly (in this respect, not significantly) different from the above one.

Although $K_{ii}^{xx}$ is certainly negative (cf. (5)), $K_{ii}^{px}$ may be positive, zero, or negative. If $K_{ii}^{px}$ is sufficiently positive—the stability conditions do not enable us to reject this possibility—the left-hand side of (20) may be positive. The same holds for the left-hand side of the equation:

$$\frac{\partial p_i}{\partial \pi_i} + p_i x_i \frac{\partial p_i}{\partial y} = p_i K_{ii}^{xp} + x_i K_{ii}^{pp} \, . \tag{21}$$

However, it is impossible that the left-hand sides of both (20) and (21) are positive, for this would imply a contradiction with (14) (cf. also (6)). So we may conclude that a compensated increase of the price coefficient $\pi_i$ cannot cause the quantity bought $x_i$ and the quality indicator $p_i$ to increase simultaneously; one of them may increase, or none.

Let us consider the $K$-terms more closely. In traditional consumption theory equations like (20) and (21) have only one such term in their right-hand side; then this term can simply be interpreted as the influence of a compensated increment of the price of commodity $i$ (considered as a datum) upon the quantity bought of $i$. Moreover, especially when these terms have different subscripts, they can be used for simple substitution and complementarity definitions.

In (20) and (21), however, we have two $K$-terms in the right-hand side. This is not surprising in view of the following heuristic considerations. In traditional theory an increase of the price of commodity $i$ causes the factor by which $x_i$ is multiplied in the side relation to be changed. On the other hand, in our approach an increase of the price coefficient $\pi_i$ causes both the factor by which $x_i$ is multiplied in (2), viz., $\pi_i p_i$, and the factor by which $p_i$ is multiplied in (2), viz., $\pi_i x_i$, to be changed. So it is indeed not surprising to find two different $K$-terms in the right-hand sides of (20) and of (21).

We could give a simple meaning to these $K$-terms, if it were possible to express them explicitly in terms of partial derivatives. However, this is impossible. There are only two equations, viz., (20) and (21), whereas there are three unknowns, viz., $K_{ii}^{xx}$, $K_{ii}^{px} = K_{ii}^{xp}$ and $K_{ii}^{pp}$. That there are not more equations for these unknowns follows directly from the fact that only the symmetry conditions (7) yield equations, whereas the stability conditions are all inequalities. So we cannot find these $K$-terms by calculating the partial derivatives of the left-hand sides of (20) and (21); *a fortiori* it is impossible to test the equation $K_{ii}^{px} = K_{ii}^{xp}$, as Schultz could try to do for traditional theory.[18] We could only solve the $K$-terms explicitly if we could compensate the changes of the multipliers of $p_i$ and $x_i$ in (2) for (20) and (21) respectively; but our approach does not enable us to do so.

We shall now consider the equations:

[18] Cf. H. Schultz (1938, ch. 19).

$$\frac{\partial x_i}{\partial \pi_j} + p_j x_j \frac{\partial x_i}{\partial y} = p_j K_{ji}^{xx} + x_j K_{ji}^{px} \tag{22}$$

$$\frac{\partial p_i}{\partial \pi_j} + p_j x_j \frac{\partial p_i}{\partial y} = p_j K_{ji}^{xp} + x_j K_{ji}^{pp} \tag{23}$$

$$\frac{\partial x_j}{\partial \pi_i} + p_i x_i \frac{\partial x_j}{\partial y} = p_i K_{ij}^{xx} + x_i K_{ij}^{px} \tag{24}$$

$$\frac{\partial p_j}{\partial \pi_i} + p_i x_i \frac{\partial p_j}{\partial y} = p_i K_{ij}^{xp} + x_i K_{ij}^{pp} \tag{25}$$

These four equations are the only ones in which $K$-terms with subscripts $i$ and $j$ occur. It follows from the symmetry conditions that there are four different $K$-terms of this type. Four equations are available; however, they are not independent. The relation of dependence is (12), as the reader may verify. So it is not possible to solve these unknowns in terms of the partial derivatives of (22), (23), (24) and (25).

As a matter of fact, the $K$-terms cannot be found even if all partial derivatives:

$$\frac{\partial x_i}{\partial \pi_j}, \frac{\partial p_i}{\partial \pi_j}, \frac{\partial x_i}{\partial y}, \frac{\partial p_i}{\partial y} \quad (i, j = 1, \ldots, n)$$

are known with whatever accuracy; the $K$-terms are not identifiable by means of these derivatives.[19] However, nothing can prevent us from defining complementarity and substitution in a way analogous to the one in traditional theory, viz., according to the sign of the $K$-term. So we shall say that a quantity $x_i$ is complementary with a quantity $x_j$, if $K_{ji}^{xx} < 0$; that a quantity $x_i$ is a substitute of a quality indicator $p_j$, if $K_{ji}^{px} > 0$; etc. This way of defining has consequences closely related to those in traditional theory; we may refer to the Mathematical Appendix of *Value and Capital*. The following may be noted:

(a) If $x_i$ is complementary with $p_j$, the $p_j$ is complementary with $x_i$, etc. (both substitution and complementarity are symmetric relations).

(b) $x_i$ is complementary with itself, etc. (complementarity is reflexive).

(c) If $x_i$ is complementary with both $x_j$ and $p_j$, then a compensated increase of $\pi_j$ causes $x_i$ to be reduced, etc.

(d) If $x_i$ is complementary with $x_j$ and a substitute for $p_j$, then a compensated increase of $\pi_j$ may increase or decrease $x_i$; if the "amount of substitution" to $p_j$ (viz., $|K_{ji}^{px}|$)

---

[19] Cf. T.C. Koopmans, H. Rubin and R.B. Leipnik, (1950).

is sufficiently small in relation to the "amount of complementarity" to $x_j$ (viz., $|K_{ji}^{xx}|$), then $x_i$ will be reduced, etc.[20]

(e) If $x_i$ is complementary to $p_i$, then a compensated increase of $\pi_i$ causes $x_i$ to be reduced; the same is true, if $x_i$ is a substitute of $p_i$, provided the amount of substitution is sufficiently small.

(f) It is also possible to define substitution and complementarity relations between two commodities $i$ and $j$ (just as in traditional theory) viz., according to the sign of:

$$p_i p_j K_{ji}^{xx} + p_i x_j K_{ji}^{px} + p_j x_i K_{ji}^{xp} + x_i x_j K_{ji}^{pp} ,$$

an expression which is equal to each of the sides of equation (12); it follows from (6) that a commodity is complementary to itself. We may add that this expression is identifiable by means of partial derivatives.

## 3. Empirical Results

### 3.1 PREVIOUS EMPIRICAL INVESTIGATIONS

Before rendering an account of our empirical findings it may be useful to call attention to two other investigations.

F.V. Waugh (1929) made an interesting inquiry into the price formation in an American vegetable market; a subject related to ours.[21] Waugh's theoretical approach has some resemblance to that of section 2.2.

H.S. Houthakker and S.J. Prais (1951) used budget data in order to find income elasticities of the average prices paid for certain commodities in several countries; their approach is more in accordance with that of section 2.1. A section below will be devoted to a comparison of one of their hypotheses—which came to our attention just before this paper was completed—with our results.

### 3.2 THE MATERIAL; THE VARIABLES; THE EQUATIONS

During the period March, 1934 - February, 1935, a budget enquiry was held in Amsterdam. The number of participating families was 184; a part of them consisted of clerical families, the remaining part being composed of families of manual workers.

[20] It will be observed that these $K$-terms are not invariant against changes of scale; this requires only an unimportant modification.

[21] Quoted in P. J. Verdoorn (1950, pp. 192-196).

Unpublished material contains the quantities bought (in units of 100 grams) and the amounts spent on several food commodities.[22] The following commodities were considered: sweet biscuits, cake, tea, coffee, cocoa, chocolate, cheese, meat and meat products. By dividing the amounts spent by the quantities bought we obtained average prices (in cents per unit of 100 grams). One may assume that the constituent quality prices of these commodities did not alter materially during the budget year.

In order to simplify the computations we considered only those families who consumed a positive amount of each of these commodities. After omitting the families the incomes of which were unknown, we had ninety-two clerical families and sixty-two families of manual workers.

It is plausible that the average commodity prices (just as the quantities) are dependent on family size. The larger a family is, the more it is inclined to buy cheaper qualities of a commodity, because it needs larger quantities of, e.g., clothes and food. Hence family size as well as income have to enter into the equations describing the quantities bought and the average prices paid.

We measured family size by means of the Amsterdam scale of consumption units. This scale gives 0.15 unit to children of age zero; 0.20 unit to children of one year; 0.30 unit to children of two years; for each further year an additional 0.05 unit is given; the maximum number for women is 0.90, which is reached at the age of 14; men of 15 years and older represent one unit.

Let us denote the income of family $i$ by $y_i$, the sum total of the consumption units of its members by $S_i$, the quantity bought by $x_i$ and the average price paid by $p_i$. Then for each of both groups we postulate that preferences are identical for all families, apart from differences in family size ($S$) and from random disturbances. This implies that $x_i$ and $p_i$ are functions of $y_i$, $S_i$, and the disturbances $u_i$ and $u_i'$ respectively:

$$x_i = f^x(y_i, S_i, u_i)$$

$$p_i = f^p(y_i, S_i, u_i') \ .$$

These general forms have been specified by the following linear relationships:

$$x_i = a + \beta y_i + \gamma S_i + u_i \tag{26}$$

$$p_i = a' + \beta' y_i + \gamma' S_i + u_i' \tag{27}$$

[22] The author is indebted to the Director of the Amsterdam Municipal Bureau of Statistics, who put this material at his disposal.

in which $a$, $\beta$, $\gamma$, $a'$, $\beta'$, $\gamma'$ are parameters. These parameters have been estimated by means of the method of least squares.

The computations have been performed by Messrs. E. Bakker, econ. cand., and D. Woudhuysen, econ. cand.

## 3.3 THE BEHAVIOR PATTERN OF THE FAMILIES INVESTIGATED

3.3.1 *Discussion of some of the results.* The main results of the computations have been summarized in Table I (for clerical workers) and Table II (for manual workers), which are to be found below. They contain the following results:

(1) The average values of $x$ and $p$ over all ninety-two and sixty-two families respectively.

(2) The income elasticities of quantities bought and of prices paid in the center of gravity of the observed point sets ($e_1$), viz.:

$$b\frac{\bar{y}}{\bar{x}} \quad \text{and} \quad b'\frac{\bar{y}}{\bar{p}}$$

($b$ being the least squares estimate of $\beta$), together with their standard errors $s_{e_1}$ computed by means of Mosak's formula.[23]

(3) The family size elasticities $e_2$ defined in the same way, together with their standard errors $s_{e_2}$.

(4) The multiple correlation coefficients $R$ of the equations (26) and (27) respectively.

Let us first compare the corresponding average values $\bar{x}$ and $\bar{p}$ for the clerical and the manual workers. It appears that only a part of the differences can be explained by income differences (the average family size $S$ is for both groups virtually the same); some differences must be due to sociological causes as to the habits of spending. It is found, e.g., that the quantities bought of tea, coffee, and meat-products are larger for workers' families than for clerical families, in spite of the fact that the average income of the former group is less than one-half of the average income of the latter group. On the other hand, the average values of the $p$'s show a much more regular pattern; they are all higher for clerical than for workers' families. The reader will observe, of course, that part of the differences in commodity prices is due to price differences in the richer and poorer quarters of the town. This is not necessarily a new element entering into the picture, for the last-mentioned price differences are usually accompanied by differences in service, etc., so that we can speak of different qualities (cf. section 1). Nevertheless, we must say that the elasticities to be considered describe long-run relationships, which hold when a family's income is sufficiently changed, so that it removes to another quarter.

[23] Cf. J. L. Mosak (1939).

**TABLE I.** Clerical Workers
(Average income f4,385; average family size ($\bar{S}$) 3.44)

| | $\bar{x}$ / $\bar{p}$ | $e_1$ | $(s_{e_1})$ | $e_2$ | $(s_{e_2})$ | $R$ |
|---|---|---|---|---|---|---|
| Sweet biscuits | 214.91 | 0.012 | (0.049) | 0.294 | (0.113) | 0.315 |
| | 12.01 | 0.206 | (0.025) | -0.139 | (0.057) | 0.668 |
| Cake | 93.16 | 0.307 | (0.086) | 0.279 | (0.195) | 0.484 |
| | 15.45 | 0.132 | (0.030) | -0.012 | (0.069) | 0.462 |
| Tea | 67.52 | 0.087 | (0.048) | 0.694 | (0.114) | 0.667 |
| | 27.81 | 0.040 | (0.020) | -0.027 | (0.047) | 0.207 |
| Coffee | 73.10 | 0.255 | (0.073) | 0.306 | (0.166) | 0.501 |
| | 14.62 | 0.099 | (0.038) | -0.088 | (0.087) | 0.267 |
| Cocoa | 14.18 | 0.294 | (0.150) | 0.353 | (0.340) | 0.311 |
| | 15.68 | 0.103 | (0.040) | -0.071 | (0.092) | 0.268 |
| Chocolate | 74.05 | 0.128 | (0.127) | 0.302 | (0.292) | 0.211 |
| | 13.24 | 0.157 | (0.028) | -0.214 | (0.065) | 0.504 |
| Cheese | 214.89 | 0.086 | (0.069) | 0.830 | (0.166) | 0.584 |
| | 7.94 | 0.144 | (0.023) | -0.171 | (0.052) | 0.558 |
| Meat | 951.27 | 0.071 | (0.043) | 0.973 | (0.106) | 0.790 |
| | 11.56 | 0.217 | (0.026) | -0.123 | (0.058) | 0.686 |
| Meat-products | 184.11 | -0.107 | (0.027) | 1.258 | (0.068) | 0.576 |
| | 14.71 | 0.212 | (0.021) | -0.180 | (0.048) | 0.733 |

**TABLE II.** Manual Workers
(Average income f1,996; average family size ($\bar{S}$) 3.46)

| | $\frac{\bar{x}}{\bar{p}}$ | $e_1$ | $(s_{e_1})$ | $e_2$ | $(s_{e_2})$ | $R$ |
|---|---|---|---|---|---|---|
| Sweet biscuits | 193.09<br>9.19 | 0.056<br>0.574 | (0.241)<br>(0.106) | 0.626<br>-0.309 | (0.190)<br>(0.083) | 0.497<br>0.569 |
| Cake | 54.30<br>12.86 | 1.184<br>0.261 | (0.483)<br>(0.168) | -0.423<br>-0.126 | (0.366)<br>(0.130) | 0.313<br>0.197 |
| Tea | 68.25<br>24.89 | 0.127<br>0.205 | (0.253)<br>(0.079) | 0.528<br>-0.184 | (0.199)<br>(0.061) | 0.444<br>0.370 |
| Coffee | 89.48<br>12.14 | -0.090<br>0.325 | (0.381)<br>(0.145) | 0.810<br>-0.299 | (0.304)<br>(0.113) | 0.391<br>0.330 |
| Cocoa | 13.77<br>12.81 | 0.091<br>0.314 | (0.536)<br>(0.188) | 0.398<br>-0.240 | (0.419)<br>(0.146) | 0.173<br>0.226 |
| Chocolate | 43.84<br>11.68 | 1.017<br>0.050 | (0.466)<br>(0.088) | -0.471<br>-0.061 | (0.357)<br>(0.069) | 0.274<br>0.110 |
| Cheese | 212.25<br>7.41 | 0.490<br>0.298 | (0.342)<br>(0.091) | 0.210<br>-0.163 | (0.265)<br>(0.071) | 0.317<br>0.382 |
| Meat | 826.26<br>9.09 | 0.631<br>0.348 | (0.203)<br>(0.068) | 0.542<br>-0.333 | (0.158)<br>(0.053) | 0.700<br>0.634 |
| Meat-products | 212.22<br>12.31 | 0.803<br>0.281 | (0.309)<br>(0.082) | 0.833<br>-0.172 | (0.243)<br>(0.064) | 0.675<br>0.405 |

With the exception of the family size elasticities of the quantities bought, most elasticities are smaller in absolute value for the clerical families than for the other families; see Table III below.

**TABLE III.** Average Values of the Elasticities

| | *Clerical workers* | *Manual workers* |
|---|---|---|
| Income elasticities of $x$ | 0.126 | 0.479 |
| of $p$ | 0.146 | 0.295 |
| Family size elasticities of $x$ | 0.588 | 0.339 |
| of $p$ | -0.114 | -0.210 |

The averages have been taken over the nine commodities investigated. The results contained in this table suggest that clerical families are more saturated with respect to the quantities and quality indicators considered than the other families with their much smaller incomes. Only six of the twenty-seven income elasticities (of quantities bought and prices paid) and family size elasticities of prices paid (i.e. their absolute values) are smaller for the families of manual workers than the corresponding elasticities for the clerical families.

Two income elasticities are negative: the one of the quantity of coffee for manual workers (which is not significantly negative) and the income elasticity of the quantity of meat-products for the clerical families. The latter elasticity differs significantly from zero. But the income elasticity of the amount spent on this commodity—which is simply the sum of the $e_1$'s of the $x$- and the $p$-equation—is positive because of the larger effect of income on the average price paid.

It appears from Table III that the average value of the family size elasticities of quantities bought is smaller for manual workers than for clerical workers. The former group shows even negative values for two of these elasticities, viz., for cake and for chocolate, but these are not significantly negative.

All income and family size elasticities of the average prices paid, for both sets of families, have the sign that can ordinarily be expected, viz., positive and negative respectively. However, there is a number of cases in which the significance is not well-established.

It is of some interest to compare the income elasticities of the quantities bought with the income elasticities of the corresponding average prices paid, because such a comparison reveals which part of the income elasticity of the amount spent on a commodity has to be ascribed to a change in the average price paid. Table I reveals that for the following commodities the estimate $e_1$ of the quantity equation is smaller than $e_1$ for the price equation: sweet biscuits, chocolate, cheese, meat, meat-products. For the manual workers this holds for: sweet biscuits, tea, coffee, cocoa. Hence, apart from sampling errors, about one-half of the commodities investigated show income elasticities of average prices paid that are larger than the corresponding income elasticities of the quantities bought. Though this group of commodities is by no means identical for both sets of families, it is clear that one cannot say that income elasticities of average prices paid are generally small as compared with the corresponding elasticities of the quantities bought.

Let us also compare the family size elasticities of the quantity and the price equations. Their algebraic sum represents the influence of family size on the amount spent on the commodity. Table I shows that this sum is always positive for clerical families. For the other set of families the same holds with two exceptions, viz., cake and chocolate, for which the $e_2$'s of the quantity equations are negative. Of course, some caution is necessary in view of the disturbing influence of sampling errors.

3.3.2 *Further Discussion of the Elasticities of the Price Equations.* In their empirical analysis Houthakker and Prais assumed that the average price paid for a certain commodity is a function of the ratio of income to the number of consumption units (i.e., of income per consumption unit). This implies that they assume that the family size elasticity is equal to minus the corresponding income elasticity. Although their consumption units are different from those used in this paper (their $S$ is equal to the number of persons per family), it is of some interest to test the corresponding hypothesis with our consumption units for the material investigated here; one must, however, be conscious of the fact that the Houthakker-Prais hypothesis is not strictly identical with the present one.

If the hypothesis is correct, the sum of the elasticities $e_1 + e_2$ for the price equations must vanish, apart from sampling errors. So we computed the standard errors of these sums, $s_{e_1+e_2}$, and obtained the ratios $(e_1 + e_2)/s_{e_1+e_2}$. These ratios can be found in Table IV below.

**TABLE IV.** $(e_1 + e_2)/s_{e_1+e_2}$ for the Average Prices Paid

| | *Clerical workers* | *Manual workers* |
|---|---|---|
| Sweet biscuits | 1.34 | 3.15 |
| Cake | 2.00 | 1.02 |
| Tea | 0.33 | 0.34 |
| Coffee | 0.14 | 0.23 |
| Cocoa | 0.40 | 0.50 |
| Chocolate | -1.02 | -0.16 |
| Cheese | -0.59 | 1.89 |
| Meat | 1.81 | 0.28 |
| Meat-products | 0.76 | 1.68 |

Although these ratios are not significant for almost all of the commodities considered (the only exception being sweet biscuits for manual workers and possibly cake for clerical families) it is highly probable that the hypothesis is not correct for the material as a whole, because so few ratios have negative values. As the probability of obtaining only three values of one sign out of a sample of eighteen—under the hypothesis that the probability of each sign is one-half—is equal to 0.0075, we must conclude that family size elasticities are often smaller than income elasticities.[24] This is clearly illustrated in Diagram 3: almost all observed points $(e_1, e_2)$ lie above the line $e_1 = -e_2$. But this diagram shows another important fact, viz., that the line $e_1 = -4/3\ e_2$ gives a much better fit to these points, especially for the manual workers whose elasticities have a much larger range than those of the clerical workers.

So the hypothesis that the parent value of $e_1$ is minus 4/3 times the parent value of $e_2$ is more acceptable than the hypothesis that these parent values are equal, apart from sign; as a matter of fact, the former hypothesis cannot be rejected on the basis of the observations. If it is true, we can describe the average prices paid as a function, not of $y/S$, but of $y/S^{3/4}$, at least in the neighborhood of the center of gravity.

[24] It will be clear that use has been made of the (maintained) hypothesis that these ratios are independent for the different commodities.

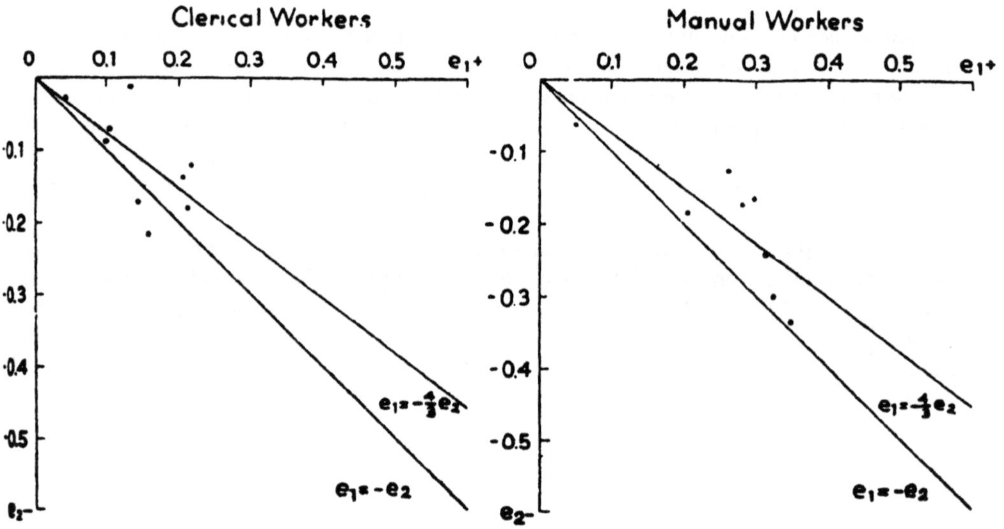


Diagram 3

Let us assume that this hypothesis is true. Then we have two estimates of the income elasticities of the average prices paid, viz., $e_1$ and -4/3 $e_2$. This implies that a more efficient estimate can be obtained by computing a weighted average of these estimates, viz.:

$$e_{12} = \lambda e_1 - \frac{4}{3}(1 - \lambda) e_2 \ ,$$

**TABLE V.** Revised Income Elasticities of the Average Prices Paid

| | *Clerical workers* | | *Manual workers* | |
|---|---|---|---|---|
| | $e_{12}$ | $(s_{e_{12}})$ | $e_{12}$ | $(s_{e_{12}})$ |
| Sweet biscuits | 0.208 | (0.024) | 0.501 | (0.097) |
| Cake | 0.141 | (0.029) | 0.219 | (0.154) |
| Tea | 0.040 | (0.020) | 0.223 | (0.073) |
| Coffee | 0.098 | (0.037) | 0.358 | (0.133) |
| Cocoa | 0.104 | (0.039) | 0.317 | (0.173) |
| Chocolate | 0.147 | (0.027) | 0.064 | (0.081) |
| Cheese | 0.138 | (0.022) | 0.262 | (0.084) |
| Meat | 0.221 | (0.025) | 0.391 | (0.062) |
| Meat-products | 0.210 | (0.021) | 0.258 | (0.075) |

in which $\lambda$ and $(1 - \lambda)$ are weights; $\lambda$ has been chosen such that the sampling variance of $e_{12}$ is a minimum.[25] The results are shown in Table V.

It appears that the income elasticities for the clerical workers are fairly precisely determined; for the manual workers the standard errors $s_{e_{12}}$ are still rather large, which is not surprising in view of the large difference of the income ranges of both groups.

The correlation between the revised income elasticities of both sets of families is not high (viz., 0.36, which is not significantly different from zero). This implies that the degree of saturation with respect to quality indicators reached by the clerical workers is, in relation to the degree reached by the manual workers, rather different for different commodities.

3.3.3 *Substitution Between Quantities and Quality Indicators.* Let us assume that the following situation may be considered as an indication of the existence of a substitution relationship between the quantity bought of a certain commodity, $x$, and its average price, $p$:[26] those families whose $x$'s have larger values than those computed by means of the regression equation (26) have generally smaller $p$'s and the $p$'s computed by means of (27), and vice versa. Simpler: there is an indication of substitution between $x$ and $p$, if families who buy large quantities pay relatively low prices. Of course, the danger exists that such an effect has nothing to do with substitution, only with price reductions granted by a retailer in order to stimulate large-scale buying. It is, however, not plausible that this effect has any real importance for the commodities investigated here.

The criterion stated above can be quantified by means of the correlation coefficients between the residuals $u$ and $u'$ of the equations (26) and (27); they can be found in Table VI below.

**TABLE VI.** Correlation Coefficients between the Residuals of the Quantity and the Price Equations

| | *Clerical workers* | *Manual workers* |
|---|---|---|
| Sweet biscuits | -0.185 | -0.065 |
| Cake | -0.133 | -0.220 |
| Tea | -0.052 | -0.222 |
| Coffee | -0.193 | -0.118 |
| Cocoa | -0.225 | -0.040 |
| Chocolate | -0.097 | -0.245 |
| Cheese | -0.119 | -0.676 |
| Meat | -0.053 | -0.212 |
| Meat-products | -0.720 | -0.191 |

[25] This caused the weight $(1 - \lambda)$ for the clerical workers to be slightly negative, as the covariance between $e_1$ and $e_2$ is of great importance in this group. For the covariance between $b$ and $c$, on which the former covariance is based, see H. Cramer (1946, p. 552).

[26] See especially R.G.D. Allen and A.L. Bowley (1935, pp. 89-96).

The correlation coefficient of meat-products for clerical workers and that of cheese for manual workers are highly significant.[27] The significance of those coefficients that are somewhat above -1/4 is doubtful. However, for both sets of correlation coefficients as a whole it is practically certain that significance exists, even if we omit the seven coefficients that are smaller than -0.2, which are individually significant or nearly significant, because of the absence of positive values. So, if we accept negative correlation between residuals as an indication of substitution, we may conclude that substitution between a quantity and the corresponding quality indicator is a realistic but not an obvious phenomenon.

The author wants to express his indebtedness to Mr. P. de Wolff for his stimulating and constructive criticism.

## References

Allen, R.G.D.: 1938, *Mathematical Analysis for Economists*, Macmillan, London.

Allen, R.G.D.: 1942, Expenditure Patterns of Families of Different Types, in: O Lange, F. McIntyre and Th. Yntema, eds., *Studies in Mathematical Economics and Econometrics in Memory of Henry Schultz*, University of Chicago Press, Chicago, 190-207.

Allen. R.G.D., and A.L. Bowley: 1935, *Family Expenditure*, P.S. King and Son, Ltd., London, 1935.

Brems, H.: 1951, *Product Equilibrium under Monopolistic Competition*, Harvard University Press, Cambridge, Massachusetts.

Cramer, H.: 1946, *Mathematical Methods of Statistics*, Princeton University Press, Princeton, New Jersey.

David, F.N.: 1938, *Tables of the Correlation Coefficient*, London.

Hicks, J.R.: 1946, *Value and Capital*, 2nd ed., Oxford University Press, London.

Houthakker, H.S., and S.J. Prais: 1951, "Quantities and Qualities in Family Budgets," Paper delivered at the Louvain Meeting of the Econometric Society (to be published in *Economie Appliquée*).

[27] Cf. F. N. David (1938).

Koopmans, T.C., H. Rubin, and R.B. Leipnik: 1950, "Measuring the Equation Systems of Dynamic Economics," in T.C. Koopmans, ed., *Statistical Inference in Dynamic Economic Models*, John Wiley and Sons Inc., New York, 53-238.

Mosak, J.L.: 1939, "The Least-squares Standard Error of the Coefficient of Elasticity of Demand," *Journal of the American Statistical Association*, **34**, 353-361.

Samuelson, P.A.: 1948, *Foundations of Economic Analysis*, Harvard University Press, Cambridge, Massachusetts.

Schultz, H.: 1938, *The Theory and Measurement of Demand*, University of Chicago Press, Chicago, Illinois.

Stone, J.R.N.: 1950, "The Demand for Food in the United Kingdom," Paper delivered at the Varese Meeting of the Econometric Society.

Veblen, T.: 1924, *The Theory of the Leisure Class*, Macmillan Company, London.

Verdoorn, P.J.: 1950, *Grondslagen en Techniek der Marktanalyse,* Leiden, The Netherlands.

Waugh, F.V.: 1929, *Quality as a Determinant of Vegetable Prices*, Columbia University Press, New York.

CHAPTER 35

# SUBSTITUTION, COMPLEMENTARITY, AND THE RESIDUAL VARIATION AROUND ENGEL CURVES*

HENRI THEIL
*Netherlands School of Economics (now Erasmus University), Rotterdam, The Netherlands*

HEINZ NEUDECKER
*Netherlands School of Economics (now Erasmus University), Rotterdam, The Netherlands*

## 1. Introduction

It is well-known that the empirical determination of substitution and complementarity relationships among pairs of consumption goods is hampered by serious difficulties. The time series analysis which is necessary for the estimation of the underlying price and income elasticities is characterised by the problems of small samples, multicollinearity among the explanatory variables, etc., so that rather large standard errors of the resulting estimates is a normal result. It is understandable, therefore, that alternative procedures have been devised in order to determine substitution and complementarity relations. The present paper is concerned with one of these procedures, which is based on budget data. The number of observations in budget enquiries is usually very much larger than in the case of time series analysis, but there is of course the disadvantage that no adequate price variation among the observational units exists.[1] The procedure followed implies then that, for any pair of commodities for which one wants to establish a substitution or complementarity relationship, the two Engel curves are derived, after which the two sets of residuals around these curves are correlated with each other. A positive residual correlation is then regarded as a *prima facie* indication of complementarity, a negative correlation as an indication of a substitution relationship. Allen and Bowley (1935) (to whom, as far as the present authors are aware, this method is due) computed thirty-eight residual correlations for pairs of expenditure groups and arrived at figures ranging from -0.94 (for butter and margarine) to 0.73 (for fresh fruit and vegetables), most of them being negative. Following their lead, one of the authors (Theil, 1952-1953) computed eighteen residual correlations belonging to an Engel curve for the total quantity bought of a particular commodity group and to the corresponding curve for the average price paid

* This article first appeared in *The Review of Economic Studies*, **25** (1957-1958), 114-123. Reprinted with the permission of Elsevier Science Publishers B.V. (North-Holland).

[1] There is of course price variation in the sense that different families pay different prices for the "same" commodity because of differences in quality; a reference to this phenomenon is made in a later part of this section. This kind of price variation is not suitable for the determination of price elasticities.

for this same group.[2] These correlations, which are concerned with substitution relationships between "quality" and "quantity" of single commodity groups, turned out to be all negative. This dominance of negative values is in accordance with the theoretically established dominance of substitution over complementarity relationships.

It seems obvious that this approach is of interest for the empirical determination of substitution relationships, provided it is indeed true that the residual correlations measure what they are supposed to measure. For the only thing which one has to do is to divide the consumer's budget into an appropriate number (say $n$) of categories, after which the $(n/2)$ residual correlations indicate, for each pair of categories, whether there is substitution or complementarity, and perhaps also the strength of the relationship. However, the proviso mentioned above is not of a simple kind, as Allen and Bowley observed already in their work. Later research by Prais (1953) did not result in particularly hopeful suggestions.[3] Since it is unclear at present what is really measured by the residual correlations, it seems worth-while to explore this matter in more detail. This is the primary purpose of this paper; a second purpose is that of the economic interpretation of the "disturbances" of Engel curves - a subject which is largely, but undeservedly, neglected in the analysis of these and most other econometric relations.

The main result of the analysis which follows is that, on the one hand, it is possible (under certain conditions) to express the residual variances and covariances in terms of the classical substitution terms of consumer's analysis, whereas, on the other hand, it appears that the covariance for one pair of commodities is not solely determined by the substitution term of this pair, but by substitution terms of other pairs as well. This is explained in the next six sections, after which the results are summarized in more detail in section 8. This concluding section contains also a suggestion on a method of deriving substitution terms from the matrix of all residual variances and covariances.

## 2. Substitution and Complementarity Re-Stated

We shall base ourselves on the classical theory of consumer's demand, for which reference can be made to, e.g., Hicks (1946). The present section is devoted to the definition of symbols.

First, we have the utility function

---

[2] Allen's and Bowley's analysis is confined to food items, and the explanatory variable in the Engel curves is total food consumption per equivalent adult (not income). The dependent variables of their regressions are the expenditures per equivalent adult. In the quantity-quality analyses no division took place by the number of equivalent adults, but this number was introduced as an additional explanatory variable besides income.

[3] Also, cf. Prais and Houthakker (1955), p. 102. Prais did not compute residual correlations, but he introduced the consumption of the competing commodity as an additional explanatory variable in the Engel regression. Essentially, this procedure is not different from computing residual correlations.

$$u = u(x_1 \, , \, \ldots \, , \, x_n) = u(x) \; , \tag{2.1}$$

$x_1, x_2, \ldots,$ being the quantities bought of the various commodities (or $x$ as a column vector). This function is to be maximized subject to the budget constraint:

$$\sum_i p_i x_i = M \; , \tag{2.2}$$

the $p$'s being prices and $M$ income.

Let us write:

$$u_{ij} = \frac{\partial^2 u}{\partial x_i \partial x_j} \tag{2.3}$$

for the derivatives of the utility function of the second order. An essential role in the second-order maximum condition is played by the matrix of these derivatives, bordered by (negative) prices:

$$U = \begin{bmatrix} u_{11} & \ldots & u_{1n} & -p_1 \\ \ldots & \ldots & \ldots & \ldots \\ u_{n1} & \ldots & u_{nn} & -p_n \\ -p_1 & \ldots & -p_n & 0 \end{bmatrix} . \tag{2.4}$$

The inverse of this matrix is written as

$$U^{-1} = \begin{bmatrix} c_{11} & \ldots & c_{1n} & c_1 \\ \ldots & \ldots & \ldots & \ldots \\ c_{n1} & \ldots & c_{nn} & c_n \\ c_1 & \ldots & c_n & c_0 \end{bmatrix} \tag{2.5}$$

or in partitioned form:

$$U^{-1} = \begin{bmatrix} C & c \\ c' & c_0 \end{bmatrix} , \tag{2.6}$$

$C$ being a symmetric and negative semi-definite matrix (its rank being $n$ - 1), $c$ a column vector, $c'$ its transpose, and $c_0$ a scalar. The matrix $C$ is called the *substitution matrix.*

Two commodities $i$ and $j$ are said to be each other's substitutes from the point of view of the consumer if their *substitution term* $c_{ij} > 0$; complementary if $c_{ij} < 0$.

## 3. The Relevance of Quadratic Utility Assumptions

Our starting point will be the assumption of a quadratic utility function:

ASSUMPTION I. *The consumers' utility function* (2.1) *has the specification*

$$u(x) = a'x + \frac{1}{2}x'Bx = \sum a_i x_i + \frac{1}{2}\sum\sum b_{ij}x_i x_j , \tag{3.1}$$

*the a's and b's being coefficients which are independent of the quantities bought.*

The relevance of this assumption for our present purposes is easily seen. For suppose that the utility function is not quadratic. In that case the second-order derivatives of $u$ are no longer constants, as they are in the quadratic case ($u_{ij}$ - $b_{ij}$). Since the substitution terms are derived by inverting the bordered matrix of these derivatives, these terms are then dependent on the quantities bought and hence on prices and income. The dependence on prices is not serious if we make the conventional (though not necessarily realistic) assumption that they are constant during the budget period and the same for all consumers of the budget survey. The dependence on income is more serious, however. The point is not so much that the income of a particular family may change during the budget survey; but it is that, if the utility function is not quadratic, two commodities may be substitutes or complementary depending on income, so that for two families with different income in the same budget survey the question of substitution or complementarity for this pair of goods may be answered differently. Clearly, a residual correlation cannot take account of such divergencies, because this is a quantity which is derived for a budget survey as a whole. To give the residual correlation as a measure of substitution or complementarity any chance at all, we should exclude such possibilities by assuming that the matrix $B$ is the same for all families of the survey, so that they all have identical substitution matrices.[4]

ASSUMPTION II. *Assumption I applies to all families of the budget survey; and their matrices B, as well as the prices, are identical for all of them.*

[4] If one prefers expressions that are invariant against monotonic transformations of the utility function, we should say that the $B$-matrices are identical except possibly for a multiplicative scalar.

This assumption implies that the preferences of all consumers of the survey are supposed to be *perfectly homogeneous* as regards the coefficients of the quadratic terms of their preference functions. We shall not suppose that this also applies to the coefficients of the linear terms; if we would do so, the Engel curves would have no residual variation at all.

## 4. The Engel Curves Under the Assumptions of Section 3

The first-order maximum conditions of consumer's equilibrium are derived by differentiating

$$a'x + \frac{1}{2}x'Bx - \lambda(p'x - M) ,$$

$\lambda$ being a Lagrange multiplier and $p$ the price vector. The result is

$$Bx - p\lambda = -a , \tag{4.1}$$

which, when combined with the budget constraint,

$$-p'x = -M \tag{4.2}$$

gives the following solution for $x$ and $\lambda$:

$$\begin{bmatrix} x \\ \lambda \end{bmatrix} = U^{-1}\begin{bmatrix} -a \\ -M \end{bmatrix} . \tag{4.3}$$

Using (2.5) we find:

$$x_i = -\sum_h c_{ih} a_h - c_i M , \tag{4.4}$$

or in matrix form:

$$x = -Ca - cM . \tag{4.5}$$

The relations (4.4) and (4.5) can be regarded as Engel curves. The coefficients $c_i$ and $c_{ih}$ are the same for all families, as follows from Assumption II, so that the slopes of these curves ($-c_i$) are identical for all of them. The constant terms, $-\Sigma c_{ih} a_h$, are not the same, because the $a$'s are assumed to differ from family to family. Let us then write $\alpha_h$ for the mean value of the $a_h$'s of all families in the survey and write (4.4) as:

$$x_i = -\sum_h c_{ih}\alpha_h - c_i M - \sum_h c_{ih}(a_h - \alpha_h) . \tag{4.6}$$

The first two terms in the right-hand side are the same for all consumers (except of course for the values taken by the variable $M$); and the third, viz.:

$$v_i = -\sum_h c_{ih}(a_h - \alpha_h) , \tag{4.7}$$

can be regarded as a disturbance. It is seen that this disturbance contains two types of factors, viz., substitution terms and the deviations of the linear preference coefficients from their average. The occurrence of substitution terms points indeed to a relationship between the residual variation around Engel curves and substitution and complementarity phenomena.

Suppose then that the following assumption is satisfied:

ASSUMPTION IIIa. *For each family participating in the budget survey, the deviation of its linear preference coefficient $a_h$ from the group average $\alpha_h$ can be regarded as a random drawing from a universe with zero mean and a finite covariance matrix which is common to all families; and no correlation exists between this deviation and income over the set of all families, for $h = 1, \cdots, n$.*

If this assumption is indeed satisfied, then the disturbances $v_i$ of the Engel curves are subject to a probability distribution, and they are uncorrelated with income. The latter condition will be weakened in section 7. The first part of Assumption IIIa implies that the families are supposed to be *stochastically homogeneous* with respect to their linear preference coefficients.

## 5. The Residual Variation in the Case of Uncorrelated Linear Preference Coefficients

Let us write:

$$\text{var } v_i = E v_i^2 \tag{5.1}$$

for the variance of the disturbances of the Engel curve for $x_i$ over the set of families participating in the survey. The mean value of $v_i$ is of course zero because of Assumption IIIa. Applying (4.7) we find:

$$\operatorname{var} v_i = \sum_h \sum_k c_{ih} c_{ik} \operatorname{cov}(a_h, a_k) , \tag{5.2}$$

where

$$\operatorname{cov}(a_h, a_k) = E[(a_h - \alpha_h)(a_k - \alpha_k)]$$

is the covariance of the linear preference coefficients $a_h$ and $a_k$, which is, according to assumption IIIa, the same for all families. To make further progress, it is necessary to make an assumption concerning these covariances. The simplest is:

ASSUMPTION IVa. *The linear preference coefficients $a_1, \cdots, a_n$ are all uncorrelated:*

$$\operatorname{cov}(a_h, a_k) = 0 \qquad \text{if } h \neq k . \tag{5.3}$$

In that case (5.2) reduces to:

$$\operatorname{var} v_i = \sum_h c_{ih}^2 \sigma_h^2 , \tag{5.4}$$

where

$$\sigma_h^2 = \operatorname{var} a_h . \tag{5.5}$$

Similarly, we find for the covariance of the disturbances $v_i$ and $v_j$ corresponding to the Engel curves for $x_i$ and $x_j$ :

$$\operatorname{cov}(v_i, v_j) = \sum_h \sum_k c_{ih} c_{jk} \operatorname{cov}(a_h, a_k) , \tag{5.6}$$

which reduces under Assumption IVa to:

$$\operatorname{cov}(v_i, v_j) = \sum_h c_{ih} c_{jh} \sigma_h^2 . \tag{5.7}$$

The residual correlation is then found by dividing (5.7) by the geometric average of (5.4) and the similar expression for var $v_j$. If our interest is restricted to the qualitative distinctions of positive and negative correlations and of substitution and complementarity, we can confine ourselves to the covariance (5.7). It is seen that the sign of this covariance is not determined by the substitution term $c_{ij}$ (which ought to be the case if the conjecture of the first paragraph of section 1 were correct), but that it is determined by all substitution terms in which one of the commodities $i$ and $j$ enters. More precisely, this covariance is obtained by considering all commodities $h = 1, \ldots, n$ of the entire budget, multiplying the substitution terms $i$ and $j$ with such a commodity with each other, weighting the product with the variance $\sigma_h^2$, and adding. In other words, a large positive covariance indicates that the two commodities $i$ and $j$ "agree" with each other by being both substitutes of or both complementary with most of the commodities of the budget; and this does not necessarily imply that $i$ and $j$ are complementary. Conversely, a large negative covariance indicates that they disagree in the sense that, if one of them is a substitute of $h$, the other is usually complementary with $h$; which does not necessarily imply that $i$ and $j$ are substitutes. It is to be noted, however, that the two terms corresponding to $h = i$ and $j$ in the summation contribute to the expected sign: both $c_{ii}c_{ij}\sigma^2$ and $c_{ij}c_{jj}\sigma_j^2$ have signs opposite to $c_{ij} = c_{ji}$, so that their contribution to the covariance is negative when $i$ and $j$ are substitutes, positive when they are complementary. Furthermore, it will be noted that the weighting by $\sigma_h^2$ implies that those substitution terms $c_{ih}, c_{jh}$ are heavily weighted which belong to a commodity $h$ for which the linear preference coefficients $a_h$ have large variance.

The following alternative interpretation is also instructive. Suppose we write:

$$\sigma_h^2 = 1 \qquad \text{for} \qquad h = 1, \cdots, n. \tag{5.8}$$

This is always possible when suitable units for the quantities of the various commodities are chosen; in the case of a large variance of certain linear preference coefficients $a_h$ it implies that the corresponding quantities $x_h$ are measured in relatively small units. Combining (5.8) and (5.4), we find:

$$\operatorname{var} v_i = \sum_h c_{ih}^2, \tag{5.9}$$

which is a diagonal element of the product matrix $CC'$; or, given the symmetry of the substitution matrix, of $C^2$. Similarly, combining (5.8) and (5.7):

$$\operatorname{cov}(v_i, v_j) = \sum_h c_{ih} c_{jh} \,, \tag{5.10}$$

which is the element in the $i$th row and $j$th column of $C^2$.[5] Hence we have found that, given the assumptions made and given an adequate choice of units, the covariance matrix of the disturbances around the $n$ Engel curves equals the square of the substitution matrix. The presumption of the first paragraph of section 1 was different: from the remarks made there we might have expected that—given an adequate choice of units, etc.—this covariance matrix equals $-C$, substitution corresponding to negative and complementarity to positive residual correlations.

## 6. The Residual Variation in a Case of Correlated Linear Preference Coefficients

It can be maintained that Assumption IVa is not very realistic. For, if a consumer's linear preference coefficient $a_h$ exceeds the group average $\alpha_h$, this can be regarded as an indication that this consumer values $h$ more than the average consumer does; and, if $h$ and $k$ are substitutes, it seems likely that he will value $k$ less than the average consumer does. This argument suggests that $a_h$ and $a_k$ are negatively correlated when $h$ and $k$ are substitutes, and positively correlated when they are complementary. In that case we should replace (5.4) by:

$$\operatorname{var} v_i = \sum_h \sum_k c_{ih} c_{ik} \sigma_h \sigma_k \rho_{hk} \,, \tag{6.1}$$

where the correlation:

$$\rho_{hk} = \frac{\operatorname{cov}(a_h, a_k)}{\sigma_h \sigma_k} \tag{6.2}$$

does no longer vanish for $h \neq k$, but is positive if $h$ and $k$ are complementary ($c_{hk} < 0$) and negative if they are substitutes ($c_{hk} > 0$). To make further progress, it is necessary to make more specific assumptions of the following kind. The correlation $\rho_{hk}$ is of course confined to the interval (-1, 1); similarly, the substitution term $c_{hk}$ is smaller in absolute value than $\sqrt{c_{hh}\, c_{kk}}$, as follows from the semi-definiteness of the substitution matrix. Since it is plausible that $\rho_{hk}$ is an algebraically decreasing function of $c_{hk}$, it seems worthwhile to analyse the implications of:

ASSUMPTION IVb. *The correlations between the linear preference coefficients, as defined in* (6.2), *are given by*

---

[5] $x'CCx = y'y \geq 0$; because $C$ is singular, it is possible to find $x \neq 0$, satisfying $Cx = y = 0$, so that $C^2$ is positive semi-definite.

$$\rho_{hk} = \frac{-c_{hk}}{\sqrt{c_{hh}\, c_{kk}}} \tag{6.3}$$

Combining (6.3) and (6.1), we find:

$$\operatorname{var} v_i = \sum_h \sum_k c_{ih}\, c_{ik}\, \sigma_h\, \sigma_k \frac{-c_{hk}}{\sqrt{c_{hh}\, c_{kk}}} . \tag{6.4}$$

This expression can be simplified if we write:

$$\sigma_h \Big/ \sqrt{-c_{hh}} = 1 \qquad \text{for } h = 1 \ , \ \ldots \ , n \ , \tag{6.5}$$

which is possible by the choice of adequate units. Then (6.4) reduces to:

$$\operatorname{var} v_i = -\sum_h \sum_k c_{ih}\, c_{ik}\, c_{hk} \ , \tag{6.6}$$

which is a diagonal element of the matrix $-C^3$. Similarly, we find for the covariance:

$$\operatorname{cov}(v_i, v_j) = \sum_h \sum_k c_{ih}\, c_{jk}\, \sigma_h\, \sigma_k \frac{-c_{hk}}{\sqrt{c_{hh}\, c_{kk}}} \ , \tag{6.7}$$

or, using (6.5),

$$\operatorname{cov}(v_i, v_j) = -\sum_h \sum_k c_{ih}\, c_{jk}\, c_{hk} \ , \tag{6.8}$$

which is the $(i,j)$-th element of $-C^3$. So we have found that, under the present assumptions, the covariance matrix of the disturbances around the $n$ Engel curves is neither $-C$, nor $C^2$, but $-C^3$.[6]

The economic interpretation of this result is more complicated than that of section 5. The sign of the covariance is no longer determined by the degree to which $i$ and $j$

---

[6] $-C^3$ is positive semi-definite, because it is possible to write $-x'C^3x$ as $-z'Cz$, which is positive semi-definite.

the budget. Instead, we should consider the substitution terms in which $i$ enters together with all commodities $h$, and also the terms in which $j$ enters with all $k$. In section 5 $h$ and $k$ were identical commodities, but this is no longer the case. The substitution terms $c_{ih}$ and $c_{ik}$ are linked together by the third term $c_{hk}$, and the resulting product $c_{ih}c_{jk}c_{hk}$ is to be summed over all $h$ and $k$. What we can say is this: if, for those pairs of commodities $h$, $k$ which are substitutes, $i$ and $j$ are both usually complementary with or substitutes of $h$ and $k$, respectively; and if, for those pairs $h$ and $k$ which are complementary, $i$ is usually a substitute of $h$ and $j$ complementary with $k$ or *vice versa*; then the covariance of $v_i$ and $v_j$ tend to be negative. A similar statement can be given for the case of a positive covariance. Comparing this with the result of section 5, we must say that the distance between this covariance and the simple substitution term $c_{ij}$ has become larger.

## 7. The Case of Correlation Between Linear Preference Coefficients and Income

In this section we shall remove the assumption that no correlation exists between the linear preference coefficients $a_1, a_2, \ldots$ and income. The simplest alternative assumption is that of linear dependence:

$$a_h - \alpha_h = q_h(M - \bar{M}) + w_h , \qquad (7.1)$$

$\bar{M}$ being the average income of the families participating in the budget survey and $w_h$ a disturbance. More precisely:

ASSUMPTION IIIb. *For each family participating in the budget survey, the deviation of its linear preference coefficient $a_h$ from the group average $\alpha_h$ can be described as a stochastic linear function of its income in the budget period in accordance with* (7.1), *where $q_h$ is a coefficient independent of the particular family and $w_h$ a random disturbance with zero mean and a finite covariance matrix which is common to all families; and no correlation exists between $w_h$ and income over the set of all families, for $h = 1, \ldots n$.*

Applying this to (4.4), we find:

$$x_i = -\sum_h c_{ih}(\alpha_h - q_h\bar{M}) - \left(c_i + \sum_h c_{ih}q_h\right)M - \sum_h c_{ih}w_h , \qquad (7.2)$$

where $-(c_i + \Sigma c_{ih}q_h)$ is the new slope of the Engel curve for the set of all families, and

$$v_i^* = -\sum_h c_{ih} w_h \tag{7.3}$$

the new disturbance. It is seen that the new slope differs from the value $-c_i$ which describes the rate of change of consumption with respect to income when the income of the individual consumer varies. We can say that the new slope is biased relative to $-c_i$, the bias being due to the substitution terms and the $q$'s in $-\Sigma c_{ih} q_h$.

The variance of the disturbance $v_i^*$ can be derived as follows:

$$\begin{aligned}
\operatorname{var} v_i^* &= \sum_h \sum_k c_{ih} c_{ik} E(w_h w_k) \\
&= \sum_h \sum_k c_{ih} c_{ik} E\left[\left\{a_h - \alpha_h - q_h (M - \bar{M})\right\} \times \left\{a_k - \alpha_k - q_k (M - \bar{M})\right\}\right] \\
&= \sum_h \sum_k c_{ih} c_{ik} \left\{\operatorname{cov}(a_h, a_k) + q_h q_k \operatorname{var} M - q_h \operatorname{cov}(M, a_k) - q_k \operatorname{cov}(M, a_h)\right\} \\
&= \sum_h \sum_k c_{ih} c_{ik} \{ \operatorname{cov}(a_h, a_k) - q_h q_k \} \operatorname{var} M \ ,
\end{aligned} \tag{7.4}$$

because

$$q_h \operatorname{cov}(M, a_k) = q_k \operatorname{cov}(M, a_h) = q_h q_k \operatorname{var} M \ .$$

In the same way:

$$\operatorname{cov}(v_i^*, v_j^*) = \sum_h \sum_k c_{ih} c_{jk} \{ \operatorname{cov}(a_h, a_k) - q_h q_k \} \operatorname{var} M \ . \tag{7.5}$$

Evidently, if the linear preference coefficients cease to be uncorrelated with income, two effects are of importance for the sign of the residual correlations. First, the variance of the income distribution plays a determining role. Secondly, just because of the presence of the term $-q_h q_k$ var $M$, it is no longer true that the terms $c_{ih} c_{jk}$ for $h \neq k$ are absent in the case of uncorrelated linear preference coefficients, cov$(a_h, a_k) = 0$. More specific results require additional assumptions about the $q$'s, which will not be pursued here.

## 8. Conclusion and Summary

The result of the analysis is negative in the sense that no conditions have been found under which the residual correlation of the Engel curves of two commodities, or at least the sign of this correlation, is determined by the substitution term corresponding to this pair of commodities. Indeed, it is plausible that no simple conditions of this kind exist.

The result is positive, however, in the sense that the residual correlation has been expressed in the theoretical concepts of consumption analysis; at least under certain conditions, the most important of which is that the utility function be quadratic, the coefficients of the quadratic terms being the same for all consumers. Under these conditions the residuals around Engel curves can be said to be determined by substitution terms and by the coefficients of the linear part of the utility functions, provided that these coefficients are not correlated with the consumers' incomes. If this proviso is not fulfilled, the following effects occur: first, the slopes of the Engel curves are biased by the presence of substitution terms; second, the variance of the income distributions plays a role in the residual variances and covariances of the Engel curves; third, the relatively simple result which occurs in the special case of uncorrelated linear preference coefficients (to be considered below) is then no longer applicable.

If the above proviso is fulfilled, a distinction should be made between the case in which the coefficients of the linear part of the preference functions are correlated over the set of all families participating in the budget survey, and that in which they are not correlated. In the latter case the result is, in qualitative terms, the following: the sign of the residual correlation for any pair of Engel curves is not determined by the question whether the two commodities are substitutes or complementary, but by the degree to which these commodities agree by being both substitutes of or complementary with all commodities of the budget, including these two. However, it can be shown that the substitution or complementarity relationship between the two commodities themselves contribute to a correctness of the presumption of section 1 in the sense that they tend to make the residual correlation negative in the case of substitution, positive in the case of complementarity. Hence, if there is only little substitution or complementarity between either of these commodities and all other commodities, this tendency may be sufficient to determine the sign of the residual correlation.

The results are more complicated when the linear preference coefficients are correlated. For the special case considered in section 6 it was found that the sign of the residual correlation for two commodities $i$ and $j$ is not uniquely determined by their substitution term $c_{ij}$ (which is the presumption of section 1), nor even by the terms $c_{ih}$ and $c_{jh}$ in which at least one of the two commodities $i$ and $j$ participate (which is the case of uncorrelated linear preference coefficients), but that a determining role is played by the substitution terms $c_{hk}$ of all pairs of commodities $h, k$ of the entire budget. More precisely, whereas the presumption of section 1 was that—given a choice of appropriate units for the quantities of the various commodities—the covariance matrix of the disturbances around the set of all Engel curves equals $-C$, $C$ being the substitution matrix, we found that this matrix is $C^2$ for the uncorrelated case of the preceding paragraph and $-C^3$ for the correlated case considered here.

It is conceivable that this result is used to determine $-C$ itself. A theorem in matrix algebra[7] states that, if $V$ is a real symmetric and positive semi-definite matrix, there is

[7] See, e.g, Zurmühl (1950), p. 166, for a detailed treatment.

a unique positive semi-definite symmetric matrix $W$, for each positive integer $m$, such that:

$$W^m = V \ .$$

On the basis of this theorem it may be possible to determine $-C$, either starting from $C^2$ or from $-C^3$. A comparison of the alternative outcomes is obviously interesting, but this is largely an empirical subject which will not be pursued here.

**References**

Allen, R.G.D., and A.L. Bowley: 1935, *Family Expenditure*, P.S. King and Son, Ltd., London.

Hicks, J.R.: 1946, *Value and Capital*, 2nd ed., Oxford University Press, London.

Prais, S.J.: 1953, "Non-Linear Estimates of the Engel Curves," *The Review of Economic Studies*, **20**, 98.

Prais, S.J., and H.S. Houthakker, H.S.: 1955, *The Analysis of Family Budgets*, Cambridge University Press, Cambridge.

Theil, H.: 1952-53, "Quantities, Prices and Budget Enquiries," *The Review of Economic Studies*, **19**, 146.

Zurmühl, R.: 1950, *Matrizen*, Springer-Verlag, Berlin/Göttingen/Heidelberg.

CHAPTER 36

# THE INFORMATION APPROACH TO DEMAND ANALYSIS*

HENRI THEIL
*Netherlands School of Economics*
*(Now Erasmus University)*
*Rotterdam, The Netherlands*

ABSTRACT. This article approaches demand analysis in a probabilistic manner. The main ingredient is the value share (the proportion of total expenditure spent on a particular commodity), which can be regarded as a probability in view of the fact that it is nonnegative and adds up to one when summed over all commodities. This ingredient is used for the formulation of price and quantity index numbers and demand equations, partly in the light of information theory.

## 1. Introduction

If we select at random a dollar of a consumer's or a company's budget, what is the chance that it will be spent on the *i*th commodity? The answer is evidently that this is the value or budget share $w_i=p_iq_i/\mu$, where $p_i$ is the price and $q_i$ the quantity bought of that commodity and $\mu$ is income or total expenditure.

This probabilistic question is not very usual in demand analysis, but it does have some merits. First, we note that it stresses that value shares, like probabilities, should be nonnegative and add up to one. This corresponds to the nonnegativity of the $q$'s and with the adding-up criterion in ordinary demand analysis, which are issues that are not handled completely satisfactorily in all forms of demand analysis. Secondly, it is easily seen that, under the usual assumption of given prices and income, knowledge of value shares implies and is implied by knowledge of quantities. The classical analysis in terms of the $q$'s is therefore equivalent to an analysis in terms of the $w$'s. Thirdly, an analysis of value shares opens the possibility of using some of the results of information theory. The present article is in particular concerned with this aspect in its relation to classical demand theory.

The order of discussion is as follows: Section 2 contains an elementary introduction to information theory concepts as far as this is necessary for our purposes. Section 3 considers a simple pair of geometric chain index numbers for prices and quantities which does not satisfy the factor reversal test; the discrepancy with respect to this test is treated analytically with information theory concepts and is considered empirically in section 5. The intermediate section 4 shows that the price index is a

* This article first appeared in *Econometrica*, **33** (1965), 67-87. Reprinted by permission of Elsevier Science Publishers B.V. (North Holland). The author is indebted to Messrs. C.T. Leenders and G.A.C. Beerens for their remarks on an earlier draft of this paper and their computational assistance.

piecewise quadratic approximation to a constant-utility price index, while section 6 shows that the contribution of each commodity to the quantity index is a convenient dependent variable in demand equations. Such demand equations contain real income and relative prices as explanatory variables, but income and prices are deflated by two different indices. Following Barten (1964), we take for the income deflator the price index just mentioned, which represents the income effect of price changes; and for the price deflator, we take another price index which represents the "general" substitution effect of price changes and which approximates the constant-marginal-utility-of-income price index in the same way as the other index approximates the constant-utility price index. This is considered in section 7. Section 8 contains some further extensions.

## 2. Some Concepts of Information Theory

One of the basic intuitive ideas underlying information theory can be described as follows. Suppose that it is known that some event $E$ will occur with probability 0.99 so that it is practically certain that $E$ will take place. Then, if one is told later that $E$ has indeed occurred, this statement contains little information compared with what was known before, viz., that $E$ would take place with probability 0.99. Conversely, suppose that it is known that some other event $E'$ will take place with probability 0.01. If in that case one is later told that $E'$ has nevertheless occurred, one will regard such a statement as containing a good deal of information.

The information concept of the preceding paragraph is an intuitive one, but information theory uses a more precise (and, in fact, quantitative) concept. In accordance with our examples, this concept is defined as a decreasing function of the probability that the event considered will occur. In principle one can take any decreasing function, but there are certain advantages in using the logarithm of the reciprocal of the probability (equal to the negative of the logarithm of the probability itself). The main reason for choosing the logarithmic measure is its additivity for independent events: when $E$ and $E'$ are stochastically independent, the information that both occur is then equal to the information that $E$ occurs plus the information that $E'$ occurs.

Consider now the case in which we have an arbitrary but finite number of possible outcomes. They exclude each other pairwise and one of them will be realized; we write $x_1, x_2, \ldots$ for their probabilities. The information gained by the knowledge that the $i$th event has occurred is then

$$\log\,(1/x_i) = -\log x_i\,. \tag{2.1}$$

We now define the average or expected information as

$$\sum_i x_i \log\,(1/x_i) = -\sum_i x_i \log x_i\,, \tag{2.2}$$

i.e., we weight the individual terms (2.1) according to their probabilities. The expected information is nonnegative and is zero if and only if one of the probabilities is 1 and all others 0. (We interpret $x_i \log x_i = 0$ if $x_i = 0$.) This is a natural result, because we can expect no information from the statement that one of a certain set of events has occurred if it is known in advance that one event has probability 1. The expected information takes its maximum value when all probabilities $x_i$ are equal. This is natural too, for we are then completely in the dark as to the question of which event will occur; the answer to this question will bring more light than in any other situation. It will be noted that in (2.1) and (2.2) the base of the logarithms determines the unit in which information is measured. A widespread procedure is to choose 2 as the base, but this has no advantages for our analysis. All logarithms of this article should be regarded as natural logarithms.[1]

The next step implies that we assume that a certain message is received which changes our ideas about the likelihood of the various events. For example, if the $x_i$ are value shares of consumption this year and if somebody (whom we trust) tells us that income will decrease next year, whereas we had originally expected that income and prices would remain constant, then our ideas about value shares next year will change. Specifically, we expect value shares for "necessities" to be greater and for other commodity groups to be smaller. Let us write $y_1, y_2, \ldots$ for the probabilities attached to the various outcomes after the message changes our probabilities from $x_i$ to $y_i$, how should we measure the expected information content of this message? The answer given by information theory is

$$I(y : x) = \sum_i y_i \log \frac{y_i}{x_i}. \tag{2.3}$$

This measure satisfies the requirement that it should be equal to the reduction of uncertainty caused by the message in the special case when the outcomes were originally equally likely ($x_1 = x_2 = \ldots$). "Reduction of uncertainty" is to be interpreted here as reduction of expected information (in accordance with the ideas set forth in the first paragraph of this section). It is also easily verified that $I(y : x)$ is always nonnegative and zero if and only if $x_i = y_i$ holds for all $i$.[2]

It was just observed that information and uncertainty are related concepts. In fact, there are more such relatives, the oldest being the entropy or disorder concept in physics. In the nineteen-forties and later, a rapid development of information theory in the communication area took place, stimulated particularly by Shannon. Another area of application is mathematical statistics, e.g., Kullback (1958). We may wish to test whether

[1] This has the advantage that the price and quantity index numbers of section 3 and the trend terms of our demand equations in section 6 have a simple percentage-change interpretation.

[2] Consider the numbers $x_i / y_i$; their arithmetic average is 1 if $y_i$ is the frequency of $x_i / y_i$. But $-I(y:x)$ is the logarithm of their geometric mean. The geometric mean of positive numbers (not all equal to each other) is always below the arithmetic mean, hence this logarithm is below $\log 1 = 0$ and therefore $-I(y:x) < 0$ (but $= 0$ if $x_i = y_i$ for all $i$).

a distribution has probabilities $x_i$ or $y_i$; and $I(y:x)$ may then be regarded as the expected information (per observation) in favor of the $y$-hypothesis. We can attach an analogous means to $I(x:y)$, and

$$J(x,y) = I(x:y) + I(y:x) \tag{2.4}$$

is known as the divergence of the two hypotheses. It can be regarded as a measure of the difficulty of discriminating between them and, like its two components, it is obviously nonnegative.

There exists an extensive literature on information theory. A brief and lucid introduction has been provided by Koopman and Kimball (1959).

## 3. On Certain Geometric Index Numbers

We shall now introduce a pair of price and quantity indices by way of chain index numbers. The introduction will be completely heuristic, but a justification of the price index will follow in section 4 and of the quantity index in section 6; the relationship with the information concepts of section 2 will be considered at the end of the present section.

Our starting point is the relative change in price and quantity of commodity $i$ in any given period (compared with the preceding period), where $i = 1, ..., n$. Hence $\Delta(\log p_i)$ and $\Delta(\log q_i)$ are the basic ingredients of this section, where $\Delta$ stands for the operator of first (backward) differences. Following the line of thought with which we started at the beginning of section 1, we can say that the probability associated with the $i$th commodity is the value share $w_i$. Since we are comparing prices (and quantities) of this period with those of the preceding period, an obvious choice is the average of the value shares of the two periods. This leads to:

$$\begin{aligned} \Delta(\log p) &= \sum_i \frac{w_i + (w_i)_{-1}}{2} \Delta(\log p_i), \\ \Delta(\log q) &= \sum_i \frac{w_i + (w_i)_{-1}}{2} \Delta(\log q_i), \end{aligned} \tag{3.1}$$

where $w_i$ is the current and $(w_i)_{-1}$ last period's value share. Equation (3.1) defines a pair of price and quantity index numbers: their log-change is the weighted mean of the corresponding individual log-changes and the weights are the averages of the relevant value shares of the two successive periods. It is easily seen that these index numbers satisfy the time reversal test.[3]

Let us write

$$\mu = \sum_i p_i q_i \tag{3.2}$$

for total expenditure. Then, by adding $\Delta(\log p)$ and $\Delta(\log q)$ we obtain

$$\begin{aligned}\Delta(\log pq) &= \sum_i \frac{w_i + (w_i)_{-1}}{2} \Delta(\log w_i \mu) \\ &= \Delta(\log \mu) + \sum_i \frac{w_i + (w_i)_{-1}}{2} \Delta(\log w_i),\end{aligned}$$

which can also be written as

$$\Delta(\log \mu) = \Delta(\log p) + \Delta(\log q) - \frac{I(w : w_{-1}) - I(w_{-1} : w)}{2}. \tag{3.3}$$

In other words: if we accept the price and quantity indices (3.1), then the factor reversal test is violated; instead, *the log-change in total expenditure is equal to the log-change in the price level plus the log-change in volume minus half the difference between this period's expected information about last period's allocation and last period's expected information about this period's allocation*. In what follows we shall indicate the last term as the "information component" of the log-change in total expenditure. It is tempting to consider physical analogies, but this is beyond the scope of this article.

## 4. On Constant-Utility Price Indices

We shall now give a constant-utility interpretation to the price index whose log-change is given in (3.1). The argument is as follows. The decision as to how money is spent on the various commodities is considered as the result of the maximization of a utility function,

---

[3] Note that the indices (3.1) are similar to Fisher's "ideal" indices to the extent that both are geometric means of Laspeyres-type and Paasche-type index numbers. Fisher's indices, however, are a rather curious mixture of linearity (the underlying Laspeyres and Paasche indices being ratios of linear forms) and log-linearity (the geometric mean), whereas (3.1) is completely log-linear. Note also that (3.1) is closely related to Divisia's approach. Divisia writes $\Sigma(dp_i)q_i / \Sigma p_i q_i$ for the infinitesimal change in the price index; this can also be written as $\Sigma w_i d(\log p_i)$.

$$u = u(q_1, ..., q_n), \tag{4.1}$$

subject to the constraint (3.2), the $p$'s and $\mu$ being regarded as given constants. This leads under certain general conditions to $q$'s which are unique functions of the $p$'s and $\mu$ (the demand equations). Substituting these into (4.1), we obtain utility as a function of the $p$'s and $\mu$, which can be interpreted as the highest utility level attainable given the $p$'s and $\mu$; in what follows $\mu$ will be called "income" for the sake of convenience. Then, for any given set of prices, $p_1^0, ..., p_n^0$, there exists a certain minimum income which enables the consumer to attain any given utility level. This is "real income." For any other set of prices, $p_1^1, ..., p_n^l$, we can in principle compute the income which enables the consumer in this new situation to attain the original preference level. When dividing this income by the real income just mentioned, we obtain the constant-utility price index $f$. It is well known[4] that the elasticity of this index with respect to each individual price is equal to the corresponding value share:

$$\frac{\partial(\log f)}{\partial(\log p_i)} = w_i \qquad (i = 1, ..., n). \tag{4.2}$$

Suppose now that we decide to approximate $\log f$ by a quadratic function of the logarithms of the individual prices. Introducing a temporary change of notation, we write $\psi = \log f$, $a = [(\log p_i)_{-1}]$ for the $n$-element column vector of the logs of last period's prices, $b = [\Delta(\log p_i)]$ for the column vector of the log-changes in prices, $\psi_a$ for the column vector of derivatives of $\psi$ evaluated at last period's prices, and $\Psi$ for the matrix of second-order derivatives. Then we have

$$\psi(a + b) = \psi(a) + \psi_a' b + \tfrac{1}{2} b'\Psi b = \psi(a) + \tfrac{1}{2}[\psi_a + (\psi_a + \Psi b)]'b,$$

which should be interpreted in the sense that the change in the logarithm of $f$, $\Delta(\log f) = \psi(a + b) - \psi(a)$ is equal to the inner product of $b$ and the average of $\psi_a$ and $\psi_a + \Psi b$. But (4.2) specifies that $\psi_a$ is the vector $[(w_i)_{-1}]$; and $\psi_a + \Psi b$ is the vector of derivatives of $\psi$ evaluated at $a + b$ and hence is the vector of current value shares, $[w_i]$. It follows that the inner product just mentioned is nothing else than $\frac{1}{2}\Sigma[w_i + (w_i)_{-1}]\Delta(\log p_i)$. Therefore, $\Delta(\log f) = \Delta(\log p)$ as defined in (3.1); in other words, the price index whose log-change is given in (3.1) is a *period-to-period piecewise quadratic approximation to the constant-utility index*, where "quadratic" means quadratic

[4] See, for example, V. Rajaoja (1958, p. 51). (I am indebted to Professor H.S. Houthakker of Harvard University, who called my attention to Miss Rajoaja's monograph.) Note that the analysis carried out here implies, strictly speaking, that real income remains unchanged. This will in general lead to minor discrepancies, given that we consider period-to-period changes only.

in logarithms (of the index as well as of the individual prices). It seems reasonable to suppose that this approximation will usually be rather accurate. Also the index has the advantage that it does not involve any unknown parameters.

## 5. Some Empirical Evidence

Now that a theoretical justification of the price index (3.1) has been obtained, it is useful to go back to the decomposition (3.3) in order to gain an impression of the order of magnitude of the various components in observed time series. Four cases are considered in the table which follows. Two deal with imports and exports of The Netherlands in 1921-1936; these are divided into fifteen commodity groups. The two other groups are consumption in the interwar period (1921-1939) and the postwar period (1948-1958). The number of commodity groups is here fourteen.[5]

The table shows that there is a substantial difference between the price and volume components on the one hand and the information component on the other hand. The medians (disregarding sign) of the former components are of the order of five per cent per year, those of the latter about one hundredth of one per cent in the case of exports and even smaller for consumption and imports. The largest observed value of the information component is -0.0008, which is associated with the war transition between the years 1939 and 1948. It is obvious that the difference in "disorder" of such years should be relatively large. Nevertheless, even in that case the information component is small compared with the usual values of the other two components.

One may therefore ask, given that the information component is numerically so unimportant, whether it is possible to eliminate it altogether. This can indeed be done. Instead of weighting by $\frac{1}{2}[w_i + (w_i)_{-1}]$ as we did in (3.1) we can use $\theta w_i + (1-\theta)(w_i)_{-1}$ and adjust $\theta$ so that the resulting information component vanishes. This component then becomes $\theta I(w : w_{-1}) - (1 - \theta) I(w_{-1} : w)$, and in order that it vanish we should select

$$\theta = \frac{I(w_{-1} : w)}{J(w_{-1}, w)}, \qquad 1 - \theta = \frac{I(w : w_{-1})}{J(w_{-1}, w)}. \tag{5.1}$$

This implies a price index whose log-change is defined as

$$\sum_i \frac{w_i I(w_{-1} : w) + (w_i)_{-1} I(w : w_{-1})}{J(w_{-1}, w)} \Delta(\log p_i), \tag{5.2}$$

[5] The import and export data used have been published by Kloek and De Wit (1961) and those on consumption by Barten and Vorst (1962). Total consumer expenditure is taken here as excluding rents and "other goods and services."

| | Decomposition of Value Change | | | | | | | | | | |
|---|---|---|---|---|---|---|---|---|---|---|---|
| | $\Delta(\log \mu)$ | $\Delta(\log p)$ | $\Delta(\log q)$ | Information Component | $\theta$ | $\Delta(\log \mu)$ | $\Delta(\log p)$ | $\Delta(\log q)$ | Information Component | $\theta$ | |
| | Imports | | | | | Exports | | | | | |
| 1921-22 | -100 | -215 | 115 | 0.059 | 0.498 | -115 | -232 | 117 | -0.003 | 0.500 | 1921-22 |
| 22-23 | -9 | -20 | 11 | -0.015 | 0.501 | 65 | -44 | 108 | -0.019 | 0.502 | 22-23 |
| 23-24 | 162 | 15 | 147 | -0.006 | 0.501 | 242 | 49 | 193 | -0.006 | 0.500 | 23-24 |
| 24-25 | 38 | -35 | 73 | -0.001 | 0.501 | 85 | -37 | 122 | 0.246 | 0.481 | 24-25 |
| 25-26 | -5 | -79 | 73 | 0.015 | 0.498 | -33 | -81 | 49 | 0.314 | 0.481 | 25-26 |
| 26-27 | 43 | 11 | 32 | -0.004 | 0.501 | 83 | 5 | 77 | 0.106 | 0.492 | 26-27 |
| 27-28 | 52 | 28 | 24 | -0.007 | 0.501 | 45 | 4 | 41 | 0.090 | 0.493 | 27-28 |
| 28-29 | 25 | -8 | 33 | -0.085 | 0.509 | 2 | 4 | -1 | 0.463 | 0.479 | 28-29 |
| 29-30 | -129 | -131 | 2 | -0.029 | 0.503 | -146 | -88 | -58 | 0.014 | 0.497 | 29-30 |
| 30-31 | -245 | -193 | -52 | -0.016 | 0.504 | -270 | -17 | -97 | -0.046 | 0.504 | 30-31 |
| 31-32 | -376 | -204 | -172 | -0.066 | O.505 | -438 | -254 | -184 | -0.090 | 0.506 | 31-32 |
| 32-33 | -72 | -74 | 2 | 0.041 | 0.496 | -154 | -129 | -25 | 0.231 | 0.482 | 32-33 |
| 33-34 | -153 | -80 | -72 | -0.094 | 0.508 | -19 | -10 | -9 | -0.158 | 0.519 | 33-34 |
| 34-35 | -104 | -21 | -83 | -0.042 | 0.506 | -53 | -10 | -43 | 0.248 | 0.482 | 34-35 |
| 35-36 | 83 | 75 | 8 | 0.070 | 0.488 | 99 | 21 | 77 | -0.013 | 0.504 | 35-36 |

Decomposition of Value Change (continued)

| | Δ(log μ) | Δ(log p) | Δ(log q) | Information Component | θ | Δ(log μ) | Δ(log p) | Δ(log q) | Information Component | θ | |
|---|---|---|---|---|---|---|---|---|---|---|---|
| | Consumption Prewar | | | | | Consumption Postwar | | | | | |
| 1921-22 | -11 | -123 | 112 | 0.030 | 0.496 | 814 | 934 | -121 | -0.803 | 0.510 | 1939-48 |
| 22-23 | -58 | -27 | -31 | -0.000 | 0.500 | 148 | 65 | 83 | -0.169 | 0.508 | 48-49 |
| 23-24 | 19 | 7 | 12 | 0.020 | 0.494 | 129 | 101 | 28 | 0.169 | 0.489 | 49-50 |
| 24-25 | -6 | 4 | -10 | -0.009 | 0.504 | 91 | 115 | -24 | 0.000 | 0.500 | 50-51 |
| 25-26 | 2 | -48 | 49 | 0.003 | 0.498 | -4 | -8 | 4 | -0.024 | 0.503 | 51-52 |
| 26-27 | 25 | -20 | 45 | -0.007 | 0.503 | 49 | -12 | 61 | 0.005 | 0.495 | 52-53 |
| 27-28 | 40 | 9 | 31 | 0.000 | 0.500 | 103 | 26 | 77 | 0.002 | 0.499 | 53-54 |
| 28-29 | 17 | -19 | 37 | -0.006 | 0.503 | 76 | 10 | 66 | 0.012 | 0.496 | 54-55 |
| 29-30 | -9 | -56 | 47 | -0.001 | 0.501 | 105 | 9 | 96 | -0.007 | 0.504 | 55-56 |
| 30-31 | -73 | -110 | 37 | 0.006 | 0.498 | 43 | 47 | -4 | 0.002 | 0.500 | 56-57 |
| 31-32 | -103 | -126 | 23 | -0.003 | 0.501 | 9 | 6 | 3 | -0.002 | 0.502 | 57-58 |
| 32-33 | -39 | -16 | -23 | -0.017 | 0.506 | | | | | | |
| 33-34 | -45 | -30 | -14 | 0.030 | 0.493 | | | | | | |
| 34-35 | -35 | -34 | -1 | -0.001 | 0.501 | | | | | | |
| 35-36 | 2 | -12 | 14 | -0.000 | 0.500 | | | | | | |
| 36-37 | 62 | 63 | -0 | 0.030 | 0.482 | | | | | | |
| 37-38 | 25 | 11 | 14 | -0.002 | 0.501 | | | | | | |
| 38-39 | 86 | 5 | 81 | 0.014 | 0.497 | | | | | | |

* All figures (except the θ-values) are multiplied by 1000.

and a volume index defined similarly. The table contains the θ-values of (5.1) for all three sets of data and all years, all of which are very close to ½, so that one should not expect much difference in the values taken by index numbers of the type (5.2) compared with those of (3.1). The procedure (5.2) can be used if one insists upon the satisfaction of the factor reversal test; nevertheless, I do not recommend it wholeheartedly because of the difficulties to which it leads in case one wants to construct partial index numbers. For let us take some subset $S$ of commodities. Applying (3.1), we find for the log-change of its (partial) price index:

$$\Delta(\log p_s) = \frac{\sum_{i\in S} \frac{w_i + (w_i)_{-1}}{2} \Delta(\log p_i)}{\sum_{i\in S} \frac{w_i + (w_i)_{-1}}{2}} .$$

If we imagine that the set of all commodities is divided into such subsets $S$, $S'$, $S''$, ..., and if we decide to construct a price index number for the entire set based on such partial index numbers while following the method (3.1), then, as is easily seen, we obtain precisely the same $\Delta(\log p)$ as we do when we start with the separate commodities. This desirable property is not satisfied by the more complicated index numbers of the type (5.2).

There is some clarifying value in expressing some of these measures in terms of moments of the distribution of value share changes. Let us write $a_i$ for the average of $w_i$ and $(w_i)_{-1}$ and $\delta_i$ for their difference relative to $a_i$:

$$w_i = a_i(1 + \tfrac{1}{2}\delta_i), \quad (w_i)_{-1} = a_i(1 - \tfrac{1}{2}\delta_i), \quad \sum_i a_i = 1, \quad \sum_i a_i\delta_i = 0 . \tag{5.3}$$

Let us also write $m_h$ for the $h$th moment of the δ's:

$$m_h = \sum_i a_i \delta_i^h . \tag{5.4}$$

Then we have:

$$\begin{aligned} I(w : w_{-1}) &= \sum_i a_i(1 + \tfrac{1}{2}\delta_i) \log \frac{a_i(1 + \frac{1}{2}\delta_i)}{a_i(1 - \frac{1}{2}\delta_i)} \\ &= \tfrac{1}{2}m_2 + \tfrac{1}{12}m_3 + \tfrac{1}{24}m_4 + \tfrac{1}{80}m_5 + \tfrac{1}{160}m_6 + \dots , \end{aligned} \tag{5.5}$$

where use is made of the fact that the expansion of log $(1 \pm \frac{1}{2}\delta_i)$ converges since $|\frac{1}{2}\delta_i| < 1$ whenever $w_i$, $(w_i)_{-1} > 0$. In the same way one can derive

$$I(w_{-1} : w) = \frac{1}{2}m_2 - \frac{1}{12}m_3 + \frac{1}{24}m_4 - \frac{1}{80}m_5 + \frac{1}{160}m_6 - \ldots, \tag{5.6}$$

and hence:

$$J(w_{-1}, w) = m_2 + \frac{1}{12}m_4 + \frac{1}{80}m_6 + \ldots,$$

$$\frac{I(w : w_{-1}) - I(w_{-1} : w)}{2} = \frac{1}{12}m_3 + \frac{1}{80}m_5 + \ldots . \tag{5.7}$$

The information component of (3.3) involves only odd moments; hence it vanishes when the distribution of the δ's is symmetric. There is no special reason to assume that it is symmetric in general, but even in case of asymmetry it will usually be small. Take, for example, the situation in which the largest $|\delta_i|$ is 20 per cent; then $\frac{1}{12}m_3$, which is the leading term of the information component, is certainly less than 0.001 in absolute value.

## 6. Consumer Demand Analysis

We continue the discussion which we started in section 4, where it was assumed that the quantities are determined by the maximization of a utility function subject to a budget constraint. The exposition will be simplified by the use of matrix algebra, hence the utility function is written as $u(q)$ and the budget constraint as $p'q = \mu$, where $p$ and $q$ are column vectors of prices and quantities, respectively. The classical approach implies that one considers the Lagrangean expression $u(q) - \lambda(p'q - \mu)$, where the Langrangean multiplier $\lambda$ is known as the marginal utility of income. Maximization with respect of $q_i$ gives the familiar proportionality of marginal utilities and prices:

$$\frac{\partial u}{\partial q_i} - \lambda p_i = 0 . \tag{6.1}$$

These are $n$ equilibrium conditions; together with the budget constraint they are sufficient in number to determine the $q$'s and $\lambda$ as functions of $\mu$ and the $p$'s.

We proceed to consider the derivatives of these functions with respect to their arguments. They are obtained by differentiating the $n$ conditions (6.1) and the budget constraint successively. We write the result in the form

$$\begin{bmatrix} U & p \\ p' & 0 \end{bmatrix} \begin{bmatrix} q_\mu & Q_p \\ -\lambda_\mu & -\lambda'_p \end{bmatrix} = \begin{bmatrix} 0 & \lambda I \\ 1 & -q' \end{bmatrix}, \tag{6.2}$$

where $U = [\partial^2 u/\partial q_i \partial q_j]$ is the Hessian of the utility function and $q_u$, $Q_p$, $\lambda_\mu$, and $\lambda_p$ are derivatives with respect to their index: $q_\mu = [\partial q_i/\partial \mu]$, $Q_p = [\partial q_i/\partial p_j]$, $\lambda_\mu = \partial \lambda/\partial \mu$, and $\lambda_p = [\partial \lambda/\partial p_j]$. By inverting the first matrix on the left of (6.2), we obtain explicit solutions for these derivatives. On the assumption that the Hessian is nonsingular we can write the inverse as

$$\begin{bmatrix} U & p \\ p' & 0 \end{bmatrix}^{-1} = \frac{1}{p'U^{-1}p} \begin{bmatrix} (p'U^{-1}p)U^{-1} - (U^{-1}p)(U^{-1}p)' & U^{-1}p \\ (U^{-1}p)' & -1 \end{bmatrix}$$

and the solution of (6.2) is then:

$$\begin{bmatrix} q_\mu & Q_p \\ -\lambda_\mu & -\lambda'_p \end{bmatrix} \tag{6.3}$$

$$= \begin{bmatrix} \dfrac{1}{p'U^{-1}p} U^{-1}p & \lambda U^{-1} - \dfrac{\lambda}{p'U^{-1}p}(U^{-1}p)(U^{-1}p)' - \dfrac{1}{p'U^{-1}p} U^{-1}pq' \\ -\dfrac{1}{p'U^{-1}p} & \dfrac{\lambda}{p'U^{-1}p}(U^{-1}p)' + \dfrac{1}{p'U^{-1}p} q' \end{bmatrix}.$$

This result can also be written in the following more convenient form:

$$q_\mu = \lambda_\mu U^{-1}p, \tag{6.4}$$

$$Q_p = \lambda U^{-1} - (\lambda/\lambda_\mu) q_\mu q'_\mu - q_\mu q', \tag{6.5}$$

$$\lambda_\mu = (p'U^{-1}p)^{-1}, \tag{6.6}$$

$$\lambda_p = -\lambda q_\mu - \lambda_\mu q \,. \tag{6.7}$$

Consider in particular (6.5), which specifies the matrix of price derivatives of the demand functions as the sum of three terms. The third, $-q_\mu q'$, represents the well-known income effect, the first two represent jointly the substitution effect. For reasons to be given in section 7, we shall indicate the first term, $\lambda U^{-1}$, as the specific substitution effect, the second as the general substitution effect. It will prove instructive to write (6.5) in elasticity form:

$$\frac{\partial(\log q_i)}{\partial(\log p_j)} = \varepsilon_{ij} - \varphi\eta_i\eta_j w_j - \eta_i w_j \,, \tag{6.8}$$

where

$$\varepsilon_{ij} = \frac{\lambda u^{ij} p_j}{q_i}, \; [u^{ij}] = U^{-1}, \; \eta_i = \frac{\partial(\log q_i)}{\partial(\log \mu)},$$

$$\varphi = \frac{1}{\lambda_\mu(\mu/\lambda)} = \frac{\dfrac{1}{\partial(\log\lambda)}}{\partial(\log\mu)} \,. \tag{6.9}$$

Thus, $\eta_i$ is the income elasticity of the demand for the $i$th commodity and $\varphi$ is the reciprocal of the income elasticity of the marginal utility of income, the income flexibility for short.[6]

We now return to the log-changes of section 3 and consider explicit demand equations. Applying a Taylor expansion in logarithms and taking leading terms only, we have for the log-change in the $i$th quantity:

[6] The terminology is unfortunately not completely clear on this concept. Frisch (1959) uses the term "money flexibility," which is defined by him as the reciprocal of our $\varphi$. Houthakker (1960) uses "income flexibility," which is defined by him as $\varphi$ times income, $\mu$; its reciprocal measures the relative change in the marginal utility of income resulting from a small absolute (not relative) income increase.

$$\begin{aligned}\Delta(\log q_i) &= \frac{\partial(\log q_i)}{\partial(\log \mu)}\Delta(\log \mu) + \sum_j \frac{\partial(\log q_i)}{\partial(\log p_j)}\Delta(\log p_j) \\ &= \eta_i \Delta(\log \mu) + \sum_j (\varepsilon_{ij} - \varphi\eta_i\eta_j w_j - \eta_i w_j)\Delta(\log p_j) \\ &= \eta_i[\Delta(\log \mu) - \sum_k w_k \Delta(\log p_k)] + \sum_j (\varepsilon_{ij} - \varphi\eta_i\eta_j w_j)\Delta(\log p_j)\,.\end{aligned} \tag{6.10}$$

This means that we use the income effect as a deflator for income. In the same way we are able to use the general substitution effect as a deflator for prices, which can be shown as follows. By postmultiplying the specific substitution effect in (6.5), $\lambda U^{-1}$, by $(\lambda_\mu/\lambda)p$ we obtain $q_\mu$ [see (6.4)]. For the $i$th row of $\lambda U^{-1}$ this is equivalent to

$$\frac{\lambda_\mu}{\lambda}\sum_j \lambda u^{ij} p_j = \frac{\partial q_i}{\partial \mu}\,,$$

which in turn is equivalent to

$$\sum_j \varepsilon_{ij} = \varphi\eta_i\,, \tag{6.11}$$

see (6.9). On combining this with the last term of (6.10) we obtain:

$$\begin{aligned}\Delta(\log q_i) &= \eta_i[\Delta(\log \mu) - \sum_k w_k \Delta(\log p_k)] \\ &+ \sum_j \varepsilon_{ij}[\Delta(\log p_j) - \sum_k w_k \eta_k \Delta(\log p_k)]\,.\end{aligned} \tag{6.12}$$

The second price index uses the weights

$$w_k\eta_k = \frac{\partial(p_k q_k)}{\partial \mu}\,; \tag{6.13}$$

i.e., its weights are the marginal propensities to consume — contrary to the weights $w_k$ of the first index, which are the average propensities to consume.

Equation (6.12) forms the basis of Barten's recent estimates of Dutch demand functions [1]. He added constant terms to allow for gradual shifts in preferences and estimated these together with the $\eta$'s and $\varepsilon$'s subject to constraint (6.11) and to the following additional constraints:

$$\sum_{i=1}^{n} w_i \eta_i = 1 ; \quad w_i \varepsilon_{ij} = w_j \varepsilon_{ji} , \quad \text{for all pairs } (i,j) , \tag{6.14}$$

where use is made of (6.9) and of the symmetry of the Hessian $U$. The value shares of (6.12) and (6.14) were taken as constant and put equal to the average of the observed shares in the sample period.

The analysis of the preceding pages enables us to handle this value share problem in a more satisfactory manner. First we observe that it is preferable to replace the fixed-weight price index which is used for income deflation, $\Sigma w_k \Delta(\log p_k)$, by the price index (3.1). This follows directly from the constant-utility results of section 4. Secondly, suppose that we multiply both sides of (6.12) by the average of $w_i$ and $(w_i)_{-1}$. This means that the income elasticity which is the first term following the equation sign becomes the elasticity multiplied by the average value share of the two consecutive periods, which has two consequences: the sum of these coefficients is 1, see (6.14), and at the same time this coefficient becomes the weight of $p_i$ in the price index which acts as a deflator for the price term of (6.12). The same multiplication implies also that the $\varepsilon_{ij}$ behind the summation sign becomes $\varepsilon_{ij}$ multiplied by the average value share of the $i$th commodity in the two consecutive periods, which is symmetric in $i$ and $j$ according to (6.14). I therefore suggest the following form of demand function:

$$\frac{w_i + (w_i)_{-1}}{2} \Delta(\log q_i) = A_i + B_i \Delta(\log \bar{\mu}) + \sum_j C_{ij} \Delta(\log \bar{p}_j) + \mu_i , \tag{6.15}$$

where $\bar{\mu}$ is real income and $\bar{p}_j$ is the deflated price of the $j$th commodity:

$$\bar{\mu} = \frac{\mu}{p} , \quad \bar{p}_j = \frac{p_j}{p*} , \quad \Delta(\log p*) = \sum_i B_i \Delta(\log p_i) , \tag{6.16}$$

the price index $p$ being defined in (3.1). It is seen that the dependent variable of the regression (6.15) is *the contribution of the ith commodity to the log-change in the volume index defined in* (3.1). We have from (6.14):

$$\sum_{i=1}^{n} B_i = 1 ; \quad C_{ij} = C_{ji} \quad \text{for all pairs } (i,j) . \tag{6.17}$$

Further, on multiplying both sides of (6.11) by the average of $w_i$ and $(w_i)_{-1}$, we find

$$\sum_j C_{ij} = \varphi B_i \quad (i=1, ..., n) . \tag{6.18}$$

Let us now consider the sum of all $n$ demand equations (6.15):

$$\begin{aligned}\Delta(\log q) &= \sum_i A_i + \Delta(\log \bar{\mu}) + \sum_i \sum_j C_{ij} \Delta(\log \bar{p}_j) + \sum_i u_i \\ &= \sum_i A_i + \Delta(\log \bar{\mu}) + \sum_j (\sum_i C_{ji}) \Delta(\log \bar{p}_j) + \sum_i u_i ,\end{aligned} \quad (6.19)$$

where use has been made of (6.17). Now the sum over $i$ of $C_{ji}$ is $\varphi B_j$ according to (6.18); hence the price term of (6.19) can be written as

$$\begin{aligned}\varphi \sum_j B_j \Delta(\log \bar{p}_j) &= \varphi \sum_j B_j [\Delta(\log p_j) - \sum_k B_k \Delta(\log p_k)] \\ &= \varphi \sum_j B_j \Delta(\log p_j) - \varphi(\sum_j B_j) \sum_k B_k \Delta(\log p_k) = 0 .\end{aligned}$$

Using $\Delta(\log \bar{\mu}) = \Delta(\log \mu) - \Delta(\log p)$, we can therefore conclude that (6.19) may be written in the form:

$$\Delta(\log p) + \Delta(\log q) - \Delta(\log \mu) = \sum_i A_i + \sum_i u_i . \quad (6.20)$$

The left-hand side, however, is nothing else then the *information component* of (3.3), which under the demand specification (6.15) turns out to be *independent of income and prices and equal to the sum of the constant terms and the disturbances of all demand equations.*

The empirical evidence supplied in section 5 suggests that the information component is generally very small. If one is willing to assume that it is generated by a stochastic process with zero mean, one can impose

$$\sum_i A_i = 0 \quad (6.21)$$

as an additional constraint, thus reducing the number of unknown parameters by one. For the information components of the consumption data of section 5 we obtain observed means over time, both prewar and postwar (disregarding the war transition 1939-48), which are less than $5 \times 10^{-6}$ in absolute value. It does not seem unreasonable to assume that this can be replaced by 0 for practical purposes, which can be argued as follows. In order that the trend term of log $q_i$ be of any importance, it should be of the order of 1 percent or more in absolute value. Now the change in log $q_i$ is multiplied by a value share, which is on the average about 0.07 if we have fourteen commodity groups. Hence the $A_i$ which are of any real significance must be at least 0.0005, say, in absolute value.

If their mean over $i$ is estimated as less than 1 percent of that value absolutely, this is effectively zero.

We conclude by noting that the demand equations (6.15) can be written completely in terms of price coefficients (apart from trend and disturbance terms).

Writing

$$C_{i.} = \sum_j C_{ij} \quad \text{and} \quad C_{..} = \sum_i C_{i.} = \sum_i \sum_j C_{ij}, \tag{6.22}$$

we find from (6.17) and (6.18):

$$\varphi = C_{..} \quad \text{and} \quad B_i = C_{i.}/C_{..}, \tag{6.23}$$

and therefore

$$\frac{w_i + (w_i)_{-1}}{2} \Delta(\log q_i) = A_i + \frac{C_{i.}}{C_{..}} \Delta(\log \bar{\mu}) + \sum_j C_{ij} \Delta(\log \bar{p}_j) + u_i, \tag{6.24}$$

where

$$\bar{p}_j = p_j / p*, \quad \Delta(\log p*) = \sum_i \frac{C_{i.}}{C_{..}} \Delta(\log p_i). \tag{6.25}$$

## 7. Further Discussion of the Price Term of the Consumer Demand Equations

The demand equation (6.15) is invariant under monotonic transformations of the utility function except for the price term, $\Sigma C_{ij} \Delta(\log \bar{p}_j)$. The price term as a whole is of course invariant (otherwise at least one other term would not be invariant either); but the coefficients $C_{ij}$ change in general when we shift from one utility function to the next, and the same applies to the income flexibility $\varphi$. Whatever utility function we decide to select for the representation of a given preference ordering, it is always true that the sum of $\varepsilon_{ij}$ (over all $j$) is equal to $\varphi$ times $\eta_i$; also, the sum over $j$ of $C_{ij}$ is equal to $\varphi$ times $B_i$; but the $\varepsilon$'s and $C$'s and $\varphi$ are different for different utility functions, whereas $\eta_i$ and $B_i$ are invariant. Thus, let us replace $u$ by $F(u)$ such that the derivative $F'(u)$ is always positive. Then $\lambda$ is replaced by $F'\lambda$ and the income elasticity of the marginal utility of income becomes [see (6.1)]:

$$\frac{\partial(\log F'\lambda)}{\partial(\log\mu)} = \frac{\partial(\log\lambda)}{\partial(\log\mu)} + \frac{\partial(\log F')}{\partial(\log\mu)}$$
$$= \frac{1}{\varphi} + \frac{\mu}{F'}F''\sum_i \frac{\partial u}{\partial q_i}\frac{\partial q_i}{\partial\mu} = \frac{1}{\varphi} + \frac{F''\lambda\mu}{F'}. \tag{7.1}$$

Apart from the case of linear transformations ($F'' \equiv 0$) this will be different from the reciprocal of the original $\varphi$.

In the last few decades there has been a tendency to regard statements which are not invariant against monotonic transformations of the utility function with some suspicion. This is a perfectly acceptable point of view insofar as one wants to guard himself against statements which make no sense; but it is at least conceivable that by doing so one forgets to examine particular utility functions with particularly interesting properties. In fact, one can mention several such functions. One deals with the case in which the object of evaluation is a probability distribution of outcomes rather than a sure prospect; it was shown by von Neumann and Morgenstern that under relatively weak conditions a utility function exists which handles this situation conveniently in the sense that the consumer (or, more generally, the decision maker) acts as if he maximizes expected utility. Such a utility function may be replaced by a linear increasing function of itself without losing the property just mentioned, but not by an arbitrary increasing function of itself. Another interesting function is real income. This is an indirect utility function, the $q$'s being replaced by $p$'s and $\mu$; and it is invariant against homogeneous linear transformations since it has effectively only one degree of freedom, namely, the unit in which income is expressed.

The utility function which we have in mind for the estimation of $\varphi$ and the $C$'s differs from these two and is much more closely related to the recent work of Frisch (1959), Strotz (1957), Houthakker (1960), and Barten (1964). Suppose that the consumer's preference ordering can be described by an additive utility function:

$$u(q) = \sum_i u_i(q_i). \tag{7.2}$$

Then, for this particular utility function the Hessian and its inverse are diagonal; the same applies to $[\varepsilon_{ij}]$ and $[C_{ij}]$, see (6.9), so that each demand equations contains only one explicit price variable, the effect of all other prices being handled by deflation. It may be that (7.2) is too simple, but it can be generalized fairly easily, as Strotz and Barten have shown. The Hessian and its inverse may be block diagonal; then for each $i$ there is only a limited number of $C_{ij}$'s different from zero. Another case is that of a Hessian whose off-diagonal elements are mostly zero and small (relative to the geometric mean of the corresponding diagonal elements) whenever they are not zero. In such a case of "almost additivity" the inverse of the Hessian has zero elements (approximately) in the corresponding places, and the same applies to $[C_{ij}]$.

The utility function which we suggest for the estimation of $\varphi$ and the $C$'s has nothing to do with decision making under certainty, nor with the construction of cost-of-living index numbers, but with a description of quantities bought in terms of income and prices. It is simply a matter of scientific efficiency that this description should be made by means of the smallest possible number of parameters. Suppose then that the preference ordering can be represented by an additive utility function, (7.2); we see from (6.8) that this implies

$$\frac{\partial(\log q_i)}{\partial(\log p_j)} = -\varphi\eta_i\eta_j w_j - \eta_i w_j, \tag{7.3}$$

for all pairs $(i,j)$, $i \neq j$. In other words, there exists a number $\varphi$ such that (7.3) holds for all these pairs, and the price terms of (6.15) contain then only $n$ unknown parameters ($C_{ij}$) for all demand equations combined (which is the minimum number attainable). Note that the existence of such a $\varphi$ can be verified by means of observations under ideal conditions. Note also that this makes utility unique up to a linear transformation, because other transformations lead to a different value of $\varphi$ (see (7.1)).

It may be that there exists no $\varphi$-value such that (7.3) holds for all pairs $(i,j)$. But, in principle at least, one can always compare the left hand side with the right hand side for alternative values of $\varphi$ and choose that $\varphi$ for which (7.3) holds for the largest number of pairs $(i,j)$. This is the procedure which we recommend: for purposes of demand analysis *use that utility function* (unique up to a linear transformation given that $\varphi$ is fixed)[7] *for which* (7.3) *is true for the maximum number of pairs* $(i,j)$, *and the associated* $C_{ij}$ *are then zero.* When (7.3) holds for any particular pair $(i,j)$, the substitution effect for this pair involves only the "general" term $-\varphi\eta_i\eta_j w_j$; it does not involve anything that depends on the combination $(i,j)$, only quantities that are specific for $i$ and $j$ separately ($\eta_i$, $\eta_j$, $w_j$, and also $\varphi$ which refers to all commodities simultaneously). It is therefore not unreasonable to call $-\varphi\eta_i\eta_j w_j$ the general substitution effect (as Houthakker, 1960 suggested), and the procedure suggested here amounts to an effort to minimize the number of specific substitution effects. In most practical cases one will have to decide a priori about the substitution effects which are admitted to be nonzero (rather than to estimate all $n^2$ price elasticities and find the appropriate $\varphi$). This requires some intuition (possibly introspection), but the use of intuition prior to analysis is common in most empirical work. In fact, we can say that the present approach gives some guidance to intuition as to which prices should be introduced into the demand equations (viz., by means of the inverted Hessian). The approach which confines itself to statements which are invariant against monotonic transformations of the utility function gives very little guidance; for example, it does not make clear why the price of butter is more promising than the price of sugar as an explanatory variable in the demand equation for margarine.

The final point to be considered here is the nature of the price deflator $p^*$ used in obtaining (6.15). We found that the income deflator is the price index defined in (3.1),

[7] It may be that there are two (or more) $\varphi$'s which maximize the number of pairs $(i,j)$ for which (7.3) holds. This leads to different, but equivalent, descriptions of the quantities bought in terms of income and prices.

that the left hand variable is the contribution of the $i$th commodity to the volume index defined in (3.1), and that the sum of all demand equations leads directly to the information component; all these concepts are familiar from section 3, but the price deflator is not. We may compare the two deflators ($p$ and $p^*$) as follows. The log-change of the income deflator is the expected value of the log-changes of the individual prices when the probabilities attached to the latter are the average of this period's and last period's value shares. This is a statistical interpretation which is completely in line with what has been said at the beginning of section 1. The log-change of the price deflator is the expected value of the same individual log-changes but the probabilities are now the marginal propensities to consume, see (6.13). They answer the question: if we raise the consumer's income by a certain (small) amount and if we pick at random a dollar of this increase, what is the chance that it is spent on the $i$th commodity? Evidently, the two indices are quite similar from this point of view; the main difference is that the probabilities of $p^*$ may have the unusual property of being negative, viz., when a commodity is inferior ($\eta_i$, $B_i < 0$).

To analyze the economic interpretation of the price deflator it is useful to go back to (6.7), which specifies

$$\frac{\partial \lambda}{\partial p_i} = -\lambda \frac{\partial q_i}{\partial \mu} - \lambda_\mu q_i \,.$$

On multiplying both sides by $p_i / \lambda$ we obtain

$$\frac{\partial (\log \lambda)}{\partial (\log p_i)} = -\frac{\partial (p_i q_i)}{\partial \mu} - \frac{w_i}{\varphi} \,.$$

Recalling that $1/\varphi$ is the income elasticity of $\lambda$, we conclude

$$d(\log \lambda) = \frac{1}{\varphi} d(\log \mu) - \sum_i \left( \frac{\partial (p_i q_i)}{\partial \mu} + \frac{w_i}{\varphi} \right) d(\log p_i) \,,$$

which can be written in the following more convenient form:

$$d(\log\lambda) + \sum_i \frac{\partial (p_i q_i)}{\partial \mu} d(\log p_i) = \frac{1}{\varphi} [d(\log\mu) - \sum_i w_i d(\log p_i)] \,. \tag{7.4}$$

Note that $d(\log \lambda)$ is an invariant concept. We are now working with a utility function which is unique up to a linear transformation. Hence $\lambda$ is unique up to a multiplicative constant, so that log $\lambda$ is unique up to an additive constant, which drops out when we taken the differential.

It is easily seen that the right hand side (7.4) is effectively $1/\varphi$ times the change in log $\bar{\mu}$ when we consider period-to-period changes. In the same way the left hand side is then the change in log $(\lambda p^*)$, see (6.16). Hence *the dependence of the marginal utility of income on prices and income is, as far as prices are concerned, determined by two indices: the income deflator and the price deflator*. Going back to section 4, we see that if money income, $\mu$, changes, the utility level is affected unless the $\mu$-change is compensated for by a change in prices such that $\mu/f$ remains constant; and we therefore say that $f$ is the constant-utility price index. In precisely the same way we see from (7.4) that if *real* income changes, the marginal utility of income, $\lambda$, is affected unless this change is compensated for by such a change in prices that the price term on the left of (7.4) is equal to the right hand side of that equation. But we just found how this price term is related to our price deflator. Therefore, *the price deflator $p^*$ approximates the constant-marginal-utility-of-income index as the income deflator p approximates the constant-utility index.*

The log-change of the index $p^*$ is derived from the log-changes of the individual prices by weighting proportionally to the marginal propensities to consume. This index is not at all new and, in fact, dates back to the early nineteen-thirties. Frisch (1932, pp. 74-77) called it the "marginal living index." Returning again to section 4, we have the following alternative interpretation. Starting from any given set of prices $p_i^0$ and a given preference level, we defined real income as the minimum income that enables the consumer when confronted with these prices to attain that utility level. Then we considered another set of prices, $p_i^1$, and computed the income which in the new situation enables the consumer to attain the same utility level. The constant-utility index is defined as a ratio; and the price deflator (the "marginal index") is the derivative of the latter income with respect to real income.[8]

## 8. Some Further Extensions

The preceding pages have shown that information theory is useful for demand analysis in more than one respect. It suggests useful definitions for price and quantity index numbers and also a promising specification of demand equations which takes constraints on coefficients of different equations into account. The approach can be extended even further. Statistically speaking, we can regard the log-changes of our price and quantity index numbers as expected values of the underlying distributions of individual price and quantity log-changes. We can also consider higher moments. The variance of the logarithmic price and quantity changes measure the extent to which the price and quantity structure changes from one year to the next, "structure" being defined as the set of ratios

---

[8] For details, see V. Rajaoja (1958, pp. 26-26). In chapter IV of her monograph, Miss Rajaoja considers cases related to additivity and obtains results which are similar to those of the authors mentioned in the third paragraph of this section. We may also refer to a similar approach by I.F. Pearce (1961, p. 512).

of the individual prices and quantities to the index value. In the same way we have the covariance of the logarithmic price and quantity changes, which is generally negative due to the tendency to substitute in favor of commodities which have become relatively cheaper. These second-order moments, which are closely related to the divergence $J(w_{-1}, w)$ of the value shares of the two years, were analyzed recently by Kloek and Theil (1965) in a comparison of different countries (rather than successive years).

Another extension deals with the definition of a volume index whose log-change is defined as the weighted average of the individual log-changes with the $B$'s (rather than the $w$'s) as weights. This is analogous to the way in which the logarithmic price changes are weighted in the price deflator. The difference between the log-change in this volume index and that of (3.1),

$$\sum_{i=1}^{n} \left( B_i - \frac{w_i + (w_i)_{-1}}{2} \right) \Delta (\log q_i) , \tag{8.1}$$

can be regarded as the log-change in a "luxury index." The expression (8.1) is positive when on the average the quantities of luxuries ($B_i > \frac{1}{2}[w_i + (w_i)_{-1}]$) increase more or decrease less than the quantities of necessities. In the special case of additive preferences the log-change in the luxury index can be expressed easily and elegantly in prices and income. It turns out that the variance of the income elasticities is of special importance for this index. Reference is made to Theil (1964).

A subject which we did not consider in the previous pages is to what extent it is possible to apply information theory *itself* to demand analysis; that is, whether we can measure the information content of messages on changes in income and prices when these changes are substituted into demand equations. This subject will be considered in a later publication, but it is appropriate to make some remarks on it in order to avoid the impression that some of the *concepts* of information theory are useful for the specification of demand equations but the information *idea* is not. Suppose then that a complete system of demand equations (6.15) has been specified (with numerical coefficients $A_i$, $B_i$, $C_{ij}$). Suppose also that we have forecasts of the changes in income and prices during the next year. Then we can predict the changes in quantities and in value shares and hence obtain predicted value shares $\hat{w}_i$, ..., $\hat{w}_n$ for next year. These forecasts will differ from the corresponding observed value shares $w_i$, ..., $w_n$ for several reasons:

(1) The predicted income and price changes differ from the changes that will be observed.

(2) The numerical specification of the coefficients $A_i$, $B_i$, $C_{ij}$ is subject to sampling errors.

(3) The demand equations are subject to random disturbances, which are replaced by their conditional expectations — given the available data — for prediction purposes.

(4) Finally, we have the possibility of specification errors in the model and of measurement errors in the variables. These can in principle be combined with the

disturbances mentioned under (3), although such a combination implies that the disturbances cease to have their classical statistical properties.

Information theory enables us to evaluate the merits of the predicted value shares in the light of the observed shares, the idea being the following. We regard the observed shares as a posterior message, obtained after the predicted shares (the prior message) became available. The information obtained from this posterior message, given the prior message, is

$$\sum_{i=1}^{n} w_i \log \frac{w_i}{\hat{w}_i} \, . \tag{8.2}$$

If this information takes a large value, this means that the posterior message (the observed value shares) differs substantially from the prior message (the predicted value shares), so that the forecasts are highly inaccurate. Conversely, if the information supplied by the observed values, given the forecasts, is very small, the latter are accurate predictions. This is the reason why the expression (8.2) was proposed by Tilanus and Theil (1965) as the *information inaccuracy* of the forecasts $\hat{w}_i$, ..., $\hat{w}_n$. It is in principle possible to decompose the information inaccuracy according to the various causes of the forecast errors mentioned above.

We conclude by noting that when the relative prediction errors are small, the information inaccuracy is very close to a quadratic criterion. (These relative errors will be small in general, because the value shares themselves do not change very much from one year to the next.) Let us write

$$\varepsilon_i = \frac{\hat{w}_i - w_i}{w_i} \tag{8.3}$$

for the relative error; then the information inaccuracy (8.2) can be expanded as follows:

$$\begin{aligned} \sum w_i \log \frac{w_i}{w_i(1+\varepsilon_i)} &= -\sum w_i \log(1+\varepsilon_i) \\ &= -\sum w_i (\varepsilon_i - \tfrac{1}{2}\varepsilon_i^2 + \tfrac{1}{3}\varepsilon_i^3 - \ldots) \\ &= \tfrac{1}{2}\sum w_i \varepsilon_i^2 - \tfrac{1}{3}\sum w_i \varepsilon_i^3 + \ldots \, . \end{aligned} \tag{8.4}$$

This procedure (which is analogous to that of section 5) shows that in first approximation the information inaccuracy is equal to half the weighted variance of the relative forecast errors, the weights being equal to the corresponding "true" value shares.

**References**

Barten, A.P.: 1964, "Consumer Demand Equations under Conditions of Almost Additive Preferences," *Econometrica*, **32**, 1-38.

Barten, A.P., and J.I. Vorst: 1962, "De consumptieve uitgaven van gezinshuishoudingen in Nederland," Report 6202 of the Econometric Institute of the Netherlands School of Economics, Rotterdam, The Netherlands.

Frisch, R.: 1932, *New Methods of Measuring Marginal Utility*. Volume 3 of *Beiträge zur Ökonomischen Theorie*, J.C.B. Mohr, Tübingen, Germany.

Frisch, R.: 1959, "A Complete Scheme for Computing All Direct and Cross Elasticities in a Model with Many Sectors," *Econometrica*, **27**, 177-196.

Houthakker, H.S.: 1960, "Additive Preferences," *Econometrica*, **28**, 244-257.

Kloek, T., and G.M. De Wit: 1961, "Best Linear and Best Linear Unbiased Index Numbers," *Econometrica*, **29**, 602-616. (The underlying data were not published in this article but in the corresponding Report 6006 of the Econometric Institute of the Netherlands School of Economics.)

Kloek, T., and H. Theil: 1965, "International Comparisons of Prices and Quantities Consumed," *Econometrica*, **33**, 535-556.

Koopman, B.O., and G.E. Kimball: 1959, "Information Theory," in *Notes on Operations Research 1959*, assembled by the Operations Research Center, M.I.T., The Technology Press, Massachusetts Institute of Technology, pp. 188-210.

Kullback, S.: 1958, *Information Theory and Statistics*, John Wiley and Sons, New York and London.

Pearce, I.F.: 1961, "An Exact Method of Consumer Demand Analysis," *Econometrica*, **29**, 499-516.

Rajaoja, V.: 1958, *A Study in the Theory of Demand Functions and Price Indexes*, Societas Scientiarum Fennica, Helsinki, Finland.

Strotz, R.H.: 1957, "The Empirical Implications of a Utility Tree," *Econometrica*, **25**, 269-280.

Theil, H.: 1964, "Simultaneous Estimation of Complete Systems of Demand Equations," Mimeographed lecture notes, University of Chicago Press, Chicago, Illinois.

Tilanus, C.B., and H. Theil: 1965, "The Information Approach to the Evaluation of Input-Output Forecasts," *Econometrica*, **33**, 847-862.

# SECTION 3.2: INDEX NUMBERS

CHAPTER 37

# BEST LINEAR INDEX NUMBERS OF PRICES AND QUANTITIES*

HENRI THEIL[1,2]
*Netherlands School of Economics, (now Erasmus University), Rotterdam, The Netherlands* and *Stanford University California, U.S.A.*

ABSTRACT. This article deals with the construction of price and quantity index numbers for an arbitrary number of periods (or geographical units) which satisfy the requirement that the total sum of squares of the discrepancies between true and index-constructed cross-values is minimized. Special attention is paid to the aggregation problem which arises when this method is applied to a group of commodities as well as to subgroups.

## 1. Introduction

The subject of index numbers is one of the oldest in statistics and also, as regards the more specialized subject of cost of living index numbers, an old one in economics. There are two distinct lines of approach to this subject, as was stressed by Professor Frisch in his still inspiring Annual Survey (1936) in the January, 1936 issue of *Econometrica*: there is a statistical approach which is concerned with the specification of a central tendency of price and quantity ratios that is optimal in some statistical sense, and there is an economic approach which tries to specify price indices of varying batches of consumer goods corresponding with a constant level of satisfaction.

The present article is of the statistical type, but it differs from the usual formulation insofar as it is not (at least not necessarily) concerned with one single pair of periods. Normally, one takes a "base year" and a "current year" and formulates an index number for the latter year with the former as a base. This procedure can be repeated for several different current years but it is generally true that in each of these the index numbers are uniquely determined by prices and quantities of that year and of the base year. Here we shall consider index numbers for an arbitrary number of periods; they are determined by the prices and quantities of all separate periods. This implies that the procedure is "ex-

* This article first appeared in *Econometrica*, **28** (1960), 464-480. Reprinted with the permission of The Econometric Society.

[1] This work was supported by the Office of Naval Research under Task NR 047-004 and will be included in the Reprint Series of the Stanford Institute for Mathematical Studies in the Social Sciences.

[2] The author is indebted to Professor Kenneth J. Arrow of Stanford University, to Mr. P.J.M. van den Bogaard of the Econometric Institute of the Netherlands School of Economics, and to Mr. J. van IJzeren of the Technical University of Eindhoven for their valuable comments.

post," since it can be applied only after the individual prices and quantities for the whole period have become available. The procedure can therefore be applied for a computation of price and quantity indices to be used for the estimation of an econometric model. It can also be applied, however, on a current basis when one is interested in price and quantity comparisons of different geographical units, the reason being that it is immaterial from a mathematical point of view whether the symbol $t$ (to be used from section 3 on) refers to geographical or to time units. This alternative application seems to become of increasing importance in view of the interest shown in price and quantity comparisons of different countries in recent years. The exposition will, however, be largely confined to variation over time.

The order of discussion is as follows. The approach is introduced geometrically in section 2 and pursued algebraically in section 3. It is a "linear" approach in the sense that the price index vector is a linear function of the matrix of individual prices, and it is "best" in the sense that the linear function is chosen such that a quadratic form in certain discrepancies is minimized; it is therefore closely related to principal-component analysis.[3] Sections 2 and 3 deal with prices only, but for quantities the approach is completely analogous, as will be explained in section 4. After this, prices and quantities are combined in sections 5 and 6. Section 7 deals with a fitting index which measures the statistical quantity of the price and quantity index vectors; section 8 deals with partial index numbers and problems of aggregation; and section 9 contains some concluding remarks.

## 2. A Geometric Picture

Suppose there are $n$ commodities and $T$ periods, the price of the $i$th commodity in the $t$th period being $p_i(t)$. For each period, we can represent all $n$ prices by a point or a vector in an $n$ dimensional cartesian space. This leads to $T$ "price points" $P_1, P_2, \ldots, P_T$ and to $T$ "price vectors" $OP_1, OP_2, \ldots, OP_T$. If all prices would move proportionally, these points would lie on a straight line (the "price line") through the origin, the parametric representation of which is:

$$p_i = a_i p \qquad (i = 1, \ldots, n) , \tag{2.1}$$

the $a_i$ being positive constants. In general, however, this is not more than approximately true, in which case we obtain a picture like the one sketched below for $n = 2$. No single straight line then goes through the origin and all $T$ price points simultaneously. So we have to *fit* a price line through the origin, to project the price points on this line (this projection being not necessarily orthogonal), and to take the lengths of the projection

[3] There is a difference from the usual type of principal-component analysis in that we consider here two sets of variables, viz., prices and quantities.

vectors $OP_1'$, $OP_2'$, . . . , $OP_T'$ as index numbers. This will be worked out algebraically in the next section.

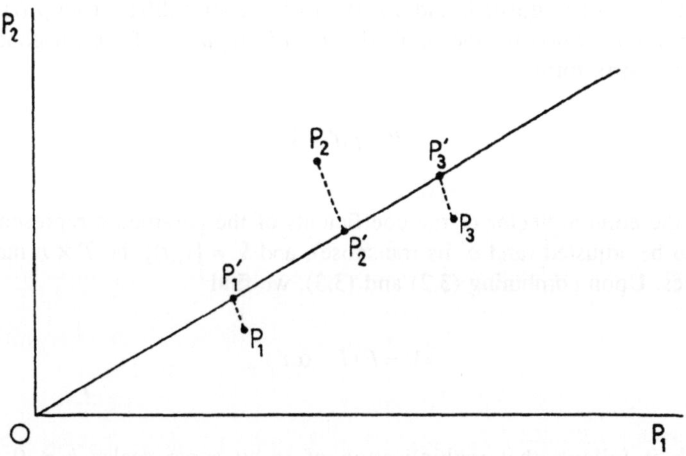


Figure 1

## 3. General Best Linear Price Index Numbers

The individual prices $p_i(t)$ and the values $p(t)$ taken by the price index number can be conveniently written in matrix form:

$$P = \begin{bmatrix} p_1(1) & \dots & p_n(1) \\ \dots & \dots & \dots \\ p_1(T) & \dots & p_n(T) \end{bmatrix}; \quad p = \begin{bmatrix} p(1) \\ \vdots \\ p(T) \end{bmatrix}. \tag{3.1}$$

Our problem is that of an appropriate description of the columns of $P$ by a single column $p$ subject to the constraint that each component $p(t)$ of $p$ be the same linear function of the corresponding row of $P$:

$$p = P\alpha, \tag{3.2}$$

$\alpha$ being a column vector of $n$ components. This implies that our price index has fixed weights.

It follows from the remarks made at the end of section 2 that the parametric representation (2,1) does not in general hold without errors. In fact, the implied value of the $i$th price in the $t$th period according to this representation is $a_i p(t)$, $a_i$ being determined by the price line to be adjusted; and $a_i p(t)$ will in general differ from $p_i(t)$. Let us then write $v_i(t) = p_i(t) - a_i p(t)$ for the implied *price discrepancy* of the $i$th good and the $t$th period; or in matrix form

$$P = pa' + V \ , \tag{3.3}$$

where $a$ is the column vector of the coefficients of the parametric representation of the price line to be adjusted (and $a'$ its transpose), and $V = [v_i(t)]$ the $T \times n$ matrix of price discrepancies. Upon combining (3.2) and (3.3), we find

$$V = P(I - \alpha a') \ , \tag{3.4}$$

from which it follows that multiplication of $\alpha$ by some scalar $k \neq 0$ followed by multiplication of $a$ by $1/k$ does not affect $V$. Hence, if our goal is to minimize the elements of $V$ in some sense, this can at most lead to a specification of $\alpha$ and $a$ except for two multiplicative scalars which are reciprocal to each other.

Our procedure will be to choose $\alpha$ and $a$ such that we minimize the following quadratic form in the $V$-elements:[4]

$$\sum_{i,j} g_{ij} \sum_t v_i(t) v_j(t) = \operatorname{tr}(GV'V) \ , \tag{3.5}$$

where G = $[g_{ij}]$ is a symmetric and positive-definite or semi-definite matrix of order $n$. Combining (3.4) and (3.5), we see that this implies a minimum with respect of $\alpha$ and $a$ of

$$\begin{aligned} \operatorname{tr}(GV'V) &= \operatorname{tr}(GP'P) - \operatorname{tr}(Ga\alpha'P'P) - \operatorname{tr}(GP'P\alpha a') + \operatorname{tr}(Ga\alpha'P'P\alpha a') \\ &= \operatorname{tr}(GP'P) - 2\alpha'P'PGa + (\alpha'P'P\alpha)(a'Ga) \ . \end{aligned} \tag{3.6}$$

Partial differentiation of (3.6) with respect to $\alpha$ and $a$ gives:

---

[4] The trace of some square matrix $A$ (tr$A$), which is used rather frequently in what follows, is defined as the sum of the diagonal elements of $A$. The following simple properties are applied: tr($AB$) = tr($BA$) if the product matrices $AB$ and $BA$ both exist; tr($A + B$) = tr$A$ + tr$B$ if $A + B$ exists; tr$k$ = $k$ if $k$ is a scalar.

$$\frac{1}{2}\frac{\partial\,\mathrm{tr}(GV'V)}{\partial\,\alpha} = -P'PGa + (a'Ga)P'Pa = 0 \tag{3.7}$$

and

$$\frac{1}{2}\frac{\partial\,\mathrm{tr}(GV'V)}{\partial\,a} = -GP'P\alpha + (\alpha'P'P\alpha)Ga = 0\ . \tag{3.8}$$

Premultiplying (3.8) by $P'P$ and applying (3.7) gives

$$-P'PGP'P\alpha + (\alpha'P'P\alpha)(a'Ga)P'P\alpha = 0\ ,$$

which can be written in two alternative forms:

$$[P'PG - (\alpha'P'P\alpha)(a'Ga)I]P'P\alpha = 0\ ; \tag{3.9}$$

$$P'P[GP'P - (\alpha'P'P\alpha)(a'Ga)I]\alpha = 0\ . \tag{3.10}$$

Similarly, after premultiplying (3.7) by $G$ and applying (3.8), we obtain

$$[GP'P - (\alpha'P'P\alpha)(a'Ga)I]Ga = 0\ ; \tag{3.11}$$

$$G[P'PG - (\alpha'P'P\alpha)(a'Ga)I]a = 0\ . \tag{3.12}$$

From (3.9) we conclude that either $P'P\alpha = 0$, or $P'P\alpha$ is a characteristic vector of the matrix $P'PG$; similarly, from (3.11), that either $Ga = 0$, or $Ga$ is a characteristic vector of $GP'P$. To find out which of these alternatives is relevant for our purpose, we substitute (3.7) [or (3.8)] in (3.6) and obtain

$$\mathrm{Min}\,[\mathrm{tr}(GV'V)] = \mathrm{tr}(GP'P) - (\alpha'P'P\alpha)(a'Ga)\ , \tag{3.13}$$

$\alpha$ and $a$ being here the optimal vectors. From (3.13) it follows that, if we take $P'P\alpha = 0$ or $Ga = 0$, then $\mathrm{tr}(GV'V) = \mathrm{tr}(GP'P)$; but if we take for $PP\alpha$ and $Ga$ the characteristic vectors of $P'PG$ and $GP'P$, respectively corresponding to the largest root, then we arrive at a lower value of $\mathrm{tr}(GV'V)$ provided that this root is positive. Now it is well known that $P'PG$ and $GP'P$ have the same roots,[5] and that this also applies to the roots of $PGP'$.[6]

[5] When two matrices $A$ and $B$ (like $P'P$ and $G$) are square and of the same order, then $AB$ and $BA$ have the same roots. See, e.g., Zurmühl (1958, p. 162).

But the last matrix is positive-definite or positive semidefinite, so that its largest root is positive except when it is a zero matrix; and this exception can be easily excluded.[7] Therefore, $P'P\alpha$ is a characteristic vector of $P'PG$, and $Ga$ is a characteristic vector of $GP'P$; they both correspond with the largest root, which has the same value in the two cases. We shall write this root as

$$\lambda^2 = (\alpha' P' P \alpha)(a' G a) \ , \tag{3.14}$$

$\alpha$ and $a$ being again the optimal vectors here.

To analyze the weights of the price index number (the vector $\alpha$), we consider (3.10) and write

$$c = [GP'P - (\alpha' P' P \alpha)(a' G a) I]\alpha \ . \tag{3.15}$$

Then (3.10) states that $P'Pc = 0$, which implies that $c = 0$ or that $c$ is a non-zero vector which describes the linear dependence of the columns of $P'P$. The latter alternative is obviously inapplicable when $P'P$ is non-singular; in that case, therefore, it is certain that $c = 0$, which implies that $\alpha$ is (just as $Ga$) a characteristic vector of $GP'P$ corresponding with the largest root. In the alternative case when $P'P$ is singular it is not necessarily true that $\alpha$ must be chosen as a characteristic vector of $GP'P$ corresponding with root $\lambda^2$; but it is easily shown that we attain the goal of minimization if we do so. For it follows from (3.13) that $\mathrm{tr}(GV'V)$ is minimized if we make $(\alpha' P' P \alpha)(a' Ga)$ as large as possible; and we found in the preceding paragraph that this largest value is the largest root of $GP'P$. Clearly, we may specify $\alpha$ in any manner provided this condition is not violated; and it follows then from (3.10) that the choice of $\alpha$ as a characteristic vector of $GP'P$ corresponding with root $\lambda^2$ does satisfy this condition. In the same way, it follows from (3.12) that $a$ is (just as $P'P\alpha$) a characteristic vector of $P'PG$ corresponding with root $\lambda^2$ if $G$ is a positive-definite matrix, and that we attain the goal of minimization if we choose $a$ in this way even when $G$ is positive semidefinite.

The discussion of the preceding paragraph shows that there is an indeterminacy as to $\alpha$ in the case when $P'P$ is singular. To see what is at stake, we write $Pc = 0$ instead of $P'Pc = 0$, which are equivalent statements.[8] Then the alternative to $\alpha$ as a characteristic vector of $GP'P$, viz., $Pc = 0$ and $c \neq 0$, implies a linear dependence of the columns of the matrix of individual prices. This, in turn, simply implies that the price of one of the commodities depends on the prices of the other commodities, the relationship

---

[6] More precisely, when $P'PG$ and $PGP'$ are of the same order, they have equal roots; and if the order of one of them exceeds that of the other by $k$ (say), then the former has $k$ additional zero roots. This, of course, does not affect the largest root. See Zurmühl, *loc. cit.*

[7] In what follows we shall consider in particular the case in which $G$ is a matrix of positive elements. Then $PGP'$ is a zero matrix only if $P$ is zero.

[8] Proof: premultiplying $P'Pc = 0$ by $c'$, we obtain $c'P'Pc = (Pc)'Pc = 0$, which implies $Pc = 0$.

being linear with constant coefficients. It is then clear that in such a case an infinite number of weighting systems exists which all lead to the same price index vector.

The price index vector just mentioned is not characterized by any indeterminacy of this kind. This is seen immediately if we write $Pc = 0$ in the form

$$[PGP' - (\alpha'P'P\alpha)(a'Ga)I]P\alpha = 0 \ , \tag{3.16}$$

which shows that $P\alpha = p$ is a characteristic vector of $PGP'$ corresponding to the largest root $(\lambda^2)$.[9]

## 4. The Quantity Side

Quantities are dealt with in a manner which is perfectly similar, both geometrically and algebraically. The present section is therefore exclusively devoted to the definition of relevant symbols.

We write $Q = [q_i(t)]$ for the $T \times n$ matrix of quantities of the various goods in the various periods, and $q$ for the column vector of the $T$ values of the quantity index. Then

$$q = Q\beta \quad \text{and} \quad Q = qb' + W \ , \tag{4.1}$$

which state that the quantity index is a fixed-weight index ($\beta$ being the vector of weights), that there are $T\,n$ *quantity discrepancies* which are arranged in a matrix $W$, and that $b$ is the coefficient vector of the parametric quantity representation. Our purpose is to choose $\beta$ and $b$ such that $\mathrm{tr}(HW'W)$ is minimized, where $H$ is some symmetric and positive-definite or semidefinite matrix of order $n$. The minimal value is

$$\mathrm{Min}\,[\mathrm{tr}(HW'W)] = \mathrm{tr}(HQ'Q) - (\beta'Q'Q\beta)(b'Hb) \ , \tag{4.2}$$

where $\beta$ and $b$ are subject to the following restrictions:

$$[Q'QH - (\beta'Q'Q\beta)(b'Hb)I]Q'Q\beta = 0 \ , \tag{4.3}$$

$$Q'Q\,[HQ'Q - (\beta'Q'Q\beta)(b'Hb)I]\beta = 0 \ , \tag{4.4}$$

[9] There is no problem of multiple roots, because the largest root of a matrix of positive elements (see footnote 7) is single. See e.g., Zurmühl (1958, p. 212).

$$[HQ'Q - (\beta'Q'Q\beta)(b'Hb)I\,]Hb = 0 \ , \tag{4.5}$$

$$H\,[Q'QH - (\beta'Q'Q\beta)(b'Hb)I\,]b = 0 \ , \tag{4.6}$$

So we find solutions for $\beta$ and $Hb$ by taking a characteristic vector of $HQ'Q$ corresponding to the largest root; the same applies to $b$ and $Q'Q\beta$ with respect to the matrix $Q'QH$. Corresponding to (3.16), finally, we find

$$[QHQ' - (\beta'Q'Q\beta)(b'Hb)I\,]q = 0 \ , \tag{4.7}$$

implying that the quantity index vector can be found as a characteristic vector of $QHQ'$ corresponding with the largest root.

## 5. Symmetric Best Linear Price and Quantity Index Numbers

A rather obvious approach is to formulate price and quantity index numbers which are symmetric. A little reflection shows that this goal is attained if we specify

$$G = Q'Q \qquad \text{and} \qquad H = P'P \ , \tag{5.1}$$

which imply that the price index vector is then a characteristic vector of $PQ'QP'$ and the quantity index vector is a characteristic vector of $QP'PQ'$, both corresponding to the largest root. The results (3.9) - (3.12), (4.3) - (4.6) can then be arranged in two groups, viz.,

$$\begin{cases} [P'PQ'Q - (\alpha'P'P\alpha)\,(a'Q'Qa)I\,]P'P\alpha = 0 \ , \\ Q'Q\,[P'PQ'Q - (\alpha'P'P\alpha)\,(a'Q'Qa)I\,]a = 0 \ , \\ [P'PQ'Q - (b'P'Pb)\,(\beta'Q'Q\beta)I\,]P'Pb = 0 \ , \\ Q'Q\,[P'PQ'Q - (b'P'Pb)\,(\beta'Q'Q\beta)I\,]\beta = 0 \ , \end{cases} \tag{5.2}$$

and

$$\begin{cases} [Q'QP'P - (\alpha'P'P\alpha)(a'Q'Qa)I]Q'Qa = 0 \ , \\ P'P[Q'QP'P - (\alpha'P'P\alpha)(a'Q'Qa)I]\alpha = 0 \ , \\ [Q'QP'P - (b'P'Pb)(\beta'Q'Q\beta)I]Q'Q\beta = 0 \ , \\ P'P[Q'QP'P - (b'P'Pb)(\beta'Q'Q\beta)I]b = 0 \ . \end{cases} \tag{5.3}$$

It follows that the vectors

$$P'P\alpha , \quad a , \quad P'Pb , \quad \beta \tag{5.4}$$

are then all characteristic vectors of $P'PQ'Q$; similarly, that

$$Q'Qa , \quad \alpha , \quad Q'Q\beta , \quad b \tag{5.5}$$

are all characteristic vectors of $Q'QP'P$; finally, that these vectors all correspond to the largest latent root, which has the same value for the two matrices. Since the largest root is necessarily a single root, we can conclude that the four vectors (5.4) must all be equal to each other apart possibly from multiplicative scalars; and similarly for (5.5). But it was observed earlier[10] that we may multiply either $\alpha$ or $a$ by some constant without affecting the argument. As the same applies to $\beta$ and $b$, we may therefore write without loss of generality

$$a = \beta \quad \text{and} \quad b = \alpha \ , \tag{5.6}$$

which means that the quantity weights ($\beta$) are identical with the corresponding coefficients of the parametric price representation ($a$), and *vice versa*, prices and quantities being interchanged. The relation between the price weights ($\alpha$) and the quantity weights ($\beta$) is also easily established. Applying the equality (except for scalar multipliers) of the vectors (5.4) and (5.5), we obtain

$$P'P\alpha = k_1\beta \quad \text{and} \quad Q'Q\beta = k_2\alpha \ . \tag{5.7}$$

Combining these results, we find $Q'QP'P\alpha = k_1k_2\alpha$, so that

[10] See the end of the second paragraph of section 3.

$$k_1 k_2 = (\alpha' P' P \alpha)(a' Q' Q a) = (\alpha' P' P \alpha)(\beta' Q' Q \beta) = \lambda^2 \tag{5.8}$$

in view of (5.3), (5.6), and the definition of $\lambda^2$ as the largest latent root of $GP'P = Q'QP'P$. It follows that (5.7) can be written as $P'P\alpha = k_1\beta$, $Q'Q\beta = (\lambda^2/k_1)\alpha$, so that one degree of freedom ($k_2$) is lost. We shall remove the other as well by taking $k_1 = \lambda$, which means

$$P'P\alpha = \lambda\beta \qquad \text{and} \qquad Q'Q\beta = \lambda\alpha \, , \tag{5.9}$$

or in words: premultiplying the price weights by the moment matrix of individual prices gives $\lambda$ times the vector of quantity weights, and premultiplying the quantity weights by the moment matrix of individual quantities gives $\lambda$ times the price weights, where $\lambda$ is the positive square root of the largest latent root of the products ($P'PQ'Q$ and $Q'QP'P$) of these two moment matrices.

Premultiplying the first equation of (5.9) by $q'Q$ and the second by $p'P$, we obtain $q'QP'P\alpha = q'QP'p = \lambda q'Q\beta = \lambda q'q$ and $p'PQ'Q\beta = p'PQ'q = \lambda p'P\alpha = \lambda p'p$. But $q'QP'p = p'PQ'q$, so that $p'p = q'q$. As it follows further from (5.8) that $p'p \cdot q'q = \lambda^2$, we have

$$p'p = q'q = \lambda \, , \tag{5.10}$$

or in words: $\lambda$ is the squared length of both the price index vector and the quantity index vector.[11] Also, if we premultiply the first equation of (5.9) by $\alpha'$, we obtain $\alpha'P'P\alpha = p'p = \lambda = \lambda\alpha'\beta$ and hence

$$\alpha'\beta = 1 \, , \tag{5.11}$$

or in words: the inner product of the price and quantity weights is unity.

Finally, if we premultiply the first equation (5.9) by $Q$ and the second by $P$, we obtain $QP'p = \lambda q$ and $PQ'q = \lambda p$. If is of some interest to consider the matrix

$$C = PQ' \, , \tag{5.12}$$

which will be termed the *cross-value matrix*; its elements measure the aggregate value of the quantities of any period at the prices of any period. Hence the relations just described can be written as

---

[11] This is, of course, not the usual way of normalization. Normally, the average of the price index numbers for some periods is put equal to 1, while quantity index numbers are taken as values at such average prices. Here, however, it will prove convenient to treat prices and quantities completely symmetrically.

$$C'p = \lambda q \qquad \text{and} \qquad Cq = \lambda p \ , \tag{5.13}$$

or in words: premultiplying the price index vector by the transpose of the cross-value matrix gives $\lambda$ times the quantity index vector, and premultiplying the latter vector by the cross-value matrix gives $\lambda$ times the former vector. We also note that

$$p'Cq = \lambda^2 \qquad \text{and} \qquad p'C'Cq = \lambda^2 p'q \ . \tag{5.14}$$

The first relation is derived by premultiplying $Cq = \lambda p$ by $p'$, the second follows from the fact that $q$ is a characteristic vector of $C'C$ corresponding to root $\lambda^2$.

## 6. The Optimal Character of Symmetric Best Linear Index Numbers

The symmetric variant of the preceding section was introduced primarily because of its mathematical elegance; but it can be shown that it has a fundamental optimal property as well. Let us therefore consider the well-known "factor reversal test,"[12] which implies that if we take $t_0$ as a basis for both prices and quantities (so that $p(t_0) = q(t_0) = 1$), the product $p(t)q(t)$ should measure correctly the aggregate value in period $t$ relative to the aggregate value in $t_0$. Applying our matrix notation, this implies that corresponding diagonal elements of the matrices

$$pq' \qquad \text{and} \qquad PQ' = C \tag{6.1}$$

should be equal, apart possibly from a common multiplicative scalar.[13]

It is easily seen that this test cannot be fulfilled in general because the number of restrictions implied by it depends on the number of periods, and the number of coefficients ($\alpha$, $a$, $\beta$, $b$, $G$, $H$) that can be handled in order to attain this goal depends on the number of commodities. Furthermore, it is difficult to see why we should confine ourselves to the equality of the diagonal elements of the matrices (6.1). For example, we may require that on the basis 1920 = 100, say, the 1925 price index multiplied by the 1930 quantity index measures correctly the aggregate value of the quantities of 1930 at the prices of 1925. This is clearly a much more ambitious requirement than the equality of the diagonal elements of $pq'$ and $PQ'$.

---

[12] The "proportionality test" and the "circular test" are satisfied by B.L. index numbers because of the constancy of the weights ($\alpha$ and $\beta$). These tests are, of course, not satisfied in the sense that they hold identically in all individual prices and quantities; but this is not our problem, since we take $P$ and $Q$ as they are and try to find the most satisfactory column representations $p$ and $q$ of these *given* matrices.

[13] In fact, it is easily seen that the normalization (5,6) implies that this scalar is unity. Hence the components of $pq'$ have the dimensions of money value (possibly per unit of time).

Nevertheless, Symmetric Best Linear index numbers do achieve something in this respect. To show this, we postmultiply (3.3) by $Q'$:

$$PQ' = pa'Q' + VQ' = pq' + VQ' \ , \tag{6.2}$$

where use has been made of $Qa = Q\beta = q$ [see (5.6)]. Hence

$$E = VQ' \tag{6.3}$$

can be called the matrix of *cross-value discrepancies*. Each such discrepancy is equal to the difference between the aggregate value of the quantities in $t$ valued at the prices of $t'$ computed by means of index numbers and the same cross-value computed on the basis of the individual data. Now it can be shown that the sum of squares of these discrepancies is minimized by Symmetric B.L. index numbers. For this sum of squares is[14]

$$tr[(VQ')(VQ')'] = tr(VQ'QV') = tr(Q'QV'V) \ ,$$

which is precisely the quadratic form (3.5) under the specification (5.1). In other words: Symmetric Best Linear (B.L.) index numbers minimize certain quadratic forms in the price and quantity discrepancies such that these indices implicitly minimize the sum of squares of the cross-value discrepancies.

It is well known that, in ordinary regression theory, the least-squares principle implies that the residual vector is orthogonal to the vectors of values taken by the explanatory variables. We have a similar result here. Postmultiplying $E$ by $q$, we obtain

$$Eq = PQ'q - pq'q = \lambda p - \lambda p = 0$$

because of (5.13). A similar result is obtained when $E'$ is postmultiplied by $p$; hence

$$E'p = 0 \qquad \text{and} \qquad Eq = 0 \ , \tag{6.4}$$

or in words: If we take all cross-value discrepancies involving the quantities of $t$, then the resulting $T$ discrepancies have a zero cross-moment with the price index vector, for any $t = 1, \ldots, T$; and similarly, if we take all cross-value discrepancies involving the prices of any given $t$, then the resulting $T$ discrepancies have a zero cross-moment with the quantity index vector.

[14] For any matrix $M$, tr($MM'$) is the sum of squares of all elements of $M$. This sum is sometimes called the norm of $M$; see, e.g., Bowker (1947) for an analysis of its properties.

## 7. A Fitting Index

Symmetric B.L. index numbers are computed very easily. Once the individual prices and quantities are available, one computes the cross-value matrix $C = PQ'$, after which the price and quantity index vectors are obtained by taking the characteristic vectors — corresponding with the largest root — of $CC'$ and $C'C$. It is interesting to note that this root can be used as an indicator of the "statistical quality" of the indices. Consider (3,13) and apply (5.1) and (5.10):

$$\text{Min}\,[\text{tr}(Q'QV'V)] = \text{tr}(Q'QP'P) - \lambda^2 \,, \tag{7.1}$$

$\lambda^2$ being the largest root of $QQ'P'P$. But $\text{tr}(Q'QP'P)$ is the sum of all the roots of $Q'QP'P$, and these roots are all nonnegative.[15] Hence an adequate measure of our "success" in minimizing $\text{tr}(Q'QV'V)$ is the *fitting index* $I$ which is the positive square root[16] of

$$I^2 = \frac{\lambda^2}{tr(Q'QP'P)} = \frac{\lambda^2}{tr(CC')} = \frac{\lambda^2}{tr(C'C)} \,. \tag{7.2}$$

This index takes the value 1 if we have succeeded in reducing all cross-value discrepancies to zero, which implies that the largest root $\lambda^2$ absorbs then the whole trace, all other roots being zero. The minimum value of $I^2$ is $1/r$, where $r$ is either $n$ or $T$, whichever is smaller. This is because the largest root can never be smaller than any of the other positive roots, and the number of positive roots of the matrices $Q'QP'P$ and $QP'PQ'$ exceeds neither $n$ nor $T$.[17]

Two things are of some interest with respect to this index. First, it should be stressed that the fitting index refers to both the price and the quantity index vector; it does not measure some average of the statistical qualities of these two vectors. This follows immediately from the fact that $I^2$ is both equal to the ratio of the largest root of $CC'$ to the trace of this matrix (the corresponding characteristic vector being $p$) and to the ratio of the largest root to the trace of $CC'$ (the characteristic vector being here $q$). Second, $I^2 \le 1$ is equivalent to saying that the sum of squares of the elements of the cross-value matrix $pq'$ based on the index vectors is smaller than or equal to the sum of squares of the elements of the cross-value matrix $C$ based on the individual data:

---

[15] This is because $Q'QP'P$ and the positive-definite (or semi-definite) matrix $QP'PQ'$ have the same roots, except possibly for a number of zero roots; see footnote 6.

[16] We take the square root of the ratio defined in (7,2) because it is essentially a squared quantity. In fact, it is easily seen that $I^2$ is analogous to a squared multiple correlation coefficient because its denominator is the sum of squares of the "dependent" values ($\Sigma\Sigma c_{tt'}^2$, where $c_{tt'}$ is an element of $C$), while the numerator is the sum of squares of that part of these dependent values that is "explained" by the index numbers; see (7,3) below.

[17] If one prefers an index whose limits are 0 and 1, one can replace $I^2$ by $r(I^2 - 1/r)/(r - 1)$.

$$1 \geq I^2 = \frac{p'pq'q}{tr(CC')} = \frac{tr[(pq')(pq')']}{tr(CC')} = \frac{\sum_t \sum_{t'} \{p(t)q(t')\}^2}{\sum_t \sum_{t'} c_{tt'}^2} , \tag{7.3}$$

where $c_{tt'}$ is an element of $C$.

## 8. Partial Index Numbers and Aggregation Problems

A convenient formulation of B.L. index numbers is the following. We start from the cross-value matrix $C = PQ'$ and construct vectors $p$, $q$ in such a way that $p'p = q'q = \lambda$ where $\lambda^2$ is the largest root of $C'C$, and that $E'p = Eq = 0$ where $E = C - pq'$. As a whole, these are $2T$ conditions determining the $2T$ elements of $p$ and $q$.

Now it will be clear that such index numbers can be applied, not only to a given group of commodities, but also to subsets of such a group. Let us then partition the price and quantity matrices $P$ and $Q$ conformably in $s$ submatrices corresponding to $s$ commodity groups:

$$P = [P_1 \;\cdots\; P_s] \quad \text{and} \quad Q = [Q_1 \;\cdots\; Q_s] . \tag{8.1}$$

For each group $h$ (= 1 , . . . , $s$), we can then compute "partial" B.L. index vectors $p_h$ and $q_h$. Following the formulation of the preceding paragraph, we can say that $p_h$ and $q_h$ are based on the "partial" cross-value matrix

$$C_h = P_h Q_h' ; \tag{8.2}$$

that the squared length of $p_h$ and $q_h$ is equal to $\lambda_h$ which is the square root of the largest latent root of $C_h'C_h$,

$$p_h' p_h = q_h' q_h = \lambda_h ; \tag{8.3}$$

and that the columns of the corresponding matrix of cross-value discrepancies are all orthogonal to $p_h$ while the rows are orthogonal to $q_h$:

$$E_h' p_h = 0 \quad \text{and} \quad E_h q_h = 0 , \tag{8.4}$$

where

$$E_h = C_h - p_h q_h' . \tag{8.5}$$

In addition, the sum of the partial cross-value matrices is the original matrix $C$:

$$\sum C_h = C \ , \tag{8.6}$$

where $\Sigma$ is to be read (here as well as in the remainder of this section) as "sum over all $s$ commodity groups."

The following problem of aggregation then arises. Suppose we have computed B.L. index numbers for a certain set of commodity groups; suppose also that we want to use these partial index numbers as a basis for the construction of B.L. index numbers of the entire group. Will such "aggregative" index numbers be identical with the corresponding B.L. index numbers based on individual data? The answer is negative, which is easily understood by means of the following heuristic argument. For the construction of the B.L. price index vector $p$ based on the individual data, we use $G = Q'Q$, which is the matrix of the quadratic form in the price discrepancies that is minimized. Supposing that the commodity group is divided into two subgroups, we can partition

$$Q'Q = \begin{bmatrix} Q_1'Q_1 & Q_1'Q_2 \\ Q_2'Q_1 & Q_2'Q_2 \end{bmatrix} . \tag{8.7}$$

The construction of the partial index vectors $p_1$ and $p_2$ is based on $Q_1'Q_1$ and $Q_2'Q_2$, respectively; it is not based on $Q_1'Q_2$ and $Q_2'Q_1$ which are determining factors of the overall index vector $p$. It is true that the construction of the B.L. price index vector based on the partial vectors $p_1$ and $p_2$ does take account of the interrelationships between the quantities of the two groups; but it does so in an aggregative manner, not in a detailed manner as prescribed by the off-diagonal submatrices of (8.7).

We can obtain approximate statements about the aggregation errors by applying the formulation of the first paragraph of this section. Let us write $p + \delta$ and $q + \varepsilon$ for the B.L. price and quantity index vectors, respectively, which are obtained when the partial B.L. index vectors $p_1, \ldots, p_s, q_1, \ldots, q_s$ are taken as a starting point instead of $P$, $Q$. Hence $\delta$ is the vector of aggregation errors for prices, and $\varepsilon$ for quantities. The underlying cross-value matrix is now

$$C^* = \sum p_h q_h' \ ; \tag{8.8}$$

and the vectors $p + \delta$, $q + \varepsilon$ have the same squared length $\lambda^*$ which is the square root of the largest latent root of $C^{*\prime}C^*$:

$$(p + \delta)'(p + \delta) = (q + \varepsilon)'(q + \varepsilon) = \lambda^* \ . \tag{8.9}$$

In addition, the columns and rows of $E^*$ (the corresponding matrix of cross-value discrepancies) are orthogonal to $p + \delta$ and $q + \varepsilon$, respectively:

$$E^{*\prime}(p + \delta) = 0 \qquad \text{and} \qquad E^{*}(q + \varepsilon) = 0 \ , \tag{8.10}$$

where

$$E^{*} = C^{*} - (p + \delta)(q + \varepsilon)' \ . \tag{8.11}$$

In what follows we shall confine ourselves to terms which are linear in the aggregation errors; we shall neglect their squares and higher powers. Then (8.9) implies

$$p'\delta = q'\varepsilon \ . \tag{8.12}$$

Further, applying (8.11), (8.8), (8.6), and (8.5), we have

$$E^{*} = E - \sum_h E_h - p\varepsilon' - \delta q' \ . \tag{8.13}$$

Then $E^{*}(q + \varepsilon) = 0$ [see (8.10)] can be written as

$$\Big(E - \sum_h E_h\Big)\varepsilon - \sum_h E_h q - p\varepsilon' q - \delta q' q = 0 \ . \tag{8.14}$$

But $p\varepsilon' q = pp'\delta$ in view of (8.12) and $\delta q' q = \lambda\delta$, so that $p\varepsilon' q + \delta q' q = (\lambda I + pp')\delta$. Furthermore, let us write

$$p_h = p + \delta_h \qquad \text{and} \qquad q_h = q + \varepsilon_h \ , \tag{8.15}$$

so that $\Sigma E_h q = \Sigma E_h (q_h - \varepsilon_h) = - \Sigma E_h \varepsilon_h$ in view of (8.4). Then (8.14) can be simplified to

$$\Big(E - \sum_h E_h\Big)\varepsilon + \sum_h E_h \varepsilon_h - (\lambda I + pp')\delta = 0 \ ,$$

from which it follows that

$$\begin{aligned} \delta &= (\lambda I + pp')^{-1}\Big[\sum_h E_h \varepsilon_h + \Big(E - \sum_h E_h\Big)\varepsilon\Big] \\ &= \frac{1}{\lambda^2}\Big(\lambda I - \frac{1}{2}pp'\Big)\Big[\sum_h E_h \varepsilon_h + \Big(E - \sum_h E_h\Big)\varepsilon\Big] \ . \end{aligned} \tag{8.16}$$

In exactly the same way, we find for the quantity aggregation errors

$$\varepsilon = \frac{1}{\lambda^2}\left(\lambda I - \frac{1}{2}qq'\right)\left[\Sigma E_h{}'\delta_h + \left(E - \Sigma E_h\right)'\delta\right]. \tag{8.17}$$

Combining (8.16) and (8.17), and neglecting terms involving squares and products of cross-value discrepancies, we find that (8.16) can be simplified to

$$\begin{aligned}\delta &= \frac{1}{\lambda^2}\left(\lambda I - \frac{1}{2}pp'\right)\Sigma E_h \varepsilon_h = \frac{1}{\lambda}\Sigma E_h \varepsilon_h - \frac{1}{2\lambda^2}\left(\Sigma p' E_h \varepsilon_h\right)p \\ &= \frac{1}{\lambda}\Sigma E_h \varepsilon_h + \frac{1}{2\lambda^2}\left(\Sigma \delta_h{}' E_h \varepsilon_h\right)p ,\end{aligned} \tag{8.18}$$

so that the price index vector based on partial B.L. index numbers becomes

$$p + \delta = \left(1 + \frac{1}{2\lambda^2}\Sigma \delta_h{}' E_h \varepsilon_h\right)p + \frac{1}{\lambda}\Sigma E_h \varepsilon_h , \tag{8.19}$$

while the corresponding expression for the quantity index vector is

$$q + \varepsilon = \left(1 + \frac{1}{2\lambda^2}\Sigma \delta_h{}' E_h \varepsilon_h\right)q + \frac{1}{\lambda}\Sigma E_h{}'\delta_h . \tag{8.20}$$

Therefore we can say that to our order of approximation (squares of aggregation errors and of cross-value discrepancies being neglected), the aggregative B.L. index vectors are subject to a proportional error and to an additive error. The latter term is different for the two vectors; for the aggregative price index vector it is a linear combination of the deviations between the partial quantity index vectors and the over-all quantity vector (based on individual data), for the aggregative quantity index vector it is a similar combination of price deviations. The proportional error is the same for the two vectors; it is bilinear in the deviations between the partial and the over-all index vectors. Whether or not these aggregation errors are large in practice is an empirical matter which will not be pursued here.

## 9. Concluding Remarks

(i) If the fitting index is low, one may feel inclined to use the characteristic vector corresponding to the second largest latent root in addition to the vector of the first root. We then have two price index vectors and two quantity index vectors, the former as well as the latter being pairwise orthogonal; and combined they account for a greater part of the variation of the individual prices and quantities than do the index vectors corresponding to the largest root. Also, their orthogonality is an advantage when such index vectors are used as explanatory variables in a regression analysis. The index vectors corresponding to the second largest root, however, have a feature which is rather unusual for index numbers; some of their elements are negative. This follows from the theorem[18] which states that any square matrix whose elements are positive has the property that the characteristic vector corresponding to the largest root consists of positive elements only,[19] while the characteristic vectors corresponding to any other root all have at least one negative element. It will be clear that this implies positive signs, not only for the price and quantity index vectors, but also for their weights ($\alpha$ and $\beta$) and for the vectors of the parametric representation ($a$ and $b$). In the case of the second largest root all these vectors have at least one negative element.

(ii) If $T = 2$, the present approach boils down to the conventional approach; so let us designate $t = 1$ as the "base period," $t = 2$ as the "current period." Furthermore, we write $P_L$ for the Laspeyres price index, $Q_L$ for the Laspeyres quantity index, and

$$P_P = P_L(1 + \eta) \tag{9.1}$$

for the Paasche price index. Disregarding squares and higher powers of $\eta$, we find after some algebraic rearrangements for the symmetric B.L. price index number of the second period with the first as base:

$$P = P_L\left(1 + \eta\,\frac{Q_L^2}{1 + Q_L^2}\right). \tag{9.2}$$

Hence the symmetric B.L. price index number is halfway between the Laspeyres and Paasche when the quantities are the same in the two periods according to their Laspeyres index, and it is closer to the Paasche (Laspeyres) when the quantities in the current period are larger (smaller) — except, of course, for higher-order terms in $\eta$. It can also be shown that the squared fitting index $I^2$ deviates from 1 only to the order of $\eta^2$:

$$\sqrt{1 - I^2} = \eta\,\frac{P_L Q_L}{\left(1 + P_L^2\right)\left(1 + Q_L^2\right)}, \tag{9.3}$$

squares and higher powers of $\eta$ being neglected.

(iii) It will happen sometimes that there is a particular year which is to be considered as an "outlying observation." For example, rationing may have disturbed the normal development of quantities, or a price control or a deviation may have disturbed the normal development of prices. One can, of course, leave such a year out of

[18] See, e.g., Zurmühl (1958, p. 212).

[19] Or only negative values (because any characteristic vector may be multiplied by a negative scalar without losing the property of being a characteristic vector); but this is obviously an uninteresting alternative.

consideration; but it is also possible to apply a weighting procedure which treats different periods differently in a manner which resembles Aitken's (1934-1935) method of generalized least-squares. Let us therefore minimize, not (3.5), but

$$\sum_{i,j} g_{ij} \sum_{t,t'} \psi_{tt'} v_i(t) v_j(t') = \mathrm{tr}(GV'\Psi V) = \mathrm{tr}[G(I - a\alpha')P'\Psi P(I - \alpha a')] , \quad (9.4)$$

where $\Psi = [\psi_{tt'}]$ is some symmetric and positive-definite or semidefinite matrix of order $T$. All results of section 3 remain valid if we replace $P'P$ by $P'\Psi P$. In the same way, we minimize for the quantities $\mathrm{tr}(HW'\Omega W)$, $\Omega$ being also a symmetric and positive- definite or semidefinite matrix. The symmetric variant of this generalized procedure is obtained by specifying

$$G = Q'\Omega Q \qquad \text{and} \qquad H = P'\Psi P , \quad (9.5)$$

which leads to the same results as those of section 5, except that we should replace $P'P$ and $Q'Q$ by $P'\Psi P$ and $Q'\Omega Q$, respectively. The optimal property of the resulting indices is slightly different from that sketched in section 6. To show this, we introduce square matrices $A$ and $B$ such that

$$A'A = \Psi \qquad \text{and} \qquad B'B = \Omega ; \quad (9.6)$$

the positive-definiteness (or semidefiniteness) of $\Psi$ and $\Omega$ ensures that such matrices exist. We proceed to pre- and postmultiply (3.3) by $A$ and $Q'B'$ respectively:

$$APQ'B' = Apa'Q'B' + AVQ'B' = Apq'B' + AVQ'B' .$$

Hence,

$$AVQ'B' = A(PQ' - pq')B' = AEB' . \quad (9.7)$$

Now $AVQ'B'$ is precisely the matrix the sum of squares of the elements of which is minimized:

$$\begin{aligned} \mathrm{tr}[(AVQ'B')(AVQ'B')'] &= \mathrm{tr}(AVQ'B'BQV'A') \\ &= \mathrm{tr}(Q'B'BQV'A'AV) = \mathrm{tr}(Q'\Omega Q \cdot V'\Psi V) . \end{aligned}$$

Hence, we do no longer minimize the simple sum of squares of the cross-value discrepancies, but we minimize some quadratic form in these discrepancies. A special case is that in which $A = B = \hat{D}$, where $\hat{D}$ is a diagonal matrix. Then we minimize $\Sigma\Sigma(d_t d_{t'} e_{tt'})^2$, where $d_t$ is the $t$th diagonal element of $\hat{D}$. This variant may be useful for price and quantity comparisons of different countries, because the $d$'s can then be chosen such that the cross-value discrepancies involving small countries are smaller on the average than those involving large countries.[20] I hope to come back to this topic on a later occasion.

## References

Aitken, A.C.: (1934-35), "On Least-Squares and Linear Combination of Observations," *Proceedings of the Royal Society of Edinburgh*, **55**, 42-48.

Bowker, A.H.: 1947, "On the Norm of a Matrix," *Annals of Mathematical Statistics*, **18**, 285-288.

Frisch, R.: 1936, "Annual Survey of General Economic Theory: The Problem of Index Numbers," *Econometrica*, **4**, 1-38.

IJzeren, J. van: 1956, "Three Methods of Comparing the Purchasing Power of Currencies," *Statistical Studies*, **7**, 3-35.

Zurmühl, R.: 1958, *Matrizen*, 2nd ed., Berlin-Göttingen-Heidelberg.

[20] For a related contribution to the problem of price and quantity comparisons of different countries (also in terms of characteritic equations), see van IJzeren (1956).

CHAPTER 38

# ON THE GEOMETRY AND THE NUMERICAL APPROXIMATION OF COST OF LIVING AND REAL INCOME INDICES*

HENRI THEIL
*University of Chicago*
*Chicago, Illinois, USA*

ABSTRACT. The economic theory of the "true" cost of living and real income index numbers is described and illustrated geometically in the logarithmic price-income space. Special attention is paid to the real income index evaluated at the geometric means of the prices in the two periods and to the cost of living index evaluated at the utility level which is associated with these geometric mean prices and geometric mean income. It is shown that this particular pair of index numbers is the only pair which satisfies a certain simple set of axioms. It is also shown how these index numbers can be approximated on the basis of observable price-quantity data. The approximation is accurate up to the second order in price and income log-changes.

## 1. Introduction

The economic theory of index numbers is based on the indirect utility function and its income solution. This theory can be summarized briefly as follows. A consumer is supposed to maximize his utility function $u = u(q)$ subject to his budget constraint $p'q = m$, where $m$ is his income or total expenditure and $p$ and $q$ are $n$-element column vectors of the prices and quantities, respectively, of the $n$ commodities. If we assume that income and prices are fixed and given from the consumer's point of view and that the utility function satisfies certain regularity conditions, the result of this conditional maximization is a vector of demand functions $q^0 = q(m, p)$ which express the optimal quantities in terms of income and prices. We substitute these demand functions into the utility function:

$$u = u(q(m,p)) = u_I(m,p) \tag{1.1}$$

The function $u_I()$ is the indirect utility function; it measures the highest utility level that can be attained when income is $m$ and prices are $p$. Next we fix utility at a certain level $U$ and ask the following question: How large an income does the consumer need to attain the utility level $U$ when the prices are $p$? The answer is obtained by equating $u_I(m, p)$ to $U$ and solving for $m$. The result is the income solution of the indirect utility function:

* This article first appeared in *De Economist*, **116** (1968) 677-689. Reprinted with the permission of H.E. Stenfert Kroese B.V.

$$m = m_I(U,p) \tag{1.2}$$

and it is shown in the Appendix that the price elasticities of this function are of the following form:

$$\frac{\partial[\log m_I(U,p)]}{\partial(\log p_i)} = \frac{p_i q_i^0(U,p)}{m_I(U,p)} = w_i^0(U,p) \qquad i = 1, ..., n \tag{1.3}$$

where $q_i^0(U,p)$ is the optimal value of the $i^{th}$ quantity when prices are $p$ and when income is such that the consumer's maximum utility level in this price situation is $U$. Equation (1.3) thus states that, if the price of the $i^{th}$ commodity goes up by 1 per cent, while all other prices remain unchanged, the income which the consumer needs to attain a fixed utility level $U$ goes up by $w_i^0(U,p)$ per cent, where $w_i^0(U,p)$ is the budget share of the $i^{th}$ commodity in the price-utility situation described above. It goes without saying that this result is related to the familiar income effect of a price change.

The "true" cost of living index and the "true" real income index are both defined as ratios of such income solutions $m_I(\ )$, but with different arguments. Let $p_t$ be the current price vector and $p_{t-1}$ that of the previous period;[1] then the true cost of living price index comparing these periods evaluated at the utility level $U$ is defined as

$$P(p_t, p_{t-1} \mid U) = \frac{m_I(U,p_t)}{m_I(U,p_{t-1})} \tag{1.4}$$

Thus, if the income which is currently needed to attain the utility level $U$ exceeds by 10 per cent the income that was needed last year to attain the same utility level, the cost of living has gone up by that much: $P(p_t, p_{t-1} \mid U) = 1.1$. Note that this figure will in general change when we choose a different utility level. In the same way, when the consumer's current utility level is $U_t$ and that of the previous period $U_{t-1}$, the true index of real income for these periods evaluated at the price vector $p$ is defined as

$$Q(U_t, U_{t-1} \mid p) = \frac{m_I(U_t,p)}{m_I(U_{t-1},p)} \tag{1.5}$$

Thus, if the income which enables the consumer to enjoy the present utility level $U_t$ at prices $p$ exceeds by 5 per cent the income which he would have needed for last period's utility level at the same prices, his real income has gone up by that much: $Q(U_t,U_{t-1} \mid p) = 1.05$. Note that this figure will in general change when we choose a

---

[1] For the sake of definiteness we consider variations of income and prices over time, but regional comparisons can be made in a completely analogous way.

different price vector. Both $U$ in (1.4) and $p$ in (1.5) are subject to choice; there is no special reason to specify $U = U_t$ or $U = U_{t-1}$ or $p = p_t$ or $p = p_{t-1}$.

The above paragraphs summarize some classical features of the economic theory of index numbers. The objective of the present article is to discuss these indices geometrically, to choose a convenient utility level for the cost of living comparison (1.4) and a convenient price vector for the real income comparison (1.5), and to discuss approximations to the resulting special indices which can be computed directly from observable price-quantity data. The subject has a long history; the more immediate sources of inspiration for the author were a monograph by Miss V. Rajaoja (1958) and T. Kloek's Ph.D. thesis (1966), part of which were described and extended in Sections 6.7, 6.8, 6.B and 7.9 of Theil (1967). The present approach differs from the earlier one to the extent that it works systematically with the logarithms of income and prices rather than these variables themselves. This seems a natural modification, because index numbers are concerned with relative changes in prices and income, and it leads to rather substantial theoretical improvements as will be shown below.

## 2. General Geometric Discussion of the Two Indices

If we take (natural) logarithms on both sides of (1.4) and (1.5), we make the price and real income comparisons additive rather than multiplicative:

$$\log P(p_t, p_{t-1} \mid U) = \log m_I(U, p_t) - \log m_I(U, p_{t-1}) \tag{2.1}$$

$$\log Q(U_t, U_{t-1} \mid p) = \log m_I(U_t, p) - \log m_I(U_{t-1}, p) \tag{2.2}$$

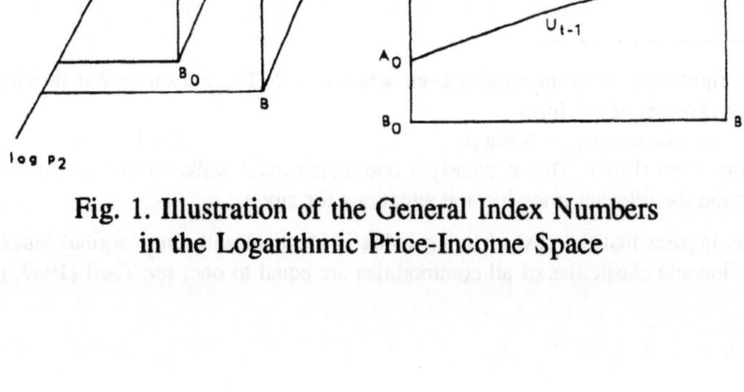


Fig. 1. Illustration of the General Index Numbers in the Logarithmic Price-Income Space

Consider now the $(n+1)$-dimensional logarithmic price-income space, which is illustrated in the left-hand diagram of Figure 1 for $n = 2$. The current point is indicated by $A$, that of the previous period by $A_0$, and their projections in the logarithmic price plane by $B$ and $B_0$, respectively. Since $A$ and $A_0$ define two price-income situations, they also define two utility levels, $U_t = u_t(m_t, p_t)$ for $A$ and $U_{t-1} = u_t(m_{t-1}, p_{t-1})$ for $A_0$, where $m_{t-1}$ and $m_t$ are the incomes of the successive periods. This is pursued in more detail in the right-hand diagram, which contains the vertical plane through $A_0$, $B_0$, $B$ and $A$.[2] The curve through $A_0$ is the locus of all points in this plane where the attainable utility level is $U_{t-1}$; the curve through $A$ contains all points with utility $U_t$. Consider now the logarithmic cost of living index (2.1) and imagine that we evaluate it at $U = U_{t-1}$, recalling that the vertical axis of Figure 1 meaures the logarithm of income. The logarithmic index is obviously $CB - A_0B_0$. But if we evaluate $\log P$ at $U_t$, the result is $AB - DB_0$. Clearly, the cost of living comparison is invariant against different choices of the utility level at which it is made only if every pair of indifference curves in the vertical plane is characterized by the same vertical distance everywhere. But this is a very serious restriction.[3]

Next consider the logarithmic real income index (2.2). If we evaluate it at last period's price vector ($p = p_{t-1}$), it is equal to $DB_0 - A_0B_0 = DA_0$, and if it is evaluated at $p_t$, it becomes $AC$. [Note that cost of living comparisons are always made on the same indifference curve and real income comparisons always on the same vertical price line.] The conclusion is that precisely the same restrictive condition is needed to guarantee that the real income index be independent of the price vector $p$.

## 3. A Special Pair of Indices

In many practical situations one will prefer to work with indices which take certain numerical values rather than indices which vary parametrically with a utility level or a price vector. This simply means that the utility level and the price vector have to be fixed at certain convenient levels. What is convenient is to a large extent a matter of taste, but the following approach has considerable appeal, at least to the author.

In most cases one will want to treat the two periods symmetrically, which means that the prices at which the real income comparison is made should be "halfway" between the prices of the two periods and that, similarly, the $U$ of the cost of living index should be "halfway" between $U_{t-1}$ and $U_t$. Recall that the axes of Figure 1 all measure logarithms of prices or income. Therefore, the midpoint of the line segment $B_0B$ in Figure 1

---

[2] Note that the right-hand diagram applies even when $n > 2$. The reason is that moving from $B_0$ to $B$ amounts to price changes of the form

$$(1 - \theta) \log p_{i,t-1} + \theta \log p_{it} \qquad i = 1, ..., n$$

where $\theta$ increases from 0 to 1. This is clearly a one-dimensional walk, so that a two-dimensional plane suffices to describe the relevant price-income situations for any $n$.

[3] The restriction implies that the cost of living index is identical with the marginal index, which in turn implies that the income elasticities of all commodities are equal to one; see Theil (1967, p. 216).

(indicated by $B^*$ in Figure 2) corresponds with the geometric means of the prices in the two successive periods.

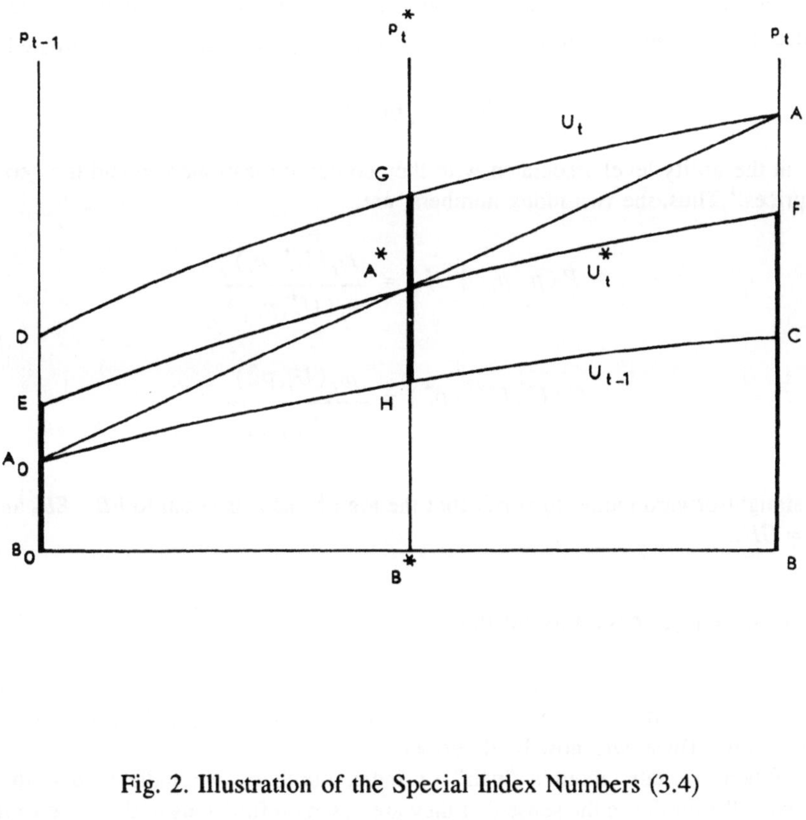


Fig. 2. Illustration of the Special Index Numbers (3.4)

If we indicate the price vector associated with $B^*$ by $p_t^*$, its elements are thus of the form

$$p_{it}^* = \sqrt{p_{i,t-1}\, p_{it}} \qquad i = 1,...,n \tag{3.1}$$

Pursuing this line of approach, we define the geometric mean income of the two periods:

$$m_t^* = \sqrt{m_{t-1}\, m_t} \tag{3.2}$$

Since the vertical axes of Figures 1 and 2 measure the logarithm of income, we may conclude that log $m_t^*$ is equal to the distance between the midpoint of the line segment $A_0A$ and the line $B_0B$; and, therefore, that log $m_t^* = A^*B^*$ in Figure 2.

The special index numbers to be considered here are the real income index evaluated at the geometric mean prices $p_t^*$ and the cost of living index evaluated at

$$U_t^* = u_I(m_t^*, p_t^*) \tag{3.3}$$

that is, at the utility level associated with the geometric mean income and the geometric mean prices.[4] Thus, the two index numbers are:

$$\begin{aligned} P(p_t, p_{t-1} \mid U_t^*) &= \frac{m_I(U_t^*, p_t)}{m_I(U_t^*, p_{t-1})} \\ Q(U_t, U_{t-1} \mid p_t^*) &= \frac{m_I(U_t, p_t^*)}{m_I(U_{t-1}, p_t^*)} \end{aligned} \tag{3.4}$$

It is a straightforward matter to verify that the log of this $P$ is equal to $FB$ - $EB_0$ and that log $Q = GH$.

## 4. The Uniqueness of the Special Pair

The advantage of the index pair (3.4) is not only that it lends itself to a neat picture. It can be shown that it is the only pair for the periods ($t$-1, $t$), provided that we accept certain axioms. These will now be described.

When we talk about a "pair" of index numbers, we indicate that they are mathematically similar in the sense that they are based on functions of the same form. We must choose a utility level $U = u_I(m, p)$ for the cost of living index and a price vector $p$ for the real income index; so our first axiom is that the argument $p$ of $u_I()$ of the former index should be the same as the $p$ of the latter. Furthermore, note that the only observed income values are $m_t$ and $m_{t-1}$ and that the only observed price vectors are $p_{t-1}$ and $p_t$. We

[4] The intermediate utility level used in Theil (1967, pp. 217-219) is defined implicitly and is slightly different. The intermediate prices used in Theil (1967, pp. 225-226) are identical with (3.1); the only (geometric) difference is that the corresponding vertical price line cannot be indicated on the line $B_0B$ of Figure 6.1 of Theil (1967, p. 212), since the axes of that figure are metric rather than logarithmic.

shall pursue the idea of mathematical similarity by requiring as a second axiom that the argument $m$ of $u_I(\ )$ be of the form $f(m_{t-1}, m_t)$ and that the $i^{th}$ element of $p$ be of the form $f(p_{i,t-1}, p_{it})$, where $f(\ )$ is defined for any pair of positive arguments. The price vector at which the real income comparison is made is then

$$[f(p_{1,t-1}, p_{1t}) \ldots f(p_{n,t-1}, p_{nt})]$$

and the utility level of the cost of living comparison is

$$u_I(f(m_{t-1}, m_t), f(p_{1,t-1}, p_{1t}), \ldots, f(p_{n,t-1}, p_{nt}))$$

The function $f(\ )$ should take values between its two arguments. An obvious third axiom is therefore:

$$f(x,x) \equiv x \qquad x > 0 \tag{4.1}$$

In addition, we shall want to treat the two periods symmetrically. This leads to the fourth axiom:

$$f(x,y) \equiv f(y,x) \qquad x,y > 0 \tag{4.2}$$

These four axioms are not sufficient to conclude that we should take the geometric means (3.1)-(3.2); it is easily verified that they are also satisfied when we take arithmetic means. But imagine now that the income and all prices of one of the two periods (say, the current period $t$) change proportionally, so that the associated utility level $U_t$ is unaffected.[5] Nothing changes in the other period; hence both $U_{t-1}$ and $U_t$ remain as they are. Our objective for the cost of living index is to specify a utility level between $U_{t-1}$ and $U_t$, and since there are no fundamental changes, it would be disturbing to find that the utility level at which the cost of living comparison is made is affected. But that is the case when arithmetic means are used. The utility level of the cost of living comparison is then

$$u_I\left(\frac{m_{t-1} + cm_t}{2}, \frac{p_{1,t-1} + cp_{1t}}{2}, \ldots, \frac{p_{n,t-1} + cp_{nt}}{2}\right)$$

where $c$ is the proportionality factor. Consider the special case $p_{it} = p_{i,t-1}$ for each $i$ but $m_t \neq m_{t-1}$ and imagine that $c$ takes larger and larger values. Then the ratios of all prices which enter as arguments of the indirect utility function remain unchanged, but this does

[5] For example, on some bright day old francs are replaced by new francs, each of which is worth 100 old francs. Then all incomes and prices are suddenly multiplied by .01.

not apply to the ratio of any such price to $(m_{t-1} + cm_t)/2$. Hence the associated utility level $u_t(\ )$ changes with $c$.

To prevent that this undesirable phenomenon will occur we shall impose the following fifth axiom. Suppose that the income and all prices of the current period are multiplied by any $c > 0$.[6] This means that $f(x, y)$ becomes $f(x, cy)$, where $(x, y)$ is either $(m_{t-1}, m_t)$ or $(p_{i,t-1}, p_{it})$ for any $i$. Then we require that the arguments $m$ and $p$ of the utility $u_t(\ )$ at which the cost of living index is evaluated are also affected proportionally, which guarantees that the value of $u_t(\ )$ remains unchanged as it should.[7] The proportionality constant is obviously a function of $c$. Hence the fifth axiom is

$$f(x, cy) \equiv F(c) f(x, y) \qquad c, x, y > 0 \tag{4.3}$$

and our next task is to find the form of $F(c)$. Consider then proportional changes in income and prices both in period $t$-1 and in $t$ and apply axiom (4.2) twice:

$$\begin{aligned} f(c_1 x, c_2 y) &\equiv F(c_2) f(c_1 x, y) \equiv F(c_2) f(y, c_1 x) \\ &\equiv F(c_1) F(c_2) f(y, x) \equiv F(c_1) F(c_2) f(x, y) \end{aligned} \tag{4.4}$$

In particular, consider the case $x = y$, $c_1 = c_2 = c$ and apply axiom (4.1) twice:

$$cx \equiv f(cx, cx) \equiv [F(c)]^2 f(x, x) \equiv [F(c)]^2 x$$

from which we conclude

$$F(c) \equiv \sqrt{c} \tag{4.5}$$

We use this result to simplify (4.4):

$$f(c_1 x, c_2 y) \equiv \sqrt{c_1 c_2}\, f(x, y) \tag{4.6}$$

The easiest way to find the form of $f(\ )$ is by taking logarithms, which will be indicated by Greek symbols:

---

[6] The axiom may also be formulated in terms of proportional income and price changes of the previous period; this makes no real difference in view of the symmetry axiom (4.2).

[7] The proportional development of the arguments of $u_t(\ )$ is a sufficient, not a necessary, condition for the value of $u_t(\ )$ to remain unchanged. So we can in principle relax this requirement, but in fact only when knowledge about the form of $u_t(\ )$ is available.

$$\xi = \log x \qquad \eta = \log y \qquad \gamma_i = \log c_i \qquad (i = 1,2)$$

Then $f(x, y) = f(e^{\xi}, e^{\eta})$, the logarithm of which is

$$\log f(e^{\xi}, e^{\eta}) \equiv \phi(\xi, \eta) \text{ say}$$

In logarithmic terms, (4.6) takes the form

$$\phi(\xi + \gamma_1, \eta + \gamma_2) \equiv \phi(\xi, \eta) + \tfrac{1}{2}\gamma_1 + \tfrac{1}{2}\gamma_2$$

which shows immediately that $\phi(\,)$ must be linear in the two arguments and that both slopes are $\frac{1}{2}$. Returning to the original variables, we conclude that $f(x, y) = A\sqrt{xy}$. Application of (4.1) shows that $A$ must be one, which proves that the geometric mean is the only solution compatible with the axioms.[8]

## 5. The Approximation of the Index Numbers by Means of Observed Price-Quantity Data

In this section we shall formulate a simple approximation to the index pair (3.4) based on the observed price-quantity data of the two periods. The approximation will be such that the error is of the third order of smallness in the price and quantity changes. Since the logarithmic index numbers themselves are of the first order in these changes, the relative error is therefore of the second order. Given that the data on such changes are usually of limited accuracy, this order of smallness would seem to be satisfactory for most applications.

The procedure will be based on the following simple lemma, proved in Section 6.A of Theil (1967). Let $f(\,)$ be a real-valued function of a vector of real-valued arguments. If it has continuous derivatives up to the third order, then

$$f(x) - f(y) = \tfrac{1}{2}(f_x + f_y)'(x - y) + O_3 \tag{5.1}$$

where $f_x$ and $f_y$ are the gradients of $f(\,)$ evaluated at $x$ and at $y$, respectively, and $O_3$ is a remainder term whose leading term is of the third degree in the elements of the vector $x$-$y$. The lemma thus states that, if the arguments change from $y$ to $x$, the change in the value of the function is equal to the inner product of the change in the arguments and the

[8] Note that the real income index defined in (3.4) is also invariant against multiplication of $m_t$ and $p_t$ by $c > 0$. It does not affect $U_t$ and $U_{t-1}$ but $p_t^*$ is now multiplied by $\sqrt{c}$. Since the income needed to attain any given utility level at prices $\sqrt{c}\, p_t^*$ increases proportionally with $\sqrt{c}$ (given that $p_t^*$ is fixed), the effects on the numerator and the denominator cancel against each other.

average of the two gradients, apart from an approximation error of the third order. The ordinary Taylor expression uses the gradient in one point and the error term is then of the second order ($O_2$). The importance of lemma (5.1) is that we can reduce this error to the third order and still use an expression which is linear in $x$-$y$, provided that we take the average of the two gradients.

As a simple example, take the share of the $i^{th}$ commodity, $w_i = p_i q_i / m$, and consider it as a function of the *logarithms* of $p_i$, $q_i$ and $m$. The gradient consists of three elements:

$$\frac{\partial w_i}{\partial (\log p_i)} = w_i \qquad \frac{\partial w_i}{\partial (\log q_i)} = w_i \qquad \frac{\partial w_i}{\partial (\log m)} = -w_i \tag{5.2}$$

Then apply (5.1) to the change from period $t$-1 to $t$ and use $\Delta$ for the first-difference operator:

$$\Delta w_{it} = \frac{1}{2}(w_{i,t-1} + w_{it})\Delta(\log p_{it}) + \frac{1}{2}(w_{i,t-1} + w_{it})\Delta(\log q_{it}) - $$
$$-\frac{1}{2}(w_{i,t-1} + w_{it})\Delta(\log m_t) + O_3$$

where $O_3$ is of the third degree in the log-changes in $p_i$, $q_i$ and $m$. When we write $w_{it}^*$ for the average of the $i^{th}$ share in the two periods and $D$ for the log-change operator:

$$w_{it}^* = \frac{1}{2}(w_{i,t-1} + w_{it}) \qquad D = \Delta(\log \quad ) \tag{5.3}$$

our result is simplified to

$$\Delta w_{it} = w_{it}^* D p_{it} + w_{it}^* D q_{it} - w_{it}^* D m_t + O_3 \tag{5.4}$$

This shows that the change in the $i^{th}$ share can be decomposed — apart from a third-order error term — into three terms dealing with the changes in $p_i$, $q_i$ and $m$ separately.

Consider now the line segment $A^*B^*$ of Figure 2. Its length is

$$\log m_I(U_t^*, p_t^*) = \log m_t^* = \log m_{t-1} + \frac{1}{2} D m_t \tag{5.5}$$

where the second equality sign is based on the fact that $m_t^*$ is the geometric mean of $m_{t-1}$ and $m_t$. Imagine that the consumer moves from $A^*$ to $F$ in Figure 2. The change in the value of log $m_I(\ )$ is then $\log m_I(U_t^*, p_t) - \log m_I(U_t^*, p_t^*) = \log m_I(U_t^*, p_t) - \log m_{t-1} - \frac{1}{2}Dm_t$. The left-hand side indicates that the utility level remains constant at the level $U_t^*$ but that the logarithm of the $i^{th}$ price increases by $\frac{1}{2}Dp_{it}$ (since $p_{it}^*$ is the geometric mean of $p_{i,t-1}$ and $p_{it}$). We apply lemma (5.1) as well as (1.3) to conclude:

$$\log m_t(U_t^*, p_t) = \log m_{t-1} + \tfrac{1}{2}Dm_t + \sum_{i=1}^{n} \frac{R_i + S_i}{2} (\tfrac{1}{2}Dp_{it}) + O_3 \tag{5.6}$$

where

$$R_i = w_i^0(U_t^*, p_t) \qquad S_i = w_i^0(U_t^*, p_t^*) \tag{5.7}$$

Next imagine that the consumer moves from $A^*$ to $E$. A similar procedure shows that we have

$$\log m_t(U_t^*, p_{t-1}) = \log m_{t-1} + \tfrac{1}{2}Dm_t + \sum_{i=1}^{n} \frac{S_i + T_i}{2} (-\tfrac{1}{2}Dp_{it}) + O_3 \tag{5.8}$$

where

$$T_i = w_i^0(U_t^*, p_{t-1}) \tag{5.9}$$

We now return to the cost of living index defined in (3.4) and observe that its logarithm is obtained by subtracting the left-hand sides of (5.6) and (5.8). Hence:

$$\log P(p_t, p_{t-1} \mid U_t^*) = \sum_{i=1}^{n} \frac{R_i + 2S_i + T_i}{4} Dp_{it} + O_3 \tag{5.10}$$

Our next task is thus to evaluate $R_i + 2S_i + T_i$. We apply a linear Taylor expansion to $R_i$ and $T_i$ around $(U_t^*, p_t^*)$:

$$R_i = S_i + \sum_{j=1}^{n} \frac{\partial}{\partial(\log p_j)} w_i^0(U_t^*, p_t^*)(\tfrac{1}{2}Dp_{jt}) + O_2$$

$$T_i = S_i + \sum_{j=1}^{n} \frac{\partial}{\partial(\log p_j)} w_i^0(U_t^*, p_t^*)(-\tfrac{1}{2}Dp_{jt}) + O_2$$

Adding the two equations gives $R_i + T_i = 2S_i + O_2$, which means that the average of $R_i$ and $T_i$ is equal to $S_i$ apart from a second-order error term. Hence:

$$R_i + 2S_i + T_i = 4S_i + O_2 \tag{5.11}$$

Consider also $w_{i,t-1}$ and $w_{it}$, the budget shares prevailing in $A_0$ and in $A$, respectively, and recall that $A^*$ is exactly halfway between these two points. A little reflection shows that, when we apply linear Taylor expansions in the logarithms of income and prices to the stretches $A^*A_0$ and $A^*A$, we obtain, after adding the two results:

$$w_{i,t-1} + w_{it} = 2S_i + O_2 \tag{5.12}$$

and hence, on combining (5.10)-(5.12):

$$\log P(p_t, p_{t-1} \mid U_t^*) = \sum_{i=1}^{n} \frac{w_{i,t-1} + w_{it} + O_2}{2} Dp_{it} + O_3$$

Since $Dp_{it}$ is $O_1$, we may merge the $O_2$ term in the numerator with the $O_3$ term at the end. On applying the $w_{it}^*$ notation of (5.3), we thus obtain

$$\log P(p_t, p_{t-1} \mid U_t^*) = \sum_{i=1}^{n} w_{it}^* Dp_{it} + O_3 \tag{5.13}$$

which means that, except for a third-order term in the price and income log-changes, the logarithm of the cost of living index defined in (3.4) is equal to a weighted average of the individual price log-changes with weights equal to the averages of the corresponding budget shares in the two periods. Note that the contribution of the $i^{th}$ commodity to this weighted average is equal to the price component of the value share change given in (5.4).

The weighted average of price log-changes is exactly the same as the price index used in Theil (1967) and applied extensively there.[9] Therefore, although the utility levels at which the cost of living comparisons are made are not the same, there is no real difference up to the second order. The real income indices used here and in Theil (1967) are evaluated at the same price vector ($p_{it}^* = \sqrt{p_{i,t-1} p_{it}}$ , $i = 1, ..., n$). So we confine ourselves to quoting the results:

$$\log Q(U_t, U_{t-1} \mid p_t^*) = Dm_t - \sum_{i=1}^{n} w_{it}^* Dp_{it} + O_3 = \sum_{i=1}^{n} w_{it}^* Dq_{it} + O_3 \tag{5.14}$$

The expression in the middle indicates that the log-change in income is deflated by the price index given in the right-hand of (5.13). The expression after the second equality sign is a weighted average of the log-changes of the individual quantities. The two expressions are equivalent up to the second order.

[9] This should not be regarded as a claim of originality: Törnqvist (1936) was a strong advocate of this particular index, it was listed as index No. 123 by Irving Fisher (1922, p. 473), and perhaps it dates back even earlier.

## References

Fisher, I.: 1922, *The Making of Index Numbers*, Houghton Mifflin Company, Boston-New York.

Kloek, T.: 1966, *Indexcijfers: Enige Methodologische Aspecten*, Ph.D. dissertation, Rotterdam.

Rajaoja, V.: 1958, *A Study in the Theory of Demand Functions and Price Indexes*, Societas Scientiarum Fennica, Helsinki.

Theil, H.: 1967, *Economics and Information Theory*, Rand McNally & Company, Chicago and North-Holland Publishing Company, Amsterdam.

Törnqvist, L.: 1936, "The Bank of Finland's Consumption Price Index," *Bank of Finland Monthly Bulletin*, **10**, 1-8.

## Appendix

By differentiating the identity (1.1) with respect to $m$ we obtain

$$\frac{\partial u_I}{\partial m} = \sum_{j=1}^{n} \frac{\partial u}{\partial q_j} \frac{\partial q_j}{\partial m} = \lambda \sum_{j=1}^{n} p_j \frac{\partial q_j}{\partial m} = \lambda \qquad \text{(A.1)}$$

The second equality sign is based on the familiar proportionality of marginal utilities and prices with $\lambda$ (the marginal utility of income) as proportionality constant. The third equality sign follows from the fact that, if we differentiate both sides of the budget constraint with respect to $m$, we obtain $1 = 1$. Similarly, by differentiating (1.1) with respect to $p_i$, we find

$$\frac{\partial u_I}{\partial p_i} = \sum_{j=1}^{n} \frac{\partial u}{\partial q_j} \frac{\partial q_j}{\partial p_i} = \lambda \sum_{j=1}^{n} p_j \frac{\partial q_j}{\partial p_i} = -\lambda q_i \qquad \text{(A.2)}$$

The last equality sign is verified by differentiating the budget constraint with respect to $p_i$.

Equate $u_I(m, p)$ to $U$ and substitute $m_I(U, p)$ for $m$:

$$U = u_I(m_I(U,p),p) \qquad \text{(A.3)}$$

Differentiate both sides with respect to $p_i$ and apply (A.1) and (A.2):

$$0 = \frac{\partial u_I}{\partial m}\frac{\partial m_I}{\partial p_i} + \frac{\partial u_I}{\partial p_i} = \lambda\frac{\partial m_I}{\partial p_i} - \lambda q_i \tag{A.4}$$

Hence $\partial m_I / \partial p_i = q_i$, from which the result (1.3) follows immediately. The notation $q_i^0(U, p)$ is used in the text to indicate explicitly that it is the optimal quantity of the $i^{th}$ commodity in the utility-price situation $(U, p)$.

CHAPTER 39

# A NEW INDEX NUMBER FORMULA*

HENRI THEIL
*University of Chicago*
*Chicago, Illinois, U.S.A.*

Several years ago (1965, 1967) I started working with price and quantity index numbers, advocated particularly by the Finnish econometrician Törnqvist (1936), whose log-changes are defined as

$$\sum_{i=1}^{n} \bar{w}_{it} \log \frac{p_{it}}{p_{i,t-1}} \quad \text{and} \quad \sum_{i=1}^{n} \bar{w}_{it} \log \frac{q_{it}}{q_{i,t-1}} \tag{1.1}$$

where $p_1,...,p_n$ are prices of the $n$ commodities, the $q$'s are quantities, $m = \Sigma_i p_i q_i$ is total expenditure, $w_i = p_i q_i / m$ is total expenditure share of the $i^{\text{th}}$ commodity, while the subscripts $t-1$ and $t$ refer to two successive periods and

$$\bar{w}_{it} = \frac{1}{2}(w_{it} + w_{i,t-1}) \tag{1.2}$$

is the arithmetic average expenditure share of the $i^{\text{th}}$ commodity in the two successive periods. All logarithms are natural logarithms.

More recently these index numbers were applied by Christensen and Jorgenson (1970) to the United States national accounts, who noted that they have several advantages: they are symmetric in the data of the successive periods [Pierson's (1896) time reversal test] and they are consistent in aggregation. Also, if the $n$ commodities are consumer goods, the indexes have an attractive economic interpretation Theil (1968, 1975-1976): the quantity index is identical with the true index of real income evaluated at the geometric mean prices of $t$ and $t$ - 1, and the price index is identical with the true cost of living index evaluated at the utility level which corresponds to the geometric mean income and prices of $t$ and $t$ - 1, both apart from a relative error term of the second order of smallness. In addition, given that the indexes (1.1) are

* This article first appeared in *The Review of Economics and Statistics*, **55** (1973), 498-502. Reprinted with the permission of Elsevier Science Publishers, B.V. (North Holland). Research supported in part by the National Science Foundation under grant GS-30084. The writer is indebted to Howard Kaikow, programmer-analyst of the Center for Mathematical Studies in Business and Economics of the University of Chicago, for his work on the computations reported in this note.

weighted means of price and quantity log-changes, there is a natural extension to second-order moments which measure the dispersion of price and quantity changes around these means.

But the indexes (1.1) have some disadvantages also. Suppose that the $i^{\text{th}}$ quantity vanishes in one of the two periods ($t$ or $t$ - 1) and that it is positive in the other. The logarithmic change in the $i^{\text{th}}$ quantity is then infinitely large. The same applies to the quantity index because the $i^{\text{th}}$ weight ($\bar{w}_{it}$) is positive. This very awkward phenomenon will rarely occur when annual data are used, but it will not be unusual for monthly or quarterly data on seasonal commodities. Also, the factor reversal test is not exactly satisfied. To explain this we write $D$ for the log-change operator, so that the indexes (1.1) become

$$\sum_{i=1}^{n} \bar{w}_{it} Dp_{it} \quad \text{and} \quad \sum_{i=1}^{n} \bar{w}_{it} Dq_{it}, \tag{1.3}$$

while their sums can be written as

$$\begin{aligned} \sum_{i=1}^{n} \bar{w}_{it}(Dp_{it} + Dq_{it}) &= \sum_{i=1}^{n} \bar{w}_{it} D(p_{it}q_{it}) \\ &= \sum_{i=1}^{n} \bar{w}_{it} D(w_{it}m_t) \\ &= \sum_{i=1}^{n} \bar{w}_{it}(Dw_{it} + Dm_t) \\ &= Dm_t + \sum_{i=1}^{n} \bar{w}_{it} Dw_{it} . \end{aligned} \tag{1.4}$$

The factor reversal test requires that the sum of the log-changes in the price and quantity indexes be equal to the log-change in total expenditure ($Dm_t$), but (1.4) shows that there is a discrepancy, equal to the weighted mean of the log-changes in the expenditure shares. The following result is proved in appendix A:

$$\sum_{i=1}^{n} \bar{w}_{it} Dw_{it} = \frac{1}{12} \sum_{i=1}^{n} \bar{w}_{it} \left( \frac{\Delta w_{it}}{\bar{w}_{it}} \right)^3 + O_5 . \tag{1.5}$$

The first term on the right, which may be viewed as one-twelfth of the third moment of the relative changes in the expenditure shares (relative to their arithmetic means), is evidently of the third order of smallness; the $0_5$ term is a remainder term of the fifth order. Normally, such a third-order term will be quite small. But again, suppose that we have monthly or quarterly data on seasonal commodities, with large relative changes in expenditure shares. The discrepancy may then be much larger, so that an effort to reduce it to a higher order of smallness becomes worthwhile.

Around the turn of the century, Walsh (1901) suggested the use of weights in (1.1) which are proportional to the geometric rather than the arithmetic mean expenditure shares. This amounts to replacing $\overline{w}_{it}$ by

$$\frac{(w_{it}\,w_{i,t-1})^{1/2}}{\sum_{j=1}^{n} (w_{jt}\,w_{j,t-1})^{1/2}} \,. \tag{1.6}$$

This modification implies that the $i^{\text{th}}$ weight vanishes when the $i^{\text{th}}$ quantity vanishes in either $t$ or $t$ - 1. Hence, when defining O log O as O in accordance with the limit of x log x for x → O, we avoid the problem of infinite index changes by replacing $\overline{w}_{it}$ by (1.6). Both indexes, the one based on $\overline{w}_{it}$ and that based on (1.6), are described by Fisher (reprinted 1967, pp. 473, 483).

The factor reversal test applied to the indexes based on (1.6) can be analyzed along the lines of (1.4). This leads to a discrepancy equal to the weighted mean of log-changes in the expenditure shares with (1.6) for $i = 1, ..., n$ as weights. Its leading term is equal to minus one-half of the leading term shown in (1.5). This suggests that by taking a weighted mean of $\overline{w}_{it}$ and the geometric mean share, with weights one-third and two-thirds respectively, we will succeed in eliminating this leading term. Specifically, my proposal is

$$\tilde{w}_{it} = \frac{(\overline{w}_{it}\,w_{it}\,w_{i,t-1})^{1/3}}{\sum_{j=1}^{n} (\overline{w}_{jt}\,w_{jt}\,w_{j,t-1})^{1/3}} \,. \tag{1.7}$$

Both (1.6) and (1.7) vanish when the $i^{\text{th}}$ quantity vanishes in either $t$ or $t$-1, so that there is no problem of infinite index changes. Also, as is proved in appendix A,

$$\sum_{i=1}^{n} \tilde{w}_{it} Dw_{it} = -\frac{1}{720} \sum_{i=1}^{n} \overline{w}_{it} \left( \frac{\Delta w_{it}}{\overline{w}_{it}} \right)^5 + O_7 \tag{1.8}$$

which confirms that the discrepancy in the factor reversal test has been reduced to the fifth order of smallness. Since the other terms occurring in (1.4) are all of the first order of smallness, the relative error is of the second order for $\overline{w}_{it}$ and of the fourth for $\tilde{w}_{it}$. We can write (1.8) in the equivalent form

$$\sum_{i=1}^{n} \tilde{w}_{it} Dw_{it} = -\frac{1}{720} \sum_{i=1}^{n} \tilde{w}_{it} (Dw_{it})^5 + O_7 \,. \tag{1.9}$$

This means that when the $\tilde{w}$'s are used as weights, the log-changes in the expenditure shares have a mean which is approximately equal to a negative fraction -1/720 of their fifth moment. The aggregation properties of the indexes based on $\tilde{w}_{it}$ are straightforward; they are summarized in appendix B.

We shall illustrate this procedure for Dutch data on 16 commodity groups, listed in Table I,

**TABLE I.** Data on 16 Commodity Groups, The Netherlands, 1939-1948

| | $Dp_{it}$ | $Dq_{it}$ | $w_{i,t-1}$ | $w_{it}$ | $\bar{w}_{it}$ | $\tilde{w}_{it}$ |
|---|---|---|---|---|---|---|
| 1. Groceries | .6430 | -.3051 | .0622 | .0439 | .0530 | .0529 |
| 2. Dairy products | .7911 | .1527 | .0690 | .0893 | .0791 | .0793 |
| 3. Vegetables and fruit | 1.2402 | -.2656 | .0400 | .0534 | .0467 | .0467 |
| 4. Meat | .8149 | -.6362 | .0652 | .0393 | .0522 | .0515 |
| 5. Fish | .9363 | .1397 | .0070 | .0104 | .0087 | .0087 |
| 6. Bread | .4221 | -.1173 | .0461 | .0315 | .0388 | .0386 |
| 7. Confectionery | .9357 | .0033 | .0305 | .0393 | .0349 | .0350 |
| 8. Tobacco | 1.0008 | -.0732 | .0309 | .0394 | .0351 | .0352 |
| 9. Beverages | .7704 | -.0401 | .0254 | .0266 | .0260 | .0262 |
| 10. Textiles | 1.0829 | -.2208 | .1250 | .1492 | .1371 | .1378 |
| 11. Footwear | 1.1168 | .1252 | .0125 | .0218 | .0171 | .0168 |
| 12. Household durables | 1.1883 | -.5675 | .0666 | .0625 | .0645 | .0650 |
| 13. Other durables | .9340 | -.0690 | .0176 | .0210 | .0193 | .0194 |
| 14. House rent | .0000 | .0732 | .1064 | .0577 | .0820 | .0802 |
| 15. Water, light, heat | .4848 | -.1349 | .0594 | .0425 | .0509 | .0509 |
| 16. Other goods and services | .6906 | .1370 | .2363 | .2724 | .2543 | .2558 |

concerning the transition from 1939 to 1948. Hence $t$ should be interpreted as 1948 and $t$ - 1 as 1939; no data are available on the intervening years. The price and quantity log-changes are shown in the first two columns. There were substantial price increases, but the development was evidently far from proportional, and most of the quantity log-changes were negative. The difference between corresponding expenditure shares, shown in the next two columns, is also substantial in several cases. The largest $Dw_{it}$ is that of House rent ($i$ = 14), the share of which was reduced by almost one-half; the major cause was rent control ($Dp_{14,t}$ = 0). The last two columns contain $\bar{w}_{it}$ and $\tilde{w}_{it}$. Their pairwise differences are small, even for House rent.

**TABLE II.** First and Second-Order Moments of Log-Changes in Prices, Quantities and Expenditure Shares, 1939-1948

| | $\bar{w}_{it}$ | $\tilde{w}_{it}$ |
|---|---|---|
| Means: | | |
| price log-changes | .7722 | .7740 |
| quantity log-changes | -.0887 | -.0886 |
| expenditure share log-changes | -.001873 | .000011 |
| Variances: | | |
| price log-changes | .1008 | .0997 |
| quantity log-changes | .0583 | .0582 |
| expenditure share log-changes | .0924 | .0914 |
| Covariance: | | |
| price and quantity log-changes | -.0333 | -.0332 |

The first two lines of Table II contain the log-changes in the price and quantity index numbers. The difference between the two weighing methods is slight. Using 1939 = 100 as a base, we obtain a price index in 1948 of 216.5 using $\bar{w}_{it}$ and of 216.8 using $\tilde{w}_{it}$. The third line of the table contains the discrepancies (1.5) and (1.9) in six decimal places. The $\bar{w}$ weighting satisfies the factor reversal test to two decimal places, the $\tilde{w}$ weighting to four. The leading terms in the right-hand sides of (1.5) and (1.9) are both close to the expressions which they serve to approximate.

The remainder of Table II contains second-order moments. If we write

$$DP_t = \sum_{i=1}^{n} w_i DP_{it}, \qquad DQ_t = \sum_{i=1}^{n} w_i Dq_{it},$$

$$DW_t = \sum_{i=1}^{n} w_i Dw_{it}$$

for the means, where $w_i$ is either $\bar{w}_{it}$ or $\tilde{w}_{it}$, then the corresponding variances of the price and quantity log-changes are

$$\Pi_t = \sum_{i=1}^{n} w_i (Dp_{it} - DP_t)^2 \quad \text{and}$$
$$K_t = \sum_{i=1}^{n} w_i (Dq_{it} - DQ_t)^2$$

while their covariance is

$$\Gamma_t = \sum_{i=1}^{n} w_i (Dp_{it} - DP_t)(Dq_{it} - DQ_t) .$$

Also consider

$$\begin{aligned} Dw_{it} - DW_t &= Dp_{it} + Dq_{it} - Dm_t - DW_t \\ &= Dp_{it} - DP_t + Dq_{it} - DQ_t \\ &\quad + (DP_t + DQ_t - Dm_t - DW_t) . \end{aligned}$$

The expression in parentheses vanishes; this follows from (1.4), which also holds when $\bar{w}_{it}$ is replaced by $\tilde{w}_{it}$. Hence:

$$Dw_{it} - DW_t = (Dp_{it} - DP_t) + (Dq_{it} - DQ_t) .$$

By squaring both sides and weighting with expenditure shares we obtain a decomposition of the variance of the log-changes in these shares:

$$\sum_{i=1}^{n} w_i (Dw_{it} - DW_t)^2 = \Pi_t + K_t + 2\Gamma_t .$$

The three variances occurring in this decomposition and the covariance are shown in Table II with $w_i$ specified as $\bar{w}_{it}$ and as $\tilde{w}_{it}$. The results are pairwise close to each other.

**References**

Christensen, L.R., and D.W. Jorgenson: 1970, "U.S. Real Product and Real Factor Input, 1929-1967," *The Review of Income and Wealth*, Series 16, 19-50.

Fisher, I.: 1922, *The Making of Index Numbers*, Houghton Miffin Company, Boston; third edition (1927) was reprinted in 1967 by Augustus M. Kelley, Publishers, New York.

Pierson, N.G.: 1896, "Further Considerations on Index-Numbers," *The Economic Journal*, **6**, 127-131.

Theil, H.: 1965, "The Information Approach to Demand Analysis," *Econometrica*, **33**, 67-87.

Theil, H.: 1967, *Economics and Information Theory*, American Elsevier Publishing Company, New York, and North-Holland Publishing Company, Amsterdam.

Theil, H.: 1968, "On the Geometry and the Numerical Approximation of Cost of Living and Real Income Indices," *De Economist*, **116**, 677-689.

Theil, H.: 1975-1976, *Theory and Measurement of Consumer Demand*, Elsevier/North Holland, Inc., New York, and North Holland Publishing Company, Amsterdam, chapters 3 and 10.

Törnqvist, L.: 1936, "The Bank of Finland's Consumption Price Index," *Bank of Finland Monthly Bulletin*, no. 10, 1-8.

Walsh, C.M.: 1901, *The Measurement of General Exchange-Value*, The Macmillan Company, New York.

## APPENDIX

### (A) *Derivations*

The log-change in the $i^{th}$ expenditure share may be written as

$$Dw_{it} = \log \frac{w_{it}}{w_{i,t-1}} = \log\left(1 + \frac{\Delta w_{it}}{2\bar{w}_{it}}\right) - \log\left(1 - \frac{\Delta w_{it}}{2\bar{w}_{it}}\right).$$

By expanding the two logarithms in the third member we obtain

$$Dw_{it} = \frac{\Delta w_{it}}{\bar{w}_{it}} + \frac{1}{12}\left(\frac{\Delta w_{it}}{\bar{w}_{it}}\right)^3 + \frac{1}{80}\left(\frac{\Delta w_{it}}{\bar{w}_{it}}\right)^5 + O_7 . \tag{A.1}$$

Multiplication by $\bar{w}_{it}$ and summation over $i$ gives

$$\sum_{i=1}^{n} \bar{w}_{it} Dw_{it} = \frac{1}{12}\sum_{i=1}^{n} \bar{w}_{it}\left(\frac{\Delta w_{it}}{\bar{w}_{it}}\right)^3 + \frac{1}{80}\sum_{i=1}^{n} \bar{w}_{it}\left(\frac{\Delta w_{it}}{\bar{w}_{it}}\right)^5 + O_7 , \tag{A.2}$$

which proves (1.5).

We shall also need:

$$\left(\sqrt{w_{it}} - \sqrt{w_{i,t-1}}\right)^2 = \frac{1}{4}\bar{w}_{it}\left(\frac{\Delta w_{it}}{\bar{w}_{it}}\right)^2 + \frac{1}{64}\bar{w}_{it}\left(\frac{\Delta w_{it}}{\bar{w}_{it}}\right)^4 + O_6 , \tag{A.3}$$

which may be proved by means of

$$\left(\sqrt{w_{it}} - \sqrt{w_{i,t-1}}\right)^2\left(\sqrt{w_{it}} + \sqrt{w_{i,t-1}}\right)^2 = (\Delta w_{it})^2 \tag{A.4}$$

and

$$\left(\sqrt{w_{it}} + \sqrt{w_{i,t-1}}\right)^2 = 2\,(w_{it} + w_{i,t-1}) - \left(w_{it} + w_{i,t-1} - 2\sqrt{w_{it}w_{i,t-1}}\right)$$

$$= 4\bar{w}_{it} - \left(\sqrt{w_{it}} - \sqrt{w_{i,t-1}}\right)^2 .$$

Substitute this in (A.4):

$$-\left(\sqrt{w_{it}} - \sqrt{w_{i,t-1}}\right)^4 + 4\bar{w}_{it}\left(\sqrt{w_{it}} - \sqrt{w_{i,t-1}}\right)^2 - (\Delta w_{it})^2 = 0 .$$

This is a quadratic equation in $\left(\sqrt{w_{it}} - \sqrt{w_{i,t-1}}\right)^2$, of which the relevant root is

$$2\bar{w}_{it} - \tfrac{1}{2}\,[\,16\bar{w}_{it}^2 - 4\,(\Delta w_{it})^2\,]^{1/2}$$

$$= 2\bar{w}_{it} - 2\bar{w}_{it}\left[1 - \left(\frac{\Delta w_{it}}{2\bar{w}_{it}}\right)^2\right]^{1/2}$$

$$= 2\bar{w}_{it} - 2\bar{w}_{it}\left[1 - \tfrac{1}{2}\left(\frac{\Delta w_{it}}{2\bar{w}_{it}}\right)^2 - \tfrac{1}{8}\left(\frac{\Delta w_{it}}{2\bar{w}_{it}}\right)^4\right] + O_6$$

which gives (A.3).

Next consider

$$\bar{w}_{it} - \sqrt{w_{it}w_{i,t-1}} = \tfrac{1}{2}\,(w_{it} + w_{i,t-1}) - \sqrt{w_{it}w_{i,t-1}}$$

$$= \tfrac{1}{2}\left(\sqrt{w_{it}} - \sqrt{w_{i,t-1}}\right)^2 ,$$

which implies

$$\frac{\sqrt{w_{it} w_{i,t-1}}}{\bar{w}_{it}} = 1 - \frac{\left(\sqrt{w_{it}} - \sqrt{w_{i,t-1}}\right)^2}{2\bar{w}_{it}} .$$

This is used in

$$\begin{aligned} (\bar{w}_{it} w_{it} w_{i,t-1})^{1/3} &= \bar{w}_{it} \left( \frac{\sqrt{w_{it} w_{i,t-1}}}{\bar{w}_{it}} \right)^{2/3} \\ &= \bar{w}_{it} \left[ 1 - \frac{\left(\sqrt{w_{it}} - \sqrt{w_{i,t-1}}\right)^2}{2\bar{w}_{it}} \right]^{2/3} . \end{aligned} \tag{A.5}$$

It follows from (A.3) that the expression in brackets differs from 1 to the order of $O_2$. When we raise it to the power 2/3, we obtain

$$1 - \frac{\left(\sqrt{w_{it}} - \sqrt{w_{i,t-1}}\right)^2}{3\bar{w}_{it}} - \frac{\left(\sqrt{w_{it}} - \sqrt{w_{i,t-1}}\right)^4}{36\bar{w}_{it}^2} + O_6 ,$$

which becomes, after substituting (A.3),

$$1 - \frac{1}{12} \left( \frac{\Delta w_{it}}{\bar{w}_{it}} \right)^2 - \frac{1}{144} \left( \frac{\Delta w_{it}}{\bar{w}_{it}} \right)^4 + O_6 .$$

Hence (A.5) becomes

$$(\bar{w}_{it} w_{it} w_{i,t-1})^{1/3} = \bar{w}_{it} - \frac{1}{12} w_{it} \left( \frac{\Delta w_{it}}{\bar{w}_{it}} \right)^2 - \frac{1}{144} \bar{w}_{it} \left( \frac{\Delta w_{it}}{\bar{w}_{it}} \right)^4 + O_6 . \tag{A.6}$$

Now multiply (A.6) by $Dw_{it}$ and sum over $i$. The right-hand side of the equation thus obtained can be written as the sum of three terms, the first of which is $\Sigma_i \bar{w}_{it} Dw_{it}$ given in (A.2). Using (A.1), we write the second term as

$$
\begin{aligned}
&- \frac{1}{12} \sum_{i=1}^{n} \bar{w}_{it} \left( \frac{\Delta w_{it}}{\bar{w}_{it}} \right)^2 \left[ \frac{\Delta w_{it}}{\bar{w}_{it}} + \frac{1}{12} \left( \frac{\Delta w_{it}}{\bar{w}_{it}} \right)^3 \right] + O_7 \\
&= - \frac{1}{12} \sum_{i=1}^{n} \bar{w}_{it} \left( \frac{\Delta w_{it}}{\bar{w}_{it}} \right)^3 - \frac{1}{144} \sum_{i=1}^{n} \bar{w}_{it} \left( \frac{\Delta w_{it}}{\bar{w}_{it}} \right)^5 + O_7 .
\end{aligned}
\tag{A.7}
$$

The third is

$$
- \frac{1}{144} \sum_{i=1}^{n} \bar{w}_{it} \left( \frac{\Delta w_{it}}{\bar{w}_{it}} \right)^5 + O_7 . \tag{A.8}
$$

By adding (A.2), (A.7), and (A.8) we obtain

$$
\sum_{i=1}^{n} ( \bar{w}_{it} w_{it} w_{i,t-1} )^{1/3} Dw_{it} = - \frac{1}{720} \sum_{i=1}^{n} \bar{w}_{it} \left( \frac{\Delta w_{it}}{\bar{w}_{it}} \right)^5 + O_7 . \tag{A.9}
$$

The left-hand side of (A.9) is identical to that of (1.8) except for the denominator in (1.7). It follows from (A.6) that this denominator differs from 1 to the order $O_2$, so that (1.8) and (A.9) are equivalent apart from a remainder term $O_7$. The equivalence of (1.8) and (1.9) apart from an $O_7$ term, follows from the fact that the difference between $\tilde{w}_{it}$ and $\bar{w}_{it}$ and that between $Dw_{it}$ and $\Delta \bar{w}_{it} / w_{it}$ are both $O_2$.

## (B) *Indexes for Commodity Groups*

Let each of the $n$ commodities belong to one of $G$ commodity groups, $S_1, \ldots, S_G$. The expenditure share of $S_g$ in $t$ is $W_{gt} = \Sigma w_{it}$ and the group extension of $\tilde{w}_{it}$ is $\tilde{W}_{gt} = \Sigma\, \tilde{w}_{it}$, where the summations are over $i \varepsilon S_g$. The following conditional shares are used for the indexes of $S_g$:

$$\frac{\tilde{w}_{it}}{\tilde{W}_{gt}} = \frac{(\bar{w}_{it} w_{it} w_{i,t-1})^{1/3}}{\sum_{j \in S_g} (\bar{w}_{jt} w_{jt} w_{j,t-1})^{1/3}} \cdot \qquad i \in S_g \tag{B.1}$$

The log-changes in the price and quantity indexes of $S_g$ are therefore

$$DP_{gt} = \sum_{i \in S_g} \frac{\tilde{w}_{it}}{\tilde{W}_{gt}} Dp_{it} \text{ and } DQ_{gt} = \sum_{i \in S_g} \frac{\tilde{w}_{it}}{\tilde{W}_{gt}} Dq_{it} . \tag{B.2}$$

The price indexes of the groups satisfy

$$\sum_{g=1}^{G} \tilde{W}_{gt} DP_{gt} = \sum_{i=1}^{n} \tilde{w}_{it} Dp_{it} ,$$

which shows that they are consistent in aggregation. The same obviously holds for the quantity indexes.

By adding $DP_{gt}$ and $DQ_{gt}$ we obtain

$$\sum_{i \in S_g} \frac{\tilde{w}_{it}}{\tilde{W}_{gt}} D(p_{it} q_{it}) = \sum_{i \in S_g} \frac{\tilde{w}_{it}}{\tilde{W}_{gt}} D\left( \frac{w_{it}}{W_{gt}} W_{gt} m_t \right)$$

$$= \sum_{i \in S_g} \frac{\tilde{w}_{it}}{\tilde{W}_{gt}} \left[ D\left( \frac{w_{it}}{W_{gt}} \right) + D(W_{gt} m_t) \right],$$

which implies

$$DP_{gt} + DQ_{gt} = D(W_{gt} m_t) + \sum_{i \in S_g} \frac{\tilde{w}_{it}}{\tilde{W}_{gt}} + D\left( \frac{w_{it}}{W_{gt}} \right). \tag{B.3}$$

The first term on the right is the log-change in the expenditure on $S_g$. A comparison with (B.1) and (1.7) shows that the second term is the conditional version of $\Sigma_i \bar{w}_{it} Dw_{it}$, so that (1.9) may be applied in conditional form:

$$\sum_{i \in S_g} \frac{\bar{w}_{it}}{\bar{W}_{gt}} D\left(\frac{w_{it}}{W_{gt}}\right) = -\frac{1}{720} \sum_{i \in S_g} \frac{\bar{w}_{it}}{\bar{W}_{gt}} \left[D\left(\frac{w_{it}}{W_{gt}}\right)\right]^5 + O_7 . \tag{B.4}$$

For the variances and covariance of the price and quantity log-changes, discussed at the end of the text, there is a groupwise decomposition of the classical analysis-of-variance (and covariance) type.

# SECTION 3.3: MODELLING THE DISTURBANCES IN DEMAND SYSTEMS

CHAPTER 40

# AN ECONOMIC THEORY OF THE SECOND MOMENTS OF DISTURBANCES OF BEHAVIORAL EQUATIONS*

HENRI THEIL
*University of Chicago*
*Chicago, Illinois, U.S.A.*

Applied econometricians have known for a long time that the smooth curves in economics texts which pretend to be the geometric representations of behavioral equations present an over-simplified picture of the real world. It almost never occurs that data fit a simple theoretical relation exactly, and an explicit method of interpreting and handling the deviations from such relations is therefore needed. In the early days of econometrics it was frequently assumed that observational errors were the only or at least the main cause of the occurrence of deviations, but this idea was later rejected on the ground that even when the data are perfect, deviations will continue to be found because there are very few economic agents who react exactly according to some simple mathematical law. The "neglected factors" entered into the picture; their combined influence came to be regarded as a random disturbance with zero mean and unknown variance.

It is important to realize that this disturbance variance is as much an unknown parameter of the model as the coefficients of the explanatory variables are. Typically, however, the economic theorist concentrates his efforts exclusively on these variables and their coefficients. He assumes that the decision maker whose behavior is described by the equation maximizes or minimizes a criterion function;

$$f(x) = f(x_1, ..., x_n), \tag{1}$$

where $x = [x_i, ..., x_n]'$ is a vector of decision variables, and that the extremum is sought subject to a set of $q$ constraints:

$$g_h(x) = 0 \qquad h = 1, ..., q. \tag{2}$$

Under appropriate conditions on the form of the functions (1) and (2), he will obtain as the solution a vector $\bar{x}$ which expresses each decision variable uniquely in terms of the parameters that determine the functions $f(\,)$, $g_1(\,)$, ..., $g_q(\,)$. Consumer demand theory is a classical example; then (1) is the utility function and (2) is the budget constraint, and

*This article first appeared in the *American Economic Review*, **61** (1971), 190-194. Reprinted by permission of the American Economic Association.

the decision variables $x_1, ..., x_n$ are the quantities bought which are expressed by the demand functions (the behavioral equations) in terms of income and prices (the $n$+1 parameters of the budget constraint).

The disturbing thing about this approach is that it leaves no room for a random disturbance. It is undoubtedly true that there are factors which are neglected by the approach, so that discrepancies between the behavior predicted by the equation(s) and the observed behavior must be expected, but it is equally true that the economic theory in this form has nothing to say about the variance of such discrepancies. This problem has gained in importance in the last few decades since the introduction of simultaneous equation systems and "seemingly unrelated regressions," which require consideration of the disturbance variances of several equations and also of their contemporaneous covariances. When there are $L$ such equations and when the $j$th contains $N_j$ unknown coefficients, their total number is

$$N_1 + N_2 + ... + N_L \tag{3}$$

and the total number of variances and contemporaneous covariances (taking account of the symmetry of their matrix) is

$$(\tfrac{1}{2})\, L\, (L + 1)\,. \tag{4}$$

When $L$ is moderately large, the number (4) may be of the same order of magnitude as the number (3) or even larger.

Economic theory in its conventional form focuses on the expectational part of behavioral equations by making more or less explicit statements on the coefficients whose number is given in (3). The question arises whether it is possible to extend this theory in such a way that it can also be brought to bear on the second moments whose number is given in (4). The objective of this article is to show that, if a set of behavioral equations refers to one single decision maker (as in the consumer demand case discussed following (2)), a plausible argument can be made for the proposition that the Hessian matrix[1] of the criterion function is the crucial determinant of the covariance matrix of the disturbances.[2] Basically, the idea in the case of one single decision variable is that, if the second-order derivative at the point of the extremum is close to zero, the loss incurred by a decision which deviates from the optimum to a moderate extent is very small, and the disturbance of the corresponding behavioral equation may then be expected to have a large variance.

---

[1] The matrix of second-order derivatives.

[2] The reader who is statistically oriented will recognize the formal similarity with the asymptotic covariance matrix of maximum-likelihood estimators, which is related to the Hessian matrix of the logarithmic likelihood function.

## 1. The Unconstrained Case

We start with the case in which there are no constraints, $q$ of (2) being zero, and assume that $f(\,)$ of (1) is to be minimized. In many economic theories, this is a smooth and well-behaved function and we shall confine ourselves to this type by assuming that it can be approximated to a sufficient degree of accuracy by a quadratic function around the minimum:

$$f(x) = a'x + (\tfrac{1}{2})\,x'Ax \tag{5}$$

where the constant term is disregarded because it is irrelevant from the viewpoint of minimization. The matrix $A$ is the (symmetric) Hessian matrix of $f(\,)$ evaluated at the point of the minimum; it will be assumed to be positive definite. The decision vector which minimizes $f(\,)$ is then

$$\bar{x} = -A^{-1}a\,. \tag{6}$$

Consider any decision $x$ which differs from $\bar{x}$. The associated value $f(x)$ of the criterion function will exceed $f(\bar{x})$ and the excess is the following quadratic form:

$$\begin{aligned} f(x) - f(\bar{x}) &= \tfrac{1}{2}(x - \bar{x})'A(x - \bar{x}) \\ &= \tfrac{1}{2}\xi'A\xi \end{aligned} \tag{7}$$

where

$$\xi = x - \bar{x} = x + A^{-1}a \tag{8}$$

is the decision discrepancy vector. Given that $A$ is symmetric and positive definite, there exists a nonsingular matrix $P$ such that

$$P'P = A\,. \tag{9}$$

It follows from (7) that the excess can be written as

$$f(x) - f(\bar{x}) = \tfrac{1}{2}\xi'P'P\xi = \tfrac{1}{2}\eta'\eta\,, \tag{10}$$

where

$$\begin{aligned}\eta &= P\xi = Px + PA^{-1}a \\ &= Px + P(P'P)^{-1}a \\ &= Px + (P')^{-1}a \quad .\end{aligned} \tag{11}$$

The second and third steps in (11) are based on (8) and (9), respectively.

Equation (10) shows that minimizing $f(\,)$ is equivalent to the minimization of the sum of squares of the elements of $\eta$. This is the simplest possible reduction of the extremum problem, and we shall therefore refer to the $\eta$ elements as the *elementary decision variables*. If the decision maker definitely wants to minimize $f(\,)$, he should put each of these variables equal to zero. If he behaves differently, the loss which he incurs—the excess of $f(\,)$ over the minimum value—is equal to one-half of the squared length of $\eta$.

To introduce the stochastic element we suppose that the vector $a$ of the linear part of $f(\,)$ in (5) fluctuates randomly, while the matrix $A$ of the quadratic part remains fixed as before.[3] It follows from (6) that the optimal vector $\bar{x}$ then becomes a linear function of random variables, so that it is also random. The vector $\bar{x}$ is then no longer feasible as a decision vector. Furthermore, when $x$ is the (nonrandom) decision which is actually made, $\eta$ of (11) is equal to the sum of the random vector $(P')^{-1}a$ and the nonrandom vector $Px$. In other words, the decision maker has no longer full control over his elementary decision variables. Part of each such variable is controlled, but the rest is a linear function of random variables.

The minimization of $f(\,)$ no longer suffices as a criterion of this stochastic situation. The criterion to be developed here rests on the assumption that the decision maker is interested in a simple mechanism to control the situation. This seems reasonably realistic, given that the decision makers involved are typically consumers or entrepreneurs who have little inclination toward formal analysis. Specifically, consider the following:

(1) Given that $\eta$ is random, the decision maker no longer controls this vector, but he can at least adjust the decision vector $x$ over time so that he controls the *distribution* of $\eta$. It follows from (10) that the loss associated with any decision is equal to $\frac{1}{2}\eta'\eta$, which is a random variable. We assume that the decision maker is interested in controlling its average value, $\frac{1}{2}E(\eta'\eta)$, and this implies that the only feature of the distribution of $\eta$ which is relevant is the matrix of its second-order moments.

(2) Since the criterion $\frac{1}{2}E(\eta'\eta)$ concerns only the squares of the elementary decision variables, not their products, there is no gain in designing a particular cross-moment pattern. The simplest solution is then to arrange a diagonal moment matrix $E(\eta\eta')$.

---

[3] The simplest way to visualize the case of a stochastic vector $a$ and a nonstochastic matrix $A$ is by interpreting $f(\,)$ as a cost function. Then all marginal cost functions are subject to additive random shocks. If the matrix $A$ were also random, the marginal cost functions would be subject to both additive and multiplicative random shocks, which is much more difficult to handle.

(3) For each of the elementary decision variables, the loss associated with a nonzero value is equal to one-half of its square. There is therefore no reason to let any such variable have a larger mean square than any other, which leads to the specification of equal diagonal elements in the moment matrix $E(\eta\eta')$. On combining this with the conclusion reached under (2) we obtain

$$E(\eta\eta') = \sigma^2 I \tag{12}$$

where $\sigma^2$ is a measure for the loss which the decision maker is willing to incur on the average. The criterion mentioned under (1), $\frac{1}{2}E(\eta'\eta)$, is then $\sigma^2$ multiplied by one-half the number of decision variables.

It follows from (8) and (11) that the difference between the actual decision $x$ and the theoretically optimal[4] decision $\bar{x}$ is $\xi = P^{-1}\eta$. This difference is the disturbance vector of the equation system which describes the decision maker's behavior with respect to the variables which he controls. Given the specification (12), we obtain the following moment matrix for this disturbance vector:

$$\begin{aligned} \upsilon(x - \bar{x}) &= P^{-1}E(\eta\eta')(P')^{-1} \\ &= \sigma^2(P'P)^{-1} = \sigma^2 A^{-1} \end{aligned} \tag{13}$$

which thus turns out to be a positive multiple of the inverse of the Hessian matrix of the criterion function.

When there is only one decision variable, this result implies a disturbance variance which is inversely proportional to the second-order derivative $d^2f/dx^2$ evaluated at the point of the minimum.[5] As stated at the end of the introduction, this simply means that the disturbance variance is larger (smaller) when the loss associated with a given discrepancy $x - \bar{x}$ is smaller (larger). When we have two decision variables, the moment matrix (13) becomes

$$\sigma^2 \begin{bmatrix} a_{11} & a_{12} \\ a_{12} & a_{22} \end{bmatrix}^{-1} = \frac{\sigma^2}{a_{11}a_{22} - a_{12}^2} \begin{bmatrix} a_{22} & -a_{12} \\ -a_{12} & a_{11} \end{bmatrix}. \tag{14}$$

This indicates that, when the two decision variables do not interact in the criterion function (5) in the sense that $a_{12}$ vanishes, the associated disturbances have a zero cross-

[4] Theoretically optimal in the sense of optimal under nonstochastic conditions.

[5] When the criterion function is not quadratic, the derivative is a function of $x$ and its value at $\bar{x}$ is random when $\bar{x}$ is random. One may then decide to take the expectation to obtain an approximate value. Note further that the word "variance" used here in the text is applicable only when the disturbances have zero mean. This condition is usually satisfied due to the presence of a constant term in the equation.

moment. If they do interact, the cross-moment has a sign opposite to that of $a_{12}$. If they interact to a sufficient degree, $a_{12}^2$ being close to $a_{11}a_{22}$, the moments are all large in absolute value and the moment matrix is close to singularity. These results are intuitively plausible.

We conclude by noting that the model developed above treats the decision which is actually made ($x$) as nonstochastic and the theoretically optimal decision and its determining factors ($\bar{x}$ and $a$) as random variables, whereas it is customary in the standard linear regression model to treat the dependent variable (our decision variable) as random and the explanatory variables (the determining factors) as taking fixed values. This difference is not essential, however, because the conditional distribution of $x - \bar{x}$ given $\bar{x}$ has the same moment matrix as the conditional distribution given $x$.

## 2. The Constrained Case

Next assume that there are $q>0$ constraints (2) subject to which the function (5) is to be minimized. We shall linearize these constraints in the same way as the criterion function is quadratized:

$$Bx = b \,, \tag{15}$$

where the elements of $B$ are to be interpreted as first-order partial derivatives of the functions $g_1(\,), \ldots, g_q(\,)$ defined in (2), evaluated at the point of the constrained minimum. It is assumed that $B$ has full row rank (i.e., rank $q$), so that the possibility of inconsistent or linearly dependent constraints is excluded.

One way of solving this more general problem is by using the constraints (15) to eliminate $q$ of the $x$'s and then proceeding along the lines of the previous section. However, a more elegant extension can be formulated on the basis of the Lagrangian function:

$$\begin{aligned} F(x,\lambda) &= f(x) + \lambda'(Bx - b) \\ &= [a' \;\; -b'] \begin{bmatrix} x \\ \lambda \end{bmatrix} + \tfrac{1}{2}[x' \;\; \lambda'] \begin{bmatrix} A & B' \\ B & 0 \end{bmatrix} \begin{bmatrix} x \\ \lambda \end{bmatrix} . \end{aligned} \tag{16}$$

The new decision vector is $[x' \ \lambda']'$ rather than $x$, the coefficient vector of the linear part is now $[a' \ {-b'}]$,[6] and the original Hessian matrix is bordered by $q$ rows and $q$ columns. It is readily seen that the extension of the moment matrix result (13) to the present case amounts to $\sigma^2$ times the inverse of the bordered Hessian matrix, and that the leading sub-matrix (corresponding to $A$ in the bordered Hessian before inversion) of this inverse gives the moment matrix of the disturbance vector corresponding to $x$. Application of the standard rules for partitioned inversion gives:

$$\upsilon(x - \bar{x}) = \sigma^2 [A^{-1} - A^{-1}B'(BA^{-1}B')^{-1}BA^{-1}]. \tag{17}$$

The matrix (17) is zero in the special case of a square nonsingular $B$. This is as it should be, because the decision vector can then be solved from the constraint (15). Note further that premultiplication of the moment matrix (17) by $B$ gives a zero matrix, which is also in agreement with (15).

## 3. Application to Consumer Demand Theory

Consider a consumer whose objective is to maximize a utility function $u(x)$ subject to the budget constraint $p'x = m$, where $p$ and $x$ are $n$-element vectors of prices and quantities, respectively, and $m$ is total expenditure (or income). It is assumed that $p$ and $m$ are fixed and given from the consumer's point of view. This amounts to the following specification of the more general model described above: $f(\,) = -u(\,)$, $B = p'$, $b = m$. Write $U$ for the Hessian matrix of $u(\,)$ in the constrained maximum, so that $A$ is specified as $-U$. The moment matrix (17) then becomes

$$-\sigma^2\left(U^{-1} - \frac{1}{p'U^{-1}p}U^{-1}pp'U^{-1}\right), \tag{18}$$

which is a positive semi-definite matrix of order $n \times n$ and rank $n - 1$ when $U$ is negative definite. The singularity of the moment matrix is due to the budget constraint $p'x = m$.

The matrix (18) is precisely the same as the moment matrix which I derived earlier on the basis of *ad hoc* considerations.[7] These considerations do add to the plausibility of the general model, however, and it is therefore worthwhile to summarize them here briefly without going into mathematical details:

(1) When equating $-f(x)$ of (5) to $u(x)$, we obtain

---

[6] The form of this coefficient vector indicates that the vector $b$ can be allowed to fluctuate randomly over time, just as $a$.

[7] See Theil (1967), pp. 228-233.

$$-a_i + \tfrac{1}{2}\sum_j u_{ij}x_j \tag{19}$$

for the marginal utility of the $i$th commodity, $a_i$ and $u_{ij}$ being the $i$th element of $a$ and the $(i, j)$th element of $U$, respectively. The assumption of a random vector $a$ implies that the marginal utilities are subject to additive random shocks. Assume that they have zero expectation. The main problem, to be considered under (2), is the specification of the $n$x$n$ covariance matrix of these shocks.

(2) Consider the case $u_{ij} = 0$, so that the $i$th and $j$th marginal utilities do not depend on $x_j$ and $x_i$, respectively. This indicates that the two commodities satisfy unrelated wants, so that it seems reasonable to assume that the random shocks of their marginal utilities are uncorrelated. Next consider the case of a *negative* $u_{ij}$. The $i$th marginal utility then decreases with $x_j$, which may be interpreted in the sense that the two commodities satisfy similar wants. When the marginal utilities are subject to random fluctuations, those corresponding to similar wants will usually be of the same sign and will therefore be *positively* correlated. Third, consider a commodity with a large negative $u_{ii}$, so that its marginal utility is unstable in the sense of being sensitive to small changes in $q_i$. It is then plausible that it is also unstable in the sense that the random shocks of its marginal utility have a large variance. All three cases ($u_{ij} = 0$, $u_{ij} < 0$, $-u_{ii}$ large) are covered when it is assumed that the covariance matrix of the random shocks is a negative multiple of the Hessian matrix $U$, and this leads directly to the matrix (18).

## Reference

Theil, H.: 1967, *Economics and Information Theory*, North Holland Publishing Co., Amsterdam, Holland.

## CHAPTER 41

# A THEORY OF RATIONAL RANDOM BEHAVIOR*


HENRI THEIL
*University of Chicago,*
*Chicago, Illinois, USA*



ABSTRACT: It is shown that, under general conditions, rational random behavior (appropriately defined) is equivalent to large-sample maximum-likelihood estimation of the theoretically optimal decision. Some supporting evidence, based on Dutch and American consumption data, is presented. The approach can also be used as a statistical basis for the delegation of authority.


## 1. The Problem

Consider a decision maker who controls $n$ variables, to be written as a column vector $x$. Our starting point is the assumption that this decision maker wants to maximize a criterion function $f(x)$ with continuous third-order derivatives and a unique maximum at $\bar{x}$. A Taylor expansion around $\bar{x}$ gives

$$f(\bar{x}) - f(x) = -\frac{1}{2}(x - \bar{x})'A(x - \bar{x}) + O_3 , \qquad (1.1)$$

where $A$ is the Hessian matrix of $f(\,)$ at $\bar{x}$ and $O_3$ is a remainder term of the third order of smallness in the elements of $x - \bar{x}$. The left side of (1.1) is the loss associated with any decision $x$, i.e., the amount by which the value of the criterion function is depressed below the attainable maximum. The equation states that, apart from an $O_3$ remainder term, this loss is equal to a quadratic form in the decision discrepancy vector $x - \bar{x}$. The matrix of this form is $-\frac{1}{2}A$, which is symmetric positive definite because $f(\,)$ has a unique maximum by assumption.

There is not much need to explain that few real-life decision makers behave in strict agreement with the maximization of a criterion function $f(\,)$. Classical economic theory postulates that housewives maximize a utility function, but there are few who take this advice literally. Decision makers of larger organizations are subject to numerous

---


* This article first appeared in the *Journal of the American Statistical Association*, **69** (1974), 310-314. Reprinted with the permission of The American Statistical Association. Henri Theil is university professor and director, Center for Mathematical Studies in Business and Economics, Graduate School of Business/Department of Economics, University of Chicago, Chicago, IL, 60637. Research for this article was supported in part by the National Science Foundation under Grant GS-30084. Valuable comments by an associate editor and a referee are gratefully acknowledged.

pressures. For example, they receive suggestions from subordinates and they will frequently give a go-ahead even when the implications are not fully in agreement with a maximum *f*( ), for various reasons, such as lack of time for explaining why the implications are wrong or a desire to keep subordinates enthusiastic.

It is in principle possible to include such considerations in the criterion function, but it is doubtful whether this will lead to a more accurate description of actual behavior. Instead, let us look at the way in which econometricians and other social scientists formulate behavioral equations. They introduce only the more important factors as explanatory variables and they consider all other factors (the "neglected variables") as one factor in the sense that their combined effect on the dependent variable is treated as a random variable, known as the disturbance of the equation. Next consider the decision maker for whom this dependent variable is a decision variable. The number of factors relevant to his decision is too large to take them into account individually. So, similar to what the econometrician does, he divides these factors into two groups, one consisting of a limited number of major factors and the other of all less important (minor) factors. His decision problem is accordingly divided into two stages, to be called the *planning stage* and the *implementation stage*:

1. In the planning stage the decision maker confines himself to the major factors, which we assume are substituted in the criterion function *f*( ). [For example, in the consumer's case with a utility function and a budget constraint, we imagine that the constraint is substituted in the utility function, so that *f*( ) involves decision variables (quantities bought) as well as income and prices.] Since only some of the factors are considered at this stage, maximization of *f*( ) is not the criterion for actual behavior. I will therefore refer to *f*( ) as the *theoretical criterion function* and, similarly, to $\bar{x}$ as the *theoretically optimal decision*. In the planning stage the decision maker does not formulate a particular decision but only, as we shall shortly see, a *decision distribution*.
2. In the implementation stage the decision maker faces all previously unscheduled factors, which he considers as realization of random variables. The actions designed to handle such factors are therefore random from the viewpoint of the planning stage. Thus, the planning stage provides the decision distribution, and which particular decision is drawn from this distribution depends on the minor factors which determine subsequent actions. In the housewife's case, such factors include her mood when she is on a shopping trip, whether she meets a friend, the availability of favorite brands, etc.

It is worthwhile to add that the person in charge of the planning stage need not be the same as the person in charge of the implementation stage. The decision maker may formulate a decision distribution based on the major factors and he may leave the implementation at the level of the actual decisions to one or several subordinates, who take care of the minor factors. The approach thus provides a statistical basis for the delegation of authority, which may be extended to several layers: the implementation stage of Mr. A's boss provides the planning stage for Mr A. himself, and A's implementation stage provides the planning stage for his subordinates. In such a hierarchy nobody is told which precise actions to take, but everyone below the top is told that his actions should adhere to a certain statistical pattern. Note that we have the same situation in the housewife's case as discussed in the previous paragraph when we imagine that the decision distribution results from deliberations of the husband-wife team.

The analysis which follows concerns the planning stage, so that the actual decision ($x$) is viewed as a random vector. Equivalently, this $x$ may be considered as consisting of a nonstochastic component, which is the theoretically optimal decision $\bar{x}$, and a random discrepancy vector $x - \bar{x}$. This particular way of looking at the problem has the advantage that $x - \bar{x}$ can be identified with the random disturbance vector of the set of behavioral equations which describe the decision maker's actions in terms of the major determining factors. We shall pursue this in section 3. The approach formulated here should also be compared with earlier methodological considerations by Marschak and Andrews (1944) and by Bentzel and Hansen (1955), who relate distributions of disturbances to statistical estimation procedures for the parameters of behavioral equations. The latter authors state (p. 167) that ". . . the whole discussion about the appropriateness of different estimation procedures seems futile . . . as long as we have no 'economic theory of disturbances.'" In this article we provide such a theory, but with the addition that the subject area need not be confined to economics.

Given that $x$ is a random decision vector, the question arises how "rational random behavior" can be defined. In an earlier article (Theil, 1971) I argued along the following lines.[1] If the decision $x$ differs from $\bar{x}$, the decision maker incurs a loss with respect to the theoretical criterion function. As (1.1) shows, this loss is a quadratic form in $x - \bar{x}$ apart from an $O_3$ term. Supposing that the decision maker ignores this $O_3$ term, we write the expected loss as perceived by him as

$$L = -\frac{1}{2}\mathscr{E}\left[(x-\bar{x})'A(x-\bar{x})\right]. \tag{1.2}$$

We assume that this expected loss summarizes the decision maker's attitude with respect to the major factors; also, that he prefers a small $L$ to a large $L$.

As to the minor factors, we assume that the decision maker prefers a large dispersion of the decision distribution to a small dispersion. The rationale is that an increase in dispersion raises his ability to cope with the unscheduled factors; in the case of delegation of authority such an increase is equivalent to more freedom of action for the subordinates. Let us agree to measure dispersion by the generalized variance. If $V$ is the covariance matrix of $x$, the generalized variance is the determinant value of $V$, to be written $|V|$. The decision maker's criterion function for the selection of his decision

[1] The exposition which follows is an adaptation based on the formulation used in this article. In the original formulation I used a linear transformation of the decision variables, but this approach is equivalent to that without such a transformation based on the generalized variance. Also, I required in the earlier article that the expectation of $x - \bar{x}$ vanishes, which is unnecessary. The zero value of this expectation is implied, which can be proved along the lines of remark (4) of section 2.

distribution involves only two variables, $L$ for the major factors and $|V|$ for the minor factors, and it is an increasing function of $|V|$ and a decreasing function of $L$; no further specifications are needed. It can be shown that maximization of this criterion function implies

$$V = -kA^{-1} \tag{1.3}$$

where $k$ is a positive scalar. This equation states that the covariance matrix of the random decision vector is negatively proportional to the inverse of the Hessian matrix of the theoretical criterion function.

The objective of this article is to modify the approach so that the form of the decision distribution is obtained, and to discuss some evidence.

## 2. A Theorem

A standard way of measuring dispersion is by means of the *entropy* of the distribution.[2] If $g(x)$ is the density function of the $n$-variate decision distribution, the associated entropy is defined as

$$H = -\int_{-\infty}^{\infty} \cdots \int_{-\infty}^{\infty} g(x) \log g(x)\, dx_1 \ldots dx_n , \tag{2.1}$$

where log (here and elsewhere) stands for natural logarithm. The following theorem is proved in the appendix.

*Theorem*: Let each of the $n$ elements of the random decision vector $x$ have range $(-\infty, \infty)$. Then the distribution of $x$ which maximizes any function $\phi(H,L)$ that satisfies

[2] A convenient axiomatic approach is along the following lines. A large dispersion of a distribution is equivalent to great uncertainty as to the value of a random drawing from this distribution. Great uncertainty may also be viewed as equivalent to a large expected information of the message which states the outcome of such a random drawing. In information theory, the information content of the message which states that event $E$ occurred is defined as $-\log p$, where $p$ is the probability of $E$ before the message arrived. [This definition can be derived from certain axioms, the crucial one being that of additivity under independence: if $E$ and $F$ are stochastically independent events, the information content of the message which states that both $E$ and $F$ occurred is equal to the sum of the information values of the messages involving the two events separately.] Given the definition $-\log p$ for information, the expected information (commonly known as the entropy) of a complete set of mutually exclusive events becomes the expectation of minus the logarithm of the probability, $-\Sigma_i p_i \log p_i$. For continuous distribution this is extended to the expectation of minus the logarithm of the density, as shown in (2.1). For further details on axioms see, e.g., Theil (1972, pp. 11-13).

$$\begin{aligned} \phi(H_1,L) &< \phi(H_2,L) \quad \text{if} \quad H_1 < H_2 \\ \phi(H,L_1) &> \phi(H,L_2) \quad \text{if} \quad L_1 < L_2 \end{aligned} \tag{2.2}$$

is $n$-variate normal with mean vector $\bar{x}$ and covariance matrix $V$ of the form (1.3) for some $k > 0$, where $\bar{x}$, $A$, and $L$ are given in (1.2) and $H$ in (2.1).

**Remarks**

(1) The condition that the elements of $x$ have range $(-\infty,\infty)$ is essential. Many economic variables are strictly positive (prices, quantities, expenditures), so that the theorem is not applicable to these. However, frequently the logarithms of such variables are considered more important because changes in logarithms represent proportionate effects. The theorem is applicable to logarithms, which have range $(-\infty,\infty)$; the implication is that the original variables (the antilogs) are log-normally distributed.

(2) We also prove in the appendix the interesting result that the marginal rate of substitution between $H$ and $L$ is inversely proportional to $L$:

$$\left(\frac{dH}{dL}\right)_{\phi = \text{constant}} = \frac{n}{2L} \ . \tag{2.3}$$

Equivalently, the indifference curves (contour lines) of $\phi(\ )$ in the $(H, \log L)$-plane are parallel straight lines. For every one percent additional expected loss which the decision maker is willing to incur, he can afford a constant entropy increase without changing the value of $\phi(\ )$.

(3) The variable $L$ measures the expected loss. For an individual random decision $x$ the associated loss is also random. In other words, random behavior according to the theorem implies that the loss incurred is subject to a distribution, to be called the *loss distribution*. It is shown in the Appendix that this distribution is $(L/n)\chi^2(n)$ when the $O_3$ term in (1.1) is ignored, where $L$ is the value of the expected loss which results from maximizing $\phi(\ )$.

(4) Note that the theorem implies that $x - \bar{x}$ has zero mean. To show more explicitly why this is so we consider the entropy,

$$H = \frac{1}{2} \log |2\pi e \Sigma| \tag{2.4}$$

of the normal distribution with mean vector $\mu$ and covariance matrix $\Sigma$, and we write (1.2) as

$$L = \frac{1}{2} \operatorname{tr}(-A) \mathscr{E}\left[(x - \bar{x})(x - \bar{x})'\right]. \tag{2.5}$$

The expectation on the right equals $\Sigma + \mu\mu'$ for this normal distribution. Given $\Sigma$, $L$ of (2.5) is thus minimized if and only if $\mu = 0$, whereas $H$ of (2.4) does not involve $\mu$. Hence maximizing $\phi(\ )$ requires $\mu = 0$.

(5) It is of considerable interest, particularly for the case of several decision variables ($n \geq 2$), to compare the theorem with statistical estimation according to the maximum likelihood method. Write $T$ for the size of the sample used for the estimation and interpret $\bar{x}$ as the parameter vector to be estimated and $f(\ )$ as $1/T$ times the log-likelihood function. It is well known that under appropriate regularity conditions and for a sufficiently large $T$, the maximum likelihood estimator is approximately normally distributed with a mean vector equal to the parameter vector ($\bar{x}$ in this case) and a covariance matrix equal to the inverse of the information matrix. This information matrix, to be written $R$, is defined as minus the matrix of the expected second-order derivatives of the log-likelihood function. The elements of $R$ are of order $T$; hence, given that $f(\ )$ is identical with $1/T$ times the log-likelihood function, the matrix $T^{-1}R$, with elements of order 1, may be identified with $-A$ of (1.1).

Equivalently, the asymptotic covariance matrix $R^{-}$ of the maximum likelihood estimator may be identified with $-(TA)^{-1}$. On comparing this result and the asymptotic normality of the estimator with the lines below (2.2), we conclude that *random behavior according to the theorem is equivalent to large-sample maximum likelihood estimation of the theoretically optimal decision.*

Also, the theorem states that the covariance matrix of $x$ equals $-kA^{-1}$, and the result $R = -(TA)^{-1}$ thus implies that $k$ may be identified with $1/T$. Since lowering $k$ reduces both the expected loss and the entropy, we thus find that *making the expected loss smaller by allowing the entropy to decrease is equivalent to drawing a larger sample for the maximum likelihood procedure.*

Finally, note that the normal distribution of the maximum likelihood estimator is only an approximate result. There is convergence toward normality as $T \to \infty$, which seems in conflict with the theorem in which no convergence is mentioned. Yet there is no real conflict. The clue to this problem is our assumption that the decision maker ignores the $O_3$ term in (1.1) when he considers the expected loss. It follows from the previous paragraph that, as $k \to 0$ (which is equivalent to $T \to \infty$), the expected loss (1.2) also converges to zero. This expected loss corresponds to the quadratic term in (1.1), which is $O_2$. As $k \to 0$, so that $x - \bar{x}$ converges in probability to a zero vector, the $O_3$ term in (1.1) disappears relative to this $O_2$ term. Therefore, *ignoring the $O_3$ term in the expected loss is equivalent to the replacement of the true distribution of the maximum likelihood estimator by its large-sample (normal) approximation.*

## 3. Evidence

One way of interpreting the theorem of section 2 is normative, as a prescription on how people "should" behave. Another interpretation is that of a model for actual behavior. In this section evidence is discussed relating to this model, for which purpose two preliminary remarks are in order.

(1) Ignoring the $O_3$ term in (1.1) implies that the theoretical criterion function is approximated by a quadratic function around $\bar{x}$.

$$f(x) = a'x + \frac{1}{2}x'Ax \, , \tag{3.1}$$

where the constant term is deleted (which is irrelevant). The function (3.1) has a maximum at $\bar{x} = -A^{-1}a$. Hence, the set of behavioral equations describing the decision maker's actions may be written as

$$x = -A^{-1}a + (x - \bar{x}) \, , \tag{3.2}$$

where $-A^{-1}a$ is the systematic (first-moment) component of the equations and $x - \bar{x}$ is the disturbance vector. Note the presence of the inverted Hessian in the first-moment component, which implies that the coefficients of the variables in the equations depend on this inverted Hessian. Since the theorem states that the covariance matrix of the disturbances is proportional to the same inverted Hessian, we thus have a direct relationship between this covariance matrix and the first-moment coefficients, as will now be explained for the case of consumer demand analysis.

(2) The theory of consumer demand postulates that the consumer maximizes a utility function $f(x)$ subject to a budget constraint $p'x = m$, where $x$ is the quantity vector, $p$ the price vector and $m$ the given amount of total expenditure. This leads to an extension of the theorem, which can be accomplished by using the budget constraint to eliminate one of the decision variables (one of the $n$ quantities). The result amounts to bordering the Hessian matrix by prices,

$$\begin{bmatrix} A & p \\ p' & 0 \end{bmatrix},$$

after which the leading $n \times n$ submatrix of the inverse of this bordered matrix takes the role of $A^{-1}$ in the theorem.[3] The particular parameterization used here is that of the Rotterdam model, which has the convenient property that its price coefficients are directly linked to the Hessian matrix of the utility function. The implication is that the variances and covariances of the disturbances of the demand equations are negatively proportional to the Slutsky coefficients, which measure the effect of price changes on demand when real income remains constant. Therefore, these variances and covariances involve only one parameter (the proportionality constant) in addition to the first-moment coefficients.[4]

Figures A and B supply visual evidence of this implication. Estimated Slutsky coefficients are measured horizontally, multiplied by -1 because of the negative sign of the proportionality, and mean squares and products of residuals vertically. Figure A is from Paulus' dissertation (Paulus, 1972), in which he estimated a complete system of 14 demand equations for Dutch commodity groups in 1922-39 and 1951-63. The 14 groups are of quite different size, leading to mean squares of residuals that are also of quite different magnitude. For this reason, Figure A uses a double-log scale. Since many mean products are negative and hence cannot be represented on such a scale, only mean squares are shown and related to the corresponding own-price coefficients. A double-log transformation changes a proportionality into a linear relation with unit slope. The figure shows that the 14 observations are indeed scattered around such a straight line.

Figure B, derived from Finizza's dissertation (Finizza, 1971), concerns a conditional demand model for beef, pork, chicken and lamb, based on American data for 1950-66. (The word "conditional" should be interpreted as " given the total demand for meat.") The scale used in this figure is metric and all ten mean squares and products are related to the corresponding Slutsky coefficient. The ten points are evidently close to a straight line through the origin, as the proportionality predicts.

An obvious next step is to estimate the model subject to the proportionality constraint. This has been done for the case of Figure B by means of the maximum likelihood method, but the derivations are beyond the scope of this article; they are given in my forthcoming book on consumer demand analysis. A likelihood ratio test has been applied,

[3] When there are several (possibly nonlinear, but differentiable) constraints, there is a bordering row and column for each constraint and the elements of these vectors are coefficients of the linear Taylor expansion of the corresponding constraint at the point of the theoretical optimum.

[4] The model used takes the form of (1.3) of Theil (1967, p. 227) with the price coefficient $v_{ij}$ replaced by the Slutsky coefficient $\pi_{ij} = v_{ij} - \phi\mu_i\mu_j$, where $\phi$ is the income flexibility (the reciprocal of the income elasticity of the marginal utility of income) and $\mu_i = \partial(p_i q_i)/\partial m$ is the $i$th marginal share (the marginal propensity to spend on the $i$th commodity). The theorem of section 2 implies that the covariance of the disturbances of the $i$th and $j$th demand equations is equal to a negative multiple of $\pi_{ij}$. This is equivalent to the covariance specifications given in (1.17) of Theil (1967, p. 232), which was derived there along different lines. The estimated Slutsky coefficients measured along the horizontal axes of Figures A and B are obtained by means of the constrained gėneralized least-squares method, with Slutsky symmetry ($\pi_{ij} = \pi_{ji}$) as constraint. The case of Figure B is a conditional version as shown in (2.10) of Theil (1967, p. 236).

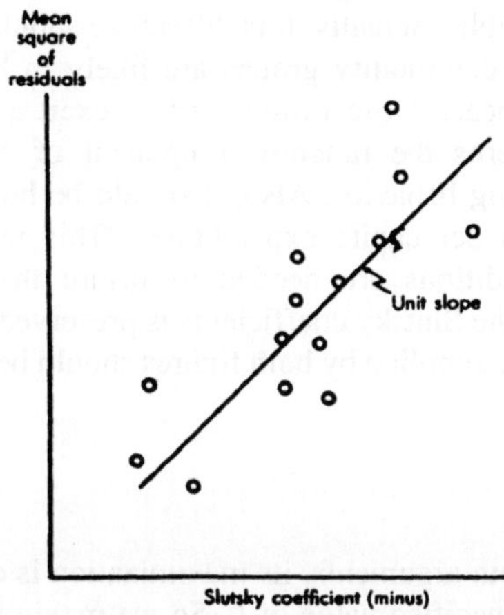


*Figure A.* The Case of 14 Commodity Groups.

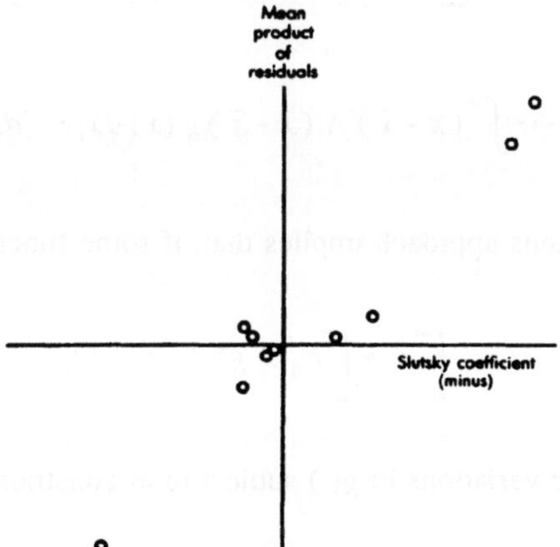


*Figure B.* The Case of Meats

which accepts the proportionality for Figure B at the five percent significance level. The case of Figure A is less favorable. Actually, this difference should cause no surprise, since the Dutch data on 14 broad commodity groups are likely to be less accurate than the American data on the four meats. Observational errors exert a disturbing influence; the theorem of Section 2 concerns the random component of behavior, not random or nonrandom errors in measuring behavior. Also, it should be borne in mind that the data discussed here are based on per capita expenditures. This involves aggregation over consumers, and special conditions are needed to insure that the proportionality of disturbance covariances and the Slutsky coefficients is preserved at this aggregative level. For these reasons the evidence supplied by both figures should be considered encouraging.

## Appendix

Since $\phi(\ )$ is monotonic in both arguments, its maximization is equivalent to maximizing $H$ for a given appropriately specified value of $L$. So we maximize $H$ defined in (2.1) for variations in $g(\ )$ subject to two constraints,

$$\int_{-\infty}^{\infty} \cdots \int_{-\infty}^{\infty} g(x)\, dx_1 \cdots dx_n = 1 \tag{A.1}$$

$$\frac{1}{2} \int_{-\infty}^{\infty} \cdots \int_{-\infty}^{\infty} (x - \bar{x})'A\,(x - \bar{x})\, g(x)\, dx_1 \cdots dx_n = -L\ . \tag{A.2}$$

The calculus-of-variations approach implies that, if some function

$$\int_{-\infty}^{\infty} \cdots \int_{-\infty}^{\infty} F_0(x,g)\, dx_1 \cdots dx_n$$

is to be maximized for variations in $g(\ )$ subject to $m$ constraints,

$$\int_{-\infty}^{\infty} \cdots \int_{-\infty}^{\infty} F_i(x,g)\, dx_1 \ldots dx_n = c_i, \quad i = 1, \cdots, m\ ,$$

where the $c_i$'s are constraints, the solution of $g(\ )$ is obtained from

$$\frac{\partial F_0}{\partial g} + \lambda_1 \frac{\partial F_1}{\partial g} + \cdots + \lambda_m \frac{\partial F_m}{\partial g} = 0$$

with the $\lambda$'s interpreted as undetermined multipliers. Application to (2.1), (A.1), and (A.2) gives

$$-\log g - 1 + \lambda_1 + \frac{1}{2}\lambda_2 (x - \bar{x})' A (x - \bar{x}) = 0 , \tag{A.3}$$

which implies

$$g(x) = e^{\lambda_1 - 1} \exp\left\{-\frac{1}{2}(x - \bar{x})' (-\lambda_2 A) (x - \bar{x})\right\} . \tag{A.4}$$

Use (A.1) to express $\lambda_1$ in terms of $\lambda_2$ and $A$:

$$g(x) = (2\pi)^{-n/2} |-\lambda_2 A|^{1/2} \exp\left\{-\frac{1}{2}(x - \bar{x})' (-\lambda_2 A) (x - \bar{x})\right\} . \tag{A.5}$$

This is the density function of the $n$-variate distribution with mean $\bar{x}$ and covariance matrix $(-\lambda_2 A)^{-1}$. To determine $\lambda_2$ we use (2.5), which gives $L = n/2\lambda_2$. Hence, the covariance matrix is

$$(-\lambda_2 A)^{-1} = (2L/n)(-A)^{-1} \tag{A.6}$$

and the associated entropy follows from (2.4):

$$H = \frac{1}{2} \log \left| \frac{4\pi e L}{n} (-A)^{-1} \right| = \frac{n}{2} \log L + \text{constant} , \tag{A.7}$$

where the constant on the right refers to factors beyond the decision maker's control, given his theoretical criterion function (which determines $n$ and $A$). Equation (A.7) specifies the maximum entropy for a fixed expected loss and it proves (2.3).

When the $O_3$ term is ignored, the loss (1.1) becomes

$$-\frac{1}{2}(x - \bar{x})' A (x - \bar{x}) = \frac{L}{n}(x - \bar{x})' \left(-\frac{n}{2L} A\right)(x - \bar{x}) .$$

The right side is a multiple of $L/n$ of a quadratic form in the normal vector $x - \bar{x}$ with matrix equal to the inverse of the covariance matrix of this vector. The distribution of this quadratic form is $\chi^2(n)$, which proves remark (3) of section 2.

## Remarks

(1) Equation (A.3) shows clearly that the use of both the entropy and the quadratic loss is essential for the normal result. The entropy is the integral of $-g \log g$; differentiation of this integrand with respect to $g$ gives $-\log g$ plus a constant. The expected loss is shown as an integral in (A.2); differentiation of the integrand with respect to $g$ gives a quadratic form in $x$. It is this *combination* of $-\log g$ and the quadratic form which generates the normal decision distribution.

(2) It is appropriate to compare the theorem of section 2 with the well-known proposition that out of all distributions with range $(-\infty, \infty)$ and given nonsingular covariance matrix $\Sigma$, the normal distribution is the one with the largest entropy. The entropy is then maximized subject to $\frac{1}{2}n(n+1)$ constraints (all elements of the symmetric matrix $\Sigma$); here there is only one constraint (A.2), in addition to the normalizing condition (A.1). Also, the present theorem specifies the mean vector of $x - \bar{x}$ to be zero, whereas the other leaves it unspecified.

## References

Bentzel, R., and Bent Hansen: 1955, "On Recursiveness and Interdependency in Economic Models," *Review of Economic Studies*, **22**, No. 59, 153-168.

Finizza, Anthony J.: 1971, "Estimation of Demand Equations for a Subgroup of Meat Commodities," Unpublished Ph.D. dissertation, Graduate School of Business, University of Chicago.

Marschak, Jacob and W.H. Andrews, Jr.: 1944, "Random Simultaneous Equations and the Theory of Production," *Econometrica*, **12**, 143-205.

Paulus, John D.: 1972, "The Estimation of Large Systems of Consumer Demand Equations Using Stochastic Prior Information," Unpublished Ph.D. dissertation, Graduate School of Business, University of Chicago.

Theil, Henri: 1967, *Economics and Information Theory*, New York: American Elsevier Publishing Company, New York, and North-Holland Publishing Company, Amsterdam.

Theil, Henri: 1971, "An Economic Theory of the Second Moments of Disturbances of Behavioral Equations," *The American Economic Review*, **61**, New York, 190-194.

Theil, Henri: 1972, *Statistical Decomposition Analysis with Applications in the Social and Administrative Sciences*, American Elsevier Publishing Company, New York, and North-Holland Publishing Company, Amsterdam.

# SECTION 3.4: THE ECONOMETRICS OF DEMAND SYSTEMS

CHAPTER 42

# THE EFFECT OF MEASUREMENT ERRORS ON THE ESTIMATION OF DEMAND SYSTEMS*

HENRI THEIL
*University of Chicago*
*Chicago, Illinois, U.S.A.*

ABSTRACT. Statistical inference in complete demand systems is usually based on imperfect data. This letter explores some of the implications of these imperfections, in particular for the estimates of income elasticities.

## 1. Introduction

The econometrics of measurement errors in independent variables is notoriously difficult. This has induced many analysts to proceed as if there are no such errors even when it is obvious that this assumption is unrealistic. Statistical inference in demand equation systems is no exception to this rule.[1] This note analyzes certain consequences of three kinds of observational errors.

## 2. Real-Income Errors in Cross-Country Demand Systems

The Working (1943)-Leser (1963) model describes the budget share $w_i$ of good $i$ as a linear function of the natural log of total expenditure $M$ (income for short),

$$w_i = \alpha_i + \beta_i \log M . \tag{1}$$

This model was applied by Clements and Theil (1979) and Suhm (1979) to data on 15 countries published by Kravis et al. (1978). Budget shares can be obtained from data in local currency, but the specification of $M$ in (1) requires a comparison of per capita incomes of different countries. There can be no doubt that the figures produced by Kravis et al. (volumes per capita at international prices) are superior to income comparisons at

* This article first appeared in *Economics Letters*, 3 (1979), 373-376. Reprinted with the permission of Elsevier Science Publishers B.V. (North-Holland). Research supported in part by NSF Grant SOC76-82718.

[1] Klevmarken (1979) provided some evidence on the fragile quality of certain consumption data; his paper is in part responsible for section 3 below, but he should not be held responsible for the restrictive assumptions made in that section. See also Houthakker (1979) on the possibility that price-quantity covariances are spuriously negative due to measurement errors.

official exchange rates, but superiority is not equivalent to perfection. When $M$ in (1) is subject to random observational error, the LS estimator of $\beta_i$ (obtained from a regression of $w_i$ on log $M$) is biased in zero direction; see, for example, Theil (1971, section 12.2). Under (1) the marginal share of $\theta_i = \partial(p_i q_i)/\partial M$ equals $w_i + \beta_i$.[2] Since the ratio $\theta_i/w_i$ is identical to the income elasticity of the demand for good $i$ this elasticity equals $1 + \beta_i/w_i$ under (1) and the bias of the $\beta_i$ estimate toward zero is equivalent to a bias of the elasticity estimate toward 1. In other words, the effect of real-income errors in (1) is to understate the dispersion of the income elasticities.

## 3. A Uniform Overstatement of Inflation

For $n$ goods the absolute price version of the Rotterdam model with homogeneity imposed takes the form[3]

$$\bar{w}_{it} Dq_{it} = \theta_i DQ_t + \sum_{j=1}^{n-1} \pi_{ij} (Dp_{jt} - Dp_{nt}) + \varepsilon_{it} . \tag{2}$$

We assume that the expenditures on all goods are measured correctly (so that $\bar{w}_{it}$ and $DP_{it} + Dq_{it}$ are known) but that the observed price log-changes algebraically exceed the true values because technological improvements are ignored. More precisely, let $Dp_{it} + \alpha$ for some unknown $\alpha > 0$ be the observed $Dp_{it}$ and hence $Dq_{it} - \alpha$ the observed $Dq_{it}$, for each $(i, t)$. Then (2), when expressed in observables, becomes

$$\bar{w}_{it} (Dq_{it} - \alpha) = \alpha(\theta_i - \bar{w}_{it}) + \theta_i (DQ_t - \alpha) + \sum_{j=1}^{n-1} \pi_{ij} (Dp_{jt} - Dp_{nt}) + \varepsilon_{it} , \tag{3}$$

where $DQ_t - \alpha = \Sigma_i \bar{w}_{it}(Dq_{it} - \alpha)$ is the observed value of the Divisia volume index.

Note that the substitution term is not affected by the observational error and that (3) contains an extra term $\alpha(\theta_i - \bar{w}_{it})$. If $\bar{w}_{it}$ does not change very much during the sample period, this extra term behaves approximately as a constant term which is positive for luxuries $(\theta_i > \bar{w}_{it})$ and negative for necessities $(\theta_i < \bar{w}_{it})$. Since (3) is in first differences, such a constant term represents an upward or downward trend. A comparison of (2) and (3) shows that when such constant terms are introduced, the overstatement of

---

[2] *Proof.* Multiplication of (1) by $M$ yields $p_i q_i = \alpha_i M + \beta_i M \log M$, after which differentiation with respect to $M$ gives $\partial(p_i q_i)/\partial M = \alpha_i + \beta_i + \beta_i \log M$, which equals $w_i + \beta_i$ in view of (1).

[3] In (2), $\bar{w}_{it}$ is the arithmetic average of the $i$th budget share in $t - 1$ and $t$, $D$ stands for log-change (the change in the natural logarithm), $DQ_t = \Sigma_i \bar{w}_{it} Dq_{it}$ is the finite-change Divisia volume index, $\pi_{ij}$ is a Slutsky coefficient, and $\varepsilon_{it}$ is a random disturbance. For further details, see Theil (1975-76, 1979); for an interpretation of (2) in terms of per capita data, see Barnett (1979).

inflation produces a spurious upward trend for the consumption of luxuries and a spurious downward trend for that of necessities.

When we ignore the term $\alpha(\theta_i - \bar{w}_{it})$ in (3), we commit a specification error in the form of an omitted variable which is positive for luxuries and negative for necessities. It seems likely that the LS regression of the left variable on those on the right will absorb at least part of this omitted variable in the real-income term, because most samples show positive real-income changes. The result is that $\theta_i$ for luxuries is subject to an upward bias and for necessities to a downward bias. This amounts to an overstatement of the dispersion of the income elasticities, which should be contrasted with the understatement described at the end of section 2. However, the situation may be more complicated because $Dp_{jt} - Dp_{nt}$ in (3) may also be predominantly of one sign for some $j$, reflecting an increasing or decreasing trend of certain price ratios. In that case part of the omitted variable could be absorbed by $Dp_{jt} - Dp_{nt}$ ; this might adversely affect the test for Slutsky symmetry $(\pi_{ij} = \pi_{ji})$.[4]

## 4. Random Errors in Prices and Quantities

Under preference independence we can write the relative price version of the Rotterdam model as

$$\bar{w}_{it} Dq_{it} = \theta_i DQ_t + \phi\theta_i (Dp_{it} - DP'_t) + \varepsilon_{it}, \tag{4}$$

where $\phi$ is the income flexibility (the reciprocal of the income elasticity of the marginal utility of income) and $DP'_t = \Sigma_i \theta_i Dp_{it}$ is the Frisch price index.

Again we assume that all expenditures are measured correctly, but we now introduce random measurement errors in the log-changes, $Dp_{it} + \eta_{it}$ being the observed $Dp_{it}$ and $Dq_{it} - \eta_{it}$ being the observed $Dq_{it}$, with $\eta_{it}$ an error which we assume to have zero mean. Then we can write (4) in observables as

$$\bar{w}_{it}(Dq_{it} - \eta_{it}) = \theta_i (DQ_t - \sum_{j=1}^{n} \bar{w}_{jt}\eta_{jt}) + \phi\theta_i (Dp_{it} - DP'_t + \eta_{it} - \sum_{j=1}^{n} \theta_j \eta_{jt}) \tag{5}$$

plus an error term of the form

---

[4] A more extensive analysis would require the auxiliary regressions of specification analysis. For a given set of data this is a rather straightforward matter [see Theil (1971, section 11.2)], but it is not fruitful to pursue this further in abstract terms.

$$\varepsilon_{it} - (\bar{w}_{it} + \phi\,\theta_i)\eta_{it} + \theta_i \sum_{j=1}^{n} (\bar{w}_{jt} + \phi\,\theta_j)\eta_{jt}\,. \qquad (6)$$

Since this case is more complicated than the previous ones, we shall confine ourselves to pointing out where the main trouble spots are under the assumption that the $\eta_{it}$'s are uncorrelated across goods. Then the error component $\Sigma_j \theta_j \eta_{jt}$ of the Frisch price index has a variance equal to $\Sigma_j \theta_j^2$ var $\eta_{jt}$ and the variance of the error component of the Divisia volume index equals $\Sigma_j \bar{w}_{jt}^2$ var $\eta_{jt}$ . These variances are both small when $n$ is not small and when no good dominates the others in terms of marginal or budget shares. This suggests that we can ignore the error component in the real-income term of (5) and that we can simplify the substitution term to $Dp_{it}$ - $DP'_t$ + $\eta_{it}$ multiplied by $\phi\theta_i$. The crucial matter is then the correlation of $\eta_{it}$ in this term with

$$-(1 - \theta_i)(\bar{w}_{it} + \phi\theta_i)\eta_{it}\,, \qquad (7)$$

which is the relevant component of the error term (6). Note that (7) vanishes if $\theta_i / \bar{w}_{it} = -1/\phi$, i.e., if the income elasticity of good $i$ equals that of the marginal utility of income in absolute value. Therefore, the main trouble spots are the substitution terms of those goods whose income elasticities deviate substantially from $-1/\phi$. Since empirical evidence indicates that $\phi$ is between 0 and -1, this applies particularly to necessities. If $i$ is a necessity, the leading error component $\eta_{it}$ of the deflated price change in (5) is negatively correlated with the error term (6).

**References**


Barnett, W.A.: 1979, "Theoretical Foundations for the Rotterdam model," *Review of Economic Studies*, **46**, 109-130.

Clements, K.W., and H. Theil: 1979, "A Cross-country Analysis of Consumption Patterns," Report no. 7924, Center for Mathematical Studies in Business and Economics, University of Chicago, Chicago, Illinois.

Houthakker, H.S.: 1979, "Growth and Inflation: Analysis by Industry," *Brookings Papers on Economic Activity*, **1**, 241-257.

Klevmarken, N.A.: 1979, "On the Complete Systems Approach to Demand Analysis," Research Report no. 1979:2, Department of Statistics, University of Göteborg, Göteborg, Sweden.

Kravis, I.B., A.W. Heston and R. Summers: 1978, *International Comparisons of Real Product and Purchasing Power*, Johns Hopkins University Press, Baltimore, Maryland.

Leser, C.E.V.: 1963, "Forms of Engel Functions," *Econometrica*, **31**, 694-703.

Suhm, F.E.: 1979, "A Cross-country Analysis of Divisia Covariances of Prices and Quantities Consumed," *Economics Letters*, **3**, 373-376.

Theil, H.: 1971, *Principles of Econometrics*, Wiley, New York.

Theil, H.: 1975-76, *Theory and Measurement of Consumer Demand*, Two vols., North-Holland, Amsterdam.

Theil, H.: 1979, *The System-wide Approach to Microeconomics*, University of Chicago Press, Chicago, Illinois.

Working, H.: 1943, "Statistical Laws of Family Expenditure," *Journal of the American Statistical Association*, **38**, 43-56.

CHAPTER 43

# THE TWO PERILS OF SYMMETRY-CONSTRAINED ESTIMATION OF DEMAND SYSTEMS*

DENZIL G. FIEBIG
*University of Sydney,*
*Sydney, Australia*

HENRI THEIL
*University of Chicago,*
*Chicago, Illinois, U.S.A.*

ABSTRACT. When the error covariance matrix $\Sigma$ of a demand system is unknown and is estimated, (1) symmetry-constrained estimates based on such a $\Sigma$ estimate may have large mean squared errors, and (2) the conventionally computed standard errors may seriously underestimate the variability of these estimates. Several procedures are compared; the conventional one (which uses a $\Sigma$ estimate consisting of mean squares and products of LS residuals) performs worst.

The work of Laitinen (1978), Meisner (1979), and Bera et al. (1981) has illustrated the deficiencies of asymptotically valid tests of demand homogeneity and Slutsky symmetry. Meisner (1981) conducted a simulation experiment based on data for 15 countries to verify the performance of symmetry-constrained estimators; the objective of this paper is to extend the analysis for other estimators using the same data. The homogeneity-constrained demand model takes the form

$$y_{ic} = \alpha_i + \beta_i x_{0c} + \sum_{j=1}^{n-1} \pi_{ij}(x_{jc} - x_{nc}) + \varepsilon_{ic} , \tag{1}$$

where $y_{ic}$ is consumption of good $i$ in country $c$, $x_{0c}$ is total consumption, $x_{jc}$ is the price of good $j$, $\varepsilon_{ic}$ is a random error and $\alpha_i$, $\beta_i$, $\pi_{ij}$ are unknown parameters. Slutsky symmetry amounts to $\pi_{ij} = \pi_{ji}$. The design of the experiment is exactly as Meisner (1981); we have $n = 8$ goods.[1]

We write (1) for all countries ($c = 1, \ldots, 15$) in the form $y_i = X\delta_i + \varepsilon_i$ and Slutsky symmetry as $R\delta = 0$, where $\delta$ is a vector with $\delta_i$ as $i$th subvector ($i = 1, \ldots, 7$) and $R$ is a matrix whose elements are all 0 or $\pm$ 1, each row of $R$ corresponding to $\pi_{ij} = \pi_{ji}$ for some $(i, j)$. The LS estimator of $\delta_i$ is $d_i = (X'X)^{-1}X'y_i$; we write $d$ for the vector with $d_i$

* This article first appeared in *Economics Letters*, 13 (1983), 105-111. Reprinted with the permission of Elsevier Science Publishers V.B. (North-Holland). Research supported in part by the McKethan-Matherly Eminent Scholar Chair, University of Florida.

[1] The eight goods are food, clothing, rent, furniture, medical care, transport, recreation and education, other expenditure.

as $i$th subvector. This $d$ does not satisfy Slutsky symmetry. The BLU estimator of $\delta$ constrained by symmetry is

$$\hat{\delta}(\Sigma) = d - C(\Sigma)R'\left[RC(\Sigma)R'\right]^{-1}Rd \tag{2}$$

and the covariance matrix of this estimator is

$$C(\Sigma) - C(\Sigma)R'\left[RC(\Sigma)R'\right]^{-1}RC(\Sigma)\ , \tag{3}$$

where $C(\Sigma) = \Sigma \otimes (X'X)^{-1}$, $\Sigma$ being the $7 \times 7$ 'contemporaneous' covariance matrix of the $\varepsilon_{ic}$'s.

If $\Sigma$ is known, as is the case in our simulation experiment, we can apply (2) and (3). The results are shown in columns (2) to (4) of Table I for 500 trials. The estimated bias is close to zero, as it should be. The RMSE in column (3) is close to the root-mean-squared standard error [the RMSSE, computed from (3)] in column (4).

In the next three columns we recognize that $\Sigma$ is typically unknown and must somehow be estimated. The estimator used is the unbiased LS estimator,

$$S = \frac{1}{15-9}Y'\left[I - X(X'X)^{-1}X'\right]Y\ , \tag{4}$$

where $Y = [y_1 \ . \ . \ . \ y_7]$. We thus substitute $S$ for $\Sigma$ in both (2) and (3). Column (5) shows that bias is not much of a problem, but columns (3) and (6) indicate that $\hat{\delta}(S)$ has a serious statistical inefficiency problem. Also, column (7) shows that the conventional standard errors, computed from the diagonal elements of (3) but with $\Sigma$ replaced by $S$, grossly understate the actual variability of $\hat{\delta}(S)$ as measured by the RMSEs in column (6).

The results discussed in the two previous paragraphs confirm Meisner's (1981) findings. Columns (8) to (10) concern $\hat{\delta}(I)$, which amounts to unweighted symmetry-constrained least squares. The RMSE's in column (9) tend to be smaller than those of $\hat{\delta}(S)$ in column (6). A more convenient summary of these results is given in the left half of Table II. For each of the 35 multiplicative coefficients of the model (corresponding to the 35 lines of Table I) the ratio of the RMSE using $\Sigma$ to the RMSE using $S$ is computed; the figures 0.67, 0.74, 0.81 in the second row of Table II are the quartiles of these 35 ratios, while 0.73, 0.77, 0.83 in the third row are the quartiles when $I$ rather than $S$ is used. The larger values of the latter quartiles indicate that we gain in efficiency by using unweighted symmetry-constrained least squares.

**TABLE I.** Symmetry-Constrained Estimation, 500 trials[a]

| | True value (1) | Using Σ Bias (2) | RMSE (3) | RMSSE (4) | Using $S$ Bias (5) | RMSE (6) | RMSSE (7) |
|---|---|---|---|---|---|---|---|
| *Coefficients* $\beta_i$ | | | | | | | |
| $i = 1$ | -1526 | 6 | 216 | 218 | -7 | 309 | 172 |
| $i = 2$ | 42 | 2 | 81 | 86 | 3 | 117 | 70 |
| $i = 3$ | 261 | 5 | 121 | 124 | 6 | 135 | 117 |
| $i = 4$ | 266 | 0 | 153 | 150 | 15 | 240 | 105 |
| $i = 5$ | 258 | -3 | 59 | 58 | -6 | 74 | 49 |
| $i = 6$ | 210 | 0 | 144 | 147 | -8 | 173 | 131 |
| $i = 7$ | 243 | -5 | 116 | 112 | 3 | 174 | 84 |
| *Diagonal Slutsky coefficients* $\pi_{ii}$ | | | | | | | |
| $i = 1$ | -1061 | -26 | 801 | 823 | -75 | 1109 | 636 |
| $i = 2$ | -502 | -3 | 175 | 174 | 2 | 223 | 134 |
| $i = 3$ | -785 | -11 | 303 | 304 | -8 | 331 | 277 |
| $i = 4$ | -546 | -19 | 495 | 480 | -56 | 818 | 309 |
| $i = 5$ | -492 | -3 | 74 | 77 | -3 | 94 | 63 |
| $i = 6$ | -580 | 9 | 447 | 459 | 4 | 510 | 404 |
| $i = 7$ | -713 | 5 | 220 | 211 | -15 | 339 | 148 |
| *Off-diagonal Slutsky coefficients* $\pi_{ij}$ | | | | | | | |
| $i = 1,\ j = 2$ | 121 | 9 | 271 | 270 | 3 | 385 | 199 |
| $i = 1,\ j = 3$ | 203 | 9 | 314 | 324 | 16 | 379 | 272 |
| $i = 1,\ j = 4$ | 133 | 22 | 499 | 495 | 66 | 805 | 338 |
| $i = 1,\ j = 5$ | 119 | 9 | 183 | 182 | 1 | 238 | 140 |
| $i = 1,\ j = 6$ | 142 | -10 | 470 | 450 | -28 | 546 | 362 |
| $i = 1,\ j = 7$ | 181 | -20 | 306 | 309 | -4 | 486 | 209 |
| $i = 2,\ j = 3$ | 82 | 8 | 142 | 145 | 7 | 176 | 125 |
| $i = 2,\ j = 4$ | 54 | -13 | 198 | 196 | -20 | 313 | 133 |
| $i = 2,\ j = 5$ | 48 | 8 | 83 | 83 | 16 | 115 | 63 |
| $i = 2,\ j = 6$ | 58 | 4 | 196 | 201 | 20 | 243 | 163 |
| $i = 2,\ j = 7$ | 73 | -7 | 141 | 138 | -13 | 212 | 96 |
| $i = 3,\ j = 4$ | 90 | -5 | 200 | 195 | -5 | 256 | 169 |
| $i = 3,\ j = 5$ | 80 | -2 | 97 | 98 | -5 | 120 | 85 |
| $i = 3,\ j = 6$ | 96 | 3 | 257 | 260 | 0 | 287 | 225 |
| $i = 3,\ j = 7$ | 123 | -5 | 158 | 157 | -5 | 201 | 138 |
| $i = 4,\ j = 5$ | 53 | 0 | 124 | 127 | 4 | 184 | 91 |
| $i = 4,\ j = 6$ | 63 | 9 | 283 | 293 | 24 | 411 | 222 |
| $i = 4,\ j = 7$ | 80 | 12 | 244 | 244 | -11 | 408 | 148 |
| $i = 5,\ j = 6$ | 56 | -15 | 134 | 141 | -17 | 172 | 113 |
| $i = 5,\ j = 7$ | 72 | 3 | 92 | 93 | 11 | 128 | 71 |
| $i = 6,\ j = 7$ | 86 | 8 | 206 | 209 | 28 | 280 | 162 |

[a] All entries are to be divided by $10^4$.

| Using $I$ | | | Using $S_\Delta$ | | | Using $\hat{\Sigma}$ | | |
|---|---|---|---|---|---|---|---|---|
| Bias (8) | RMSE (9) | RMSSE (10) | Bias (11) | RMSE (12) | RMSSE (13) | Bias (14) | RMSE (15) | RMSSE (16) |
| 5 | 273 | 275 | 5 | 245 | 233 | 19 | 235 | 328 |
| 2 | 105 | 112 | 3 | 95 | 93 | -1 | 90 | 85 |
| 9 | 131 | 133 | 7 | 125 | 125 | 2 | 123 | 133 |
| -1 | 203 | 205 | 1 | 185 | 168 | 1 | 155 | 143 |
| -3 | 76 | 74 | -4 | 69 | 63 | -5 | 65 | 81 |
| 3 | 171 | 171 | 0 | 158 | 150 | 4 | 154 | 147 |
| -11 | 155 | 159 | -8 | 140 | 132 | -26 | 123 | 115 |
| | | | | | | | | |
| -32 | 909 | 934 | -37 | 860 | 846 | 1 | 854 | 1294 |
| -10 | 224 | 220 | -10 | 204 | 200 | 12 | 174 | 154 |
| -11 | 305 | 303 | -13 | 306 | 303 | -27 | 312 | 296 |
| -18 | 677 | 663 | -23 | 620 | 568 | 0 | 497 | 411 |
| -3 | 96 | 101 | -4 | 89 | 93 | 8 | 80 | 108 |
| 9 | 490 | 518 | 4 | 473 | 482 | -30 | 463 | 395 |
| 19 | 311 | 308 | 13 | 284 | 269 | 52 | 240 | 208 |
| | | | | | | | | |
| 2 | 363 | 371 | 11 | 312 | 283 | 2 | 310 | 290 |
| 11 | 323 | 327 | 12 | 335 | 305 | -1 | 366 | 464 |
| 39 | 676 | 676 | 39 | 601 | 554 | 11 | 517 | 505 |
| 16 | 262 | 253 | 17 | 217 | 192 | 8 | 197 | 281 |
| -3 | 513 | 491 | -6 | 512 | 441 | -10 | 536 | 535 |
| -19 | 446 | 460 | -19 | 373 | 348 | -54 | 320 | 339 |
| 15 | 175 | 189 | 7 | 158 | 148 | 10 | 144 | 130 |
| -17 | 253 | 252 | -18 | 248 | 213 | -21 | 200 | 168 |
| 9 | 106 | 111 | 9 | 107 | 90 | -2 | 88 | 86 |
| 16 | 277 | 276 | 13 | 233 | 203 | 15 | 197 | 170 |
| -9 | 192 | 193 | -10 | 181 | 160 | 7 | 148 | 129 |
| -16 | 242 | 239 | -11 | 225 | 207 | 10 | 197 | 181 |
| -9 | 156 | 153 | -7 | 119 | 101 | -4 | 111 | 123 |
| 4 | 271 | 273 | 2 | 279 | 248 | 6 | 255 | 229 |
| -17 | 214 | 206 | -12 | 178 | 166 | -8 | 164 | 149 |
| -3 | 161 | 168 | -2 | 152 | 143 | 0 | 131 | 127 |
| -8 | 374 | 381 | -1 | 336 | 313 | 24 | 295 | 254 |
| 22 | 345 | 353 | 17 | 322 | 285 | 15 | 242 | 216 |
| -18 | 207 | 219 | -22 | 162 | 147 | -4 | 156 | 151 |
| 6 | 120 | 122 | 9 | 116 | 104 | 5 | 100 | 98 |
| 4 | 288 | 304 | 13 | 252 | 227 | -7 | 207 | 193 |

Another advantage of this procedure is that more accurate standard errors are easily computed. The covariance matrix of $\hat{\delta}(I)$ is $AC(\Sigma)A'$, where

$$A = I - C(I)R'\left[RC(I)R'\right]^{-1}R \,. \tag{5}$$

We can estimate the matrix $AC(\Sigma)A'$ unbiasedly by $AC(S)A'$, from which we can compute standard errors by taking the square roots of the diagonal elements.[2] The corresponding RMSSEs over 500 trials are shown in column (10) of Table I; note that they are close to the corresponding RMSEs in column (9). Also, for each of the 35 coefficients we can compute the ratio of the RMSSE to the RMSE. The right half of Table II contains the quartiles of these 35 ratios for each estimation method. In the first and third lines, where we consider $\hat{\delta}(\Sigma)$ and $\hat{\delta}(I)$, these quartiles are satisfactorily close to 1, but the second line which concerns $\hat{\delta}(S)$ shows that on the average (medianwise) the standard errors are as much as 40 per cent below the RMSEs.

Although $\hat{\delta}(I)$ represents an improvement over $\hat{\delta}(S)$, it is the case that medianwise its RMSE exceeds that of $\hat{\delta}(\Sigma)$ by a factor 1/(0.77), or about 30 percent. To verify whether further improvements are possible we consider $\hat{\delta}(S_\Delta)$, where $S_\Delta$ is the diagonal matrix whose diagonal is identical to that of $S$. This amounts to weighted least squares, the weights being designed so as to take into consideration that demand equations for different goods may have different error variances. Column (12) of Table I shows that for most of the 35 coefficients the RMSE of $\hat{\delta}(S_\Delta)$ is below that of $\hat{\delta}(I)$. In fact, a comparison of the second to fourth rows of the left half of Table II indicates that the efficiency improvement of $\hat{\delta}(S_\Delta)$ over $\hat{\delta}(I)$ exceeds that of $\hat{\delta}(I)$ over $\hat{\delta}(S)$.

Standard errors of $\hat{\delta}(S_\Delta)$ present a more complicated problem because $S_\Delta$ is random. Let us first consider $\hat{\delta}(\Sigma_\Delta)$, where $\Sigma_\Delta$ is the diagonal matrix whose diagonal is identical to that of $\Sigma$. The covariance matrix of $\hat{\delta}(\Sigma_\Delta)$ is $BC(\Sigma)B'$, where

$$B = I - C(\Sigma_\Delta)R'\left[RC(\Sigma_\Delta)R'\right]^{-1}R \,, \tag{6}$$

so that $BC(S)B'$ is an unbiased estimator of the covariance matrix of $\hat{\delta}(\Sigma_\Delta)$. For $\hat{\delta}(S_\Delta)$ we use $\hat{B}C(S)\hat{B}$, as an approximate covariance matrix, where $\hat{B}$ is obtained from (6) by substituting $S_\Delta$ for $\Sigma_\Delta$. A comparison of columns (12) and (13) of Table I shows that the RMSSEs implied by this approximation tend to be below the corresponding RMSEs. However, the quartile picture of $\hat{\delta}(S_\Delta)$ in the right half of Table II is not nearly as bad as that of $\hat{\delta}(S)$.

[2] The use of unbiased but inefficient estimators whose covariances matrices are estimated unbiasedly is reminiscent of the procedures developed by White (1980). He formalizes a consistent estimator of the covariance matrix of LS in the face of an unknown heteroscedastic error structure. However, the use of $\hat{\delta}(I)$ is motivated by the problem of estimating $\Sigma$ rather than in specifying that matrix.

**TABLE II.** Efficiency and RMSSE Comparisons

| | Efficiency comparison | | | RMSSE comparison | | |
|---|---|---|---|---|---|---|
| | Lower[a] (1) | Median (2) | Upper[b] (3) | Lower[a] (4) | Median (5) | Upper[b] (6) |
| Using $\Sigma$ | [c] | [c] | [c] | 0.99 | 1.01 | 1.02 |
| Using $S$ | 0.67 | 0.74 | 0.81 | 0.48 | 0.59 | 0.69 |
| Using $I$ | 0.73 | 0.77 | 0.83 | 0.99 | 1.01 | 1.03 |
| Using $S_\Delta$ | 0.82 | 0.84 | 0.90 | 0.89 | 0.92 | 0.95 |
| Using $\hat{\Sigma}$ | 0.92 | 0.95 | 0.99 | 0.89 | 0.94 | 1.06 |

[a] Lower quartile.
[b] Upper quartile.
[c] Identically equal to 1.

Meisner (1981) proposed a $\Sigma$ estimator based on the Theil-Laitinen (1980) maximum entropy (*ME*) distribution which exploits the relationship between the error covariance matrix $\Sigma$ and the canonical correlation coefficients of the dependent and the independent variables of the demand system. The estimator $\hat{\Sigma}$ considered in the last three columns of Table I is an improved version of Meisner's estimator.[3] For most of the 35 coefficients, $\hat{\delta}(\hat{\Sigma})$ has the smallest RMSE among the four estimators which do not use the true $\Sigma$ (see also the last row of Table II), but this must be weighted against the greater burden of computing $\hat{\Sigma}$ and also against the less than perfect performance of the standard errors. The most interesting conclusion is that the conventional procedure which uses $S$ is by far the worst.

## References

Bera, A.K., R.P. Byron and C.M. Jarque: 1981, "Further Evidence on Asymptotic Tests for Homogeneity and Symmetry in Large Demand Systems," *Economics Letters*, **8**, 101-105.

Laitinen, K.: 1978, "Why is Demand Homogeneity So Often Rejected?" *Economics Letters*, **1**, 187-191.

Meisner, J.F.: 1979, "The Sad Fate of the Asymptotic Slutsky Symmetry Test for Large Systems," *Economics Letters*, **2**, 231-233.

[3] $\hat{\Sigma}$ is based on the hybrid covariance matrix (which consists of sample variances on the diagonal and of *ME* covariances outside the diagonal). Also, $\hat{\Sigma}$ in contrast to Meisner's estimator is symmetric in all $n$ dependent variables (so that it is immaterial which of the $n$ equations is deleted). For further details see Theil and Fiebig (1985).

Meisner, J.F.: 1981, Appendix to Theil and Suhm (below).

Theil, H. and D.G. Fiebig: 1985, "Small Samples and Large Equation Systems," in: J. Hannan, P.R. Krishnaiah, and M.M. Rao, eds., *Handbook of Statistics*, Vol. 6, North-Holland, Amsterdam.

Theil, H. and K. Laitinen: 1980, "Singular Moment Matrices in Applied Econometrics," in: P.R. Krishnaiah, ed., *Multivariate Analysis*-V, North-Holland, Amsterdam, 629-649.

Theil, H. and F.E. Suhm: 1981, *International Consumption Comparisons: A System-Wide Approach*, North-Holland, Amsterdam.

White, H.: 1980, "A Heteroskedasticity-Consistent Covariance Matrix Estimator and a Direct Test for Heteroskedasticity," *Econometrica*, **48**, 817-838.

CHAPTER 44

# A SIMPLE AND EFFICIENT ESTIMATION METHOD FOR A NON-LINEAR DEMAND SYSTEM[1]

HENRI THEIL
*University of Florida,*
*Gainesville, Florida, U.S.A.*

ERIC M. DIAMOND
*University of Florida,*
*Gainesville, Florida, U.S.A.*

BALDEV RAJ
*University of Florida,*
*Gainesville, Florida, U.S.A., and*
*Wilfrid Laurier University,*
*Waterloo, Ontario, Canada*

ABSTRACT. A least-squares-type estimation method appears to be about as efficient as maximum likelihood with a known contemporaneous covariance matrix.

Rosalsky, Finke and Theil (1984) performed a simulation experiment in order to verify the merits of maximum likelihood (ML) estimation of non-linear demand systems. They selected Laitinen's (1978) experimental design, which is based on the Rotterdam model for $n = 14$ goods with $T = 31$ observations under the assumption of preference independence with a constant income flexibility $\phi$. Apart from this $\phi$, the parameters to be estimated are the marginal budget shares $\theta_1, \ldots, \theta_n$. Columns (1) and (2) of Table I list these coefficients and their true values. The next four columns summarize the results of ML estimation for 100 independent trials under the assumption that the $T$ error vectors of the demand system are independent and multivariate normal with zero mean vector and a constant covariance matrix $\Sigma$. In columns (3) and (4) this matrix is assumed to be known to the analyst. In columns (5) and (6) this $\Sigma$ is unknown and is estimated by ML. The means in columns (3) and (5) are close to the true values in column (2), thus indicating that bias is not much of a problem, but the RMSEs (around the true value) in column (6) are mostly about 20 to 30 percent larger than those in column (4). This shows that ML estimation of the coefficients of an equation system can be seriously deficient in terms of efficiency when the error covariance matrix $\Sigma$ is unknown.[1] A major cause of this deficiency is the instability of the ML estimator of $\Sigma^{-1}$ in successive sampling.

[1] This article first appeared in *Economics Letters*, **20** (1986), 351-353. Reprinted with the permission of Elsevier Science Publishers B.V. (North-Holland). Research supported in part by the McKethan-Matherly Eminent Scholar Chair, University of Florida and Wilfrid Laurier University (Ontario, Canada).

[1] Rosalsky et al. (1984) also considered the performance of asymptotic standard errors of ML estimates, but this is not a topic of the present paper.

**TABLE I.** ML Estimation of a Non-Linear Demand Model: Results for 100 trials.[a]

| | | Σ known | | Σ unknown | |
|---|---|---|---|---|---|
| Parameter (1) | True value (2) | Mean (3) | RMSE (4) | Mean (5) | RMSE (6) |
| $\theta_i$, $i = 1$ | 55 | 56 | 24 | 55 | 30 |
| $i = 2$ | 266 | 265 | 47 | 266 | 56 |
| $i = 3$ | 369 | 382 | 72 | 372 | 84 |
| $i = 4$ | 296 | 291 | 45 | 290 | 60 |
| $i = 5$ | 661 | 650 | 73 | 648 | 90 |
| $i = 6$ | 45 | 41 | 18 | 42 | 24 |
| $i = 7$ | 352 | 352 | 51 | 353 | 63 |
| $i = 8$ | 234 | 237 | 45 | 241 | 55 |
| $i = 9$ | 272 | 276 | 59 | 278 | 63 |
| $i = 10$ | 2371 | 2345 | 138 | 2338 | 169 |
| $i = 11$ | 237 | 234 | 41 | 228 | 53 |
| $i = 12$ | 2125 | 2139 | 145 | 2154 | 195 |
| $i = 13$ | 478 | 479 | 71 | 478 | 90 |
| $i = 14$ | 2240 | 2252 | 200 | 2260 | 237 |
| $\phi$ | -6000 | -5993 | 402 | -5973 | 510 |

[a] All entries to be divided by $10^4$. *Source*: Rosalsky et al. (1984).

The question arises whether we can improve on the ML estimator of $\phi$ and the $\theta_i$'s by disregarding $\Sigma^{-1}$ altogether. In the case of Laitinen's (1978) experimental design this can be done in a rather obvious manner. Given the assumption of preference independence, we may write the demand equation for good $i$ as

$$\bar{w}_{it} DQ_{it} = \theta_i DQ_t + \phi\theta_i (Dp_{it} - DP'_t) + \varepsilon_{it} , \tag{1}$$

where $DP'_t = \Sigma_{i=1}^{n} \theta_i Dp_{it}$ is the Frisch price index. Let us simplify (1) to

$$y_{it} = \theta_i x_{it} + \varepsilon_{it} , \tag{2}$$

where $y_{it} = \bar{w}_{it} Dq_{it}$ and

$$x_{it} = DQ_t + \phi (Dp_{it} - DP'_t) . \tag{3}$$

We proceed to estimate $\theta_i$ in (2) by least squares (LS),

**TABLE II.** The RMSEs of an Alternative Estimator.[a]

| Parameter (1) | | RMSEs ML, $\Sigma$ unknown (2) | RMSEs Alternative estimator (3) | Ratio (2)/(3) (4) |
|---|---|---|---|---|
| $\theta_i$, | $i = 1$ | 28 | 23 | 1.22 |
| | $i = 2$ | 54 | 45 | 1.20 |
| | $i = 3$ | 77 | 60 | 1.28 |
| | $i = 4$ | 59 | 44 | 1.34 |
| | $i = 5$ | 93 | 66 | 1.41 |
| | $i = 6$ | 22 | 17 | 1.29 |
| | $i = 7$ | 72 | 57 | 1.26 |
| | $i = 8$ | 65 | 53 | 1.23 |
| | $i = 9$ | 56 | 50 | 1.12 |
| | $i = 10$ | 169 | 152 | 1.11 |
| | $i = 11$ | 47 | 36 | 1.31 |
| | $i = 12$ | 192 | 147 | 1.31 |
| | $i = 13$ | 85 | 75 | 1.13 |
| | $i = 14$ | 237 | 207 | 1.14 |
| $\phi$ | | 498 | 405 | 1.23 |

[a] All entries in columns (2) and (3) to be divided by $10^4$.

$$\hat{\theta}_i'(\phi) = \frac{\sum_{t=1}^{T} x_{it} y_{it}}{\sum_{t=1}^{T} x_{it}^2} \, . \tag{4}$$

Two qualifications are in order. First, $x_{it}$ in (3) depends on $\phi$, so that the LS estimator (4) is conditional on $\phi$; this is indicated by writing $\phi$ in parentheses on the left. Second, $DP_t'$ in (3) depends on the unknown $\theta_i$'s. The latter problem will be handled in the following iterative manner. Initially the $\theta_i$'s determining $DP_t'$ are replaced by the averages of the observed budget shares $w_{it}$ over the $T = 31$ observations. Next we normalize the marginal shares thus obtained from (4) so that they add up to one:

$$\hat{\theta}_i''(\phi) = \frac{\hat{\theta}_i'(\phi)}{\sum_{j=1}^{n} \hat{\theta}_j'(\phi)} \, . \tag{5}$$

Thereafter we specify $DP_t'$ in (3) as $\Sigma_{i=1}^{n}\hat{\theta}_i''(\phi)Dp_{it}$ and substitute this into (4), yielding $\hat{\theta}_i'''(\phi)$, which we normalize as in (5). This iterative procedure is continued until convergence. The converged values are written $\hat{\theta}(\phi)$, without primes.

Note that these converged values are conditional estimates given $\phi$. To estimate $\phi$ we minimize the total residual sum of squares. Going back to (2) and (3), this amounts to minimizing

$$\sum_{i=1}^{n}\sum_{t=1}^{T}\left(y_{it}-\hat{\theta}_i(\phi)\left[DQ_t+\phi\left\{Dp_{it}-\sum_{j=1}^{n}\hat{\theta}_j(\phi)\,Dp_{jt}\right\}\right]\right)^2 \tag{6}$$

with respect to $\phi$. The minimizing value $\hat{\phi}$ is the estimate of $\phi$, and $\hat{\theta}_i(\hat{\phi})$ is the unconditional estimate of $\theta_i$.

The simplicity of this alternative estimation method should be noted. The marginal share estimate which starts with (4) and (5) is an iterative and normalized version of a simple regression coefficient. The $\phi$ estimate which results from (6) is a single coefficient which results from non-linear LS. Table II provides simulation results for another batch of 100 trials. Note that column (2) of this table is close to column (6) of Table I, as it should be. Also note that column (5) contains appreciably smaller elements. In fact, these elements are fairly close to those in column (4) of Table I, thus suggesting that the alternative procedure is about as good as ML when $\Sigma$ is known. The experiment summarized in Table II was repeated for an independent set of 500 trials with about the same results.

## References

Laitinen, K.: 1978, "Why is Demand Homogeneity So Often Rejected?" *Economics Letters*, **1**, 187-191.

Rosalsky, M.C., R. Finke and H. Theil: 1984, "The Downward Bias of Asymptotic Standard Errors of Maximum Likelihood Estimates of Non-linear Systems," *Economics Letters*, **14**, 207-211.

# SECTION 3.5: THE INDEPENDENCE TRANSFORMATION

CHAPTER 45

# THE INDEPENDENCE TRANSFORMATION: A REVIEW AND SOME FURTHER EXPLORATIONS*

HENRI THEIL
*University of Chicago*
*Chicago, Illinois, U.S.A.*

KENNETH LAITINEN
*University of Chicago*
*Chicago, Illinois, U.S.A*

## 1. Introduction

The objective of this chapter is to discuss the relationship between the technique of principal components, first applied to economic data in the pioneering paper by Stone (1947), and the analysis of consumer demand.

The purpose of principal component analysis in statistics is to formulate a set of variables that are in some way 'more basic' than the observed variables. Factor analysis has a similar objective. Starting in 1956, Gorman and his associates (Boyle *et al.*, 1977; Gorman, 1956; 1959; 1976b) applied these statistical techniques to consumer demand in order to assess the consumer's basic wants, while Lancaster (1966, 1971) and Becker (1965) pursued similar goals by extending the economic theory of the consumer rather than using statistical tools. The independence transformation, which originated with Theil (1967; 1975-76; 1977), Brooks (1970), and Laitinen and Theil (1978), is related to both approaches and is in fact 'between' them. The transformation requires no extension of the theory of the utility-maximizing consumer, although it can handle such extensions without difficulty (see the example on leisure in section 2). At the same time, the transformation has a simple statistical interpretation, viz., that of a constrained principal component transformation.

To provide adequate motivation, we discuss some examples in section 2. Sections 3 and 4 describe the preference independence transformation and the underlying differential approach to consumption theory. Section 5 gives a brief discussion of similar results in the theory of the firm. A comparison with principal components follows in section 6, after which the article concludes with two sections (7 and 8) on strong and weak separability. To simplify the exposition, the more complicated mathematics has been put into the appendix. The account which follows is largely expository, but there are some new results, in particular on the independence transformation under weak separability (section 8) and the case in which the consumer's utility function has a Hessian matrix that is not definite (appendix B).

---

* This article first appeared in A. S. Deaton, ed., *Essays in Theory and Management of Consumer Behavior*, Cambridge University Press, 1981, 73-112. Reprinted here with the permission of Cambridge University Press. Research supported in part by NSF Grant SOC 76-82718.

## 2. Three examples

### 2.1 TRANSFORMED MEATS

The consumer is assumed to maximize a utility function $u(q)$ subject to the budget constraint $p'q = M$, where $p = [p_i]$ and $q=[q_i]$ are $n$-element price and quantity vectors and $M$ is total expenditure (or, for short, income). One specification of the utility function, known as the Klein-Rubin (1948) or the Stone (1954)-Geary (1950) utility function, is

$$u(q) = \sum_{i=1}^{n} \theta_i \log (q_i - c_i) \tag{2.1}$$

where the $c_i$s are constants and the $\theta_i$s positive constants with unit sum. Note that (2.1) implies that the marginal utility of each good is independent of the consumption of every other good. More generally, if the consumer's preferences can be represented by an additive utility function,

$$u(q) = \sum_{i=1}^{n} u_i(q_i) \tag{2.2}$$

then the marginal utility of the $i$th good equals $du_i/dq_i$, which is independent of all $q_j$s with $j \neq i$. We shall refer to the preference structure (2.2) as preference independence.

It is unlikely that preference independence is realistic for narrowly defined goods. Indeed, when we analyze the demand for beef, pork, and chicken in the United States from 1950 to 1972, we find that the data contradict the additive structure (2.2).[1] But we can ask whether it is possible to transform these three observed meats so that each transformed meat has a marginal utility that is independent of the consumption of the other transformed meats. The answer is affirmative: the procedure to be used is the preference independence transformation. A major tool is the composition matrix which describes the expenditure on each transformed meat in terms of the expenditures on all observed meats and vice versa. The following is a bordered composition matrix for these meats:

| | | | | |
|---|---|---|---|---|
| 0.148 | 0.383 | 0.202 | 0.734 | $(T_1)$ |
| 0.296 | -0.092 | 0.000 | 0.204 | $(T_2)$ |
| 0.037 | 0.095 | -0.070 | 0.063 | $(T_3)$ |
| 0.481 | 0.387 | 0.133 | 1 | |
| (beef) | (pork) | (chicken) | | |

(2.3)

[1] The numerical results in the discussion which follows are from chapters 7 and 13 of Theil (1975-76).

The composition matrix consists of the nine figures above the horizontal line and to the left of the vertical line. The last row contains the column sums of this matrix. The figures in this row are the expenditures on the observed meats measured as fractions of the expenditure on the three-meat group. Thus, 48.1 per cent of this total expenditure is allocated to beef, 38.7 per cent to pork, and 13.3 per cent to chicken. These percentages obviously change as time proceeds. This means that, in general, the results of the preference independence transformation are time-dependent. The composition matrix (2.3) is based on data for the mid 1950s.

The row sums in the last column of (2.3) are the expenditure shares of the transformed meats, each of which has (by construction) a marginal utility that is independent of the consumption of the other transformed meats. One of these, labelled $T_1$, accounts for 73.4 per cent of the expenditure on the three-meat group. The positive sign of the elements in the first row of the composition matrix implies that the three observed meats all contribute positively to $T_1$, suggesting that this transformed meat corresponds to the consumer's basic want for meat. However, it will appear that $T_1$ has the smallest income elasticity of the three transformed meats; these elasticities provide information on transformed goods beyond that provided by the composition matrix (see sections 4 and 7). Since a small income elasticity is indicative of modest quality, we conclude that $T_1$ corresponds to the consumer's basic want for affordable meat.

The transformed meats in the second and third rows of (2.3) are both contrasts between observed meats. Thus, $T_2$ is a contrast between beef and pork, every two dollars' worth of $T_2$ consisting of (approximately) three dollars' worth of beef minus one dollar's worth of pork which is given up. The associated basic want is the consumer's desire to eat beef rather than pork; it is the most luxurious want (see section 7). The third transformed meat, finally, is a contrast between beef and pork on one hand and chicken on the other.

## 2.2 TRANSFORMED GOODS INVOLVING LEISURE

The occurrence of contrasts is a standard feature of the independence transformation. We shall illustrate this with some results obtained by Flinn (1978) for a demand system that includes the demand for leisure; this system was derived from Barnett's study (1974) and is based on US data for the period 1890-1955. Taking leisure into account implies that $M$ must be interpreted as full income, including the market value of the household's time. As before, there are three goods which are relevant for the independence transformation: semi-durables, durables, and leisure in this case. The bordered composition matrix for the early 1950s is as follows:

| | | | | |
|---|---|---|---|---|
| 0.082 | 0.117 | 0.795 | 0.994 ($T_1$) | |
| 0.018 | 0.016 | -0.028 | 0.006 ($T_2$) | |
| 0.004 | -0.005 | 0.002 | 0.000 ($T_3$) | (2.4) |
| 0.104 (semi-durables) | 0.127 (durables) | 0.769 (leisure) | 1 | |

A comparison of (2.3) and (2.4) reveals a similar numerical structure except that (2.4) is more extreme. In the case of (2.4), $T_2$ and $T_3$ are contrasts, but they account for only a very small fraction of the expenditure on the group. As we shall see in section 7, the income elasticities (with respect to full income) of $T_2$ and $T_3$ are substantially larger than that of $T_1$. Given that all three observed goods including leisure are positively represented in the first row of (2.4), and that many durables are time-saving goods, it seems reasonable to conclude that $T_1$ corresponds to the household's basic want for affordable free time. About 99 per cent of the expenditure on the three-good group is allocated to this want. The negative contribution of leisure to $T_2$ means that household members give up leisure (and hence go to work) when they buy this transformed good.

## 2.3 TRANSFORMED INPUTS

The preference independence transformation changes observed consumer goods into transformed goods so that the marginal utility of each is independent of the consumption of all other transformed goods. The input independence transformation in the theory of the firm is similar in that it changes observed inputs into transformed inputs so that the elasticity of output with respect to each transformed input is independent of the quantities of all other transformed inputs.

We shall illustrate the input independence transformation for a translog production function,

$$\log z = \text{constant} + \alpha \log K + \beta \log L + \xi(\alpha\beta)^{1/2} \log K \log L \tag{2.5}$$

where $z$ is output, $K$ is capital, $L$ is labour, and $\alpha$, $\beta$, and $\xi$ are constants ($\alpha, \beta > 0$). The elasticities of output with respect to the two inputs are

$$\frac{\partial \log z}{\partial \log K} = \alpha + \xi(\alpha\beta)^{1/2} \log L \tag{2.6}$$

$$\frac{\partial \log z}{\partial \log L} = \beta + \xi(\alpha\beta)^{1/2} \log K \tag{2.7}$$

If $\xi=0$, the elasticity of output with respect to each input is independent of the other input; the technology (2.5) is then said to be input independent. If $\xi \neq 0$, (2.5) is not input independent, in which case we apply the input independence transformation.

This transformation takes a simple form when we select units so that $K = L = 1$ holds at the point of the firm's optimum. We write $f_K$ and $f_L$ for the factor shares of capital and labour: the expenditures on these inputs measured as fractions of total input expenditure ($f_K + f_L = 1$). The following is the composition matrix of the input independence transformation for the technology (2.5):

$$\begin{bmatrix} \frac{1}{2}(f_K + (f_K f_L)^{1/2}) & \frac{1}{2}(f_L + (f_K f_L)^{1/2}) \\ \frac{1}{2}(f_K - (f_K f_L)^{1/2} & \frac{1}{2}(f_L - (f_K f_L)^{1/2}) \end{bmatrix} \tag{2.8}$$

The sums of the elements in the two columns are the factor shares $f_K$ and $f_L$ of the two observed inputs. These should be compared with the expenditure shares 0.481, 0.387, and 0.133 of the observed meats in (2.3). The row sums of (2.8) are the factor shares of the transformed inputs: $\frac{1}{2} + (f_K f_L)^{1/2}$ and $\frac{1}{2} - (f_K f_L)^{1/2}$. For example, when we specify $f_K = 0.2$ and $f_L = 0.8$ and indicate the transformed inputs by $T_1$ and $T_2$, (2.8) yields the following bordered composition matrix:

| | | | |
|---|---|---|---|
| 0.3 | 0.6 | 0.9 | ($T_1$) |
| -0.1 | 0.2 | 0.1 | ($T_2$) |
| 0.2 | 0.8 | 1 | |
| (capital) | (labour) | | |

(2.9)

Both observed inputs are positively represented in $T_1$, whereas $T_2$ is a contrast between labour and capital. Buying more $T_2$ means that the firm's operation becomes more labour-intensive, each dollar spent on $T_2$ being equivalent to two dollars' worth of labour compensated by one dollar's worth of capital services which is given up.

## 3. The Differential Approach to Consumption Theory

### 3.1 A DEMAND EQUATION SYSTEM IN DIFFERENTIAL FORM

The simplest formulation of the preference independence transformation is in terms of the differential approach to the theory of the consumer. This approach should be contrasted with that which postulates a particular algebraic form of the utility function such as (2.1). When we maximize (2.1) subject to the budget constraint, we obtain (after minor rearrangements) demand equations of the following form:

$$p_i q_i = p_i c_i + \theta_i \left( M - \sum_{j=1}^{n} p_j c_j \right) \tag{3.1}$$

This is the linear expenditure system, which is probably the most popular demand system since Stone (1954) introduced it in 1954. Differentiation of (3.1) with respect to $M$ shows that $\theta_i$ can be interpreted as the marginal expenditure share of the $i$th good:

$$\theta_i = \frac{\partial(p_i q_i)}{\partial M}, \quad \sum_{i=1}^{n} \theta_i = 1 \tag{3.2}$$

These marginal shares should be contrasted with the 'average' expenditure shares or budget shares:

$$w_i = \frac{p_i q_i}{M}, \quad \sum_{i=1}^{n} w_i = 1 \tag{3.3}$$

The differential approach to consumption theory considers infinitesimal displacements and does not restrict itself to a particular algebraic form of the utility function. Divisia indexes (1925) play an important role in this approach. We write the differential of the budget constraint as $dM = \Sigma_i q_i dp_i + \Sigma_i p_i dq_i$. Division by $M$ and use of (3.3) give

$$d(\log M) = d(\log P) + d(\log Q) \tag{3.4}$$

where log stands for natural logarithm (here and elsewhere) and $d(\log P)$ and $d(\log Q)$ are the consumer's Divisia price and volume indexes in differential form:

$$d(\log P) = \sum_{i=1}^{n} w_i d(\log p_i) \tag{3.5}$$

$$d(\log Q) = \sum_{i=1}^{n} w_i d(\log q_i) \tag{3.6}$$

We shall find it advantageous to write (3.4) in the equivalent form

$$d(\log Q) = d\left(\log \frac{M}{P}\right) \tag{3.7}$$

with the expression on the right interpreted as $d(\log M) - d(\log P)$. Equation (3.7) states that the Divisia volume index is equal to the logarithmic change in money income deflated by the Divisia price index.

We assume that the consumer's utility function is appropriately differentiable and that the Hessian matrix of this function, $U = [\partial^2 u/\partial q_i \partial q_j]$, is symmetric negative definite.[2] The equilibrium conditions consist of the budget constraint and the proportionality of marginal utilities and prices. Since these conditions hold identically in income and prices, we can differentiate them with respect to the latter variables, the result of which can be written in the form of Barten's (1964) fundamental matrix equation. By solving this equation we obtain

$$\frac{\partial q_i}{\partial p_j} = \lambda u^{ij} - \frac{\lambda}{\partial\lambda/\partial M}\frac{\partial q_i}{\partial M}\frac{\partial q_j}{\partial M} - \frac{\partial q_i}{\partial M}q_j \tag{3.8}$$

where $\lambda$ is the marginal utility of income and $u^{ij}$ is the $(i, j)$th element of $U^{-1}$. The last term in (3.8) represents the income effect of the change in $p_j$ on $q_i$, while the two preceding terms jointly represent the substitution effect. The firm term ($\lambda u^{ij}$) describes the specific substitution effect and the second the general substitution effect. The latter effect deals with the general competition of all goods for an extra dollar of the consumer's income whereas the former is concerned with the utility interaction of the $i$th and $j$th goods. The distinction between these two components of the substitution effect is from Houthakker (1960).

The differential approach uses (3.8) to describe the change in the demand for the $i$th good in terms of the changes in income and all prices. A convenient result is obtained

[2] The negative definiteness of $U$ guarantees the existence of a budget-constrained utility maximum, but a weaker condition is sufficient for this existence. In appendix B we analyse some implications of this weaker condition.

when we specify the left-hand variable as $w_i d(\log q_i)$, which is the contribution of the $i$th good to the Divisia volume index [see (3.6)]. The result is then

$$w_i d(\log q_i) = \theta_i d\left(\log \frac{M}{P}\right) + \phi \sum_{j=1}^{n} \theta_{ij} d\left(\log \frac{p_j}{P'}\right) \tag{3.9}$$

which is the $i$th equation of the differential demand system. It should be contrasted with the linear expenditure system (3.1) that is obtained from the utility function (2.1).

## 3.2 DISCUSSION OF THE DIFFERENTIAL DEMAND SYSTEM

Before explaining the various symbols in (3.9) we note that the deflator which transforms money income into real income is not the same as the deflator which transforms absolute prices into relative prices. Income is deflated by the income effect of the price changes; this is equivalent to the use of the Divisia price index as deflator [see (3.5) and (3.7)]. In the substitution term of (3.9) it is the specific substitution effect of the price changes which is deflated by the general substitution effect. The deflator involved is the Frisch price index (1932, pp. 74-82),

$$d(\log P') = \sum_{i=1}^{n} \theta_i d(\log p_i) \tag{3.10}$$

which uses marginal rather than budget shares as weights.

It is readily verified from (3.2) and (3.3) that the ratio of a marginal share to the corresponding budget share is the income elasticity:

$$\frac{\theta_i}{w_i} = \frac{\partial \log q_i}{\partial \log M} \tag{3.11}$$

A comparison of (3.10) and (3.5) shows that luxuries (goods with income elasticities larger than 1) have a larger weight in the Frisch price index than in the Divisia price index, whereas the opposite is true for necessities (with income elasticities smaller than 1). If a good is inferior ($\theta_i < 0$), an increase in its price has a downward effect on the Frisch price index.

We proceed to discuss (3.9) term by term. The expression on the left is not only the contribution of good $i$ to the Divisia volume index (3.6) but also the quantity component of the change in its budget share. This may be verified by taking the differential of $w_i = p_i q_i / M$:

$$dw_i = w_i d(\log p_i) + w_i d(\log q_i) - w_i d(\log M) \tag{3.12}$$

Hence the change in a budget share consists of a price, a quantity, and an income component. Using the *quantity component* of this change as the left-hand variable of a demand equation emphasizes the fact that the quantities bought are the consumer's decision variables. Using a component of the change in a *budget share* emphasizes the fact that consumption theory is basically an allocation theory: it is concerned with the allocation of the fixed amount of total expenditure to the individual goods, given this amount and the prices of these goods. Equation (3.9) emphasizes the allocation character of consumer demand, which may be clarified when we use (3.7) to write the equation as

$$w_i d(\log q_i) = \theta_i d(\log Q) + \phi \sum_{j=1}^{n} \theta_{ij} d\left(\log \frac{p_j}{P'}\right) \tag{3.13}$$

This equation describes the contribution of good $i$ to the Divisia volume index in terms of this index and relative price changes. When we sum (3.13) over $i$, we obtain $d(\log Q) = d(\log Q)$ in view of $\Sigma_i \theta_i = 1$ [see (3.2)] and the zero sum of the substitution term of (3.13).[3]

The first term on the right in (3.13) is the real-income component of the change in the demand for the $i$th good, with real income measured by the Divisia volume index. This index is multiplied by the marginal share $\theta_i$ which also occurs in the linear expenditure system (3.1). However, there is an important difference in that $\theta_i$ is a constant in the linear expenditure system, whereas the differential approach postulates no constancy. This approach allows all coefficients [$\theta_i$, $\phi$, and $\theta_{ij}$ in (3.13) to depend on the levels of income and prices.

The coefficient $\phi$ in the substitution term of (3.13) is defined as the reciprocal of the income elasticity of the marginal utility of income:

$$\frac{1}{\phi} = \frac{\partial \log \lambda}{\partial \log M} \tag{3.14}$$

We shall refer to $\phi$ as the income flexibility; it is negative because of the negative definiteness of $U$.[4] The coefficient $\theta_{ij}$ in (3.13) is

---

[3] This may be verified by writing the substitution term of (3.13) as a multiple $\phi$ of $\Sigma_j \theta_{ij} d(\log p_j) - \theta_i d(\log P')$ [see (3.16)]. Summation of this expression over $i$ yields zero because of the symmetry of $[\theta_{ij}]$, (3.16), and $\Sigma_i \theta_i = 1$.

[4] The derivative $\partial\lambda/\partial M$ equals the reciprocal of $p'U^{-1}p$, which is obtained by solving Barten's fundamental matrix equation. This matrix equation and its solution are given in appendix B.

$$\theta_{ij} = \frac{\lambda}{\phi M} p_i u^{ij} p_j \tag{3.15}$$

where $u^{ij}$, as in (3.8), is the $(i, j)$th element of $U^{-1}$. It follows from $\phi < 0$ and the symmetric negative definiteness of $U$ that $\theta_{ij}$ is an element of a symmetric positive definite matrix $[\theta_{ij}]$. Also, the $\theta_{ij}$s in each equation add up to the corresponding marginal share,[5]

$$\sum_{j=1}^{n} \theta_{ij} = \theta_i \tag{3.16}$$

When we sum both sides of (3.16) over i and use $\Sigma_i \theta_i = 1$, we find that the sum of all $\theta_{ij}$s equals 1. Thus, we shall refer to the $\theta_{ij}$s as the normalized price coefficients of (3.13). Each $\theta_{ij}$ is the coefficient of the logarithmic change in a relative price.

When we write (3.15) in $n$ x $n$ matrix form and invert both sides, we obtain

$$\theta^{ij} = \frac{\phi M}{\lambda} \frac{\partial^2 u}{\partial(p_i q_i)\partial(p_j q_j)} \tag{3.17}$$

where $\theta_{ij}$ is the $(i, j)$th element of $[\theta_{ij}]^{-1}$. The derivative on the right describes the change in the marginal utility of a dollar spent on the $i$th good which is caused by an extra dollar spent on the $j$th. So we may conclude from (3.17) that the *normalized* price coefficient matrix of the differential demand system (3.13) is inversely proportional to the Hessian matrix of the utility function in expenditure terms.

## 3.3 PREFERENCE INDEPENDENCE AND SPECIFIC SUBSTITUTES AND COMPLEMENTS

Under the preference independence condition (2.2) the Hessian $U$ is diagonal. Its inverse is then also diagonal, so that $\theta_{ij} = 0$ whenever $i \neq j$ in view of (3.15), while (3.16) is simplified to $\theta_{ii} = \theta_i$. Therefore, under preference independence (3.13) becomes

[5] Equation (3.16) follows from (3.15) and $\theta_i = (\lambda/\phi M)p_i \Sigma_j u^{ij} p_j$, which is obtained by solving Barten's fundamental matrix equation.

$$w_i d(\log q_i) = \theta_i d(\log Q) + \phi \theta_i d\left(\log \frac{p_i}{P'}\right) \tag{3.18}$$

which contains only one relative price. Inferior goods cannot occur under preference independence because $\theta_i = \theta_{ii} > 0$, the > sign being based on the positive definiteness of the matrix $[\theta_{ij}]$. Inferior goods are also excluded by the linear expenditure system (3.1).

Following Houthakker (1960), we call the *i*th and *j*th goods specific substitutes (complements) when $\theta_{ij}$ is negative (positive).[6] We conclude from (3.13) and $\phi < 0$ that an increase in the *j*th relative price raises (lowers) the demand for the *i*th good when the two goods are specific substitutes (complements). Also, (3.18) shows that under preference independence no good is a specific substitute or complement of any other. The preference independence transformation may be viewed as an annihilator of all specific substitution and complementarity relations so that demand equations of the form (3.18) emerge, each containing one relative price.

## 4. The Preference Independence Transformation

### 4.1 THE MAIN RESULTS OF THE TRANSFORMATION

The preference independence transformation diagonalizes the Hessian matrix $U$ (and hence also the normalized price coefficient matrix $[\theta_{ij}]$) subject to the constraint that the consumer's income and the associated Divisia indexes (3.5) and (3.6) are invariant. The main results are stated below. An outline of the derivations is given in appendix A.

We write $\Theta$ for the matrix $[\theta_{ij}]$ and $W$ for the $n$ x $n$ diagonal matrix with the budget shares on the diagonal. The transformation involves a diagonalization of $\Theta$ relative to $W$,

$$(\Theta - \lambda_i W)x_i = 0 \tag{4.1}$$

where $i = 1, ..., n$. The $\lambda_i$s are latent roots and the $x_i$s are characteristic vectors normalized so that $x_i' W x_j = 0$ for $i \neq j$ and $x_i' W x_i = 1$. We can implement (4.1) in the more convenient form

$$(D^{-1}\Theta D^{-1} - \lambda_i I)Dx_i = 0 \tag{4.2}$$

[6] This definition differs from Hicks' which is based on the total substitution effect. Houthakker's definition is more useful for our present purposes.

where $D$ is the diagonal matrix with the square roots of the budget shares on the diagonal. Both diagonalizations, (4.1) and (4.2), are unique when the roots $\lambda_1, ..., \lambda_n$ are all distinct. These roots are all real and positive because $D^{-1}\Theta D^{-1}$ in (4.2) is symmetric positive definite.

A third equivalent diagonalization is also useful. We introduce the $n \times n$ matrix $X$ whose $i$th column is the characteristic vector $x_i$ and the $n \times n$ diagonal matrix $\Lambda$ whose $i$th diagonal element is the latent root $\lambda_i$. Then the normalization rules $x_i'Wx_j = 0$ for $i \neq j$ and $x_i'Wx_i = 1$ can be written as $X'WX = I$, while (4.1) for all $i$ can be written in the form $\Theta X = WX\Lambda$. On premultiplying by $X'$ we obtain $X'\Theta X = X'WX\Lambda$, or $X'\Theta X = \Lambda$ because $X'WX = I$. Therefore,

$$X'\Theta X = \Lambda, \quad X'WX = I \tag{4.3}$$

which shows that (4.1) combined with the normalization rule on the characteristic vectors can be viewed as a simultaneous diagonalization of $\Theta$ and $W$, $\Theta$ being transformed into $\Lambda$ and $W$ into $I$.

The $\lambda_i$s are the income elasticities of the transformed goods, i.e. the transformed versions of $\theta_i/w_i$ [see (3.11)]. Thus, the fact that the transformation is unique when the $\lambda_i$s are distinct is equivalent to the proposition that *transformed goods are identified by their income elasticities*. Later we shall explore what happens when two $\lambda_i$s are equal or almost equal. The fact that the $\lambda_i$s are all positive implies that transformed goods can never be inferior goods. The income elasticities of the transformed meats described in section 2 are directly related to these $\lambda_i$s, but a more complete discussion is postponed until section 7 because this application is confined to the expenditure on meat rather than consumption as a whole.

The composition matrix of the transformation takes the form

$$T = (X^{-1}\iota)_\Delta X^{-1} \tag{4.4}$$

where $\iota$ is a column vector consisting of $n$ unit elements and $(X^{-1}\iota)_\Delta$ stands for the vector $X^{-1}\iota$ written in the form of a diagonal matrix. The column sums of $T$ are the budget shares of the observed goods and the row sums are the budget shares of the transformed goods. We cannot exclude the possibility that the vector $X^{-1}\iota$ contains a zero element. If this happens, $(X^{-1}\iota)_\Delta$ contains a zero row and so does the composition matrix in view of (4.4). This means that there is a transformed good which receives no contribution from any observed good so that nothing is spent on that transformed good. It is shown in appendix A how this can be explained in terms of the consumer's preferences.

The invariance of total expenditure and its Divisia indexes is imposed, but several other coefficients and variables can also be shown to be invariant, including the income flexibility $\phi$ and the Frisch index (3.10). Also, when the prices (quantities) of all observed goods change proportionately, the price (quantity) of each transformed good changes in the same proportion, which is a desirable property.

## 4.2 THE TRANSFORMATION UNDER CHANGING BUDGET SHARES

Even when $\Theta$ is a matrix of constant elements (which need not be the case), the diagonalization (4.1) will yield results that vary over time because the budget shares in the diagonal of $W$ will typically change. The analysis of such variations is frequently interesting. For example, the composition matrix for meats [see (2.3)] changed from the early 1950s until the early 1970s in several respects, one of which was the fact that $T_1$ (affordable meat) was gradually 'beefed up' in the sense that the contribution of beef to $T_1$ increased by more than 100 per cent. Since beef has the largest income elasticity of the three observed meats, this also raised the income elasticity of $T_1$ relative to those of the other transformed meats. Suppose that during this process two such income elasticities become equal. It is then no longer possible to separate the associated transformed goods because these are identified by their income elasticities. But is it possible to trace the transformed goods during that process? We shall answer this question for

$$\Theta = 10^{-10}\begin{bmatrix} 6553660128 & -57241262 & -433379614 \\ -57241262 & 3594930590 & -38381041 \\ -433379614 & -38381041 & 909413116 \end{bmatrix} \tag{4.5}$$

When we specify the budget shares of the observed goods as

$$[\,w_1 \quad w_2 \quad w_3\,] = [\,0.6 \qquad 0.3+\varepsilon \qquad 0.1-\varepsilon\,] \tag{4.6}$$

we obtain $\lambda_1 = \lambda_2 = 1.2$ and $\lambda_3 = 0.8$ for $\varepsilon = 0$. The upper part of table 1 shows the bordered composition matrices and $\lambda_i$s for $\varepsilon = -10^{-5}$, $\varepsilon = 0$, and $\varepsilon = 10^{-5}$. The results show that the changes are very gradual and that there is no difficulty in tracing the behaviour of the first and second transformed goods in spite of the multiple root problem.

Next, for the same $\Theta$, consider

$$[\,w_1 \quad w_2 \quad w_3\,] = [\,0.6+2\varepsilon \qquad 0.3-\varepsilon \qquad 0.1-\varepsilon\,] \tag{4.7}$$

Again there is no difficulty in tracing the behaviour of the transformed goods when $\varepsilon$ takes the values $-10^{-5}$, 0, and $10^{-5}$ (see the lower part of table 1), but note that (4.6) and (4.7) are identical for $\varepsilon = 0$ and that the associated second and fifth composition matrices in the table are not identical at all except for the last row. This illustrates the indeterminacy caused by the multiple roots. Also, the different behaviour of the first two transformed goods in the upper and lower half of the table illustrates that this behaviour depends on the path of the budget shares of the observed goods. In the case of (4.6) and (4.7) this path is linear, but there are more complicated cases (see appendix A).

## 5. Extensions to the Theory of the Firm

Although this volume deals with the consumer, it is appropriate to pay some attention to the firm also. One reason is the increased awareness of the role of duality theory in these areas; see Deaton (1979), Diewert (1974), Gorman (1976a), and McFadden (1978). An even more important reason in the present context is the fact that the differential approach to the demand and supply side of the firm yields interesting extensions of the results obtained for the consumer. For an integrated treatment see Theil (1980); the remarks which follow summarize the highlights.

(1) Consider a single-product firm whose objective is to minimize the total expenditure on $n$ inputs by varying these inputs subject to a technology constraint for given input prices and output. This objective implies (under appropriate regularity conditions) a system of $n$ equations, each describing the demand for an input in terms of input prices and output. Theil (1977) formulated a differential version of this input demand system which is similar but not identical to the demand system (3.13) for the consumer. The difference results from the fact that the firm's problem is not an allocation problem [see the discussion preceding (3.13)]. The firm does not take the total amount of input expenditure as given; it wants to minimize this amount.

(2) The gap between the firm and the consumer can be eliminated by summing the input demand equations over all inputs. This yields a proportionality between the Divisia input volume index and the change in output which describes the aggregate input change needed to produce the given output change. Then, by substituting this proportionality into the $i$th input demand equation, we obtain

$$f_i d(\log q_i) = \theta_i d(\log Q) - \psi \sum_{j=1}^{n} \theta_{ij} d\left(\log \frac{p_j}{P'}\right) \tag{5.1}$$

This is the input allocation decision for input $i$, which should be compared with (3.13). On the left, $f_i = p_i q_i/C$ is the factor share of input $i$ ($C$ = total cost). On the right, $d(\log Q)$ is the Divisia input volume index [equal to $\Sigma_i f_i d(\log q_i)$] and $\theta_i$ is the share of input $i$ in marginal cost.[7] The marginal shares $\theta_1, ..., \theta_n$ are the weights of the logarithmic input price changes in the Frisch price index which occurs as a deflator in the last term [compare (3.10)].

---

[7] That is, $\theta_i$ equals the ratio of $\partial(p_i q_i)/\partial z$ to $\partial C/\partial z$, where $z$ = output. If the firm maximizes profit under competitive conditions on the supply side, $\theta_i$ equals the additional expenditure on input $i$ caused by an extra dollar of output revenue, which is more directly comparable to (3.2). The $\Psi$ in (5.1) is a curvature measure of the logarithmic cost function; it is positive, implying $-\Psi < 0$ in (5.1), to be compared with $\phi < 0$ in (3.13).

**Table 1**. Multiple Roots

| Bordered composition matrix | | | | $\lambda_i$ | $\theta_{Ti}$ |
|---|---|---|---|---|---|
| *First perturbation* | | | | | |
| 0.343530 | 0.013662 | -0.085974 | 0.271218 | 1.199967 | 0.325452 |
| -0.027698 | 0.261164 | -0.004612 | 0.228854 | 1.200040 | 0.274634 |
| 0.284168 | 0.025164 | 0.190596 | 0.499928 | 0.799942 | 0.399913 |
| 0.600000 | 0.299990 | 0.100010 | 1 | | |
| 0.343465 | 0.013664 | -0.085975 | 0.271153 | 1.200000 | 0.325384 |
| -0.027705 | 0.261164 | -0.004612 | 0.228847 | 1.200000 | 0.274616 |
| 0.284240 | 0.025173 | 0.190587 | 0.500000 | 0.800000 | 0.400000 |
| 0.600000 | 0.300000 | 0.100000 | 1 | | |
| 0.343401 | 0.013665 | -0.085976 | 0.271089 | 1.200033 | 0.325316 |
| -0.027713 | 0.261163 | -0.004611 | 0.228839 | 1.999960 | 0.274598 |
| 0.284312 | 0.025182 | 0.190578 | 0.500072 | 0.800058 | 0.400087 |
| 0.600000 | 0.300010 | 0.099990 | 1 | | |
| *Second perturbation* | | | | | |
| 0.030777 | 0.303726 | -0.021018 | 0.313485 | 1.199959 | 0.376169 |
| 0.285064 | -0.028885 | -0.069567 | 0.186612 | 1.199997 | 0.223934 |
| 0.284139 | 0.025169 | 0.190595 | 0.499903 | 0.799949 | 0.399897 |
| 0.599980 | 0.300010 | 0.100010 | 1 | | |
| 0.030796 | 0.303721 | -0.021027 | 0.313490 | 1.200000 | 0.376188 |
| 0.284964 | -0.028894 | -0.069560 | 0.181510 | 1.200000 | 0.223811 |
| 0.284240 | 0.025173 | 0.190587 | 0.500000 | 0.800000 | 0.400000 |
| 0.600000 | 0.300000 | 0.100000 | 1 | | |
| 0.030815 | 0.303716 | -0.021035 | 0.313496 | 1.200041 | 0.376208 |
| 0.284863 | -0.028903 | -0.069553 | 0.186407 | 1.200003 | 0.223689 |
| 0.284342 | 0.025177 | 0.190579 | 0.500097 | 0.800051 | 0.400103 |
| 0.600020 | 0.299990 | 0.099990 | 1 | | |

(3) The $\theta_{ij}$s in (5.1) are normalized price coefficients which form a symmetric positive definite matrix. We extend the definitions given at the end of section 3 by calling inputs $i$ and $j$ specific substitutes (complements) when $\theta_{ij}$ is negative (positive). For (2.5), $[\theta_{ij}]$ is a positive scalar multiple of

$$\begin{bmatrix} f_K & \xi(f_K f_L)^{1/2} \\ \xi(f_K f_L)^{1/2} & f_L \end{bmatrix} \begin{matrix} \text{(capital)} \\ \text{(labour)} \end{matrix} \tag{5.2}$$

which shows that capital and labour are specific substitutes (complements) when the elasticity of output with respect to either input is a decreasing (increasing) function of the other input [see (2.6) and (2.7)].

(4) The input independence transformation changes observed inputs into transformed inputs as stated in the paragraph preceding (2.5). This transformation diagonalizes $[\theta_{ij}]$ relative to the diagonal factor share matrix, which means that total cost and its Divisia indexes are invariant. The composition matrix (2.8) is obtained from (4.3) and (4.4) after appropriate reinterpretations. By dividing (5.1) by $f_i$ we find that $\theta_i/f_i$ is the $i$th Divisia elasticity, i.e. the elasticity of $q_i$ with respect to the Divisia input volume index, which is the input version of an income elasticity. The diagonal of $\Lambda$ in (4.3) contains here the Divisia elasticities of the transformed inputs.

(5) Laitinen and Theil (1978) extended the above results for a firm which makes $m$ products. They also formulated profit maximizing supply equations in differential form under the condition that the firm takes the product prices as given. These equations describe the change in supply in terms of the changes in the $m$ product prices, each deflated by a Frisch input price index. Output independence is the case in which the firm's cost function is additive in the $m$ outputs; in that case the change in the supply of each product does not involve the price of any other product.[8] The output independence transformation changes observed products into transformed products so that the firm's cost function is additive in the latter products. The mathematics of this transformation are identical to those of its two predecessors.

## 6. Constrained Principal Components

A comparison of principal components with the independence transformation is appropriate for several reasons, one of which is that both techniques diagonalize a square matrix. The principal component transformation changes a set of $n$ correlated variables into a set of $n$ uncorrelated variables. This transformation is not unique because it depends

[8] Hall (1973) has shown that under output independence the multi-product firm can be split up into $m$ single-product firms, each making one of the products of the multi-product firm, in such a way that when the single-product firms independently maximize profits, they supply the same rate of output and use the same total quantity of each input as the multi-product firm.

on the units of measurement of the former variables.[9] To make it unique statisticians frequently standardize these variables so that they all have unit variance. Let $V$ be the covariance matrix prior to the standardization and $\hat{V}$ the diagonal matrix whose diagonal is identical to that of $V$ so that $\hat{V}^{-1/2}V\hat{V}^{-1/2}$ is the covariance matrix after the standardization. The principal component technique involves the derivation of latent roots ($\lambda_i$) from the determinantal equation

$$|\hat{V}^{-1/2}V\hat{V}^{-1/2} - \lambda_i I| = 0 \tag{6.1}$$

for $i = 1, ..., n$. Having obtained these $\lambda_i$s, we can derive the principal components and various weight vectors directly, but these are irrelevant for our present purposes.

In (6.1) we pre- and post-multiply $V$ by $\hat{V}^{-1/2}$, $\hat{V}$ being the diagonal matrix whose diagonal is identical to that of $V$. In (4.2) we pre- and post-multiply $\Theta$ by $D^{-1}$ and $D$ is also a diagonal matrix, but its diagonal has nothing to do with the diagonal of $\Theta$. The diagonal elements of $V$ and $\hat{V}$ are variances. The diagonal of $D$ consists of square roots of budget shares, whereas the diagonal elements of $\Theta$ are the $\theta_{ii}$s which describe the change in the demand for a good caused by a change in its own relative price [see (3.13)]. Both $D$ and $\Theta$ occur in (4.2) because $\Theta$ is diagonalized relative to $W$ in (4.1). The presence of $W$ results from the budget constraint that is imposed on the transformed goods. This constraint takes the form of an invariance constraint on $M$ and its Divisia indexes via the logarithmic change in $M$ [see (3.4)]. Thus, the preference independence transformation may be viewed as an income-constrained principal component transformation: the input independence transformation of the firm is a cost-constrained and the output independence transformation is a revenue-constrained principal component transformation. Such constraints are more natural than the rather arbitrary standardization convention.

A second reason why a comparison of principal components and the independence transformation is appropriate is that it is not difficult to introduce randomness into demand and supply systems. Imagine that we add a random disturbance $\varepsilon_i$ to the right-hand sides of (3.13) and (5.1). Does the independence transformation yield uncorrelated disturbances? The answer is yes under the theory of rational random behaviour, provided that account is taken of the fact that both demand equations are obtained by optimization subject to a constraint. The theory of rational random behaviour is beyond the scope of this article (see Theil, 1980, chapters 7 and 8).

Although a comparison with principal components is illuminating, we should not conclude that the usual interpretations of such components are applicable to the independence transformation. It is common among statisticians to arrange the $\lambda_i$s of (6.1) in descending order and to use the first $r < n$ principal components as an approximate description of the behaviour of the variables. We could follow this practice by considering

---

[9] This problem does not arise when all variables are expressed in the same unit. (This applies to Stone's (1947) application in which all variables are in dollars per year.) However, even in that case we obtain different results when we measure the variables from their natural zeros or from their means.

only the transformed goods with the largest income or Divisia elasticities, but we do not recommend this. If we applied this idea to the meats of section 2 with $r = 2$, we would miss $T_1$, which accounts for over 70 per cent of the expenditure on the three-meat group [see (2.3)]. If we followed the same procedure for (2.4), we would miss even more. The objective of the independence transformation is not a reduction of the number of dimensions. Its objective is to present the consumer's preferences and the firm's technology in the simplest form. The preference independence transformation makes utility additive around the point of maximum utility. The output independence transformation makes the cost function additive in the outputs around the point of maximum profit. The input independence transformation makes the logarithm of output additive in the inputs around the point of minimum input expenditure.

## 7. Groups of Goods and Strong Separability

### 7.1 THE INDEPENDENCE TRANSFORMATION FOR STRONGLY SEPARABLE GROUPS

Let there be $G$ groups of goods, $S_1, \ldots, S_G$, so that each good falls under exactly one group. Let the consumer's utility function be the sum of $G$ functions, one for each group,

$$u(q) = u_1(q_A) + u_2(q_B) + \ldots \tag{7.1}$$

where $q_A, q_B, \ldots$ are subvectors of $q$, $q_A$ containing the $q_i$s of $S_1$, $q_B$ those of $S_2$, and so on. The utility structure of (7.1) is known as strong separability or as block-independence; the marginal utility of each good is then independent of all goods that belong to different groups. When the goods are appropriately numbered, the Hessian matrix $U$ and its inverse are block-diagonal, and so is $[\theta_{ij}]$ in view of (3.15). Therefore, if the $i$th good belongs to $S_g$, (3.13) becomes

$$w_i d(\log q_i) = \theta_i d(\log Q) + \phi \sum_{j \in S_g} \theta_{ij} d\left(\log \frac{p_j}{P'}\right) \tag{7.2}$$

where the summation in the substitution term is confined to $j \in S_g$. We conclude that under (7.1) no good is a specific substitute or complement of any good that belongs to a different group. Preference independence is a special case of (7.1) with all groups consisting of one good.

If (7.1) holds, can we apply the preference independence transformation to each group of goods separately? The answer is yes, which we shall illustrate for the case of two groups. We write (4.3) in partitioned form as

$$\begin{bmatrix} X'_A & 0 \\ 0 & X'_B \end{bmatrix} \begin{bmatrix} \Theta_A & 0 \\ 0 & \Theta_B \end{bmatrix} \begin{bmatrix} X_A & 0 \\ 0 & X_B \end{bmatrix} = \begin{bmatrix} \Lambda_A & 0 \\ 0 & \Lambda_B \end{bmatrix} \tag{7.3}$$

$$\begin{bmatrix} X'_A & 0 \\ 0 & X'_B \end{bmatrix} \begin{bmatrix} W_A & 0 \\ 0 & W_B \end{bmatrix} \begin{bmatrix} X_A & 0 \\ 0 & X_B \end{bmatrix} = \begin{bmatrix} I & 0 \\ 0 & I \end{bmatrix} \tag{7.4}$$

where $\Theta_A$ and $\Theta_B$ are the principal submatrices of $\Theta$ which correspond to the two groups, $\Lambda_A$ and $\Lambda_B$ are the principal matrices of $\Lambda$ (both $\Lambda_A$ and $\Lambda_B$ are diagonal), and $W_A$ and $W_B$ are principal submatrices (both diagonal) of $W$. Clearly, (7.3) and (7.4) are satisfied by $X'_A\Theta_A X_A = \Lambda_A$, $X'_A W_A X_A = I$, and by a similar equation pair with subscript $B$. A comparison with (4.3) shows that the independence transformation can be applied to each group separately.

## 7.2 THE DEMAND FOR GROUPS AND CONDITIONAL DEMAND

For the developments which will follow in section 8 it is useful to explore the implications of (7.1) further. We write $W_g$ for the combined budget share of the goods of group $S_g$ and $d(\log Q_g)$ for the Divisia volume index of this group:

$$W_g = \sum_{i \in S_g} w_i, \quad d(\log Q_g) = \sum_{i \in S_g} \frac{w_i}{W_g} d(\log q_i) \tag{7.5}$$

The ratio $w_i/W_g$ is the expenditure of the $i$th good measured as a fraction of the total expenditure on the group to which this good belongs. We shall refer to this ratio as the $i$th conditional budget share.

We write $\Theta_g$ for the combined marginal share of the goods of $S_g$ and $d(\log P'_g)$ for the Frisch price index of this group,

$$\Theta_g = \sum_{i \in S_g} \theta_i, \quad d(\log P'_g) = \sum_{i \in S_g} \frac{\theta_i}{\Theta_g} d(\log p_i) \tag{7.6}$$

where $\theta_i/\Theta_g$ is the conditional marginal share of good $i$. Note that this share exists because $\Theta_g$ is positive under (7.1). To prove this we use the block-diagonal structure of $[\theta_{ij}]$ to write (3.16) as

$$\sum_{j \in S_g} \theta_{ij} = \theta_i \quad \text{if} \quad i \in S_g \tag{7.7}$$

By summing (7.7) over $i \in S_g$ we obtain $\Theta_g$ on the right and the double sum of $\theta_{ij}$ over $i, j \in S_g$ on the left. This double sum is positive because of the positive definiteness of $[\theta_{ij}]$.[10]

Summation of (7.2) over $i \in S_g$ yields, after minor rearrangements,

$$W_g d(\log Q_g) = \Theta_g d(\log Q) + \phi\, \Theta_g d\left(\log \frac{P_g'}{P'}\right) \tag{7.8}$$

which is a composite demand equation for $S_g$ as a group. Next we multiply (7.8) by $\theta_i/\Theta_g$ and subtract the result from (7.2), so that $d(\log Q)$ disappears. After rearrangements we obtain

$$w_i d(\log q_i) = \frac{\theta_i}{\Theta_g} W_g d(\log Q_g) + \phi \sum_{j \in S_g} \theta_{ij} d\left(\log \frac{p_j}{P_g'}\right) \tag{7.9}$$

which is a conditional demand equation for the $i$th good within its group. By dividing (7.9) by $W_g$ we find

$$\frac{w_i}{W_g} d(\log q_i) = \frac{\theta_i}{\Theta_g} d(\log Q_g) + \frac{\phi}{W_g} \sum_{j \in S_g} \theta_{ij} d\left(\log \frac{p_j}{P_g'}\right) \tag{7.10}$$

which is the within-group version of (7.2).

The expression on the left in (7.10) is the quantity component of $d(w_i/W_g)$, i.e. of the change in the conditional budget share of the $i$th good,[11] and it is also the contribution of this good to the Divisia volume index of the group [see (7.5)]. The first term on the right in (7.10) is the volume component and the second is the substitution component. The normalized price coefficients in the latter component are identical to

[10] Also note that when the group indexes in (7.5) and (7.6) are weighted with the group budget and marginal shares $W_g$ and $\Theta_g$, respectively, we obtain the indexes (3.6) and (3.10) which refer to the budget as a whole.

[11] The other components are $(w_i/W_g)d(\log p_i)$ and $-(w_i/W_g)d(\log W_g M)$. The first of these is the price component of the change in the conditional budget share and the second is the component which is attributable to the change in the amount spent on the group. This result should be viewed as a within-group version of (3.12).

those of (7.2), but the price deflator in (7.10) is the Frisch price index of the group. Similarly, the volume component in (7.10) takes the form of the Divisia volume index of the group multiplied by the *i*th conditional marginal share, whereas the corresponding term in (7.2) is the Divisia volume index of the consumer's total expenditure multiplied by the (unconditional) marginal share $\theta_i$. A further discussion of (7.8) to (7.10) is postponed until section 8, where we will discuss more general results under a condition weaker than (7.1).

## 7.3 MEATS AND LEISURE REVISITED

The implementation of (7.10) does not require any data on goods outside $S_g$.[12] Since the preference independence transformation can be directly applied to such a group, the procedure is straightforward. For example, take the meats of section 2 and recall from the discussion following (7.7) that the $\theta_{ij}$s of $S_g$ have a sum equal to $\Theta_g$. Hence the price coefficients of the goods of $S_g$ normalized within the group are of the form $\theta_{ij}/\Theta_g$. The maximum-likelihood estimate of the matrix of these coefficients is

$$\begin{bmatrix} 0.863 & -0.131 & -0.018 \\ -0.131 & 0.396 & -0.046 \\ -0.018 & -0.046 & 0.131 \end{bmatrix} \begin{matrix} \text{(beef)} \\ \text{(pork)} \\ \text{(chicken)} \end{matrix} \tag{7.11}$$

The negative off-diagonal elements in (7.11) indicate that the three meats are specific substitutes of each other. The simultaneous diagonalization (4.3) can then be applied with $\Theta$ specified as the matrix (7.11), but note that $W$ has now the conditional budget shares on the diagonal. Also, given that the matrix (7.11) is normalized within the group, its row and column sums are conditional marginal shares. Therefore, the income elasticity shown in (3.11) is now replaced by

$$\frac{\theta_i/\Theta_g}{w_i/W_g} = \frac{\theta_i/w_i}{\Theta_g/W_g} \tag{7.12}$$

which is the conditional income elasticity of good *i* within its group. By dividing (7.8) by $W_g$ we find that $\Theta_g/W_g$ is the income elasticity of the demand for the group $S_g$. Hence (7.12) implies that the conditional income elasticity of a good is equal to its unconditional income elasticity $\theta_i/w_i$ divided by the group income elasticity.

[12] The implementation does require a parametrization; see appendix C for this matter.

The application of (4.3) to (7.11) also involves the interpretation of the diagonal elements of $\Lambda$ as the conditional income elasticities of the transformed goods. In the case of meats these are the income elasticities of the three transformed meats divided by the income elasticity of the demand for the three-meat group. The $\Lambda_i$s associated with the composition matrix (2.3) are $\Lambda_1 = 0.74$, $\Lambda_2 = 1.90$, and $\Lambda_3 = 1.17$. This confirms that $T_1$ (affordable meat) has the smallest and $T_2$ (the beef-pork contrast) the largest income elasticity.

Using conditional demand equations is one procedure for the implementation of the independence transformation, but it is not the only one. Barnett (1974) considered the system (3.13) for all $n$ goods including leisure and specified $n = 5$: services, perishables, semi-durables, durables, and leisure. He then simplified his system as far as his data permitted and concluded that the additive specification (7.1) is acceptable for three groups. Two groups consist of one good each (services and perishables) and the third group consists of three goods: semi-durables, durables, and leisure. Flinn's (1978) maximum-likelihood estimate of the matrix of price coefficients of the last group (normalized within the group) is

$$\begin{bmatrix} 0.501 & 0.042 & -0.342 \\ 0.042 & 0.560 & -0.419 \\ -0.342 & -0.419 & 1.378 \end{bmatrix} \quad \begin{matrix} \text{(semi-durables)} \\ \text{(durables)} \\ \text{(leisure)} \end{matrix} \tag{7.13}$$

The off-diagonal elements indicate that semi-durables and durables are both specific substitutes of leisure and that the two former goods are specific complements of each other. Application of (4.3) to (7.13) is straightforward, but the interpretation of the $\lambda_i$s as conditional income elasticities must be amended; they are conditional full income elasticities because of the inclusion of leisure. Below the composition matrix (2.4) we mentioned that the full income elasticities of $T_2$ and $T_3$ are substantially larger than that of $T_1$. This is confirmed by the $\lambda_i$s associated with (2.4): $\lambda_1 = 0.97$, $\lambda_2 = 5.8$, $\lambda_3 = 4.2$. The unconditional full income elasticities of the three transformed goods are much smaller because the full income elasticity of the group is well below 1.

## 8. Weak Separability

### 8.1 DIFFERENTIAL DEMAND EQUATIONS UNDER WEAK SEPARABILITY

An assumption which is weaker than (7.1) is that the utility function is some function $f(\ )$, rather than the sum, of $G$ group utility functions:

$$u(q) = f(u_1(q_A), u_2(q_B),...) \tag{8.1}$$

To clarify this utility structure we consider $\partial u/\partial(p_i q_i)$, the marginal utility of a dollar spent on the $i$th good, and $\partial^2 u/\partial(p_i q_i)\partial(p_j q_j)$, the change in this marginal utility caused by an additional dollar spent on the $j$th good. This second derivative vanishes under (7.1) when $i$ and $j$ belong to different groups, but it does not vanish under (8.1). However, it can be shown that at the point of maximum utility this second derivative takes the same value for all $i$ and $j$ in two different groups and that this value depends only on these groups. Thus, if food and clothing are two such groups, an extra dollar spent on either bread or butter has the same effect on the marginal utility of a dollar spent on any good of the clothing group. This means that the utility interaction of goods belonging to different groups is a matter of the groups rather than the individual goods. Accordingly, we can refer to the utility structure (8.1) as 'blockwise dependence,' although 'weak separability' is used more often.[13]

It should be clear that the Hessian $U$ is no longer block-diagonal. Hence $[\theta_{ij}]$ is not block-diagonal either, which means that the $i$th demand equation differs from (7.2) in that it contains changes in relative prices of goods that do not belong to $S_g$. However, it contains such prices only in the form of Frisch price indexes of groups, thus illustrating blockwise dependence at the level of differential demand equations.

To clarify this further we must note that under (8.1) Frisch price indexes cannot be defined as shown in (7.6). The reason is that if (7.1) is replaced by (8.1), the ratio $\theta_i/\Theta_g$ need not exist because $\Theta_g$ may vanish. But if $\Theta_g$ vanishes, so does $\theta_i$ for each $i \in S_g$ and the conditional marginal share $\theta_i^g$ exists for each $i \in S_g$. Accordingly, we define the Frisch price index of $S_g$ as

$$d(\log P_g') = \sum_{i \in S_g} \theta_i^g d(\log p_i) \tag{8.2}$$

The $i$th demand equation ($i \in S_g$) under (8.1) can now be written in the form (7.2) except that

$$\phi\, \theta_i^g \sum_{h \neq g} \Theta_{gh}\, d\left(\log \frac{P_h'}{P'}\right) \tag{8.3}$$

must be added on the right, where

[13] The analogous constraint on the input structure of a firm was considered by MaCurdy (1975).

$$\Theta_{gh} = \sum_{i\in S_g} \sum_{j\in S_h} \theta_{ij} \quad g, h = 1, ..., G \tag{8.4}$$

We conclude that under (8.1) the substitution term is the sum of two terms, one containing the prices of the individual goods of the same group and the other the Frisch price indexes of all other groups.

Additional insight is obtained when we sum the demand equation over $i \in S_g$, which yields a composite demand equation for the group:

$$W_g d(\log Q_g) = \Theta_g d(\log Q) + \phi \sum_{h=1}^{G} \Theta_{gh} d\left(\log \frac{P_h'}{P'}\right) \tag{8.5}$$

This is a generalization of (7.8) because we have

$$\sum_{h=1}^{G} \Theta_{gh} = \Theta_g \tag{8.6}$$

which becomes $\Theta_{gg} = \Theta_g$ when the $G$ x $G$ matrix $[\Theta_{gh}]$ is diagonal, as is the case under (7.1). Note that (7.8), (8.5), and (8.6) are simply 'uppercase versions' of (3.18), (3.13), and (3.16) respectively. Thus, under (8.1) we obtain composite demand equations for groups of goods that take the general form (3.13) of differential demand equations, while under (7.1) such composite equations take the form (3.18) of preference independence.[14]

We obtained the conditional demand equation (7.9) by multiplying the equation for the group by $\theta_i/\Theta_g$ and subtracting the result from the $i$th unconditional equation. When we proceed similarly here, replacing $\theta_i/\Theta_g$ by $\theta_i^g$, we find

$$w_i d(\log q_i) = \theta_i^g W_g d(\log Q_g) + \phi \sum_{j\in S_g} \theta_{ij} d\left(\log \frac{p_j}{P_g'}\right) \tag{8.7}$$

and, after dividing both sides by $W_g$,

[14] Additional 'uppercase extensions' can be formulated. We may define $S_g$ and $S_h$ as specific substitutes (complements) when $\Theta_{gh}$ in (8.5) is negative (positive). Under (7.1) no group is a specific substitute or complement of any other group. Also, no group can be inferior under (7.1) because $\Theta_g > 0$, but inferior groups can exist under (8.1).

$$\frac{w_i}{W_g}\, d(\log q_i) = \theta_i^g d(\log Q_g) + \frac{\phi}{W_g} \sum_{j \in S_g} \theta_{ij} d\left(\log \frac{p_j}{P_g'}\right) \tag{8.8}$$

These two equations are identical to (7.9) and (7.10) except for the different notations of the conditional marginal shares.

The composite demand equations for groups and the conditional demand equations for goods within their groups enable the consumer to apply a two-stage budgeting procedure. First, he uses (8.5) for the change in the allocation of total expenditure to the $G$ groups, which requires knowledge of the volume index $d(\log Q)$ and the price indexes of the groups.[15] Second, he uses (8.7) or (8.8) for the change in the allocation of the amount available for each group to the goods of this group. This requires knowledge of the volume index $d(\log Q_g)$ which is available from the first step, and of the price changes of the individual goods.[16] It is easy to visualize a more extensive hierarchy, groups being divided into sub-groups and these into goods, but we shall not pursue this matter here.

## 8.2 THE INDEPENDENCE TRANSFORMATION UNDER WEAK SEPARABILITY

We know from section 7 that under condition (7.1) the preference independence transformation can be applied to each group separately. The question arises whether a similar result holds for the weaker condition (8.1). It is obviously not sufficient to apply the transformation to the $\theta_{ij}$s of each group, because such a procedure would not eliminate the $p_j$s that are represented by the Frisch price indexes of groups in (8.3). But these indexes are multiplied by $\Theta_{gh}$s, the normalized price coefficients of the composite demand equations for groups [see (8.5)], which suggests that the independence transformation under (8.1) might be implemented as some combination of a transformation for groups (based on the $\Theta_{gh}$s) and $G$ transformations for goods within their groups, one for each group. This problem has been the subject of numerous blackboard discussions in Chicago during many years.

Before proceeding we should mention that there is no problem at all in applying the independence transformation; the question to be considered is whether we can *simplify* this transformation by means of transformations between and within groups. It follows

[15] The required price indexes of the groups include both Divisia and Frisch price indexes. The reason is that the logarithmic change in the amount spent on $S_g$ equals $d(\log P_g) + d(\log Q_g)$, where $d(\log P_g)$ (no prime!) is the Divisia price index of $S_g$. This index is obtained by substituting $p_i$ for $q_i$ in (7.5).

[16] When random disturbances are added to the demand equations, the separation of the allocation into two steps requires the disturbances of the composite demand equations for groups of goods to be uncorrelated with those of the conditional equations. It can be shown that this is indeed the case under rational random behaviour; this theory implies that disturbances of conditional demand equations of different groups are also uncorrelated.

from (8.2) that the normalized price coefficient for the $j$th relative price ($j \in S_h$, $h \neq g$) in (8.3) is of the form $\Theta_{gh}\theta_i^g\theta_j^h$. This is an element of the matrix $\Theta_{gh}\tilde{\theta}_g\tilde{\theta}_h'$, where $\tilde{\theta}_g$ is the vector of conditional marginal shares of the goods of $S_g$. Thus, the $n \times n$ normalized price coefficient matrix for $i \in S_g$ and $g = 1, ..., G$ can be written as

$$\Theta = \begin{bmatrix} A_1 & \Theta_{12}\tilde{\theta}_1\tilde{\theta}_2' & \cdots & \Theta_{1G}\tilde{\theta}_1\tilde{\theta}_G' \\ \Theta_{21}\tilde{\theta}_2\tilde{\theta}_1' & A_2 & \cdots & \Theta_{2G}\tilde{\theta}_2\tilde{\theta}_G' \\ \cdot & \cdot & & \cdot \\ \cdot & \cdot & & \cdot \\ \cdot & \cdot & & \cdot \\ \Theta_{G1}\tilde{\theta}_G\tilde{\theta}_1' & \Theta_{G2}\tilde{\theta}_G\tilde{\theta}_2' & \cdots & A_G \end{bmatrix} \tag{8.9}$$

where $A_1$, ..., $A_G$ are the principal submatrices of $\Theta$ which contain the $\theta_{ij}$s with $i, j \in S_g$ for $g = 1, ..., G$. Note that the submatrices in (8.9) outside the diagonal blocks all have unit rank. This has led to the conjecture that the composition matrix under (8.1) might also have off-diagonal submatrices of unit rank, which would mean that the transformation treats observed goods of different groups in a 'blockwise' manner.

Suppose that we apply the independence transformation to (8.7) or (8.8) for each $S_g$. This is always possible and it amounts to a transformation of the matrix (8.9) so that $A_1$, ..., $A_g$ are changed into diagonal matrices. Since the sum of the elements of $A_g$ equals $\Theta_{gg}$ [see (8.4)] and since the row and column sums of $A_g$ are proportional to the marginal shares of the goods of $S_g$, $A_g$ thus becomes $\Theta_{gg}(\tilde{\theta}_g)_\Delta$, where $(\tilde{\theta}_g)_\Delta$ stands for the conditional marginal share vector $\tilde{\theta}_g$ written in the form of a diagonal matrix.[17] Hence (8.9) now takes the following form:

[17] Strictly speaking, we should use a notation indicating that these conditional marginal shares refer to goods obtained from the independence transformation applied to the group, but we prefer not to do so to simplify the notation. It is, of course, possible that the $G$ group utility functions (8.1) are additive in their arguments, in which case (8.9) takes the form (8.10) without any intermediate transformation. This special case was considered particularly by Pearce (1961; 1964). In the discussion later in this section we shall proceed as if (8.10) refers to observed goods.

$$\Theta = \begin{bmatrix} \Theta_{11}(\tilde{\theta}_1)_\Delta & \Theta_{12}\tilde{\theta}_1\tilde{\theta}_2' & \cdots & \Theta_{1G}\tilde{\theta}_1\tilde{\theta}_G' \\ \Theta_{21}\tilde{\theta}_2\theta_1' & \Theta_{22}(\tilde{\theta}_2)_\Delta & \cdots & \Theta_{2G}\tilde{\theta}_2\tilde{\theta}_G' \\ \cdot & \cdot & & \cdot \\ \cdot & \cdot & & \cdot \\ \cdot & \cdot & & \cdot \\ \Theta_{G1}\tilde{\theta}_G\theta_1' & \Theta_{G2}\tilde{\theta}_G\tilde{\theta}_2' & \cdots & \Theta_{GG}(\tilde{\theta}_G)_\Delta \end{bmatrix} \tag{8.10}$$

Is it possible to apply a second transformation, based on the diagonalization of the $G$ x $G$ price coefficient matrix $[\Theta_{gh}]$ of the groups, so that (8.10) is changed into a diagonal matrix?

To answer this question we should recognize that it involves observed and transformed groups because the preference independence transformation applied to $[\Theta_{gh}]$ changes observed groups into transformed groups. In the case of (7.3) and (7.4) this is trivial; the transformation for groups is the identity transformation and each transformed good is associated with one observed group. But it is not trivial for (8.9) and (8.10). When we apply the independence transformation to either matrix, the computer provides us with transformed goods arranged in the order of increasing or decreasing income elasticities. How can we decide whether a particular transformed good is associated with a particular observed group? This is possible when the transformed goods of a group have certain characteristics in common. One conjecture, based on the proposition that transformed goods are identified by their income elasticities, is that when the transformation is applied to (8.10), the conditional income elasticities of the transformed goods of each group are invariant; that is, if $i$ and $j$ belong to the same group, $\lambda_i/\lambda_j$ equals the ratio of some $\theta_i/w_i$ to some $\theta_j/w_j$. This would enable us to relate each transformed good to one of the goods represented by a row and a column of the matrix (8.10).

## 8.3 NUMERICAL EXPLORATIONS

We are not ashamed to admit that the uncertainty as to the existence of transformed groups that can be related to the observed groups has induced us to proceed numerically. We start with a case of two groups consisting of two goods each. The conditional budget shares of the first group are 0.4 and 0.6 and the conditional marginal shares are 0.34 and 0.66 so that the conditional income elasticities are 0.85 and 1.1. The conditional budget shares of the second group are 0.9 and 1.9. The budget and marginal shares of the first group are $W_1 = 0.8$ and $\Theta_1 = 0.6$ and those of the second $W_2 = 0.2$ and $\Theta_2 = 0.4$. Hence the income elasticities of the groups are $\Theta_1/W_1 = 0.75$ and $\Theta_2/W_2 = 2$, while those of the four goods are 0.6375, 0.825, 1.8, and 3.8. These elasticities are in ascending order and also in the order in which we introduced the goods, which is convenient. The normalized price coefficient matrix is as shown in (8.10) for $G = 2$ with the $\Theta_{gh}$s specified as

$$[\Theta_{gh}] = \begin{bmatrix} 0.6 + \varepsilon & -\varepsilon \\ -\varepsilon & 0.4 + \varepsilon \end{bmatrix} \tag{8.11}$$

When ε vanishes, $[\Theta_{gh}]$ is diagonal and so is Θ of (8.10). When we put ε equal to a value close to zero, we should be able to relate the transformed goods to the observed goods if such a relation exists. For $\varepsilon = 10^{-5}$ we obtain the following composition matrix:

$$T = 10^{-8} \begin{bmatrix} 32000257 & 0 & 237 & 20 \\ 0 & 48000590 & 548 & 42 \\ -237 & -548 & 17999215 & 0 \\ -20 & -42 & 0 & 1999937 \end{bmatrix} \tag{8.12}$$

This matrix is skew-symmetric as far as the off-diagonal elements are concerned and its 2 x 2 principal submatrices upper left and lower right are both diagonal. Clearly, in the case of (8.12) the transformed good of row *i* corresponds to the observed good of column *i*.

To verify that we are not caught by the special numerical structure of one example we shall consider a second with three groups, the first consisting of two goods, the second of three, and the third of four.[18] The price coefficient matrix of the groups is now of order 3 x 3 and is specified as

$$[\Theta_{gh}] = \begin{bmatrix} 0.24 - \varepsilon & 3\varepsilon & -2\varepsilon \\ 3\varepsilon & 0.36 - 2\varepsilon & -\varepsilon \\ -2\varepsilon & -\varepsilon & 0.40 + 3\varepsilon \end{bmatrix} \tag{8.13}$$

The bordered composition matrix is shown in the upper half of table 2 for $\varepsilon = 10^{-5}$ and in the lower half for $\varepsilon = -10^{-5}$. Both matrices reveal the same regularity as (8.12) does. The change in the sign of ε causes the off-diagonal elements to change in sign also. The diagonal elements are all virtually identical to the geometric mean of the corresponding

[18] The budget shares of the groups are specified as 0.6, 0.3, and 0.1; the marginal shares implied by (8.13) are 0.24, 0.36, and 0.40 for any value of ε, so that the income elasticities are 0.4, 1.2, and 4. The conditional budget shares are specified as 0.9 and 0.1 for the first group; 0.6, 0.3, and 0.1 for the second; and 0.20, 0.35, 0.30, and 0.15 for the third. The conditional marginal shares are 0.81 and 0.19 for the first group; 0.54, 0.30, and 0.16 for the second; and 0.12, 0.28, 0.33, and 0.27 for the third. The unconditional income elasticities are 0.36, 0.76, 1.08, 1.20, 1.92, 2.4, 3.2, 4.4, and 7.2. As in the earlier example, these elasticities are in ascending order and also in the order in which the goods are introduced.

row and column sums, which is the maximum value that any element of a composition matrix can take.[19]

The regularities described above indicate that groups continue to exist after the independence transformation as long as the utility structure (8.1) is sufficiently close to the additive specification (7.1). Also, the conditional income elasticities appear to be invariant under that condition. For example, consider (8.13) for $\varepsilon = 0$ so that the observed and transformed goods are identical. The income elasticities of the two goods of the first group are then 0.36 and 0.76. Next take $\varepsilon = 10^{-5}$, which yields the composition matrix in the upper half of table 2. The income elasticities of the transformed goods corresponding to the first two rows of this matrix are 0.35998499 and 0.75996833, both of which are 0.00417 percent below the corresponding value for $\varepsilon = 0$. For the three goods of the second group the percentage reductions are all equal to 0.00556. For the four goods of the third group the income elasticities at $\varepsilon = 10^{-5}$ exceed those at $\varepsilon = 0$ and the percentage excess is 0.00750 for each of the four. The uniform changes of the unconditional income elasticities of the goods of each group imply that the conditional elasticities remain unchanged.[20]

The changes in the unconditional elasticities appear to be identical to those of the groups. For example, the income elasticities of the three groups are 0.4, 1.2, and 4 in the three-group case. When we select $\varepsilon = 10^{-5}$ and apply the independence transformation to the groups (rather than the individual goods), we obtain the following income elasticities of the transformed groups: 0.39998333, 1.19993334, and 4.00030000. These figures imply percentage deviations from the values 0.4, 1.2, and 4 equal to -0.00417, -0.00556, and 0.00750, respectively. The latter figures are identical to the percentage deviations discussed in the previous paragraph, which suggests that the income elasticities of the transformation for the groups can be used to obtain the (unconditional) income elasticities of the individual transformed goods.

Also, the composition matrix of the independence transformation for groups is similar to that of the individual goods in that it is skew-symmetric with respect to the off-diagonal elements. For example, when we select $\varepsilon = 10^{-5}$ in (8.13), we obtain the following bordered composition matrix (multiplied by $10^8$) of the three groups:

[19] When we divide each element of the composition matrix by the geometric mean of the corresponding row and column sums, an orthogonal matrix emerges. The elements of such a matrix are all between -1 and 1. See Theil (1975-76, section 12.3).

[20] The conditional budget and marginal shares are not invariant. One might surmise that these shares are invariant, given that the conditional demand equations take the same form under weak and strong separability, but this conjecture is not correct. For example, when we change $\varepsilon$ from zero to $10^{-5}$ in (8.13), the unconditional budget share of the first transformed good declines by 0.0092 per cent and that of the second (which belongs to the same group) by 0.0436 per cent. The invariance of the conditional budget shares would require these two percentage changes to be equal.

| | | | |
|---|---|---|---|
| 59996805 | -3750 | 555 | 59993610 |
| 3751 | 30004107 | 357 | 30008215 |
| -555 | -357 | 9999087 | 9998175 |
| 60000000 | 30000000 | 10000000 | 100000000 |

Unfortunately, this composition matrix does not agree with the matrix of the individual goods. When we sum the elements of each submatrix of the composition matrix in the upper part of table 2, we obtain

| | | | |
|---|---|---|---|
| 59996203 | -4369 | 573 | 59992408 |
| 4370 | 30004787 | 419 | 30009576 |
| -573 | -419 | 9999008 | 9998017 |
| 60000000 | 30000000 | 10000000 | 100000000 |

The row sums of this array are not equal to the budget shares of the transformed groups. Also, it is not true that the off-diagonal submatrices of the composition matrix for the individual goods have unit rank. A visual inspection of (8.12) and table 2 is sufficient to verify this.

Until now we have discussed the case in which the off-diagonal elements of $[\Theta_{gh}]$ are close to zero. Table 3, which is based on the two-group example, provides some information on what happens when $\epsilon$ in (8.11) moves away from zero. The composition matrices on the left show that the 2 x 2 principal submatrices corresponding to the two groups cease to be diagonal when $\epsilon$ takes increasing positive values, but that the diagonal elements of these submatrices continue to dominate the off-diagonal elements. The skew-symmetry displayed by the off-diagonal submatrices continues in approximate form until $\epsilon = 0.01$, but it is much less noticeable at $\epsilon = 0.1$ and even less so at $\epsilon = 0.2$.

The $\epsilon$s in the right half of the table are all negative and show a more substantial impact, particularly the larger negative $\epsilon$s. This is not surprising because the matrix (8.11) becomes singular at $\epsilon = -0.24$ but remains positive definite at $\varepsilon = 0.24$. The composition matrix for $\epsilon = -0.2$ contains a negative diagonal element and the smallest root ($\lambda_1 = 0.189$) is much smaller than that at $\varepsilon = -0.1$. The behaviour of the $\lambda_i$s as functions of $\epsilon$ is otherwise very smooth. When $\epsilon$ moves toward -0.24, $\lambda_1$ converges to zero, which implies that the conditional income elasticities cannot be invariant when $\epsilon$ is not close to zero.

The numerical evidence discussed above suggests that when weak separability is treated by means of a Taylor expansion from the point of strong separability, the leading term (but not the next terms) of this expansion has a blockwise structure. The mathematical form of this structure merits a further investigation.

**Table 2.** Two Composition Matrices under Weak Separability

*Composition matrix for* $\varepsilon = 10^{-5}$

| | | | | | | | | | |
|---|---|---|---|---|---|---|---|---|---|
| 53997511 | 0 | -1822 | -868 | -249 | 95 | 160 | 132 | 64 | 53995023 |
| 0 | 5998692 | -962 | -389 | -79 | 28 | 44 | 34 | 16 | 5997385 |
| 1823 | 962 | 18002982 | 0 | 0 | 49 | 71 | 54 | 24 | 18005964 |
| 868 | 389 | 0 | 9001373 | 0 | 30 | 42 | 31 | 14 | 9002747 |
| 249 | 79 | 0 | 0 | 3000432 | 40 | 35 | 21 | 8 | 3000865 |
| -95 | -28 | -49 | -30 | -40 | 1999758 | 0 | 0 | 0 | 1999516 |
| -160 | -44 | -71 | -42 | -35 | 0 | 3499648 | 0 | 0 | 3499297 |
| -132 | -34 | -54 | -31 | -21 | 0 | 0 | 2999727 | 0 | 2999455 |
| -64 | -16 | -24 | -13 | -8 | 0 | 0 | 0 | 149987<br>5 | 1499749 |
| 54000000 | 6000000 | 18000000 | 9000000 | 3000000 | 2000000 | 3500000 | 3000000 | 150000<br>0 | 10000000<br>0 |

*Composition matrix for* $\varepsilon = -10^{-5}$

| | | | | | | | | | |
|---|---|---|---|---|---|---|---|---|---|
| 54002488 | 0 | 1823 | 868 | 249 | -95 | -160 | -132 | -64 | 54004976 |
| 0 | 6001307 | 962 | 389 | 79 | -28 | -44 | -34 | -16 | 6002614 |
| -1822 | -962 | 17997017 | 0 | 0 | -49 | -71 | -54 | -24 | 17994035 |
| -868 | -389 | 0 | 8998627 | 0 | -30 | -42 | -31 | -13 | 8997255 |
| -249 | -79 | 0 | 0 | 2999568 | -40 | -35 | -21 | -8 | 2999135 |
| 95 | 28 | 49 | 30 | 40 | 2000242 | 0 | 0 | 0 | 2000484 |
| 160 | 44 | 71 | 42 | 35 | 0 | 3500352 | 0 | 0 | 3500703 |
| 132 | 34 | 54 | 31 | 21 | 0 | 0 | 3000273 | 0 | 3000545 |
| 64 | 16 | 24 | 14 | 8 | 0 | 0 | 0 | 150012<br>5 | 1500251 |
| 54000000 | 6000000 | 18000000 | 9000000 | 3000000 | 2000000 | 3500000 | 3000000 | 150000<br>0 | 10000000<br>0 |

Note: All entries are to be multiplied by $10^{-8}$.

**Table 3**. Bordered Composition Matrices and Income Elasticities of Transformed Goods under Weak Separability

| Bordered composition matrix | | | | | $\lambda_i$ | Bordered composition matrix | | | | | $\lambda_i$ |
|---|---|---|---|---|---|---|---|---|---|---|---|
| | | ε=0.001 | | | | | | ε=-0.001 | | | |
| 32026 | 0 | 24 | 2 | 32052 | 0.639 | 31975 | 0 | -24 | -2 | 31949 | 0.636 |
| -1 | 48058 | 55 | 4 | 48117 | 0.826 | -1 | 47940 | -55 | -4 | 47880 | 0.824 |
| -24 | -54 | 17922 | 0 | 17844 | 1.805 | 24 | 55 | 18079 | 0 | 18158 | 1.796 |
| -2 | -4 | 0 | 1994 | 1988 | 3.810 | 2 | 4 | 0 | 2006 | 2013 | 3.791 |
| 32000 | 48000 | 18000 | 2000 | 100000 | | 32000 | 48000 | 18000 | 2000 | 100000 | |
| | | ε=0.01 | | | | | | ε=-0.01 | | | |
| 32290 | 43 | 233 | 20 | 32585 | 0.648 | 31777 | 46 | -243 | -21 | 31560 | 0.627 |
| -50 | 48505 | 536 | 41 | 49033 | 0.838 | -54 | 47318 | -558 | -43 | 46664 | 0.811 |
| -220 | -508 | 17231 | -1 | 16502 | 1.845 | 255 | 591 | 18800 | -1 | 19645 | 1.755 |
| -19 | -40 | 0 | 1939 | 1881 | 3.895 | 22 | 45 | 0 | 2065 | 2131 | 3.705 |
| 32000 | 48000 | 18000 | 2000 | 100000 | | 32000 | 48000 | 18000 | 2000 | 100000 | |
| | | ε=0.1 | | | | | | ε=-0.1 | | | |
| 36833 | 3601 | 2353 | 208 | 42995 | 0.732 | 33007 | 8747 | -4523 | -382 | 36849 | 0.507 |
| -3539 | 47301 | 3774 | 305 | 47841 | 0.935 | -5872 | 27882 | -3673 | -276 | 18061 | 0.642 |
| -1170 | -2648 | 11858 | -38 | 8001 | 2.283 | 4455 | 10520 | 26110 | -253 | 40832 | 1.410 |
| -123 | -253 | 15 | 1524 | 1163 | 4.756 | 409 | 852 | 86 | 2911 | 4259 | 2.860 |
| 32000 | 48000 | 18000 | 2000 | 100000 | | 32000 | 48000 | 18000 | 2000 | 100000 | |
| | | ε=0.2 | | | | | | ε=-0.2 | | | |
| 42217 | 12745 | 5330 | 484 | 60776 | 0.804 | 17513 | 22225 | -11203 | -1092 | 27444 | 0.189 |
| -8755 | 38480 | 4214 | 354 | 34293 | 1.023 | 2281 | -2301 | 277 | 20 | 277 | 0.468 |
| -1297 | -2886 | 8422 | -70 | 4169 | 2.803 | 9749 | 22888 | 27452 | -2110 | 57978 | 1.147 |
| -166 | -339 | 34 | 1232 | 762 | 5.720 | 2457 | 5188 | 1473 | 5183 | 14300 | 1.971 |
| 32000 | 48000 | 18000 | 2000 | 100000 | | 32000 | 48000 | 18000 | 2000 | 100000 | |

Note: All elements of the bordered composition matrices (not the $\lambda_i$s) are to be multiplied by $10^{-5}$.

## Appendix

### A. Derivations for the Preference Independence Transformation

#### A.1 INVARIANCE CONSTRAINTS

Let each dollar spent on the $j$th observed good imply $r_{ij}$ dollars spent on the $i$th transformed good, where $r_{ij}$ is to be determined but is not yet defined. When $p_j q_j$ dollars are spent on the $j$th observed good, the expenditure on the $i$th transformed good is thus $r_{ij}p_j q_j$ dollars insofar as this expenditure originates with the $j$th observed good. Summation over $j$ yields $\Sigma_j r_{ij}p_j q_j$, which is the total amount spent on the $i$th transformed good. Next, by summing this over $i$, we obtain $\Sigma_j (\Sigma_i r_{ij})p_j q_j$, the total amount spent on all $n$ transformed goods. We require the total amount spent to be invariant (equal to $M = \Sigma_j p_j q_j$), which implies $\Sigma_i r_{ij} = 1$ for each $j$ or

$$\iota' R = \iota' \tag{A.1}$$

where $\iota' = [1 \ldots 1]$ and $R$ is the $n \times n$ matrix $[r_{ij}]$.

Since the amount spent on the $i$th transformed good is $\Sigma_j r_{ij}p_j q_j$, its budget share equals $\Sigma_j r_{ij}p_j q_j / M = \Sigma_j r_{ij}w_j$. We write this as

$$W_T \iota = RW\iota \tag{A.2}$$

where $W_T$ is the diagonal matrix with the budget shares $w_{T1}, \ldots, w_{Tn}$ of the transformed goods on the diagonal.

We write $\pi$ and $\kappa$ for the $n$-element column vectors whose $i$th elements are $d(\log p_i)$ and $d(\log q_i)$, respectively. Let the logarithmic price and quantity changes of the transformed goods be linear transformations of their observed counterparts,

$$\pi_T = S\pi, \quad \kappa_T = S\kappa \tag{A.3}$$

in such a way that the Divisia indexes (3.5) and (3.6) are invariant.[21] The index (3.5) equals $\iota' W_\pi$ and its transformed counterpart is $\iota' W_T \pi_T = \iota' W_T S\pi$, which is equal to $\iota' WR' S\pi$ in view of (A.2). The invariance of this index thus amounts to

---

[21] It is possible to proceed under the weaker condition that the two transformations may be different: $\pi_T = S_1\pi$ and $\kappa_T = S_2\kappa$. However, when both Divisia indexes are constrained to be invariant, both $S_1$ and $S_2$ must be equal to the inverse of R′ and, hence, equal to each other.

$$R'S = I \tag{A.4}$$

which implies $R' = S^{-1}$. Since $R'\iota = \iota$ follows from (A.1), this yields $S^{-1}\iota = \iota$ and hence, after premultiplication by $S$,[22]

$$S\iota = \iota \tag{A.5}$$

Note that (A.4) requires $R$ to be nonsingular. The singular case will be considered at the end of this section.

## A.2 THE DIAGONALIZATION

We write (3.16) as $\Theta\iota = \theta$, where $\theta = [\theta_i]$ is the marginal share vector. The Frisch price index (3.10) can then be written as $\theta'\pi = \iota'\Theta\pi$ and the demand system (3.13) for $i = 1, \ldots, n$ as

$$W\kappa = (\iota'W\kappa)\Theta\iota + \phi\,\Theta(I - \iota\iota'\Theta)\pi \tag{A.6}$$

where $\iota'W\kappa = d(\log Q)$. We premultiply (A.6) by $R$:

$$RW\kappa = (\iota'W\kappa)R\Theta\iota + \phi\,R\Theta(I - \iota\iota'\Theta)\pi$$

The left-hand side equals $RWR'S\kappa = RWR'\kappa_T$ [see (A.3) and (A.4)]. When we proceed similarly on the right, using (A.1) also, we obtain

$$RWR'\kappa_T = (\iota'W\kappa)(R\Theta R')\iota + \phi R\Theta R'[I - \iota\iota'(R\Theta R')]\pi_T \tag{A.7}$$

Since the Divisia volume index is invariant by construction ($\iota'W\kappa = \iota'W_T\kappa_T$), (A.7) is a demand system of the same form as (A.6), with price and quantity changes $\pi_T$ and $\kappa_T$, provided $RWR'$ on the left can be identified with the diagonal budget share matrix $W_T$. The new normalized price coefficient matrix is $R\Theta R'$,[23] which occurs in the same three

[22] When the prices of all observed goods change proportionately, $\pi$ is a scalar multiple of $\iota$ so that (A.3) and (A.5) imply that $\pi_T$ is equal to the same scalar multiple of $\iota$. This proves the statement on proportionate price changes at the end of the first subsection of section 4.

[23] This matrix is indeed normalized because $\iota'R\Theta R'\iota = \iota'\Theta\iota = 1$.

places in (A.7) as $\Theta$ does in (A.6). Therefore, two conditions are required in order that (A.7) be a differential demand system in preference independent form:

$$RWR' = W_T, \quad R\Theta R' = \text{diagonal} \tag{A.8}$$

These are two conditions on $R$, which must satisfy (A.1) also.

We proceed to prove that these three conditions are satisfied by

$$R = (X^{-1}\iota)_\Delta X' \tag{A.9}$$

where $X$ and $(X^{-1}\iota)_\Delta$ are defined as in the first subsection of section 4. Condition (A.1) in the form $R'\iota = \iota$ is satisfied by (A.9) because $X(X^{-1}\iota)_\Delta\iota = XX^{-1}\iota = \iota$. Also, $RWR' = (X^{-1}\iota)_\Delta X'WX(X^{-1}\iota)_\Delta = (X^{-1}\iota)^2_\Delta$, where the last step is based on (4.3). Therefore, the first condition in (A.8) is satisfied in the following form:

$$RWR' = W_T = (X^{-1}\iota)^2_\Delta = \text{diagonal} \tag{A.10}$$

The second condition is satisfied in the form

$$R\Theta R' = (X^{-1}\iota)^2_\Delta\Lambda = \text{diagonal} \tag{A.11}$$

which follows from (A.9) and $\Theta = (X')^{-1}\Lambda X^{-1}$ [see (4.3)]. The first term on the right in (A.7) shows that $(R\Theta R')\iota$ is the marginal share vector of the transformed goods; hence the diagonal elements of the matrix product (A.11) are these marginal shares.

To verify the composition matrix (4.4) we recall from the discussion preceding (A.1) that the expenditure on the $i$th transformed good is $r_{ij}p_jq_j$ dollars insofar as it originates with the $j$th observed good. By dividing this by $M$ we obtain $r_{ij}w_j$, which is the budget share of the $i$th transformed good insofar as it originates with the $j$th observed good. This $r_{ij}w_j$ is the $(i, j)$th element of the composition matrix $T$ and obviously also the $(i, j)$th element of $RW$, so that $T=RW$. We then obtain (4.4) from $RW=(X^{-1}\iota)_\Delta X'(X')^{-1}X^{-1} = (X^{-1}\iota)_\Delta X^{-1}$, where use is made of (A.9) and $W=(X')^{-1}X^{-1}$ [see (4.3)]. Post-multiplication of $T=RW$ by $\iota$ gives $T\iota = RW\iota = W_T\iota$ [see (A.2)]; hence the row sums of $T$ are the budget shares of the transformed goods. Also, $\iota'T = \iota'RW = \iota'W$, which proves that the column sums of $T$ are the budget shares of the observed goods.

## A.3 MULTIPLE ROOTS AND NEAR-MULTIPLE ROOTS

The solution (A.9) is unique when there are no multiple roots [i.e. no equal diagonal elements in $\Lambda$ in (4.3)].[24] We proceed to consider a pair of multiple roots, $\lambda_1 = \lambda_2 \neq \lambda_i$ for $i > 2$. The characteristic vectors $x_1$ and $x_2$ associated with the multiple root are not uniquely determined; we may post-multiply $[x_1 \;\; x_2]$ by an arbitrary 2 x 2 orthogonal matrix and the two vectors which emerge satisfy (4.1) and the normalization rules. This indeterminacy of $x_1$ and $x_2$ implies a similar indeterminacy of the budget and marginal shares of the two transformed goods. If $\lambda_3, ..., \lambda_n$ are distinct, the budget and marginal shares of the last $n$ - 2 transformed goods are well defined, so that the combined budget share and the combined marginal share of the first two are also well defined. Also, the first two rows of the composition matrix are indeterminate, although constrained by the fact that their sum is determinate. This means that the two transformed goods with equal income elasticities are identical or, equivalently, that they behave like one good so that there are only $n$ - 1 transformed goods.

We proceed to discuss the perturbations of table 1, the last column of which contains the marginal shares of the transformed goods. We perturb $W$ by a diagonal matrix $dW$; this matrix must satisfy $\iota'(dW)\iota = 0$ because the budget shares add up to 1. The perturbed version of (4.1) is

$$[\Theta-(\lambda_i + d\lambda_i)(W + dW)](x_i + dx_i) = 0 \tag{A.12}$$

Using (4.1) and ignoring products of differentials, we obtain

$$(\Theta - \lambda_i W)dx_i = (d\lambda_i)Wx_i + \lambda_i(dW)x_i \tag{A.13}$$

which we premultiply by $x_i'$ to obtain

$$d\lambda_i = -\lambda_i x_i'(dW)x_i \tag{A.14}$$

If $dW_i$ is multiplied by -1, so is $d\lambda_i$ in view of (A.14) and so is $dx_i$ in view of (A.13). This explains why the two perturbations of table 1 have an approximately linear effect on the $\lambda_i$s, $\theta_{Ti}$s, and the elements of the bordered composition matrix.

The nature of this effect can be conveniently illustrated geometrically (Figure 1) for $n = 3$. Point $W$ in the triangle below corresponds to $w_1 = 0.6$, $w_2 = 0.3$, $w_3 = 0.1$, which is the point at which $\lambda_1 = \lambda_2$ in table 1. The first perturbation keeps $w_1$ at 0.6 but lets $w_2$ increase at the expense of $w_3$. This path is indicated by the horizontal arrow

[24] This statement is subject to the qualification that the right-hand side of (A.9) may be pre-multiplied by an arbitrary permutation matrix. The only effect of such a multiplication is a change in the order in which the transformed goods are listed.

through $W$. The second perturbation is orthogonal to the first and raises $w_1$ while reducing $w_2$ and $w_3$ equally. This path corresponds to the vertical arrow through $W$. Any other linear path through $W$ would have the same characteristics as the two displayed in table 1, but the path need not be linear. A non-linear path is shown in the lower part of the triangle with $W'$ the point at which $\lambda_1 = \lambda_2$. In this case $\theta_{T1}$ and $\theta_{T2}$ and the first two rows of the bordered composition matrix will change quickly; how quickly depends on the degree of curvature of the path. Tracing the behaviour of the transformed goods will now be much more difficult.

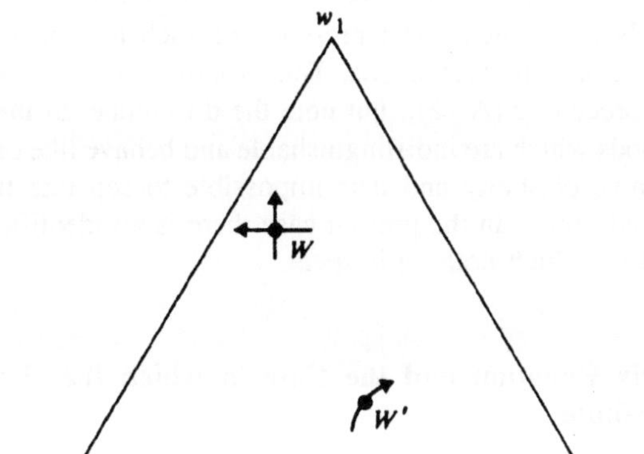


Figure 1

## A.4 THE TRANSFORMATION IN THE SINGULAR CASE

We write $\pi_T = S_\pi$ [see (A.3)] in scalar form as

$$d(\log p_{Ti}) = \sum_{j=1}^{n} s_{ij} d(\log p_j) \qquad \text{(A.15)}$$

where $d(\log p_{Ti})$ is the $i$th element of $\pi_T$ and $s_{ij}$ is the $(i, j)$th element of $S$. It follows from (A.4) and (A.9) that

$$S = (X^{-1}\iota)_\Delta^{-1} X^{-1} \qquad \text{(A.16)}$$

but this solution does not apply when $(X^{-1}\iota)_\Delta$ is singular. This occurs when $X^{-1}\iota$ contains a zero element so that $R$ is singular and no $S$ exists which satisfies (A.4).

To interpret this we start with the case in which all elements of $X^{-1}\iota$ are non-zero. Hence (A.15) applies with $[s_{ij}] = S$ defined as in (A.16). Next we consider a perturbation of the consumer's preferences so that the $i$th element of $X^{-1}\iota$ moves toward zero.[25] It follows from (A.16) that the $i$th row of $S$ will consist of elements that increase beyond bounds, so that (A.15) implies that the logarithmic price change of the $i$th transformed good moves toward $\pm\infty$. If the move is toward $\infty$, this good is priced out of the market and nothing is spent on it in the limit. If the move is toward $-\infty$, the good becomes free and, again, nothing is spent on it in the limit. Thus, a transformed good on which nothing is spent can be viewed as a limiting case with either zero or infinite price that results from the consumer's preferences. The presence of such a good implies that there are effectively only $n$ - 1 transformed goods. This is similar to the case of a multiple root [see the paragraph preceding (A.12)], but note the difference. In the latter case we have two transformed goods which are indistinguishable and behave like one good because they have the same income elasticity and it is impossible to separate their compositions in terms of the observed goods. In the present case there is no identification problem; there is simply one good on which nothing is spent.

## B. Barten's Matrix Equation and the Case in which the Hessian of the Utility Function is not Definite

### B.1 A MATRIX EQUATION AND ITS SOLUTION

By differentiating the budget constraint $p'q = M$ with respect to $M$ and $p'$ we obtain

$$p'\frac{\partial q}{\partial M} = 1, \quad p'\frac{\partial q}{\partial p'} = -q' \tag{B.1}$$

where $\partial q/\partial p'$ is the $n \times n$ matrix $[\partial q_i/\partial p_j]$. Next, by differentiating the proportionality of marginal utilities and prices, $\partial u/\partial q_i = \lambda p_i$ where $\lambda$ is the marginal utility of income, with respect to $M$ and $p'$ we find

$$U\frac{\partial q}{\partial M} = \frac{\partial \lambda}{\partial M}p, \quad U\frac{\partial q}{\partial p'} = \lambda I + p\frac{\partial \lambda}{\partial p'} \tag{B.2}$$

We can combine (B.1) and (B.2) in partitioned matrix form,

[25] The simplest way to visualize such a perturbation is in terms of the Hessian matrix of the utility function. A change in this Hessian affects the matrix $[\theta_{ij}]$ in view of (3.15) and hence also $X$ [see (4.3)].

$$\begin{bmatrix} U & p \\ p' & 0 \end{bmatrix} \begin{bmatrix} \partial q/\partial M & \partial q/\partial p' \\ -\partial\lambda/\partial M & -\partial\lambda/\partial p' \end{bmatrix} = \begin{bmatrix} 0 & \lambda I \\ 1 & -q' \end{bmatrix} \tag{B.3}$$

which is Barten's fundamental matrix equation.

If $U$ is negative definite, the inverse of the bordered Hessian on the far left in (B.3) can be written as

$$\frac{1}{p'U^{-1}p} \begin{bmatrix} (p'U^{-1}p)U^{-1} - U^{-1}p(U^{-1}p)' & U^{-1}p \\ (U^{-1}p)' & -1 \end{bmatrix} \tag{B.4}$$

Pre-multiplication of (B.3) by the matrix (B.4) yields

$$\frac{\partial\lambda}{\partial M} = \frac{1}{p'U^{-1}p}, \quad \frac{\partial q}{\partial M} = \frac{1}{p'U^{-1}p} U^{-1}p \tag{B.5}$$

$$\frac{\partial q}{\partial p'} = \lambda U^{-1} - \frac{\lambda}{p'U^{-1}p} U^{-1}p(U^{-1}p)' - \frac{1}{p'U^{-1}p} U^{-1}pq' \tag{B.6}$$

after which (3.8) follows from (B.6) and some rearrangements based on (B.5).

## B.2 WHAT HAPPENS IF THE HESSIAN IS NOT DEFINITE?

The assumption of a negative definite $U$ guarantees that utility is maximized subject to the budget constraint, but this assumption is stronger than necessary. A sufficient condition is

$$x'Ux < 0 \quad \text{for all} \quad x \neq 0 \quad \text{satisfying} \quad x'p = 0 \tag{B.7}$$

which is constrained negative definiteness.[26] We define

$$A = -P^{-1}UP^{-1} \tag{B.8}$$

[26] It was shown by Barten, Kloek, and Lempers (1969) that the bordered Hessian matrix on the far left in (B.3) continues to be non-singular under this weaker condition so that (B.3) can still be solved.

where $P$ is the diagonal matrix with $p_1, ..., p_n$ on the diagonal. For $y = Px$ we have $x'p = y'P^{-1}p = y'\iota$, so that (B.7) is equivalent to

$$y'Ay > 0 \quad \text{for all} \quad y \neq 0 \quad \text{satisfying } y'\iota = 0 \tag{B.9}$$

It follows from (3.17) and (B.8) that if $U$ and hence $\Theta$ are nonsingular,

$$A = k\Theta^{-1} \tag{B.10}$$

where $k = -\phi M/\lambda$. However, $U$ and $A$ may be singular semi-definite or indefinite under (B.7) and (B.9). Examples of a semi-definite $A_1$ and an indefinite $A_2$ satisfying (B.9) are

$$A_1 = \begin{bmatrix} 0.8 & 0.4 \\ 0.4 & 0.2 \end{bmatrix}, \quad A_2 = \begin{bmatrix} 0.8 & 0.45 \\ 0.45 & 0.2 \end{bmatrix} \tag{B.11}$$

which may be verified from the fact that (B.9) for $n = 2$ implies a $y$ vector of the form $[y_1 \quad -y_1]'$ for some non-zero scalar $y_1$.

The possible nonexistence of $\theta$ (due to the singularity of $U$) does not by itself exclude the preference independence transformation. The objective of this transformation is to make utility additive; this requires a diagonalization of $U$, which can be performed even if $U$ is singular. It will be convenient to proceed under the temporary assumption that $U$ is non-singular so that $\Theta$ exists. We premultiply (4.1) by $\Theta^{-1}$, which yields $(I - \lambda_i\Theta^{-1}W)x_i = 0$. This can be written as

$$\left(\Theta^{-1} - \frac{1}{\lambda_i} W^{-1}\right) Wx_i = 0 \tag{B.12}$$

which shows that $1/\lambda_i$ is a latent root, and $Wx_i$ a characteristic vector associated with this root, of the diagonalization of $\Theta^{-1}$ relative to $W^{-1}$. When we normalize according to $(Wx_i)'W^{-1}(Wx_j) = 0$ for $i \neq j$ and $(Wx_i)'W^{-1}(Wx_i) = 1$, we obtain $X'WX = I$ as before.

Since (B.10) shows that $A$ is inversely proportional to $\Theta$ if $\Theta$ exists, (B.12) suggests a diagonalization of $A$ relative to $W^{-1}$:

$$(A - \delta_i W^{-1})Wx_i = 0 \tag{B.13}$$

If $A$ is singular, one $\delta_i$, say $\delta_1$, will be zero. If $A$ is indefinite, $\delta_1$ will be negative. The former case could be viewed as a limiting case in which one transformed good has an income elasticity that increases beyond bounds ($\lambda_1 \to \infty$). In the latter case there would be an inferior transformed good ($\lambda_1 < 0$). Such goods could be considered acceptable if nothing were spent on them. Unfortunately, this is not true.

To prove this we define $\Delta$ as the diagonal matrix with $\delta_1, ..., \delta_n$ on the diagonal. We can then write (B.13) for $i = 1, ..., n$ in the form $AWX = X\Delta$. We postmultiply this by $X'$, $AWXX' = X\Delta X'$, implying

$$A = X\Delta X' \tag{B.14}$$

because $WX = (X')^{-1}$ follows from $X'WX = I$. On combining (B.14) with (B.9) we obtain $y'X\Delta X'y > 0$ for any $y \neq 0$ satisfying $y'\iota = 0$. We define $z = X'y$ and conclude that $z'\Delta z > 0$ holds for any $z \neq 0$ which satisfies $z'X^{-1}\iota = 0$. This is equivalent to the proposition that if $z \neq 0$ and $z'\Delta z \leq 0$, then $z'X^{-1}\iota \neq 0$. We specify $z$ as the first column of the $n$ x $n$ unit matrix; then $z'\Delta z \leq 0$ becomes $\delta_1 \leq 0$ and $z'X^{-1}\iota \neq 0$ becomes the statement that the top element of $X^{-1}\iota$ is non-zero. But this element is a square root of $w_{T1}$ in view of (A.10), so that a positive amount is spent on the transformed good with $\delta_1 \leq 0$. Ironically, the *only* good for which it is possible to prove that a positive amount is spent is that which we would like to have zero expenditure!

This result suggests that a replacement of the negative definiteness of $U$ by the weaker assumption (B.7) is unsatisfactory from the viewpoint of the preference independence transformation. It is appropriate to add that (B.7) is not very much weaker when we require it to be satisfied for *any* price vector $p$. This stronger version of (B.7) is still somewhat weaker than unconstrained negative definiteness, because all elements of $p$ must be positive. The issue is probably of minor importance, since the application of the transformation to statistical data typically involves groups of goods under the assumption of strong separability and this assumption involves unconstrained negative definiteness.

## C. Finite Change Parametrizations

The application of differential consumer demand systems to data requires a finite change parametrization. We define $Dx_t = \log (x_t/x_{t-1})$ as the log-change in any positive variable $x$ from $t$ - 1 to $t$. The most popular finite-change version of (3.13) is

$$\bar{w}_{it} Dq_{it} = \theta_i DQ_t + \sum_{j=1}^{n} \nu_{ij} \left( Dp_{jt} - \sum_{k=1}^{n} \theta_k Dp_{kt} \right) + \varepsilon_{it} \tag{C.1}$$

where $\bar{w}_{it} = (w_{i,t-1} + w_{it})/2$, $DQ_t = \Sigma_i \bar{w}_{it} Dq_{it}$, $\nu_{ij} = \phi\theta_{ij}$, and $\varepsilon_{it}$ is a random disturbance. The $\nu_{ij}$s are not identifiable without additional restrictions; this problem is related to their lack of invariance under monotone transformations of the utility function (see Theil, 1975-76, section 2.5). One way of solving this problem consists of writing the substitution term of (C.1) as $\sum_j \pi_{ij} Dp_{jr}$, where $\pi_{ij} = \nu_{ij} - \phi\theta_i\theta_j$ is the $(i, j)$th Slutsky coefficient, which is invariant. The next step is to simplify the model in the direction of preference independence as much as the data permit. See also Barnett (1979) for an interesting contribution to the aggregated (per capita) version of this model.

In the case of conditional systems, (C.1) can be implemented in two alternative forms, one based on (7.9) and the other on (7.10). Both versions were applied to meats and (7.10) was used because of its better fit. Details can be found in Theil (1975-76, chapter 7).

**References**


Barnett, W.A.: 1974, *Labor Supply and the Allocation of Consumption Expenditure*, Doctoral dissertation, Carnegie-Mellon University.

Barnett, W.A.: 1979, "Theoretical Foundations for the Rotterdam Model," *Review of Economic Studies.*

Barten, A.P.: 1964, "Consumer Demand Functions Under Conditions of Almost Additive Preferences," *Econometrica*, **32**, 1-38.

Barten, A.P., Kloek, T. and Lempers, F.B.: 1969, "A Note on a Class of Utility and Production Functions Yielding Everywhere Differentiable Demand Functions," *Review of Economic Studies*, **36**, 109-111.

Becker, G.S.: 1965, "A Theory of the Allocation of Time," *Econometric Journal*, **75**, 493-517.

Boyle, J.R., Gorman, W.M., and Pudney, S.E.: 1977, "Demand for Related Goods: A Progress Report," in M.D. Intriligator, ed., *Frontiers of Quantitative Economics*, Vol. IIIA, North-Holland Publishing Company, Amsterdam, 87-101.

Brooks, R.B.: 1970, *Diagonalizing the Hessian Matrix of the Consumer's Utility Function*, Doctoral dissertation, The University of Chicago.

Deaton, A.S.: 1979, "The Distance Function and Consumer Behaviour with Applications to Index Numbers and Optimal Taxation," *Review of Economic Studies*, **46**, 391-405.

Diewert, W.E.: 1974, "Applications of Duality Theory," in M.D. Intriligator and D.A. Kendrick, eds., *Frontiers of Quantitative Economics*, Vol. II, North-Holland Publishing Company, Amsterdam, 106-171.

Divisia, F.: 1925, "L'indice monétaire et la théorie de la monnaie," *Revue d'Economie Politique*, **39**, 980-1008.

Flinn, C.: 1978, "A Preference Independence Transformation Involving Leisure," Report 7847 of the Center for Mathematical Studies in Business and Economics, The University of Chicago.

Frisch, R.: 1932, *New Methods of Measuring Marginal Utility*, J.C.B. Mohr, Tübingen.

Geary, R. C. (1950) "A Note on A Constant Utility Index of the Cost of Living," *Review of Economic Studies*, **18**, 65-66.

Gorman, W.M.: 1956, "Demand for Related Goods," Journal Paper J3129, Iowa Agricultural Experiment Station.

Gorman, W.M.: 1959, "Demand for Fish: An Application of Factor Analysis," Birmingham Discussion Paper A6.

Gorman, W.M.: 1976a, "Tricks with Utility Functions," in M.J. Artis and A.R. Nobay, eds., *Essays in Economic Analysis*, Cambridge University Press, 211-243.

Gorman, W.M.: 1976b, "A Possible Procedure for Analysing Quality Differentials in the Egg Market," Discussion Paper No. B4 of the London School of Economics and Political Science.

Hall, R.E.: 1973, "The Specification of Technology with Several Kinds of Output," *Journal of Political Economy*, **81**, 878-892.

Houthakker, H.S.: 1960, "Additive Preferences," *Econometrica*, **28**, 244-257; errata, **30** (1962), 633.

Klein, L.R., and Rubin, H.: 1948, "A Constant-Utility Index of the Cost of Living," *Review of Economic Studies*, **15**, 84-87.

Laitinen, K., and Theil, H.: 1978, "Supply and Demand of the Multiproduct Firm," *European Economic Review*, **11**, 107-154.

Lancaster, K.J.: 1966, "A New Approach to Consumer Theory," *Journal of Political Economy*, **74**, 132-157.

Lancaster, K.J.: 1971, *Consumer Demand: A New Approach*, Columbia University Press, New York.

MaCurdy, T.: 1975, "The Firm's Demand for Inputs When These Inputs Are Blockwise Dependent," Report 7539 of the Center for Mathematical Studies in Business and Economics, The University of Chicago.

McFadden, D.: 1978, "Cost, Revenue, and Profit Functions," in M. Fuss and D. McFadden, eds., *Production Economics: A Dual Approach to Theory and Applications*, North-Holland Publishing Company, Amsterdam.

Pearce, I.F. 1961, "An Exact Method of Consumer Demand Analysis," *Econometrica*, **29**, 499-516.

Pearce, I.F.: 1964, A Contribution to Demand Analysis, Oxford University Press.

Stone, R.: 1947, "On the Interdependence of Blocks of Transactions," Supplement, *Journal of the Royal Statistical Society*, **9**, 1-45.

Stone, R.: 1954, "Linear Expenditure Systems and Demand Analysis: An Application to the Pattern of British Demand," *Economic Journal*, **64**, 511-527.

Theil, H.: 1967, *Economics and Information Theory*, North-Holland Publishing Company, Amsterdam.

Theil, H.: 1975-76, *Theory and Measurement of Consumer Demand*, two volumes, North-Holland Publishing Company, Amsterdam.

Theil, H.: 1977, "The Independent Inputs of Production," *Econometrica*, **45**, 1303-1327.

Theil, H.: 1980, *The System-Wide Approach to Microeconomics*, University of Chicago Press.

**Note added in proof:** Several theoretical and empirical developments have occurred since this article was written in 1978. Rossi (1979) proved that when all $n$ observed goods are specific substitutes (complements), the independence transformation yields one transformed good in which all observed goods are positively represented, viz., the transformed good with the smallest (largest) income or Divisia elasticity, all $n$ - 1 other transformed goods being contrasts between observed goods. Chang (1980) derived an interesting result for the *maximal* degree of dependence among observed consumer goods, inputs or outputs. Theil (1979) introduced the notion of equicorrelated substitutes and a similar concept for Nasse's (1970) extension of the linear expenditure system. The independence transformation based on this extension takes a particularly simple form; it was applied by Meisner and Clements (1979) to Australian data. Offenbacher (1980) applied the input independence transformation to the demand for money by US firms. Theil (1980) proved that when the consumer's tastes are close to preference independence, each transformed good is uniquely associated with one observed good. Also, corresponding off-diagonal elements of the composition matrix are then equal apart from sign and are inversely proportional to the difference between the income elasticities of the two associated observed goods. A blockwise extension of this result (see Section 8 above) would be appropriate.

Chang, F.R.: 1980, "The Maximal Degree of Dependence Among Inputs, Outputs, and Consumer Goods," *Economics Letters*, 5, 93-96.

Meisner, J.F., and Clements, K.W.: 1979, "Specific Complements and the Demand for Money in Australia," *Economics Letters*, 3, 207-210.

Nasse, P.: 1970, "Analyse des effets de substitution dans un système complet de fonctions de demande," *Annales de l'Insée*, **5**, 81-110.

Offenbacher, E.K.: 1980, "The Basic Functions of Money: An Application of the Input Independence Transformation," *Economics Letters*, 5, 353-357.

Rossi, P.E.: 1979, "The Independence Transformation of Specific Substitutes and Specific Complements." *Economics Letters*, **2**, 299-301.

Theil, H.: 1979, "Equicorrelated Substitutes and Nasse's Extension of the Linear Expenditure System." *Economics Letters*, **3**, 81-84.

Theil, H.: 1980, "The Independence Transformation under Almost Additivity," *Economics Letters*, **5**, 145-148.

CHAPTER 46

# THE INDEPENDENCE TRANSFORMATION UNDER ALMOST ADDITIVITY*

HENRI THEIL
*University of Chicago*
*Chicago, Illinois, U.S.A.*

**ABSTRACT. When the consumer's tastes are close to preference independence, each transformed good is uniquely associated with one observed good. The off-diagonal elements of the composition matrix of the transformation are equal apart from sign and are inversely proportional to the difference between the income elasticities of the corresponding observed goods.**

## 1. Introduction

The independence transformation in microeconomic theory changes observed goods into transformed goods subject to invariance constraints on the dollar amount of these goods and the Divisia decomposition of this amount. For example,[1] in consumption theory the transformation yields (locally) strong additivity in the sense that the marginal utility of each transformed good has zero rates of change for variations in the quantities of all other such goods. The procedure may be briefly summarized as follows.

For $n$ observed goods, let $p_i$, $q_i$, and $w_i = p_i q_i / M$ be the price, quantity, and budget share of good $i$ ($M = \Sigma_i p_i q_i$ = total expenditure). The $i$th demand equation can then be written in differential form as

$$w_i d(\log q_i) = \theta_i d(\log Q) + \phi \sum_{j=1}^{n} \theta_{ij} d\left(\log \frac{p_j}{P'}\right),$$

where $\theta_i = \partial(p_i q_i)/\partial M$, $d(\log Q)$ = Divisia volume index and $d(\log P')$ = Frisch price index,[2] and $\theta_{ij}$ is an element of the $n \times n$ matrix $\Theta$ which is a negative multiple of the

* This article first appeared in *Economics Letters*, **5** (1980), 281-284. Reprinted with the permission of Elsevier Science Publishers B.V. (North-Holland). Research supported in part by NSF Grant SOC76-82718.

[1] The exposition will be confined to consumption theory for reasons of space limitations, but the results of this paper also apply to the inputs of a firm and the outputs of a multiproduct firm. Details on the input and output independence transformations can be found in chapters 10 and 11 of Theil (1980) and the references quoted there.

[2] That is $d(\log Q) = \Sigma_i w_i d(\log q_i)$ and $d(\log P') = \Sigma_i \theta_i d(\log p_i)$ while $\phi$ is the reciprocal of the income elasticity of the marginal utility of income. For further details on the differential approach of consumption theory see chapter 2 and Appendix B of Theil (1980).

Hessian matrix of the utility function in expenditure terms. This Hessian is assumed to be symmetric negative definite so that $\Theta$ is symmetric positive definite.

Preference independence means that the consumer's tastes can be described by a utility function which is the sum of $n$ functions, one for each good. The Hessian of the utility function is then diagonal and so is $\Theta$. When there is no preference independence among the observed goods, we can apply the transformation described in the first paragraph. A major tool in the interpretation of this transformation is the $n \times n$ composition matrix whose rows describe the composition of the budget shares of transformed goods in terms of those of observed goods and whose columns describe the composition of the budget shares of the latter in terms of those of the former.[3]

## 2. The Composition Matrix under Almost Additivity

When there is preference independence among the observed goods, the transformation reduces to the identity transformation and each transformed good can be identified (trivially) with one observed good. When there is no preference independence among the observed goods, each transformed good refers to all observed goods jointly, not to any one in particular. The purpose of this paper is to show that there is an exception to this rule when the off-diagonal elements of $\Theta$ differ from zero only infinitesimally; we refer to this situation as almost additivity.[4] Let there be preference independence among the observed goods initially (so that $\Theta$ is diagonal) and imagine that tastes are slightly perturbed so that $\Theta$ becomes $\Theta + d\Theta$ with $d\theta_{ij} = d\theta_{ji}$ for $i \neq j$.[5] It is shown in section 3 that this yields a composition matrix of the form

$$T + dT = \begin{bmatrix} w_1 + \Sigma_{j\neq 1} a_{1j} & a_{12} & \cdots & a_{1n} \\ a_{21} & w_2 + \Sigma_{j\neq 2} a_{2j} & \cdots & a_{2n} \\ \cdot & \cdot & & \cdot \\ \cdot & \cdot & & \cdot \\ \cdot & \cdot & & \cdot \\ a_{n1} & a_{n2} & \cdots & w_n + \Sigma_{j\neq n} a_{nj} \end{bmatrix}, \qquad (1)$$

where

[3] For examples of composition matrices, see Barnett (1981), Meisner and Clements (1979), Offenbacher (1980), and Theil (1976, ch. 13).

[4] This concept was originally introduced by Barten (1964), although in a slightly different context.

[5] Only the off-diagonal $d\theta_{ij}$'s matter. We will assume that $d\theta_{ii} = -\Sigma_{j\neq i} d\theta_{ij}$ so that the marginal share $\theta_i = \theta_{i1} + ... + \theta_{in}$ is not affected by the perturbation.

$$a_{ij} = \frac{d\theta_{ij}}{\eta_i - \eta_j}, \qquad i \neq j, \tag{2}$$

with $\eta_i = \theta_i / w_i$, which is the income elasticity of observed good $i$.

The $w_i$'s on the diagonal in (1) correspond to $T$ on the left (which is a diagonal matrix), while the expressions involving the $a_{ij}$'s are the elements of $dT$. The $i$th row sum in (1) equals $w_i + 2\ \Sigma_{j \neq i} a_{ij}$; this is the budget share of the $i$th transformed good. Since $a_{ij} = -a_{ji}$ [see (2)], the $i$th column sum in (1) is $w_i$, as it should. The taste perturbation thus changes the budget share of the $i$th transformed good by $2\ \Sigma_{j \neq i}\ a_{ij}$, and the diagonal elements in (1) show that the corresponding observed good accounts for one-half of this change. The off-diagonal elements in (1) are equal apart from sign [see (2)]. Thus, for $i \neq j$, if observed good $i$ contributes positively to transformed good $j$, observed good $j$ contributes negatively to transformed good $i$ and the two contributions are equal in absolute value. These contributions are proportional to the displacement $d\theta_{ij}$ and inversely proportional to the difference between the income elasticities of the observed goods.[6]

## 3. Derivations

The preference independence transformation involves a simultaneous diagonalization of $\Theta$ and $W$ (the diagonal budget share matrix), $X'\Theta X = \Lambda$ and $X'WX = I$, where $\Lambda$ is a diagonal matrix with the income elasticities $\lambda_1, ..., \lambda_n$ (all positive) of the transformed goods on the diagonal and $X$ is an $n \times n$ matrix of characteristic column vectors $x_1, ..., x_n$. It was shown by Theil (1976, pp. 240, 246) that the $i$th row of $T$ equals $(x_i' W\iota) x_i' W$, where $\iota$ is a column of $n$ unit elements, and that when $\Theta$ is subject to a symmetric displacement $d\Theta$, the displacement of $x_i$ equals $dx_i = \Sigma_j \zeta_{ij} x_j$, where $\zeta_{ii} = 0$ and

$$\zeta_{ij} = \frac{x_i'(d\,\Theta)x_j}{\lambda_i - \lambda_j} \qquad \text{if } i \neq j. \tag{3}$$

The displacement of the $i$th row $(x_i' W\iota) x_i' W$ of $T$ is then

$$[(dx_i)'W\iota]x_i'W + (x_i'W\iota)(dx_i)'W, \tag{4}$$

with $dx_i = \Sigma_{j \neq i} \zeta_{ij} x_j$ and $\zeta_{ij}$ defined in (3).

---

[6] The skew-symmetry of the off-diagonal elements in (1) confirms the results of simulation experiments described by Theil and Laitinen (1980). Also, (2) shows that if $d\theta_{ij}$ is positive (negative) for all $i \neq j$, which means that the observed goods are all pairwise specific complements (substitutes) after the taste perturbation, the transformed good with the highest (lowest) income elasticity receives positive contributions from all observed goods. This agrees with Rossi's (1979) result.

When there is preference independence among the observed goods prior to the taste perturbation, $X'\Theta X = \Lambda$ and $X'WX = I$ are satisfied by $X = W^{-1/2}$ and $\lambda_i = \eta_i$ so that (3) becomes

$$\zeta_{ij} = \frac{d\theta_{ij}}{(\eta_i - \eta_j)\sqrt{w_i w_j}} \qquad \text{if } i \neq j \tag{5}$$

and $x_i'W = \sqrt{w_i}\; e_i'$, where $e_i'$ in the $i$th row of the $n \times n$ unit matrix. Also, using this result and (5),

$$(dx_i)'W = \sum_{j \neq i} \zeta_{ij} x_j'W = \frac{\iota}{\sqrt{w_i}} \sum_{j \neq i} \frac{d\theta_{ij}}{\eta_i - \eta_j} e_j' \tag{6}$$

so that the second term in (4) is a row with zero as $i$th element and $d\theta_{ij}/(\eta_i - \eta_j)$ as $j$th for each $j \neq i$. This confirms the off-diagonal elements in (1). For the first term in (4) we postmultiply (6) by $\iota$ using $e_j'\iota = 1$ and then postmultiply by $x_i'W = \sqrt{w_i e_i'}$, which confirms the diagonal elements in (1).

## References

Barnett, W.A.: 1981, *Consumer Demand and Labor Supply*, North-Holland, Amsterdam and New York.

Barten, A.P.: 1964, "Consumer Demand Functions under Conditions of Almost Additive Preferences," *Econometrica*, **32**, 1-38.

Meisner, J.F., and K.W. Clements: 1979, "Specific Complements and the Demand for Money in Australia," *Economics Letters*, **3**, 207-210.

Offenbacher, E.K.: 1980, "Disaggregated Monetary Asset Demand Systems: Estimation and an Application of the Preference Independence Transformation," Paper read at the Denver meetings of the American Economic Association.

Rossi, P.: 1979, "The Independence Transformation of Specific Substitutes and Specific Complements," *Economics Letters*, **2**, 299-301.

Theil, H.: 1976, *Theory and Measurement of Consumer Demand*, Vol. 2, North-Holland, Amsterdam.

Theil, H.: 1980, *The System-wide Approach to Microeconomics*, University of Chicago Press, Chicago, Illinois.

Theil, H., and K. Laitinen: 1981, "The Independence Transformation: A Review and some Further Explorations," in: A. Deaton, ed., *Essays in the Theory and Measurement of Consumer Behaviour*, Cambridge University Press, Cambridge, 73-112.

# PART FOUR: INFORMATION THEORY

## SECTION 4.1: DEMAND ANALYSIS

## CHAPTER 47

# BUDGET SHARE TRANSITIONS IN THE NETHERLANDS, 1952–1977*

RENATE FINKE
*University of Florida,*
*Gainesville, Florida, U.S.A.*

HENRI THEIL
*University of Florida,*
*Gainesville, Florida, U.S.A.*

ABSTRACT. Budget share transitions and their components are displayed for 10 broad consumer goods. The decrease in the budget share of food is dramatic, the increase in the share of medical care is quite substantial.

Theil (1980, section 12.6) formulated gross flows and net flows among pairs of consumer goods under preference independence (or after the preference independence transformation has been applied). Here we summarize such flows for finite changes. Let $Dp_{it}$ and $Dq_{it}$ be the price and quantity log-changes of good $i$ and let $w_{it}$ be its budget share. Then, approximately,

$$\Delta w_{it} = \bar{w}_{it}(Dp_{it} - DP_t) + \bar{w}_{it}(Dq_{it} - DQ_t) \ . \tag{1}$$

where $\Delta w_{it} = w_{it} - w_{i,t-1}$ and $\bar{w}_{it} = (w_{it} + w_{i,t-1})/2$, while $DP_t = \Sigma_{j=1}^{n} \bar{w}_{jt} Dp_{jt}$ and $DQ_t = \Sigma_{j=1}^{n} \bar{w}_{jt} Dq_{jt}$ are the Divisia price and volume indexes. Thus, (1) shows that $\Delta w_{it}$ equals a price component plus a volume component. The *gross budget share flow* from $j$ to $i$ is required to be some proportion $A_{jt}$ of the price component of $\Delta w_{it}$ plus some proportion $B_{jt}$ of the corresponding volume component,

$$A_{jt}\bar{w}_{it}(Dp_{it} - DP_t) + B_{jt}\bar{w}_{it}(Dq_{it} - DQ_t) \ , \tag{2}$$

where $\Sigma_{j=1}^{n} A_{jt} = \Sigma_{j=1}^{n} B_{jt} = 1$. The *net flow* from $j$ to $i$ equals the gross flow (2) minus the same expression with $i$ and $j$ interchanged. This net flow is required to be independent of all price changes $Dp_{kt}$, $i \neq k \neq j$. It is then easily shown (see Theil, 1980, p. 146) that this implies $A_{jt} = \bar{w}_{jt}$ and $B_{jt}$ = marginal share of $j$ (see below).

We proceed to apply this result to annual Dutch data on $n$ = 10 goods, listed in column (1) of Table I, for the period 1952-1977. The model used is Working's (1943),

* This article first appeared in *Economics Letters*, **16** (1984), 7-13. Reprinted with the permission of Elsevier Science Publishers B.V., (North-Holland).

**TABLE I.** Data on 10 Goods.

| Good (1) | $\beta_i$ (2) | Budget shares | | | Components of budget share change | | | |
|---|---|---|---|---|---|---|---|---|
| | | 1952 (3) | 1977 (4) | Change (5) | Income (6) | Substi-tution (7) | Direct price (8) | Residual (9) |
| Food | -0.1543 | 0.337 | 0.181 | -0.155 | -0.167 | 0.007 | -0.022 | 0.027 |
| Beverages, tobacco | 0.0008 | 0.069 | 0.052 | -0.017 | 0.001 | 0.010 | -0.016 | -0.011 |
| Clothing, footwear | -0.0046 | 0.169 | 0.110 | -0.060 | -0.005 | 0.018 | -0.028 | -0.044 |
| Gross rent, fuel | 0.0315 | 0.108 | 0.125 | 0.017 | 0.034 | -0.016 | 0.028 | -0.028 |
| House furnishings, operations | 0.0253 | 0.100 | 0.122 | 0.022 | 0.027 | 0.039 | -0.056 | 0.012 |
| Medical care | 0.0237 | 0.033 | 0.112 | 0.079 | 0.026 | -0.042 | 0.062 | 0.034 |
| Transport, communication | 0.0295 | 0.050 | 0.093 | 0.043 | 0.032 | 0.011 | -0.012 | 0.012 |
| Recreation | 0.0193 | 0.031 | 0.041 | 0.010 | 0.021 | -0.009 | 0.013 | -0.014 |
| Education | -0.0040 | 0.022 | 0.042 | 0.021 | -0.004 | -0.007 | 0.016 | 0.016 |
| Other expenditures | 0.0328 | 0.081 | 0.121 | 0.040 | 0.036 | -0.009 | 0.017 | -0.003 |

which implies that the marginal share of good $j$ (mentioned at the end of the previous paragraph) exceeds the budget share $\bar{w}_{jt}$ by a constant $\beta_j$. These $\beta$'s are specified numerically in column (2) of Table I; a positive (negative) $\beta_j$ implies that $j$ is a luxury (necessity). Working's model is extended by means of a substitution term under the assumption of preference independence with a constant income flexibility $\phi$ which is specified as -0.5259; see Theil and Finke (1984) for further details.

The net flow from $j$ to $i$ during the transition from year $t$ - 1 to year $t$ can now be expressed as the sum of four components:

$$\text{real-income component} = (\bar{w}_{jt}\,\beta_i - \bar{w}_{it}\,\beta_j)DQ_t\,,$$

$$\text{substitution component} = \phi\,(\bar{w}_{it} + \beta_i)\,(\bar{w}_{jt} + \beta_j)\,(Dp_{it} - Dp_{jt})\,,$$

$$\text{direct price component} = \bar{w}_{it}\,\bar{w}_{jt}\,(Dp_{it} - Dp_{jt})\,,$$

$$\text{residual component} = (\bar{w}_{jt} + \beta_j)\,\varepsilon_{it} - (\bar{w}_{it} + \beta_i)\,\varepsilon_{jt}\,.$$

The real-income component implies that an increase (decrease) in real income generates a positive net flow to the good with the larger (smaller) income elasticity. The substitution component implies that an increase in the relative price of either good generates a positive net flow to the other good. The third component is also a price term but of opposite sign. This component results from the price term in (1); we refer to it as the direct price component of the net flow. (The substitution component is an 'indirect' component; it results from the price effect on the quantities consumed.) The last component is residual because it concerns the error terms $\varepsilon_{it}$ of the demand equations.

The net flows and their components can be arranged in the form of matrices of order 10 × 10. Since there are 25 pairs of successive years in the period 1952-1977, this yields 125 matrices. We can obtain a more manageable picture by summing the net flows and their components over these 25 years. This yields Table II which will be discussed in the next paragraph. Here we consider the summary picture in columns (3) to (9) of Table I. Note the drastic decline of the budget share of food from 1952 to 1977 [first row of Table I, columns (3) to (5)]; it is largely caused by the substantial negative real-income component. Also note the considerable increase in the budget share of medical care (sixth row of Table I); as column (8) indicates, this has a great deal to do with the direct price component.

In Table II all entries have been multiplied by 100 so that they provide net flows and their components in percentage form. By reordering the 10 goods slightly it is possible to obtain a net-flow matrix with positive elements above the diagonal. The result is shown at the top of Table II. Thus, during the aggregate transition from 1952 to 1977 (obtained by summing the entries of the 25 annual transitions) food contributed positively to the budget shares of the nine other goods, clothing contributed positively to the budget shares of all except food, and so on. Note in particular the large net flows toward medical care: in each row above the diagonal, the largest element is that in the last column.

**TABLE II**. Net Flows Among 10 Goods and Their Components, 1952-1977[a]

| Food | Clothing, Footwear | Beverages, tobacco | Gross rent, fuel | Recreation | House furnishings, operations | Other expenditures | Transport, communi-cations | Education | Medical care | |
|---|---|---|---|---|---|---|---|---|---|---|
| *Net flows* | | | | | | | | | | |
| 0 | 1.27 | 0.63 | 2.54 | 1.08 | 1.88 | 2.54 | 1.65 | 0.88 | 3.06 | Food |
| -1.27 | 0 | 0.17 | 0.95 | 0.41 | 1.23 | 1.24 | 1.10 | 0.48 | 1.67 | Clothing |
| -0.63 | -0.17 | 0 | 0.28 | 0.14 | 0.36 | 0.44 | 0.41 | 0.19 | 0.65 | Beverages |
| -2.54 | -0.95 | -0.28 | 0 | 0.05 | 0.26 | 0.32 | 0.52 | 0.16 | 0.72 | Rent |
| -1.08 | -0.41 | -0.14 | -0.05 | 0 | 0.07 | 0.09 | 0.19 | 0.04 | 0.25 | Recreation |
| -1.88 | -1.23 | -0.36 | -0.26 | -0.07 | 0 | 0.16 | 0.37 | 0.27 | 0.82 | Furnishings |
| -2.54 | -1.24 | -0.44 | -0.32 | -0.09 | -0.16 | 0 | 0.25 | 0.09 | 0.48 | Other |
| -1.65 | -1.10 | -0.41 | -0.52 | -0.19 | -0.37 | -0.25 | 0 | 0.03 | 0.15 | Transport |
| -0.88 | -0.48 | -0.19 | -0.16 | -0.04 | -0.27 | -0.09 | -0.03 | 0 | 0.10 | Education |
| -3.06 | -1.67 | -0.65 | -0.72 | -0.25 | -0.82 | -0.48 | -0.15 | -0.10 | 0 | Medical |
| *Real-income components* | | | | | | | | | | |
| | 2.36 | 1.10 | 2.70 | 1.12 | 2.81 | 2.52 | 1.95 | 0.40 | 1.76 | Food |
| | | 0.05 | 0.56 | 0.33 | 0.47 | 0.58 | 0.51 | -0.05 | 0.42 | Clothing |
| | | | 0.21 | 0.13 | 0.16 | 0.22 | 0.20 | -0.03 | 0.16 | Beverages |
| | | | | 0.11 | -0.13 | 0.06 | 0.12 | -0.15 | 0.06 | Rent |
| | | | | | -0.17 | -0.08 | -0.03 | -0.08 | -0.05 | Recreation |
| | | | | | | 0.18 | 0.22 | -0.14 | 0.14 | Furnishings |
| | | | | | | | 0.07 | -0.15 | 0.01 | Other |
| | | | | | | | | -0.13 | -0.04 | Transport |
| | | | | | | | | | 0.11 | Education |

[a] All entries to be divided by 100.

| | | | | | | | | | |
|---|---|---|---|---|---|---|---|---|---|
| *Substitution components* | | | | | | | | | |
| 0.21 | 0.02 | -0.35 | -0.13 | 0.24 | -0.19 | 0.05 | -0.07 | -0.45 | Food |
| | 0.00 | -0.50 | -0.21 | 0.27 | -0.32 | 0.01 | -0.12 | -0.68 | Clothing |
| | | -0.25 | -0.12 | 0.10 | -0.21 | -0.04 | -0.08 | -0.39 | Beverages |
| | | | -0.06 | 0.76 | 0.04 | 0.28 | -0.07 | -0.48 | Rent |
| | | | | 0.35 | 0.07 | 0.15 | -0.01 | -0.15 | Recreation |
| | | | | | -0.66 | -0.23 | -0.22 | -1.03 | Furnishings |
| | | | | | | 0.22 | -0.07 | -0.47 | Other |
| | | | | | | | -0.10 | -0.52 | Transport |
| | | | | | | | | -0.05 | Education |
| *Direct price components* | | | | | | | | | |
| -0.65 | -0.20 | 1.08 | 0.41 | -1.07 | 0.67 | -0.15 | 0.44 | 1.67 | Food |
| | -0.01 | 0.75 | 0.26 | -0.45 | 0.45 | -0.04 | 0.27 | 0.94 | Clothing |
| | | 0.36 | 0.15 | -0.15 | 0.30 | 0.06 | 0.16 | 0.55 | Beverages |
| | | | 0.06 | -0.94 | -0.04 | -0.28 | 0.11 | 0.53 | Rent |
| | | | | -0.36 | -0.07 | -0.13 | 0.02 | 0.14 | Recreation |
| | | | | | 0.78 | 0.27 | 0.39 | 1.23 | Furnishings |
| | | | | | | -0.22 | 0.11 | 0.51 | Other |
| | | | | | | | 0.15 | 0.52 | Transport |
| | | | | | | | | 0.08 | Education |
| *Residual components* | | | | | | | | | |
| -0.65 | -0.28 | -0.89 | -0.32 | -0.10 | -0.46 | -0.20 | 0.12 | 0.08 | Food |
| | 0.13 | 0.13 | 0.04 | 0.94 | 0.54 | 0.61 | 0.38 | 0.98 | Clothing |
| | | -0.04 | -0.02 | 0.25 | 0.13 | 0.19 | 0.14 | 0.33 | Beverages |
| | | | -0.07 | 0.56 | 0.26 | 0.40 | 0.28 | 0.61 | Rent |
| | | | | 0.25 | 0.16 | 0.19 | 0.12 | 0.31 | Recreation |
| | | | | | -0.15 | 0.12 | 0.24 | 0.48 | Furnishings |
| | | | | | | 0.18 | 0.19 | 0.44 | Other |
| | | | | | | | 0.11 | 0.18 | Transport |
| | | | | | | | | -0.04 | Education |

[a] All entries to be divided by 100.

Since the matrices of net flows and their components are skew-symmetric, it is sufficient to show the elements above the diagonal. This procedure is followed for the four component matrices in Table II. Note that the real-income components are mostly positive; this is so because the ordering of the 10 goods in Table II is close to the ordering according to increasing income elasticities (education and recreation are the major exceptions). The real-income components tend to be larger than the three others. Counting those components that exceed 1 percent, we have eight for real income (all originating from food), four direct price components (all originating from food or going to medical care), one substitution component (going to medical care), and no residual component. Nevertheless, many residual components are not particularly small. This should not surprise us, since the $\varepsilon_{it}$'s in these components are summed over 25 values of $t$. If the $\varepsilon_{it}$'s are serially independent, this summation yields variances which are 25 times larger than the variances of the individual $\varepsilon_{it}$'s.[1]

## References

Theil, H.: 1980, *The System-Wide Approach to Microeconomics*, University of Chicago Press, Chicago, Illinois.

Theil, H. and R. Finke: 1984, "A Time Series Analysis of a Demand System Based on Cross-Country Coefficient Estimates," *Economics Letters*, **15**, nos. 3-4, 245-250.

Working, H.: 1943, "Statistical Laws of Family Expenditure," *Journal of the American Statistical Association*, **38**, 43-56.

[1] Also note that the residual components shown (those above the diagonal) are predominantly positive. This is a spurious effect (at least in part) due to the ranking of the goods so that the net flows above the diagonal are positive.

# SECTION 4.2: ECONOMIC INEQUALITY AND INTERNATIONAL COMPARISONS

CHAPTER 48

# INTERNATIONAL INEQUALITIES AND GENERAL CRITERIA FOR DEVELOPMENT AID*

HENRI THEIL
*Netherlands School of Economics*
*(now Erasmus University)*
*Rotterdam, The Netherlands*

Translated from Dutch[1] by S.J. Wells

## I

The study of the distribution of income forms one of the most traditional branches of econometrics. In the last century, when the term 'econometrics' was still unknown, investigators like Pareto carefully analysed many distribution patterns; their work is of great interest even today because of the light which it throws upon the problems of social inequality of that time. However, these problems all concern relationships within single national units, and much less consideration has been given to the differences of welfare between national units. A rough idea of these differences can be obtained by looking at the distribution of *per capita* incomes as between different countries. Such a comparison is hardly possible before 1949, but for that year the Statistical Office of the United Nations has made estimates (expressed in U.S. dollars) of the national and *per capita* incomes of seventy countries which between them accounted for about 90 per cent of the world population.[2] This is the subject which I intend to discuss here. I will compare the distribution of *per capita* incomes between countries with the classical distributions of individual incomes within single countries; I shall also try to show how in principle the

* This translation of the article (from Dutch) first appeared in *International Economic Papers*, **10** (1960), 42-63. Reprinted with the permission of MacMillan Publishing, United Kingdom.

[1] "Enige Kwantitatieve Aspecten van het Probleem der Hulpverlening aan Onderontwikkelde Landen," *De Economist*, Vol. 101, **11** (November 1953), pp. 721-749.

The author obtained his doctorate at the University of Amsterdam in 1951 and was appointed Professor of Econometrics at the Nederlandsche Economische Hoogeschool at Rotterdam in 1953; the present paper is a translation of the inaugural address which he gave on taking up his chair. He was a staff member of the Central Planning Bureau at The Hague from 1952 to 1955, and in 1956 he became Director of the Econometrisch Instituut at the Hoogeschool. During the last five years he has also been a visiting professor at Chicago, Stanford and Harvard. Professor Theil is the author of two books, *Linear Aggregation of Economic Relations* (1954) and *Economic Forecasts and Policy* (1958).

[2] *National and Per Capita Incomes of Seventy Countries in 1949, Expressed in U.S. Dollars*, Statistical Papers, Series E, No. 1, Statistical Office of the United Nations, New York, 1950.

distribution of *per capita* incomes can be modified, and how an econometrician would treat such a process of modification.

## II

It is scarcely necessary to stress that the data of the Statistical Office are in a number of cases little more than rough approximations. In particular, in the underdeveloped countries much relevant information is either unobtainable or available only in part; in addition, as a result of the underlying differences between the economic structures of the various countries the statistics are far from completely comparable. If, however, we can assume in the first instance that the published data are largely correct, it is evident that world incomes are distributed unevenly to a really alarming degree. The twenty-five poorest countries, which between them embrace 54 per cent of world population as considered in this paper, together have an income that does not amount to more than 9 per cent of the total. On the other hand, the eight richest countries include 11 per cent of world population but collectively enjoy an income amounting to 56 per cent of the total. In the poorest countries the standard of living is deplorably low; for the group of twenty-five countries in this category the income level is below $100 per head, and for the group of the poorest twelve countries it is even below $50.

One might perhaps wonder how human beings can exist at all at such a low standard of living. In the Netherlands and likewise in other developed countries it would clearly be impossible. But in countries which are less privileged it is possible to keep oneself alive on a diet which is very cheap, little varied and extremely inferior in quality. The effects of catering for physical needs in such a way can be imagined; in a country like India, for instance, infant mortality is such that the average expectation of life is only thirty years, as against seventy in the Netherlands. It should, however, be noted in this connection that for the poorest countries the estimate of the level of income per head is probably somewhat on the low side. In these countries a number of non-monetary transactions take place, and one can easily overlook items under this heading which are of relatively great importance in a poor area, whereas the same items would be insignificant in a more developed country.[3] However, even if these divergences are relatively important, one cannot expect the actual pattern of the distribution of *per capita* incomes to be characterized by a small or even a moderate dispersion.

It would seem rather obvious to base a statement about the degree of inequality of *per capita* incomes as between different countries upon our empirically derived knowledge of the distribution of individual incomes within single countries. However, the distribution of *per capita* incomes and the distribution of incomes between individuals are somewhat different in character. Evidently, the former is not the distribution of individual incomes all over the world. Such a distribution would have little practical value, for problems concerning the distribution of incomes between individuals are usually

---

[3] *National and Per Capita Incomes of Seventy Countries ..., op. cit.*

considered at a national rather than at an international level. On the contrary, in the international field it is more fruitful to deal with international problems of the distribution of income between individuals in two stages — inequalities between countries and inequalities within countries. It is therefore appropriate to examine the distribution of *per capita* incomes and the distribution of incomes between individuals separately; this introduces a conceptual distinction which accords with political reality.[4]

We shall examine first some quantitative aspects of the distribution of income between individuals. It has now been recognized for a considerable time that this distribution can in many cases be approximately described by a simple mathematical relationship called the Pareto distribution. Such distributions are characterized by a parameter known as the Pareto coefficient, which is a measure of the way in which individual incomes are grouped round their mean. If one is dealing with considerable inequalities the Pareto coefficient is low; in the opposite case, it is high. In most cases the values for these coefficients have been found to lie in the neighbourhood of $1\frac{1}{2}$ to 2; e.g., a value of about 2 was calculated for the distribution obtained in the Netherlands in 1948.

If we wish to compare the *per capita* income distribution between countries on similar lines, certain striking facts appear. In the first place, the Pareto distribution turns out to be not quite accurate as a representation of *per capita* incomes, yet given the quality of the income data it is not a bad approximation. In the second place, and this is more important, the appropriate Pareto coefficient is markedly lower than has ever been found for distributions of incomes between individuals; this points to much greater inequalities between countries than are usually found within a country, for the Pareto coefficient of the *per capita* income distribution is as low as two-thirds. Against this one can plead that owing to the somewhat conservative nature of the income estimates for the poor countries the difference is presumably overstated. It must, however, be remembered that the actual *per capita* income distribution will approach closely to the distribution of incomes between individuals only if the estimates are very much too low. Assume, for example, that *per capita* incomes in the richest countries are correctly calculated, that those of the poorest countries are underestimated to such an extent that their actual *per capita* income levels are twice as high as those which appear in the data, and that for the remaining countries the size of the error depends upon their relative position in the income scale; if the corresponding adjustments are made, the Pareto coefficient would be raised from two-thirds to about four-fifths. An increase to unity implies that the incomes of the poorest countries are estimated at only one quarter of what they really are, and yet a Pareto coefficient as low as unity is never found for the income distribution within a

[4] At the same time this way of looking at the problems takes care of a possible objection, namely, that the distribution of *per capita* incomes depends upon the way in which individuals are grouped within national units, and that the approach is thus of only relative value. For instance, one can think of South Africa as being divided into a white and a coloured part so that the present-day level of South African income per head would be replaced by a higher average level for the white part and a lower one for the coloured part, with greater inequality in *per capita* incomes as a result. The answer to this is that quite clearly defined national units are recognized by political reality.

country. Only if really unacceptable adjustments are made, will one arrive at a distribution of *per capita* incomes between countries which shows any resemblance to the normal pattern of the distribution of income within countries. Accordingly, one cannot avoid the conclusion that income differences within national frontiers are small in comparison with those existing between national entities. But this is not all. For the pattern of the distribution of income between individuals the Pareto distribution is a valid approximation only for incomes above a certain boundary. Below that boundary the number of income recipients is always lower than this distribution would imply, so that a higher boundary indicates a less frequent incidence of poverty. In principle the same holds for the distribution of *per capita* incomes, but the great difference is that the boundary below which the Pareto curve loses it validity now lies much lower than it does when the Pareto distribution is applied to the incomes of individuals. Thus, not only the difference between the Pareto coefficients but also the different degree of validity of the Pareto distribution point to markedly greater income inequalities between countries than within countries.[5]

## III

So much for the present situation. Next we have the important problem of the trend of income differences over time; to begin with, let us look at the development of individual incomes. Over the last decades a gradual levelling process has taken place in economically developed countries; this has meant that the value of the Pareto coefficients has been raised to a level higher than that ruling hitherto. It is true that this has not been an uninterrupted process; inequalities have constantly been subject to cyclical fluctuations - in times of depression higher incomes have been affected more than lower incomes - but on the whole the process has been clearly marked even if we eliminate the effects of mounting progressive taxation. Some quantitative information on this point can be drawn from Colin Clark's *The Conditions of Economic Progress* in which about 150 Pareto coefficients are set out, ranging from that of Italy in Cicero's time and England in 1688 to those of Burma and the United States at the present time. If one selects from this material the data for those countries which are now economically developed, one gets the impression that in the period from the beginning of the Industrial Revolution to the first World War income inequalities were in general somewhat, but not much, less than in the preceding period, while after 1919 the levelling process was markedly speeded up. If we then set next to this the Pareto coefficients for the countries which are still underdeveloped, we get a picture of striking contrast to the position of developed countries in the modern world, a picture which suggests that present-day inequalities in the poor countries are of the same order of magnitude as inequalities in the developed

[5] See Appendix A.1.1 for the histogram of the distribution of income per head and — for comparison — that of the distribution of income within the Netherlands in 1948. This is followed by the two distribution patterns expressed on a double logarithmic scale, from which the Pareto coefficients can be read off.

countries when these stood on the threshold of the Industrial Revolution.[6] The movement towards greater equality that has been so marked in the developed countries has scarcely begun in the poor countries.

An obvious question is how this development of the distribution of income between individuals in the advanced countries compares with the development of the world's *per capita* income distribution. Of course it is not easy to estimate the *per capita* distribution in Cicero's time and I shall therefore limit myself to the last hundred years. Even this, however, is far from straightforward because relevant data for a period as long as this are notoriously scarce. On the other hand, detailed information is not really necessary in order to form an overall impression of the trend of *per capita* incomes. One can assume that it is hardly conceivable that in the poorest countries poverty could have been much more serious a century ago than it is today. Certainly this is true of the non-urban population, and in such countries the rural workers make up the greater part of the population even today. Not that national income has failed to rise in these countries, but the increase has frequently been absorbed in large measure by population growth, so that *per capita* incomes have in many cases not increased or have increased only slightly. By contrast, the improvement of the standard of living in North America and in Western Europe is so evident that it is hardly necessary to point it out. We must conclude that the present-day distribution of *per capita* incomes is the result of a process which — certainly during the last hundred years — has implied growing divergences. This development is, therefore, in a wholly different direction from that taken by individual inequalities within economically developed countries.

The question arises whether the process will continue to be marked by such divergences in the future. The answer to this question is necessarily of a somewhat speculative character, but with the aid of published plans and forecasts one can obtain some general impressions. Thus, in the Paley Report which dealt with the prospective supplies of raw materials for United States consumption in 1975 it was estimated that the national product of the United States would be about doubled, while the increase in population would continue to be on a much more limited scale (even though it is quite important). Calculations of the Central Planning Bureau for the Netherlands relating to the year 1970 likewise assume that there will be a substantial increase in income and consumption per head. By contrast, the Indian Five-Year Plan is much more pessimistic. In India they will be forced to try raising their living standards with the aid of domestic investment, but it is not expected that in the first ten to fifteen years this will lead to any considerable improvement in the general standard of living. The reasons for this are obvious. On the one hand, in the case of a poor country only a small percentage of the national income is (normally) devoted to increasing the supply of capital goods, so that the rate of increase of national income remains limited. On the other hand, the size of the population in a country like India is all the time increasing at a rapid rate, so that the greater part of even a moderate expansion in output of capital goods is of necessity absorbed by the increase in population, and therefore the standard of living based on this

[6] See Appendix A.1.2 for the relevant histograms of the Pareto coefficients.

expansion is not much higher than that of the initial population. An obvious retort is, perhaps, that in these countries there is a marked shortage of capital, and if this reflected itself in a high average rate of interest, capital funds would automatically be attracted from the more developed countries. However, in spite of the fact that the import of capital from abroad includes significant sums of money, flows of this kind are limited by the distinct degree of uncertainty which is a marked characteristic of external economic relations. This question is particularly relevant at the present time, since a large number of underdeveloped countries have gained their independence and thus have really become regarded as "foreign." All in all, it would not be surprising if the *per capita* income distribution in the years immediately ahead, and perhaps even for decades, were to continue to develop along the lines followed up to the present — that is, in the direction of continually increasing inequality.

As against this, however, one important point must be remembered. A feature of recent years has been the growth of various forms of investment from other, non-private, sources. The United Nations organization has offered technical aid to the underdeveloped territories. The Americans have launched their *Point Four Programme*, the British their *Colombo Plan*, the Norwegians have contributed to the development of the Indian fisheries and the Netherlands have set up the *Institute of Social Studies*, where students from the underdeveloped countries can gain a share of some of the knowledge which such countries often so sadly lack; and so one can go on.

Such programmes are important and valuable not only because they form a supplement to the long-established flow of private capital, but also because of the new atmosphere which this new source of capital has created. The question arises, however, whether the scope of these programmes is sufficient — sufficient with respect to certain alternative objectives which can be laid down. This problem of the relationship between means and ends with regard to aid for underdeveloped countries is one which I should like to elaborate a little further. Naturally this is a problem with many facets, and it is scarcely possible for me in this survey to treat the matter very fully. I shall accordingly limit myself as far as possible to the quantitative aspects.

A remark on the nature of the objective seems called for. If it is desired to help underdeveloped and thus poor countries, then this will in general imply that living standards in these countries are to be raised to a certain minimum level. One can express this more precisely by saying that the *per capita* incomes of the poorest countries must be raised within a certain time to a stipulated level. The resources necessary for this must be obtained from these countries themselves and possibly also from the richest countries which will accordingly have to make certain sacrifices. The relationship between results and sacrifices should be the basis for answering the question whether or not any measures should be taken, and if so, which measures. This decision should be determined mainly by ethical and political considerations. However, the relationship between results and sacrifices itself clearly has quantitative aspects, and an econometric model, describing the development of incomes in the different countries as influenced by alternative measures, is accordingly an appropriate means of obtaining an insight into this relationship.

## IV

An econometric model in its usual form is a system of algebraic equations which describe the process by which certain economic variables are determined numerically. That such a description is in a simplified and approximate form must necessarily be the case, and as such it speaks for itself. A description of a social process, whether in words or in symbols, cannot in every respect be close to reality. However, this in any case is not necessary. In each investigation one considers certain well defined aspects of the problem, and those matters which are not of immediate concern are given less attention. In the case of the problem at hand it is the level of incomes per head and their growth over time which are of preponderant significance; they are of more significance than, for example, the differences between the incomes of individuals within countries. Attention is accordingly concentrated on the growth of incomes and, in particular, on long-term growth, for one would not expect that in the short run, i.e., within the space of a few years, much could be done for the relief of the poorest countries. I may add that the possibility of constructing adequate models for development objectives is still limited; therefore, in order not to create the impression that I propose to do more than is practicable, I shall limit myself to the simple specifications of the Harrod-Domar type when there are no compelling reasons for preferring more complicated forms.

We consider first the relatively rich industrialized countries, and begin with their national incomes or national products measured at constant prices. This aggregate is made up of consumption (interpreted in a wide sense), net investment, and possibly a contribution for the development of poor countries. Taking a long-term view one can regard consumption as approximately proportionate to income after the subtraction of the amount of the aid. Similarly one can regard the long run stock of capital goods (of which net investments represent the annual increment) as being proportional to the national product. These are two macro-economic behavioural relationships. It is then necessary to specify the amount of the aid. It seems rather obvious to make this quantity dependent upon the rate of growth of national income and to put it, say, equal to a fixed percentage of the trend value of national income — a percentage which can be determined at a round table conference and which can in principle differ from country to country. Finally, an assumption must be made regarding the trend of population growth; this is necessary in order to reduce the aggregate quantities to a *per capita* basis. The simplest assumption is that of a constant annual percentage increase; by choosing a suitable average of different annual percentage rates of increase a rough idea of the course of demographic trends is obtained.

Together with the identities this gives a model of six equations from which the rate of growth of income, of consumption and of aid can be determined. The growth of income appears to be closely dependent upon that part of national income which is invested and, furthermore, upon the ratio of capital to output. The percentage that is devoted to aid seems to be of hardly any significance, at least so long as it remains within certain limits. This must be so, since productive capacity does not appear in the long run to be in any marked degree influenced by a switch in selling to hitherto unspecified purchasers. However, these sales have to be financed internally, and this influences consumption. The sacrifices of the contributing countries must therefore be looked for in the field of consumption rather than in production. For example, a contribution equivalent to 2 per cent of the national income lowers the level of consumption by slightly more than 2 per cent but has practically no effect upon the growth of income. Thus as income itself continues to grow undisturbed, the volume of aid will grow in proportion to the income trend. It will rise at the same percentage rate from year to year depending upon the ratio of income to investment and to the stock of capital. If these ratios are the same for all the contributing countries, the contribution from each one will rise at the same percentage rate, and so will the total aid which is made available. Very broadly speaking this condition is fulfilled, and hence the following conclusion is justified: if a number of economically developed countries each year set aside a fixed percentage of the trend value of their national incomes, then the total contribution that becomes available in this way will rise from year to year at about the same rate as that at which the income of *each* of these countries rises.

A steadily growing contribution would thus become available and should be used for the development of the poorest countries. The effect of this can likewise be traced by means of a model — this time a model relating to the poor, underdeveloped areas. It is noteworthy that although the economic structure of these countries is so different, some fundamental macro-economic characteristics appear to show a certain similarity to those of the more developed countries. For example, the ratio of capital to output seems to be of the same order of magnitude. On the other hand, there are some other aspects, such as demographic development, where in the past differences have been obvious. An improvement in the standards of living leads to a fall of mortality and not, at least in the short run, to a fall in the birth rate. On the other hand, it is true that the Indian government, for example, is well aware of this process and has even been considering the adoption of measures designed to limit the percentage rate of population increase. One has not much experience to fall back on in this field, and accordingly the assumption of a constant percentage rate of increase seems the best available. In this way a macro-economic model is built which — as in the case of the developed countries — consists of six equations, but there are certain differences. In particular, the contribution which in the developed countries has to be set aside for the granting of aid is now absent; in its place there is a contribution which the poor countries receive and which is earmarked for economic development. It therefore seems obvious to devote this contribution to productive purposes. The increase in the supply of capital goods can then be regarded as being made up of two factors — net investment out of domestic output and finance received from external sources.

With the aid of this model it is possible to form some idea of trends in the economies of the underdeveloped countries. However, it is useful to make a distinction between two alternative possibilities with regard to investment out of domestic resources. One can in the first place assume that this investment will amount to a fixed and unchanged percentage of national income; generally this would be lower than the corresponding percentage for the developed countries. It can secondly be assumed that the governments of the underdeveloped countries would wish to push this percentage to a higher level, e.g., through raising the present relatively low rate of taxation on high incomes and devoting the proceeds to the finance of investment projects. From the model it can be seen that in the first case — when the poor countries are assumed to save less than the rich countries — the national incomes of the poor countries certainly increase in an absolute sense, but not relatively to the growth of income in the richer countries, unless aid contributions from the rich countries compensate for the difference in the rate of savings. There is thus a possibility that the inequality of the *per capita* income distribution might increase rather than diminish. A more rapid development of the poorest countries could be brought about in two ways — by action taken in the countries in question to raise the level of savings in such a way that other things being equal their rate of growth keeps in step with that of the richest countries, and by the receipt of a contribution from external sources. This would permit a higher rate of growth and thereby enable these countries gradually to gain ground. Assume, for example, that as a result of an increase in savings national incomes were to grow by 2 per cent a year in the absence of external help and that this rate of savings amounts to 10 per cent of income. If the amount of help received in the first year is equivalent to 5 per cent of the national income, i.e., half the volume of savings, then the percentage rate of increase of the national income would also be raised by one-half, i.e., from 2 to 3 per cent. This percentage would gradually decrease because the amount of aid would not rise as rapidly as income, the amount of the aid bearing always a constant ratio to the trend value of income in the developed countries, which is growing relatively more slowly. However, the percentage remains higher than that obtained in the richer countries. With respect to income the situation is thus favourable. Consumption, on the other hand, will grow less fast, at least in the first years, because the raising of the level of saving implies that relatively fewer resources can be allocated to consumption.

## V

So much for the assumptions and for some general results of the models. In order to arrive at numerical conclusions it is necessary to be somewhat more specific about targets. No advantage is served by letting the amounts of aid received and granted depend upon the outcome of negotiations with, e.g., an international body; the danger of this is the high degree of arbitrariness which is reflected in the results of such negotiations. It is preferable first to formulate a general criterion, in which particular countries are not named. Once this criterion has been established, discussion can take place in a more objective manner. The results can then be applied to particular countries, naturally after the opportunity has been taken to make any necessary corrections.

In the framework of a general analysis of means and ends it is not very satisfactory to choose a single numerical aim or criterion, and it is much more sensible to consider a group of alternative objectives. One rather obvious group of this kind can be described in the following terms. The countries with the lowest *per capita* incomes are the most eligible for aid. One can then decide upon a certain minimum level of subsistence, a marginal level below which human life is considered intolerable. One might take, for example, $100 a year per head, the average standard of living of the Japanese.

However, in framing long-term policies the adoption of this level must not be interpreted too rigidly. Two centuries ago, when even an English queen did not see any one of her seventeen children survive to the age of eleven years, people's ideas with respect to the minimum standard of living were without doubt different from what they are today. In modern times progress is rapid, and in proposing a target it is advisable to take predictable changes of aims into account. We must therefore conceive of a flexible marginal income level, for instance, one that grows in step with the *per capita* incomes in the wealthier countries. The target then becomes this: to lift the standard of living in the countries which now find themselves below the adopted minimum to this marginal level in a given time. For example, if we accept for the present an income level of $100 per head, the *per capita* income level in Japan, as the minimum, and if we envisage a time limit of 50 years, then the target is the following: to raise within 50 years the *per capita* incomes of all countries which are at present poorer than Japan to the level that Japan will herself have reached after 50 years. The range of objectives within which a choice can be made is thus determined by the initial value of the minimum income level and by the time period in which it is to be reached; the further movement of the minimum level over time is then no longer subject to choice since it rises proportionally to the *per capita* incomes of the richer countries.

The objective thus specified determines the amount of resources which are necessary for its realization. If calculations are based on the study of the United Nations Statistical Office and therefore confined to the countries covered by this investigation, it is found that an annual sum of around $5 thousand million (at 1949 prices) is required if the poor countries are to reach a minimum income level initially fixed at $100 within a period of 50 years. This amount must be shared by about half the world's population. The question now arises which countries should contribute. It seems natural to select for this purpose those countries (of which the Netherlands is one) in which the level of income per head amounts to at least, say, $400 to $500 a year. In either case, the total incomes of these countries together come to about $300 thousand million — i.e., the required amount of about $5 thousand million represents something less than 2 per cent of their total national output. On the other hand, if we keep the same minimum income level but now require it to be reached in 25 years, $10 to $11 thousand million are necessary, i.e., about $3\frac{1}{2}$ per cent of the total national incomes of the contributing countries. The same percentage being paid over a 50-year period would permit the *per capita* income level of Yugoslavia to be reached, corresponding to an initial level of $150; in 75 years a level initially fixed at $200 would be attained. The significance of all these percentages can be described most clearly in terms of the amount of consumption sacrificed by the richer countries. The model shows that for every one per cent of national income sacrificed for the needs of underdeveloped countries the rate of growth of *per capita* consumption will be held back for a period of about eight months. For example, a contribution of $3\frac{1}{2}$ per cent means that the trend value of *per capita* consumption will at any period of time be at the level which but for these contributions would have been reached two years earlier.[7] In this way one can always picture the sacrifices of the richer countries as a deliberate postponement of the enjoyment of the fruits of their economic progress.

It is necessary to examine further the position of particular countries. The Communist countries hardly play a role in these considerations because the standard of living of their people is such that they are not eligible for the receipt of aid, nor are they required to grant it — in the pattern of world *per capita* incomes these countries all belong to the middle group. There is one important exception — China. She is the largest country in the world and at the same time one of the poorest of all. Should China hold aloof, then the annual amount of aid required to reach the Japanese or Yugoslav level can be reduced by about one half. The contributing countries would thus be able to halve their percentages without harming the rest of the poorer countries. If, however, the United States should stand apart, the picture would again be wholly different. The United states is by far the richest country and at the same time is one of the largest. In 1949 her *per capita* income amounted to almost $1,500, whereas that of the next richest country, Canada, failes to reach even $900 — 40 per cent less. If we further confine our list of developed countries to a limit of $500 per head, one is left with a group of ten countries which together with Canada have a smaller total number of inhabitants than has the United States alone. It is accordingly hardly surprising that America's national income accounts for about 70 per cent of the total income of all countries which are potentially eligible to make contributions. This more than anything else indicates the key position which the United States holds in these matters. It also throws light on the significance of President Eisenhower's offer in April of this year[8] under certain conditions to put part of the funds currently earmarked for military objectives into the aid programme for underdeveloped territories. At present military expenditure accounts for 15 to 20 per cent of the national income of the United States; a mere fraction of this would be quite sufficient to achieve noteworthy results.

## VI

It is worthwhile pointing out that if the economically developed world were in fact willing to surrender substantial sums, the magnitude of these amounts would be limited as much by the absorptive capacity of the underdeveloped countries as by the readiness of the richer countries to make these sacrifices. So long as the amounts involved are as small as is now the case, no problem arises; they are indeed so small that one can expect them to be effective only in the very long run. However, with aid on a large scale this would be different; for example, if one finds that the poorest countries would need to receive annually a sum greater than their present national income in order to reach within 25 years a minimum income level initially fixed at $200 a year, then one can only

[7] This result is based on certain numerical assumptions (see Appendix A.2.4).

[8] 1953.

conclude that for these countries such a programme is not at present feasible. One would then have to adopt a more modest objective, for example, the attainment by the poorest countries of this target somewhat later than by the less poor ones. Such adjustments will inevitably have to be made in any case. It may therefore be desirable to introduce the initial aid gradually. After all, a certain amount of preparation is necessary in order to raise the absorptive capacity, and this can take several years. Furthermore, certain adjustments must be made in our results arising from divergences in population trends, and in making estimates it must be remembered that the results of all these calculations are affected by errors in the measurement of present-day *per capita* incomes. The implication is that if in comparison with the *per capita* incomes of the richer countries those of the poorest countries have been underestimated, given objectives can be attained with the same resources in a shorter period.[9] A careful interpretation of the results of the model is accordingly desirable. An important advantage of the use of such models is, however, that with their aid one can directly infer the effects of any adjustments.

In the present state of economic knowledge we cannot predict the consequences of our actions with perfect precision. There is no Laplace formula by means of which one can foretell without error the course of events in the distant future; indeed, this will never be the case. However, we do have ready to hand the theory of probability, with the aid of which numerical probabilities can be attached to alternative outcomes. In principle, one has to make decisions with as full an insight into their consequences as is attainable, and this often amounts to the use of the probability distribution of possible outcomes. In practice this is a complicated procedure; in building models one generally limits oneself to the mean values of these distributions. However, it can be shown that under certain assumptions (which in most cases are only slightly limiting) such a short cut leads to the same choice of decisions as does the more complicated procedure.[10] This should be regarded as an adequate justification of the use of models which merely systematize. Their forecasts are approximations, sometimes rough approximations, but the actual policies based on these forecasts are less likely to go wrong due to a neglect of possible errors in the forecasts than are the original forecasts themselves.

---

[9] One should not make too much out of this "advantage." If it is decided to choose as a minimum the *per capita* income of those countries which according to the U.N. statisticians have an annual *per capita* income of, say, $100, then the numerical value of this minimum income level is also subject to observational errors. Nevertheless, if the degree of underestimation for the still poorer countries is relatively greater, some residual favourable effect will remain.

[10] See H. Theil: 1954, "Econometric Models and Welfare Maximization," *Weltwirtschaftliches Archiv*, **72**, 60-83.

## Appendix

### A.1. The Distribution of *Per Capita* Incomes and Some Distributions of Income Between Individuals

#### A.1.1. THE DISTRIBUTION OF PER CAPITA INCOMES (1949) AND THE DISTRIBUTION OF INCOME IN THE NETHERLANDS (1948)

Figure 1 is the histogram of the *per capita* income distribution derived from the study of the United Nations Statistical Office (see footnote 1). *Per capita* income (in U.S. dollars) is marked off on the horizontal axis and the area of the bars is proportional to the total number of inhabitants of the countries in which the level of *per capita* income falls in the relevant interval. By way of comparison we have in Figure 2 the histogram of the distribution of income in the Netherlands in 1948.

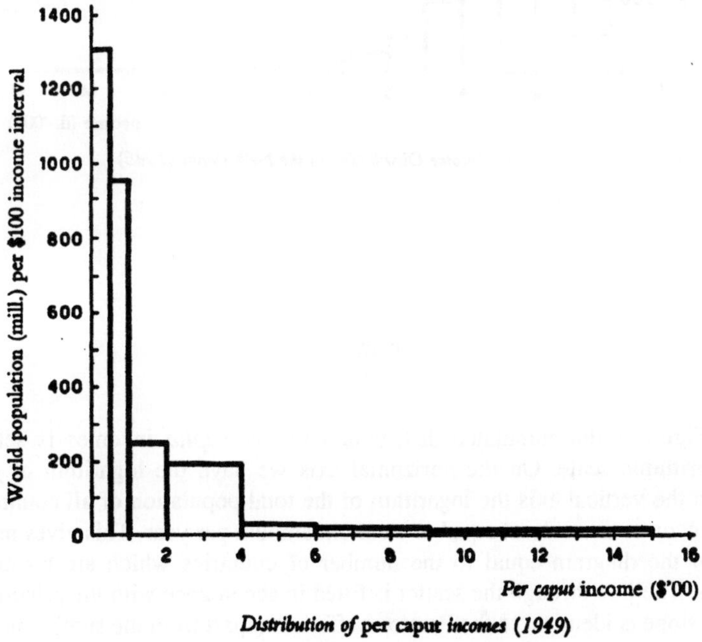


*Distribution of* per caput *incomes (1949)*

**Figure 1**

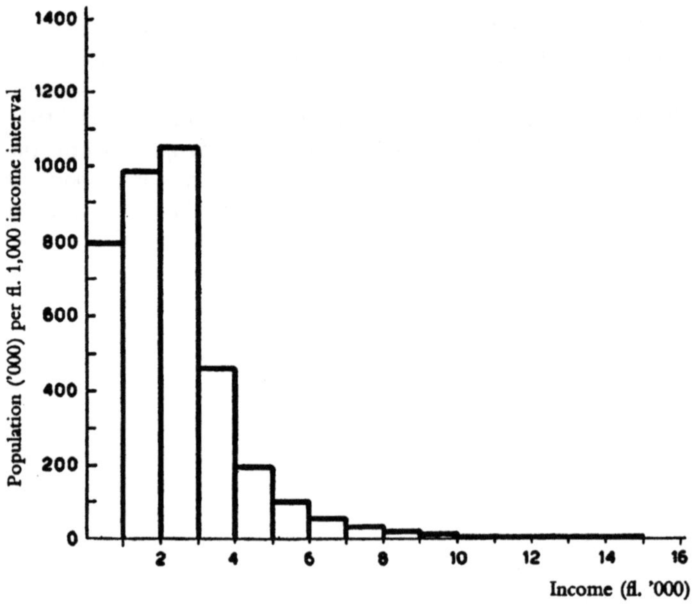


*Income Distribution in the Netherlands (1948)*

**Figure 2**

In Figure 3 the cumulated distribution of *per capita* incomes is set out on a double-logarithmic scale. On the horizontal axis we have the logarithm of *per capita* incomes, on the vertical axis the logarithm of the total population of all countries whose *per capita* incomes are at least equal to a certain amount per year. This gives us a number of points in the diagram equal to the number of countries which are covered by the calculations. The line through the scatter is fitted in accordance with the principle of least squares. Its slope is identical to the Pareto coefficient (apart from the sign) which amounts to 0.66. For the purpose of comparison the analogous scatter for the distribution of income in the Netherlands is plotted in Figure 4. The line through this scatter clearly has a markedly steeper slope.

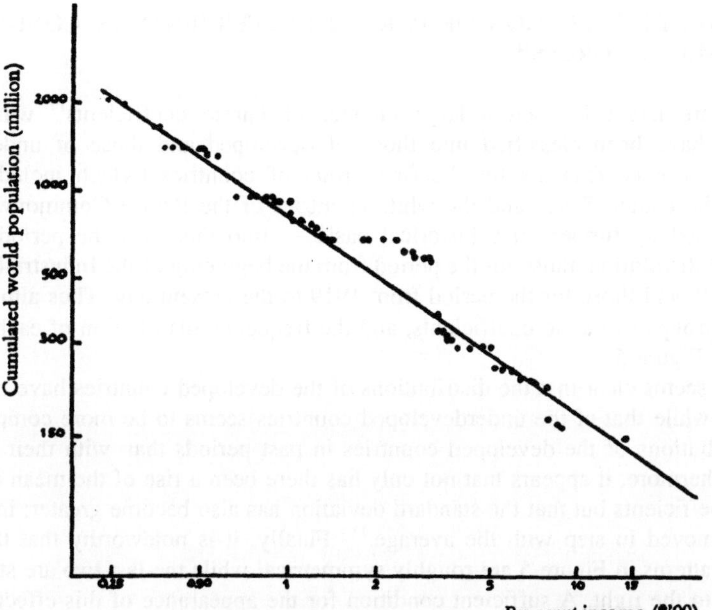


*Cumulated distribution of* per caput *incomes (1949)*

**Figure 3**

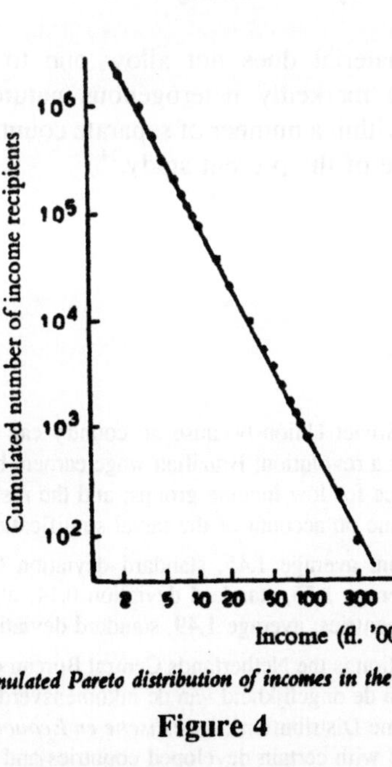


*Cumulated Pareto distribution of incomes in the Netherlands (1948)*

**Figure 4**

## A.1.2. THE DISTRIBUTION OF PARETO COEFFICIENTS IN CONDITIONS OF ECONOMIC PROGRESS[11]

Colin Clark has calculated a large number of Pareto coefficients[12] which for our purposes have been classified into those of developed and those of underdeveloped countries. The coefficients for the first group of countries (which includes Western Europe, the United States and the white countries of the British Commonwealth) have been divided up further on a historical basis — into those for the period before the Industrial Revolution, those for the period from the beginning of the Industrial Revolution up to 1919, and those for the period from 1919 to the present day. Thus altogether there are four groups of Pareto coefficients, and the frequency distribution of each of these is shown in Figure 5.

It seems clear that the distributions of the developed countries have moved up to the right while that of the underdeveloped countries seems to be more comparable with the distributions of the developed countries in past periods than with their present-day one. Furthermore, it appears that not only has there been a rise of the mean value of the Pareto coefficients but that the standard deviation has also become greater; indeed, it has roughly moved in step with the average.[13] Finally, it is noteworthy that the first two income patterns in Figure 5 are roughly symmetrical while the last two are steeper to the left than to the right. A sufficient condition for the appearance of this effect is that low Pareto coefficients increase more slowly than higher ones — i.e., measured in terms of the movement of Pareto coefficients the levelling process made more rapid progress in countries in which the inequality was already moderate than in countries with greater inequalities.

Otherwise Clark's material does not allow one to draw more than tentative conclusions since it is of a markedly heterogenous nature. An investigation of the development of inequalities within a number of separate countries is a preferable approach but this lies outside the scope of the present study.[14]

[11] Pp. 533-537.

[12] Omitted from the sample: the Soviet Union because no country can be expected to have a "normal" pattern of income distribution after a revolution; Brazilian wage earners because the Pareto approximation can have only a limited significance for low income groups; and the results for different racial groups in South Africa and in former Palestine on account of the racial stratification of these countries.

[13] Before the Industrial Revolution: average 1.45, standard deviation 0.18; from the beginning of the Industrial Revolution to 1919: average 1.55, standard deviation 0.14; after 1919: average 1.88, standard deviation 0.24. Underdeveloped countries: average 1.49, standard deviation 0.19.

[14] An example of such an investigation is the Netherlands Central Bureau of Statistics study "Een statistisch onderzoek naar de veranderingen in de ongelijkheid van de inkomensverdeling" [A Statistical Examination of Changes in Inequalities of Income Distribution], *Statistische en Econometrische Onderzoekingen*, 1946, pp. 55-67. This study is concerned with certain developed countries and relatively short time periods.

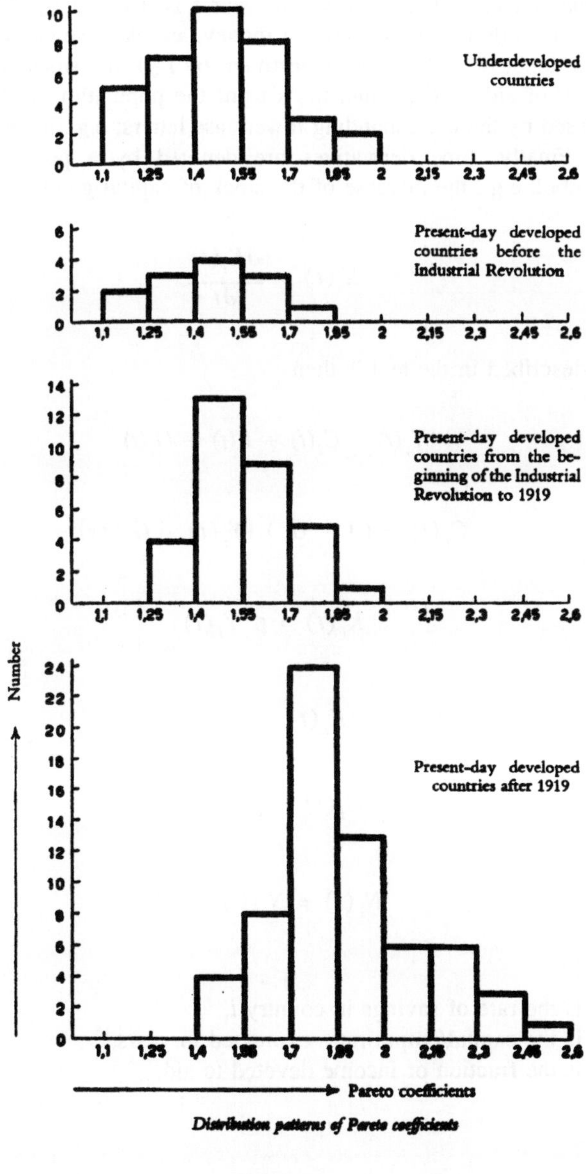


*Distribution patterns of Pareto coefficients*

**Figure 5**

## A.2. The Granting and the Receiving of Aid

### A.2.1. A MODEL FOR DEVELOPED COUNTRIES

The real national income of a country $i$ in year $t$ is denoted by $Y_i(t)$; all subsequent variables, in so far as they relate to sums of money, are likewise expressed in real terms. Consumption is denoted by $C_i(t)$, net investment by $I_i(t)$, the stock of capital goods by $K_i(t)$, the amount of aid by $G_i(t)$, and the size of the population by $N_i(t)$. Amounts per head are expressed by the corresponding lower case letters; e.g., income per head is $y_i(t)$ [$= Y_i(t)/N_i(t)$]. Finally, time derivatives are denoted by a point placed above the appropriate symbol, e.g., the increase of the stock of capital goods is written as

$$\dot{K}_i(t) = \frac{\partial K_i(t)}{\partial t}$$

The model as described in the text is then

$$Y_i(t) = C_i(t) + I_i(t) + G_i(t) \tag{1.1}$$

$$C_i(t) = (1 - \sigma_i)\{Y_i(t) - G_i(t)\} \tag{1.2}$$

$$K_i(t) = \rho_i Y_i(t) \tag{1.3}$$

$$\dot{K}_i(t) = I_i(t) \tag{1.4}$$

$$G_i(t) = \gamma_i Y_i(t) \tag{1.5}$$

$$N_i(t) = N_i(0)e^{\nu_i t}\,. \tag{1.6}$$

where

- $\sigma_i$ is the rate of savings in country $i$,
- $\rho_i$ is the capital/output ratio expressed in years,[15]
- $\gamma_i$ is the fraction of income devoted to aid,

[15] $K$ is a stock of money, $Y$ is an amount per period of time, their ratio thus has a time dimension.

$\nu_i$ is the annual increase in population, measured as a fraction of the existing population,

$t = 0$ is the date from which the arrangements decided upon [cf. (1.5)] are to operate.

From this model one can derive

$$Y_i(t) = Y_i(0) \exp \frac{\sigma_i (1 - \gamma_i) t}{\rho_i} \tag{1.7}$$

where exp $x$ stands for $e^x$. In this way the growth trend of the national income is described. From (1.5) we further derive the growth of the amount of aid made available,

$$G_i(t) = \gamma_i Y_i(0) \exp \frac{\sigma_i (1 - \gamma_i) t}{\rho_i} \tag{1.8}$$

and the total of all contributions is then

$$\Sigma G_i(t) = \Sigma \gamma_i Y_i(0) \exp \frac{\sigma_i (1 - \gamma_i) t}{\rho_i} \tag{1.9}$$

where the summation is extended over all the contributing countries.

As a rough approximation one may say that $\sigma_i$ is of the order of 0.1 and $\rho_i$ is about four years.[16] The ratio $\sigma_i/\rho_i$ is thus about 0.025 per year and the multiplication factor $(1-\gamma_i)$ has little influence on this, so long as the contribution does not amount to more than, say, 5 per cent of income. We shall, therefore, proceed to neglect this factor. If we further assume that the $\sigma$'s and the $\rho$'s of the contributing countries are of roughly the same order of magnitude,[17] the exponent can be brought outside the summation and we can describe the relationship as follows:

$$\Sigma G_i(t) = \{\Sigma \gamma_i Y_i(0)\} \exp \frac{\sigma t}{\rho} \tag{1.10}$$

[16] See, e.g., C.M. Palvia, *An Econometric Model for Development Planning* (Dissertation, Rotterdam, 1953), p. 81.

[17] In the event of different ratios $\sigma_i/\rho_i$, the adoption of the ratio applicable to the United States (which is by far the most important of the contributing countries) is advisable in (1.9).

Given the numerical assumptions made above it follows from this that the total amount which becomes available increases by roughly $2\frac{1}{2}$ per cent per annum.

## A.2.2. A MODEL FOR UNDERDEVELOPED COUNTRIES

Underdeveloped countries will be indicated by the index $j$. The amount that $j$ receives in the year $t$ is written $H_j$(t). We shall require that aid receipts and contributions are equal to one another in each annual period.

$$\Sigma G_i(t) = \Sigma H_j(t) \tag{2.1}$$

An obvious way to satisfy this requirement is to make the individual receipts proportional to $\Sigma G$. This implies

$$H_j(t) = H_j(0) \exp \frac{\sigma t}{\rho} \tag{2.2}$$

which is one of the equations of the model of this section. The remaining equations are analogous to those of the model in A.2.1. Only (1.5) disappears and so does the $G$ term in (1.1), while (1.4) is replaced by

$$\dot{K}_j(t) = I_j(t) + H_j(t)$$

The model then gives two alternative results for the growth of income; the respective validity of these depends on whether the ratios $\sigma_j/\rho_j$ and $\sigma/\rho$ are identical or not identical. If they are not identical, then

$$Y_j(t) = Y_j(0) \exp \frac{\sigma_j t}{\rho_j} + \frac{\rho H_j(0)}{\sigma \rho_j - \sigma_j \rho} \left\{ \exp \frac{\sigma t}{\rho} - \exp \frac{\sigma_j t}{\rho_j} \right\} \tag{2.3}$$

If, on the other hand, they are identical and if we also assume that $\rho_j = \rho$, then we obtain

$$Y_j(t) = Y_j(0) \left\{ 1 + \frac{\delta_j t}{\rho} \right\} \exp \frac{\sigma t}{\rho} \tag{2.4}$$

where $\delta_j$ is the amount of aid in the first year, expressed as a fraction of the incomes of that year $[H_j(0)/Y_j(0)]$. Since the assumption $\rho_j = \rho$ is not unrealistic and since the equality $\sigma_j = \sigma$ represents the raising of the savings rate as described in the text, it is desirable to examine the implications of both variants. As to (2.3) it can be shown that in this case the ratio of the national incomes of a poor country $j$ and of a rich country $i$ can be approximately given as

$$\frac{Y_j(t)}{Y_i(t)} = \frac{Y_j(0)}{Y_i(0)} \left[ \left\{ 1 - \frac{\delta_j}{\sigma - \sigma_j} \right\} \exp \frac{(\sigma_j - \sigma)\,t}{\rho} + \frac{\delta_j}{\sigma - \sigma_j} \right] \tag{2.5}$$

in the case where $\rho_j = \rho$. Now if $\sigma_j < \sigma$, the exponent of (2.5) is a decreasing function of time. The income ratio thus rises only if the coefficient of the exponent has a negative sign, viz., if $\delta_j + \sigma_j > \sigma$; in words: if the difference in the savings rate is compensated by the receipt of aid. In the case (2.4) the income ratio is an increasing linear function of time:

$$\frac{Y_j(t)}{Y_i(t)} = \frac{Y_j(0)}{Y_i(0)} \left\{ 1 + \frac{\delta_j t}{\rho} \right\} \tag{2.6}$$

This variant has been chosen for reasons explained in the text.

### A.2.3. CRITERIA AND NUMERICAL RESULTS

We choose a "marginal" country (with the index $g$) whose *per capita* income grows as follows:

$$y_g(t) = y_g(0) \exp[(\sigma/\rho - \nu)\,t] \tag{3.1}$$

The assumptions here employed are (i) that for this country $\sigma$ and $\rho$ are respectively equal to the corresponding parameters of the rich and poor countries considered above (the $\sigma_j$ having been raised to the $\sigma$ level), (ii) that the difference between the percentage increases of the populations of the various countries can be ignored. The last assumption in particular calls for refinement; in this connection, however, it is useful to point out that in the period 1937-1947 the percentage growth of the populations of various countries was not in any close degree correlated with their welfare.[18] It appears that the high birth rates of the poor countries have been offset to such an extent by their high death rates that the

[18] See L.D. Stamp: 1953, *Our Undeveloped World*, London, p. 26.

difference between the two tends to be of the same order of magnitude as that in the richer countries, at least on the average.

In a poor country income per head grows as follows [from (2.4)]:

$$y_j(t) = y_j(0)\left\{1 + \frac{\delta_j t}{\rho}\right\} \exp[(\sigma/\rho - \nu_j)t] \tag{3.2}$$

Accordingly, if $\nu_j = \nu$, the ratio of this income to the minimum level described in (3.1) is

$$\frac{y_j(t)}{y_g(t)} = \frac{y_j(0)}{y_g(0)}\left\{1 + \frac{\delta_j t}{\rho}\right\} \tag{3.3}$$

Country $j$ will reach the minimum level in period $T$, when the relationship $y_j(T) = y_g(T)$ will hold. Now $T$ is subject to choice, and once this choice has been made, the fraction $\delta_j$ which the country will have to receive is determined. This is derived from (3.3)

$$\delta_j = \frac{\rho}{T}\,\frac{y_g(0) - y_j(0)}{y_j(0)} \tag{3.4}$$

The amount which country $j$ receives at the outset, $H_j(0) = \delta_j Y_j(0)$ is then

$$H_j(0) = \frac{\rho}{T} N_j(0)\,[y_g(0) - y_j(0)]$$

and the total of all these amounts is

$$\Sigma H_j(0) = \frac{\rho}{T} \Sigma N_j(0)\,[y_g(0) - y_j(0)] \tag{3.5}$$

where the summation has taken place for all the countries $j$ for which $y_j(0) < y_g(0)$ holds. The amount of aid is therefore proportional to the capital/output ratio and to the aggregate amount by which the poor countries at the outset fall below the minimum income level, and is inversely proportional to the time that it is decided to allow for the process.

Tables 1 and 2 contain estimates of the total amount (3.5) required under alternative assumptions concerning $T$ and $y_g(0)$; $\rho$ is fixed at four years. The sum of \$300 thousand million referred to in these tables is the total income of all countries in 1949

**TABLE 1.** Initial payments of aid
(1) in absolute amounts
(2) as percentages of the total income of the paying countries

| | $T$ = 25 | | $T$ = 50 | | $T$ = 75 | |
|---|---|---|---|---|---|---|
| | (1) $ thousand million | (2) % of $300 thousand million | (1) $ thousand million | (2) % of $300 thousand million | (1) $ thousand million | (2) % of $300 thousand million |
| $y_g(0) = 100$ | 10.7 | 3.6 | 5.3 | 1.8 | 3.6 | 1.2 |
| $y_g(0) = 150$ | 21.2 | 7.1 | 10.6 | 3.5 | 7.1 | 2.4 |
| $y_g(0) = 200$ | 32.3 | 10.8 | 16.1 | 5.4 | 10.8 | 3.6 |

**TABLE 2.** As Table 1 but excluding China

| | $T$ = 25 | | $T$ = 50 | | $T$ = 75 | |
|---|---|---|---|---|---|---|
| | (1) $ thousand million | (2) % of $300 thousand million | (1) $ thousand million | (2) % of $300 thousand million | (1) $ thousand million | (2) % of $300 thousand million |
| $y_g(0) = 100$ | 5.3 | 1.8 | 2.6 | 0.9 | 1.8 | 0.6 |
| $y_g(0) = 150$ | 12.1 | 4.0 | 6.1 | 2.0 | 4.0 | 1.3 |
| $y_g(0) = 200$ | 19.4 | 6.5 | 9.7 | 3.2 | 6.5 | 2.2 |

whose *per capita* income as calculated in the study of the United Nations Statistical Office appears to have amounted to $500 or more; the total incomes of countries with a *per capita* income of between $400-500 amounted only to about $20 thousand million. These figures, as also those shown below, are naturally confined to the countries for which data are available in the U.N. study.

With the aid of the data given the receipts of single countries can be directly read off, using (3.4). For the sake of brevity we confine ourselves to mentioning that if a minimum level of $100 is to be reached in a period of 50 years, this implies for the poorest countries (Indonesia, China, South Korea, etc.) a $\delta_j$ of about 0.3 to 0.5. This result suggests that it may be necessary to choose a higher value for $T$ for the poorest countries than for those which are less poor (see text).

## A.2.4. THE EFFECT ON PER CAPITA CONSUMPTION

The argument so far has been concerned mostly with the growth of income. It is clear that an increase in the rate of growth is obtained at the expense of consumption.

We consider first consumption in the developed countries. From (1.2), (1.5) and (1.7) we have

$$C_i(t) = (1 - \sigma)(1 - \gamma_i) Y_i(0) \exp \frac{\sigma t}{\rho}$$

For consumption per head we then have

$$c_i(t) = (1 - \sigma)(1 - \gamma_i) y_i(0) \exp[(\sigma/\rho - \nu_i)t] \tag{4.1}$$

We now derive the level of consumption per head which would obtain in period t′ if the measures referred to in (1.5) had not been taken; writing this as $\bar{c}_i(t')$, we have

$$\bar{c}_i(t') = (1 - \sigma) y_i(0) \exp[(\sigma/\rho - \nu_i)t'] \tag{4.2}$$

If we now put $c_i(t) = \bar{c}_i(t')$, we obtain the difference $(t\text{-}t')$ which corresponds to the period of postponement in the growth of consumption as discussed in the text. From (4.1) and (4.2) it follows that the equation implies

$$(1 - \gamma_i) \exp[(\sigma/\rho - \nu_i)(t - t')] = 1$$

or approximately

$$t - t' = \frac{\gamma_i}{\sigma/\rho - \nu_i} \tag{4.3}$$

If $\sigma = 0.1$, $\rho = 4$ years, and $\nu_i = 0.01$ per annum, an amount of 1 per cent ($\gamma_i = 0.01$) implies a period of postponement $(t\text{-}t')$ of two-thirds of a year or 8 months.

For the development of *per capita* consumption in underdeveloped countries we easily find

$$c_j(t) = (1 - \sigma) y_j(0) \left\{ 1 + \frac{\delta_j t}{\rho} \right\} \exp\left[ (\sigma/\rho - \nu_j) t \right] \tag{4.4}$$

Without the measures discussed *per capita* consumption in $t'$ would be

$$\bar{c}_j(t') = (1 - \bar{\sigma}) y_j(0) \exp\left[ (\bar{\sigma}/\rho - \nu_j) t' \right] \tag{4.5}$$

when $\bar{\sigma}$ is a savings rate lower than $\sigma$. The equation $c_j(t) = \bar{c}_j(t')$ implies

$$\frac{1 - \sigma}{1 - \bar{\sigma}} \left\{ 1 + \frac{\delta_j t}{\rho} \right\} \exp\left[ (\sigma/\rho - \nu_j)(t - t') + \frac{(\sigma - \bar{\sigma}) t'}{\rho} \right] = 1$$

or approximately

$$t - t' = \left( \frac{\sigma + \delta_j}{\rho} - \nu_j \right)^{-1} \left[ \sigma - \bar{\sigma} - \frac{\delta_j + \sigma - \bar{\sigma}}{\rho} t' \right] \tag{4.6}$$

In this case, therefore, the period of postponement is a decreasing function of time; after a certain interval this period becomes negative, and the trend level of *per capita* consumption becomes higher than it would have been without the arrangements we have outlined — which is only to be expected. If $\sigma = 0.1$, $\bar{\sigma} = 0.05$, $\rho = 4$ years, $\nu_j = 0.01$ per annum, and $\delta_j = 0.04$, this effect appears after $t' = 2.2$ years.

CHAPTER 49

# INTERNATIONAL COMPARISONS OF PRICES AND QUANTITIES CONSUMED*

TEUN KLOEK
*Netherlands School of Economics*
*(now Erasmus University)*
*Rotterdam, The Netherlands*

HENRI THEIL[1]
*Netherlands School of Economics*
*(now Erasmus University)*
*Rotterdam, The Netherlands*

## 1. Introduction

The importance of international comparisons in the area of prices and consumption has increased substantially in the last decade due to the increase of tourism and of work carried out abroad. The problem is not at all new; it has been considered fairly recently by, for example, Gilbert and Kravis (undated).

In the present article we propose a number of comparison standards based on logarithms of prices and quantities. This logarithmic approach can be justified by pointing to the fact that one is usually interested in *relative* differences. In addition to the conventional problem of differences in "average" price and volume levels we shall also consider dispersion problems. These arise because some prices are relatively much higher or much lower in a particular country than "average." The variance of logarithmic price differences and of logarithmic quantity differences and also their covariance provide natural measures for describing this phenomenon. Further, it will be shown that these measures are closely related to the divergence between the two sets of value shares of two countries, where "divergence" is defined in the way in which it is done in information theory.

The order of discussion is as follows. In section 2 we consider the problem of price and quantity level comparison. The procedure proposed there is applied in section 4 to data on coal miner families in the European Coal and Steel Community, which are described in section 3. The result is a set of pairwise comparisons. In section 5 a simple least-squares approach is formulated which transforms these pairwise comparisons into one scale. Section 6 discusses the dispersion and the divergence measures, which are subsequently applied in section 7 and interpreted as squared distances in section 8. The Appendix, finally, presents disaggregated material for 21 commodity groups and a comparison of some of the results of this paper with some classical index numbers.

* This article first appeared in *Econometrica*, 33 (1965), 535-556. Reprinted with the permission of The Econometric Society.

[1] The authors are indebted to Mr. B. Kok of BULL Nederland N.V. and to Mr. A. Kunstman for programming the computations and to Mr. J. N. J.Th. Kloes for his assistance in the evaluation of the results and his work on additional computations.

## 2. The Decomposition of the Logarithmic Differences in Total Expenditure

Let us write $p_{ia}$ for the price of the $i$th commodity in the $a$th region, where $i = 1, \ldots, n$ (the number of commodities) and $a = 1, \ldots, N$ (the number of regions). We write $q_{ia}$ for the corresponding quantity consumed per family, so that

$$m_a = \sum_{i=1}^{n} p_{ia} q_{ia} \tag{2.1}$$

is total expenditure per family in the $a$th region. The value shares are

$$w_{ia} = \frac{p_{ia} q_{ia}}{m_a} . \tag{2.2}$$

Finally, in view of the frequent appearance of logarithms we introduce

$$\pi_{ia} = \log p_{ia}, \qquad \kappa_{ia} = \log q_{ia}, \qquad \mu_a = \log m_a . \tag{2.3}$$

Natural logarithms will be used throughout.

The price ratio of the $i$th commodity in any two regions is of the form $p_{ia}/p_{ib}$ and its logarithm is $\pi_{ia} - \pi_{ib}$. We define the (average) logarithmic price difference between the two regions as follows:

$$\Pi_{ab} = \sum_{i=1}^{n} w_{iab} (\pi_{ia} - \pi_{ib}), \qquad w_{iab} = \frac{w_{ia} + w_{ib}}{2} . \tag{2.4}$$

Thus, the logarithmic price difference is a weighted average of the individual logarithmic price differences; and the weights are of the form $w_{iab}$, i.e., they are the average of the corresponding value shares in the two regions. In original symbols rather than logarithms:

$$e^{\Pi_{ab}} = \sqrt{\prod_{i=1}^{n} (p_{ia}/p_{ib})^{w_{ia}} \prod_{i=1}^{n} (p_{ia}/p_{ib})^{w_{ib}}} .$$

That is, the ratio of the two price levels is defined as the geometric average of two weighted geometric averages. The latter averages are both averages of individual price ratios and one of them uses the value shares of the $a$th region as weights, the other those of the $b$th region.

To justify the use of $\Pi_{ab}$, we consider the time series counterpart of (2.4):

$$\log \frac{p}{p_{-1}} = \sum_{i=1}^{n} \frac{w_i + (w_i)_{-1}}{2} \log \frac{p_i}{(p_i)_{-1}} , \tag{2.5}$$

where $p_i$ is the price of the $i$th commodity in the current period, $(p_i)_{-1}$ that of the preceding period, $w_i$ and $(w_i)_{-1}$ the corresponding value shares, and $p/p_{-1}$ the ratio of the price levels in the two successive periods. Now it was shown by one of the authors (Theil, 1965, 1964) that the price index whose log-change is defined in (2.5) is a local quadratic approximation to the constant-utility price index if real income does not change. The interpretation of the cross-section analogue (2.4) is similar except, of course, that one might expect a larger discrepancy due to the possibility of a more serious violation of this condition. That is, whereas in successive periods the difference in real income is usually small (when the periods are not too large), this difference may be more substantial in the comparison of two regions. This disadvantage should be weighted against the advantage of the very simple linear form of $\Pi_{ab}$. It is an ordinary average and the natural extension to second moments (see section 6 below) provides interesting additional insight into the price and quantity structure.

The average logarithmic quantity difference between the two regions is defined similarly:

$$K_{ab} = \sum_{i=1}^{n} w_{iab} (\kappa_{ia} - \kappa_{ib}) . \tag{2.6}$$

The time series analogue, which is obtained from (2.5) by replacing $p$ and $p_i$ by $q$ and $q_i$, respectively, has an interesting interpretation in demand analysis. For it can be shown that the contribution of the $i$th commodity to the log-change of this volume index,

$$\frac{w_i + (w_i)_{-1}}{2} \log \frac{q_i}{(q_i)_{-1}} ,$$

is approximately equal to the change in the $i$th value share; in infinitesimal rather than finite terms:

$$\begin{aligned} dw_i &= w_i d(\log q_i) && \text{(due to quantity change)} \\ &+ w_i d(\log p_i) && \text{(due to price change)} \\ &- w_i d(\log m) && \text{(due to total expenditure change)} . \end{aligned}$$

Further, the contribution of the $i$th commodity to the log-change is also a convenient dependent variable in the demand equation for the $i$th commodity. Reference is made to Theil (1965, 1964).

An interesting question is whether the logarithmic differences of the price and volume levels add up to the logarithmic difference in total expenditure; that is, whether it is true that

$$\Pi_{ab} + K_{ab} = \log \frac{m_a}{m_b} = \mu_a - \mu_b \; .$$

The answer is that this is not the case. When using $\pi_{ia} + \kappa_{ia} = \log w_{ia} m_a = \mu_a + \log w_{ia}$ we obtain

$$\Pi_{ab} + K_{ab} = \mu_a - \mu_b + \sum_{i=1}^{n} w_{iab} \log \frac{w_{ia}}{w_{ib}}$$

or

$$\mu_a - \mu_b = \Pi_{ab} + K_{ab} + \Delta_{ab} \; , \tag{2.7}$$

where

$$\Delta_{ab} = -\sum_{i=1}^{n} w_{iab} \log \frac{w_{ia}}{w_{ib}} = -\sum_{i=1}^{n} \frac{w_{ia} + w_{ib}}{2} \log \frac{w_{ia}}{w_{ib}} \; . \tag{2.8}$$

The term $\Delta_{ab}$ is called the *information difference component* of the log-change in total expenditure.[2] For what follows it will prove to be of considerable importance to consider this term in more detail. It is minus half the difference between

$$I(w_a; w_b) = \sum_{i=1}^{n} w_{ia} \log \frac{w_{ia}}{w_{ib}} \tag{2.9}$$

and

$$I(w_b; w_a) = \sum_{i=1}^{n} w_{ib} \log \frac{w_{ib}}{w_{ia}} \; . \tag{2.10}$$

[2] In (Theil, 1965) the term "information component" was introduced, but this is abandoned here because it suggests something which cannot be negative.

In information theory the expression (2.9) is called the information gained by the message $(w_{1a}, \ldots, w_{na})$, given the "prior" fractions $(w_{1b}, \ldots, w_{nb})$. In the same way (2.10) is the information gained by $(w_{1b}, \ldots, w_{nb})$. Such concepts are applied in information theory to probabilities, but it is easily seen that our value shares can be regarded as such, since they are necessarily non-negative and add up to 1. Both expressions (2.9) and (2.10) are positive except when $w_{ia} = w_{ib}$ for all $i$, in which case they vanish. The information difference component may be positive or negative. Reference is made to Theil (1965, 1964).

## 3. Description of the Data

We shall apply the decomposition of the log-change in total expenditure implied by (2.7) to household data of coal miner families (all with two children below 14 years) in six countries: Germany (Federal Republic, excluding Saarland), Belgium, France, Italy, Netherlands, and the Saarland.[3] A list of the coal mining areas in these countries is presented in Table I. It appears that all coal miners except the Italians and a minority of the French live within an equilateral triangle with sides of a little over 300 km and angle points in or near Dortmund, Lille, and Saarbrücken; thus, a rather small area, which is divided, however, by a number of national and linguistic borders.

The price survey was held by the Statistical Office of the European Communities[4] in 1958 and covers 177 commodities. The average price of each commodity was determined for each region and then weighted (see the weights of Table I) to obtain national averages. In addition, data on house rents were obtained from the national statistical offices, so that 178 prices were available for each country. For details see (Bureau voor de Statistiek der Europese Gemeenschappen, 1960b).

The High Authority of the European Coal and Steel Community organized a budget survey in the period May 1956—May 1957; see (Bureau voor de Statistiek der Europese Gemeenschappen, 1960a). The value shares obtained from that survey have been taken as a starting point for the derivation of the $w$'s and, therefore, the price and volume comparisons. Since many of the shares are very small (and specified only in units of one tenth of one per cent) the 178 commodities have been aggregated to 21 commodity groups. This aggregation is such that each commodity group has a value of at least 2 per cent in at least four of the six regions. A list of these groups is given in Table II, together with their value shares. The shares below 2 per cent are marked by an asterisk.

---

[3] The Saarland (part of Germany before and in the Second World War) was occupied by the French army after the war. From 1947-1956 it was autonomous to a certain extent, but economically closely related to France. On January 1, 1957 it was politically reunited with the Federal Republic of Germany, but its economic integration into Germany was postponed until the summer of 1959. This explains why it has been taken as a separate country here.

[4] I.e., the European Atomic Energy Community, the European Coal and Steel Community, and the European Economic Community.

**TABLE I.** Regions and Their Weights Within Each Country

| Region | Weight |
|---|---|
| *Germany** | |
| Aix-la-Chapelle (Aachen) | .1 |
| Ruhr area | .9 |
| *Belgium* | |
| Borinage (near Mons) | .1 |
| Charleroi | .3 |
| Center (near La Louvière) | .1 |
| Liège | .2 |
| Campine (North-East of the country) | .3 |
| *France* | |
| North (near Lille) | .6 |
| Lorraine (near Saarland border) | .2 |
| Upper Loire Valley (near Saint Etienne) | .1 |
| Cevennes | .1 |
| *Italy* | |
| Sulcis (Isle of Sardinia) | |
| *Netherlands* | |
| South Limburg (South-East of the country) | |

* Federal Republic excluding Saarland

Formula (2.4) was then applied to obtain average logarithmic price differences for all pairs of countries and for each of the 21 commodity groups (where, of course, $w_{iab}$ should be interpreted as the share of the individual commodity in the group to which it belongs). There are no volume data at the individual commodity level, so (2.7) was applied to obtain average logarithmic volume differences for each commodity group. At this group level $m_a$ and $m_b$ are interpreted as the amounts spent on the particular commodity group; the information difference component is thus neglected within the groups. Reference is made to the Appendix for more details.

**TABLE II.** Commodity Groups and Value Shares (x 1000)

| | Commodity groups | Ger-many | Bel-gium | France | Italy | Nether-lands | Saar-land |
|---|---|---|---|---|---|---|---|
| 1. | Bread, rice, spaghetti, and other | | | | | | |
| | wheat products | 60 | 59 | 61 | 120 | 74 | 54 |
| 2. | Meat, meat products, and fish | 114 | 121 | 134 | 103 | 101 | 107 |
| 3. | Butter, margarine, and other fats | | | | | | |
| | and oils | 45 | 73 | 73 | 42 | 34 | 71 |
| 4. | Milk, cheese, and eggs | 66 | 52 | 55 | 70 | 77 | 56 |
| 5. | Vegetables, potatoes, and fruit | 63 | 55 | 64 | 77 | 60 | 55 |
| 6. | Other foods | 40 | 27 | 28 | 28 | 44 | 26 |
| 7. | Drinks (alcoholic and | 60 | 59 | 97 | 77 | 41 | 50 |
| | nonalcoholic) | 33 | 21 | 29 | 34 | 34 | 25 |
| 8. | Tobacco and tobacco products | 35 | 35 | 32 | 32 | 41 | 41 |
| 9. | Men's clothing | 38 | 28 | 29 | 14* | 38 | 40 |
| 10. | Women's clothing | | | | | | |
| 11. | Other clothing (incl. children's | 36 | 38 | 41 | 28 | 40 | 48 |
| | clothing) | 27 | 27 | 27 | 29 | 28 | 33 |
| 12. | Footwear | 55 | 38 | 51 | 36 | 58 | 64 |
| 13. | Furniture and linens | 42 | 34 | 35 | 25 | 38 | 37 |
| 14. | Household appliances | | | | | | |
| 15. | Earthenware, glass, etc. and | 25 | 41 | 19* | 12* | 32 | 53 |
| | house repairs | 56 | 62 | 47 | 79 | 59 | 49 |
| 16. | Coal, gas and electricity | 78 | 79 | 50 | 101 | 65 | 57 |
| 17. | House rent | 24 | 21 | 26 | 20 | 28 | 26 |
| 18. | Cleaning and repairs of clothing | 24 | 28 | 20 | 17* | 23 | 21 |
| 19. | Personal and medical care | 48 | 37 | 47 | 34 | 47 | 48 |
| 20. | Education and recreation | 31 | 65 | 35 | 22 | 38 | 39 |
| 21. | Private and public transportation | | | | | | |

## 4. Pairwise Comparisons of Price and Volume Levels

From now on we shall confine ourselves to the 21 commodity groups ($i = 1, 2, \ldots, 21, = n$). We have prices and quantities for each of these groups (as described in the preceding section) and also total expenditure. Prices and expenditure are expressed in local currency in the original publications, but for the purpose of this study they have been converted according to the official rates of exchange. This makes the comparison of purchasing power parities and official exchange rates easier.[5]

The decomposition of the logarithmic differences of total expenditure in terms of $\Pi_{ab}$, $K_{ab}$, and $\Delta_{ab}$ is presented in Table III. The results are given in the form of matrices which are all skew-symmetric. The figures shown are multiplied by one hundred. Given that natural logarithms are used this means that these figures correspond approximately

[5] Reference is made to the Appendix for details. It is easily seen from (2.4) that any other conversion has only additive implications. It also follows from (2.4) and (2.6) that a change in the unit of measurement of some quantity has no effect whatever.

with percentage differences. Hence, the second figure in the first row (-13.93) means that the average German coal miner's family spends about 13 per cent less than its Belgian counterpart at the official rates of exchange. We conclude that the Saarland is a comparatively expensive place, all elements of its $\Pi_{ab}$ row being positive; that things are cheap in The Netherlands; that real income is comparatively high in Belgium and low in Italy, and so on.[6] Note in particular that the information difference component is very small, viz., less than 1 per cent in all comparisons.

**TABLE III**. Decomposition of the Logarithmic Difference in Total Expenditure (x $10^2$)

| | Germany | Belgium | France | Italy | Netherlands | Saarland |
|---|---|---|---|---|---|---|
| | | | *Total Expenditure* ($\mu_a$ - $\mu_b$) | | | |
| Germany | 0 | -13.93 | -10.24 | 16.75 | 13.61 | -15.85 |
| Belium | 13.93 | 0 | 3.69 | 30.68 | 27.54 | -1.92 |
| France | 10.24 | -3.69 | 0 | 26.98 | 23.85 | -5.61 |
| Italy | -16.75 | -30.68 | -26.98 | 0 | -3.14 | -32.59 |
| Netherlands | -13.61 | -27.54 | -23.85 | 3.14 | 0 | -29.46 |
| Saarland | 15.85 | 1.92 | 5.61 | 32.59 | 29.46 | 0 |
| | | | *Price level* ($\Pi_{ab}$) | | | |
| Germany | 0 | 2.85 | -6.82 | 4.38 | 20.25 | -11.05 |
| Belgium | -2.85 | 0 | -9.23 | 1.21 | 17.03 | -12.15 |
| France | 6.82 | 9.23 | 0 | 9.45 | 25.92 | -2.53 |
| Italy | -4.28 | -1.21 | -9.45 | 0 | 14.53 | -12.61 |
| Netherlands | -20.25 | -17.03 | -25.92 | -14.53 | 0 | -30.99 |
| Saarland | 11.05 | 12.15 | 2.53 | 12.61 | 30.99 | 0 |
| | | | *Real Income* ($K_{ab}$) | | | |
| Germany | 0 | -16.94 | -3.47 | 12.45 | -6.62 | -4.94 |
| Belgium | 16.94 | 0 | 13.09 | 30.07 | 10.66 | 10.23 |
| France | 3.47 | -13.09 | 0 | 17.28 | -1.63 | -3.21 |
| Italy | -12.45 | -30.07 | -17.28 | 0 | -17.90 | -20.63 |
| Netherlands | 6.62 | -10.66 | 1.63 | 17.90 | 0 | 1.40 |
| Saarland | 4.94 | -10.23 | 3.21 | 20.63 | -1.40 | 0 |
| | | | *Information difference component* ($\Delta_{ab}$) | | | |
| Germany | 0 | 0.16 | 0.05 | -0.08 | -0.02 | 0.14 |
| Belgium | -0.16 | 0 | -0.17 | -0.60 | -0.14 | 0.00 |
| France | -0.05 | 0.17 | 0 | 0.25 | -0.44 | 0.13 |
| Italy | .08 | 0.60 | -0.25 | 0 | 0.23 | 0.64 |
| Netherlands | .02 | 0.14 | 0.44 | -0.23 | 0 | 0.13 |
| Saarland | -0.14 | -0.00 | -0.13 | -0.64 | -0.13 | 0 |

[6] These numerical conclusions (and those of section 5 below) are in qualitative accordance with those of (Bureau voor de Statistiek der Europese Gemeenschappen, 1960b).

## 5. A Single Scale

An obvious question,[7] given the pairwise results obtained in the previous section, is whether these results can be written in such a way that a single scale is obtained. The answer is that this is not the case, at least not exactly; it would require that $\Pi_{ab} + \Pi_{bc} = \Pi_{ac}$ holds for all triples of countries (similarly for the quantities) and formulas (2.4) and (2.6) do not satisfy that property. But in many cases the discrepancy will be small. To analyze this, we note that the fulfilment of this circular test requires that one should be able to write $\Pi_{ab}$ in the form $\pi_a - \pi_b$; or in matrix terms, $[\Pi_{ab}] = \pi\iota' - \iota\pi'$, where $\pi$ is the $N$-element column vector $[\pi_a]$ and $\iota$ a column of $N$ units. ($N$ is the number of countries.) For the observed $[\Pi_{ab}]$ one must therefore write

$$\left[\Pi_{ab}\right] = \pi\iota' - \iota\pi' + U , \tag{5.1}$$

where $U$ is an $N \times N$ matrix of residual errors. An obvious procedure is to select $\pi$ such that the sum of squares of all residuals is minimized. This implies minimization of tr $U'U$, where tr (trace) stands for the sum of the diagonal elements. Using the ordinary rules of trace algebra (and the fact that $\Pi_{ab}$ is skew-symmetric) we obtain

$$\operatorname{tr} U'U = \operatorname{tr}\left[\Pi_{ab}\right]\left[\Pi_{ab}\right]' + 4\,\iota'\left[\Pi_{ab}\right]\pi - 2\,(\pi'\iota)^2 + 2N\pi'\pi \ .$$

This expression has to be minimized with respect to $\pi$. Note that an index vector like $\pi$ has always one additive "degree of freedom." This can be used to impose a certain constraint on $\pi$, e.g., $\pi'\iota = 0$ (which means that the geometric average of the $N$ price index numbers is 1). Doing so we obtain after differentiation:

$$\pi_a = \frac{1}{N}\sum_{b=1}^{N} \Pi_{ab} \ ; \tag{5.2}$$

that is, the logarithmic price index number of the $a$th country is obtained by taking the average of all elements of the $a$th row of $[\Pi_{ab}]$.

---

[7] That is to say, obvious to most applied workers. At the level of economic theory the problem is not without difficulties (see, e.g, Mouchez, 1964); but we shall not go into these, because the results to be presented here show that a single scale can account for the pairwise logarithmic differences to a very large extent.

The procedure for the volumes is completely analogous. The result is:

| | Germany | Belgium | France | Italy | Netherlands | Saarland |
|---|---|---|---|---|---|---|
| Price: | .0160 | -.0100 | .0815 | -.0219 | -.1812 | .1155 |
| Quantity: | -.0325 | .1350 | .0047 | -.1639 | .0282 | .0286 |

and in anti-logs:

| | Germany | Belgium | France | Italy | Netherlands | Saarland |
|---|---|---|---|---|---|---|
| Price: | 1.016 | .990 | 1.085 | .978 | .834 | 1.122 |
| Quantity: | .968 | 1.145 | 1.005 | .849 | 1.029 | 1.029 |

After substituting the $\pi_a$ thus obtained into (5.1) we obtain the residual matrix $U$. This matrix (and also the corresponding matrix of the quantities) are given in Table IV. The results show that the residuals are at most 1.5 per cent in absolute value. This is small compared with the pairwise differences of Table III from which they are derived. It is, of course, hardly necessary to add that the results of this procedure will change somewhat when a country is added or deleted.[8]

It is worth-while to consider the single-scale index numbers in somewhat more detail. Regarding prices we observe that there are three groups of countries: (*i*) France and the Saarland where prices are relatively high, (*ii*) Germany, Belgium, and Italy with average price levels, and (*iii*) The Netherlands, with very low prices. It is interesting to note that the French (and the Saarland) franc was devaluated 17.55 per cent at the end of 1958, three months after the price survey. The low prices in The Netherlands, on the other hand, were a result of purposive government policy in order to stimulate exports. As a result, it has been profitable for many years to work (and earn) in Germany and to buy in The Netherlands, and many people from both sides of the border have benefited financially from this situation.

[8] It will be noted that corresponding price and quantity residuals of Table IV are, in general, of the same order of magnitude but of opposite sign. For example, in the Germany-Belgium comparison: .25 and -.19 ($\times 10^{-2}$). This is due to the fact that minus the sum of such a pair of residuals is equal to

$$\Delta_{ab} - \frac{1}{N}\left(\sum_a \Delta_{ab} + \sum_b \Delta_{ab}\right) ;$$

and these information difference components are generally small.

**TABLE IV.** Single-Scale Residuals (x $10^2$) for Prices and Quantities

| | Germany | Belgium | France | Italy | Netherlands | Saarland |
|---|---|---|---|---|---|---|
| | | | *Prices* | | | |
| Germany | 0 | .25 | -.27 | .59 | .53 | -1.10 |
| Belium | -.25 | 0 | -.08 | .02 | -.09 | .40 |
| France | .27 | .08 | 0 | -.88 | -.35 | .88 |
| Italy | -.59 | -.02 | .88 | 0 | -1.40 | 1.13 |
| Netherlands | -.53 | .09 | .35 | 1.40 | 0 | -1.31 |
| Saarland | 1.10 | -.40 | -.88 | -1.13 | 1.31 | 0 |
| | | | *Quantities* | | | |
| Germany | 0 | -.19 | .25 | -.68 | -.55 | 1.17 |
| Belgium | .19 | 0 | .06 | .18 | -.03 | -.41 |
| France | -.25 | -0.06 | 0 | .42 | .72 | -.83 |
| Italy | .68 | -.18 | -.42 | 0 | 1.31 | -1.38 |
| Netherlands | .55 | .03 | -.72 | -1.31 | 0 | 1.44 |
| Saarland | -1.17 | .41 | .83 | 1.38 | -1.44 | 0 |

Regarding real income, the Belgian coal miners took first position. In the middle group, the Saarland and The Netherlands (almost indistinguishable) were only a little ahead of France and Germany. The Italian miners, however, were far below this level.

## 6. Divergence of Value Shares and Price-Quantity Dispersion and Correlation: Theoretical Discussion

The difference between corresponding value shares in different countries is really the fundamental problem in the type of comparisons which we are considering here. For if $w_{ia}$ would be equal to $w_{ib}$ for each $i$ and all pairs $(a, b)$, the information difference component would vanish and the single-scale approach (5.1) would hold with zero residuals. In other words, the factor reversal test and the circular test would be satisfied. It is, therefore, appropriate to consider the value shares in more detail. Doing so, we shall find that it leads to other interesting aspects as well.

We return to (2.9) and (2.10), which specify the information gained by one set of value shares given the other set. The information difference component is half their difference. We now consider their sum:

$$J(w_a, w_b) = \sum_{i=1}^{n} (w_{ia} - w_{ib}) \log \frac{w_{ia}}{w_{ib}} , \tag{6.1}$$

which is a symmetric expression in $w_{ia}$ and $w_{ib}$ (not skew-symmetric!) known as the *divergence* of the two sets of value shares. To analyze the nature of this measure we introduce the difference between corresponding value shares measured as a fraction of their average:

$$\varepsilon_{iab} = \frac{w_{ia} - w_{ib}}{\frac{1}{2}\left(w_{ia} + w_{ib}\right)} = \frac{w_{ia} - w_{ib}}{w_{iab}}, \tag{6.2}$$

so that the divergence can be written as

$$J(w_a, w_b) = \sum_{i=1}^{n} w_{iab}\, \varepsilon_{iab} \log \frac{w_{ia}}{w_{ib}}. \tag{6.3}$$

Now $w_{ia}/w_{ib}$ can be written as the ratio of $1 + \frac{1}{2}\varepsilon_{iab}$ to $1 - \frac{1}{2}\varepsilon_{iab}$. Writing $e^x$ for $w_{ia}/w_{ib}$ and hence $x$ for $\log(w_{ia}/w_{ib})$, we then have

$$\varepsilon_{iab} = \frac{2(e^x - 1)}{e^x + 1} = x\, \frac{2 + x + \frac{1}{3}x^2 + \cdots}{2 + x + \frac{1}{2}x^2 + \cdots} \approx x\left(1 - \frac{1}{12}x^2\right), \tag{6.4}$$

which shows that $\varepsilon_{iab}$ is equal to $x = \log(w_{ia}/w_{ib})$ apart from a relative error term which is of the order of the square of the logarithmic difference between the value shares $w_{ia}$ and $w_{ib}$. Hence, from (6.3) and (6.4),

$$J(w_a, w_b) \approx \sum_{i=1}^{n} w_{iab}\, x^2 \left(1 - \frac{1}{12}x^2\right), \tag{6.5}$$

which, on neglecting the term in brackets, becomes

$$J(w_a, w_b) \approx \sum_{i=1}^{n} w_{iab} \left(\log \frac{w_{ia}}{w_{ib}}\right)^2. \tag{6.6}$$

In other words, when the value shares of the two countries are not too far from each other, the divergence is approximately equal to the second moment of their logarithmic differences. It is interesting to compare this with the information difference component (2.8), which is minus the first moment of these differences.

Let us now consider $x = \log(w_{ia}/w_{ib})$. Using $w_{ia} = p_{ia}q_{ia}/m_a$, we can decompose it as follows:

$$\log\frac{w_{ia}}{w_{ib}} = \pi_{ia} + \kappa_{ia} - \mu_a - \pi_{ib} - \kappa_{ib} + \mu_b \tag{6.7}$$
$$= (\pi_{ia} - \pi_{ib} - \Pi_{ab}) + (\kappa_{ia} - \kappa_{ib} - K_{ab}) + (\Pi_{ab} + K_{ab} - \mu_a + \mu_b) .$$

On squaring and weighting by $w_{iab}$:

$$\sum_{i=1}^{n} w_{iab}\left(\log\frac{w_{ia}}{w_{ib}}\right)^2 = A_{ab} + B_{ab} + 2C_{ab} + \Delta_{ab}^2 , \tag{6.8}$$

where $\Delta_{ab}^2$ is the squared information difference component, $A_{ab}$ is the variance of the logarithmic price differences:[9]

$$A_{ab} = \sum_{i=1}^{n} w_{iab}(\pi_{ia} - \pi_{ib} - \Pi_{ab})^2 , \tag{6.9}$$

$B_{ab}$ is the variance of the logarithmic quantity differences:

$$B_{ab} = \sum_{i=1}^{n} w_{iab}(\kappa_{ia} - \kappa_{ib} - K_{ab})^2 , \tag{6.10}$$

and $C_{ab}$ is their covariance:

$$C_{ab} = \sum_{i=1}^{n} w_{iab}(\pi_{ia} - \pi_{ib} - \Pi_{ab})(\kappa_{ia} - \kappa_{ib} - K_{ab}) . \tag{6.11}$$

Finally, when we now combine (6.5) and (6.8), we obtain

$$J(w_a, w_b) = A_{ab} + B_{ab} + 2C_{ab} + \text{error term} , \tag{6.12}$$

[9] After this article was completed we found out that the logarithmic price variance $A_{ab}$ had been proposed and applied by Leo Törnqvist (1936) as early as 1936.

where the error term is approximately equal to

$$\Delta_{ab}^2 - \frac{1}{12}\sum_{i=1}^{n} w_{iab}\left(\log\frac{w_{ia}}{w_{ib}}\right)^4 . \tag{6.13}$$

The result is, therefore, that the divergence between the two sets of value shares is approximately equal to the logarithmic price variance plus the logarithmic quantity variance plus twice the logarithmic price-quantity covariance, apart from an error whose leading term is given in (6.13).

## 7. Divergence, Dispersion, and Correlation: Application

The divergences and their decomposition according to (6.12) are presented in Table V. All figures are multiplied by $10^4$. Since the divergence is essentially a variance concept, its square root corresponds to the dimension of our basic data (logarithmic differences in prices, quantities, and value shares). By taking square roots of the figures of Table V (so that the multiplication factor $10^4$ is reduced to $10^2$) we obtain percentage differences.

Let us first consider the logarithmic variances. For prices they range from 0.01 to slightly more than 0.05, which corresponds to standard deviations between 10 and 20-25 per cent. The median standard deviation of the logarithmic price differences is slightly below 20 per cent. The logarithmic quantity variances are substantially larger and range from more than 0.03 to 0.23 (corresponding to standard deviations between almost 20 and about 50 per cent, respectively). The median standard deviation of the logarithmic quantity differences is between 30 and 40 per cent. The covariance term ($2C_{ab}$) is sizable too. Its sign is mostly negative, which could be expected in view of the tendency to substitute in favour of commodities which are comparatively cheap. The error component is small (less than 0.01 in absolute value apart from two cases) but it is systematically negative. Evidently, the squared information difference component in (6.13) is dominated by the negative term.

Turning to the divergence itself, we find that it ranges from less than 0.03 to almost 0.3. By far the largest values are those of Italy, whose divergences exceed all others in every row of Table V. It seems that the Sardinian miners stand more or less on their own. If we strike out the Italian figures, the maximum divergence is reduced to less than 0.13 and is thus more than halved.

**TABLE V.** Divergences and Their Decompositions (x $10^4$)

| | Germany | Belgium | France | Italy | Netherlands | Saarland |
|---|---|---|---|---|---|---|
| | | | *Divergence* [$J(w_a, w_b)$] | | | |
| Germany | 0 | 777 | 634 | 1322 | 254 | 644 |
| Belium | 777 | 0 | 879 | 2008 | 1062 | 599 |
| France | 634 | 879 | 0 | 1693 | 1257 | 878 |
| Italy | 1322 | 2008 | 1693 | 0 | 1640 | 2722 |
| Netherlands | 254 | 1062 | 1257 | 1640 | 0 | 719 |
| Saarland | 644 | 599 | 878 | 2722 | 719 | 0 |
| | | | *Price variance* ($A_{ab}$) | | | |
| Germany | 0 | 442 | 536 | 338 | 175 | 393 |
| Belgium | 442 | 0 | 337 | 348 | 327 | 395 |
| France | 536 | 337 | 0 | 471 | 319 | 105 |
| Italy | 338 | 348 | 471 | 0 | 376 | 470 |
| Netherlands | 175 | 327 | 319 | 376 | 0 | 191 |
| Saarland | 393 | 395 | 105 | 470 | 191 | 0 |
| | | | *Quantity Variance* ($B_{ab}$) | | | |
| Germany | 0 | 971 | 1225 | 2004 | 311 | 470 |
| Belgium | 971 | 0 | 911 | 2217 | 1016 | 440 |
| France | 1225 | 911 | 0 | 1486 | 1802 | 1127 |
| Italy | 2004 | 2217 | 1486 | 0 | 2044 | 2302 |
| Netherlands | 311 | 1016 | 1802 | 2044 | 0 | 441 |
| Saarland | 470 | 440 | 1127 | 2302 | 441 | 0 |
| | | | *Twice the price-quantity covariance* ($2C_{ab}$) | | | |
| Germany | 0 | -618 | -1118 | -974 | -231 | -205 |
| Belgium | -618 | 0 | -347 | -439 | -256 | -228 |
| France | -1118 | -347 | 0 | -218 | -816 | -312 |
| Italy | -974 | -439 | -218 | 0 | -722 | 136 |
| Netherlands | -231 | -256 | -816 | -722 | 0 | 106 |
| Saarland | -205 | -228 | -312 | 136 | 106 | 0 |
| | | | *Error Term* | | | |
| Germany | 0 | -19 | -9 | -47 | -1 | -14 |
| Belgium | -19 | 0 | -22 | -119 | -25 | -8 |
| France | -9 | -22 | 0 | -47 | -49 | -42 |
| Italy | -47 | -119 | -47 | 0 | -58 | -187 |
| Netherlands | -1 | -25 | -49 | -58 | 0 | -18 |
| Saarland | -14 | -8 | -42 | -187 | -18 | 0 |

There are several other interesting things that can be read from Table V. For example, the extremely small logarithmic price variance for France and the Saarland (not surprising in view of their economic ties!) is accompanied by a logarithmic quantity variance which is not at all so small. When this is combined with the rather small difference in real income (see Table III) the conclusion is tempting that preferences must be different. In fact the Saarland-Germany quantity variance is much smaller in spite of a much larger price variance compared with the Saarland-France case. As to the covariances, Table VI contains the corresponding correlations, which appear not to be very large; the median value is about -0.3. The largest positive value (0.18) is that of the Saarland and The Netherlands. The data presented in the Appendix reveal that this is in particular due to two commodity groups. One is butter, margarine, etc. which is comparatively more expensive in the Saarland but also comparatively more consumed. The other commodity group is "other foods" (consisting of, *inter alia*, sugar, jam, salt, chocolate, cocoa, and dried soups) which are heavily consumed by Dutchmen in spite of a relatively high price. Here again there is some indication that differences in tastes may play an important role.

**TABLE VI.** Correlations of the Logarithmic Differences of Prices and Quantities

| | Germany | Belgium | France | Italy | Netherlands | Saarland |
|---|---|---|---|---|---|---|
| Germany | . | -.472 | -.690 | -.591 | -.494 | -.239 |
| Belgium | -.472 | . | -.313 | -.250 | -.222 | -.274 |
| France | -.690 | -.313 | . | -.130 | -.538 | -.453 |
| Italy | -.591 | -.250 | -.130 | . | -.412 | .066 |
| Netherlands | -.494 | -.222 | -.538 | -.412 | . | .183 |
| Saarland | -.239 | -.274 | -.453 | .066 | .183 | . |

## 8. Interpretation of Divergences and Variances as Squared Distances

It is rather natural to consider the price and quantity variances and the divergences as the squares of *distances* between a number of points in a Euclidian space of an appropriate number of dimensions. Each such point corresponds with one country and the squared distance between two such points measures the logarithmic price or quantity variance between the two corresponding countries or the divergence between their value shares. It is easily seen that such a geometric representation is always possible for the price and quantity variance if we would be willing to proceed under the assumption that the $w_{ia}$ of (6.9) and (6.10) are independent of $a$ for each $i$, and if we choose a space of as many dimensions as there are commodities. But we are not interested in that specialized assumption, nor are we interested in a geometric picture of that many dimensions.

We proceed as follows. When there are $N$ countries ($N = 6$ in our case), we can represent these as points in an $(N - 1)$-space such that the $\frac{1}{2}N(N - 1)$ squared distances are equal to the appropriate divergences (or, for that matter, to the price or quantity variances). For example, put Germany in the origin and Belgium on the first axis. Then, all of Belgium's coordinates are zero except the first, which is equal to the positive or negative square root of the Germany-Belgium divergence. Then, put France in the plane determined by the first two axes, so that all of France's coordinates vanish except the first two. These are determined by using the Germany-France and the Belgium-France divergences, which is a matter of solving simple quadratic equations. In this way one goes on by giving each "new" country an additional nonzero coordinate. The solutions of the successive quadratic equations are not unique; this reflects the fact that the mere specification of distances do not specify the location of the points completely. Note that the "triangle inequality" has to be satisfied (the distance from $A$ to $B$ plus that from $B$ to $C$ should not be less than that from $A$ to $C$); otherwise the quadratic equations produce complex roots. There are no such cases in our application, neither with the divergences nor with the price and quantity variances.

Such a representation in the $(N - 1)$-space is always possible (under the proviso just mentioned) but not very convenient except when, say, $N = 3$ or 4. The question thus arises whether the divergences can also be (approximately) represented by squared distances in a space of a *smaller* number of dimensions.

We shall adopt the following orthogonal regression procedure. First, we remove Germany from the origin and shift the axes parallel to themselves such that the center of gravity of the $N$ points coincides with the origin. (This does not affect distances, of course.) Each point can thus be described by a column vector $y_i$ of $N - 1$ components; and the sum of $y_i$ over $i$ is a zero vector. We introduce a vector $v$ in this space (of unit length: $v'v = 1$) and the projection of $y_i$ on $v$. That is, our first effort is to reduce the $(N - 1)$-space to a *one*-dimensional space, viz., the straight line defined by the vector $v$. Let us write $y_i = \lambda_{1i}v + u_i$, where $\lambda_{1i}$ is a scalar. Both $\lambda_{1i}$ and $v$ are determined in such a way that the sum of squares of all residuals $\Sigma u_i'u_i$, is minimized. This problem of an extremum under constraint ($v'v = 1$) is solved by straightforward differentiation.

The result is that $v$ is the characteristic vector of $\Sigma y_i y_i'$ corresponding with the largest root. Note that the matrix $\Sigma y_i y_i'$ is positive semi-definite, so that its roots are either zero or positive. When only one root is positive, this is necessarily the largest and at the same time $y_i = \lambda_{1i}v$ holds with zero residuals. This is the case when all $N$ points are located on a straight line in the $(N - 1)$-space. This is generally not the case, of course, and the ratio of the largest root to the sum of all roots is then a natural measure for the degree to which the straight line representation accounts for the location of the $N$ points in the $(N - 1)$-space. Note that the sum of all roots can be easily determined as the sum of all diagonal elements of the matrix (known as the trace, tr $\Sigma y_i y_i'$).

When the ratio just mentioned is not considered to be sufficiently close to 1, one can proceed to a two-dimensional representation $y_i = \lambda_{1i}v + \lambda_{2i}w + u_i$, where $w$ is a vector (also of unit length, $w'w = 1$) which is orthogonal to $v$, i.e., $v'w = 0$. Minimization of the sum of squares of the residuals leads to the result that $w$ is the characteristic vector of $\Sigma y_i y_i'$ corresponding to the second largest root, whereas $v$ remains as described in the preceding paragraph. This result implies that the $N$ points are now represented by their projections in the two-dimensional space spanned by the vectors $v$ and $w$; furthermore, the two axes (those of $v$ and $w$) are perpendicular to each other and the $v$-coordinates are precisely the same as those of the preceding paragraph when we considered the one-dimensional representation. The degree to which the two-dimensional representation accounts for the location of the points is measured by the *sum* of the two largest roots divided by the sum of all roots. The coefficients $\lambda_{1i}$, $\lambda_{2i}$ are determined from $\lambda_{1i} = v'y_i$, $\lambda_{2i} = w'y_i$. (These equations follow directly from the minimization procedure.)

**TABLE VII.** Coordinates in Spaces of Closest Fit (× $10^2$)

| | Germany | Belgium | France | Italy | Netherlands | Saarland | Proportion accounted for |
|---|---|---|---|---|---|---|---|
| | | | | *Divergence* | | | |
| $\lambda_1$ | .07 | 9.41 | 2.04 | -32.53 | 1.84 | 19.17 | .534 |
| $\lambda_2$ | 6.68 | -8.83 | -15.66 | -1.61 | 17.88 | 1.53 | .777 |
| $\lambda_3$ | 5.22 | -15.08 | 12.60 | -3.70 | 1.34 | -.38 | .928 |
| $\lambda_4$ | 5.50 | 4.30 | 1.31 | -3.82 | 1.63 | -8.91 | .980 |
| $\lambda_5$ | 5.33 | -.63 | -2.32 | .41 | -4.44 | 1.65 | 1.000 |
| | | | | *Price variance* | | | |
| $\lambda_1$ | 9.30 | .53 | -11.05 | 8.67 | 1.22 | -8.67 | .414 |
| $\lambda_2$ | 7.70 | -9.46 | -1.89 | -6.91 | 6.48 | 4.09 | .712 |
| $\lambda_3$ | 1.29 | 8.50 | -2.62 | -7.95 | 3.07 | -2.28 | .894 |
| $\lambda_4$ | 4.64 | .39 | 2.66 | -1.58 | -5.39 | -.72 | .964 |
| $\lambda_5$ | .07 | .95 | -3.17 | .14 | -2.02 | 4.03 | 1.000 |
| | | | | *Quantity variance* | | | |
| $\lambda_1$ | 9.76 | 7.51 | -11.48 | -31.84 | 12.45 | 13.60 | .523 |
| $\lambda_2$ | 8.05 | -13.41 | -18.17 | 10.77 | 14.98 | -2.22 | .818 |
| $\lambda_3$ | 10.42 | -11.78 | 9.93 | -4.75 | -1.08 | -2.73 | .938 |
| $\lambda_4$ | 5.12 | 5.42 | -1.42 | -.36 | -.57 | -8.20 | .978 |
| $\lambda_5$ | 3.77 | .17 | -2.82 | 1.36 | -5.78 | 3.30 | 1.000 |

In this way one can go on until, finally, an ($N$ - 1)-dimensional representation is used which is, of course, identical with the original one. It is equally obvious that the ratio which describes the "fit" is then 1. The results are shown in Table VII, both for the divergences and for the logarithmic price and quantity variances. It turns out that in each of these three cases a one-dimensional representation accounts for only 40 or 50 per cent of the location of the $N$ points in the ($N$ - 1)-space, but also that a three-dimensional representation raises this percentage to about 90 per cent and up. So let us consider the three-dimensional approach for the quantity variances, which is the most interesting case.[10] The two main axes (corresponding to the two largest roots) are represented by the plane which is drawn below and which contains the center of gravity. The third axis is perpendicular to this plane. Each country is indicated by its initial (*G* is Germany, *B* is Belgium, etc.) and its projection in the plane by its initial and a prime (*G*′, *B*′, . . . ). It is of some interest to observe that the two-dimensional representation bears some resemblance to Europe's map: Italy in the South, France Northwest of Italy, Belgium North of France, and Germany North of Italy and East of Belgium. The similarity does not apply to the Saarland and The Netherlands, the latter country being located somewhere in the Baltic Sea; but its third coordinate indicates that it is slightly below sea level, which is realistic.

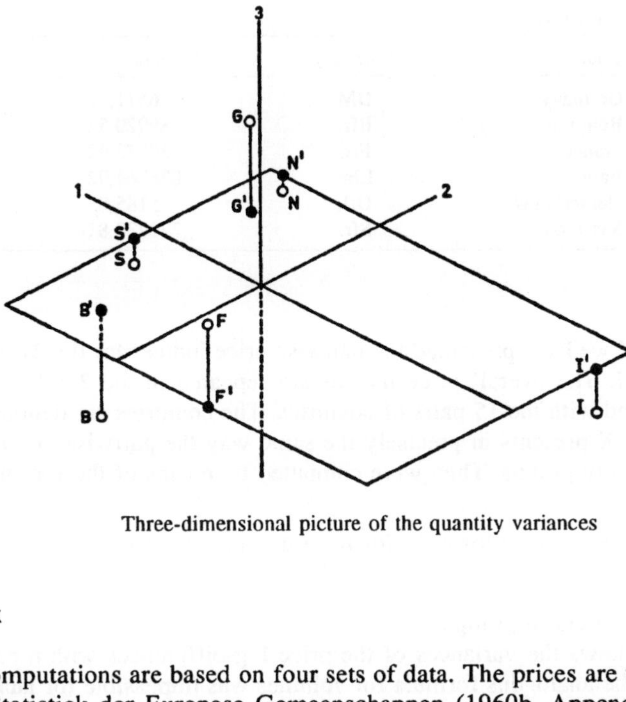


Three-dimensional picture of the quantity variances

## Appendix

All our computations are based on four sets of data. The prices are taken from Bureau voor de Statistiek der Europese Gemeenschappen (1960b, Appendix IV), the house rents from Bureau voor de Statistiek der Europese Gemeenschappen (1960b, Table III), the value shares from Bureau voor de Statistiek der Europese Gemeenschappen (1960b, Appendix V). The total expenditures were computed form the amounts given in Bureau voor de Statistiek der Europese Gemeenschappen (1960a, Tables III-1, III-10, III-14, III-24, III-39, and III-47) by subtracting the items which clearly had not been

[10] The picture of the divergences is roughly the same as that of the quantity variances. For the price variances it is different. The two-dimensional representation amounts to a table in the form of an ellipse with the Latin countries (France, Belgium, and Italy) sitting on one side and the three other countries on the other side.

considered in the price survey.[11] The results of this subtraction are given in Table VIII. The official rates of exchange were taken from Bureau voor de Statistiek der Europese Gemeenschappen (1960b, Tables 9-14). The matrix of their logarithms was made skew-symmetric by taking averages of the absolute values of the elements $(a, b)$ and $(b, a)$. After that the single-scale procedure described in Section 5 was applied to it. Otherwise the matrix $[\mu_a - \mu_b]$ (see Table III) would have lost its skew-symmetric and single-scale properties which it had before the exchange-rate correction.

**TABLE VIII.** Total Expenditure Amounts per Annum for Typical Miner's Families in Six Countries

| Country | Currency | Amount |
|---|---|---|
| Germany | DM | 6571,52 |
| Belgium | Bfr. | 89920,52 |
| France | Ffr. | 730572,92 |
| Italy | Lire | 826264,92 |
| Netherlands | Dfl. | 5185,85 |
| Saarland | Sfr. | 772730,81 |

In Table IX we have presented the pairwise price indices for the 21 commodity groups of Table II. The overall price indices are repeated in the 22nd row. The 15 columns correspond with the 15 pairs of countries. The countries are denoted by their first letters. Table X presents in precisely the same way the pairwise volume indices for the 21 commodity groups. They were computed by means of the formula

$$\kappa_{ga} - \kappa_{gb} = \log w_{ga} - \log w_{gb} + \mu_a - \mu_b - \pi_{ga} + \pi_{gb} \tag{A.1}$$

where the index $g$ refers to groups.

Table XI shows the variances of the price log-differences within each group. (Computation of the analogous formula for volumes was impossible for lack of micro quantity data.) It reveals that for some commodity groups much is lost if one works with group data, rather than on micro level. An example is the .53 variance for the countries Germany-Belgium and the group personal and medical care. The zero variances of group 17 (house rents) is simply due to the fact that this group consists of only one commodity.

[11] These were the items (in the code used in Bureau voor de Statistiek der Europese Gemeenschappen 1960a): 0620, 09, 10, 11, 14, 15, and 16. Neither social insurance premiums nor taxes were included.

**TABLE IX.** Price Indices for 21 Commodity Groups and for All Groups Together (× $10^2$)

| Group number | GB | GF | GI | GN | GS | BF | BI | BN | BS | FI | FN | FS | IN | IS | NS |
|---|---|---|---|---|---|---|---|---|---|---|---|---|---|---|---|
| 1 | 13.04 | .99 | 16.57 | 33.77 | 6.56 | -15.31 | 1.27 | 19.78 | -4.92 | 16.04 | 34.41 | 5.11 | 16.66 | -7.12 | -27.75 |
| 2 | 8.12 | -21.00 | 2.62 | 13.33 | -21.21 | -26.57 | -1.12 | 1.99 | -29.90 | 24.13 | 28.95 | 1.02 | 2.74 | -28.33 | -33.57 |
| 3 | 3.97 | -9.04 | -10.37 | 50.96 | -16.65 | -6.58 | -26.27 | 49.79 | -17.02 | -15.54 | 62.82 | -8.81 | 43.43 | 6.22 | -70.88 |
| 4 | -1.81 | -5.29 | -17.36 | 20.08 | -15.54 | -2.96 | -17.12 | 21.43 | -13.78 | -12.73 | 26.41 | -11.64 | 39.25 | .01 | -34.76 |
| 5 | 7.17 | -6.62 | 22.64 | 25.35 | -16.01 | -14.10 | 15.90 | 14.62 | -21.59 | 32.30 | 27.78 | -6.22 | 1.96 | -36.55 | -36.59 |
| 6 | 25.98 | 30.00 | 34.71 | 28.18 | 11.31 | 9.35 | 12.53 | 2.72 | -11.16 | 11.11 | -18.15 | -15.13 | -27.34 | -20.04 | -13.96 |
| 7 | 20.66 | 9.50 | -21.40 | 21.68 | 12.49 | -10.69 | -43.01 | 4.00 | -8.05 | -36.08 | 17.81 | .27 | 47.28 | 35.71 | -11.84 |
| 8 | 100.10 | 60.78 | 48.84 | 55.25 | 48.86 | -47.65 | -58.70 | -49.63 | -59.18 | -21.90 | -7.64 | -21.23 | 10.73 | -.99 | -10.53 |
| 9 | -28.21 | -31.13 | -2.04 | 6.00 | -34.88 | -2.89 | 28.42 | 34.73 | -4.81 | 30.69 | 37.85 | -2.10 | 9.10 | -32.00 | -40.54 |
| 10 | -4.23 | -23.13 | -.01 | 15.70 | -19.99 | -19.28 | .62 | 19.16 | -16.56 | 19.07 | 38.52 | 2.99 | 15.44 | -18.83 | -35.00 |
| 11 | -10.72 | -17.57 | 5.48 | 19.59 | -17.24 | -5.97 | 11.94 | 29.44 | -7.72 | 19.44 | 35.78 | .67 | 14.47 | -20.87 | -36.44 |
| 12 | -5.93 | -15.79 | 13.83 | 5.98 | -27.46 | -10.78 | 20.67 | 11.35 | -21.99 | 31.78 | 21.90 | -11.31 | -9.30 | -42.70 | -33.14 |
| 13 | -5.26 | -35.46 | -1.01 | 5.31 | -33.26 | -28.84 | 5.33 | 9.46 | -26.87 | 35.29 | 35.86 | 3.66 | 5.79 | -31.92 | -35.92 |
| 14 | -14.03 | -39.36 | -17.77 | -.63 | -41.04 | -23.81 | -.12 | 15.89 | -23.31 | 24.57 | 40.82 | -1.98 | 16.57 | -27.65 | -43.05 |
| 15 | 1.21 | -32.72 | 7.73 | .01 | -39.70 | -30.06 | 6.95 | 2.20 | -38.70 | 40.47 | 31.23 | -7.88 | -7.74 | -46.23 | -39.33 |
| 16 | -28.14 | -19.98 | -26.67 | 15.23 | 7.31 | 6.82 | 2.19 | 36.42 | 36.21 | -6.45 | 27.97 | 26.78 | 38.31 | 33.10 | -10.77 |
| 17 | -8.78 | 32.92 | 1.89 | 33.82 | 15.27 | 41.70 | 10.68 | 42.61 | 24.05 | -31.03 | .90 | -17.65 | 31.93 | 13.37 | -18.56 |
| 18 | 4.88 | -13.79 | 1.16 | 21.24 | -15.49 | -19.83 | -6.37 | 17.83 | -19.38 | 13.19 | 35.56 | -.05 | 21.85 | -14.97 | -35.89 |
| 19 | 16.82 | -13.87 | 10.74 | 14.36 | -13.89 | -12.94 | -14.06 | 7.02 | -13.44 | 13.60 | 30.15 | 5.36 | 8.29 | -16.35 | -27.28 |
| 20 | -1.30 | -14.26 | -.96 | 12.79 | -17.30 | -13.91 | 3.50 | 11.94 | -15.98 | 13.26 | 26.33 | -2.17 | 12.33 | -12.79 | -29.98 |
| 21 | -1.84 | -8.55 | 29.80 | 16.35 | 7.04 | -4.21 | 36.01 | 15.24 | 8.61 | 38.30 | 24.08 | 12.54 | -18.50 | -26.57 | -10.40 |
| All groups | 2.85 | -6.82 | 4.38 | 20.25 | -11.05 | -9.23 | 1.21 | 17.03 | -12.15 | 9.45 | 25.92 | -2.53 | 14.53 | -12.61 | -30.99 |

**TABLE X**. Quantity Indices for 21 Commodity Groups and for All Groups Together ($\times 10^2$)

| Group number | GB | GF | GI | GN | GS | BF | BI | BN | BS | FI | FN | FS | IN | IS | NS |
|---|---|---|---|---|---|---|---|---|---|---|---|---|---|---|---|
| 1 | -25.29 | -12.88 | -69.14 | -41.13 | -11.87 | 15.67 | -41.59 | -14.89 | 11.86 | -56.72 | -29.88 | 1.47 | 28.55 | 54.38 | 29.80 |
| 2 | -28.01 | -5.40 | 24.27 | 12.39 | 11.70 | 20.05 | 47.91 | 43.62 | 40.28 | 29.16 | 23.17 | 15.87 | -3.92 | -7.57 | -1.66 |
| 3 | -66.28 | -49.58 | 34.02 | -9.32 | -44.80 | 10.28 | 112.22 | 54.17 | 17.89 | 97.81 | 37.43 | 5.98 | -25.44 | -91.31 | -32.21 |
| 4 | 11.72 | 13.29 | 28.23 | -21.88 | 16.12 | 1.04 | 18.07 | -33.15 | 4.45 | 15.60 | -36.21 | 4.22 | -51.91 | -10.29 | 37.15 |
| 5 | -7.52 | -5.19 | -25.96 | -6.86 | 13.74 | 2.64 | -18.87 | 4.22 | 19.67 | -23.81 | 2.52 | 15.76 | 19.85 | 37.61 | 15.83 |
| 6 | 4.72 | 15.93 | 73.81 | -17.60 | 14.74 | 10.75 | 70.05 | -25.29 | 9.91 | 63.06 | -39.16 | 1.53 | -95.61 | -60.90 | 34.99 |
| 7 | -38.23 | -88.28 | -42.91 | 23.51 | -8.93 | -55.37 | -8.48 | 61.21 | 25.80 | 38.96 | 128.11 | 75.79 | 87.23 | 30.63 | -35.34 |
| 8 | -68.83 | -58.09 | -35.08 | -44.63 | -36.95 | 19.07 | 41.20 | 28.99 | 39.83 | 32.98 | 15.58 | 30.46 | -13.87 | -.86 | 11.82 |
| 9 | 14.28 | 29.86 | 27.74 | -8.22 | 3.21 | 15.55 | 11.22 | -23.01 | -12.92 | -3.71 | -38.79 | -28.30 | -37.02 | -25.38 | 11.09 |
| 10 | 20.83 | 39.92 | 116.61 | -2.09 | -.98 | 19.47 | 99.37 | -22.16 | -21.03 | 80.73 | -41.70 | -40.76 | -118.43 | -118.75 | .41 |
| 11 | -8.62 | -5.67 | 36.39 | -16.52 | -27.38 | 2.07 | 49.27 | -7.02 | -17.56 | 45.68 | -9.46 | -22.04 | -53.27 | -65.63 | -11.25 |
| 12 | -8.00 | 5.56 | -4.23 | 3.99 | -8.46 | 14.47 | 2.87 | 12.55 | .00 | -11.94 | -1.69 | -14.37 | 9.68 | -2.82 | -12.75 |
| 13 | 28.30 | 32.78 | 60.14 | 2.99 | 2.25 | 3.11 | 30.76 | -24.21 | -27.18 | 62.52 | -24.87 | -31.98 | -56.62 | -58.21 | -3.38 |
| 14 | 21.23 | 47.35 | 86.39 | 24.25 | 37.87 | 24.60 | 61.54 | .53 | 12.94 | 36.06 | -25.19 | -9.19 | -61.57 | -44.15 | 16.26 |
| 15 | -64.61 | 49.93 | 82.41 | -11.09 | -51.29 | 110.67 | 146.59 | 50.13 | 11.11 | 32.46 | -59.51 | -100.31 | -93.48 | -134.90 | -40.59 |
| 16 | 4.03 | 27.26 | 9.01 | -6.84 | -9.81 | 24.58 | 4.26 | -3.92 | -14.60 | -18.49 | -26.86 | -36.55 | -12.26 | -17.93 | -.12 |
| 17 | -6.42 | 1.31 | -10.99 | -1.98 | .25 | 7.73 | -4.57 | 4.44 | 6.67 | -12.30 | -3.29 | -1.06 | 9.00 | 11.24 | 2.23 |
| 18 | -5.45 | -4.45 | 33.82 | -23.04 | -8.36 | 2.17 | 41.93 | -19.06 | -3.89 | 40.03 | -19.12 | -5.56 | -58.63 | -43.87 | 13.84 |
| 19 | -46.17 | 21.86 | 40.49 | 3.50 | 11.39 | 50.28 | 94.64 | 40.20 | 40.29 | 29.64 | -20.27 | -15.85 | -41.65 | -37.38 | 6.91 |
| 20 | 13.40 | 6.13 | 52.19 | 2.92 | 1.45 | -6.31 | 35.63 | -8.32 | -11.96 | 46.10 | -2.49 | -5.55 | -47.85 | -54.29 | -1.58 |
| 21 | -86.13 | -13.82 | 21.24 | -23.10 | -45.84 | 69.81 | 103.00 | 65.99 | 40.55 | 35.11 | -8.45 | -28.97 | -39.29 | -63.28 | -21.66 |
| All groups | -16.94 | -3.47 | 12.45 | -6.62 | -4.94 | 13.09 | 30.07 | 10.66 | 10.23 | 17.28 | -1.63 | -3.21 | -17.90 | -20.63 | 1.40 |

**TABLE XI.** Variances of Log-Differences of Prices Within 21 Commodity Groups and for All Groups Together ($\times 10^2$)

| Group number | GB | GF | GI | GN | GS | BF | BI | BN | BS | FI | FN | FS | IN | IS | NS |
|---|---|---|---|---|---|---|---|---|---|---|---|---|---|---|---|
| 1 | 10.94 | 7.01 | 7.42 | 5.15 | 7.25 | 1.30 | 8.17 | 1.57 | 2.42 | 2.41 | .57 | 1.03 | 5.06 | 10.31 | 1.27 |
| 2 | 2.63 | 4.15 | 2.51 | 2.81 | 2.05 | 2.15 | 2.42 | 1.97 | 1.89 | 2.10 | 5.57 | 1.80 | 5.22 | 2.58 | 3.02 |
| 3 | 5.08 | 1.07 | 8.67 | .74 | .84 | 2.18 | 6.61 | 8.22 | 1.69 | .76 | 4.03 | .22 | 25.32 | 3.12 | 2.70 |
| 4 | 2.89 | 1.17 | 3.10 | 2.47 | .81 | 2.23 | .31 | 2.00 | 6.15 | 1.28 | 5.54 | 1.36 | 4.09 | 5.44 | 5.82 |
| 5 | 7.80 | 3.04 | 34.65 | 7.75 | 3.18 | 9.53 | 29.39 | 8.34 | 11.41 | 26.21 | 10.22 | 1.22 | 26.10 | 27.57 | 11.40 |
| 6 | 10.15 | 15.89 | 8.61 | 3.54 | 11.68 | 10.64 | 10.48 | 4.25 | 7.05 | 17.60 | 13.33 | 1.94 | 2.62 | 16.25 | 7.59 |
| 7 | 11.47 | 5.23 | 10.37 | 16.01 | 2.83 | 4.00 | 25.48 | 7.91 | 4.61 | 12.22 | 14.25 | 1.95 | 54.03 | 9.62 | 13.15 |
| 8 | .65 | 6.16 | 12.69 | 3.45 | 9.26 | 13.31 | 26.18 | 8.73 | 21.15 | 3.88 | .23 | 1.90 | 4.54 | .13 | 2.53 |
| 9 | 2.44 | 1.87 | 3.16 | .79 | 1.28 | 2.58 | 2.60 | 1.40 | 2.87 | 1.31 | 1.47 | 1.96 | 1.93 | 2.43 | 1.64 |
| 10 | 1.54 | 1.85 | 5.83 | 2.06 | 1.22 | 1.04 | 3.75 | 1.69 | 1.69 | 3.35 | .83 | .55 | 5.20 | 4.27 | 1.91 |
| 11 | 3.48 | 1.28 | 2.27 | 4.31 | 1.97 | 4.32 | 5.27 | 2.70 | 6.87 | 2.47 | 4.48 | 1.38 | 2.82 | 4.29 | 7.44 |
| 12 | .72 | 1.04 | 3.45 | 1.03 | 1.02 | .53 | 1.88 | .10 | .20 | 4.14 | .92 | .48 | 1.38 | 2.86 | .25 |
| 13 | 2.17 | 8.29 | 4.21 | 4.11 | 1.76 | 2.69 | 4.42 | 1.44 | 1.69 | 6.84 | 3.13 | 4.45 | 6.94 | 3.46 | 1.79 |
| 14 | 1.46 | 1.43 | 2.54 | 1.70 | 1.51 | 3.79 | 4.62 | 3.94 | 3.95 | 2.93 | 2.49 | .17 | 2.16 | 3.69 | 2.28 |
| 15 | 3.32 | 10.69 | 7.42 | 4.41 | 6.27 | 6.09 | 1.54 | 4.70 | 3.49 | 8.27 | 6.95 | 1.55 | 10.28 | 4.70 | 4.49 |
| 16 | .30 | .92 | 1.66 | 1.78 | .72 | .40 | 1.33 | 1.36 | 1.18 | 1.75 | 3.09 | 2.23 | 6.17 | 1.31 | 4.21 |
| 17 | 0 | 0 | 0 | 0 | 0 | 0 | 0 | 0 | 0 | 0 | 0 | 0 | 0 | 0 | 0 |
| 18 | 1.93 | 1.40 | .44 | .89 | .88 | 1.99 | 2.58 | 2.67 | 1.46 | 2.90 | .91 | .72 | 1.43 | 1.40 | .20 |
| 19 | 52.92 | 21.93 | 2.19 | 8.09 | 11.41 | 31.77 | 55.10 | 26.65 | 42.50 | 25.92 | 13.06 | 3.03 | 4.67 | 13.02 | 7.71 |
| 20 | 7.24 | 3.05 | 6.70 | 8.00 | 2.63 | 11.33 | 9.44 | 2.68 | 13.12 | 5.35 | 15.23 | 1.45 | 11.41 | 10.22 | 16.41 |
| 21 | 4.04 | 14.69 | 8.07 | 13.22 | 15.48 | 9.88 | 8.98 | 5.24 | 9.93 | 1.51 | 18.84 | 3.57 | 12.77 | 5.38 | 10.40 |
| All groups | 9.84 | 9.89 | 10.26 | 6.03 | 7.27 | 8.04 | 12.41 | 7.23 | 9.38 | 10.58 | 9.17 | 2.61 | 13.63 | 11.10 | 6.87 |

Table XII, finally, gives a comparison of the index numbers defined in (2.4) and (2.6) and the natural logarithms of some classical index numbers. The logarithms of the Paasche and Laspeyres price indices for the pair of regions $(a, b)$ are defined as

$$\log \frac{\sum p_{ia} q_{ia}}{\sum p_{ib} q_{ia}} \quad \text{and} \quad \log \frac{\sum p_{ia} q_{ib}}{\sum p_{ib} q_{ib}},$$

respectively. The logarithm of the Fisher index is the average of these two expressions. The quantity index numbers are defined in an analogous manner. It is seen that the differences between Laspeyres and Paasche are positive in all cases and substantial in many cases. Also, the index numbers presented in the present paper are fairly close to the corresponding Fisher index numbers.

**TABLE XII.** Comparison of Logarithmic Price and Quantity Indices (× $10^2$)

| Pairs of Regions | Prices | | | | Quantities | | | |
|---|---|---|---|---|---|---|---|---|
| | Paasche | Fisher | (2.4) | Laspeyres | Paasche | Fisher | (2.6) | Laspeyres |
| GB | -1.22 | 3.92 | 2.85 | 9.06 | -23.07 | -17.93 | -16.94 | -12.80 |
| GF | -11.29 | -5.88 | -6.82 | -0.47 | -9.17 | -3.76 | -3.47 | 1.65 |
| GI | -4.29 | 5.53 | 4.38 | 15.36 | 1.71 | 11.54 | 12.45 | 21.36 |
| GN | 16.60 | 20.10 | 20.25 | 23.60 | -10.18 | -6.68 | -6.62 | -3.18 |
| GS | -12.19 | -10.12 | -11.05 | -8.06 | -7.19 | -5.13 | -4.94 | -3.07 |
| BF | -12.26 | -8.90 | -9.23 | -5.54 | 9.91 | 13.27 | 13.09 | 16.63 |
| BI | -8.17 | 0.91 | 1.21 | 10.00 | 21.08 | 30.17 | 30.07 | 39.26 |
| BN | 12.79 | 15.94 | 17.03 | 19.10 | 8.34 | 11.49 | 10.66 | 14.64 |
| BS | -17.12 | -12.65 | -12.15 | -8.17 | 6.93 | 11.41 | 10.23 | 15.88 |
| FI | 4.75 | 9.32 | 9.45 | 13.89 | 12.82 | 17.39 | 17.28 | 21.96 |
| FN | 17.50 | 23.83 | 25.92 | 30.16 | -7.10 | -0.77 | -1.63 | 5.56 |
| FS | -4.53 | -2.45 | -2.53 | -0.38 | -5.23 | -3.16 | -3.21 | -1.08 |
| IN | -0.53 | 12.20 | 14.53 | 24.92 | -28.57 | -15.85 | -17.90 | -3.12 |
| IS | -17.75 | -12.41 | -12.61 | -7.07 | -25.25 | -19.91 | -20.63 | -14.57 |
| NS | -33.40 | -29.83 | -30.99 | -26.25 | -2.42 | 1.15 | 1.40 | 4.73 |

## References

Bureau voor de Statistiek der Europese Gemeenschappen: 1960a, "Huishoudrekeningen van de arbeiders der E.G.K.S. 1956-57," *Statistische Mededelingen* (Serie Sociale Statistiek, No. 1). (Published in Dutch, German, French, and Italian.)

Bureau voor de Statistiek der Europese Gemeenschappen: 1960b, "Reële inkomens E.G.K.S. 1954-58," *Statistische Mededelingen* (Serie Sociale Statistiek, No. 2). (Published in Dutch, German, French, and Italian.)

Gilbert, M., and I. B. Kravis: undated, *An International Comparison of National Products and the Purchasing Power of Currencies*, Organization for European Economic Cooperation, Paris.

Mouchez, PH.: 1961, *Les indices de prix*, Editions Cujas, Paris.

Theil, H.: 1965, "The Information Approach to Demand Analysis," *Econometrica*, **33**, No. 1.

Theil, H.: 1964, "Simultaneous Estimation of Complete Systems of Demand Equations," Lecture Notes, Center for Mathematical Studies in Business and Economics, University of Chicago, Chapter 1-3.

Törnqvist, L.: 1936, "The Bank of Finland's Consumption Price Index," *Bank of Finland Monthly Bulletin.*

CHAPTER 50

# REGIONAL PER CAPITA INCOMES AND INCOME INEQUALITIES: POINT ESTIMATES AND THEIR STANDARD ERRORS*

HENRI THEIL
*The University of Chicago,*
*Chicago, Illinois, U.S.A.*

YORAM FRIEDMAN
*University of Tel-Aviv,*
*Tel-Aviv, Israel.*

ABSTRACT. A simple statistical model is developed to assess the implications of random measurement errors in reported per capita incomes and of the bias caused by the use of official exchange rates for (1) regional per capita incomes and (2) regional income inequality. It appears that regional per capita incomes can be estimated with a fair degree of accuracy, provided that the measurement errors of the reported per capita incomes of individual countries are not too highly positively correlated. The measurement of regional inequality is characterized by considerable uncertainty.

## 1. Errors in Per Capita Income Estimates

Economists, statisticians and laymen agree that per capita income data are imperfect. One reason is conceptual: gross national product is not identical with economic welfare, and we refer to the effort made by Nordhaus and Tobin (1972) to transform GNP into a "measure of economic welfare." A second reason is more statistical in nature. Even if per capita income measures in principle what we want to be measured, it does so imperfectly, particularly when the objective is to compare different countries. The present article concerns this statistical problem.

More generally, economic data are not fully accurate; sometimes they are very inaccurate. When it is impossible to improve on their quality, it is at least desirable that explicit statements be made on the statistical structure of their observational error. This is unfortunately rarely done. The major objective of this article is to show how it can be done and how this sometimes leads to the conclusion that ignorance prevails. To accomplish this goal we shall consider data on per capita gross domestic product (for short, per capita income) published by Hagen and Hawrylyshyn (1969).

The main statistical tools to be used in our analysis can be summarized as follows:

* This article first appeared in *Journal of the American Statistical Association*, **68** (1973), 531-539. Reprinted with the permission of the American Statistical Association.

Henri Theil is a professor and director, Centre for Mathematical Studies in Business and Economics, The University of Chicago, Ill. 60637. Mr. Friedman is lecturer, The Leon Recanati Graduate School of Business, The University of Tel-Aviv, Israel. Research for this article was supported in part by the National Science Foundation under Grant G8-30084, carried out at the Center for Mathematical Studies in Business and Economics of The University of Chicago. The authors are indebted to Professor Everett E. Hagen of the Massachusetts Institute of Techology for clarification of their statistical data.

1. On the average, the relative errors of the reported per capita incomes of low-income countries are larger than those of more developed countries. Write $y_i$ for the reported per capita income of the $i$th country, $\eta_i$ for the error-free value, and let us measure the size of the relative error by the variance of the natural logarithm of $y_i/\eta_i$. The following model formalizes this statement on the behavior of relative errors:

$$\text{var}\left(\log \frac{y_i}{\eta_i}\right) = \alpha_0 + \alpha\left(\log \frac{\eta_1}{\eta_i}\right)^2 \qquad \alpha_0, \alpha > 0 \tag{1.1}$$

where $\eta_1$ on the right is the error-free per capita income of the U.S. ($i = 1$). This model implies that the variances of the logarithmic errors of all countries exceed that of the U.S., but that the excess is minor for countries whose per capita incomes are only moderately less than that of the U.S.[1]

2. Systematic errors are made when per capita incomes are compared on the basis of official exchange rates. It is beyond the scope of this article to go into the causes, but real-income comparisons based on these exchange rates systematically underestimate the relative incomes of low-income countries. To handle this problem, write $Y_i$ for the error-free value of country $i$'s per capita income which measures what it would be worth in the U.S., and $\hat{Y}_i$ for the corresponding observed value; this $\hat{Y}_i$ is a function of the observed $y$'s whereas $Y_i$ involves the $\eta$'s. To correct for the bias just described, we compute $\hat{Y}_i$ from

$$\log \frac{\hat{Y}_i}{y_i} = \theta \log \frac{y_1}{y_i} . \qquad 0 < \theta < 1 \tag{1.2}$$

This means that $\hat{Y}_i$ is a weighted geometric mean of the per capita incomes of the U.S. and of the $i$th country with weights equal to $\theta$ and $1 - \theta$, respectively:

$$\hat{Y}_i = y_1^{\theta} y_i^{1-\theta} . \tag{1.3}$$

Hence the per capita incomes of all countries are corrected in the direction of that of the U.S., and the relative corrections are larger for low-income countries than for medium-income countries. The dependence of the error-free $Y_i$ on the $\eta$'s will be considered in section 4.

[1] Two countries (Kuwait and Qatar) have per capita incomes exceeding the U.S. value; the model (1.1) implies that their error variances are also larger than that of the U.S. This is of minor importance but probably realistic.

The specifications (1.1) and (1.2) involve simple functions of logarithmic income ratios. There are no doubt other specifications which accomplish approximately the same objectives, but simplicity and tractability should weigh heavily in the present state of art.

## 2. Regional Per Capita Incomes

### 2.1 DESCRIPTION OF THE DATA

Hagen and Hawrylyshyn estimated the per capita incomes of almost all countries (including non-self-governing areas) in 1960 and 1965. Our interest is in regional per capita incomes and regional income inequality, and we shall therefore make no effort to be so exhaustive. The following are five (more or less) homogeneous regions, mostly consisting of neighboring countries:

$R_1$, North America and Europe, consisting of 22 countries with a total population of 537 million in 1965;
$R_2$, Latin America, 31 countries, 242 million (1965)[2];
$R_3$, Central Africa, 34 countries, 210 million (1965);
$R_4$, North Africa and Middle East, 21 countries, 152 million (1965);
$R_5$, Asia, 25 countries, 1003 million (1965).

A complete list of all 133 countries is given in Appendix A. The five regions do not include Communist countries (except Cuba which is part of $R_2$). The exclusion of Communist countries is motivated by the large margins of error of their income estimates in dollars. The non-Communist countries not represented are Australia, New Zealand, the countries in the southern tip of Africa, small islands in various oceans, and small countries elsewhere which Hagen and Hawrylyshyn combined into "Others" groups. There exists no reasonable way of grouping these countries into regions. Their total population in 1965 is about 40 million, which is quite small compared with the total population of these five regions. We shall refer to the combination of these regions as "the world" from now on, and we shall continue to assign the subscript $i$ = 1 to the U.S. (which is part of $R_1$) in agreement with the notation used in section 1.

### 2.2 ESTIMATES OF THE WORLD AND REGIONAL PER CAPITA INCOMES

Write $p_i$ for the population of the $i$th country, measured as a fraction of the world total. Similarly, write $P_g = \Sigma\, p_i$, where the summation is over $i \in R_g$, for the population share of region $R_g$. Then the uncorrected per capita income of the world and of $R_g$ are, respectively,

[2] There are two printing errors in Hagen's and Hawrylyshyn's Table 5A: the populations of Barbados and Bolivia in 1960, listed as .11 and .23 million, should be .23 and 3.46 million, respectively.

$$\sum_{i=1}^{133} p_i y_i \quad \text{and} \quad \sum_{i \in R_g} \frac{p_i}{P_g} y_i \tag{2.1}$$

whereas the estimates of the corrected values are

$$\hat{Z} = \sum_{i=1}^{133} p_i \hat{Y}_i \quad \text{and} \quad \hat{Z}_g = \sum_{i \in R_g} \frac{p_i}{P_g} \hat{Y}_i \; . \tag{2.2}$$

The implementation of these corrections requires a numerical specification of the parameter $\theta$ in (1.2). The following values will be used for $\theta$ and for the parameters of (1.1):

$$\theta = \frac{1}{3} \qquad \alpha_0 = .002 \qquad \alpha = .004 \; . \tag{2.3}$$

The value of $\theta$ implies for $y_1 = 3{,}000$ (the approximate U.S. per capita income in dollars per year) that a reported per capita income of $y_i = 100$ is corrected to $\hat{Y}_i \approx 310$. The value of $\alpha_0$ implies in view of (1.1) that the standard error of the U.S. per capita income is about four or five percent. The lowest reported per capita incomes are around 50 dollars per year, which gives a natural logarithm of $\eta_1/\eta_i$ of the order of four. Using (1.1) and the $\alpha$ of (2.3), we obtain a variance of the logarithm of $y_i/\eta_i$ between .06 and .07, which amounts to a standard deviation of the error of the per capita income of a very poor country of the order of 25 percent. These numerical values are in approximate agreement with conjecture made by Hagen and Hawrylyshyn on the quality of their data (1969, pp. 4-7 and 9-10). Needless to say, such numbers are subjective. To handle this problem, we shall present decompositions in the discussion of standard errors (section 4) which enable the reader to substitute his own preferred numbers.

The uncorrected values (2.1) are shown in the first two columns of Table I and the estimates (2.2) of the corrected values in the last two. As could be expected, the correction raises the per capita income estimates of all regions, particularly for Central Africa and Asia.[3] The figures in parentheses in the last two columns are standard errors. Their derivation as well as the assumptions underlying the derivation are described in section 4. It should be stressed here that one of these assumptions states that the logarithmic errors of the reported (uncorrected) per capita incomes of different countries are uncorrelated. There are reasons for believing that this assumption is not entirely

[3] To obtain an impression of the effect of alternative values of $\theta$ we note from (1.2) that log $\hat{Y}_i$ is a linear function of $\theta$ with slope log $(y_1/y_i)$. Hence, for $y_1 = 3{,}000$ and $y_i = 100$, an increase of $\theta$ from ⅓ to .4 raises log $\hat{Y}_i$ by about .23, and hence $\hat{Y}_i$ by about 25 percent. The figure $y_i = 100$ roughly applies to most countries of Central Africa in 1965, so that its regional per capita income in this year under $\theta = .4$ becomes about \$400.

satisfactory, particularly for less developed countries. In many cases the estimates of the per capita incomes of such countries are obtained indirectly, by means of a comparison with other countries in the same region. This may easily lead to a situation in which the observational errors of the per capita incomes of the former countries have the same sign as the income errors of the latter, which implies a positive correlation. The matter is pursued in Appendix B, where it appears that such a positive correlation can have a noticeable (upward) effect on the standard errors of the regional per capita income estimates.

## 3. Income Inequality Among and Within Regions

### 3.1 AN INFORMATIONAL MEASURE OF INCOME INEQUALITY

We write $p_1, \ldots, p_{133}$ for the population shares as before and we introduce the countries' income shares, to be written $q_1, \ldots, q_{133}$. Each $q_i$ measures a country's gross domestic product as a fraction of the world total. A simple measure for the degree to which the per capita incomes differ, based on the elementary concepts of information theory,[4] is

$$I = \sum_{i=1}^{133} p_i \log \frac{p_i}{q_i} . \tag{3.1}$$

**TABLE I.** World and Regional Per Capita Incomes[a]

| Per capita income of | 1960 | 1965 | 1960 | | 1965 | |
|---|---|---|---|---|---|---|
| | Uncorrected | | Corrected | | | |
| World | 565 | 737 | 795 | (35) | 1021 | (43) |
| Regional | | | | | | |
| Europe and N. America | 1717 | 2304 | 1955 | (62) | 2590 | (80) |
| Latin America | 332 | 412 | 663 | (41) | 824 | (51) |
| Central Africa | 82 | 98 | 261 | (35) | 315 | (43) |
| N. Africa and Middle East | 212 | 269 | 483 | (39) | 607 | (49) |
| Asia | 122 | 180 | 326 | (39) | 439 | (49) |

[a] Dollars per year

[4] The measure (3.1) is the expected information of the "message" which transforms the income shares of the 133 countries as "prior probabilities" into their population shares as "posterior probabilities." It was discussed by Theil (1967, pp. 125-128). An alternative procedure consists of interchanging the roles of the $p$'s and $q$'s in (3.1); we rejected this alternative because it would lead to a greater dependence on the income shares (the $q$'s) which are known much less accurately than the $p$'s. For other applications of information measures to income inequality see Fishlow (1972) and Theil (1972).

To express $q_i$ in terms of the concepts used in section 2 we write $N_i$ for the population of the $i$th country and $N$ for the world's population. The income shares based on corrected per capita incomes are then

$$q_i = \frac{N_i Y_i}{NZ} = p_i \frac{Y_i}{Z} \qquad i = 1, \ldots, 133 \tag{3.2}$$

so that the inequality measure (3.1) can be written as

$$I = \sum_{i=1}^{133} p_i \log \frac{Z}{Y_i} = \log Z - \sum_{i=1}^{133} p_i \log Y_i \,. \tag{3.3}$$

This shows that $I$ is simply the logarithmic ratio of arithmetic mean per capita income to geometric mean per capita income, both means being weighted means with weights equal to the population shares.

One of the major attractive features of the informational income inequality measure (3.1) is the simplicity of its aggregation properties. In our analysis the 133 countries are grouped into five regions. Write $Q_g = \Sigma_i q_i$, where the summation is over $i \in R_g$, for the income share of region $R_g$, so that

$$I_0 = \sum_{g=1}^{5} P_g \log \frac{P_g}{Q_g} = \log Z - \sum_{g=1}^{5} P_g \log Z_g \tag{3.4}$$

measures the inequality among regions with respect to their (regional) per capita incomes. It is easily verified that $I$ and $I_0$ are connected by

$$I = I_0 + \sum_{g=1}^{5} P_g I_g \tag{3.5}$$

where

$$I_g = \sum_{i \in R_g} \frac{p_i}{P_g} \log \frac{p_i/P_g}{q_i/Q_g} = \log Z_g - \sum_{i \in R_g} \frac{p_i}{P_g} \log Y_i \tag{3.6}$$

measures the inequality among the countries of region $R_g$. Thus, (3.5) states that world inequality at the country level equals world inequality at the regional level plus a weighted average of the country-level inequalities of the separate regions, with weights proportional to the populations of the regions.

## 3.2 APPLICATIONS

The successive lines of Table II contain $I$, $I_0$, $\Sigma P_g I_g$, $I_1, \ldots, I_5$ for 1960 and 1965. The first two columns are based on the uncorrected per capita income figures and the last two on the estimates $\hat{Y}_i$ of the corrected values. It comes as no surprise that the correction reduces the inequalities substantially. Confining ourselves to point estimates first, we observe that there was an increase in world inequality from 1960 to 1965 wholly due to changes within regions. The $I_g$'s of the separate regions all increased except for the Europe and North America region.

The largest regional inequality in 1960 is that of Asia and its increase from 1960 to 1965 (by about 50 percent) exceeds that of any other region. This is wholly due to the rapid economic development of Japan. The first line of Table III shows that when Japan is excluded, Asia's per capita income is only barely better than that of Central Africa (see Table I). A comparison of the second line of Table III with the corresponding line of Table II indicates that the exclusion of Japan raises the inequality among regions. The third lines of these two tables show that this exclusion reduces the average within-region inequality substantially, but since the latter is so small relative to the between-region inequality, their sum (world inequality) becomes larger when Japan is excluded. The reduction of the average within-region inequality is solely due to a reduction of $\hat{I}_5$, the regional inequality of Asia. In fact, the last line of Table III shows that this inequality becomes smaller than that of any other region.

**TABLE II.** World and Regional Income Inequality[a]

| Inequality by area | 1960 | 1965 | 1960 | | 1965 | |
|---|---|---|---|---|---|---|
| | Uncorrected | | Corrected | | | |
| World | .917 | .949 | .417 | (.041) | .436 | (.040) |
| Among regions | .730 | .708 | .338 | (.041) | .338 | (.039) |
| Average within regions | .188 | .241 | .079 | (.057) | .098 | (.056) |
| Within individual regions | | | | | | |
| Europe and N. America | .181 | .132 | .086 | (.008) | .062 | (.006) |
| Latin America | .093 | .104 | .041 | (.040) | .046 | (.041) |
| Central Africa | .096 | .124 | .041 | (.116) | .052 | (.119) |
| N. Africa and Middle East | .129 | .165 | .048 | (.061) | .064 | (.061) |
| Asia | .242 | .370 | .097 | (.080) | .145 | (.075) |

[a] Natural logarithms

The statements made in the preceding paragraph are based on point estimates. When we subsequently consider their standard errors (derived in section 5), we have to conclude that many of these statements have no real validity. Several of the $\hat{I}_g$'s have standard errors that are of the same order of magnitude, which implies that the data reveal very little about the per capita income inequality among the countries of these regions;

the only exception is $\hat{I}_1$, which exceeds its standard error by a factor of 10 in both years. The result is that the estimate of the average within-region inequality is also very uncertain. We have better results for world inequality at the country level and at the regional level, but it would evidently be unwise to regard the increase in the former from 1960 to 1965 as statistically well-established.

**TABLE III.** Some Estimates with Japan Excluded

| Variables by area | 1960 | 1965 | 1960 | | 1965 | |
|---|---|---|---|---|---|---|
| | Uncorrected | | Corrected | | | |
| Per capita income of Asia[a] | 83 | 105 | 267 | (40) | 336 | (51) |
| Income inequality among regions[b] | .865 | .902 | .395 | (.052) | .415 | (.054) |
| Average within-region inequality[b] | .097 | .091 | .043 | (.059) | .040 | (.060) |
| Regional inequality of Asia[b] | .041 | .044 | .016 | (.086) | .018 | (.085) |

[a] Dollars per year
[b] Natural logarithms

## 4. Standard Errors of Per Capita Income Estimates

### 4.1 NOTATION

We define $\theta_i$ in terms of the error-free per capita incomes (corrected as well as uncorrected) of the U.S. and the $i$th country:

$$\log \frac{Y_i}{\eta_i} = \theta_i \log \frac{\eta_1}{\eta_i} . \tag{4.1}$$

By subtracting this equation from (1.2) we obtain

$$\log \frac{\hat{Y}_i}{y_i} - \log \frac{Y_i}{\eta_i} = \theta \log \frac{y_1}{y_i} - \theta_i \log \frac{\eta_1}{\eta_i}$$

or, equivalently,

$$\log \frac{\hat{Y}_i}{Y_i} = \theta \log \frac{y_1}{\eta_1} + (1 - \theta) \log \frac{y_i}{\eta_i} - (\theta_i - \theta) \log \frac{\eta_1}{\eta_i} .$$

This may be written as

$$\log \frac{\hat{Y}_i}{Y_i} = \theta\, \varepsilon_1 + (1-\theta)\, \varepsilon_i - a_i (\theta_i - \theta) \tag{4.2}$$

where

$$\varepsilon_i = \log \frac{y_i}{\eta_i} \qquad a_i = \log \frac{\eta_1}{\eta_i} \; . \tag{4.3}$$

Equation (4.2) expresses the logarithmic error of the estimate of the corrected per capita income linearly in terms of $\theta_i - \theta$ and the logarithmic errors of the uncorrected per capita incomes (the $\varepsilon$'s). Using the same notation, we can write (1.1) as

$$\operatorname{var} \varepsilon_i = \alpha_0 + \alpha\, a_i^2 \; . \tag{4.4}$$

## 4.2 THE MOMENT MATRIX OF THE CORRECTED PER CAPITA INCOMES

We proceed to derive the second-order moments of the logarithmic errors of the corrected per capita incomes under the assumption that the $\varepsilon$'s are uncorrelated. Note first that (4.2) for the U.S. ($i = 1$) reduces, in view of $a_1 = 0$, to

$$\log \frac{\hat{Y}_1}{Y_1} = \varepsilon_1 \; . \tag{4.5}$$

The second moment of the logarithmic error of the U.S. income estimate, to be written $m_{11}$, is obtained by squaring (4.5) and taking the expectation, and the cross-moment of this error and that of any other country ($m_{i1}$, $i \neq 1$) by multiplying (4.5) and (4.2) and taking the expectation. Using (4.4), we obtain

$$\begin{aligned} m_{i1} &= \alpha_0 && \text{if} \quad i = 1 \\ &= \alpha_0 \theta && \text{if} \quad i \neq 1. \end{aligned} \tag{4.6}$$

For any country other than the U.S. we use (4.2) only. Squaring both sides and taking the expectation gives

$$m_{ii} = \alpha_0 \theta^2 + (1-\theta)^2 (\alpha_0 + \alpha\, a_i^2) + a_i^2 (\theta_i - \theta)^2 \qquad i \neq 1 \; . \tag{4.7}$$

The cross-moment is obtained similarly:

$$m_{ij} = \alpha_0 \theta^2 + a_i a_j (\theta_i - \theta)(\theta_j - \theta) \qquad 1 \neq i \neq j \neq 1 \ . \tag{4.8}$$

It will prove convenient to combine (4.7) and (4.8) into

$$m_{ij} = \alpha_0 \theta^2 + a_i a_j (\theta_i - \theta)(\theta_j - \theta) + \delta_{ij}(1-\theta)^2(\alpha_0 + \alpha a_i^2) \qquad i \neq 1 \neq j \tag{4.9}$$

where $\delta_{ij}$ is the Kronecker delta.

## 4.3 DERIVATION OF THE STANDARD ERRORS

We define the error-free corrected per capita income $Z_g$ of region $R_g$ as the same function of the error-free $Y$'s as $\hat{Z}_g$ is of the $\hat{Y}$'s in (2.2). The error of $\hat{Z}_g$ can then be expressed as follows:

$$\hat{Z}_g - Z_g = \sum_{i \in R_g} \frac{p_i}{P_g} Y_i \frac{\hat{Y}_i - Y_i}{Y_i} \approx \sum_{i \in R_g} \frac{p_i}{P_g} Y_i \log \frac{\hat{Y}_i}{Y_i} \ . \tag{4.10}$$

The second moment of this error is

$$\sum_{i \in R_g} \sum_{j \in R_g} \frac{p_i}{P_g} Y_i \frac{p_j}{P_g} Y_j m_{ij} \ , \tag{4.11}$$

where $m_{ij}$ is defined in (4.6) and (4.9). Note that this procedure assumes that the population shares are error free. This simplification is justified to the extent that such shares are much less inaccurate than the income shares.

Consider first any region $R_g$ other than $R_1$, so that the United States is not included. Then $m_{ij}$ is as given in (4.9), so that the second moment (4.11) is equal to the sum of the following three terms:

$$A_g^2 = \alpha_0 \theta^2 \left( \sum_{i \in R_g} \frac{p_i}{P_g} Y_i \right)^2 \tag{4.12}$$

$$B_g^2 = \left[ \sum_{i \in R_g} \frac{p_i}{P_g} Y_i a_i (\theta_i - \theta) \right]^2 \tag{4.13}$$

$$C_g^2 = (1-\theta)^2 \sum_{i \in R_g} \left( \frac{p_i}{P_g} Y_i \right)^2 (\alpha_0 + \alpha a_i^2) \, . \tag{4.14}$$

The expression for $B_g^2$ causes complications because the right side of (4.13) involves the $\theta_i$'s of the individual countries. We shall estimate this term under the assumption that the $\theta_i$'s and $\eta_i$'s are stochastically independent over the set of countries in each region. In view of (4.1) this means that the size of the correction factor $\theta_i$ is assumed not to be systematically related to the country's per capita income prior to the correction. The distribution of the $\theta_i$'s and $\eta_i$'s is further defined by assigning a probability mass to each country proportional to its population. Finally, to simplify the analysis we assume that $\theta = ⅓$ (the value used in section 2) is the mean of the $\theta_i$'s in each region:

$$\theta = \sum_{i \in R_g} \frac{p_i}{P_g} \theta_i \qquad g = 1, \ldots, 5 \, . \tag{4.15}$$

Define then, $B_g$ as the square root of $B_g^2$, so that (4.13) gives

$$\begin{aligned} B_g &= \sum_{i \in R_g} \frac{p_i}{P_g} Y_i a_i (\theta_i - \theta) \\ &= \sum_{i \in R_g} \frac{p_i}{P_g} \eta_i \left( \frac{\eta_1}{\eta_i} \right)^{\theta_i} \left( \log \frac{\eta_1}{\eta_i} \right) (\theta_i - \theta) \, , \end{aligned} \tag{4.16}$$

where the second equality sign is based on (4.1) and (4.3).

To exploit the independence of the $\eta_i$'s and the $\theta_i$'s it is convenient to have an expectation of a product of a number of terms, each involving either $\eta_i$ or $\theta_i$ but not both. This is evidently not the case for $(\eta_1/\eta_i)^{\theta_i}$ in the second line of (4.16). So we apply a Taylor expansion around $\theta_i = \theta$ to that term:

$$\left( \frac{\eta_1}{\eta_i} \right)^{\theta_i} \approx \left( \frac{\eta_1}{\eta_i} \right)^{\theta} + (\theta_i - \theta) \left( \frac{\eta_1}{\eta_i} \right)^{\theta} \log \frac{\eta_1}{\eta_i} \, .$$

Substitution of the right side in the second line of (4.16) gives

$$B_g = \sum_{i \in R_g} \frac{p_i}{P_g} \eta_i \left(\frac{\eta_1}{\eta_i}\right)^{\theta} \left(\log \frac{\eta_1}{\eta_i}\right) (\theta_i - \theta)$$

$$+ \sum_{i \in R_g} \frac{p_i}{P_g} \eta_i \left(\frac{\eta_1}{\eta_i}\right)^{\theta} \left(\log \frac{\eta_1}{\eta_i}\right)^2 (\theta_i - \theta)^2 .$$

Using the independence of the $\eta_i$'s and $\theta_i$'s we can write the first term on the right as

$$\left[\sum_{i \in R_g} \frac{p_i}{P_g} \eta_i \left(\frac{\eta_1}{\eta_i}\right)^{\theta} \log \frac{\eta_1}{\eta_i}\right] \left[\sum_{i \in R_g} \frac{p_i}{P_g} (\theta_i - \theta)\right] ,$$

which vanishes in view of (4.15). So we obtain:

$$B_g = \sigma^2 \sum_{i \in R_g} \frac{p_i}{P_g} \eta_i \left(\frac{\eta_1}{\eta_i}\right)^{\theta} \left(\log \frac{\eta_1}{\eta_i}\right)^2 , \tag{4.17}$$

where

$$\sigma^2 = \sum_{i \in R_g} \frac{p_i}{P_g} (\theta_i - \theta)^2 \tag{4.18}$$

is the variance of the $\theta_i$'s.

For $R_1$ we need a correction because (4.9) implies that $m_{i1}$ and $m_{1i}$ for $i \neq 1$ both equal $\alpha_0 \theta^2$ (recall that $a_1$ vanishes), whereas we know from (4.6) that they are equal to $\alpha_0 \theta$ and it implies that $m_{11}$ equals

$$\alpha_0 \left[\theta^2 + (1 - \theta)^2\right] = \alpha_0 - 2\alpha_0 \theta (1 - \theta) ,$$

and we know from (4.6) that it is equal to $\alpha_0$. Hence, to obtain the second moment (4.11) for $g = 1$, we must add

$$2\alpha_0 \theta (1 - \theta) \frac{p_1}{P_1} Y_1 \sum_{i \in R_1} \frac{p_i}{P_1} Y_i = 2\alpha_0 \theta (1 - \theta) \frac{p_1}{P_1} Y_1 Z_1 \tag{4.19}$$

to $A_1^2 + B_1^2 + C_1^2$.

The computation of the standard error of the estimate of world per capita income requires a similar correction, equal to

$$2\,\alpha_0\,\theta\,(1-\theta)\,p_1\,Y_1\,Z\,.$$

In addition, the summations over $i \in R_g$ are replaced by summations over $i = 1, \ldots, 133$, and $P_g$ is replaced by 1.

## 4.4 NUMERICAL RESULTS

The results are shown in Line (1) of Table IV for 1960 and in Line (5) for 1965; the standard errors of Table I are the square roots of the figures in these two lines. The numerical specifications used are (2.3) for $\theta_1$, $\alpha_0$ and $\alpha$; $\hat{Y}_i$ and $y_i$ for $Y_i$ and $\eta_i$, respectively; and $\hat{Y}_i$ for $\eta_i(\eta_1/\eta_i)^\theta$ in (4.17). The variance (4.18) is specified as .01, implying a standard deviation $\sigma = .1$, which allows a rather wide range of variation of the $\theta_i$'s around their mean $\theta = 1/3$.

The other lines of Table IV contain the three components ($A_g^2$, $B_g^2$, $C_g^2$) but in slightly rearranged form. We combine $A_g^2$ with the $\alpha_0$ component of $C_g^2$ and with (4.19) for $g = 1$:

$$\alpha_0 \text{ component} = \alpha_0\,\theta^2\left(\sum_{i\in R_g}\frac{p_i}{P_g}Y_i\right)^2 + \alpha_0\,(1-\theta)^2\sum_{i\in R_g}\left(\frac{p_i}{P_g}Y_i\right)^2 + 2\delta_{1g}\,\alpha_0\,\theta\,(1-\theta)\,\frac{p_1}{P_1}Y_1Z_1\,, \tag{4.20}$$

where $\delta_{1g}$ is the Kronecker delta. What remains of $C_g^2$ is the $\alpha$ component:

$$\alpha \text{ component} = \alpha\,(1-\theta)^2\sum_{i\in R_g}\left(\frac{p_i}{P_g}Y_i a_i\right)^2. \tag{4.21}$$

The third component is the square of $B_g$ given in (4.17), which is called the $\sigma^2$ component. The decomposition for world income per capita is identical with that for $Z_1$ except for the replacement of $P_g$'s by 1 and the extension of the summation range to 1, . . . , 133.

**TABLE IV.** Squared Standard Errors of Point Estimates of Corrected Per Capita Incomes and Their Decomposition[a]

| Statistic | World | $R_1$ | $R_2$ | $R_3$ | $R_4$ | $R_5$ |
|---|---|---|---|---|---|---|
| | | | 1960 | | | |
| (1) Squared standard error | 1207 | 3840 | 1650 | 1194 | 1544 | 1536 |
| (2) $\alpha_0$ component | 401 | 3599 | 153 | 20 | 77 | 45 |
| (3) $\alpha$ component | 113 | 153 | 554 | 114 | 357 | 434 |
| (4) $\sigma^2$ component | 693 | 88 | 943 | 1061 | 1110 | 1057 |
| | | | 1965 | | | |
| (5) Squared standard error | 1868 | 6389 | 2571 | 1834 | 2389 | 2399 |
| (6) $\alpha_0$ component | 637 | 6091 | 234 | 29 | 121 | 85 |
| (7) $\alpha$ component | 183 | 209 | 847 | 173 | 548 | 705 |
| (8) $\sigma^2$ component | 1049 | 89 | 1490 | 1631 | 1719 | 1609 |

[a] Squares of dollars per year

The decomposition shown in Table IV should be useful for anyone who prefers a specification of $\alpha_0$, $\alpha$ or $\sigma L^2$ which differs from the one used here. For example, to have an $\alpha_0$ which is twice as large, double the figures in lines (2) and (6) and adjust lines (1) and (5) accordingly. Our specification implies that the $\alpha_0$ component is dominant for the per capita income of $R_1$, but not for the incomes of any other region. The $\sigma L^2$ component is leading in the case of the latter regions, followed by the $\alpha$ component. Evidently, the disparity of the true correction factors (the $\theta_i$'s) is responsible for most of the uncertainty as to the corrected values of the per capita incomes of $R_2, \ldots, R_5$.

## 5. Standard Errors of the Inequality Estimates

The standard errors in Table II are based on the assumptions of section 4 plus the additional assumption that the $\theta_i$'s are independent across countries. Details are provided in Appendix C; an extension to correlated $\varepsilon$'s is given in Appendix D. It appears that the squared standard errors can be decomposed (similarly to Table IV) in terms of $\alpha_0$, $\alpha$ and $\sigma^2$ components. These squared standard errors and their decompositions in percentage form are given in Table V; the percentage form is preferred because different squared standard errors are of quite different orders of magnitude.

It appears that the $\sigma^2$ component accounts for about 90 percent or more in all cases except $\hat{I}$, $\hat{I}_0$ and $\hat{I}_1$. This means that in all cases except these three the squared standard error is approximately proportional to $\sigma^4$ and hence the standard error itself is approximately proportional to $\sigma^2$. Thus, if we specify $\sigma = .07$ rather than .1, the standard errors of $\hat{I}_2, \ldots, \hat{I}_5$ are reduced by about 50 percent. Nevertheless, they are still large.

**TABLE V.** Squared Standard Errors of Inequality Estimates and Their Decompositions

| Inequality by area | Squared standard error | | Percentage Decomposition | | | | | |
|---|---|---|---|---|---|---|---|---|
| | | | $\alpha_0$ | $\alpha$ | $\sigma^2$ | $\alpha_0$ | $\alpha$ | $\sigma^2$ |
| | 1960 | 1965 | 1960 | | | 1965 | | |
| World | $17.0 \times 10^{-4}$ | $16.3 \times 10^{-4}$ | 4 | 35 | 61 | 4 | 38 | 58 |
| Among regions | $16.8 \times 10^{-4}$ | $15.3 \times 10^{-4}$ | 3 | 19 | 78 | 3 | 18 | 79 |
| Average within regions | $32.7 \times 10^{-4}$ | $30.9 \times 10^{-4}$ | 0 | 3 | 97 | 0 | 4 | 96 |
| Within individual regions | | | | | | | | |
| Europe and N. America | $68.4 \times 10^{-6}$ | $41.7 \times 10^{-6}$ | 38 | 32 | 31 | 44 | 27 | 29 |
| Latin America | $16.0 \times 10^{-4}$ | $16.8 \times 10^{-4}$ | 0 | 3 | 96 | 0 | 5 | 94 |
| Central Africa | $133.7 \times 10^{-4}$ | $141.1 \times 10^{-4}$ | 0 | 1 | 99 | 0 | 1 | 99 |
| N. Africa and Middle East | $36.9 \times 10^{-4}$ | $36.7 \times 10^{-4}$ | 0 | 1 | 99 | 0 | 2 | 98 |
| Asia | $63.6 \times 10^{-4}$ | $56.1 \times 10^{-4}$ | 1 | 7 | 93 | 1 | 10 | 89 |

## Appendix A: List of Countries

The order of countries within each region is alphabetical except that the United States, Canada and Greenland are listed prior to the European countries in $R_1$. Central Africa ($R_3$) is defined as the area south of the countries that border on the Mediterranean and north of the countries which are dominated by a native white minority (South Africa, South West Africa and Rhodesia). This also excludes the enclaves within the latter countries (Botswana, Lesotho and Swaziland).

$R_1$, *North America and Europe*: (1) United States, (2) Canada, (3) Greenland, (4) Austria, (5) Belgium, (6) Denmark, (7) Finland, (8) France, (9) Germany, (10) Greece, (11) Iceland, (12) Ireland, (13) Italy, (14) Luxembourg, (15) Malta, (16) Netherlands, (17) Norway, (18) Portugal, (19) Spain, (20) Sweden, (21) Switzerland, (22) United Kingdom.

$R_2$, *Latin America*: (23) Argentina, (24) Barbados, (25) Bolivia, (26) Brazil, (27) British Honduras, (28) Chile, (29) Colombia, (30) Costa Rica, (31) Cuba, (32) Dominican Republic, (33) Ecuador, (34) El Salvador, (35) Guadeloupe, (36) Guatemala, (37) Guyana, (38) Haiti, (39) Honduras, (40) Jamaica, (41) Martinique, (42) Mexico, (43) Netherlands Antilles, (44) Nicaragua, (45) Panama, (46) Panama Canal Zone, (47) Paraguay, (48) Peru, (49) Puerto Rico, (50) Surinam, (51) Trinidad, (52) Uruguay, (53) Venezuela.

$R_3$, *Central Africa*: (54) Angola, (55) Burundi, (56) Cameroon, (57) Central African Republic, (58) Chad, (59) Congo (Brazzaville), (60) Congo (Kinshasa), (61) Dahomey, (62) Ethiopia, (63) Gabon, (64) Gambia, (65) Ghana, (66) Guinea, (67) Ivory Coast, (68) Kenya, (69) Liberia, (70) Malagasy Republic, (71) Malawi, (72) Mali, (73) Mauritania, (74) Mozambique, (75) Niger, (76) Nigeria, (77) Portuguese Guinea, (78) Rwanda, (79) Senegal, (80) Sierra Leone, (81) Somalia, (82) Sudan, (83) Tanzania, (84) Togo, (85) Uganda, (86) Upper Volta, (87) Zambia.

$R_4$, *North Africa and Middle East*: (88) Aden, (89) Algeria, (90) Bahrain, (91) Cyprus, (92) Gaza Strip, (93) Iran, (94) Iraq, (95) Israel, (96) Jordan, (97) Kuwait, (98) Lebanon, (99) Libya, (100) Morocco, (101) Muscat and Oman, (102) Qatar, (103) Saudi Arabia, (104) Syria, (105) Tunisia, (106) Turkey, (107) United Arab Republic, (108) Yemen.

$R_5$, *Asia*: (109) Afghanistan, (110) Bhutan, (111) Brunei, (112) Burma, (113) Cambodia, (114) Ceylon, (115) China (Taiwan), (116) Hong Kong, (117) India, (118) Indonesia, (119) Japan, (120) Laos, (121) Macao, (122) Malaysia, (123) Nepal, (124) New Guinea, (125) Pakistan, (126) Papua, (127) Philippines, (128) Portuguese Timor, (129) Ryukyu Islands, (130) Singapore, (131) South Korea, (132) South Vietnam, (133) Thailand.

## Appendix B: Effect of Correlated Errors on the Standard Errors of the Regional Per Capita Income Estimates

As stated at the end of section 2, (positively) correlated ε's are particularly plausible for less developed countries in the same region, and we shall therefore concentrate our efforts on that special case. To simplify the analysis still further, we shall assume that these correlations are all equal (to ρ, say). Thus, for $i \neq j$, the correlation coefficient of $\varepsilon_i$ and $\varepsilon_j$ equals ρ when $i$ and $j$ are both in $R_g \neq R_1$, and zero otherwise. It follows from (4.2) and (4.5) that the results (4.6) and (4.7) remain unchanged, but that (4.8) has to be modified by adding

$$\rho\,(1-\theta)^2\sqrt{\left(\alpha_0+\alpha\,a_i^2\right)\left(\alpha_0+\alpha a_j^2\right)}$$

to the right side when $i$ and $j$ are both in $R_g \neq R_1$. Equivalently, (4.6) remains unchanged, but (4.9) has to be modified by the addition of

$$(1-\delta_{ij})\,\rho\,(1-\theta)^2\sqrt{\left(\alpha_0+\alpha a_i^2\right)\left(\alpha_0+\alpha a_j^2\right)} \tag{B.1}$$

to the right side when $i$ and $j$ are both in $R_g \neq R_1$, $\delta_{ij}$ being a Kronecker delta.

This modification obviously does not affect the standard error of $\hat{Z}_1$. For $\hat{Z}_g$ with $g \neq 1$, we use its second moment (4.11). The correction (B.1) implies that

$$\rho\,(1-\theta)^2\left[\left(\sum_{i\in R_g}\frac{p_i}{P_g}Y_i\sqrt{\alpha_0+\alpha\,a_i^2}\right)^2-\sum_{i\in R_g}\left(\frac{p_i}{P_g}Y_i\right)^2(\alpha_0+\alpha\,a_i^2)\right] \tag{B.2}$$

must be added to the expression for the squared standard error of $\hat{Z}_g$ which is derived in the text for the case $\rho = 0$. For the squared standard error of $\hat{Z}$ (world per capita income) the term to be added is

$$\rho\,(1-\theta)^2\sum_{g=2}^{5}\left[\left(\sum_{i\in R_g}p_iY_i\sqrt{\alpha_0+\alpha\,a_i^2}\right)^2-\sum_{i\in R_g}(p_iY_i)^2\left(\alpha_0+\alpha\,a_i^2\right)\right]. \tag{B.3}$$

For $p = ½$, the terms (B.3) and (B.2) are given in Table I′ below the squared standard errors obtained in the text for $\rho = 0$. It appears that the $\rho$ term raises the squared standard error by a percentage ranging from about 50 to 100. The effect on the standard error of world per capita income is small, no doubt because the income of $R_1$ accounts for much of world income and because the $\varepsilon$'s of $R_1$ are assumed to be uncorrelated.

**TABLE I′.** Correlated Errors and Regional Per Capita Incomes

| Statistic | World | $R_2$ | $R_3$ | $R_4$ | $R_5$ |
|---|---|---|---|---|---|
| | | | 1960 | | |
| Squared standard error, $\rho = 0$ | 1207 | 1650 | 1194 | 1544 | 1536 |
| To be added for $\rho = ½$ | 184 | 1635 | 715 | 1299 | 706 |
| Squared standard error, $\rho = ½$ | 1390 | 3285 | 1909 | 2844 | 2242 |
| Standard error,[a] $\rho = ½$ | 37 | 57 | 44 | 53 | 47 |
| | | | 1965 | | |
| Squared standard error, $\rho = 0$ | 1868 | 2571 | 1834 | 2389 | 2399 |
| To be added for $\rho = ½$ | 298 | 2551 | 1061 | 2001 | 1118 |
| Squared standard error, $\rho = ½$ | 2166 | 5122 | 2895 | 4389 | 3517 |
| Standard error,[a] $\rho = ½$ | 47 | 72 | 54 | 66 | 59 |

[a] Dollars per year. The figures in other lines of the table are in squares of dollars per year.

## Appendix C: Standard Errors of the Inequality Estimates

The error of the estimate $\hat{I}$ of the inequality defined in (3.6) is

$$\hat{I}_g - I_g = \log \frac{\hat{Z}_g}{Z_g} - \sum_{i \in R_g} \frac{p_i}{P_g} \log \frac{\hat{Y}_i}{Y_i}$$

$$\approx \frac{\hat{Z}_g - Z_g}{Z_g} - \sum_{i \in R_g} \frac{p_i}{P_g} \log \frac{\hat{Y}_i}{Y_i} .$$

Application of (4.10) indicates that this can be written as

$$\hat{I}_g - I_g \approx \sum_{i \in R_g} \frac{p_i}{P_g} \left( \frac{Y_i}{Z_g} - 1 \right) \log \frac{\hat{Y}}{Y_i} \tag{C.1}$$

with a second moment of the following form:

$$\sum_{i \in R_g} \sum_{j \in R_g} \frac{p_i}{P_g} \left( \frac{Y_i}{Z_g} - 1 \right) \frac{p_j}{P_g} \left( \frac{Y_j}{Z_g} - 1 \right) m_{ij} . \tag{C.2}$$

Consider first $R_g \neq R_1$, so that $m_{ij}$ is as specified in (4.9). The second moment (C.2) can then be written as the sum of three terms:

$$\alpha_0 \theta^2 \left[ \sum_{i \in R_g} \frac{p_i}{P_g} \left( \frac{Y_i}{Z_g} - 1 \right) \right]^2 = 0 \tag{C.3}$$

$$\left[ \sum_{i \in R_g} \frac{p_i}{P_g} \left( \frac{Y_i}{Z_g} - 1 \right) a_i (\theta_i - \theta) \right]^2 \tag{C.4}$$

$$(1 - \theta)^2 \sum_{i \in R_g} \left[ \frac{p_i}{P_g} \left( \frac{Y_i}{Z_g} - 1 \right) \right]^2 \left( \alpha_0 + \alpha a_i^2 \right) , \tag{C.5}$$

where the inequality sign in (C.3) is based on the definition of $Z_g$. The next paragraph provides an approximation to (C.4) equal to the square of

$$\sigma^2 \sum_{i \in R_g} \frac{p_i Y_i}{P_g Z_g} \left( 1 - \frac{p_i Y_i}{P_g Z_g} \right) a_i^2 . \tag{C.6}$$

Thus, the squared standard error of $\hat{I}_g$ for $g \neq 1$ is the sum of (C.5) and the square of (C.6); the latter is the $\sigma^2$ component and (C.5) can be separated into an $\alpha_0$ and an $\alpha$ component. The components with unknown parameters and variables approximated in the usual way, are shown in Table V.

As in section 4, we apply a linear Taylor expansion to $Y_i$ in (C.4). When we do the same for $Z_g$, we obtain the following expression for their ratio:

$$\frac{Y_i}{Z_g} \approx \frac{c_i [1 + a_i(\theta_i - \theta)]}{\sum_{j \in R_g} \frac{p_j}{P_g} c_j [1 + a_j(\theta_j - \theta)]} \quad \text{where} \quad c_i = \eta_i \left( \frac{\eta_1}{\eta_i} \right)^{\theta} . \tag{C.7}$$

This can be simplified to

$$\frac{Y_i}{Z_g} \approx \frac{c_i}{\sum_{j \in R_g} \frac{p_j}{P_g} c_j} \left( 1 + a_i(\theta_i - \theta) - \frac{\sum_{j \in R_g} \frac{p_j}{P_g} c_j a_j (\theta_j - \theta)}{\sum_{j \in R_g} \frac{p_j}{P_g} c_j} \right) \tag{C.8}$$

$$= \frac{c_i}{C_g} \left( 1 - \frac{p_i c_i}{P_g C_g} \right) a_i (\theta_i - \theta) + k_i ,$$

where

$$C_g = \sum_{i \in R_g} \frac{p_i}{P_g} c_i \tag{C.9}$$

and $k_i$ is a linear function of $\theta_j - \theta$ for each $j \in R_g$ excluding $j = i$.

The square root of (C.4) can thus be written as

$$\sum_{i \in R_g} \frac{p_i c_i}{P_g C_g} \left( 1 - \frac{p_i c_i}{P_g C_g} \right) a_i^2 (\theta_i - \theta)^2 + \sum_{i \in R_g} \frac{p_i}{P_g} (k_i - 1) a_i (\theta_i - \theta) \ .$$

The second term vanishes when the $\theta_i$'s are independent, and the first becomes (C.6) when we approximate $c_i$ by $Y_i$ and $C_g$ by $Z_g$.

For the standard error of $\hat{I}_1$ we need a correction similar to (4.19). It may be verified, using (C.2) that this correction is

$$2 \alpha_0 \theta (1 - \theta) \frac{p_1}{P_1} \left( \frac{Y_1}{Z_1} - 1 \right) \sum_{i \in R_1} \frac{p_i}{P_1} \left( \frac{Y_i}{Z_1} - 1 \right) . \qquad \text{(C.10)}$$

This expression vanishes, so that no correction is needed.

For the error $\hat{I} - I$ of the estimate of world inequality at the country level we obtain an expression similar to (C.1):

$$\hat{I} - I \approx \sum_{i=1}^{133} p_i \left( \frac{Y_i}{Z} - 1 \right) \log \frac{\hat{Y}_i}{Y_i} \ .$$

The resulting squared standard error is equal to the sum of (C.5), the square of (C.6), and (C.10) with the following modifications. First, the summation over $i \in R_g$ in (C.5) and (C.6) is replaced by that over $i = 1, \ldots, 133$, and $P_g$ and $Z_g$ by 1 and $Z$, respectively. Second, (C.10) becomes

$$2 \alpha_0 \theta (1 - \theta) p_i \left( \frac{Y_1}{Z} - 1 \right) \sum_{i=1}^{133} p_i \left( \frac{Y_i}{Z} - 1 \right) ,$$

which also vanishes.

Next consider the error $\hat{I}_0 - I_0$ of the world inequality estimate at the regional level:

$$\hat{I}_0 - I_0 = \log\frac{\hat{Z}}{Z} - \sum_{g=1}^{5} P_g \log\frac{\hat{Z}_g}{Z_g}$$

$$\approx \frac{1}{Z}\sum_{i=1}^{133} p_i Y_i \log\frac{\hat{Y}_i}{Y_i} - \sum_{g=1}^{5}\frac{P_g}{Z_g}\sum_{i\in R_g}\frac{p_i}{P_g} Y_i \log\frac{\hat{Y}_i}{Y_i}$$

$$= \sum_{g=1}^{5} P_g' \sum_{i\in R_g}\frac{p_i}{P_g} Y_i \log\frac{\hat{Y}_i}{Y_i} ,$$

where

$$P_g' = P_g\left(\frac{1}{Z} - \frac{1}{Z_g}\right). \tag{C.11}$$

This leads to the following second moment:

$$\sum_{g=1}^{5} P_g' \sum_{h=1}^{5} P_h' \sum_{i\in R_g}\frac{p_i}{P_g} Y_i \sum_{j\in R_h}\frac{p_j}{P_h} Y_j m_{ij} . \tag{C.12}$$

Using (4.9) for $m_{ij}$, we find that this is equal to the sum of three terms:

$$\alpha_0\theta^2\left[\sum_{g=1}^{5} P_g' \sum_{i\in R_g}\frac{p_i}{P_g} Y_i\right]^2 = \alpha_0\theta^2\left(\sum_{g=1}^{5} P_g' Z_g\right)^2 \tag{C.13}$$

$$\left[\sum_{g=1}^{5} P_g' \sum_{i\in R_g}\frac{p_i}{P_g} Y_i a_i(\theta_i - \theta)\right]^2 \tag{C.14}$$

$$(1-\theta)^2\sum_{g=1}^{5}\sum_{i\in R_g}\left(P_g'\frac{p_i}{P_g} Y_i\right)^2\left(\alpha_0 + \alpha a_i^2\right) . \tag{C.15}$$

Term (C.13) vanishes because $\Sigma_g P_g' Z_g$ follows from (C.11). Term (C.14) is the square of $\Sigma_g P_g' B_g$, where $B_g$ is the square root of (4.13), and hence equal to the square of

$$\sigma^2 \sum_{g=1}^{5} P_g' \sum_{i \in R_g} \frac{p_i}{P_g} Y_i a_i^2 \;, \tag{C.16}$$

where $Y_i$ has been substituted for $\eta_i(\eta_1/\eta_i)^\theta$ in (4.17). Term (C.15) is separated into $\alpha_0$ and $\alpha$ components:

$$\alpha_0 (1-\theta)^2 \sum_{g=1}^{5} \sum_{i \in R_g} \left[ p_i Y_i \left( \frac{1}{Z} - \frac{1}{Z_g} \right) \right]^2 \tag{C.17}$$

$$\alpha (1-\theta)^2 \sum_{g=1}^{5} \sum_{i \in R_g} \left[ p_i Y_i a_i \left( \frac{1}{Z} - \frac{1}{Z_g} \right) \right]^2 . \tag{C.18}$$

In addition, given the use of (4.9) for $m_{ij}$, we must apply the correction term $2\alpha_0\theta(1-\theta)$. This leads to

$$2\alpha_0\theta(1-\theta) P_1' \frac{p_1}{P_1} Y_1 \sum_{g=1}^{5} P_g' \sum_{i \in R_g} \frac{p_i}{P_g} Y_i = 2\,\alpha_0\theta(1-\theta) P_1' \frac{p_1}{P_1} Y_1 \sum_{g=1}^{5} P_g' Z_g \;,$$

which is zero.

Finally, consider the average within-region inequality $\Sigma\, P_g I_g$. It follows from (C.1) that its estimation error is of the form

$$\sum_{g=1}^{5} P_g \sum_{i \in R_g} \frac{p_i}{P_g} \left( \frac{Y_i}{Z_g} - 1 \right) \log \frac{\hat{Y}_i}{Y_i}$$

with the following second moment:

$$\sum_{g=1}^{5} P_g \sum_{h=1}^{5} P_h \sum_{i \in R_g} \frac{p_i}{P_g} \left( \frac{Y_i}{Z_g} - 1 \right) \sum_{j \in R_h} \frac{p_j}{P_h} \left( \frac{Y_j}{Z_h} - 1 \right) m_{ij} \;. \tag{C.19}$$

Applying (4.9) for $m_{ij}$, we find that this can be written as the sum of three terms:

$$\alpha_0 \theta^2 \left[ \sum_{g=1}^{5} P_g \sum_{i \in R_g} \frac{p_i}{P_g} \left( \frac{Y_i}{Z_g} - 1 \right) \right]^2 = 0 \tag{C.20}$$

$$\left[ \sum_{g=1}^{5} P_g \sum_{i \in R_g} \frac{p_i}{P_g} \left( \frac{Y_i}{Z_g} - 1 \right) a_i (\theta_i - \theta) \right]^2 \tag{C.21}$$

$$(1 - \theta)^2 \sum_{g=1}^{5} \sum_{i \in R_g} \left[ p_i \left( \frac{Y_i}{Z_g} - 1 \right) \right]^2 \left( \alpha_0 + \alpha a_i^2 \right) . \tag{C.22}$$

The square root of (C.21) equals a weighted average, with weights $P_1, \ldots, P_5$, of the square roots of (B.4) for $g = 1, \ldots, 5$. Applying (C.6), we thus find that (C.21) is the square of

$$\sigma^2 \sum_{g=1}^{5} P_g \sum_{i \in R_g} \frac{p_i Y_i}{P_g Z_g} \left( 1 - \frac{p_i Y_i}{P_g Z_g} \right) a_i^2 , \tag{C.23}$$

which yields after squaring the $\sigma^2$ component of the squared standard error of $\Sigma P_g \hat{I}_g$. Furthermore, given the use of (4.9) for $m_{ij}$, we have to add the correction term

$$2 \alpha_0 \theta (1 - \theta) P_1 \frac{p_1}{P_1} \left( \frac{Y_1}{Z_1} - 1 \right) \sum_{g=1}^{5} P_g \sum_{i \in R_g} \frac{p_i}{P_g} \left( \frac{Y_i}{Z_g} - 1 \right)$$

which is zero.

## Appendix D: The Effect of Correlated Errors on the Standard Errors of the Inequality Estimates

When the $\varepsilon$'s are correlated as specified in Appendix B, we must add expression (B.1) to the right side of (4.9) if $i$ and $j$ are both in $R_g \neq R_1$. Thus, in the case of the squared standard error of $\hat{I}_g$ with $g \neq 1$, using (C.2), we add

$$\rho\,(1-\theta)^2\left[\sum_{i\in R_g}\frac{p_i}{P_g}\left(\frac{Y_i}{Z_g}-1\right)\sqrt{\alpha_0+\alpha a_i^2}\,\right]^2 - \rho\,(1-\theta)^2\sum_{i\in R_g}\left[\frac{p_i}{P_g}\left(\frac{Y_i}{Z_g}-1\right)\right]^2\left(\alpha_0+\alpha a_i^2\right). \tag{D.1}$$

There are no changes in the standard error of $\hat{I}_1$. For $\hat{I}$, the estimated world inequality at the country level, we have to add the following expression to its squared standard error:

$$\rho\,(1-\theta)^2\sum_{g=2}^{5}\left[\sum_{i\in R_g}p_i\left(\frac{Y_i}{Z}-1\right)\sqrt{\alpha_0+\alpha a_i^2}\,\right]^2 - \rho\,(1-\theta)^2\sum_{g=2}^{5}\left\{\sum_{i\in R_g}\left[p_i\left(\frac{Y_i}{Z}-1\right)\right]^2\left(\alpha_0+\alpha a_i^2\right)\right\}. \tag{D.2}$$

For world inequality at the regional level we use the second moment (C.12). The expression to be added is

$$\rho\,(1-\theta)^2\sum_{g=2}^{5}(P_g')^2\left(\sum_{i\in R_g}\frac{p_i}{P_g}Y_i\sqrt{\alpha_0+\alpha a_i^2}\right)^2 - \rho\,(1-\theta)^2\sum_{g=2}^{5}(P_g')^2\sum_{i\in R_g}\left(\frac{p_i}{P_g}Y_i\right)^2\left(\alpha_0+\alpha a_i^2\right). \tag{D.3}$$

For the average within-region inequality we obtain similarly, using (C.19),

$$\rho(1-\theta)^2\sum_{g=2}^{5}P_g^2\left[\sum_{i\in R_g}\frac{p_i}{P_g}\left(\frac{Y_i}{Z_g}-1\right)\sqrt{\alpha_0+\alpha a_i^2}\,\right]^2 - \rho\,(1-\theta)^2\sum_{g=2}^{5}P_g^2\sum_{i\in R_g}\left[\frac{p_i}{P_g}\left(\frac{Y_i}{Z_g}-1\right)\right]^2\left(\alpha_0+\alpha a_i^2\right). \tag{D.4}$$

It turns out that, for $\rho = {}^1/_3$, these corrections affect the standard errors of the regional inequalities and the average within-region inequality by at most one unit in the third decimal place. The standard error of $\hat{I}$ increases from .041 to .048 in 1960 and from .040 to .048 in 1965. For the standard error of $\hat{I}_g$ these increases are from .041 to .047 (1960) and from .039 to .045 (1965).

## References

Fishlow, A.: 1972, "Brazilian Size Distribution of Income," *The American Economic Review*, **62**, 391-402.

Hagen, E.E., and O. Hawrylyshyn, O.: 1969, "Analysis of World Income and Growth, 1955-1965," *Economic Development and Cultural Change*, **18** (No. 1, Part II), 1-96.

Nordhaus, W., and J. Tobin: 1972, "Is Growth Obsolete?" *Fiftieth Anniversary Colloquium*, Vol. V., National Bureau of Economic Research, Inc., New York.

Theil, H.: 1967, *Economics and Information Theory*, American Elsevier Publishing Company, New York, and North-Holland Publishing Company, Amsterdam.

Theil, H.: 1972, *Statistical Decomposition Analysis with Applications in the Social and Administrative Sciences*, American Elsevier Publishing Company, New York, and North-Holland Publishing Company, Amsterdam.

CHAPTER 51

# INEQUALITY AND SOCIAL STATUS IN SUCCESSIVE GENERATIONS*

HENRI THEIL
*University of Chicago,*
*Chicago, Illinois, U.S.A.*

ROBERT STAMBAUGH
*University of Chicago,*
*Chicago, Illinois, U.S.A.*

**ABSTRACT. This paper attempts to model transition probabilities of intergenerational occupational mobility for British and Danish data. A bivariate normal status distribution is tried but rejected. A simple bivariate Gumbel model, with only one unknown parameter that determines the social mobility process, appears to provide a satisfactory fit for both sets of data.**

## 1. Introduction

There are various ways in which inequality among individuals can be expressed. Examples are the inequality of wealth measured in dollars and the inequality of income or consumption measured in dollars per year. Another example is the inequality of education measured in numbers of years of schooling. In this article we address ourselves to the problem of the measurement of social status, which falls under the broad category of inequality measurement because unequal status presents another form of inequality. More specifically, we want to design a model for social status in two successive generations.

The problem can be illustrated conveniently by means of British data on seven occupational groups published by Glass and Hall (1954). These groups, which consist of occupations of successively lower social status, are the following:

(1) Professional and high administrative
(2) Managerial and executive
(3) Inspectional, supervisors, and other nonmanual (higher grade)
(4) Same (lower grade)
(5) Skilled manual and routine grades of nonmanual
(6) Semi-skilled manual
(7) Unskilled manual

The first seven lines of Table I contain the number of father-son pairs observed by Glass and Hall. For example, the first column shows that there are 50 persons in the top group whose fathers were also in the top group, and 16 in the top group whose fathers were in the second group. The first seven entries in the last column are the row sums, i.e.,

* This article first appeared in *European Economic Review*, **10** (1977), 125-139. Reprinted with the permission of Elsevier Science Publishers B.V. (North Holland). Research supported in part by NSF Grant SOC76-82718.

the total numbers of fathers in the seven groups. By dividing each entry of a row by the corresponding row sum, we obtain the transition frequencies $p_{ij}$. Specifically, $p_{ij}$ is the conditional relative frequency of a person's being part of the $j$th group, given that his father was in the $i$th.

Our objective is to formulate a status model for these $p_{ij}$'s. The observed values are shown in Table I in the form of a transition matrix; they obviously satisfy $\Sigma_j p_{ij} = 1$, as indicated by the units in the last column. There is much to be said in favor of the idea of modelling the $p_{ij}$'s, because many of them are probably rather inaccurate. For example, $p_{17}$ is determined as the ratio 2/129 of the last two entries in the first row of Table I. The first two row sums (129 and 150) are small, which has obvious consequences for the accuracy of the corresponding transition frequencies.

## 2. The Exchange Matrix

The entries in the last column from 0.0228 to 0.1293 are the equilibrium proportions $\pi_1, \ldots, \pi_7$ corresponding to the observed $p_{ij}$'s, computed from

$$\sum_{i=1}^{7} \pi_i p_{ij} = \pi_j \ , \tag{1}$$

This equation shows that if the $\pi_i$'s describe the occupational distribution of some generation, the next generation has the same occupational distribution (on the basis of the observed $p_{ij}$'s). Also, $\pi_{ij}$ defined as

$$\pi_{ij} = \pi_i p_{ij} \tag{2}$$

is the associated relative frequency of a father-son pair with the father in the $i$th group and the son in the $j$th. The matrix $[\pi_{ij}]$ will be referred to as the exchange matrix and is shown in Table I. Both the row and the column sums of this matrix are equal to the equilibrium proportions.

Notice that the exchange matrix is almost symmetric. [When evaluating the degree of symmetry, the reader is advised to look particularly at the larger elements and to take into consideration that the number of decimal places shown is rather large, given the size of the samples (the entries in the last column and the first seven rows).] This is further pursued in the last seven rows of Table I, where the observed exchange matrix is symmetrized by substituting ½ $(\pi_{ij} + \pi_{ji})$ for $\pi_{ij}$; evidently, the approximation to the observed exchange matrix is close. This symmetry property is not confined to British data. Danish data from Svalastoga (1959) and two sets of American data from Rogoff (1953) also yield exchange matrices which are close to symmetry. This property was used in Theil (1972, ch. 5) to model the transition frequencies of intergenerational occupational mobility by means of 'distances' between status groups. But it can be done in a more direct way, as the account which follows will show.

**TABLE I.** British Data on Seven Status Groups

| Father's status group | Subject's status group 1 | 2 | 3 | 4 | 5 | 6 | 7 | Row sum |
|---|---|---|---|---|---|---|---|---|
| | | | | *Number of observations* | | | | |
| 1 | 50 | 19 | 26 | 8 | 18 | 6 | 2 | 129 |
| 2 | 16 | 40 | 34 | 18 | 31 | 8 | 3 | 150 |
| 3 | 12 | 35 | 65 | 66 | 123 | 23 | 21 | 345 |
| 4 | 11 | 20 | 58 | 110 | 223 | 64 | 32 | 518 |
| 5 | 14 | 36 | 114 | 185 | 714 | 258 | 189 | 1510 |
| 6 | 0 | 6 | 19 | 40 | 179 | 143 | 71 | 458 |
| 7 | 0 | 3 | 14 | 32 | 141 | 91 | 106 | 387 |
| | | | | *Transition matrix* | | | | |
| 1 | 0.388 | 0.147 | 0.202 | 0.062 | 0.140 | 0.047 | 0.016 | 1 |
| 2 | 0.107 | 0.267 | 0.227 | 0.120 | 0.207 | 0.053 | 0.020 | 1 |
| 3 | 0.035 | 0.101 | 0.188 | 0.191 | 0.357 | 0.067 | 0.061 | 1 |
| 4 | 0.021 | 0.039 | 0.112 | 0.212 | 0.431 | 0.124 | 0.062 | 1 |
| 5 | 0.009 | 0.024 | 0.075 | 0.123 | 0.473 | 0.171 | 0.125 | 1 |
| 6 | 0.000 | 0.013 | 0.041 | 0.087 | 0.391 | 0.312 | 0.155 | 1 |
| 7 | 0.000 | 0.008 | 0.036 | 0.083 | 0.364 | 0.235 | 0.274 | 1 |
| | | | | *Exchange matrix* | | | | |
| 1 | 0.0088 | 0.0034 | 0.0046 | 0.0014 | 0.0032 | 0.0011 | 0.0004 | 0.0228 |
| 2 | 0.0044 | 0.0110 | 0.0094 | 0.0050 | 0.0085 | 0.0022 | 0.0008 | 0.0414 |
| 3 | 0.0031 | 0.0089 | 0.0166 | 0.0168 | 0.0313 | 0.0059 | 0.0054 | 0.0879 |
| 4 | 0.0027 | 0.0049 | 0.0142 | 0.0270 | 0.0546 | 0.0157 | 0.0078 | 0.1269 |
| 5 | 0.0038 | 0.0098 | 0.0309 | 0.0502 | 0.1937 | 0.0700 | 0.0513 | 0.4097 |
| 6 | 0.0000 | 0.0024 | 0.0076 | 0.0159 | 0.0711 | 0.0568 | 0.0282 | 0.1820 |
| 7 | 0.0000 | 0.0010 | 0.0047 | 0.0107 | 0.0471 | 0.0304 | 0.0354 | 0.1293 |
| | | | | *Symmetrized exchange matrix* | | | | |
| 1 | 0.0088 | 0.0039 | 0.0038 | 0.0021 | 0.0035 | 0.0005 | 0.0002 | 0.0228 |
| 2 | | 0.0110 | 0.0091 | 0.0049 | 0.0092 | 0.0023 | 0.0009 | 0.0414 |
| 3 | | | 0.0166 | 0.0155 | 0.0311 | 0.0067 | 0.0050 | 0.0879 |
| 4 | | | | 0.0270 | 0.0524 | 0.0158 | 0.0093 | 0.1269 |
| 5 | | | | | 0.1937 | 0.0706 | 0.0492 | 0.4097 |
| 6 | | | | | | 0.0568 | 0.0293 | 0.1820 |
| 7 | | | | | | | 0.0354 | 0.1293 |

Before proceeding, we should mention that the above concepts have a simple interpretation under the condition that intergenerational mobility is a Markov process with a constant transition matrix $[p_{ij}]$. If each father has one son and if all sons are born to fathers of the same age, the $\pi_i$'s constitute the occupational distribution that will be reached in the limit as time proceeds. If the associated exchange matrix is symmetric, $\pi_{ij}$

$= \pi_{ji}$, the Markov chain is reversible in the sense that there exists, in the limit, a reverse Markov chain (a 'Vokram' chain) which describes the occupations of persons in terms of those of their sons with the same transition matrix.

But we need not assume that intergenerational mobility is a Markov process. Our objective is to model the observed $p_{ij}$'s, which will lead to the adjusted transition matrices shown in Tables III and IV below. Nor do we have to assume that the $\pi_i$'s constitute the occupational distribution of the present generation. As shown in (1), the $\pi_i$'s are simply a property of the observed $p_{ij}$'s.[1] Using the $\pi_i$'s has the advantage that this yields the exchange matrix with equal row and column sums. The closeness of the observed exchange matrix to symmetry is another advantage that will be exploited.

## 3. Bivariate Status Distributions

Imagine again that the $\pi_i$'s describe the occupational distributions of the two successive generations, and consider the leading element 0.0088 of the symmetrized exchange matrix in Table I. This element may be viewed as the joint relative frequency that both the father and the son belong to the top $100\pi_1 = 2.28$ percent of society. Similarly, 0.0088 + 0.0039 is the joint relative frequency that the father belongs to the top 2.28 percent and the son to the top 2.28 + 4.14 percent. Note that this interpretation is equivalent to the introduction of a status variable for the father as well as the son. Instead of using the seven groups described above, we measure status as a variable which is continuous from the bottom of society to the top.

This approach has several advantages. First, the number of status groups and the cut-off points between the groups tend to be arbitrary. This problem is avoided by the continuous approach. Second, in the distance model referred to above (Theil, 1972, ch. 5), it appears that reducing the number of status groups by combining pairs of adjacent groups reduces the average distance between groups. When we use six status groups rather than the seven of Table I, which can be done in six different ways by combining adjacent groups, there is a distance reduction in each case and the average reduction is about 10 percent. When we use five status groups rather than seven, the average distance reduction is about 20 percent. Given these results, an obvious solution is to avoid this aggregation problem by replacing the seven status groups by a continuous status variable.

We write $X$ for the status of the father and $Y$ for that of his son, both of which are random variables. We write $f(x, y)$ for the density function of $(X, Y)$ and note that the two marginal distributions must be identical because the two occupational distributions are identical by assumption. The condition for a symmetric exchange matrix is then

$$f(x,y) \equiv f(y,x) \ . \tag{3}$$

[1] The vector $[\pi_1 \cdots \pi_7]$ is the characteristic row (normalized so that its elements add up to 1) of the matrix $[p_{ij}]$ corresponding to the unit latent root. This row is unique when $[p_{ij}]$ has one single root. See also footnote 4.

## 4. The Bivariate Normal Status Distribution

One possible specification of the bivariate status distribution is the bivariate normal distribution.[2] The two means of this distribution must be equal, and the two variances also, because the marginal distributions are identical. Without loss of generality, we can equate the means to zero, so that this zero represents 'median status,' with 50 percent of the population of higher status and another 50 percent of lower status. The variances determine the scale of the status distribution and can be put equal to 1 without loss of generality. So we can write the bivariate normal status distribution in the form

$$f(x,y) = \frac{1}{2\pi\sqrt{(1-\rho^2)}} \exp\left(-\frac{1}{2}\frac{x^2+y^2-2\rho xy}{1-\rho^2}\right). \tag{4}$$

which satisfies (3). We conclude that $\rho$, the correlation coefficient of the father's status and that of his son, is the single parameter which determines the mobility process under the bivariate normal condition (4). Also, the conditional status distribution of a person, given the status of his father, is normal under (4). This normality could be justified by means of the central limit theorem; each person's status is affected by a large number of stochastically independent events that occur in his lifetime.

The implementation of (4) is a matter of using a table of the bivariate normal distribution. Since the marginal distributions associated with (4) are standardized normal, the equilibrium proportion 0.0228 of the first group (see the last column of Table I) implies that, if a person is part of this group, his status exceeds 2.00. Hence the bivariate normal distribution implies that $\pi_{11}$, the probability that the father and son are both in the first group, is equal to $P[X > 2, Y > 2]$, which depends on $\rho$ as (4) shows. Proceeding in this way, we can find the bivariate normal exchange matrix corresponding to the equilibrium proportions of Table I for any given $\rho$.[3] Three such matrices are shown in Table II below the symmetrized matrix, which is reproduced from Table I to facilitate the comparison. The results show that a large $\rho$ is needed to approximate the diagonal elements of the two top groups, and a small $\rho$ to approximate the diagonal element of the

---

[2] Svalastoga (1961, 1965) postulated a bivariate normal status distribution and estimated status correlations for successive generations, but he made no attempt to verify to what extent such a distribution fits the data. His discussion is in terms of a bivariate lognormal status distribution, but what he actually did is equivalent to using a bivariate normal distribution.

[3] The separation points between pairs of successive status groups, based on the standardized normal distribution and the seven limit proportions of Table I, are 1/2, 2.00; 2/3, 1.52; 3/4, 1.03; 4/5, 0.58; 5/6, -0.49; 6/7, -1.13 (in two places after the decimal point). Owing to limitations of the available tables of the bivariate normal distribution [NBS (1959)], these separation points had to be rounded to the nearest multiple of 0.1. This implies approximation errors of the bivariate normal exchange matrices of Table II, but such errors are small compared with the discrepancies between these matrices and the symmetrized exchange matrix at the top of Table II.

lowest group, and a $\rho$ around ½ to approximate the elements in the upper-right corner. Evidently, the normal approximation is unsatisfactory for any $\rho$.

## 5. Bivariate Status Distributions of the Gumbel Family

There are obviously other bivariate distributions besides the normal. In fact, it is not even necessary to specify the form of the distribution completely; it is sufficient to express the cumulated bivariate distribution in terms of the cumulated marginal distributions. Specifically, let $p$ be the value of the cumulated marginal status distribution of the father, measured from the bottom of society, so that $p = 0.1293$ means that the father belongs to the lowest of the seven groups and $p = 0.1293 + 0.1820$ that the father belongs to either of the two lowest groups (see the last column of Table I). Similarly, let $q$ be the value of the cumulated marginal status distribution of the son, also measured from the bottom of society. The bivariate cumulated status distribution function is $F(x, y) = \int\int f(s, t)\, ds\, dt$ [see the discussion preceding (3)]. Since $p$ and $q$ are one-to-one functions of $x$ and $y$, respectively, we can write $F(x, y)$ as $H(p, q)$. Consider then the model

$$-\log H(p,q) = \left[ (-\log p)^m + (-\log q)^m \right]^{1/m} , \tag{5}$$

where

$$m \geqq 1 . \tag{6}$$

The model (5) describes the joint status distribution in terms of the two marginal distributions. If $m = 1$, the right-hand side of (5) is the sum of -log $p$ and -log $q$, so that $H(p, q) = pq$, which is the case of stochastic independence of the father's status and that of his son. (This is usually referred to as 'perfect social mobility' in the sociological literature.) If $m$ increases beyond bounds, the right-hand side of (5) converges to the larger of -log $p$ and -log $q$, which means that the bivariate status distribution degenerates in such a way that the son's status equals that of his father with unit probability. This limit evidently corresponds to a perfect caste system.

Note that the model (5) does not specify the dependence of the cumulated marginal status distributions $p$ and $q$ on the values taken by the status variable. Gumbel (1961) considered (5) for the case in which $p$ and $q$ are logistic distributions, and Gumbel and Mustafi (1967) did this for the case in which $p$ and $q$ follow the first asymptotic distribution of the largest values. (See also Mardia, 1970, p. 78.) However, for our purpose it is sufficient to apply (5) in its present form. In fact, (5) has a straight-forward interpretation in terms of information theory, where information is defined as minus the logarithm of a probability. Both the left-hand side of (5) and -log $p$ and -log $q$ on the right are minus the logarithm of a probability. Hence (5) may be interpreted in the sense that the joint status information is a generalized sum of the status information of the father and that of his son.

**TABLE II.** The Symmetrized and Some Bivariate Normal Exchange Matrices

| Father's status group | Subject's status group | | | | | | |
|---|---|---|---|---|---|---|---|
| | 1 | 2 | 3 | 4 | 5 | 6 | 7 |
| | | | | *Symmetrized exchange matrix* | | | |
| 1 | 0.0088 | 0.0039 | 0.0038 | 0.0021 | 0.0035 | 0.0005 | 0.0002 |
| 2 | | 0.0110 | 0.0091 | 0.0049 | 0.0092 | 0.0023 | 0.0009 |
| 3 | | | 0.0166 | 0.0155 | 0.0311 | 0.0067 | 0.0050 |
| 4 | | | | 0.0270 | 0.0524 | 0.0158 | 0.0093 |
| 5 | | | | | 0.1937 | 0.0706 | 0.0492 |
| 6 | | | | | | 0.0568 | 0.0293 |
| 7 | | | | | | | 0.0354 |
| | | | | *Bivariate normal, $\rho = 0.25$* | | | |
| 1 | 0.0017 | 0.0023 | 0.0037 | 0.0036 | 0.0085 | 0.0020 | 0.0009 |
| 2 | | 0.0036 | 0.0063 | 0.0067 | 0.0177 | 0.0049 | 0.0025 |
| 3 | | | 0.0118 | 0.0132 | 0.0383 | 0.0119 | 0.0067 |
| 4 | | | | 0.0156 | 0.0492 | 0.0168 | 0.0104 |
| 5 | | | | | 0.1788 | 0.0722 | 0.0527 |
| 6 | | | | | | 0.0348 | 0.0302 |
| 7 | | | | | | | 0.0321 |
| | | | | *Bivariate normal, $\rho = 0.5$* | | | |
| 1 | 0.0041 | 0.0042 | 0.0051 | 0.0037 | 0.0051 | 0.0005 | 0.0001 |
| 2 | | 0.0060 | 0.0090 | 0.0080 | 0.0143 | 0.0021 | 0.0005 |
| 3 | | | 0.0160 | 0.0163 | 0.0362 | 0.0070 | 0.0022 |
| 4 | | | | 0.0189 | 0.0511 | 0.0126 | 0.0050 |
| 5 | | | | | 0.1952 | 0.0731 | 0.0422 |
| 6 | | | | | | 0.0419 | 0.0357 |
| 7 | | | | | | | 0.0500 |
| | | | | *Bivariate normal, $\rho = 0.75$* | | | |
| 1 | 0.0085 | 0.0063 | 0.0049 | 0.0020 | 0.0010 | 0.0000 | 0.0000 |
| 2 | | 0.0102 | 0.0128 | 0.0080 | 0.0066 | 0.0002 | 0.0000 |
| 3 | | | 0.0238 | 0.0212 | 0.0276 | 0.0015 | 0.0001 |
| 4 | | | | 0.0260 | 0.0525 | 0.0052 | 0.0007 |
| 5 | | | | | 0.2362 | 0.0712 | 0.0221 |
| 6 | | | | | | 0.0566 | 0.0382 |
| 7 | | | | | | | 0.0746 |

We emphasize that the Gumbel model (5) is similar to the bivariate normal model (4) in that it uses only *one* parameter. This should be contrasted with the more complicated model proposed by Levine (1972) and certain log-linear models described by Haberman (1974, ch. 6) and Bishop and others (1975, pp. 320-324), several of which involve distances between status groups.

## 6. Implementing the Gumbel Family

For $p = q$, (5) implies $[-\log H(p, p)]^m = 2(-\log p)^m$, which can be written as

$$\frac{-\log H(p,p)}{-\log p} = 2^{1/m} . \tag{7}$$

Since the right-hand side is independent of $p$, we can use (7) to check the validity of the Gumbel model in a simple and informal way. At the separation point between the sixth and seventh groups, Table I yields $p = 0.1293$ and $H(p, p) = 0.0354$, for which the left-hand side of (7) equals 1.63 (natural logs). When we repeat this for the separation points between all pairs of successive groups, we obtain the figures shown in (8). They are close to each other, which is what (7) predicts and, therefore, is encouraging for the Gumbel model,

$$\begin{array}{llllll} 6/7, & 1.63 & 5/6, & 1.62 & 4/5, & 1.64 \\ 3/4, & 1.61 & 2/3, & 1.60 & 1/2, & 1.63 . \end{array} \tag{8}$$

Given $m$, we can use (5) to compute the implied elements of the exchange matrix, written $\hat{\pi}_{ij}(m)$, by equating $p$ and $q$ to the relevant sums of the equilibrium proportions. For example, $\hat{\pi}_{77}(m)$ is obtained by substituting $p = q = 0.1293$ in the right-hand side of (5) and then taking the antilog and, $\hat{\pi}_{67}(m) + \hat{\pi}_{77}(m)$ is obtained by substituting $p = 0.1293 + 0.1820$ and $q = 0.1293$. Then, with $\pi_{ij}$ defined as the $(i, j)$th element of the observed (not symmetrized) exchange matrix shown in Table I, we select $m$ by minimizing the information inaccuracy (Theil, 1972, sec. 2.4),

$$I(m) = \sum_{i=1}^{n} \sum_{j=1}^{n} \pi_{ij} \log \frac{\pi_{ij}}{\hat{\pi}_{ij}(m)} , \tag{9}$$

where $n = 7$ in this case. The minimum is reached at

$$m = 1.404 , \tag{10}$$

and the minimum value equals 0.00798 (natural logarithms). To appreciate this value we note that $m = 1$ (perfect mobility) yields $\hat{\pi}_{ij}(1) = \pi_i \pi_j$, so that (9) becomes

$$I(1) = \sum_{i=1}^{n} \sum_{j=1}^{n} \pi_{ij} \log \frac{\pi_{ij}}{\pi_i \pi_j} . \tag{11}$$

This is also the expected mutual information of the exchange matrix, which is a measure of dependence from information theory (Theil, 1972, sec. 3.3). The value of $I(1)$ for the exchange matrix of Table I is 0.117. The minimum of (9) is about 7 percent of this value, so that the adjustment of one parameter ($m$) reduces the information inaccuracy of the perfect-mobility assumption by 93 percent.

Write $\hat{\pi}_{ij}$ for $\hat{\pi}_{ij}(m)$ at the $m$ value (10), and $I$ for the corresponding (minimum) value of $I(m)$. The transition probability implied by $\hat{\pi}_{ij}$ is $\hat{p}_{ij} = \hat{\pi}_{ij}/\pi_i$ in view of (2).[4] The adjusted transition matrix $[\hat{p}_{ij}]$ and exchange matrix $[\hat{\pi}_{ij}]$ are shown in Table III together with the corresponding observed matrices (reproduced from Table I). To evaluate the fit of the separate rows of the transition matrix, we write (9) at the $m$ value (10) as

$$I = \sum_{i=1}^{n} \pi_i \sum_{j=1}^{n} \frac{\pi_{ij}}{\pi_i} \log \frac{\pi_{ij}/\pi_i}{\hat{\pi}_{ij}/\pi_i} = \sum_{i=1}^{n} \pi_i \sum_{j=1}^{n} p_{ij} \log \frac{p_{ij}}{\hat{p}_{ij}} .$$

This can be written as

$$I = \sum_{i=1}^{n} \pi_i I_i , \tag{12}$$

where

$$I_i = \sum_{j=1}^{n} p_{ij} \log \frac{p_{ij}}{\hat{p}_{ij}} . \tag{13}$$

Hence the information inaccuracy of the fitted exchange matrix is equal to a weighted mean, with weights equal to the corresponding equilibrium proportions, of the information inaccuracies of the rows of the implied transition matrix. The latter inaccuracies are shown in the last column of Table III. They indicate that the fit of $(\hat{p}_{i1}, \ldots, \hat{p}_{i7})$ is worse for $i = 1$ and 2 than for the other groups; we will return to this at the end of the article.

## 7. A Prediction of the Danish Occupational Mobility Structure

An attractive check of a model derived from certain data is its application to a different set of data, for which we use Svalastoga's (1959, p. 324) Danish data on five status groups. Table IV contains five matrices, the first two consisting of numbers of observations of father-son pairs and of the implied $p_{ij}$'s (similar to Table I), while the fourth is the exchange matrix implied by these $p_{ij}$'s, with the equilibrium proportions in the last column. Note that this exchange matrix is close to symmetry.

---

[4] Note that $\hat{p}_{ij}$ is determined completely by the observed $p_{ij}$'s, given the choice of the Gumbel family (5) and the criterion (9) for the selection of the parameter $m$. The equilibrium proportions $\pi_1, \ldots, \pi_7$ which are used to construct the $\hat{p}_{ij}$'s are also determined by the $p_{ij}$'s (see footnote 1).

**TABLE III.** Observed and Adjusted Transition and Exchange Matrices

| Father's status group | Subject's status group 1 | 2 | 3 | 4 | 5 | 6 | 7 | $I_t$ |
|---|---|---|---|---|---|---|---|---|
| | | | | *Observed transition matrix* | | | | |
| 1 | 0.388 | 0.147 | 0.202 | 0.062 | 0.140 | 0.047 | 0.016 | |
| 2 | 0.107 | 0.267 | 0.227 | 0.120 | 0.207 | 0.053 | 0.020 | |
| 3 | 0.035 | 0.101 | 0.188 | 0.191 | 0.357 | 0.067 | 0.061 | |
| 4 | 0.021 | 0.039 | 0.112 | 0.212 | 0.431 | 0.124 | 0.062 | |
| 5 | 0.009 | 0.024 | 0.075 | 0.123 | 0.473 | 0.171 | 0.125 | |
| 6 | 0.000 | 0.013 | 0.041 | 0.087 | 0.391 | 0.312 | 0.155 | |
| 7 | 0.000 | 0.008 | 0.036 | 0.083 | 0.364 | 0.235 | 0.274 | |
| | | | | *Adjusted transition matrix* | | | | |
| 1 | 0.374 | 0.202 | 0.152 | 0.096 | 0.131 | 0.031 | 0.015 | 0.026 |
| 2 | 0.111 | 0.185 | 0.218 | 0.163 | 0.238 | 0.057 | 0.028 | 0.025 |
| 3 | 0.039 | 0.103 | 0.193 | 0.195 | 0.339 | 0.087 | 0.044 | 0.006 |
| 4 | 0.017 | 0.053 | 0.135 | 0.186 | 0.422 | 0.122 | 0.064 | 0.007 |
| 5 | 0.007 | 0.024 | 0.073 | 0.131 | 0.463 | 0.188 | 0.114 | 0.002 |
| 6 | 0.004 | 0.013 | 0.042 | 0.085 | 0.424 | 0.245 | 0.187 | 0.017 |
| 7 | 0.003 | 0.009 | 0.030 | 0.063 | 0.361 | 0.264 | 0.271 | 0.008 |
| | | | | *Observed exchange matrix* | | | | |
| 1 | 0.0088 | 0.0034 | 0.0046 | 0.0014 | 0.0032 | 0.0011 | 0.0004 | |
| 2 | 0.0044 | 0.0110 | 0.0094 | 0.0050 | 0.0085 | 0.0022 | 0.0008 | |
| 3 | 0.0031 | 0.0089 | 0.0166 | 0.0168 | 0.0313 | 0.0059 | 0.0054 | |
| 4 | 0.0027 | 0.0049 | 0.0142 | 0.0270 | 0.0546 | 0.0157 | 0.0078 | |
| 5 | 0.0038 | 0.0098 | 0.0309 | 0.0502 | 0.1937 | 0.0700 | 0.0513 | |
| 6 | 0.0000 | 0.0024 | 0.0076 | 0.0159 | 0.0711 | 0.0568 | 0.0282 | |
| 7 | 0.0000 | 0.0010 | 0.0047 | 0.0107 | 0.0471 | 0.0304 | 0.0354 | |
| | | | | *Adjusted exchange matrix* | | | | |
| 1 | 0.0085 | 0.0046 | 0.0035 | 0.0022 | 0.0030 | 0.0007 | 0.0003 | |
| 2 | 0.0046 | 0.0077 | 0.0090 | 0.0067 | 0.0099 | 0.0024 | 0.0012 | |
| 3 | 0.0035 | 0.0090 | 0.0170 | 0.0172 | 0.0298 | 0.0076 | 0.0038 | |
| 4 | 0.0022 | 0.0067 | 0.0172 | 0.0236 | 0.0536 | 0.0155 | 0.0081 | |
| 5 | 0.0030 | 0.0099 | 0.0298 | 0.0536 | 0.1896 | 0.0772 | 0.0467 | |
| 6 | 0.0007 | 0.0024 | 0.0076 | 0.0155 | 0.0772 | 0.0446 | 0.0341 | |
| 7 | 0.0003 | 0.0012 | 0.0038 | 0.0081 | 0.0467 | 0.0341 | 0.0350 | |

**TABLE IV.** Data on Danish Occupational Mobility

| Father's status group | Subject's status group 1 | 2 | 3 | 4 | 5 | Row sum |
|---|---|---|---|---|---|---|
| | *Numbers of observations* | | | | | |
| 1 | 13 | 8 | 5 | 4 | 1 | 31 |
| 2 | 12 | 72 | 71 | 56 | 23 | 234 |
| 3 | 11 | 68 | 191 | 177 | 84 | 531 |
| 4 | 6 | 26 | 140 | 305 | 198 | 675 |
| 5 | 3 | 11 | 67 | 184 | 234 | 499 |
| | *Observed transition matrix* | | | | | |
| 1 | 0.419 | 0.258 | 0.161 | 0.129 | 0.032 | 1 |
| 2 | 0.051 | 0.308 | 0.303 | 0.239 | 0.098 | 1 |
| 3 | 0.021 | 0.128 | 0.360 | 0.333 | 0.158 | 1 |
| 4 | 0.009 | 0.039 | 0.207 | 0.452 | 0.293 | 1 |
| 5 | 0.006 | 0.022 | 0.134 | 0.369 | 0.469 | 1 |
| | *Adjusted transition matrix* | | | | | |
| 1 | 0.374 | 0.284 | 0.188 | 0.111 | 0.043 | 1 |
| 2 | 0.084 | 0.262 | 0.330 | 0.231 | 0.093 | 1 |
| 3 | 0.020 | 0.118 | 0.326 | 0.364 | 0.172 | 1 |
| 4 | 0.007 | 0.050 | 0.220 | 0.427 | 0.296 | 1 |
| 5 | 0.004 | 0.026 | 0.134 | 0.381 | 0.455 | 1 |
| | *Observed exchange matrix* | | | | | |
| 1 | 0.0101 | 0.0062 | 0.0039 | 0.0031 | 0.0008 | 0.0241 |
| 2 | 0.0042 | 0.0250 | 0.0246 | 0.0194 | 0.0080 | 0.0812 |
| 3 | 0.0047 | 0.0291 | 0.0818 | 0.0758 | 0.0360 | 0.2274 |
| 4 | 0.0033 | 0.0145 | 0.0779 | 0.1697 | 0.1102 | 0.3756 |
| 5 | 0.0018 | 0.0064 | 0.0392 | 0.1076 | 0.1368 | 0.2917 |
| | *Adjusted exchange matrix* | | | | | |
| 1 | 0.0090 | 0.0068 | 0.0045 | 0.0027 | 0.0010 | 0.0241 |
| 2 | 0.0068 | 0.0213 | 0.0268 | 0.0188 | 0.0075 | 0.0812 |
| 3 | 0.0045 | 0.0268 | 0.0742 | 0.0827 | 0.0391 | 0.2274 |
| 4 | 0.0027 | 0.0188 | 0.0827 | 0.1604 | 0.1111 | 0.3756 |
| 5 | 0.0010 | 0.0075 | 0.0391 | 0.1111 | 0.1329 | 0.2917 |

The third and fifth matrices are the adjusted transition and exchange matrices, computed from (5) at the $m$ value (10) which minimizes the information inaccuracy for the *British* data. The information inaccuracy of the adjusted exchange matrix in Table IV, calculated from (9) with $n = 5$ and $m = 1.404$, equals 0.00357. For perfect mobility we have $I(1) = 0.117$, so that the model (5) and the $m$ value (10) reduce the information inaccuracy of the perfect-mobility assumption by about 97 percent, which is even better than the corresponding percentage for the British data. The information inaccuracies (13) for the individual rows of the adjusted transition matrix are $I_1 = 0.009$, $I_2 = 0.013$, $I_3 = 0.004$, $I_4 = 0.003$, $I_5 = 0.001$. As in the case of the British $I_i$'s shown in the last column of Table III, those of the two top groups ($i = 1$ and 2) take the largest values.[5]

## 8. Concluding Comments

Given that only one parameter ($m$) is adjusted, the fit of the model (5) as shown by the adjusted matrices of Tables III and IV may be considered reasonably close. In fact, this fit as measured by the information inaccuracy is somewhat better than that of the distance model (Theil, 1972, ch. 5) in spite of the fact that the latter model adjusts a larger number of parameters.

The most modest view of (5) is that of a naive model for transition frequencies of intergenerational occupational mobility, the fit of which should be improved by more sophisticated models. If we adopt the less modest view that the model (5) is at least approximately correct, we can use it to obtain better estimates of the transition probabilities. For this purpose recall that, for both the British and the Danish data, the two top groups ($i = 1$ and 2) have the largest information inaccuracy (13). The point is that the $p_{ij}$'s of these two groups are obtained from the smallest samples. We noted this for the British data when discussing the transition frequencies of Table I; it is even more true for the Danish data in Table IV, where $p_{15} = 0.032$ is obtained as 1/31. By contrast, the adjusted value $\hat{p}_{15} = 0.043$ is based on all Danish data, so that this estimate must be considered more trustworthy if the model (5) is at least substantially correct.

Two things should be noted when the implications of this model are discussed. First, given that the model describes social mobility as determined by one parameter ($m$), any descriptive measure of mobility must be a function of this parameter (see Boudon, 1973, for several such measures). Second, since (5) describes the bivariate status distribution in terms of the two marginal distributions, we can use any type of distribution for the latter. A convenient choice is the uniform distribution over the interval [0,1]. This is used in Figure 1, where the variable measured horizontally is the status of the father, from 0 (the bottom of society) to 1 (the top). The variable measured vertically is the subject's conditional median status, given his father's status. Five values of $m$ are displayed. For $m = 1$ the conditional median status is always ½. For $m = \infty$ the conditional status, given the father's status, equals the latter with unit probability, which yields the 45 degree line through the origin. The interesting values of $m$ are between these two limits. Note that the curves shown (for $m = 1¼$, $1½$ and 2) are asymmetric in the sense that the conditional median status approaches the father's status when the latter approaches 1, whereas the conditional median status remains well above

[5] Direct minimization of (9) for the Danish data yields a minimum of 0.00314 at $m = 1.441$. The Danish counterparts of the figures in (8) are 4/5, 1.61; 3/4, 1.60; 2/3, 1.62; 1/2, 1.59.

the father's status when the latter approaches 0. The derivation of Figure 1 is described in the appendix.

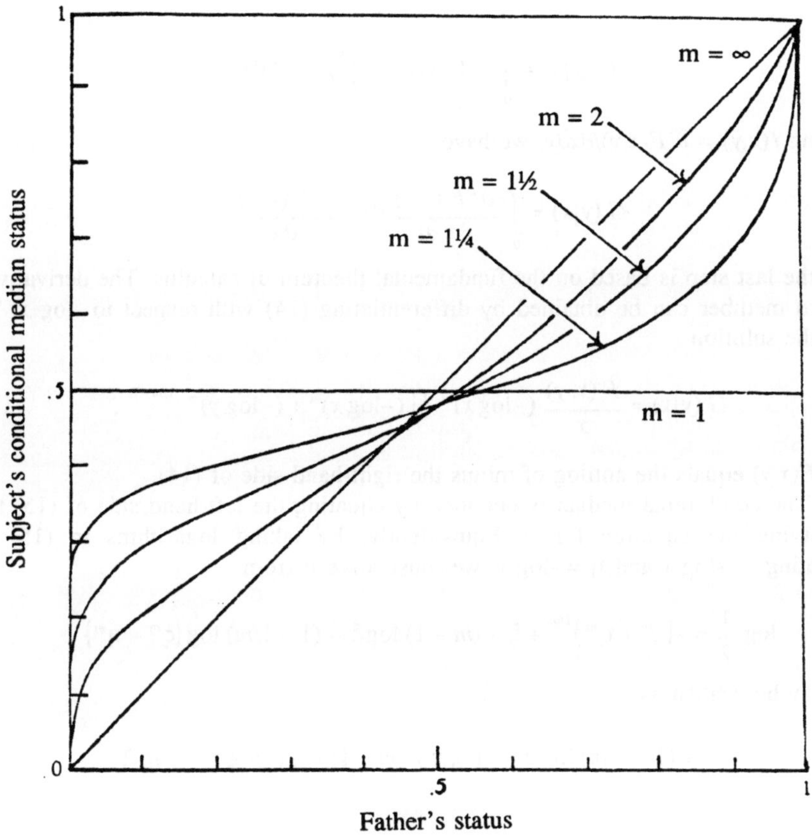


Fig. 1. A subject's conditional median status, given his father's status, based on the model (5).

## Appendix

When the marginal status distributions are both uniform over the interval [0, 1], $p$ and $q$ in (5) are equal to $x$ and $y$, respectively, and $H(p,q)$ equals $F(x,y)$, so that (5) can be written as

$$-\log F(x, y) = \left[ (-\log x)^m + (-\log y)^m \right]^{1/m} . \tag{14}$$

The density function of the bivariate status distribution is $f(x,y)$, from which the density function $g(y|x)$ of the conditional status distribution, given that the father's status equals $x$, is obtained by dividing the father's marginal status density at $x$. Since this divisor equals 1, we have $g(y|x) = f(x,y)$. Therefore, cumulated conditional status distribution equals

$$G(y|x) = \int_0^y g(t|x)\,\mathrm{d}t = \int_0^y f(x,t)\,\mathrm{d}t \ .$$

So, using $f(x,y) = \partial^2 F(x,y)/\partial x \partial y$, we have

$$G(y|x) = \int_0^y \frac{\partial^2 F(x,t)}{\partial x \partial t}\,\mathrm{d}t = \frac{\partial F(x,y)}{\partial x} \ ,$$

where the last step is based on the fundamental theorem of calculus. The derivative in the third member can be obtained by differentiating (14) with respect to -log $x$. This yields the solution

$$G(y|x) = \frac{F(x,y)}{x}(-\log x)^{m-1}\left[(-\log x)^m + (-\log y)^m\right]^{1/m-1} \ , \tag{15}$$

where $F(x,y)$ equals the antilog of minus the right-hand side of (14).

The conditional median is obtained by equating the left-hand side of (15) to ½ and solving the equation for $y$. Equivalently, by taking logarithms in (15) and substituting = -log $x$ and $\eta$ = -log $y$, we must solve $\eta$ from

$$\log\frac{1}{2} = -\left(\xi^m + \eta^m\right)^{1/m} + \xi + (m-1)\log\xi - (1 - 1/m)\log\left(\xi^m + \eta^m\right) .$$

This may be written as

$$z^{1/m} + (1 - 1/m)\log z = -\log x + (m-1)\log(-\log x) + \log 2 \ , \tag{16}$$

where

$$z = \xi^m + \eta^m = (-\log x)^m + (-\log y)^m \ , \tag{17}$$

implying

$$y = \exp\left\{-\left[z - (-\log x)^m\right]^{1/m}\right\} . \tag{18}$$

At $m$ = 1, (16) becomes $z$ = -log $x$ + log 2, so that (18) yields

$$y = \exp\left\{-\left[-\log x + \log 2 - (-\log x)\right]\right\} = \exp(-\log 2) = \frac{1}{2} \ ,$$

which agrees with the horizontal line for $m = 1$ in Figure 1. To verify the 45 degree line for $m = \infty$, $y = x$ implying $\eta = \xi$, we use (17) to obtain $z = 2(-\log x)^m$ for $x = y$, so that the left-hand side of (16) becomes

$$2^{1/m}(-\log x) + (1 - 1/m)\log 2 + (m - 1)\log(-\log x) \ .$$

This agrees with the right-hand side of (16) for $m \to \infty$, as it should.

For $m = 1\frac{1}{4}$, $1\frac{1}{2}$ and 2, (16) was solved numerically for $z$ by means of Newton's method with $x$ increasing in multiples of 0.01 from 0.01 to 0.2 and from 0.8 to 0.99, and multiples 0.05 between 0.2 and 0.8, after which $y$ was obtained from (18).

## References


Bishop, Y.M.M., S.E. Fienberg and P.W. Holland, 1975, Discrete multivariate analysis: Theory and practice (MIT Press, Cambridge, MA).

Boudon, R., 1973, Mathematical structures of social mobility (Jossey-Bass, San Francisco, CA and Elsevier Scientific Publishing Company, Amsterdam).

Glass, D.V. and J.R. Hall, 1954, Social mobility in Great Britain: A study of inter-generation changes in status, in: D.V. Glass, ed., Social mobility in Britain (The Free Press, Glencoe, IL) ch. VIII.

Gumbel, E.J., 1961, Bivariate logistic distributions, Journal of the American Statistical Association 56, 335-349.

Gumbel, E.J. and C.K. Mustafi, 1967, Some analytical properties of bivariate extremal distributions, Journal of the American Statistical Association 62, 569-588.

Haberman, S.J., 1974, The analysis of frequency data (University of Chicago Press, Chicago, IL).

Levine, J.H., 1972, A two-parameter model of interaction in father-son status mobility, Behavioral Science 17, 455-465.

Mardia, K.V., 1970, Families of bivariate distributions (Hafner Publishing Company, Darien, CT).

NBS (National Bureau of Standards), 1959, Tables of the bivariate normal distribution function and related functions, Applied Mathematics Series, vol. 50 (U.S. Government Printing Office, Washington, DC).

Rogoff, N., 1953, Recent trends in occupational mobility (The Free Press, Glencoe, IL).

Svalastoga, K., 1959, Prestige, class and mobility, William Heinemann, London.

Svalastoga, K., 1961, Gedanken zu internationalen Vergleichen sozialer Mobilität, in: D. Glass and Renée König, eds., Soziale Schichtung und soziale Mobilität, Sonderheft 5 of Kölner Zeitschrift für Soziologie und Sozialpsychologie, 284-301.

Svalastoga, K., 1965, Social mobility: The Western European model, Acta Sociologica 9, 175-182.

Theil, H., 1972, Statistical decomposition analysis with applications in the social and administrative sciences, North-Holland, Amsterdam.

CHAPTER 52

# WORLD INCOME INEQUALITY AND ITS COMPONENTS*

HENRI THEIL
*University of Southern California, Los Angeles, California, U.S.A.*
*University of Chicago, Chicago, Illinois, U.S.A.*

ABSTRACT. About 65 percent of total income inequality in the non-communist world is accounted for by international inequality, and about 35 percent by inequality within nations. More than 70 percent of international inequality is accounted for by the inequality of two major regions.

## 1. Income Inequality and Its Components

One measure of income inequality is the logarithm of the ratio of arithmetic mean income to geometric mean income.[1] When applied to the per capita incomes of $n$ countries which constitute the world, it equals

$$J_I = \sum_{i=1}^{n} p_i \log \frac{p_i}{y_i} , \tag{1}$$

where $p_i$ is the population share and $y_i$ the income share of country $i$. When countries are grouped into regions $R_1, \ldots, R_G$, we have

$$J_I = J_R + \bar{J}_I , \qquad \bar{J}_I = \sum_{g=1}^{G} P_g J_{Ig} , \tag{2}$$

where $P_g = \Sigma_{i \in R_g} p_i$ = population share of $R_g$, $J_R$ = inequality between regions, $J_{Ig}$ = inequality within $R_g$, and $\bar{J}_I$ = average inequality within regions,

* This article first appeared in *Economics Letters*, **2** (1979), 99-102. Reprinted with the permission of Elsevier Science Publishers B.V. (North-Holland). Research supported in part by NSF Grant SOC 76-82718. The author is indebted to James Meisner for his able computational assistance, and to Professor Robert Summers of the University of Pennsylvania for making Taiwan's GDP per capita available.

[1] All logarithms are natural logarithms. The inequality measure used here is one of the two informational measures which I proposed earlier [Theil (1967, app. 4.A)]; its use is preferred because of its convenient decomposition with population shares as weights. See also Cowell and Kuga (1977) and Cowell (1978).

$$J_R = \sum_{g=1}^{G} P_g \log \frac{P_g}{Y_g} \,, \qquad J_{Ig} = \sum_{i \in R_g} \frac{p_i}{P_g} \log \frac{p_i/P_g}{y_i/Y_g} \,, \tag{3}$$

where $Y_g = \Sigma_{i \in R_g} y_i$ = income share of $R_g$.

**TABLE I.**

| | | | | | | | |
|---|---|---|---|---|---|---|---|
| GDP per capita | 0.90 | 0.65 | 0.40 | 0.30 | 0.20 | 0.10 | 0.05 |
| Average inequality | 0.23 | 0.28 | 0.33 | 0.43 | 0.44 | 0.38 | 0.30 |

The preceding discussion is based on per capita incomes and thus ignores inequality within countries. This is indicated by the subscript $I$ (international inequality) in (1)-(3). But, obviously, (2) can be extended to

$$J = J_I + \bar{J}_N \,, \qquad \bar{J}_N = \sum_{i=1}^{n} p_i J(i) \,, \tag{4}$$

where $J(i)$ = inequality within country $i$ and $J$ = world inequality, which exceeds international inequality $J_I$ by the average national inequality $\bar{J}_N$. The specification of $J(i)$ for each $i$ is not feasible; instead, we use the statistical regularity observed by Paukert (1973) for average Gini ratios of income distributions within countries at different levels of per capita GDP. When we put the U.S. level at 1 and translate Gini ratios into our inequality measure,[2] we obtain Table I which is used to define $J(i)$ as 0.25 if $i$ has a per capita income exceeding 0.65, 0.30 for $i$ with a per capita income in (0.40, 0.65), 0.40 for (0.30, 0.40), 0.45 for (0.20, 0.30), 0.40 for (0.10, 0.20), and 0.30 if $i$'s per capita income is below 0.10. This procedure is highly approximate, but perhaps acceptable for a first attempt.

[2] Gini ratios are much more complicated for regional (and other) decompositions; see Pyatt (1976). Paukert approximated the upper tail of his income distributions by Pareto and the lower and middle parts lognormally. For Pareto with parameter $\alpha$, Gini's ratio equals $1/(2\alpha-1)$ and our measure equals $\log[\alpha/(\alpha-1)] - 1/\alpha$; for the lognormal distribution, Gini's ratio equals $2N(\sigma/\sqrt{2}) - 1$, and our measure equals $\frac{1}{2}\sigma^2$, where $\sigma^2$ is the variance of the logarithm of income and $N(\,)$ is the cumulated standard normal distribution [see Cowell (1977, p. 153) and Theil (1967, p. 127)]. The average inequality in table 1 is the arithmetic mean of the Pareto and lognormal translations of Paukert's average Gini ratio.

**TABLE II.**

| | Income per capita | Inequality Total | International | Average national |
|---|---|---|---|---|
| World | 0.294 | 0.91 | 0.58 | 0.32 |
| *Five regions* | | | | |
| North | 0.717 | 0.36 | 0.08 | 0.28 |
| South | 0.428 | 0.44 | 0.06 | 0.38 |
| Tropical America | 0.233 | 0.48 | 0.05 | 0.42 |
| Tropical Africa | 0.094 | 0.44 | 0.11 | 0.34 |
| Tropical Asia | 0.081 | 0.45 | 0.13 | 0.32 |
| *Two superregions* | | | | |
| North + South | 0.690 | 0.38 | 0.09 | 0.29 |
| Tropical Middle | 0.105 | 0.53 | 0.20 | 0.34 |

## 2. Discussion of the Results

Per capita incomes are approximated by the 1970 real GDP per capita values of 110 non-communist countries of Kravis et al. (1978).[3] These countries will be viewed as 'the world.' The first line of Table II contains world per capita income (U.S. per capita income = 1) and $J$, $J_I$ and $\bar{J}_N$ [see eq. (4)], which show that international inequality accounts for about 65 percent of world inequality.

The next five lines of Table II divide the world into the temperate regions of the North and South and the tropical and semitropical regions in America, Africa and Asia.[4] The figures in the last three columns represent a within-region version of (4), $J_g = J_{Ig} + \bar{J}_{Ng}$, where $J_{Ig}$ is defined in (3) and $\bar{J}_{Ng} = \Sigma_i (p_i/P_g)J(i)$. In the last two lines the first two and the last three regions are combined into two superregions. In all regions the average national inequality dominates the international inequality.

[3] The figures used are in column (2) of table 4 of Kravis et al. (1978), and the population figures are from the World Bank (1971) for 1969. Excluded countries are communist countries (but Hungary is included) and those with a population below 1 million. Taiwan's real GDP per capita equals 0.185.

[4] The North (21 countries) consists of Western Europe (incl. Hungary), U.S., Canada, Japan and Korea. The South consists of Australia, New Zealand, South Africa, Chile, Argentina and Uruguay. Tropical (and semitropical) America contains 19 countries south of the U.S. and in the Caribbean; tropical Africa consists of 36 countries, and Asia of 28 (from Turkey and the Middle East all the way to Indonesia, the Philippines and Papua). The successive population shares of the five regions are 0.293, 0.030, 0.096, 0.135 and 0.446; the income shares are 0.715, 0.044, 0.076, 0.043 and 0.122.

For the five regions, the regional inequality $J_R$ equals 0.48 and the average international inequality $\bar{J}_I$ equals 0.10, so that regional differences account for over 80 percent of total international inequality $J_I = 0.58$ [see eqs. (2), (3) and line 1 of table 2]. For the two superregions in the last two lines of table 2, the regional inequality $J_R$ equals 0.42 and the average international inequality $\bar{J}_I$ equals 0.16 so that the per capita income difference between these two regions accounts for over 70 per cent of total international inequality $J_I = 0.58$.

## References


Cowell, F.A.: 1977, *Measuring Inequality*, Wiley, New York.

Cowell, F.A.: 1978, "On the Structure of Additive Inequality Measures," Discussion Paper, London School of Economics, London.

Cowell, F.A., and K. Kuga: 1977, "Additivity and the Entropy Concept: An Axiomatic Approach to Inequality Measurement," Discussion Paper no. 96, The Institute of Social and Economic Research, Osaka University, Osaka.

Kravis, I.B., A.W. Heston and R. Summers: 1978, "Real GDP Per Capita for More Than One Hundred Countries," *Economic Journal*, **88**, 215-242.

Paukert, F.: 1973, "Income Distribution at Different Levels of Development: A Survey of Evidence," *International Labour Review*, **108**, 97-125.

Pyatt, G.: 1976, "On the Interpretation and Disaggregation of Gini Coefficients," *Economic Journal*, **86**, 243-255.

Theil, H.: 1967, *Economics and Information Theory*, North-Holland, Amsterdam.

World Bank: 1971, *World Bank Atlas*.

CHAPTER 53

# THE DEVELOPMENT OF INTERNATIONAL INEQUALITY, 1960-1985*

HENRI THEIL
*University of Florida,*
*Gainesville, Florida, U.S.A.*

ABSTRACT. Data from the International Comparison Project are used to assess the economic development in five regions of the non-Communist world: the North, the South, and three regions in the Tropical Middle (in America, Asia, and Africa). The use of an additively decomposable inequality measure is emphasized. A convenient Lorenz-type graphical procedure is presented.

## 1. Introduction

In Theil (1979) I considered world income inequality in 1970, using the real GDP per capita values published by Kravis, Heston, and Summers (1978). Their results were extended considerably by Summers and Heston (1984, 1988). In particular, the 1988 article provides annual data from 1950 to 1985 for a large number of countries. The objective of the present paper is to use these data for an analysis of income development in a regional context.

## 2. The North, the South, and the Tropical Middle

As in Theil (1979) I divide the world into three major regions: the North, the South and the Tropical Middle (to be explained below). The 'world' should be interpreted as the non-Communist world. Summers and Heston (1988) provide some data for nine centrally planned economies, but these will not be used here.

The North consists of 25 countries. These are the U.S. and Canada on the American continent, Japan and South Korea on the Western Pacific Rim, and 21 countries in Western and Southern Europe, stretching all the way from Iceland to Turkey. Further details are provided in the appendix.

The South consists of nine countries. Three of these constitute the Southern cone of the American continent: Argentina, Chile, and Uruguay. Then there are Australia and New Zealand on the Western Pacific Rim, while four are in the Southern tip of Africa: South Africa, Botswana, Lesotho, and Swaziland.

---

* This article first appeared in the *Journal of Econometrics*, **42** (1989), 145-155. Reprinted by permission of Elsevier Science Publishers B.V. (North-Holland). Research supported in part by the McKethan-Matherly Eminent Scholar Chair. Research assistance by Susan Narduzzi is gratefully acknowledged.

**TABLE I.** Population by Regions

| | | Percentage shares | | | | |
|---|---|---|---|---|---|---|
| Year (1) | World (millions) (2) | North (3) | South (4) | Tropical America (5) | Tropical Asia (6) | Tropical Africa (7) |
| 1960 | 1953 | 33.49 | 3.24 | 8.96 | 40.95 | 13.36 |
| 1965 | 2167 | 32.12 | 3.22 | 9.39 | 41.63 | 13.63 |
| 1970 | 2397 | 30.57 | 3.18 | 9.76 | 42.52 | 13.97 |
| 1975 | 2657 | 28.99 | 3.16 | 10.05 | 43.36 | 14.44 |
| 1980 | 2936 | 27.29 | 3.12 | 10.31 | 44.23 | 15.04 |
| 1985 | 3241 | 25.64 | 3.10 | 10.51 | 44.94 | 15.82 |

The North plus the South constitute the world's temperate zone. The other zone is the tropical (and subtropical) area around the equator. We divide the latter area into three regions. Tropical America consists of 21 countries; these are either in the Caribbean or on the American continent South of the U.S. border and North of the Southern cone. Tropical Asia stretches from Israel and Syria in the West to Papua New Guinea and Fiji in the East; that region consists of 23 countries. Finally, Tropical Africa consists of 38 countries. See the appendix for further details.

## 3. Population Shares and Per Capita Incomes

Summers and Heston (1988) consider 121 non-Communist countries, but for many of these the data do not go back to 1950. To solve this problem we start in 1960 (not 1950) and we delete five countries for which 1960 data are not available, so that the number of countries included is 116 rather than 121. (See the appendix for details.) Column 2 of Table I shows the world population at five-year intervals; the later columns contain the population shares of the five regions. Note that the share of the North has declined drastically and that the share of the South also declined (but not nearly as drastically). The population shares of the three tropical regions have all increased.

Table II contains world and regional per capita incomes. The underlying income concept is the Summers-Heston RGDP2 series, where RGDP stands for the real gross domestic product, while the number 2 indicates that the procedure involves a chain index. The world and regional per capita incomes are obtained from the corresponding country values by taking the weighted mean (with weights equal to the population shares).

**TABLE II.** World and Regional Per Capita Incomes

| Year (1) | World (2) | North (3) | South (4) | Tropical America (5) | Tropical Asia (6) | Tropical Africa (7) |
|---|---|---|---|---|---|---|
| 1960 | 2112 | 4565 | 3316 | 1451 | 663 | 549 |
| 1965 | 2438 | 5506 | 3768 | 1803 | 720 | 582 |
| 1970 | 2803 | 6607 | 4371 | 2172 | 811 | 629 |
| 1975 | 3097 | 7428 | 4664 | 2736 | 976 | 677 |
| 1980 | 3428 | 8581 | 4963 | 3269 | 1094 | 730 |
| 1985 | 3513 | 9348 | 4491 | 3051 | 1219 | 687 |

Column 2 of Table II shows that world per capita income has increased by almost two-thirds in the 25-year period. The other columns indicate that the ranking of the five regions according to per capita income has not changed over time; the North is richer than the South and both are richer than each of the three tropical regions; within the Tropical middle, Tropical America is first, Tropical Asia is second, Tropical Africa is last. Note the negative rank correlation of the five regions according to influence (Table II) and according to the change in population share (Table I). In fact, if the population shares of our 116 countries had been fixed at the 1960 levels, while the development of their per capita incomes remains as observed, world per capita income would have doubled rather than increased by two-thirds (see the beginning of this paragraph).

The successive entries in each column of Table II show that the income performance of the regions is quite different. In the North and in Tropical Asia these entries increase uninterruptedly, but in the three other regions there are declines at the end of the 25-year period. In the North per capita income more than doubled from 1960 to 1985, but in the South the development is much less impressive. Within the Tropical Middle, Tropical Africa shows the poorest performance.

## 4. The Measurement of Income Inequality

One measure of inequality is the natural logarithm of the ratio of arithmetic mean income to geometric mean income. When this measure is applied to the per capita incomes of our 116 countries, it can be written as

$$J = \sum_{i=1}^{116} p_i \log (p_i/y_i) \ , \qquad (1)$$

where $p_i$ is the population share of country $i$ and $y_i$ is its income share (the shares of $i$ in world population and in total world income, respectively).

The advantage of (1) is its convenient additive decomposition, which may be explained as follows. Let $R_1, \ldots, R_G$ be regions so that each country is in exactly one region. Let $P_g$ and $Y_g$ be the population and income shares of region $R_g$: $P_g = \Sigma_i p_i$ and $Y_g = \Sigma_i y_i$, where the summations are over $i \in R_g$. Then the extension of (1) to regions is

$$J_R = \sum_{g=1}^{G} P_g \log (P_g / Y_g) \ , \tag{2}$$

which measures the inequality among regions, while

$$J_g = \sum_{i \in R_g} \left( \frac{p_i}{P_g} \right) \log \left[ \left( \frac{p_i / P_g}{y_i / Y_g} \right) \right] \tag{3}$$

measures the inequality among the countries of region $R_g$. The additive decomposition is then

$$J = J_R + \bar{J} \qquad \text{where} \qquad \bar{J} = \sum_{g=1}^{G} P_g J_g \ . \tag{4}$$

Thus, total inequality among the 116 countries equals regional inequality plus the average within-region inequality, the average being a weighted average with the population shares $P_1, \ldots, P_G$ as weights. Note that these weights are identical to those of the regional per capita incomes (see the end of the second paragraph of section 3).

Since we confine ourselves to the per capita incomes of the 116 countries, we ignore the income inequality within these countries. Thus, $J$ of eq. (1) is not 'world income inequality,' but it is 'international inequality' where 'international' means that the individual incomes in each country have been replaced by that country's per capita income. We obtain world inequality from international inequality by adding the average within-country inequality; this is a decomposition similar to (4). Indeed, in Theil (1979) I provided rough estimates for such within-country terms in 1970. For further details, particularly on matters of additive decomposability, see Bourguignon (1979), Cowell and Kuga (1981), Fishlow (1972), Foster (1980), Shorrocks (1983), Summers et al. (1984), and Theil (1967, ch. 4).

## 5. Discussion

Table III contains the measures shown in eqs. (1) to (4) for the $G = 5$ regions and for each year from 1960 to 1985. Column 2 contains $J$ defined in (1); it shows a substantial increase in international inequality (from less than 0.55 in 1960 to about 0.65 in 1980 and later). Columns 3 and 4 contain the regional inequality $J_R$ and the average within-region inequality $\bar{J}$. The former dominates the latter. This is clearly illustrated by column 5, which shows that $J_R$ is almost 80 percent of $J$ in each year.

**TABLE III.** International Income Inequality By Regions

| Year (1) | International Inequality (2) | Regional inequality (3) | Average within regions (4) | (3) as a percentage of (2) (5) | Inequality within regions: North (6) | South (7) | Tropical America (8) | Tropical Asia (9) | Tropical Africa (10) |
|---|---|---|---|---|---|---|---|---|---|
| 1960 | 0.5355 | 0.4146 | 0.1209 | 77.4 | 0.1555 | 0.0693 | 0.0998 | 0.1147 | 0.0799 |
| 1961 | 0.5415 | 0.4251 | 0.1164 | 78.5 | 0.1453 | 0.0668 | 0.0620 | 0.1222 | 0.0760 |
| 1962 | 0.5487 | 0.4329 | 0.1158 | 78.9 | 0.1431 | 0.0676 | 0.0608 | 0.1269 | 0.0639 |
| 1963 | 0.5506 | 0.4367 | 0.1139 | 79.3 | 0.1362 | 0.0706 | 0.0654 | 0.1222 | 0.0780 |
| 1964 | 0.5578 | 0.4401 | 0.1177 | 78.9 | 0.1342 | 0.0680 | 0.0721 | 0.1303 | 0.0829 |
| 1965 | 0.5832 | 0.4559 | 0.1273 | 78.2 | 0.1369 | 0.0664 | 0.0777 | 0.1505 | 0.0821 |
| 1966 | 0.6069 | 0.4756 | 0.1313 | 78.4 | 0.1323 | 0.0663 | 0.0775 | 0.1676 | 0.0702 |
| 1967 | 0.6069 | 0.4785 | 0.1285 | 78.8 | 0.1273 | 0.0655 | 0.0773 | 0.1623 | 0.0778 |
| 1968 | 0.6175 | 0.4842 | 0.1333 | 78.4 | 0.1223 | 0.0706 | 0.0751 | 0.1744 | 0.0877 |
| 1969 | 0.6168 | 0.4854 | 0.1313 | 78.7 | 0.1166 | 0.0699 | 0.0727 | 0.1751 | 0.0855 |
| 1970 | 0.6124 | 0.4850 | 0.1274 | 79.2 | 0.1093 | 0.0707 | 0.0713 | 0.1727 | 0.0813 |
| 1971 | 0.6175 | 0.4835 | 0.1340 | 78.3 | 0.1038 | 0.0686 | 0.0618 | 0.1945 | 0.0808 |
| 1972 | 0.6385 | 0.4940 | 0.1445 | 77.4 | 0.1033 | 0.0696 | 0.0609 | 0.2168 | 0.0880 |
| 1973 | 0.6474 | 0.4988 | 0.1486 | 77.0 | 0.1000 | 0.0721 | 0.0575 | 0.2276 | 0.0917 |
| 1974 | 0.6437 | 0.4822 | 0.1614 | 74.9 | 0.0918 | 0.0643 | 0.0553 | 0.2624 | 0.0951 |
| 1975 | 0.6216 | 0.4660 | 0.1556 | 75.0 | 0.0860 | 0.0728 | 0.0540 | 0.2512 | 0.0973 |
| 1976 | 0.6375 | 0.4713 | 0.1662 | 73.9 | 0.0829 | 0.0728 | 0.0513 | 0.2738 | 0.1078 |
| 1977 | 0.6357 | 0.4703 | 0.1654 | 74.0 | 0.0835 | 0.0679 | 0.0510 | 0.2664 | 0.1216 |
| 1978 | 0.6366 | 0.4768 | 0.1598 | 74.8 | 0.0850 | 0.0686 | 0.0495 | 0.2527 | 0.1210 |
| 1979 | 0.6595 | 0.4822 | 0.1773 | 73.1 | 0.0849 | 0.0649 | 0.0534 | 0.2839 | 0.1424 |
| 1980 | 0.6491 | 0.4808 | 0.1683 | 74.1 | 0.0846 | 0.0627 | 0.0544 | 0.2584 | 0.1552 |
| 1981 | 0.6484 | 0.4877 | 0.1607 | 75.2 | 0.0857 | 0.0674 | 0.0584 | 0.2368 | 0.1607 |
| 1982 | 0.6514 | 0.4863 | 0.1651 | 74.6 | 0.0805 | 0.0761 | 0.0589 | 0.2458 | 0.1676 |
| 1983 | 0.6460 | 0.4814 | 0.1646 | 74.5 | 0.0819 | 0.0784 | 0.0564 | 0.2425 | 0.1707 |
| 1984 | 0.6419 | 0.4827 | 0.1592 | 75.2 | 0.0834 | 0.0843 | 0.0550 | 0.2235 | 0.1856 |
| 1985 | 0.6407 | 0.4900 | 0.1506 | 76.5 | 0.0859 | 0.0931 | 0.0580 | 0.2003 | 0.1871 |

The last five columns of Table III contain the regional inequalities $J_g$ for all regions $R_1, \ldots, R_5$. Their behavior is quite different. In 1960 the inequality in the North exceeded that in any other region, but Northern inequality declined so fast that in 1985 it was the second lowest. In contrast to the North, Tropical Africa and Asia showed substantial increases in inequality.

What is the cause of these opposite developments in these different regions? In the next three paragraphs we shall try to answer this question for the North and for Tropical Asia, which are the two largest regions in terms of population (see table I). The answer will clearly show the power of the additive decomposability of an inequality measure.

Let us guess that a major cause of the decline of the inequality in the North is that countries other than the United States (particularly in Western Europe and also Japan) have gained in affluence relative to the U.S. So we divide the North into two subregions: the United States (a single-country subregion) and the North excluding the U.S. Then we go back to equation (4), reproduced here: $J = J_R + \bar{J}$, but we interpret $J$ now as the inequality in the North, $J_R$ as the subregional inequality, and $\bar{J}$ as the average inequality within the two subregions. The results are shown in Table IV (where column 2 is reproduced from column 6 of Table III). The inequality in the North reached its lowest point in 1982; the decline from 1960 is 0.1555 - 0.0805 = 0.075. Column 3 shows that most of this decline is indeed accounted for by the decrease in the inequality between the two subregions: 0.0609 - 0.0169 = 0.044.

**TABLE IV**. Income Inequality Among the Northern Countries

| Year (1) | Inequality in the North (2) | Subregional inequality (3) | Average within subregions (4) | (3) as a percentage of (2) (5) | Inequality within non-U.S. North (6) |
|---|---|---|---|---|---|
| 1960 | 0.1555 | 0.0609 | 0.0946 | 39.2 | 0.1307 |
| 1961 | 0.1453 | 0.0543 | 0.0910 | 37.4 | 0.1260 |
| 1962 | 0.1431 | 0.0533 | 0.0898 | 37.2 | 0.1243 |
| 1963 | 0.1362 | 0.0501 | 0.0861 | 36.8 | 0.1194 |
| 1964 | 0.1342 | 0.0487 | 0.0855 | 36.3 | 0.1186 |
| 1965 | 0.1369 | 0.0502 | 0.0867 | 36.7 | 0.1203 |
| 1966 | 0.1323 | 0.0504 | 0.0819 | 38.1 | 0.1136 |
| 1967 | 0.1273 | 0.0475 | 0.0798 | 37.3 | 0.1108 |
| 1968 | 0.1223 | 0.0448 | 0.0775 | 36.6 | 0.1077 |
| 1969 | 0.1166 | 0.0399 | 0.0767 | 34.2 | 0.1065 |
| 1970 | 0.1093 | 0.0329 | 0.0764 | 30.1 | 0.1061 |
| 1971 | 0.1038 | 0.0310 | 0.0728 | 29.9 | 0.1012 |
| 1972 | 0.1033 | 0.0304 | 0.0729 | 29.4 | 0.1013 |
| 1973 | 0.1000 | 0.0283 | 0.0717 | 28.3 | 0.0996 |
| 1974 | 0.0918 | 0.0251 | 0.0667 | 27.3 | 0.0927 |
| 1975 | 0.0860 | 0.0238 | 0.0622 | 27.7 | 0.0864 |
| 1976 | 0.0829 | 0.0231 | 0.0598 | 27.9 | 0.0832 |
| 1977 | 0.0835 | 0.0249 | 0.0586 | 29.8 | 0.0816 |
| 1978 | 0.0850 | 0.0254 | 0.0596 | 29.9 | 0.0831 |
| 1979 | 0.0849 | 0.0231 | 0.0619 | 27.2 | 0.0863 |
| 1980 | 0.0846 | 0.0194 | 0.0652 | 22.9 | 0.0911 |
| 1981 | 0.0857 | 0.0206 | 0.0651 | 24.0 | 0.0909 |
| 1982 | 0.0805 | 0.0169 | 0.0636 | 21.0 | 0.0891 |
| 1983 | 0.0819 | 0.0188 | 0.0631 | 23.0 | 0.0884 |
| 1984 | 0.0834 | 0.0201 | 0.0633 | 24.1 | 0.0887 |
| 1985 | 0.0859 | 0.0219 | 0.0641 | 25.5 | 0.0899 |

The remainder of the decline of Northern inequality is accounted for by the behavior of the average inequality within the subregions. Note that the inequality within a single-country subregion is always zero. In the present case of the North, the average inequality within its two subregions is equal to the inequality within the non-U.S. North (shown in column 6 of Table IV) multiplied by the population share of this subregion within the North.

**TABLE V.** Income Inequality Among Asian[a] Countries

| Year (1) | Inequality in Asia (2) | Subregional inequality (3) | Average within subregions (4) | (3) as a percentage of (2) (5) | Inequality within Asia excl. India (6) |
|---|---|---|---|---|---|
| 1960 | 0.1147 | 0.0220 | 0.0927 | 19.2 | 0.2031 |
| 1961 | 0.1222 | 0.0299 | 0.0923 | 24.5 | 0.2018 |
| 1962 | 0.1269 | 0.0318 | 0.0951 | 25.1 | 0.2077 |
| 1963 | 0.1222 | 0.0288 | 0.0934 | 23.6 | 0.2036 |
| 1964 | 0.1303 | 0.0275 | 0.1028 | 21.1 | 0.2239 |
| 1965 | 0.1505 | 0.0416 | 0.1089 | 27.6 | 0.2367 |
| 1966 | 0.1676 | 0.0528 | 0.1148 | 31.5 | 0.2494 |
| 1967 | 0.1623 | 0.0470 | 0.1153 | 29.0 | 0.2502 |
| 1968 | 0.1744 | 0.0531 | 0.1214 | 30.4 | 0.2629 |
| 1969 | 0.1751 | 0.0526 | 0.1225 | 30.0 | 0.2650 |
| 1970 | 0.1727 | 0.0486 | 0.1241 | 28.1 | 0.2681 |
| 1971 | 0.1945 | 0.0539 | 0.1406 | 27.7 | 0.3033 |
| 1972 | 0.2168 | 0.0679 | 0.1489 | 31.3 | 0.3203 |
| 1973 | 0.2276 | 0.0792 | 0.1484 | 34.8 | 0.3187 |
| 1974 | 0.2624 | 0.1018 | 0.1606 | 38.8 | 0.3441 |
| 1975 | 0.2512 | 0.0948 | 0.1564 | 37.7 | 0.3346 |
| 1976 | 0.2738 | 0.1108 | 0.1630 | 40.5 | 0.3482 |
| 1977 | 0.2664 | 0.1077 | 0.1587 | 40.4 | 0.3387 |
| 1978 | 0.2527 | 0.1029 | 0.1498 | 40.7 | 0.3192 |
| 1979 | 0.2839 | 0.1291 | 0.1548 | 45.5 | 0.3293 |
| 1980 | 0.2584 | 0.1169 | 0.1415 | 45.2 | 0.3005 |
| 1981 | 0.2368 | 0.1063 | 0.1304 | 44.9 | 0.2765 |
| 1982 | 0.2458 | 0.1187 | 0.1272 | 48.3 | 0.2692 |
| 1983 | 0.2425 | 0.1148 | 0.1276 | 47.3 | 0.2699 |
| 1984 | 0.2235 | 0.0969 | 0.1266 | 43.4 | 0.2671 |
| 1985 | 0.2003 | 0.0839 | 0.1164 | 41.9 | 0.2449 |

[a] Asia should be interpreted as Tropical Asia.

The case of Tropical Asia is pursued in Table V. The two subregions are now India and Tropical Asia excluding India. The economic development of India lagged behind the average Asian development until the late 1970's. The subregional inequality of column 3 of Table V shows a rapid increase, from 0.02 in 1960 to 0.13 in 1979. This accounts for most of the increase in Asia's inequality (from less than 0.12 in 1960 to a little over 0.28 in 1979). Also note that the subregional inequality measured as a percentage of total Asian inequality (column 5) increased rapidly, from less than 20 percent in 1960 to about 45 percent in 1979. (This is in contrast to the corresponding development in Table IV, where the U.S./non-U.S. inequality measured as a percentage of total Northern inequality decreased from almost 40 percent in 1960 to about 20 percent in 1982).

The subregional analysis can obviously be extended. There is no reason why one subregion should contain only one country. (For example, we could add Canada to the U.S. in order to obtain a North-American subregion.) There could also be more subregions than two.

## 6. A Lorenz-type Graphical Exploration

Here we present a geometric picture of $J$ defined in (1). It will be convenient to start with an income distribution over 100 households (so that all population shares are 0.01). Let the 100 incomes $z_1, \ldots, z_{100}$ be independent and pseudo-lognormal, $\log z_j$ being pseudo-normal with zero mean and variance ½ for $j = 1, \ldots, 100$. We rank the households according to increasing income: $z_{(1)} < z_{(2)} < \ldots < z_{(100)}$. It is then readily verified that (1) can in this case be written as

$$J = (1/100)\sum_{j=1}^{100} \log\left(\bar{z}/z_{(j)}\right), \tag{5}$$

where $\bar{z}$ is the arithmetic mean of the 100 incomes.

In Figure 1 we measure $(1/100)\log(z_{(j)}/\bar{z})$ vertically; this is simply the contribution of household $j$ to $-J$ in view of (5). Since the households are arranged according to increasing affluence, the 'curve' of Figure 1 increases monotonically. If all 100 incomes had been equal, the curve would have been horizontal. The similarity to the Lorenz curve should be obvious.

Figure 2 provides an analogous picture based on the per capita income data of our 116 countries at five-year intervals. The countries are ranked according to increasing per capita incomes (these rankings may be different in different years). Obviously, the population shares $p_i$ are not the same for all countries. For example, the location of India in the left (negative) part of the figure and that of the United States on the far right are immediately visible.

The picture of Figure 2 becomes particularly attractive when the objective is to trace the income development of one country relative to that of the rest of the world. Three such countries are indicated in Fig. 2: Argentina, Japan, and Korea. The first country is an example of relative decline, while the latter two are examples of relative improvement. It should be obvious that similar figures can be constructed for countries within a region.

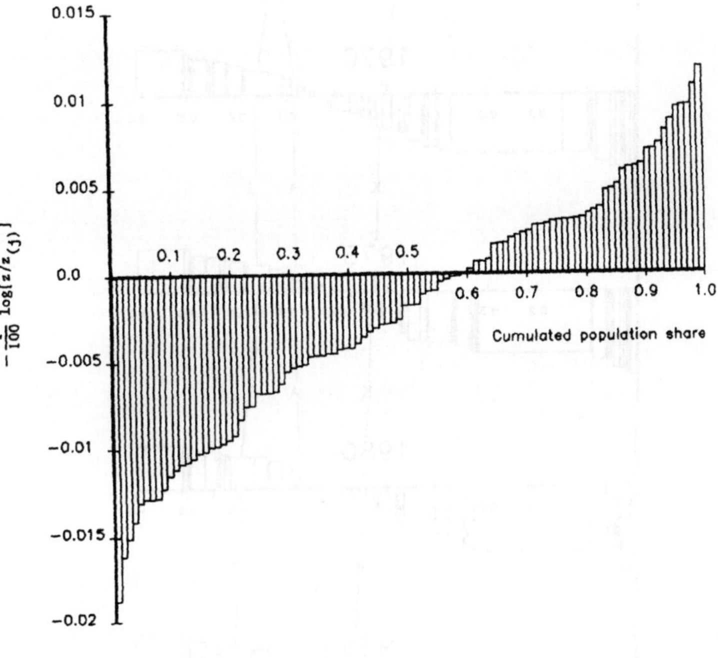


Figure 1
An inequality picture for 100 households.

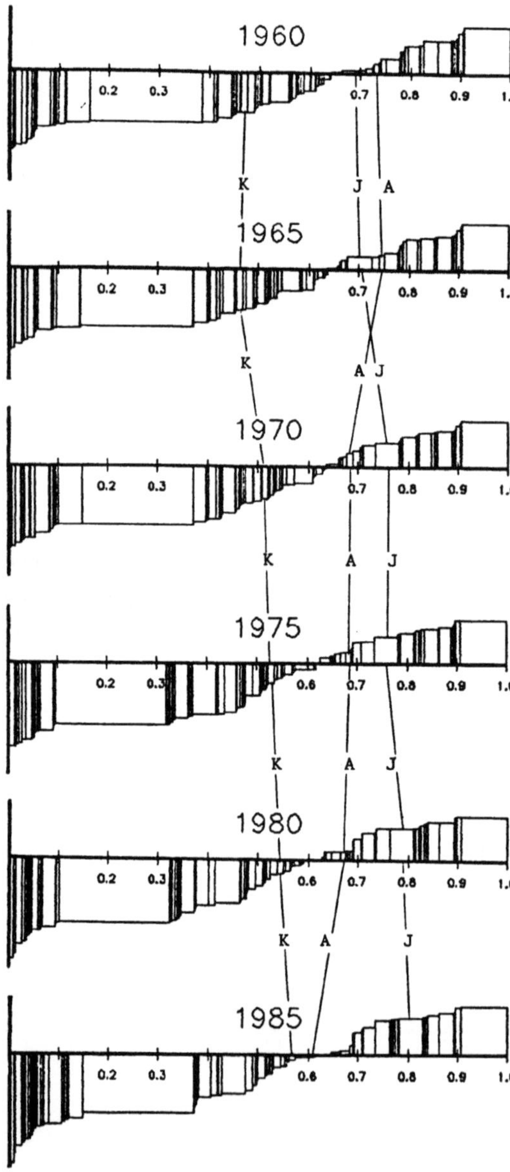


Figure 2
The economic development of Argentina (A), Japan (J), and South Korea (K) relative to that of the (non-Communist) world.

## Appendix

Five countries have data that start later than 1960. These are Burkina Faso in Africa and four countries in Asia: Bahrain, United Arab Emirates, Oman, and Yemen. Deleting these five countries reduces the 121 of Summers and Heston to the 116 used in this article.

Afghanistan and Indonesia require approximations. There are no RGDP2 data for Afghanistan in the years 1982 through 1985. These unknown numbers have been approximated by the 1981 value. There are no population data for Indonesia in 1960 and 1961. Linear extrapolation has been used, yielding 96.31 million in 1961 and 94.18 million in 1960. The approximation errors will be minor.

The 21 countries in Western and Southern Europe are Austria, Belgium, Cyprus, Denmark, Finland, France, Germany (West), Greece, Iceland, Ireland, Italy, Luxembourg, Malta, Netherlands, Norway, Portugal, Spain, Sweden, Switzerland, Turkey, and the United Kingdom.

The 21 countries in Tropical America are Barbados, Bolivia, Brazil, Columbia, Costa Rica, Dominican Republic, Ecuador, El Salvador, Guatemala, Guyana, Haiti, Honduras, Jamaica, Mexico, Nicaragua, Panama, Paraguay, Peru, Surinam, Trinidad and Tobago, and Venezuela.

The 23 countries in Tropical Asia are Afghanistan, Bangladesh, Burma, Fiji, Hong Kong, India, Indonesia, Iran, Iraq, Israel, Jordan, Kuwait, Malaysia, Nepal, Pakistan, Papua New Guinea, Philippines, Saudi Arabia, Singapore, Sri Lanka, Syrian Arab Republic, Taiwan, and Thailand.

The 38 countries in Tropical Africa are Algeria, Angola, Benin, Burundi, Cameroon, Central African Republic, Chad, Congo (People's Republic), Egypt, Ethiopia, Gabon, Gambia, Ghana, Guinea, Ivory Coast, Kenya, Liberia, Madagascar, Malawi, Mali, Mauritania, Mauritius, Morocco, Mozambique, Niger, Nigeria, Rwanda, Senegal, Sierra Leone, Somalia, Sudan, Tanzania, Togo, Tunisia, Uganda, Zaire, Zambia, and Zimbabwe.

## References

Bourguignon, F.: 1979, "Decomposable Income Inequality Measures," *Econometrica*, **47**, 901-920.

Cowell, F.A. and K. Kuga: 1981, "Additivity and the Entropy Concept: An Axiomatic Approach to Inequality Measurement," *Journal of Economic Theory*, **25**, 131-143.

Fishlow, A.: 1972, "Brazilian Size Distribution of Income," *American Economic Review*, **62**, 391-402.

Foster, J.E.: 1983, "An Axiomatic Characterization of the Theil Measure of Income Inequality," *Journal of Economic Theory*, **31**, 105-121.

Kravis, I.B., A.W. Heston, and R. Summers: 1978, "Real GDP Per Capita for More Than One Hundred Countries," *Economic Journal*, **88**, 215-242.

Shorrocks, A.F.: 1980, "The Class of Additively Decomposable Inequality Measures," *Econometrica*, **48**, 613-625.

Summers, R. and A.W. Heston: 1984, "Improved International Comparisons of Real Product and Its Composition: 1950-77," *Review of Income and Wealth*, **30**, 207-262.

Summers, R. and A.W. Heston: 1988, "A New Set of International Comparisons of Real Product and Price Levels: Estimates for 130 countries, 1950-1985," *Review of Income and Wealth*, **34**, 1-25.

Summers, R., I.B. Kravis, and A. Heston: 1984, "Changes in the World Income Distribution," *Journal of Policy Modelling*, **6**, 237-269.

Theil, H.: 1967, *Economics and Information Theory*, North-Holland, Amsterdam.

Theil, H.: 1979, "World Income Inequality and Its Components," *Economics Letters*, **2**, 99-102.

# SECTION 4.3: APPLICATIONS IN ECONOMETRICS

CHAPTER 54

# A MAXIMUM ENTROPY APPROACH TO THE SPECIFICATION OF DISTRIBUTED LAGS*

HENRI THEIL
*University of Chicago*
*Chicago, Illinois, U.S.A.*

DENZIL FIEBIG
*University of Southern California*
*Los Angeles, California, U.S.A.*

ABSTRACT. The maximum entropy (ME) criterion is used to justify three different specifications of distributed lags. For lag distributions in several dimensions, the ME criterion yields a considerable simplification.

## 1. An ME Justification of Three Distributed Lag Forms

In continuous time, a linear distributed lag specification with one explanatory variable takes the form

$$y(t) = \beta_0 + \beta\int_0^\infty f(\tau)x(t-\tau)\,d\tau + \varepsilon(t), \tag{1}$$

where $f(\cdot)$ is the density function of the lag distribution, the β's are coefficients, and $\varepsilon(t)$ is a random disturbance. The problem to be considered is that of specifying $f(\cdot)$. The principle of maximum entropy (ME) states if a statistician's problem is to fit a distribution as an estimator of some true distribution, he should formulate his prior knowledge on the latter distribution in the form of constraints on the distribution to be fitted; then he should select the most uninformative distribution subject to these constraints, with the entropy (minus the expected log of the density) used as measure of uninformativeness.

In the case of lag distributions, it is known that all mass is concentrated on the positive part of the real line. Hence, the entropy takes the form

$$H = -\int_0^\infty f(\tau)\log f(\tau)\,d\tau\,. \tag{2}$$

Suppose that we also know that the range of the lag distribution is $(0,T)$, where $T$ is finite. If that is all we know, the ME distribution is uniform over this range so that the

* This article originally appeared in *Economics Letters*, 7 (1981), 339-342. Reprinted with the permission of Elsevier Science Publishers B.V. (North-Holland).

ME principle yields a uniform distributed lag over $(0, T)$. This result can be easily extended to the range $(T_1, T_2)$, with $0 \leq T_1 < T_2 < \infty$.

Alternatively, suppose that the range is $(0, \infty)$ and that the mean lag is restricted to be equal to $\mu$, $0 < \mu < \infty$. The ME distribution is then exponential over $(0, \infty)$ with mean $\mu$, the density function being $f(\tau) = (1/\mu)e^{-\tau/\mu}$.

Next suppose that the range is $(0, \infty)$, that the mean lag is restricted to be equal to $\mu$, and the geometric mean lag to $G$, where $0 < G < \mu < \infty$. [This case does not fall under that of the previous paragraph because the exponential distribution with range $(0, \infty)$ has zero geometric mean.] The ME distribution is now the gamma distribution, with mean $\mu$ and geometric mean $G$. The density function of this distribution is

$$f(\tau) = \tau^{\alpha-1} e^{-\tau/\beta} / \beta^{\alpha} \Gamma(\alpha), \quad \alpha > 1, \quad \beta, \tau > 0, \tag{3}$$

and the mean $\mu$ of this distribution equals $\alpha\beta$ and its geometric mean $G$ is equal to the antilog of $d\,[\,\log \Gamma(\alpha)\,] / d\alpha + \log \beta$. The gamma distributed lag was proposed by Tsurumi (1971) and was further discussed by Schmidt (1974). For details on the gamma distribution, see, e.g., Johnson and Kotz (1970, ch. 17).

If the distributed lag model is formulated in discrete, rather than continuous time, the ME approach again provides a specification of the lag weights. The model now takes the form

$$y_t = \beta_0 + \beta_1 \sum_{i=0}^{q} p_i x_{t-i} + \varepsilon_t, \qquad t = 1, \ldots, N, \tag{4}$$

and the problem involves specifying $p_i$.

As one would expect, the results are analogous to the continuous time versions derived above.[1] In the case of a finite range $(0, T)$, the ME distribution is given by $p_i = 1/(T + 1)$. For known mean lag $\mu$ and range $(0, \infty)$ we obtain

$$p_i = \frac{1}{1 + \mu} \left[ \frac{\mu}{1 + \mu} \right]^i . \tag{5}$$

On substituting $\mu = \lambda / (1 - \lambda)$, (5) becomes $p_i = (1 - \lambda)\lambda^i$, which is equivalent to Koyck's (1954) specification of distributed lags.

Finally, suppose that the range is $(0, \infty)$, and that the mean lag is $\mu$ and geometric mean lag is $G$. The ME distribution is then

[1] Tribus (1969) provides derivations for the discrete ME distributions.

$$p_i = \left[ \sum_{i=0}^{\infty} i^{-\lambda_2} e^{-\lambda_1 i} \right]^{-1} i^{-\lambda_2} e^{-\lambda_1 i} . \tag{6}$$

This is equivalent to Tsurumi's (1971) formulation with $\lambda_1 = 1$ and $\lambda_2 = 1 - S$. One of Schmidt's (1974) suggestions was the relaxation of the $\lambda_1 = 1$ constraint to give a more flexible two-parameter distribution. As we have seen, this suggestion is also consistent with the ME version of the Gamma distributed lag.

We conclude that the ME principle provides a direct justification of three different forms of distributed lags depending on which type of prior information is available. Lev and Theil (1978) used the same kind of argument for straight-line and exponential depreciation of assets. The depreciation distribution is then uniform or exponential. It would be of interest to consider the gamma depreciation distribution as a third possibility; it is easily verified from (3) that the depreciation rate increases from zero until a maximum at $\tau = (\alpha - 1)/\beta$ and then decreases monotonically.

## 2. Extension to Several Explanatory Variables

When we have two explanatory variables rather than one, it is natural to consider a bivariate lag distribution. Let $f(\tau_1, \tau_2)$ be the density function of this distribution, and let $f_1(\tau_1)$ and $f_2(\tau_2)$ be the density functions of the marginal distributions. The bivariate extension of (1) including a bilinear term, is then

$$\begin{aligned} y(t) = \beta_0 &+ \beta_1 \int_0^{\infty} f_1(\tau_1) x_1(t - \tau_1)\, d\tau_1 + \beta_2 \int_0^{\infty} f_2(\tau_2) x_2(t - \tau_2)\, d\tau_2 \\ &+ \beta_{12} \int_0^{\infty} \int_0^{\infty} f(\tau_1, \tau_2) x_1(t - \tau_1) x_2(t - \tau_2)\, d\tau_1\, d\tau_2 + \varepsilon(t) . \end{aligned} \tag{7}$$

The bilinear term easily leads to problems of overparameterization, but the ME principle is useful in this respect also. Given the entropies of the two marginal distributions, the bivariate entropy is maximized under stochastic independence. Thus, when nothing is known about the lag-dependence of the two explanatory variables, the ME principle implies that $f(\tau_1, \tau_2) \equiv f_1(\tau_1) f_2(\tau_2)$ so that (7) is simplified to

$$y(t) = \beta_0 + \beta_1 X_1\{t\} + \beta_2 X_2\{t\} + \beta_{12} X_1\{t\} X_2\{t\} + \varepsilon(t) , \tag{8}$$

where $X_h\{t\} = \int_0^{\infty} \mathrm{f_h}(\tau_h) X_h(t - \tau_h)\, d\tau_h$ for $h = 1, 2$. The extension of this result to discrete time and higher dimensions is straightforward. The latter extension follows from the fact that a multivariate entropy equals the sum of all univariate marginal entropies minus the expected mutual information, the latter being positive except that it vanishes under stochastic independence.

## References

Johnson, N.L., and S. Kotz: 1970, *Continuous Univariate Distributions - 1*, Houghton Mifflin Company, Boston, Massachusetts.

Koyck, L.M.: 1954, *Distributed Lags and Investment Analysis*, North-Holland, Amsterdam.

Lev, B., and H. Theil: 1978, "A Maximum Entropy Approach to Choice of Asset Depreciation," *Journal of Accounting Research*, **16**, 286-293.

Schmidt, P.: 1974, "An Argument for the Usefulness of the Gamma Distributed Lag Model," *International Economic Review*, **15**, 247-250.

Tribus, M.: 1969, *Rational Descriptions, Decisions and Designs*, Pergamon Press, New York.

Tsurumi, H.: 1971, "A Note on Gamma Distributed Lags," *International Economic Review*, **12**, 317-324.

CHAPTER 55

# INFORMATION-THEORETIC MEASURES OF FIT FOR UNIVARIATE AND MULTIVARIATE LINEAR REGRESSIONS*

HENRI THEIL
*University of Florida,*
*Gainesville, Florida U.S.A.*

CHING-FAN CHUNG
*University of Florida,*
*Gainesville, Florida U.S.A.*

ABSTRACT. For the purpose of measuring the relative importance of independent variables in a multiple regression, Kruskal (1987) proposed an averaging procedure over all possible orderings of these variables. The present article uses this suggestion, but it is based on a different measure, from statistical information theory, and it extends the result to systems of equations.

KEY WORDS: Correlation; Information theory; Multiple regression; Systems of Equations.

## 1. Introduction

Consider a linear regression of $X_0$ on $X_1, \ldots, X_p$. Several authors have suggested measures for the importance of $X_1, \ldots, X_p$ in the "explanation" of $X_0$. Kruskal (1987) returned to this topic and proposed a measure based on simple correlations (such as $r_{01}$) and partial correlations (such as $r_{02\cdot1}$). This yields a unique answer if the independent variables have a unique ordering, $X_1$ coming before $X_2$ and so on until $X_p$. If there is no such ordering, Kruskal proposed taking the arithmetic average of this measure over all orderings, that is, over all $p!$ permutations of $1, \ldots, p$ as subscripts.

Once the idea of averaging over all orderings is accepted, other measures should also be considered. Theil (1987) proposed an information-theoretic measure based on the identity

$$1 - R^2 = (1 - r_{01}^2)(1 - r_{02\cdot1}^2)\ldots(1 - r_{0p\cdot12\ldots(p-1)}^2)\ , \tag{1}$$

where $R$ is the multiple correlation coefficient between $X_0$ and $X_1, \ldots, X_p$. The purpose of this article is expository; it covers both the multiple-regression case and the canonical-correlation extension proposed by Thiel and Chung (1988). Correlations are regarded

* This article first appeared in *The American Statistician*, **42** (November 1988), 249-252. Reprinted with the permission of The American Statistical Association.

Henri Theil is McKethan-Matherly Eminent Scholar and Ching-Fan Chung is McKethan-Matherly Post-Doctoral Fellow, Graduate School of Business Administration, University of Florida, Gainesville, Florida 32611. Research for this article was supported by the University of Florida's McKethan-Matherly Eminent Scholar Chair.

mainly as descriptive devices except in section 11 (where matters of inference are briefly discussed).

## 2. An Informational Version of Kruskal's Average

To derive a measure of information, we take the base 2 logarithm of both sides of (1) to arrive at

$$I(R^2) = I(r_{01}^2) + I(r_{02\cdot1}^2) + \ldots + I(r_{0p\cdot12\ldots(p-1)}^2) \;, \tag{2}$$

where $I(x) = -\log_2(1 - x)$ for $0 \leq x \leq 1$. For example, if $R^2 = .5$, then $I(R^2) = -\log_2(1 - .5) = 1$ bit; if $R^2 = .75$, then $I(R^2) = 2$ bits. The logarithmic function $I(\cdot)$ is a well-known measure from statistical information theory.

Theil (1987) proposed $I(R^2)$ as the information (in bits) on the behaviour of $X_0$ that is provided by all $p$ independent variables jointly. Equation (2) will then yield a unique additive decomposition of this total information in terms of the individual independent variables, provided we agree on a particular ordering of these variables. If there is no such natural ordering, Theil proposed to follow Kruskal's suggestion by averaging the information decomposition over all $p!$ orderings.

## 3. Example 1: The Demand for Textile

To illustrate the use of the measures of information we consider annual data collected in the Netherlands for 1923-1939. The variables considered for this example include the log of real income per capita, $X_1$, the log of relative textile price, $X_2$, and the dependent variable-log of textile consumption per capita, $X_0$ (for details see Theil 1971, pp. 102, 115-116, 172-180). Here $R^2 = .974$, $r_{01}^2 = .010$, $r_{02}^2 = .876$, $r_{01\cdot2}^2 = .793$ and $r_{02\cdot1}^2 = .974$. Kruskal's measure for the relative importance of income and price is based on the average of $r_{01}^2$ and $r_{01\cdot2}^2$ for income (which equals .402) and the average of $r_{02}^2$ and $r_{02\cdot1}^2$ for the relative textile price (equal to .925); he would conclude that the price is 925/402 = 2.3 times as important as income.

Theil's proposal is based on Equation (2). For $X_1$ = log of income and $X_2$ = log of price, this equation becomes, in bits,

$$5.29 = .02 + 5.27 \;. \tag{3}$$

For $X_1$ = log of price and $X_2$ = log of income, it becomes

$$5.29 = 3.02 + 2.27. \tag{4}$$

The averaging procedure yields 5.29 = ½(.02 + 2.27) + ½(5.27 + 3.02) or 5.29 = 1.14 (income) + 4.15 (price). Thus the information on the behaviour of textile consumption provided by both variables together is 5.29 bits, and the relative textile price is more than 3.6 times as important as income. The latter conclusion should be contrasted with that at the end of the previous paragraph, where the price was found to be 2.3 times as important as income.

## 4. Discussion

The additivity of informational measures is one of the axioms of statistical information theory. This additivity lends a natural support to the idea of taking the arithmetic average under Kruskal's proposal for handling the $p!$ orderings.

Note further that the decompositions (3) and (4) hold exactly for each ordering prior to the averaging procedure, whereas there are no counterparts of (3) and (4) under Kruskal's measure of relative importance (because this measure does not involve the multiple correlation $R$). Also, the "average" decomposition 5.29 = 1.14 + 4.15 discussed in Section 3 provides not only measures of relative importance but also measures of "absolute" importance because the sum (5.29 bits) is directly related to $R^2$.

Finally it may be argued that using $I(R^2)$ rather than $R^2$ provides a more natural scale. For example, the three values $R^2$ = .98, .99, and .999 are almost equidistant, whereas the associated values $I(R^2)$ are 5.64, 6.64, and 9.97 (all in bits) which present a more realistic picture. The correction of $I(R^2)$ for degrees of freedom is discussed in Section 11.

## 5. A Canonical-Correlation Extension

Next we turn to two sets of variates, $X_1, \ldots, X_p$ and $Y_1, \ldots, Y_q$, the single variate $X_0$ of our earlier discussion being replaced by $q$ new variates. Theil and Chung (1988) extended the approach of section 2 to the canonical correlations of these two sets, $R_1 \geq R_2 \geq \ldots R_m \geq 0$, where $m = \min(p, q)$. If the $p + q$ variates constitute a nonsingular distribution, the largest canonical correlation $R_1$ is strictly less than 1; we shall make this assumption here and in the next two sections.

Since $R_i$ is the correlation coefficient of the $i^{th}$ canonical variate of the $X$'s and the $i^{th}$ canonical variate of the $Y$'s, the result (2) is directly applicable in two different ways:

$$I(R_i^2) = I(r_{y_i1}^2) + I(r_{y_i2\cdot1}^2) + \ldots + I(r_{y_ip\cdot12\ldots(p-1)}^2) \tag{5}$$

and

$$I(R_i^2) = I(r_{x_i1}^2) + I(r_{x_i2\cdot 1}^2) + \ldots + I(r_{x_iq\cdot 12\ldots(q-1)}^2) \ . \qquad (6)$$

In (5), $y_i$ denotes the $i$th canonical variate of the $Y$'s, whereas the observed $X$ variates are indicated by pure numbers as in (2). In (5) we regard $I(R_i^2)$ as the information (in bits) on the $i$th canonical variate of the $Y$'s that is provided by the $p$ observed $X$ variates, whereas in (6) we view the same $I(R_i^2)$ as the information on the $i$th canonical variate of the $X$'s (indicated by $x_i$) that is provided by the observed $Y$ variates (indicated by 1, ··· , $q$). When there is neither a natural ordering of the observed $X$'s nor of the observed $Y$'s, we average over all $p!$ or $q!$ orderings; an example is provided in Section 7.

## 6. The Total Amount of Information

Since information is an additive concept, it is natural to sum $I(R_i^2)$ over $i$:

$$T = \sum_{i=1}^{m} I(R_i^2) = -\sum_{i=1}^{m} \log_2 (1 - R_i^2) \ . \qquad (7)$$

This is the total amount of information that either set of variates provides about the other.

It is of interest to add that $T$ is related to the expected mutual information for the case in which the $p + q$ variates follow a multinormal distribution. This expected mutual information, or the average uncertainty reduction of either set of variates when the other becomes known, is equal to the entropy of the $X$'s plus that of the $Y$'s minus that of the $X$'s and $Y$'s together. If the distribution is multinormal with canonical correlations $R_1, \ldots, R_m$, the expected mutual information is

$$-\frac{1}{2}\sum_{i=1}^{m} \log_e (1 - R_i^2) \ , \qquad (8)$$

which is equal to (7) apart from the factor ½ and the base of the logarithms. These differences affect only the information unit.

Both (7) and (8) are logarithmic versions of Hotelling's (1936) vector-alienation coefficient. Tinsley, Spindt, and Friar (1980) developed similar concepts for the loss of indicator information that results from the aggregation of monetary variables, although they did not provide the link (8) with canonical-correlation theory. See Theil and Fiebig (1984, pp. 114-118) for further details.

## 7. Example 2: Length and Breadth of Human Heads

Anderson (1984, pp. 500-502) described an example (due to C. R. Rao) for $m = p = q = 2$. The two $X$'s refer to the first son ($F$) in a family, the two $Y$'s to the second son ($S$). The two measurements on each son are the length ($L$) and breadth ($B$) of the head. Therefore, $(X_1, X_2) = (FL, FB)$ and $(Y_1, Y_2) = (SL, SB)$.

The canonical correlations are $R_1 = .789$ and $R_2 = .054$. Their information values are shown (in bits, in five decimal places) in the first row of Table 1, together with the total information $T$ defined in equation (7). Here the largest canonical correlation $R_1$ accounts for as much as 99.7% of $T$.

The next two rows are based on the decomposition given in equation (5), and the last two on that given in (6). Take (5) for $i = 1$. For $X_1 = FL$ and $X_2 = FB$ it takes the form 1.40257 = 1.13252 + .27005; for $X_1 = FB$ and $X_2 = FL$ it becomes 1.40257 = 1.10301 + .29956. Application of Kruskal's averaging procedure yields 1.40257 = .71604 ($FL$) + .68653 ($FB$). The last two numbers are shown in the second column. We conclude that the two measurements on the first son ($FL$ and $FB$) contribute about equally to the behaviour of the second-son canonical variate that corresponds to the larger canonical-correlation coefficient.

The other items on Table 1 are similarly obtained by means of Kruskal's averaging procedure over $p! = 2$ or $q! = 2$ orderings. As the results show, the two observed first-son variates ($FL$ and $FB$) contribute about equally to both $I(R_1^2)$ and $I(R_2^2)$, and so do the two observed second-son variates.

**TABLE I.** First Information Tableau

| | $I(R_1^2)$ | $I(R_2^2)$ | Total |
|---|---|---|---|
| | 1.40257 | .00417 | 1.40674 |
| | First son | | |
| Length ($FL$) | .71604 | .00205 | .71809 |
| Breadth ($FB$) | .68653 | .00212 | .68865 |
| | Second Son | | |
| Length ($SL$) | .69036 | .00211 | .69247 |
| Breadth ($SB$) | .71221 | .00206 | .71427 |

## 8. Extension to Linear Simultaneous-Equations Models: The Treatment of Identities

We proceed to consider the information tableau of a linear econometric system of $q$ equations in $q$ endogenous variables $Y_1, \ldots, Y_q$ and $p$ exogenous variables $X_1, \ldots, X_p$. The application of Hotelling's vector alienation coefficient (the antilog of $T$) to such systems is not new (see Theil, 1958, pp. 345-347), but Kruskal's averaging procedure provides some valuable new insights.

There is one aspect that is new compared with the developments in Sections 5 and 6: the occurrence of identities without unknown coefficients and without nonzero error terms. Let there be $k$ such identities; if they are linearly independent and if each involves both endogenous and exogenous variables, there will be $k$ canonical correlations equal to 1. This follows directly from the fact that each identity can be written as a linear combination of the $Y$'s that is equal to (and hence perfectly correlated with) a linear combination of the $X$'s.

If $R_i = 1$, then $I(R_i^2)$ is not defined; however, this is irrelevant. Since identities contain neither error terms nor unknown coefficients, they constitute the uninteresting singular part of the equation system. In the example that follows we confine ourselves to the more interesting nonsingular part of the $q - k$ equations that are not identities.

## 9. Example 3: Klein's Model I

L. R. Klein's model involves an extension of the exogenous-endogenous distinction, because variables occur both in current form and lagged one year. Current endogenous variables are called *jointly dependent*; lagged variables (both endogenous and exogenous) are called *predetermined.*

There are $q = 6$ jointly dependent variables in the model. Their symbols are listed in the first column of Table 2: $C$, consumption; $X$, private output; $I$, investment; $K$, capital stock; $P$, profits; and $W$, private wage bill.

We write $p$ for the number of predetermined variables. Here $p = 7$: $P_{-1}$ denotes profits in last year, $B$ is business taxes, $G$ is government nonwage expenditure, $X_{-1}$ is private output of last year, $V$ is government wage bill, $t$ is calendar time, and $K_{-1}$ is last year's capital stock.

The model consists of $q = 6$ equations, 3 of which are identities. Thus there are three canonical correlations equal to 1 and three less than 1: $R_1 = .992$, $R_2 = .901$, and $R_3 = .154$. Their information values $I(R_i^2)$ are shown in the first row of Table 2, together with their sum $T = 8.338$ bits. Note that $I(R_1^2)$ is not nearly as dominant as it is in Table 1.

In Table II we have ranked the variables of each of the two groups according to the declining contributions of $T$. (It is a bit ironic that we started with the assumption of no natural ordering and now end up with an ordering!) Among the predetermined variables, $P_{-1}$ and $B$ contribute most and $K_{-1}$ contributes least; among the jointly dependent variables, $C$ and $W$ are at opposite ends of the scale. Naturally, most of the variables derive most of their contributions to $T$ from their contributions to $I(R_1^2)$, but $P_{-1}$ and $I$ are major exceptions. We shall not go into further details because Klein's Model I gives a highly simplified picture of the U.S economy, but we do want to emphasize the considerable extension of the present results beyond those obtained for textile in section 3.

**TABLE II.** Information Tableau for Klein's Model I

| Variable | $I(R_1^2)$ | $I(R_2^2)$ | $I(R_3^2)$ | Total |
|---|---|---|---|---|
| | 5.899 | 2.404 | .035 | 8.338 |
| | | Predetermined variables | | |
| $P_{-1}$ | .348 | 1.198 | .003 | 1.550 |
| $B$ | 1.247 | .240 | .000 | 1.487 |
| $G$ | 1.180 | .156 | .001 | 1.337 |
| $X_{-1}$ | .668 | .505 | .006 | 1.179 |
| $V$ | .857 | .147 | .009 | 1.013 |
| $t$ | .828 | .113 | .011 | .953 |
| $K_{-1}$ | .769 | .046 | .004 | .819 |
| | | Jointly dependent variables | | |
| $C$ | 1.793 | .120 | .002 | 1.915 |
| $X$ | 1.418 | .178 | .006 | 1.602 |
| $I$ | .457 | 1.127 | .005 | 1.589 |
| $K$ | .988 | .352 | .003 | 1.343 |
| $P$ | .511 | .508 | .007 | 1.025 |
| $W$ | .732 | .121 | .011 | .864 |

## 10. A Computational Note

Table II is based on the data presented by Theil (1971, p. 456). When $p$ and $q$ are 6 and 7, as is the case here, the number of orderings ($p!$ or $q!$) is quite large and it becomes imperative to program the Kruskal averaging procedure efficiently; see Chung (1987) for this problem. See also Anderson (1984, pp. 491-492) for a useful result on the correlations between canonical variates and the components of the observed vectors.

## 11. Corrections for Degrees of Freedom

It should be intuitively obvious that when $T$ defined in (7) is based on sample moments it will be upwardly biased. Both $T$ and the underlying $R_i^2$'s are generalizations of the multiple correlation $R$. For a regression on $p$ independent variables (including a constant term) based on a sample of size $n$, a correction that is frequently used amounts to replacing $R$ by $\bar{R}$, obtained from

$$1 - \bar{R}^2 = \frac{n-1}{n-p-1}(1 - R^2) \; . \tag{9}$$

Bias corrections of canonical correlations were considered by Lawley (1956, 1959), but these are not easy to implement (see also Anderson, 1984, pp.497-498). Tinsley et al. (1980) considered the problem of correcting the expected mutual information (which is proportional to $T$ under normality), but their solution fails to recognize that this measure is symmetric in the two sets of variates.

A simple correction for canonical correlations is

$$1 - \bar{R}_i^2 = (1 - R_i^2)^{n/(n+p+q-1)} . \tag{10}$$

To explain the exponent we note that each canonical variate involves $p - 1$ or $q - 1$ multiplicative coefficients (only the ratios of these coefficients matter). This yields $p + q - 2$ for a pair of canonical variates, to which we add 1 for a constant term. (Both canonical variates have constant terms, but the covariance in the numerator of the canonical correlation is not affected when only one constant is used.)

For $q = 1$ the correction given (10) becomes $1 - \bar{R}_1^2 = (1 - R_1^2)^{n/(n+p)}$, which should be compared with the conventional correction given in (9). Note the advantage of the exponential form of (10); it guarantees that $\bar{R}_i^2$ in contrast to $\bar{R}^2$ is never negative.

Also note that (10) has the advantage of simplicity in that the only change in the information tableau is that all entries are to be multiplied by the ratio of $n$ to $n + p + q - 1$. We conducted a small simulation experiment, based on the experimental design described by Theil and Fiebig (1984, pp. 118-123), and found that (10) reduces the upward bias of $T$ substantially but not completely. Another solution is to replace the exponent of (10) by the ratio of $n - r$ or $n + r$, where $r = ½(p + q - 1)$. Such corrections can also be useful for statistical inference in equation systems that involve an unknown error covariance matrix, but this is beyond the scope of this article.

## References


Anderson, T.W.: 1984, *An Introduction to Multivariate Statistical Analysis*, 2nd ed., John Wiley, New York.

Chung, C.-F.: 1987, "On Calculating the Information-Theoretic Measure of Fit for Multivariate Linear Regressions," McKethan-Matherly Discussion Paper 28, University of Florida, College of Business Administration.

Hotelling, H.: 1936, "Relations Between Two Sets of Variates," *Biometrika*, **28**, 321-377.

Kruskal, W.: 1987, "Relative Importance by Averaging Over Orderings," *The American Statistician*, **41**, 6-10.

Lawley, D.N.: 1956, "Tests of Significance of the Latent Roots of Covariance and Correlation Matrices," *Biometrika*, **43**, 128-136.

Lawley, D.N.: 1959, "Tests of Significance in Canonical Analysis," *Biometrika*, **46**, 59-66.

Theil, H.: 1958, *Economic Forecasts and Policy*, North-Holland, Amsterdam.

Theil, H.: 1971, *Principles of Econometrics*, John Wiley, New York.

Theil, H.: 1987, "How Many Bits of Information Does an Independent Variable Yield in a Multiple Regression?" *Statistics and Probability Letters*, **6**, 107-108.

Theil, H., and Chung, C.-F.: 1988, "Relations Between Two Sets of Variates: The Bits of Information Provided by Each Variate in Each Set," *Statistics and Probability Letters*, **6**, 137-139.

Theil, H., and Fiebig, D.G.: 1984, "*Exploiting Continuity: Maximum Entropy Estimation of Continuous Distributions,*" Ballinger, Cambridge, Massachusetts.

Tinsley, P.A., Spindt, P.A., and Friar, M.E.: 1980, "Indicator and Filter Attributes of Monetary Aggregates: A Nit-Picking Case for Disaggregation," *Journal of Econometrics*, **14**, 61-91.

# SECTION 4.4: INPUT-OUTPUT ANALYSIS

CHAPTER 56

# LINEAR AGGREGATION IN INPUT-OUTPUT ANALYSIS*

HENRI THEIL
*Netherlands School of Economics*
*(now Erasmus University),*
*Rotterdam, The Netherlands*

## 1. Introduction

Recent contributions of Mrs. Balderston and Mr. Whitin (1954) and of M.E. Malinvaud (1954) have stressed the importance of the aggregation problems in input-output analysis. A solution of these problems is clearly desirable; for, although input-output analysis itself was designed in order to show certain basic relations in more detail than the "usual" type of econometric macroanalysis (in terms of regression and structural equations) does, the degree of aggregation is still considerable, even for very large input-output tables.

The Balderston-Whitin paper is primarily interesting because of its instructive examples. Malinvaud's contribution goes deeper; he is concerned with the formal characteristics of the aggregation process, and with sufficient conditions under which this process does involve any contradictions. The present paper is largely concerned with such contradictions, its approach being of the following type: If total-output predictions of certain industries are derived by means of an aggregated input-output table, what is the nature of the forecasting error that is to be ascribed to the aggregation? The general set-up, which is closely related to the author's monograph (1954), is described in sections 2, 3, and 4. Predictions are considered in sections 5 and 6, after which the main results (on the aggregation bias of input-output macro- predictions) are presented in section 7. These results are discussed thereafter, and the final section contains some remarks on the difference between input-output aggregation and the problems considered in Theil (1954).

## 2. The Microtheory

We shall say that the microtheory runs in terms of firms, and the macrotheory in terms of industries. It should be stressed that this is a terminology which is simply chosen for the sake of convenience, and that it is equally permissible to start from a microtheory in terms of separate parts of firms or of groups of firms. This generality is due to the fact that disturbances will be introduced even at the microlevel, and they may be regarded as

* This article first appeared in *Econometrica*, **25** (1957), 111-122. Reprinted with the permission of the Econometric Society. The author is indebted to Messrs. Carl F. Christ of the University of Chicago and E. Malinvaud of the I.N.S.E.E., Paris, for their comments, especially for the latter's contribution to the analysis of homogeneous input structures (section 9).

comprising all kinds of errors at this level, including those of aggregation if the microsystem itself is the result of some aggregation.

Each separate firm will be denoted by two symbols, e.g., ($\mu i$) or ($\mu' j$), of which the first refers to the industry to which it belongs ($\mu$ or $\mu'$) and the second is its number within the industry. The total number of industries is $M$, and the number of firms in industry $\mu$ is written $I_\mu$. The total number of all firms is then

$$\omega = \sum_{\mu} I_{\mu} \, . \tag{2.1}$$

We shall denote by $y_{\mu i,\mu' j}$ the output of ($\mu i$), as far as it is sold to ($\mu' j$) during the period for which we wish to make predictions. The total output sold to all firms is then

$$y_{\mu i} = \sum_{\mu', j} y_{\mu i,\mu' j} \, , \tag{2.2}$$

where the $j$-summation takes place over $1, \ldots, I_{\mu'}$ and the $\mu'$-summation over $1, \ldots, M$. When denoting by $x_{\mu i}$ the final demand for the products of ($\mu i$), the total output of this firm becomes

$$z_{\mu i} = y_{\mu i} + x_{\mu i} \, . \tag{2.3}$$

Our microtheory is, in accordance with Leontief's original set-up, that there are fixed technical coefficients which connect the interfirm deliveries with the total output of the recipient firm. As indicated in the first paragraph of this section, we shall add a disturbance, in that we obtain $\omega^2$ equations of the type

$$y_{\mu i,\mu' j} = \alpha_{\mu i,\mu' j} \, z_{\mu' j} + u_{\mu i,\mu' j} \, ; \tag{2.4}$$

and we suppose that the technical coefficients have been derived from an input-output table in some base period indicated by the superscript 0:

$$\alpha_{\mu i,\mu' j} = y^{0}_{\mu i,\mu' j} / z^{0}_{\mu' j} \, , \tag{2.5}$$

from which it follows that (2.4) holds for the base period with zero disturbance. It will not be necessary to make any assumptions about the disturbance of (2.4), so that this "microtheory" is, in fact, a set of error definitions rather than a "real" theory. Alternatively, we may say that (2.4) without the disturbance is the theory, and the disturbance its error.

## 3. The Aggregation

The aggregation is of the usual summation type (cf. Theil, 1954, p. 12) and the aggregates corresponding to the interfirm deliveries are the interindustry deliveries,

$$y_{\mu\mu'} = \sum_{i,j} y_{\mu i,\mu' j'} , \tag{3.1}$$

when the $i$-summation takes place over $1 , \ldots , I_\mu$ and the $j$-summation over $1 , \ldots , I_{\mu'}$. Here, as well as in (2.2) and in further relevant places, the summation over an index is simply denoted by dropping the index. The output sold by industry μ to all industries is then

$$y_\mu = \sum_{\mu'} y_{\mu\mu'} = \sum_i y_{\mu i} \tag{3.2}$$

and its final demand

$$x_\mu = \sum_i x_{\mu i} , \tag{3.3}$$

so that the total output of μ becomes

$$z_\mu = y_\mu + x_\mu . \tag{3.4}$$

## 4. The Macrotheory

The macrotheory, being based on the analogy approach (cf. Theil, 1954, p. 6), states that there are fixed technical coefficients in the macrosphere, and that these coefficients are derived from the input-output table in the base period:

$$y_{\mu\mu'} = \alpha_{\mu\mu'} z_{\mu'} + u_{\mu\mu'} , \tag{4.1}$$

$u_{\mu\mu'}$ being a macrodisturbance (which will be replaced by zero for prediction purposes), and

$$\alpha_{\mu\mu'} = y^0_{\mu\mu'} / z^0_{\mu'} . \tag{4.2}$$

Note that $\alpha_{\mu\mu'}$ does not equal $\Sigma\Sigma\alpha_{\mu i,\mu' j}$. Instead, we have $y^0_{\mu\mu'} = \Sigma\Sigma y^0_{\mu i,\mu' j}$, $z^0_{\mu'} = \Sigma z^0_{\mu' j}$ and hence, from (2.5) and (4.2),

$$\alpha_{\mu\mu'} = \sum_j \zeta_{\mu' j} \sum_i \alpha_{\mu i,\mu' j} , \tag{4.3}$$

where $\zeta_{\mu' j}$ is the total output of $(\mu' j)$ in the base period as a proportion of the total output of its industry,

$$\zeta_{\mu' j} = z^0_{\mu' j} / z^0_{\mu'} . \tag{4.4}$$

## 5. Micropredictions

We proceed to consider, for each firm and industry, the total output corresponding to any given final bill. When following the microanalysis, we have from (2.2), (2.3), and (2.4)

$$z_{\mu i} = \sum_{\mu', j} \alpha_{\mu i,\mu' j} z_{\mu' j} + x_{\mu i} + u_{\mu i} , \tag{5.1}$$

where $u_{\mu i}$ is the sum of $\omega$ microdisturbances:

$$u_{\mu i} = \sum_{\mu', j} u_{\mu i,\mu' j} . \tag{5.2}$$

In matrix notation, (5.1) becomes

$$(I - A_{\omega\omega}) z_\omega = x_\omega + u_\omega \tag{5.3}$$

or

$$z_\omega = (I - A_{\omega\omega})^{-1} (x_\omega + u_\omega) , \tag{5.4}$$

where $I$ is the $\omega \times \omega$ unit matrix, $A_{\omega\omega}$ the matrix of technical microcoefficients [the firms $(\mu i)$ being arranged in the order (11), (12), . . . , $(1I_1)$, . . . , $(MI_M)$], $z_\omega$ the total output vector, $x_\omega$ the vector describing the final microbill, and $u_\omega$ the vector of disturbance sums (5.2). Here, as well as in the remainder of this paper, indices attached to vectors and matrices indicate their order; if there are two indices, the first refers to the number of rows, the second to the number of columns; and all vectors are column vectors.

Predictions are based on the "systematic" part of (2.4) and hence of (5.4), excluding the disturbances. The predicted vector of total micro-output is, therefore,

$$z_\omega^* = (I - A_{\omega\omega})^{-1} x_\omega , \tag{5.5}$$

and the prediction error becomes

$$e_\omega = z_\omega^* - z_\omega = -(I - A_{\omega\omega})^{-1} u_\omega . \tag{5.6}$$

## 6. Macropredictions

Just as in many other aggregation problems, there are two ways of arriving at predictions of values of macrovariables, viz., by means of the microtheory and by means of the macrotheory. We start with the microtheory and introduce the $M \times \omega$ matrix

$$I_{M\omega} = \begin{bmatrix} 1\ldots1 & 0\ldots0 & \ldots & 0\ldots0 \\ 0\ldots0 & 1\ldots1 & \ldots & 0\ldots0 \\ \ldots & \ldots & \ldots & \ldots \\ 0\ldots0 & 0\ldots0 & \ldots & 1\ldots1 \end{bmatrix} , \tag{6.1}$$

the $\mu$th row of which has, first, $(I_1 \ldots + I_{\mu-1})$ zeros, then $I_\mu$ units, and finally $(I_{\mu+1} + \ldots + I_M)$ zeros (cf. Theil, 1954, p. 72). Obviously

$$x_M = I_{M\omega} x_\omega ; \qquad z_M = I_{M\omega} z_\omega , \tag{6.2}$$

where the vectors with index $\omega$ represent micro-outputs (of final demand and of total output, respectively) and those with index $M$ represent macro-outputs. From (5.4) and (6.2) we then obtain

$$z_M = I_{M\omega} (I - A_{\omega\omega})^{-1} (x_\omega + u_\omega) , \tag{6.3}$$

which gives the vector of industry outputs corresponding to a given final microbill (including microdisturbances).

The prediction according to the macrotheory can be derived in a way similar to that described in section 5, so that we have

$$z_M = (I - A_{MM})^{-1} (x_M + u_M) = (I - A_{MM})^{-1} (I_{M\omega} x_\omega + u_M) , \tag{6.4}$$

where $A_{MM}$ is the matrix of technical coefficients, and $u_M$ the vector of the disturbance sums of (4.1),

$$u_M = \left[ \sum_{\mu'} u_{\mu\mu'} \right] . \tag{6.5}$$

The prediction by means of the macrotheory is, therefore,

$$z_M^* = (I - A_{MM})^{-1} I_{M\omega} x_\omega , \tag{6.6}$$

and this, together with (6.3), gives the "macro-error,"

$$e_M = z_M^* - z_M = P x_\omega - I_{M\omega} (I - A_{\omega\omega})^{-1} u_\omega = P x_\omega + I_{M\omega} e_\omega \tag{6.7}$$

[cf. (5.6)], where

$$P = (I - A_{MM})^{-1} I_{M\omega} - I_{M\omega} (I - A_{\omega\omega})^{-1} . \tag{6.8}$$

It follows from (6.7) that the prediction (macro) errors are homogeneous linear combinations of the final microbill, plus the sum of corresponding micro-errors.[1]

## 7. The Fundamental Aggregation Equations

The result (6.7), (6.8) cannot be considered as final, since both $A_{MM}$ and $A_{\omega\omega}$ play a role in (6.8), and they are connected.[2] To show this, it is convenient to introduce the $M \times \omega$ matrix

[1] Summation of corresponding micro-errors means that all those elements of $e_\omega$ are added which correspond to firms in the same industry; cf. (Theil, 1954, p. 14).

[2] The relations (6.7), (6.8) are closely related to equation (7), p. 108 of Balderston and Whitin (1954), the main difference being that the latter equation contains no micro-errors. Unfortunately, however, the authors stopped when reaching this result.

$$Z_{M\omega} = \begin{bmatrix} \zeta_{11}\ldots\zeta_{1l_1} & 0\ldots0 & \ldots0 & \ldots0 \\ 0\ldots0 & \zeta_{21}\ldots\zeta_{2l_2} & \ldots0 & \ldots0 \\ \ldots & \ldots & \ldots & \ldots \\ 0\ldots0 & 0\ldots0 & \ldots & \zeta_{Ml}\ldots\zeta_{Ml_M} \end{bmatrix}, \tag{7.1}$$

which is identical with $I_{M\omega}$ as far as the zeros are concerned, but which contains the proportions $\zeta_{\mu'j}$ defined in (4.4) in those places where $I_{M\omega}$ has units.

Now we have, if $Z_{\omega M}$ is the transpose of $Z_{M\omega}$,

$$I_{M\omega} Z_{\omega M} = I \tag{7.2}$$

and

$$Z_{\omega M} I_{M\omega} = Z = \begin{bmatrix} Z_1 & 0 & \ldots & 0 \\ 0 & Z_2 & \ldots & 0 \\ \ldots & \ldots & \ldots & \ldots \\ 0 & 0 & \ldots & Z_M \end{bmatrix}, \tag{7.3}$$

where $Z_\mu$ is the square matrix

$$Z_\mu = \begin{bmatrix} \zeta_{\mu 1} & \cdots & \zeta_{\mu 1} \\ \ldots & \ldots & \ldots \\ \zeta_{\mu l \mu} & \cdots & \zeta_{\mu l \mu} \end{bmatrix}. \tag{7.4}$$

We can then re-write the equation (4.3) as

$$A_{MM} = I_{M\omega} A_{\omega\omega} Z_{\omega M}, \tag{7.5}$$

so that (6.8) becomes

$$P = (I - I_{M\omega} A_{\omega\omega} Z_{\omega M})^{-1} I_{M\omega} - I_{M\omega} (I - A_{\omega\omega})^{-1}. \tag{7.6}$$

When expanding the first term on the right-hand side, we obtain

$$I_{M\omega}\left[I + A_{\omega\omega} Z_{\omega M} I_{M\omega} + (A_{\omega\omega} Z_{\omega M} I_{M\omega})^2 + \cdots\right] = I_{M\omega}(I - A_{\omega\omega} Z)^{-1}$$

because of (7.3). Hence

$$P = I_{M\omega}\left[(I - A_{\omega\omega} Z)^{-1} - (I - A_{\omega\omega})^{-1}\right] . \tag{7.7}$$

Furthermore, when replacing the unit matrix of order $M$ in (7.6) by $I_{M\omega}Z_{\omega M}$ in accordance with (7.2),

$$P = \left[I_{M\omega}(I - A_{\omega\omega}) Z_{\omega M}\right]^{-1} I_{M\omega} - I_{M\omega}(I - A_{\omega\omega})^{-1} ,$$

and post-multiplying by $(I - A_{\omega\omega})Z_{\omega M}$, we find

$$P(I - A_{\omega\omega}) Z_{\omega M} = I - I_{M\omega} Z_{\omega M} = 0 , \tag{7.8}$$

the square zero matrix of order $M$.

By now we have gathered the following main results:

$$e_M = P x_\omega + I_{M\omega} e_\omega \quad \text{with} \quad e_\omega = -(I - A_{\omega\omega})^{-1} u_\omega ; \tag{6.7}$$

$$P = I_{M\omega}\left[(I - A_{\omega\omega} Z)^{-1} - (I - A_{\omega\omega})^{-1}\right] ; \tag{7.7}$$

$$P(I - A_{\omega\omega}) Z_{\omega M} = 0 . \tag{7.8}$$

These relations constitute what may be called "the fundamental aggregation equations of input-output analysis." They express the macroprediction error of the total outputs of $M$ industries in terms of two vectors and two matrices (we disregard the unit matrix and the summation matrix $I_{M\omega}$, which have no empirical content), the vectors being the final bill and the errors in the "technical" equations—both of them micro and belonging to the prediction period, the matrices being those of the technical coefficients and of the total-output proportions of firms within their industries—both of them again micro, but now belonging to the base period. The first equation states that the prediction error is the sum of a homogeneous linear combination of the final demand of the individual firms on the one hand, and of the sum of corresponding microprediction errors on the other, the latter errors being determined by the matrix of technical microcoefficients and by the disturbances implied by its application in the prediction period. Since the aggregation procedure cannot be blamed for any errors of the latter category, it is useful to define the other part, viz., $Px_{\omega}$, as the *aggregation bias* of the macroprediction; cf. Theil (1954, p. 122).[3] The second equation states then that the coefficient matrix $P$ of the aggregation bias is completely determined by the base period; for it contains only its technical microcoefficients and its output proportions; and the third states that the $M\omega$ elements of $P$ are interconnected by the $M^2$ linear equations

$$\sum_{\mu'',j} c_{\mu''j,\mu'} p_{\mu,\mu''j} = 0 \quad \text{for each } \mu, \mu', \tag{7.9}$$

where $c_{\mu''j,\mu'}$ is an element of the $\omega \times M$ matrix $(I - A_{\omega\omega})Z_{\omega M}$, and $p_{\mu,\mu''j}$ of the $M \times \omega$ matrix $P$. In other words, for each row of $P$ (and, therefore, for each component of the aggregation bias) the matrix $(I - A_{\omega\omega})Z_{\omega M}$ supplies $M$ sets of weights such that the resulting $M$ weighted averages of the elements of this row are all zero; and these weights apply to all rows of $P$.

## 8. Further Discussion of the Fundamental Equations

Some further remarks are useful to make the nature of the fundamental equations more transparent.

First, consider the matrix $I_{M\omega}A_{\omega\omega}$. Although this product does not appear in any of the fundamental equations explicitly, we shall meet it immediately, so that it is useful to discuss it here. We have

$$I_{M\omega} A_{\omega\omega} = \left[\sum_i \alpha_{\mu i,\mu' j}\right] = \left[\alpha_{\mu,\mu' j}\right], \text{ say.} \tag{8.1}$$

In other words, $I_{M\omega}A_{\omega\omega}$ is the matrix of technical microcoefficients which is obtained when the separate coefficients of individual supplying firms within each industry are combined by adding. This implies "half-way aggregation," viz., with respect to suppliers only, not with respect to receiving firms. We shall call the elements of $I_{M\omega}A_{\omega\omega}$ "derived technical microcoefficients."[4]

Second, consider the matrix $A_{\omega\omega}Z$, which appears in (7.7). The typical $(\mu i, \mu' j)$th element of this $\omega \times \omega$ matrix is

$$\sum_k \alpha_{\mu i,\mu' k} \zeta_{\mu' k} = \bar{\alpha}_{\mu i,\mu'}, \text{ say.} \tag{8.2}$$

[3] Note that this bias is the same for total output as for total deliveries to industries ($y_{\mu}$), since the difference, viz., final demand, is exogenous and hence not subject to aggregation bias.

[4] These coefficients are derived microparameters; cf. Theil (1954), p. 31.

This is independent of $j$. It follows that $A_{\omega\omega}Z$ is the $\omega \times \omega$ matrix of technical microcoefficients which is obtained when the separate coefficients of the individual receiving firms within each industry are replaced by their industry averages, these averages being derived by using the output proportions in the base period as weights. It will be noted that

$$\sum_i \bar{\alpha}_{\mu i,\mu'} = \alpha_{\mu\mu'} \tag{8.3}$$

in view of (4.3).

Finally, we expand the inverted matrices in (7.7),

$$P = I_{M\omega}\left[A_{\omega\omega}Z + (A_{\omega\omega}Z)^2 + \cdots - (A_{\omega\omega} + A_{\omega\omega}^2 + \cdots)\right],$$

and we take the first-order terms,

$$P_1 = I_{M\omega}(A_{\omega\omega}Z - A_{\omega\omega}) . \tag{8.4}$$

We shall call $P_1 x_\omega$ the "first-order aggregation bias." In view of (8.2) this part can be written as

$$P_1 x_\omega = \left[\sum_{\mu',j} x_{\mu'j} \sum_i (\bar{\alpha}_{\mu i,\mu'} - \alpha_{\mu i,\mu' j})\right], \tag{8.5}$$

in other words: in order to find the first-order aggregation bias for a particular industry $\mu$, we should consider all technical microcoefficients in which firms of this industry enter as suppliers, subtract them from their weighted averages (8.2), and add these deviations for all of these firms; after this, the resulting sums of deviations act as coefficients by which the final microbill is to be multiplied in order to arrive at the required bias. It is easy to see [cf. (8.3)] that, in a macronotation, (8.5) can be written as

$$P_1 x_\omega = \left[\sum_{\mu',j} x_{\mu'j}(\alpha_{\mu\mu'} - \alpha_{\mu,\mu'j})\right], \tag{8.6}$$

so that the aforementioned sums of deviations appear to be equal to the difference between technical macro and derived technical microcoefficients; in matrix notation, this follows from a substitution of (7.5) into (8.4). As to the weighted-average rules of $P_1$ (cf. the end of section 7), we have

$$P_1 Z_{\omega M} = I_{M\omega} A_{\omega\omega}(Z - I) Z_{\omega M} = I_{M\omega} A_{\omega\omega}(Z_{\omega M} I_{M\omega} Z_{\omega M} - Z_{\omega M}) = 0 , \tag{8.7}$$

which is the analogue of (7.8), and much simpler. It states that each row of the coefficient matrix by which the final bill of the firms of a particular industry $\mu'$, i.e., $x_{\mu'j}$ for $j = 1, \ldots, I_{\mu'}$, is multiplied in the first-order bias, has zero weighted average,

$$\sum_j \zeta_{\mu' j}\, p'_{\mu,\mu' j} = 0 \text{ for each } \mu, \mu', \tag{8.8}$$

where the prime of $p$ serves to stress that it is an element of $P_1$ rather than $P$. It follows that we have here one zero weighted average for each of the $M$ parts (corresponding to every industry) of each row of $P_1$, whereas we had $M$ zero weighted averages for each entire row of $P$; cf. (7.8) and (7.9).

## 9. Special Cases: (i) Concerning Technical Coefficients

A few special cases are useful to give additional insight into the fundamental aggregation equations. As the bias, being equal to $Px_\omega$ or $P_1x_\omega$ as in the first-order formulation, is composed of two entirely different quantities, viz., $P$ ($P_1$) and $x_\omega$, it is convenient to split up the discussion. This section is devoted to the $P$'s.[5]

Suppose that all technical microcoefficients $\alpha_{\mu i,\mu' j}$ are independent of both $i$ and $j$, for all pairs $\mu$, $\mu'$. This means that all industries have a "homogeneous input-output structure," i.e., an additional output of one unit of any firm belonging to industry $\mu'$ requires the same demand for the products of each firm of industry $\mu$, no matter which pair of firms in these industries is chosen. In such a case we have $A_{\omega\omega}Z = A_{\omega\omega}$, so that it follows from (7.9) that the aggregation bias is identically (i.e., for all vectors $x_\omega$) zero if all industries are characterized by a homogeneous input-output structure.

This condition can be weakened. Suppose that all derived technical microcoefficients $\alpha_{\mu,\mu' j}$ are independent of $j$, for each pair $\mu$, $\mu'$. This is the assumption of a "homogeneous input structure"; an additional output of one unit of any firm belonging to industry $\mu'$ requires the same demand for the products of the aggregate industry $\mu$. In that case the right-hand $\alpha$'s of the equality $\alpha_{\mu\mu'} = \Sigma_j\, \alpha_{\mu,\mu' j}\, \zeta_{\mu' j}$ are all equal, so that the macrocoefficient $\alpha_{\mu\mu'}$ is equal to each of them; and it follows from (8.6) that the first-order aggregation bias vanishes. But this is not all. Using the same equality, we find easily that in the case of a homogeneous input structure $I_{M\omega}A_{\omega\omega} = A_{MM}I_{M\omega}$. Subtracting this from $I_{M\omega} = I_{M\omega}$, we obtain $I_{M\omega}(I - A_{\omega\omega}) = (I - A_{MM})I_{M\omega}$; and, finally, premultiplying and postmultiplying this equation by the inverses of $(I - A_{MM})$ and $(I - A_{\omega\omega})$, respectively, we find $P = 0$ in view of (6.8). Hence there is no aggregation bias in the case of a homogeneous input structure. This result does not hold (neither $P = 0$, nor even $P_1 = 0$), if we change our assumption to that of a "homogeneous output structure," i.e., $\bar{\alpha}_{\mu i,\mu'}$ independent of $i$.

---

[5] Cf. also Malinvaud (1954), pp. 198-199.

Finally, suppose that only one particular industry, $\mu'$ say, has a homogeneous input structure, i.e., all derived coefficients $\alpha_{\mu,\mu'j}$ are independent of $j$, for this $\mu'$ and for each $\mu$. It follows then from (8.6) that the coefficients of $x_{\mu'j}$ for this $\mu'$ in the first-order bias are all zero, and hence that the contribution to the aggregation bias of the final bill vector $x_\omega$, as far as it corresponds to this industry, is of the second order; it is easily verified that the second-order contribution is not zero in general.

## 10. Special Cases: (ii) Concerning the Final Microbill

The aggregation bias, being a linear combination of the final bill, may be of the second order or even zero when the above conditions are not satisfied, viz., under certain assumptions concerning this bill; this holds especially since the coefficients of the combination obey the zero-weighted-average rules (7.8). These assumptions may be interpreted as those of absence of certain correlations, which can be shown for the first-order bias as follows. The contribution of the final microbill of industry $\mu'$ to the aggregation bias of the total output of industry $\mu$ is, according to (8.6),

$$\sum_j (\alpha_{\mu\mu'} - \alpha_{\mu,\mu'j}) x_{\mu'j} = \sum_j \zeta_{\mu'j} (\alpha_{\mu\mu'} - \alpha_{\mu,\mu'j}) \frac{x_{\mu'j}}{\zeta_{\mu'j}} . \tag{10.1}$$

As we have [cf. (8.8)]

$$\sum_j \zeta_{\mu'j} (\alpha_{\mu\mu'} - \alpha_{\mu,\mu'j}) = 0 ,$$

we may interpret (10.1) as the covariance of the deviations of the derived microcoefficients $\alpha_{\mu,\mu'j}$ from the corresponding macrocoefficients $\alpha_{\mu\mu'}$ on the one hand, and the final demand components $x_{\mu'j}$ "deflated" by the base period output proportions $\zeta_{\mu'j}$ on the other; and the "frequency" which is attached to each firm is equal to its output proportion. It follows that each component of the first-order aggregation bias is the sum of $M$ such covariances, so that the bias must be of the second order if all $M^2$ covariances vanish. A particular case is $x_{\mu'j} = 0$ for all $j$; then there are $M$ of these covariances which vanish. Actually, in that case the industry $\mu'$ does not contribute at all to the aggregation bias of any order; cf. (6.7).

Another interesting case occurs if all components of the final microbill in the prediction period are proportional to the corresponding components of the base period,

$$x_\omega = k x_\omega^0 , \tag{10.2}$$

$k$ being a scalar and $x_\omega^0$ the final microbill in the base period. As we have

$$x_\omega^0 = (I - A_{\omega\omega}) z_\omega^0 \tag{10.3}$$

(without disturbances!), the aggregation bias is

$$P x_\omega = k P (I - A_{\omega\omega}) z_\omega^0 ,$$

which is a vector of zeros because of (7.8). Hence there is no aggregation bias if the components of the final microbill change proportionally.

The same is not true if the proportionality is confined to the firms within separate industries. In that case the μth component of the first-order bias can be written as

$$\sum_{\mu'} k_{\mu'} \sum_j (\alpha_{\mu,\mu'} - \alpha_{\mu,\mu'j}) x_{\mu'j}^0 ,$$

and this is not zero in general. However, if the $M^2$ conditions

$$\sum_j (\alpha_{\mu\mu'} - \alpha_{\mu,\mu'j}) x_{\mu'j}^0 = 0 \quad \text{for each } \mu, \mu' \tag{10.4}$$

are satisfied—and this is a condition on the base period, not on the prediction period—then the aggregation bias is of the second order for any prediction period in which the final demand of the firms within each industry is proportional to the final demand in the base period, $x_{\mu'j} = k_{\mu'} x^0_{\mu'j}$.

## 11. Perfect Aggregation

In general, it is not possible to impose the conditions of the preceding two sections. The final bill is considered exogenous and, therefore, beyond control; and no way of grouping the firms to industries may exist which satisfies the homogeneity conditions. In such a case a way of eliminating the bias, for all final bill vectors, is that of perfect aggregation by means of a suitable choice of exogenous aggregates; cf. Theil (1954), Ch. VII.

Consider the total output vector $z_m$ [cf. (6.3) and (5.6)]

$$z_M = I_{M\omega} \left[ (I - A_{\omega\omega})^{-1} x_\omega - e_\omega \right] , \tag{11.1}$$

and write

$$I_{M\omega}(I - A_{\omega\omega})^{-1} = \left[a_{\mu,\mu'j}\right]. \tag{11.2}$$

Suppose we choose for the prediction of $z_\mu$ the linear combinations

$$\sum_j a_{\mu,\mu'j} x_{\mu'j} = x_{\mu'}^{\mu} \tag{11.3}$$

as aggregates for the final bill of the industries $\mu' = 1, \ldots, M$, rather than the sums $x_{\mu'}$. The prediction $z_\mu^* = \Sigma x_{\mu'}^{\mu}$ has no aggregation bias, as can be easily verified. Actually, it can be shown that this weighting procedure is the only method which reduces the aggregation bias identically to zero, for all final bill compositions (cf. Theil (1954), sections 7.5 and 7.6); except, of course, when weighting is trivial because the elements to be weighted are equal, as in the case of a homogeneous input structure.

Two prices are to be paid: the computation of the $a$'s requires the inversion of a large matrix, and the final bill aggregate of each industry $\mu'$ appropriate for the prediction of $z_\mu$ depends on $\mu$. Nothing can be done as to the latter point, but the former may sometimes be dealt with by means of an approximation: replace $a_{\mu,\mu'j}$ by

$$I_{M\omega}(I + A_{\omega\omega}) = \left[b_{\mu,\mu'j}\right].$$

If we substitute the $b$'s for the $a$'s in (11.3), the resulting aggregation bias is

$$-I_{M\omega}(A_{\omega\omega}^2 + A_{\omega\omega}^3 + \cdots)x_\omega = -I_{M\omega}A_{\omega\omega}^2(I - A_{\omega\omega})^{-1}x_\omega \approx -I_{M\omega}A_{\omega\omega}^2 z_\omega ,$$

which is always negative, but small if the successive powers of $A_{\omega\omega}$ converge to 0 sufficiently rapidly.

## 12. A Comparison with the Aggregation of Conventional Economic Relations

Although the similarity of input-output aggregation and the aggregation of "conventional" economic relations is considerable, there are certain differences which should be mentioned. The alternative ways of grouping, e.g., for a given degree of aggregation, are not equally numerous in both cases. There are many ways of grouping $\omega$ firms in $M$ industries and it is frequently difficult to say *a priori* which is the most satisfactory way; the analysis of section 9 will give, however, some hints in this direction, provided of course sufficient microeconomic information is available. On the other hand, in the case of macroeconomic regression equations the economist feels much less unsure about the question whether a particular microvariable should be included into one aggregate or another. The basic cause of this difference is the fact that in input-output analysis the variables (output volumes) have all a similar economic character, contrary to the variables of most regression equations.

Another difference is the fact that, in input-output analysis, the numerical specification of the macrotheory is entirely based on the situation of one base period, whereas for regression and structural equations there is a problem of fitting—either over time, or over "space" as in cross-section analysis. This may suggest that the latter type of aggregation is characterized by more stability, and this impression may even be correct; but the above analysis shows that input-output aggregation is characterized by certain desirable features because of its restriction of the macrotheory to one base period. First, it follows from (4.3) that the macroparameters (the technical macrocoefficients) are determined by corresponding microparameters only; i.e., no technical macrocoefficient depends on a microcoefficient of a firm in a different industry.[6] This is not true when the specification of the macrotheory is based on fitting; cf. Theil (1954), p. 14. Second, it can be shown that the aggregation bias of small industries, i.e., industries with relatively small total outputs, tend to be small in an absolute (not relative) sense; and this convenient result does not hold in the other aggregation problem (cf. Theil (1954), p. 22). To see this, consider the first-order bias

$$P_1 x_\omega = \left[ \sum_{\mu',j} (\alpha_{\mu\mu'} - \alpha_{\mu,\mu'j}) x_{\mu'j} \right] .$$

The $\alpha$'s tend to be large if $\mu$ is a large industry, small if $\mu$ is small. The differences within parentheses may be of either sign and small or large but, when disregarding the sign, we may say that they, too, tend to be large on the average if $\mu$ is large and small if $\mu$ is small. It follows that the first-order aggregation bias of a small industry is obtained by multiplying the final bill components by coefficients which are mostly closer to zero than in the case of large industries. It will be observed that this result is decisively dependent on the fact that non-corresponding technical microcoefficients do not affect macrocoefficients, for otherwise it is not permissible to say that a small industry $\mu$ is usually characterized by small macroparameters $\alpha_{\mu\mu'}$.[7]

## References

Balderston, J.B, and T.M. Whitin: 1954, "Aggregation in the Input-Output Model," in O. Morgenstern, ed., *Economic Activity Analysis*, John Wiley and Sons, Inc., New York.

---

[6] In a remote sense, there is such a dependence, viz., via the $\zeta$'s, $z^0$'s and $x^0$'s; and in this dependence all technical microcoefficients are involved. But this is clearly an inefficient and cumbersome way of describing the situation.

[7] Another interesting feature is that the weights in perfect aggregation [the $a$'s of (11.3)] are always nonnegative—which is not true in the aggregation of "conventional" equations.

Malinvaud, E.: 1954, "Aggregation Problems in Input-Output Models," in *The Structural Interdependence of the Economy*, Proceedings of an International Conference on Input-Output Analysis, Varenna, 189-202.

Theil, H.: 1954, *Linear Aggregation of Economic Relations*, North Holland Publishing Company, Amsterdam. (Vol. VII of the series "Contributions to Economic Analysis.")

CHAPTER 57

# THE INFORMATION APPROACH TO THE AGGREGATION OF INPUT-OUTPUT TABLES*

HENRI THEIL
*Netherlands School of Economics*
*(now Erasmus University)*
*Rotterdam, The Netherlands*

PEDRO URIBE
*Netherlands School of Economics*
*(now Erasmus University),*
*Rotterdam, The Netherlands*

## 1. Introduction

In a recent publication by the Czechoslovak Academy of Sciences, Jiri Skolka (1964) suggested information measures for the value of input-output tables as well as an information criterion for the aggregation of such tables.[1] When sectors are combined to groups of sectors, a smaller input-output table is the result, the information value of which (to be defined appropriately) is always less than or equal to that of the original tables. The information reduction can be decomposed into various terms, some of which were given an economic interpretation by Skolka. The objective of the present paper is to present the information decomposition for the general case of $n$ sectors aggregated to $G$ groups of sectors, to apply the result to the annual postwar input-output tables of the Netherlands, to formulate and apply an approach for partial disaggregation, and to relate the information criterion to the classical input-output problem of predicting intermediate and primary demand. These respective goals will be pursued in sections 2 through 5, 6 and 7, 8, and 9.

## 2. The Input-Output System at the Sector Level

Our starting point is an input-output table consisting of $m$ secondary sectors (industries) and $n - m$ primary sectors. We write $x_{ij}$ for the flow from the $i$th to the $j$th industry, $x_i$ for the total output of the $i$th industry, and $f_i$ for the final demand for its products. The secondary part of the input-output system is then written in the following form:

---

* This article first appeared in *The Review of Economics and Statistics*, **49** (1967), 451-462. Reprinted with the permission of Elsevier Science Publishers B.V. (North-Holland).

[1] The authors are indebted to Mr. Skolka for his comments on a first draft of this paper. He asked them to mention the name of Mr. Hajek who helped him when working on the problem. They are also much indebted to Mr. A. Kunstman of the Econometric Institute in Rotterdam who programmed the computations.

$$\begin{aligned} x_{11} + x_{12} + \ldots + x_{1m} &= x_1 - f_1 \\ x_{21} + x_{22} + \ldots + x_{2m} &= x_2 - f_2 \\ &\vdots \\ x_{m1} + x_{m2} + \ldots + x_{mm} &= x_m - f_m \,. \end{aligned} \tag{1}$$

In the same way, we write $y_{hi}$ for the flow from the $h$th primary sector to the $i$th industry, and $y_h$ for the total flow originating in the $h$th primary sector. The primary part of the input-output system is then written as follows:

$$\begin{aligned} y_{11} + y_{12} + \ldots + y_{1m} &= y_1 \\ y_{21} + y_{22} + \ldots + y_{2m} &= y_2 \\ &\vdots \\ y_{n-m,1} + y_{n-m,2} + \ldots + y_{n-m,m} &= y_{n-m} \,. \end{aligned} \tag{2}$$

Let us now divide both sides of the $n$ equations (1) - (2) by the total output (≡ total input) of all $m$ industries:

$$x = \sum_{i=1}^{m} x_i \,. \tag{3}$$

The result is that we obtain on the left of (1) the inter-industry flows measured as a fraction of aggregate output,

$$p_{ij} = \frac{x_{ij}}{x} \qquad i, j = 1, \ldots, m \,. \tag{4}$$

On the left of (2) we obtain the primary flows absorbed by the various industries, also measured as a fraction of the aggregate output:

$$p_{m+h,j} = \frac{y_{hj}}{x} \qquad h = 1, \ldots, n-m \,; \quad j = 1, \ldots, m \,. \tag{5}$$

On the right of (1) we obtain total intermediate demand for the products of each industry, measured as a fraction of aggregate output:

$$p_{i.} = \frac{x_i - f_i}{x} \qquad i = 1, \ldots, m . \tag{6}$$

On the right of (2) we obtain the total flow of each primary input, measured in the same way:

$$p_{m+h,.} = \frac{y_h}{x} \qquad h = 1, \ldots, n - m . \tag{7}$$

We have thus succeeded in expressing all elementary flows between sectors in terms of an $n \times m$ matrix $[p_{ij}]$, the elements of which are nonnegative and add up (when summed over $i$ from one through $n$ and over $j$ from one through $m$) to one. The algebra which follows will be simplified considerably when we interpret $[p_{ij}]$ as a square of order $n \times n$, which can be performed by adding an appropriate number of zeros:

$$p_{ij} = 0 \qquad i = 1, \ldots, n; \quad j = m + 1, \ldots, n . \tag{8}$$

The input-output system is thus transformed to a square system of nonnegative fractions adding up to one. The $n$ numbers $p_i$ defined in (6) and (7) are row totals. We have also $n$ column totals:

$$p_{.j} = \begin{cases} \dfrac{x_j}{x} & j = 1, \ldots, m \\ 0 & j = m + 1, \ldots, n . \end{cases} \tag{9}$$

It will be convenient to illustrate the algebraic manipulations of this article with a simple numerical example:

| Supplying Sector $i$ | Receiving Sector $j$ 1 | 2 | 3 | 4 | Sum |
|---|---|---|---|---|---|
| | | $P_{ij}$ | | | $P_{i}$ |
| 1 | 0.05 | 0.05 | 0 | 0 | 0.1 |
| 2 | 0.05 | 0.1 | 0.05 | 0 | 0.2 |
| 3 | 0.1 | 0.05 | 0.1 | 0 | 0.25 |
| 4 | 0.2 | 0.1 | 0.15 | 0 | 0.45 |
| Sum $p_{.j}$ | 0.4 | 0.3 | 0.3 | 0 | 1 |

In this example there are three industries and one primary sector. Hence, the fourth column must consist of zeros.

## 3. The Information Content of an Input-Output Table

The fractions $p_{ij}$ can be regarded as a bivariate array of probabilities. If we have $p_{ij} = p_{i.}p_{.j}$ for all pairs $(i, j)$, the array is characterized by independence. If for a particular pair of indices $p_{ij}$ exceeds $p_{i.}p_{.j}$, the flow from sector $i$ to sector $j$ may be said to be above the independence value. If $p_{ij} = p_{i.}p_{.j}$, the flow is at the independence value, and if $p_j < p_{i.}p_{.j}$, the flow is below that value. A convenient measure is

$$\log \frac{p_{ij}}{p_{i.}p_{.j}}$$

the sign of which determines whether the flow from sector $i$ to sector $j$ is above, at, or below the independence value. This logarithmic ratio is known in information theory as the mutual information of the $i$th transmitted signal and the $j$th received signal, $p_{ij}$ being the probability that the $i$th signal is transmitted and the $j$th is received (see for example Schwartz, 1963, pp. 30-31). In our present context the logarithmic ratio should be regarded as the mutual information between the supplying sector, $i$, and the receiving sector, $j$. Although these mutual information values are of different sign, their expectation is nonnegative. This expectation,

$$I = \sum_{i=1}^{n} \sum_{j=1}^{n} p_{ij} \log \frac{p_{ij}}{p_{i.}p_{.j}} \tag{10}$$

is known as the *expected mutual information*, in this case, of the input-output system. It is always positive except when there is independence, in which case it is zero.[2] If we use 2 as the base of the logarithm (so that information is expressed in binary digits or "bits"), the information of the illustrative example of section 2 is equal to

$$I = 0.05 \log \frac{0.05}{0.1 \times 0.4} + 0.05 \log \frac{0.05}{0.1 \times 0.3} + \ldots = 0.102 \text{ bit} . \tag{11}$$

It should be noted that there is the convention in information theory of interpreting 0 log 0 and 0 log ∞ as 0, which is in accordance with the limit of $x \log x$ and $x \log (1/x)$ for $x$ decreasing toward zero. This applies inter alia to those terms in (10) for which $j > m$.

The information content (10) of an input-output table was proposed by Skolka as a measure for the value of that table. If it is zero, there is independence, so that the separate flows from one sector to another can be derived directly from the corresponding marginal totals. In that case we do not need the table at all. We do need the table when the sectors are interconnected in a less trivial way, and the corresponding $I$ will then take a positive value, which becomes larger when the interconnection pattern deviates more and more from the independence pattern.

It is of some interest to consider the latter pattern from the standpoint of input-output prediction. The $(i, j)$th secondary input coefficient is

$$a_{ij} = \frac{x_{ij}}{x_j} = \frac{x_{ij}/x}{x_j/x} = \frac{p_{ij}}{p_{.j}} \qquad i, j = 1, \ldots, m ,$$

which is simplified to $a_{ij} = p_{i.}$ in the special case of independence. In words: All input coefficients are the same for each supplying industry. Now the total intermediate demand for the products of any industry is

$$z_i = \sum_{j=1}^{m} x_{ij} = \sum_{j=1}^{m} a_{ij} x_j = \sum_{j=1}^{m} p_{i.} x_j = p_{i.} x .$$

Hence $z_i$ is simply proportional to the aggregate output of all $m$ industries. The classical input-output prediction procedure takes final demand as given, not total output. We therefore sum both sides of the equation:

---

[2] The proof is as follows. Write $p_g$ for $p_{ij}$ and $p_g'$ for $p_{i.}p_{.j}$. Then $I = \Sigma p_g \log(p_g/p_g')$, where the summation over $g$ is over the $n^2$ values of the pairs $(i,j)$. Now $-I$ can be regarded as the logarithm of a weighted geometric average of the ratios $p_g'/p_g$ with the $p_g$ as weights. It is easily verified that the corresponding arithmetic average is one; since a geometric average of positive numbers is not larger than the arithmetic average, it must be $\leq 1$ and hence its logarithm $-I \leq 0$, so that $I \geq 0$. We have $I = 0$ if and only if all ratios $p_g'/p_g$ are equal and hence equal to one, which is equivalent to $p_{ij} = p_{i.}\,p_{.j}$.

$$\sum_{i=1}^{m} z_i = x - \sum_{i=1}^{m} f_i = x \sum_{i=1}^{m} p_{i.}$$

and conclude

$$x = \frac{f}{1 - \sum_{i=1}^{m} p_{i.}} = \frac{f}{\sum_{h=m+1}^{n} p_{h.}}$$

where $f = \Sigma f_i$ is the aggregate final demand for the products of all industries, while the right-hand denominator stands for the aggregate primary input absorbed by all industries, measured as a fraction of these industries' total input. The final result is

$$z_i = \frac{p_{i.}}{\sum_{h=m+1}^{n} p_{h.}} f .$$

In words: The total intermediate demand for the products of each individual industry is predicted to be proportional to aggregate final demand for the products of all industries. This is a very simple variant of the final-demand-blowup extrapolation method.

## 4. The Aggregation Procedure

We now suppose that the sectors are combined to $G$ groups, the $g$th group consisting of a set $S_g$, $g = 1, \ldots, G$. The aggregation should be such that each sector belongs to exactly one $S_g$. In addition, one will usually wish to avoid the situation in which an $S_g$ contains both primary and secondary sectors.

The fractions of the groups are obtained by summation and will be denoted by capitals:

$$P_{gh} = \sum_{i \in S_g} \sum_{j \in S_h} p_{ij} \qquad g, h = 1, \ldots, G . \tag{12}$$

This is the total flow from all sectors of the $g$th group (for short: the flow from the $g$th group) to the $h$th group, measured as a fraction of the total output of all $m$ industries. We also have marginal group fractions:

$$P_{g.} = \sum_{h=1}^{G} P_{gh} = \sum_{i \in S_g} p_{i.} \qquad g = 1, \ldots, G \tag{13}$$

$$P_{.h} = \sum_{g=1}^{G} P_{gh} = \sum_{j \in S_h} p_{.j} \qquad h = 1, \ldots, G \,, \tag{14}$$

which are the total flows originating in the $g$th group and going to the $h$th group, respectively, both measured as a fraction of the aggregate output of all $m$ industries.

The information content of the aggregated table is

$$I_0 = \sum_{g=1}^{G} \sum_{h=1}^{G} P_{gh} \log \frac{P_{gh}}{P_{g.} P_{.h}} \tag{15}$$

and the obvious question is what can be said about the relationship between $I$ and $I_0$. We shall illustrate this problem with our numerical example, assuming that the first two sectors are aggregated. Hence $S_1 = (1, 2)$, $S_2 = (3)$, $S_3 = (4)$. The array now becomes:

| Supplying Group $g$ | Receiving Group $h$ 1 | 2 | 3 | Sum |
|---|---|---|---|---|
| | | $P_{gh}$ | | $P_{g.}$ |
| 1 | 0.25 | 0.05 | 0 | 0.3 |
| 2 | 0.15 | 0.1 | 0 | 0.25 |
| 3 | 0.3 | 0.15 | 0 | 0.45 |
| Sum $P_{.h}$ | 0.7 | 0.3 | 0 | 1 |

The corresponding $I_0$ value is:

$$I_0 = 0.25 \log \frac{0.25}{0.3 \times 0.7} + 0.05 \log \frac{0.05}{0.3 \times 0.3} + \ldots = 0.030 \text{ bit} \,, \tag{16}$$

which is less than (11). This, in fact, is generally true as will be shown in the next section.

## 5. The Information Decomposition Equation of Input-Output Aggregation

To analyze the relationship between $I$ and $I_0$ we should introduce some symbols indicating halfway aggregation. When summing the $p$'s over a *row* index in a set $S_g$ we write

$$r_{gj} = \sum_{i \in S_g} p_{ij} \qquad g = 1, \ldots, G; \;\; j = 1, \ldots, n . \tag{17}$$

This is the flow from the group $S_g$ to the individual sector $j$, measured as a fraction of the total output of all industries. When summing the $p$'s over a *column* index in set $S_h$ we write

$$c_{ih} = \sum_{j \in S_h} p_{ij} \qquad i = 1, \ldots, n; \;\; h = 1, \ldots, G \tag{18}$$

which is the flow from the individual sector $i$ to the group $S_h$, measured in the same way. Note that we have

$$\sum_{g=1}^{G} r_{gj} = p_{.j} \qquad \sum_{j \in S_h} r_{gj} = P_{gh} \tag{19}$$

$$\sum_{i \in S_g} c_{ih} = P_{gh} \qquad \sum_{h=1}^{G} c_{ih} = p_{i.} \; . \tag{20}$$

We now consider the difference $I - I_0$, which can be written as follows:

$$I - I_0 = \sum_{g=1}^{G} \sum_{h=1}^{G} \sum_{i \in S_g} \sum_{j \in S_h} p_{ij} \left[ \log \frac{p_{ij}}{p_{i.}\, p_{.j}} - \log \frac{P_{gh}}{P_{g.}\, P_{.h}} \right] .$$

The logarithmic difference in brackets can be written as

$$\log \frac{c_{ih}/P_{gh}}{p_{i.}/P_{g.}} + \log \frac{r_{gj}/P_{gh}}{p_{.j}/P_{.h}} + \log \frac{p_{ij}/P_{gh}}{(c_{ih}\, r_{gj})/(P_{gh}\, P_{gh})}$$

so that we conclude:

$$I - I_0 = \sum_{g=1}^{G}\sum_{h=1}^{G}\sum_{i \in S_g} c_{ih} \log \frac{c_{ih}/P_{gh}}{p_{i.}/P_{g.}} + \sum_{g=1}^{G}\sum_{h=1}^{G}\sum_{j \in S_h} r_{gj} \log \frac{r_{gj}/P_{gh}}{p_{.j}/P_{.h}}$$

$$+ \sum_{g=1}^{G}\sum_{h=1}^{G}\sum_{i \in S_g}\sum_{j \in S_h} p_{ij} \log \frac{p_{ij}/P_{gh}}{(c_{ih} r_{gj})/(P_{gh} P_{gh})} \ .$$

This is equivalent to

$$I = I_0 + \sum_{g=1}^{G} P_{g.} I_{g.} + \sum_{h=1}^{G} P_{.h} I_{.h} + I_{..} \tag{21}$$

where $I_{g.}$ is the row effect of the $g$th group:

$$I_{g.} = \sum_{h=1}^{G} \frac{P_{gh}}{P_{g.}} \sum_{i \in S_g} \frac{c_{ih}}{P_{gh}} \log \frac{c_{ih}/P_{gh}}{p_{i.}/P_{g.}} \tag{22}$$

and the $I_{.h}$ the column effect of the $h$th group:

$$I_{.h} = \sum_{g=1}^{G} \frac{P_{gh}}{P_{.h}} \sum_{j \in S_h} \frac{r_{gj}}{P_{gh}} \log \frac{r_{gj}/P_{gh}}{p_{.j}/P_{.h}} \tag{23}$$

and $I_{..}$ a weighted average of $G^2$ cell effects:

$$I_{..} = \sum_{g=1}^{G}\sum_{h=1}^{G} P_{gh} I_{gh}$$

$$= \sum_{g=1}^{G}\sum_{h=1}^{G} P_{gh} \sum_{i \in S_g}\sum_{j \in S_h} \frac{p_{ij}}{P_{gh}} \log \frac{p_{ij}/P_{gh}}{\frac{c_{ih}}{P_{gh}} \frac{r_{gj}}{P_{gh}}} \ . \tag{24}$$

Equation (21) will be called the *information decomposition equation* of the input-output aggregation. The interpretation of the expressions (22) through (24) is as follows: We note that $I_{g.}$ is a weighted average of

$$\sum_{i \in S_g} \frac{c_{ih}}{P_{gh}} \log \frac{c_{ih}/P_{gh}}{p_{i.}/P_{g.}} \ . \tag{25}$$

This expression can be regarded (in the language of information theory) as the expected information of an indirect message which transforms the prior probabilities $p_{i.}/P_{g.}$, $i \in S_g$, to the posterior probabilities $c_{ih}/P_{gh}$, $i \in S_g$. Such an expected information is always nonnegative. It is zero if and only if

$$\frac{c_{ih}}{P_{gh}} = \frac{p_{i.}}{P_{g.}} \quad \text{or} \quad \frac{c_{ih}}{p_{i.}} = \frac{P_{gh}}{P_{g.}} \quad \text{for each } i \in S_g \; . \tag{26}$$

The ratio $c_{ih}/p_{i.}$ is the part of sector $i$'s total output which is sold to $S_h$. The ratio $P_{gh}/P_{g.}$ is the part of the total output of $i$'s group $S_g$ which is sold to $S_h$. When the ratios are equal for each $i \in S_g$, we may say that there is a uniform output distribution over the sectors of $S_g$ as far as the supplies to $S_h$ are concerned. This is the condition under which (25) vanishes. It is positive as soon as $S_g$ is characterized by some output heterogeneity with respect to the supplies to $S_h$. Since $I_{g.}$ is a weighted average of expressions of the type of (25) with weights $P_{gh}/P_{g.}$, $h = 1, \ldots, G$, we conclude that $I_{g.}$ vanishes if and only if the output distribution of $S_g$ over its sectors is homogeneous with respect to all group clients $S_1, \ldots, S_G$. In all other cases it is positive. Hence we may say that $I_{g.}$ measures the *output heterogeneity of* $S_g$ and that $\Sigma \, P_{g.} I_{g.}$ measures the *total output heterogeneity* of all groups.

In precisely the same way it can be argued that $I_{.h}$ as defined in (23) measures the *input heterogeneity of* $S_h$. It is a weighted average of

$$\sum_{j \in S_h} \frac{r_{gj}}{P_{gh}} \log \frac{r_{gj}/P_{gh}}{p_{.j}/P_{.h}} \; , \tag{27}$$

which is positive unless

$$\frac{r_{gj}}{P_{gh}} = \frac{p_{.j}}{P_{.h}} \quad \text{or} \quad \frac{r_{gj}}{p_{.j}} = \frac{P_{gh}}{P_{.h}} \quad \text{for each } j \in S_h \; , \tag{28}$$

in which case (27) vanishes. The ratio $r_{gj}/p_{.j}$ is the fraction of sector $j$'s total input which it buys from $S_h$. The ratio $P_{gh}/P_{.h}$ is the part of the total input of $j$'s group $S_h$ which it buys from $S_g$. There is a uniform input distribution of $S_h$ with respect to the supplying group $S_g$ when these ratios are equal for all $j \in S_h$. Hence $I_{.h}$ vanishes when the input distribution of $S_h$ is uniform with respect to all supplying groups, and it is positive as soon as there is some input heterogeneity. The weighted average $\Sigma \, P_{.h} I_{.h}$ is the total input heterogeneity.

Finally, we have $I_{..}$, which according to (24) is a weighted average of

$$I_{gh} = \sum_{i \in S_g} \sum_{j \in S_h} \frac{p_{ij}}{P_{gh}} \log \frac{p_{ij} / P_{gh}}{(c_{ih} r_{gj}) / (P_{gh} P_{gh})} , \tag{29}$$

which is positive unless

$$\frac{p_{ij}}{P_{gh}} = \frac{c_{ih}}{P_{gh}} \frac{r_{gj}}{P_{gh}} \quad \text{for each } i \in S_g ,\ j \in S_h , \tag{30}$$

in which case $I_{gh} = 0$. Condition (30) states that the share $p_{ij}/P_{gh}$ of the flow from sector $i$ to sector $j$ in the corresponding group flow (from $S_g$ to $S_h$, $i \in S_g$ and $j \in S_h$) is equal to the product of two marginal shares. One is the share $c_{ij}/P_{gh}$ of the flow from sector $i$ to $S_h$ in the group flow from $S_g$ to $S_h$, the other is the share $r_{gj}/P_{gh}$ of the flow from $S_g$ to sector $j$ in the same group flow. Hence (30) amounts to independence of the sector flows within the group flow from $S_g$ to $S_h$, so that $I_{gh}$ – the $(g, h)$th *cell effect* – can be said to measure the degree of dependence in the cell $(g, h)$. The *total cell effect* $I_{..}$ is equal to a weighted average of these individual cell effects with weights $P_{gh}$. We also note that a zero value of $I_{gh}$ corresponds with a zero information value of the input-output table if and only if our cell were the whole table.

We have thus succeeded in obtaining a natural decomposition of the information loss $I - I_0$ which is due to the aggregation. The total row effect, $\Sigma P_{g.} I_{g.}$, is nothing else than the aggregate effect of the heterogeneity of the output distributions of the $G$ groups, and the total column effect, $\Sigma P_{.h} I_{.h}$, is simply the aggregate effect of the heterogeneity of the input distributions of the $G$ groups. The total cell effect measures the information which is lost when we approximate the individual flows within each group flow by the values which are implied by the independence pattern. All terms on the right of (21) are nonnegative, hence $I_0 \leq I$ as stated at the end of the previous section.

In our numerical example the information loss is $I - I_0 = 0.102 - 0.030 = 0.072$ bit. It is a matter of straightforward computation to find that the total row effect is $\Sigma\, P_{g.} I_{g.} = 0.033$ bit, the total column effect $\Sigma\, P_{.h} I_{.h} = 0.034$ bit, and the total cell effect $I_{..} = 0.005$ bit. Together they account for the aggregation loss of 0.072 bit. We conclude that in this case the heterogeneity of the input and of the output distributions are equally serious, the information loss which each of them causes being about equal to the information value of the input-output table after aggregation, and that the cell effect is of minor importance.

## 6. Aggregation of the Dutch Input-Output Tables

We shall now apply the ideas set forth to the annual Dutch input-output tables in the years 1949 through 1960. These tables contain figures for 35 industries. Following C. B. Tilanus (1964) we shall aggregate these to 11 groups. Four groups consist of one sector each, seven contain two sectors or more. The following are the 11 groups:

1) *Agriculture, forestry, and fishing*, consisting of one sector that carries the same name.
2) *Foods, beverages, and tobacco*, consisting of three sectors:
   a) Food manufacturing industries (animal products)
   b) Food manufacturing industries (other products)
   c) Beverage industries and tobacco manufacturers.
3) *Textiles, footwear, and other wearing apparel*, consisting of two sectors:
   a) Textiles
   b) Footwear and other wearing apparel.
4) *Chemicals and petroleum refineries*, consisting of one sector that carries the same name
5) The *metal industry*, consisting of five sectors:
   a) Basic metal industries
   b) Metal products and machinery
   c) Electrical machinery and apparatus
   d) Transport equipment
   e) Other metal products and the diamond industry
6) *Construction*, consisting of one sector that carries the same name
7) *Electricity, gas and water*, consisting of one sector that carries the same name
8) *Other manufacturing industries*, consisting of seven sectors:
   a) Coal mining
   b) Crude petroleum and salt mining, peat cutting, etc.
   c) Wood and furniture
   d) Paper and paper products
   e) Printing, publishing and allied industries
   f) Leather and rubber products (excluding footwear)
   g) Earthenware, glass, lime, and stoneware
9) *Trade* (margins), consisting of two sectors:
   a) Wholesale trade
   b) Retail trade
10) *Transport, storage, and communication*, consisting of three sectors:
   a) Ocean and air transport
   b) Other transport
   c) Communication
11) *Other service industries*, consisting of nine sectors:
   a) Banks and other financial institutions
   b) Insurance
   c) Ownership of residential housing
   d) Medical and related services
   e) Business services
   f) Recreation services
   g) Hotels, cafes, and restaurants
   h) Other personal services
   i) Goods and services not elsewhere classified

The tables contain seven primary sectors, which are aggregated to the following three groups:

12) *Imports*, consisting of one sector that carries the same name
13) *Wages*, consisting of two sectors:
    a) Wages and salaries
    b) Employers' social insurance fees
14) *Gross profits*, consisting of four sectors:
    a) Depreciation
    b) Indirect taxes
    c) Subsidies (treated as a negative input)
    d) Other income (profits, interest, etc.)

It should be noted that the seven primary sectors will be combined to three even at the sector level (i.e., before the aggregation to be considered here). This is motivated by the fact that subsidies are negative inputs while other income is also negative in some cases. The informational approach can handle only nonnegative flows, so that a combination to a sector like gross profits is in order.[3] As a whole, therefore, we shall work with 14 groups $S_1, \ldots, S_{14}$ out of which the first 11 are secondary and the last three are primary. Four secondary groups consist of one sector each ($S_1$, $S_4$, $S_6$, $S_7$), the seven other secondary groups consist of two sectors or more. All three primary groups are regarded as consisting of one sector each. The total number of sectors is three (primary) + 35 (secondary) = 38.

## 7. The Information Decomposition, 1949-1960[4]

The information content, $I$, of each of the 12 tables is presented in Table I, together with its components as specified in equation (21). It turns out that $I$ is fairly constant and of the order of 0.9 bits. The information content $I_0$ after aggregation is, on the average, slightly larger than half a bit. The aggregation reduces the information content by a little over 40 per cent. The heterogeneity of the input structures is primarily responsible for this reduction. The total column (input) effect is on the average about 0.2 bit and accounts for almost 60 per cent of the information reduction $I - I_0$. The heterogeneity of the output structures is much less important. The total row (output) effect is less than 0.1 bit, on the average, and accounts for only one-quarter of the reduction $I - I_0$. The total cell effect accounts for less than 20 per cent of this reduction.

An obvious question is: Which groups are mainly responsible for the reduction of the information content? This question is answered in Table II, which contains the contributions $P_{g.}I_{g.}$ to the total output heterogeneity and also the contributions $P_{.h}I_{.h}$ to the

[3] In one year (1948) even gross profits is negative for one secondary sector. The table for that year has therefore been deleted from the analysis.

[4] The authors are much indebted to Mr. A. Kunstman of the Econometrics Institute in Rotterdam for programming the computations.

**TABLE I.** The Information Decomposition of Twelve Input-Output Tables

| Year of the input-output table | Information content $I$ | Information content after aggregation $I_0$ | Output heterogeneity $\Sigma P_{g.} I_{g.}$ | Input heterogeneity $\Sigma P_{.h} I_{.h}$ | Cell effect $I_{..}$ |
|---|---|---|---|---|---|
| | | In $10^{-4}$ bit | | | |
| 1949 | 8546 | 4788 | 922 | 2154 | 683 |
| 1950 | 9046 | 5228 | 869 | 2275 | 674 |
| 1951 | 9205 | 5414 | 903 | 2243 | 645 |
| 1952 | 9090 | 5336 | 919 | 2151 | 685 |
| 1953 | 8899 | 5201 | 953 | 2069 | 677 |
| 1954 | 8998 | 5202 | 932 | 2184 | 680 |
| 1955 | 8825 | 5262 | 938 | 1980 | 644 |
| 1956 | 8754 | 5170 | 949 | 1985 | 650 |
| 1957 | 8859 | 5177 | 1005 | 2023 | 654 |
| 1958 | 8705 | 5059 | 990 | 1978 | 678 |
| 1959 | 8715 | 5103 | 980 | 1958 | 673 |
| 1960 | 8588 | 5036 | 980 | 1926 | 645 |
| Average | 8853 | 5165 | 945 | 2077 | 666 |
| | | As a percentage of $I$ | | | |
| 1949 | 100 | 56 | 11 | 25 | 8 |
| 1950 | 100 | 58 | 10 | 25 | 7 |
| 1951 | 100 | 59 | 10 | 24 | 7 |
| 1952 | 100 | 59 | 10 | 24 | 8 |
| 1953 | 100 | 58 | 11 | 23 | 8 |
| 1954 | 100 | 58 | 10 | 24 | 8 |
| 1955 | 100 | 60 | 11 | 22 | 7 |
| 1956 | 100 | 59 | 11 | 23 | 7 |
| 1957 | 100 | 58 | 11 | 23 | 7 |
| 1958 | 100 | 58 | 11 | 23 | 8 |
| 1959 | 100 | 59 | 11 | 22 | 8 |
| 1960 | 100 | 59 | 11 | 22 | 8 |
| Average | 100 | 58 | 11 | 23 | 8 |
| | | As a percentage of $I - I_0$ | | | |
| 1949 | | | 25 | 57 | 18 |
| 1950 | | | 23 | 60 | 18 |
| 1951 | | | 24 | 59 | 17 |
| 1952 | | | 24 | 57 | 18 |
| 1953 | | | 26 | 56 | 18 |
| 1954 | | | 25 | 58 | 18 |
| 1955 | | | 26 | 56 | 18 |
| 1956 | | | 26 | 55 | 18 |
| 1957 | | | 27 | 55 | 18 |
| 1958 | | | 27 | 54 | 19 |
| 1959 | | | 27 | 54 | 19 |
| 1960 | | | 28 | 54 | 18 |
| Average | | | 26 | 56 | 18 |

total input heterogeneity. (Only the seven groups are considered which contain more than one sector. For the seven other groups these contributions are obviously zero.) The results indicate that the largest figures are those of the input heterogeneity of other service industries. The input heterogeneity of food, beverages, and tobacco is second, the output heterogeneity of other manufacturing industries third. These three heterogeneities jointly account for about 50 per cent of the information reduction $I - I_0$.

**TABLE II.** Contribution of Industry Groups to Input and Output Heterogeneity

| Year of the input-output table | Food, beverages, and tobacco | Textiles, footwear, and other wearing apparel | Metal industry | Other manufacturing industries | Trade (margins) | Trans-portation, storage, and communi-cations | Other service industries | Total |
|---|---|---|---|---|---|---|---|---|
| | | | | Output heterogeneity ($P_{g.}I_{g.}$ in $10^{-4}$ bit) | | | | |
| 1949 | 98 | 15 | 233 | 463 | 0 | 47 | 66 | 922 |
| 1950 | 105 | 13 | 204 | 441 | 0 | 48 | 57 | 869 |
| 1951 | 97 | 11 | 235 | 463 | 0 | 36 | 61 | 903 |
| 1952 | 104 | 13 | 231 | 467 | 0 | 42 | 62 | 919 |
| 1953 | 99 | 14 | 242 | 477 | 0 | 53 | 67 | 953 |
| 1954 | 98 | 14 | 217 | 476 | 0 | 61 | 67 | 932 |
| 1955 | 93 | 14 | 245 | 471 | 0 | 50 | 65 | 938 |
| 1956 | 90 | 13 | 271 | 468 | 0 | 44 | 62 | 949 |
| 1957 | 96 | 11 | 277 | 507 | 0 | 43 | 71 | 1005 |
| 1958 | 103 | 12 | 267 | 490 | 0 | 43 | 75 | 990 |
| 1959 | 109 | 12 | 269 | 468 | 0 | 46 | 77 | 980 |
| 1960 | 109 | 6 | 277 | 453 | 0 | 45 | 90 | 980 |
| Average | 100 | 12 | 247 | 470 | 0 | 47 | 68 | 945 |
| | | | | Input heterogeneity ($P_{.h}I_{.h}$ in $10^{-4}$ bit) | | | | |
| 1949 | 581 | 80 | 61 | 200 | 145 | 208 | 878 | 2154 |
| 1950 | 768 | 62 | 66 | 216 | 120 | 216 | 827 | 2275 |
| 1951 | 809 | 65 | 100 | 245 | 95 | 196 | 732 | 2243 |
| 1952 | 761 | 52 | 91 | 217 | 101 | 207 | 722 | 2151 |
| 1953 | 716 | 50 | 96 | 204 | 108 | 190 | 705 | 2069 |
| 1954 | 747 | 57 | 98 | 204 | 123 | 197 | 757 | 2184 |
| 1955 | 678 | 44 | 99 | 214 | 110 | 193 | 643 | 1980 |
| 1956 | 669 | 38 | 110 | 203 | 111 | 182 | 672 | 1985 |
| 1957 | 672 | 38 | 135 | 204 | 104 | 186 | 685 | 2023 |
| 1958 | 615 | 27 | 123 | 187 | 109 | 174 | 742 | 1978 |
| 1959 | 642 | 30 | 132 | 186 | 122 | 165 | 681 | 1958 |
| 1960 | 585 | 28 | 156 | 185 | 130 | 155 | 686 | 1926 |
| Average | 687 | 48 | 106 | 205 | 115 | 189 | 728 | 2077 |

The question arises of whether it is possible to have a smaller information reduction by a moderate degree of disaggregation. This is rather complicated for other service industries and other manufacturing industries, which consist of nine and seven sectors, respectively. We shall therefore confine ourselves in the next section to food, beverages, and tobacco, which will be disaggregated to two subgroups: food manufacturing of animal products and other foods, beverages, and tobacco, the latter subgroup consisting of two sectors: food manufacturing of non-animal products, and beverage industries and tobacco manufacturers.

## 8. Disaggregation of the Food Group

We shall indicate, for notational convenience, the food, beverages, and tobacco group by $S_1$. The information value $I_0$ can then be written as the sum of four terms:

$$I_0 = P_{11}\log\frac{P_{11}}{P_{1.}P_{.1}} + \sum_{h=2}^{G} P_{1h}\log\frac{P_{1h}}{P_{1.}P_{.h}} + \sum_{g=2}^{G} P_{g1}\log\frac{P_{g1}}{P_{g.}P_{.1}} + \sum_{g=2}^{G}\sum_{h=2}^{G} P_{gh}\log\frac{P_{gh}}{P_{g.}P_{.h}}\,. \quad (31)$$

of which the fourth term does not involve $S_1$. We disaggregate this group into two subgroups: food manufacturing of animal products (to be indicated by $r$ or $s$ = 1) and other foods, beverages, and tobacco ($r$ or $s$ = 2). The flows between these subgroups, measured as fractions of the total output of all secondary sectors, will be indicated by $q_{rs}$. The flows from these subgroups to $S_h$, $h = 2, \ldots, G$, will be indicated by $Q_{rh}$ (measured the same way) and the flows from $S_g$ to these subgroups by $Q_{gs}'$, $g = 2, \ldots, G$. We obviously have

$$\sum_{r=1}^{2}\sum_{s=1}^{2} q_{rs} = P_{11} \quad (32)$$

$$\sum_{r=1}^{2} Q_{rh} = P_{1h} \qquad h = 2, \ldots, G \quad (33)$$

$$\sum_{s=1}^{2} Q_{gs}' = P_{g1} \qquad g = 2, \ldots, G\,. \quad (34)$$

The informational content of the table after this partial disaggregation is then

$$I_0^* = \sum_{r=1}^{2}\sum_{s=1}^{2} q_{rs} \log \frac{q_{rs}}{Q_{r.}Q_{.s}} + \sum_{r=1}^{2}\sum_{h=2}^{G} Q_{rh} \log \frac{Q_{rh}}{Q_{r.}P_{.h}}$$
$$+ \sum_{g=2}^{G}\sum_{s=1}^{2} Q_{gs}' \log \frac{Q_{gs}'}{P_{g.}Q_{.s}} + \sum_{g=2}^{G}\sum_{h=2}^{G} P_{gh} \log \frac{P_{gh}}{P_{g.}P_{.h}} , \tag{35}$$

where

$$Q_{r.} = \sum_{s=1}^{2} q_{rs} + \sum_{h=2}^{G} Q_{rh}$$
$$Q_{.s} = \sum_{r=1}^{2} q_{rs} + \sum_{g=2}^{G} Q_{gs}' \tag{36}$$

represent the total flows from the subgroup $r$ and to the subgroup $s$, respectively.

On comparing (35) and (31) we conclude that the difference $I_0^* - I_0$ can be written as the sum of three terms:

$$I_0^* - I_0 = P_{11}\Delta_{11} + \sum_{h=2}^{G} P_{1h}\Delta_{1h} + \sum_{g=2}^{G} P_{g1}\Delta_{g1} , \tag{37}$$

where

$$\Delta_{11} = \sum_{r=1}^{2}\sum_{s=1}^{2} \frac{q_{rs}}{P_{11}} \log \frac{q_{rs}/P_{11}}{(Q_{r.}Q_{.s})/(P_{1.}P_{.1})} \tag{38}$$

deals with the information loss which is incurred when the four subgroup flows within food, beverages, and tobacco are aggregated to one group flow;

$$\Delta_{1h} = \sum_{r=1}^{2} \frac{Q_{rh}}{P_{1h}} \log \frac{Q_{rh}/P_{1h}}{Q_{r.}/P_{1.}} \tag{39}$$

deals with the information loss incurred when the two subgroup flows from $S_1$ to $S_h$ are combined, and

$$\Delta_{g1} = \sum_{s=1}^{2} \frac{Q_{gs}'}{P_{g1}} \log \frac{Q_{gs}'/P_{g1}}{Q_{.s}/P_{.1}} \tag{40}$$

deals with two subgroup flows from $S_g$ to $S_1$.

Consider then the information decomposition equation (21), which was based on aggregation to $G = 14$ groups rather than 15. When we apply partial disaggregation (13 groups plus two subgroups), the information value of the input-output table becomes $I_0^*$ instead of $I_0$; the total cell effect becomes $I_{..} - P_{11}\Delta_{11}$, which is less than or equal to the old value $I_{..}$; the total row (output) effect becomes

$$\sum_{g=1}^{G} P_{g.} I_{g.} - \sum_{h=2}^{G} P_{1h} \Delta_{1h} ,$$

which is also less than or equal to the old value; and the total column (input) effect becomes

$$\sum_{h=1}^{G} P_{.h} I_{.h} - \sum_{g=2}^{G} P_{g1} \Delta_{g1} ,$$

for which the same statement can be made.

Table III contains the three components of the information gain which is obtained by this partial disaggregation. It turns out that the input heterogeneity component due to the food group is, on the average, reduced by almost 75 per cent. This reduction amounts to about 25 per cent of the total input heterogeneity. The reduction of the output heterogeneity is of minor importance, but the cell effect is decreased more substantially. The average $P_{11}\Delta_{11}$ is about 20 per cent of the average $I$. The average information content of the 15-sector table is just below .6 bit. The average information loss due to the aggregation, which was .37 bit in the case of Table II, is now .30 bit, which amounts to a reduction of about 20 per cent.

## 9. Aggregation and Input-Output Forecasting

We shall now consider the information criterion from the standpoint of input-output forecasting of intermediate and primary demand. The forecast vector of total intermediate demand per supplying secondary sector is

**TABLE III.** The Information Gain Obtained by Partial Disaggregation of Food, Beverages, and Tobacco*

| Year of the input-output table | Reduction of: Output heterogeneity $\Sigma P_{1h}\Delta_{1h}$ | Input heterogeneity $\Sigma P_{g1}\Delta_{g1}$ | Cell effect $P_{11}\Delta_{11}$ | Information content of the 15-sector table $I_0^*$ |
|---|---|---|---|---|
| 1949 | 16 | 343 | 132 | 5279 |
| 1950 | 20 | 544 | 147 | 5939 |
| 1951 | 22 | 552 | 145 | 6133 |
| 1952 | 22 | 579 | 162 | 6099 |
| 1953 | 23 | 539 | 145 | 5908 |
| 1954 | 25 | 583 | 138 | 5948 |
| 1955 | 21 | 503 | 123 | 5909 |
| 1956 | 22 | 496 | 123 | 5811 |
| 1957 | 25 | 493 | 119 | 5814 |
| 1958 | 29 | 456 | 129 | 5673 |
| 1959 | 32 | 475 | 130 | 5740 |
| 1960 | 33 | 425 | 116 | 5610 |
| Average | 24 | 499 | 134 | 5822 |

* All figures are $10^{-4}$ bit.

$$\left[(I - A)^{-1} - I\right]f \tag{41}$$

and that of total primary demand per primary sector is

$$B\,(1 - A)^{-1} f \tag{42}$$

where $A$ is the matrix of secondary input coefficients, $B$ is that of primary input coefficients, and $f$ the vector of final demand. At the individual sector level $A$ is an $m \times m$ matrix with elements $p_{ij}/p_{.j}$ $(i, j = 1, \ldots, m)$ and $B$ is an $(n - m) \times m$ matrix with elements $p_{hj}/p_{.j}$ with $h = m + 1, \ldots, n$ and $j = 1, \ldots, m$.

The forecasts (41) and (42) are conditional, given the $f$ specification. In most applications, $A$ and $f$ will not correspond to the same period, since $A$ is normally based on the most recent input-output table and hence belongs to the past, while $f$ refers to some future year for which we wish to predict intermediate and primary demand. Therefore, if there is aggregation, two kinds of error will be committed, one of which is due to the aggregation itself and the other to a changing input structure at the individual sector level. Here we are interested in the aggregation only. It is therefore sufficient to consider the special case in which $A$, $B$, and $f$ all refer to the same year. The forecasts (41) and (42) are then trivially perfect when individual sector data are used. There will be discrepancies between forecasts and observed values when grouped data are used. These will now be analyzed empirically.

Consider any year, $t$, of the period 1949-1960. When the 35 secondary sectors are combined to 11 groups, we obtain an 11 × 11 matrix, $A$, the typical element of which is $P_{gh}/P_{.h}$, and an 11-element vector of final demand per group. Using (41) we then obtain an estimate of the intermediate demand vector whose typical element will be indicated by $\hat{z}_{gt}$ ($g = 1, \ldots, 11$). The corresponding observed value is $z_{gt}$, so that the logarithmic error is

$$e_{gt} = \log \frac{\hat{z}_{gt}}{z_{gt}} \tag{43}$$

and the mean square over all 12 years:

$$m_g = \frac{1}{12} \sum_{t=1}^{12} e_{gt}^2 . \tag{44}$$

**TABLE IV.** Mean Square Prediction Errors of Intermediate and Primary Demand Before and After Disaggregation*

| | Group or Subgroup | Mean Square Error | |
|---|---|---|---|
| | | Before Disaggregation | After Disaggregation |
| 1) | Agriculture, forestry, and fishing | 263 | 332 |
| 2) | Food, beverages, and tobacco | 471 | 472 |
| | 2a) Food manufacturing (animal products) | | 6265 |
| | 2b) Other food, beverages, and tobacco | | 398 |
| 3) | Textile, footwear, and other wearing apparel | 1186 | 1186 |
| 4) | Chemicals and petroleum refineries | 462 | 460 |
| 5) | Metal industry | 1873 | 1909 |
| 6) | Construction | 2233 | 2204 |
| 7) | Electricity, gas, and water | 3700 | 3669 |
| 8) | Other manufacturing industries | 1361 | 1363 |
| 9) | Trade (margins) | 928 | 926 |
| 10) | Transport, storage, and communication | 2218 | 2226 |
| 11) | Other service industries | 5394 | 5400 |
| 12) | Imports | 18 | 18 |
| 13) | Wages | 41 | 40 |
| 14) | Gross profits | 25 | 25 |

* All figures are to be multiplied by $10^{-10}$.

The logarithmic errors (natural logarithms) are presented in the appendix of this paper. The mean squares are given in Table IV, both for $G = 14$ and after the disaggregation of food, beverages, and tobacco. The table contains also the mean square errors of the primary demand forecasts (42), which are derived in a completely analogous manner. The results indicate that the mean square errors are hardly affected by the disaggregation. One might have expected that the figure for the food group would go down, but this is not the case at all. Actually, the figure goes up for the closely related agricultural sector.

How can we explain this effect? In other words, what is the relation between the information content of an input-output table and the input-output prediction errors? Should we not expect some kind of equivalence between the criterion of a maximum information content of the aggregated input-output table and that of a minimum mean square prediction error? We shall answer these questions with the aid of a result obtained earlier by one of the authors (Theil, 1957). It can be briefly described as follows. The intermediate demand forecasts of the input-output method (when applied at the group level) exceed the corresponding realizations by the so-called aggregation bias, which is a linear combination of the final demand vector at the micro level. The transformation matrix is rather complicated, but it can be simplified considerably when we apply an expansion according to increasing powers of the sector input coefficient matrix. If we disregard second and higher powers, we obtain the so-called first-order aggregation bias, which can thus be regarded as an approximation to the excess of the macroeconomic forecast over the observed value. In the case of the intermediate demand forecast this bias is of the following form:[5]

$$B_g = \sum_{h=1}^{F} \sum_{j \in S_h} f_j \left( \frac{P_{gh}}{P_{.h}} - \frac{r_{gj}}{p_{.j}} \right) \qquad g = 1, \ldots, F , \tag{45}$$

where $S_1, \ldots, S_F$ are the secondary groups. Now $B_g$ is measured in guilders per year. If we want to express the first-order bias as a fraction of the value to be predicted (the intermediate demand $z_g = x_g - f_g$),

$$b_g = \frac{B_g}{x_g - f_g} \qquad g = 1, \cdots, F \tag{46}$$

we obtain

[5] The derivation in Theil (1957) is in terms of final output predictions, but this does not make any real difference, because total output exceeds total intermediate demand by the amount of final demand, which is taken as given by the prediction procedure.

$$b_g = \frac{1}{P_{g.}} \sum_{h=1}^{F} \sum_{j \in S_h} (p_{.j} - p_{j.}) \left( \frac{P_{gh}}{P_{.h}} - \frac{r_{gj}}{p_{.j}} \right) \qquad g = 1, \ldots, F . \tag{47}$$

Here we made use of

$$\frac{f_j}{x} = p_{.j} - p_{j.} \qquad j = 1, \ldots, m . \tag{48}$$

See equations (6) and (9).

The crucial point is the relationship between $b_g$ and the input heterogeneity of the decomposition (21). For that purpose we consider the expression (27) under the temporary assumption that its logarithm is a natural logarithm. We shall expand that logarithm, making use of the following simple result which applies to any two sets of positive numbers $a_1, \ldots, a_n, b_1, \ldots, b_n$ such that $\Sigma a_i = \Sigma b_i = 1$:

$$\sum_{i=1}^{n} a_i \log \frac{a_i}{b_i} = - \sum_{i=1}^{n} a_i \log \left( 1 + \frac{b_i - a_i}{a_i} \right)$$

$$= - \sum_{i=1}^{n} a_i \left[ \frac{b_i - a_i}{a_i} - \frac{1}{2} \frac{(b_i - a_i)^2}{a_i^2} + \cdots \right] \approx \frac{1}{2} \sum_{i=1}^{n} \frac{(b_i - a_i)^2}{a_i}$$

$$\approx \frac{1}{2} \sum_{i=1}^{n} \frac{(b_i - a_i)^2}{b_i}$$

provided that the expansion converges, i.e., provided that the $a$'s and $b$'s are, pair-wise, sufficiently close to each other. We shally apply this expansion to (27), interpreting the $a$'s as $r_{gj}/P_{gh}$ and the $b$'s as $p_{.j}/P_{.h}$. The proviso just mentioned thus implies that there should not be too much input heterogeneity. We thus obtain

$$\sum_{j \in S_h} \frac{r_{gj}}{P_{gh}} \log \frac{r_{gj}/P_{gh}}{p_{.j}/P_{.h}} \approx \frac{1}{2} \sum_{j \in S_h} \left( \frac{((p_{.j}/P_{.h}) - (r_{gj}/P_{gh}))^2}{(p_{.j}/P_{.h})} \right)$$

$$= \frac{1}{2} \left( \frac{P_{.h}}{P_{gh}} \right) \sum_{j \in S_h} \frac{p_{.j}}{P_{.h}} \left( \frac{P_{gh}}{P_{.h}} - \frac{r_{gj}}{p_{.j}} \right)^2 ,$$

so that we conclude:

$$I_{.h} \approx \frac{1}{2}\sum_{g=1}^{G}\frac{P_{.h}}{P_{gh}}\sum_{j\in S_h}\frac{p_{.j}}{P_{.h}}\left(\frac{P_{gh}}{P_{.h}}-\frac{r_{gj}}{p_{.j}}\right)^2 . \tag{49}$$

We thus find that the input heterogeneity of $S_h$ is approximately equal to a weighted sum of the following expressions:

$$\sum_{j\in S_h}\frac{p_{.j}}{P_{.h}}\left(\frac{P_{gh}}{P_{.h}}-\frac{r_{gj}}{p_{.j}}\right)^2 \qquad g = 1, \ldots, G , \tag{50}$$

which is the second moment of the differences between the macroeconomic input coefficients $P_{gh}/P_{.h}$ and the corresponding sums of microefficients $r_{gj}/p_{.j} = (\Sigma\, p_{ij})/p_{.j}$ (sum over $i \in S_g$). Actually, the second moment is a variance because the mean vanishes:

$$\sum_{j\in S_h}\frac{p_{.j}}{P_{.h}}\left(\frac{P_{gh}}{P_{.h}}-\frac{r_{gj}}{p_{.j}}\right) = \frac{1}{P_{.h}}\left(P_{gh}-\sum_{j\in S_h}r_{gj}\right) = 0.$$

Now the first-order aggregation bias $b_g$ (see equation 47) can be written as follows:

$$b_g = \frac{1}{P_{g.}}\sum_{h=1}^{F}P_{.h}\sum_{j\in S_h}\frac{p_{.j}}{P_{.h}}\left(\frac{P_{gh}}{P_{.h}}-\frac{r_{gj}}{p_{.j}}\right)\left(1-\frac{p_{j.}}{p_{.j}}\right), \tag{51}$$

which means that it is a weighted sum of a number of covariances:

$$\sum_{j\in S_h}\frac{p_{.j}}{P_{.h}}\left(\frac{P_{gh}}{P_{.h}}-\frac{r_{gj}}{p_{.j}}\right)\left(1-\frac{p_{j.}}{p_{.j}}\right) \qquad h = 1, \ldots, F . \tag{52}$$

On comparing (52) with (50) we conclude that (52) can be regarded as a covariance of, on the one hand, the input coefficient differences whose variance is considered in (50) and, on the other hand, the ratios $p_{j.}/p_{.j}$ subtracted from unity. Now these ratios are all equal if final demand as a percentage of total output is the same for all sectors of $S_h$. In general, this will not be the case, so that the value of (52) will usually differ from zero. But when we minimize the variance (50), the covariance (52) is forced to take values in a smaller interval. This is what the criterion of a minimum input heterogeneity does. It does not guarantee smaller prediction errors as we saw in the beginning of this section.

The criterion has a minimax character: It minimizes the size of the interval in which the errors are located.

It will be noted that in (52) only the input heterogeneity of the secondary sectors plays a role. However, it can be easily verified along similar lines that the input heterogeneity with respect to primary sectors plays an analogous role when we consider primary demand predictions (see equation 42). Note further that the output heterogeneity and the cell effect of the decomposition (21) play no role at all, so that the advice is to aggregate in such a way that the input heterogeneity is minimized, not the total heterogeneity. This is simply due to the asymmetric use of the input-output table: Given the input structure (not the output structure), how can we predict given final demand?

## References

Schwartz, L.S.: 1963, *Principles of Coding, Filtering, and Information Theory*, Spartan Books, Baltimore, Maryland, and Cleaver-Hume Press, London, U.K.

Skolka, J.: 1964, *The Aggregation Problem in Input-Output Analysis*, Czechoslovakian Academy of Sciences, Prague.

Theil, H.: 1957, "Linear Aggregation in Input-Output Analysis," *Econometrica*, **25**, 111-122.

Tilanus, C.B.: 1964, "Thirteen Aggregated Input-Output Tables, The Netherlands 1948-1960," Report 6423 of the Econometric Institute of the Netherlands School of Economics, Rotterdam.

## APPENDIX

Tables A.I and A.II contain the logarithmic errors (43) before and after, respectively, the partial disaggregation of the food group. All figures of these tables are to be multiplied by $10^{-6}$.

**TABLE A.I.** Logarithmic Errors, Equation (43), 1949-1960

| | Group of Sectors | 1949 | 1950 | 1951 | 1952 | 1953 | 1954 | 1955 | 1956 | 1957 | 1958 | 1959 | 1960 |
|---|---|---|---|---|---|---|---|---|---|---|---|---|---|
| 1) | Agriculture, forestry, and fishing | 93 | -42 | 262 | 149 | 150 | 152 | -188 | -74 | -72 | -293 | 188 | -46 |
| 2) | Food, beverages, and tobacco | 183 | -357 | 219 | -138 | 125 | 293 | -300 | 10 | -107 | -170 | 121 | -302 |
| 3) | Textiles, footwear, and other wearing apparel | 299 | -17 | -643 | -332 | -175 | -63 | 315 | 568 | 270 | -383 | -228 | 287 |
| 4) | Chemicals and petroleum refineries | 125 | 258 | -263 | -60 | -373 | -159 | -96 | -189 | 224 | -217 | -265 | 150 |
| 5) | Metal industry | -562 | 288 | -783 | -766 | 523 | -203 | 243 | 252 | -415 | 118 | 134 | -86 |
| 6) | Construction | 300 | -243 | -74 | 1311 | 61 | -760 | 217 | -106 | 317 | 219 | 28 | 134 |
| 7) | Electricity, gas, and water | -46 | -16 | -833 | 945 | 244 | -704 | -229 | -664 | 319 | 429 | -931 | 806 |
| 8) | Other manufacturing industries | 254 | 351 | -759 | -153 | 499 | 93 | 296 | -404 | 101 | -147 | -443 | 331 |
| 9) | Trade (margins) | 177 | -371 | 370 | -161 | -302 | -418 | -255 | -230 | -406 | -3 | 324 | 358 |
| 10) | Transport, storage, and communication | -212 | 368 | -82 | -251 | -23 | -545 | 406 | -81 | 1102 | 217 | 507 | -651 |
| 11) | Other service industries | 265 | -611 | -993 | -351 | 313 | -25 | 640 | 205 | -1 | 1396 | -1507 | -387 |
| 12) | Imports | 10 | -47 | -95 | -27 | -1 | -11 | -58 | -18 | -57 | -38 | 8 | 34 |
| 13) | Wages | -24 | 89 | -85 | -32 | 108 | -77 | -5 | 15 | 108 | 39 | -34 | 7 |
| 14) | Gross profits | 11 | -29 | 123 | 37 | -68 | 57 | 40 | 2 | -39 | -5 | 20 | -28 |

**TABLE A.II.** Logarithmic Errors After Partial Disaggregation of Group 2

| | Group or Subgroup | 1949 | 1950 | 1951 | 1952 | 1953 | 1954 | 1955 | 1956 | 1957 | 1958 | 1959 | 1960 |
|---|---|---|---|---|---|---|---|---|---|---|---|---|---|
| 1) | Agriculture, forestry, and fishing | 198 | -122 | 240 | -30 | 102 | 237 | -190 | -27 | -27 | -279 | 291 | -139 |
| 2) | Food, beverages, and tobacco | 159 | -353 | 220 | -134 | 124 | 299 | -300 | 12 | -103 | -168 | 136 | -313 |
| | 2a) Food manufacturing (animal products) | 452 | -1067 | -713 | -1336 | 239 | 957 | -922 | 972 | 206 | 247 | 329 | -950 |
| | 2b) Other food, beverages, and tobacco | 104 | -170 | 440 | 122 | 97 | 140 | -179 | -170 | 170 | -259 | 97 | -186 |
| 3) | Textiles, footwear, and | 300 | -18 | -643 | -332 | -175 | -63 | 315 | 568 | 270 | -383 | -227 | 285 |
| | other wearing apparel | | | | | | | | | | | | |
| 4) | Chemicals and petroleum | 139 | 247 | -267 | -87 | -381 | -147 | -96 | -184 | 229 | -215 | -254 | 141 |
| | refineries | -555 | 282 | -785 | -781 | 520 | -197 | -300 | 255 | -413 | 119 | 140 | -91 |
| 5) | Metal industry | 308 | -251 | -76 | 1297 | 58 | -755 | 216 | -103 | 319 | 220 | 33 | 131 |
| 6) | Construction | -39 | -23 | -834 | 934 | 242 | -699 | -229 | -663 | 320 | 429 | -928 | 804 |
| 7) | Electricity, gas, and water | | | | | | | | | | | | |
| 8) | Other manufacturing | 255 | 350 | -760 | -153 | 499 | 94 | 296 | -404 | 102 | -146 | -443 | 332 |
| | industries | 173 | -369 | 370 | -158 | -301 | -419 | -255 | -229 | -406 | -2 | 328 | 356 |
| 9) | Trade (margins) | | | | | | | | | | | | |
| 10) | Transport, storage, and | -209 | 365 | -83 | -256 | -24 | -543 | 406 | -80 | 1104 | 217 | 511 | -654 |
| | communication | 270 | -615 | -994 | -358 | 311 | -21 | 639 | 208 | 2 | 1397 | -1503 | -392 |
| 11) | Other service industries | -10 | -33 | -91 | 1 | 6 | -22 | -58 | -24 | -62 | -39 | -3 | 44 |
| 12) | Imports | -21 | 86 | -86 | -39 | 106 | -73 | -5 | 16 | 109 | 39 | -31 | 4 |
| 13) | Wages | 19 | -36 | 121 | 25 | -71 | 63 | 40 | 5 | -36 | -4 | 25 | -33 |
| 14) | Gross profits | | | | | | | | | | | | |

CHAPTER 58

# A COMPARISON OF SHIFT-SHARE AND THE RAS ADJUSTMENT*[1]

HENRI THEIL
*University of Chicago*
*Chicago, Illinois, USA*

RIDDHI GHOSH
*University of Southern California*
*Los Angeles, California, USA*

ABSTRACT. It is argued that the RAS procedure applied to regions and industries performs a function similar to that of the shift-share technique, and that RAS has the advantage of a justification based on concepts from information theory.

An economy consists of $m$ regions and $n$ industries. We write $A_{pit}$ for the output[2] in year $t$ of industry $i$ in region $p$, $A_{.it} = \Sigma_p A_{pit}$ for the national output of industry $i$, $A_{p.t} = \Sigma_i A_{pit}$ for the total output in region $p$, and $A_{..t} = \Sigma_p \Sigma_i A_{pit}$ for total national output. The shift-share technique[3] writes the change in the output of each region and industry, measured by $A_{pit}/A_{pi,t-1} - 1$, as the sum of three terms: the national share effect $A_{..t}/A_{..t-1} - 1$; the industrial mix effect $A_{.it}/A_{.i,t-1} - A_{..t}/A_{..t-1}$; and the 'competitive' component $A_{pit}/A_{pi,t-1} - A_{.it}/A_{.i,t-1}$. The sum of the last two components is known as the shift effect.

Note that this decomposition is asymmetric in $p$ and $i$. This asymmetry would not be objectionable if it could be economically justified, but shift-share is essentially a descriptive technique without deep economic content.[4] Also note that the national share effect can be handled by the simple device of dividing all bivariate outputs by total national output. We define $a_{pit} = A_{pit}/A_{..t}$, $a_{.it} = A_{.it}/A_{..t}$, $a_{p.t} = A_{p.t}/A_{..t}$, and consider the RAS model[5]

$$\hat{a}_{pit} = r_p a_{pi,t-1} s_i \,, \tag{1}$$

* This article first appeared in *Regional Science and Urban Economics*, **10** (1980), 175-180. Reprinted with the permission of Elsevier Science Publishers, B.V.

[1] Research supported in part by NSF Grant SOC76-82718. The authors are indebted to Professor Harry Richardson for helpful comments.

[2] We may also use the number of persons employed or any other variable which takes the same dimension across regions and industries.

[3] See, e.g., Chalmers and Beckhelm (1976) and Edwards (1976).

[4] The issue of asymmetry in shift-share was considered by Klaassen and Paelinck (1972). See also Estaban-Marquillas (1972), Hewings (1977, pp. 77-83), Parakevopoulos (1974), and Sakashita (1973).

[5] See Bacharach (1970) for a description in monograph form.

where $r_1, ..., r_m, s_1, ..., s_n$ are adjusted so that $\Sigma_p \hat{a}_{pit} = a_{.it}$ for each $i$ and $\Sigma_i \hat{a}_{pit} = a_{p.t}$ for each $p$. The following remarks serve to clarify the relationship of the RAS model (1) to shift-share:

(1) In contrast to shift-share, (1) is symmetric in $p$ and $i$. A large (small) coefficient $r_p$ indicates that region $p$ has grown (declined) relative to other regions, and a large (small) $s_i$ indicates that industry $i$ has grown (declined) relative to other industries. Table 1 contains the adjustment coefficient $r_p$ for each of nine regions of the United States for each pair of successive years from 1953 to 1974, and table 2 contains the $s_i$'s of seven industry groups.[6] The last three lines of each table contain summary statistics of the (natural) logarithms of the 21 values of $r_p$ and $s_i$ for each $p$ and $i$: the arithmetic mean, the standard deviation, and the Von Neumann ratio. The standard deviations in table 2 tend to be much larger than those in table 1; this means that, over the course of time, the relative growth or decline of a region is much more steady than that of an industry.[7]

(2) Whereas shift-share provides an exhaustive description of the outputs of all industries in all regions in $t$ relative to $t$-1, (1) is an adjustment which provides an approximation $\hat{a}_{pit}$ of the true $a_{pit}$. This difference results from the fact that (1) avoids a region-industry interaction term (compare the competitive component of shift-share). A comparison of $\hat{a}_{pit}$ and $a_{pit}$ enables the analyst to verify to what extent changes from $t$-1 to $t$ can be described in terms of regional and industry effects without interaction (see also remark 4 below).

(3) The adjustment (1) can be justified in terms of informational concepts. The criterion is that of a minimum value of

$$I(\hat{a}_t : a_{t-1}) = \sum_{p=1}^{m} \sum_{i=1}^{n} \hat{a}_{pit} \log \frac{\hat{a}_{pit}}{a_{pi,t-1}}, \tag{2}$$

subject to the marginal constraints stated in the discussion following (1).[8] The measure (2) is the expected information of the message which transforms the $a_{pi,t-1}$'s into the $\hat{a}_{pit}$'s; see Theil (1967, ch. 2).

(4) We may view (2) as a measure of the degree to which the $a_{pi,t-1}$'s differ from the $\hat{a}_{pit}$'s. Therefore, the analogous expression

[6] These tables are from Theil (1977) and are based on the statistics on employees in the *Statistical Abstract of the United States*. The normalization is such that, for each pair of successive years, the weighted geometric mean of $r_1, ..., r_9$ equals the weighted geometric mean of $s_1, ..., s_7$, with weights equal to the corresponding marginal proportions.

[7] The Von Neumann ratios suggest that some of the adjustment coefficients are positively autocorrelated. However, the evidence is not very strong.

[8] This justification was first formulated by Ireland and Kullback (1968).

**TABLE 1.** Adjustment Coefficients for Regions

| | New England | Middle Atlantic | East North Central | West North Central | South Atlantic | East South Central | West South Central | Mountain | Pacific |
|---|---|---|---|---|---|---|---|---|---|
| 1953-54 | 1.0014 | 0.9996 | 0.9882 | 1.0070 | 1.0091 | 1.0096 | 0.9995 | 1.0005 | 1.0089 |
| 1954-55 | 0.9874 | 0.9835 | 1.0104 | 0.9880 | 1.0076 | 1.0026 | 1.0065 | 1.0267 | 1.0098 |
| 1955-56 | 0.9975 | 0.9886 | 0.9842 | 0.9809 | 1.0206 | 1.0002 | 1.0134 | 1.0244 | 1.0341 |
| 1956-57 | 0.9855 | 1.0072 | 0.9946 | 0.9886 | 0.9933 | 0.9980 | 1.0099 | 1.0189 | 1.0110 |
| 1957-58 | 0.9988 | 0.9979 | 0.9651 | 1.0108 | 1.0286 | 1.0104 | 1.0122 | 1.0308 | 1.0158 |
| 1958-59 | 1.0001 | 0.9813 | 1.0082 | 1.0044 | 1.0073 | 1.0045 | 0.9886 | 1.0288 | 1.0117 |
| 1959-60 | 0.9982 | 0.9937 | 0.9905 | 0.9938 | 1.0106 | 1.0089 | 0.9904 | 1.0258 | 1.0201 |
| 1960-61 | 1.0081 | 0.9940 | 0.9903 | 1.0038 | 1.0096 | 0.9993 | 1.0022 | 1.0204 | 1.0059 |
| 1961-62 | 0.9876 | 0.9876 | 0.9966 | 0.9915 | 1.0076 | 1.0131 | 1.0109 | 1.0167 | 1.0160 |
| 1962-63 | 0.9859 | 0.9835 | 0.9983 | 0.9987 | 1.0158 | 1.0139 | 1.0056 | 1.0106 | 1.0115 |
| 1963-64 | 0.9853 | 0.9921 | 1.0016 | 0.9928 | 1.0093 | 1.0143 | 1.0113 | 0.9918 | 1.0027 |
| 1964-65 | 0.9972 | 0.9896 | 1.0071 | 0.9960 | 1.0093 | 1.0102 | 1.0053 | 0.9861 | 0.9954 |
| 1965-66 | 0.9887 | 0.9843 | 1.0034 | 1.0027 | 1.0048 | 1.0089 | 1.0129 | 1.0010 | 1.0082 |
| 1966-67 | 0.9937 | 0.9893 | 0.9945 | 1.0067 | 1.0100 | 0.9962 | 1.0176 | 0.9944 | 1.0080 |
| 1967-68 | 0.9983 | 0.9892 | 0.9994 | 0.9942 | 1.0088 | 0.9994 | 1.0046 | 1.0039 | 1.0096 |
| 1968-69 | 0.9858 | 0.9952 | 0.9970 | 0.9918 | 1.0113 | 1.0038 | 1.0087 | 1.0089 | 1.0027 |
| 1969-70 | 1.0015 | 0.9955 | 0.9902 | 0.9943 | 1.0146 | 1.0126 | 0.9999 | 1.0241 | 0.9988 |
| 1970-71 | 0.9980 | 0.9856 | 0.9959 | 0.9962 | 1.0188 | 1.0199 | 1.0083 | 1.0371 | 0.9873 |
| 1971-72 | 0.9803 | 0.9764 | 0.9847 | 1.0051 | 1.0152 | 1.0250 | 1.0211 | 1.0538 | 1.0091 |
| 1972-73 | 0.9883 | 0.9722 | 0.9951 | 1.0044 | 1.0254 | 1.0115 | 1.0116 | 1.0137 | 1.0055 |
| 1973-74 | 0.9940 | 0.9805 | 0.9936 | 1.0047 | 1.0093 | 1.0051 | 1.0178 | 1.0301 | 1.0036 |
| *Logarithmic summary measures* | | | | | | | | | |
| Mean | -0.0066 | -0.0112 | -0.0053 | -0.0021 | 0.0117 | 0.0079 | 0.0075 | 0.0163 | 0.0083 |
| Standard deviation | 0.0071 | 0.0080 | 0.0097 | 0.0076 | 0.0072 | 0.0072 | 0.0080 | 0.0159 | 0.0090 |
| Von Neumann | 2.23 | 1.29 | 2.63 | 1.56 | 3.00 | 1.09 | 1.32 | 0.81 | 1.52 |

**Table 2.** Adjustment Coefficients for Industries

| | Contract construction | Manufacturing | Transportation | Trade | Finance | Services | Government |
|---|---|---|---|---|---|---|---|
| 1953-54 | 1.0114 | 0.9542 | 0.9797 | 1.0240 | 1.0556 | 1.0412 | 1.0362 |
| 1954-55 | 1.0200 | 1.0023 | 0.9765 | 0.9959 | 1.0215 | 1.0070 | 0.9953 |
| 1955-56 | 1.0149 | 0.9876 | 0.9918 | 1.0080 | 1.0184 | 1.0171 | 0.9966 |
| 1956-57 | 0.9816 | 0.9785 | 0.9881 | 1.0093 | 1.0171 | 1.0319 | 1.0178 |
| 1957-58 | 0.9869 | 0.9534 | 0.9728 | 1.0148 | 1.0431 | 1.0408 | 1.0523 |
| 1958-59 | 1.0003 | 1.0417 | 0.9718 | 0.9349 | 0.9849 | 0.9993 | 1.0309 |
| 1959-60 | 0.9708 | 0.9818 | 0.9727 | 0.9971 | 1.0354 | 1.0662 | 1.0005 |
| 1960-61 | 0.9713 | 0.9707 | 0.9725 | 0.9968 | 1.0365 | 1.0462 | 1.0338 |
| 1961-62 | 0.9852 | 1.0083 | 0.9701 | 0.9893 | 1.0003 | 1.0143 | 1.0041 |
| 1962-63 | 1.0037 | 0.9905 | 0.9798 | 0.9972 | 1.0008 | 1.0207 | 1.0107 |
| 1963-64 | 1.0147 | 0.9889 | 0.9824 | 1.0033 | 1.0028 | 1.0167 | 1.0033 |
| 1964-65 | 0.9984 | 1.0005 | 0.9813 | 0.9990 | 0.9844 | 1.0082 | 1.0060 |
| 1965-66 | 0.9788 | 1.0114 | 0.9747 | 0.9915 | 0.9706 | 0.9997 | 1.0159 |
| 1966-67 | 0.9447 | 0.9823 | 0.9950 | 0.9964 | 1.0008 | 1.0296 | 1.0280 |
| 1967-68 | 1.0026 | 0.9854 | 0.9828 | 1.0012 | 1.0173 | 1.0181 | 1.0084 |
| 1968-69 | 1.0073 | 0.9870 | 0.9922 | 1.0034 | 1.0167 | 1.0178 | 0.9980 |
| 1969-70 | 0.9707 | 0.9571 | 1.0039 | 1.0153 | 1.0263 | 1.0312 | 1.0223 |
| 1970-71 | 0.9983 | 0.9563 | 0.9896 | 1.0144 | 1.0256 | 1.0207 | 1.0270 |
| 1971-72 | 1.0374 | 0.9914 | 0.9781 | 1.0075 | 1.0038 | 1.0151 | 0.9872 |
| 1972-73 | 1.0422 | 1.0050 | 0.9797 | 1.0024 | 1.0026 | 1.0117 | 0.9741 |
| 1973-74 | 0.9730 | 0.9832 | 0.9929 | 0.9984 | 1.0099 | 1.0248 | 1.0101 |
| *Logarithmic summary measures* | | | | | | | |
| Mean | -0.0044 | -0.0138 | -0.0179 | -0.0001 | 0.0128 | 0.0224 | 0.0121 |
| Standard deviation | 0.0234 | 0.0212 | 0.0091 | 0.0172 | 0.0198 | 0.0153 | 0.0177 |
| Von Neumann | 1.54 | 2.30 | 1.21 | 2.08 | 1.42 | 2.20 | 1.74 |

$$I(a_t : \hat{a}_t) = \sum_{p=1}^{m} \sum_{i=1}^{n} a_{pit} \log \frac{a_{pit}}{\hat{a}_{pit}} \tag{3}$$

measures the inaccuracy of the RAS adjustments $\hat{a}_{pit}$ with respect to the corresponding observed $a_{pit}$'s, while

$$I(a_t : a_{t-1}) = \sum_{p=1}^{m} \sum_{i=1}^{n} a_{pit} \log \frac{a_{pit}}{a_{pi,t-1}} \tag{4}$$

measures the inaccuracy of last year's $a_{pi,t-1}$'s as approximations of the current $a_{pit}$'s. It is easily verified that[9]

$$I(a_t : a_{t-1}) = I(a_t : \hat{a}_t) + \bar{I}(\hat{a}_t : a_{t-1}) \,, \tag{5}$$

where $\bar{I}(\hat{a}_t : a_{t-1})$ is the minimum of (2). Thus, given the inaccuracy of no-change extrapolation as measured by the left-hand side of (5), the RAS adjustment provides a more accurate approximation of the true $a_{pit}$'s when the minimum value of (2) is larger, i.e. when the marginal constraints imposed on the $\hat{a}_{pit}$'s force these to differ more from the $a_{pi,t-1}$'s. Also, RAS is never less accurate than no-change extrapolation because $\bar{I}(\hat{a}_t : a_{t-1}) \geq 0$ in (5).[10]

(5) When $m$ and $n$ are moderately large, both shift-share and RAS handle large numbers of outputs of individual industries in individual regions, particularly when the analysis covers several years rather than two. It is therefore of considerable interest to use summary measures for the goodness of fit of (1) for individual regions and industries. The output distribution of region $p$ in $t$ is $a_{p1t}/a_{p.t}, \ldots, a_{pnt}/a_{p.t}$, so that the version of (3) which applies to this region, is

$$I_p(a_t : \hat{a}_t) = \sum_{i=1}^{n} \frac{a_{pit}}{a_{p.t}} \log \frac{a_{pit}/a_{p.t}}{\hat{a}_{pit}/a_{p.t}} \,, \tag{6}$$

---

[9] See Theil (1977), also for the proofs of statements made in remark 5 below.

[10] For the data of tables 1 and 2 there is only one observation (1964-65) for which $I(a_t : \hat{a}_t)$ exceeds $\bar{I}(\hat{a}_t : a_{t-1})$. When we average both sides of (5) over $t = 1, \ldots, 21$, we find that the first term on the right-hand is a little over 20 percent of the term on the left-hand side. This means that the adjustment coefficients of tables 1 and 2 account, on the average, for almost 80 percent of the observed bivariate changes from one year to the next.

which satisfies $\Sigma_p a_{p.t} I_p (a_t : \hat{a}_t) = I(a_t : \hat{a}_t)$. Hence the inaccuracy of the RAS adjustment is a weighted mean of the inaccuracies of the adjustments for the individual regions. The version of (4) which applies to region $p$ is

$$I_p(a_t : a_{t-1}) = \sum_{i=1}^{n} \frac{a_{pit}}{a_{p.t}} \log \frac{a_{pit} / a_{p.t}}{a_{pi,t-1} / a_{p.t-1}}, \tag{7}$$

which satisfies

$$\sum_{p=1}^{m} a_{p.t} I_p(a_t : a_{t-1}) = I(a_t : a_{t-1}) - \sum_{p=1}^{m} a_{p.t} \log \frac{a_{p.t}}{a_{p.t-1}}, \tag{8}$$

where the sum on the far right is the inaccuracy of no-change extrapolation of the marginal regional proportions. The extension of (2) for region $p$ yields results similar to (7) and (8). The analogous results for industries (rather than regions) are entirely similar.

## References

Bacharach, M.: 1970, *Biproportional Matrices and Input-Output Change*, Cambridge University Press, Cambridge.

Chalmers, J.A., and T.L. Beckhelm: 1976, "Shift and Share and the Theory of Industrial Location," *Regional Studies*, **10**, 15-23.

Edwards, J.A.: 1976, "Industrial Structure and Regional Change: A Shift-share Analysis of the British Columbia Economy 1961-1970," *Regional Studies*, **10**, 307-317.

Estaban-Marquillas, J.M.: 1972, "A Reinterpretation of Shift-share Analysis," *Regional Science and Urban Economics*, **2**, 249-255.

Hewings, G.J.D.: 1977, *Regional Industrial Analysis and Development*, St. Martin's Press, New York.

Ireland, C.T., and S. Kullback: 1968, "Contingency Tables with Given Marginals," *Biometrika*, **55**, 179-188.

Klaassen, L.H., and J.H.P. Paelinck: 1972, "Asymmetry in Shift- and Share Analysis," *Regional Science and Urban Economics*, **2**, 256-261.

Paraskevopoulos, C.C.: 1974, "Patterns of Regional Economic Growth," *Regional Science and Urban Economics*, **4**, 77-105.

Sakashita, N.: 1973, "An Axiomatic Approach to Shift-and-Share Analysis," *Regional Science and Urban Economics*, **3**, 263-271.

Theil, H.: 1967, *Economics and Information Theory*, North-Holland, Amsterdam.

Theil, H.: 1977, "The Information Analysis of Changes in Regional Distributions," in: C.A. van Bochoven et al., eds., *Modeling for Government and Business*, Martinus Nijhoff, Leiden, 9-32.

# SECTION 4.5: APPLICATIONS IN BUSINESS AND FINANCE

CHAPTER 59

# ON THE USE OF INFORMATION THEORY CONCEPTS IN THE ANALYSIS OF FINANCIAL STATEMENTS*

HENRI THEIL
*The University of Chicago,*
*Chicago, Illinois, U.S.A.*

ABSTRACT. Balance sheets and income statements are numerical decompositions of certain total sums: total assets, total liabilities, total sales, and total costs and expenses. The behavior of individual items measured as fractions of the corresponding total is important for the analysis of the company's financial position. It will be argued in this article that certain concepts derived from information theory are useful as summarizing descriptive devices for changes in such fractions as well as for the analysis of differences between companies of the same industry.

## 1. Introduction

The order of discussion is as follows. Section 2 describes the basic information theory concepts, which are applied in section 3 to assets and liabilities. Section 4 deals with problems of disaggregation, the various assets being divided into a larger number of more homogeneous assets (similarly for the liabilities). In section 5 we consider the two sides of the income statement, sales as well as costs and expenses, and in particular the possibility that sales are divided into groups according to two different criteria (e.g., different products and different regions in which the products are sold). This two-dimensional problem is pursued further in section 6.

In section 7 we return to balance sheets in order to handle assets and liabilities simultaneously. In a sense, this section is most closely related to conventional ratio analysis; it leads to a new type of balance sheet, the information balance sheet. Section 8 deals with a comparison of individual companies with the industry to which they belong. The last section contains some concluding remarks.

## 2. Some Concepts of Information Theory

Consider an arbitrary event $E$ whose probability is $p$ as of this moment. Suppose that at some later point of time we receive the message that $E$ has taken place; it is assumed that this message is definite and reliable. Clearly, the smaller the $p$, the more surprised we

---

* Reprinted by permission, "On the Use of Information Theory Concepts in the Analysis of Financial Statements," Henri Theil, *Management Science*, **15** (1969), 459-480. 

will be. Equivalently, the message on the realization of $E$ is *more* informative when the event was *less* likely to occur.

Information theory provides a precise and, in fact, quantitative measure of the information content of such a message, defined in terms of the probability $p$ before the arrival of the message. The discussion of the preceding paragraph shows that this measure should be a decreasing function of $p$. The function chosen is log (1/p) which decreases from $\infty$ to 0 when $p$ increases from 0 to 1. The logarithmic form is motivated by the convenient additive property of information, thus defined, which may be shown as follows. Consider two events, $E_1$ and $E_2$, as well as their joint, conditional, and unconditional probabilities, which are connected by

$$P[E_1 \text{ and } E_2] = P[E_1]P[E_2|E_1] = P[E_2]P[E_1|E_2].$$

Assume that we are first informed that $E_1$ occurred, so that the information received is log ($1/P[E1]$) and the probability that $E_2$ will occur becomes $P[E_2|E_1]$. Assume next that we are informed that $E_2$ also occurred. The total information received with the two messages is

$$\log 1/P[E_1] + \log 1/P[E_2|E_1] = \log 1/P[E_1 \text{ and } E_2]$$

which means that this total information is independent of the order of occurrence of $E_1$ and $E_2$.

Consider now that a complete system of mutually exclusive events, $E_1, \ldots, E_n$ with probabilities $p_1, \ldots, p_n$. Supposing that we receive later a message stating that $E_i$ occurred, we conclude from the previous paragraph that the information received is log ($1/p$). However, *before* the message comes in we do not know which event took place; we only know that $E_i$ has chance $p_i$. But this enables us to compute the expected value of the information to be received, if $p_i$ is the probability of $E_i$, it is also the probability that the amount of information received is log ($1/p_i$), and hence

$$H = \sum_{i=1}^{n} p_i \log 1/p_i \tag{2.1}$$

is the *expected information* of the message that states which of the events $E_1, \ldots, E_n$ occurred. It is also known as the *entropy* of the distribution of which the $p$'s are the probabilities. The minimum of $H$ is zero, which corresponds to the case of one $p_i$ equal to 1 and all the others equal to 0, and the maximum is log $n$, corresponding with the case of equal probabilities (all $p$'s being equal to $1/n$).[1] Thus, when it is known that one event

[1] The maximum is found straightforwardly by means of the Lagrangian technique applied to $H$ subject to the constraint $\sum p_i = 1$. For the minimum, note that $x \log x$ is defined as zero for $x = 0$ in accordance with the limit of $x \log x$ decreasing toward zero.

has unit probability and all others have zero probability, there is a zero amount of information to be expected from the message on what actually happened. This is intuitively plausible. When all probabilities are equal, so that we are not even able to say that one event is more likely to occur than another, we are completely in the dark and hence we expect more information from the message that tells us which event took place than in any other situation. This is in accordance with the maximum of $H$, $\log n$, for $p_i = 1/n$, $i = 1, \ldots, n$.

The unit of information is determined by the base of the logarithm. For $n = 2$ we have a maximum $\log 2$ of $H$, which becomes 1 when we choose 2 as the logarithmic base. This is frequently done in information theory and we will follow this custom in this paper. Information is then said to be measured in binary digits, or for short, *bits*. The maximum entropy for the case of two alternatives ($E_1$ and $E_2$) is hence 1 bit, and it is the actual entropy when $E_1$ and $E_2$ both have probability ½. Natural logarithms are also frequently used, particularly for continuous distributions, but this will not be done here.

We proceed to generalize the information concept to messages which are not completely definite, in the first instance for one single event ($E$). Suppose that the message states that the odds in favor of $E$ have changed (for whatever reason) such that the original probability $p$ (called prior probability in the sequel) is replaced by the posterior probability $q$. Assume that it ultimately turns out that $E$ does take place. The information received is then $\log (1/p)$ on the basis of the prior probability and $\log (1/q)$ on the basis of the posterior probability. Given the additivity of the information concept, an obvious way of defining the information associated with the message that transforms prior $p$ to posterior $q$ consists of taking the difference:

$$\log 1/p - \log 1/q = \log q/p.$$

This includes as a special case the information received with a definite message ($q = 1$). The information value is zero when $p$ and $q$ are equal, as it obviously should be. The value is negative when $q < p$, which is also understandable given that it is assumed that $E$ will ultimately take place.

But the fact of the matter is that the message which transforms prior $p$ to posterior $q$ gives no definite clue as to the question of whether or not $E$ will ultimately take place (unless $q = 0$ or 1). That is perfectly true, but the definition just given enables us to compute the expected information of this message. Consider again a complete system of mutually exclusive events, $E_1, \ldots, E_n$. Let the prior probabilities be $p_1, \ldots, p_n$ and let the message transform these to the posterior probabilities $q_1, \ldots, q_n$. If $E_i$ ultimately occurs, the information is $\log (q_i/p_i)$. The message states that the chance of $E_i$, and hence also the chance of $\log (q_i/p_i)$ bits of information, is $q_i$. Therefore,

$$I(q:p) = \sum_{i=1}^{n} q_i \log q_i/p_i \tag{2.2}$$

is the *expected information of the message which transforms the prior probabilities* $p_1, \ldots, p_n$ *to the posterior probabilities* $q_1, \ldots, q_n$. The symbols $p$ and $q$ in the left-hand side of (2.2) stand for the set of $n$ prior and that of $n$ posterior probabilities, respectively.

It is easily shown that $I(q{:}p)$ is always positive when the prior and posterior probabilities are not pairwise equal ($p_i \neq q_i$ for some $i$) and that it vanishes if and only if all prior and posterior probabilities are pairwise equal ($p_i = q_i$ for each $i$). Hence, no information is to be expected from the message when it does not change any of the prior probabilities; but as soon as there are such changes, there is a positive expected value of information. Note also that, when the message is definite in the sense that one of the $n$ events has unit posterior probability ($q_i = 1$ for some $i$, $q_j = 0$ for each $j \neq i$), the right-hand side of (2.2) reduces to log $(1/p_i)$. This is in accordance with the information definition for a definite message given in the second paragraph of this section.

This is all we need as far as information theory concepts are concerned. As we shall see in the next section, the probabilistic interpretation of these concepts can be extended considerably. The field originated with Shannon (1948), with Hartley (1928) an important forerunner. For applications of these concepts to economics see Theil (1967).

## 3. Assets Information and Liabilities Information

Our first application deals with the two sides of a balance sheet, for which purpose we take Table I as an illustrative example. This table is based on the 1964 and 1965 annual reports of Ford Motor Company and its consolidated subsidiaries, but we have simplified and guessed a few figures, particularly for sales (Section 5).

The argument underlying the application of information theory concepts is as follows. When we compare the figures for 1965 and 1964, we are struck first by the increase of the totals, from 6459 to 7596 million dollars. This increase is a measure for the company's growth in dollar terms. When all separate assets and liabilities grow in the same proportion, there is nothing more to be said. In fact, the 1964 balance sheet plus the knowledge of total assets at the end of 1965 would then enable us to compute the 1965 balance sheet straightforwardly. However, the individual assets and liabilities do not grow proportionately; some may even decrease. Equivalently, the individual items measured as a fraction of the total will change from 1964 to 1965, and an interesting problem is then how to measure the size of this change.

The ideas discussed in the previous section suggest that one may regard the individual assets in the earlier year (1964), measured as a fraction of total assets in that year, as prior probabilities:

$$\frac{3156}{6459} \qquad \frac{586}{6459} \qquad \frac{2588}{6459} \qquad \frac{129}{6459}\,.$$

**TABLE I.** Balance Sheets for 1964 and 1965 ($10^6$ Dollars)

| Assets | 1965 | 1964 | Liabilities | 1965 | 1964 |
|---|---|---|---|---|---|
| Current Assets | 3733 | 3156 | Current liabilities | 2610 | 2062 |
| Investments and noncurrent receivables | 693 | 586 | Long-term debt | 295 | 227 |
| Property, plant and equipment | 3020 | 2588 | Other liabilities and reserves | 201 | 159 |
| Taxes and other expenses allocable to future years | 150 | 129 | Stockholders' equity | 4490 | 4011 |
| Total assets | 7596 | 6459 | Total liabilities* | 7596 | 6459 |

*Including stockholders' equity

A possible objection to this interpretation is that these fractions are not probabilities in the usual sense. Two answers may be given. First, such fractions are probabilities in the conventional sense when we ask the following question: If one takes at random a dollar of the company's assets at the end of 1964, what is the chance that this dollar falls under current assets (say)? Answer: This probability is the current assets fraction 3156/6459. Second, it is not really true that information theory is exclusively concerned with the probabilities in the usual sense of the word. Basically, a measure such as the entropy (2.1) describes the degree to which some total is divided into smaller fractions. This total may be the total (unit) probability, but it may also be the total population of the United States, divided into the populations of the fifty separate states; it may be the total personal income of all U.S. residents, divided into the total incomes of the residents of the separate states; it may be the student body of a school, divided into the groups of students according to race, *etc.*[2] In this case, it is the company's amount of total assets at the end of 1964, divided into the four assets groups of Table I.

When these four fractions are the prior probabilities, we may regard the corresponding assets fractions of the later year (1965) as the posterior probabilities:

$$\frac{3733}{7596} \quad \frac{693}{7596} \quad \frac{3020}{7596} \quad \frac{150}{7596} \, .$$

Thus, the assets side of the 1965 balance sheet is considered a message which transforms the 1964 assets fractions (as prior probabilities) to the 1965 assets fractions (as posterior probabilities). We ask: How informative is this message? The answer will be given by means of formula (2.2):

[2] The interpretation in terms of the race of students leads to the concept of the racial entropy of a school as a measure of integration; see Theil and Finezza (1967). The interpretation in terms of population and income shares leads to a measure of income inequality; see Theil (1967, Chapter 6).

$$\frac{3733}{7596} \log \frac{3733/7596}{3156/6459} + \ldots + \frac{150}{7596} \log \frac{150/7596}{129/6459} = 33 \times 10^{-6} \text{ bits} . \quad (3.1)$$

This value will be called the *assets information* of 1965, given 1964, or for short the 1965 assets information. In the present case this information is positive, which means that the changes in the individual assets from 1964 to 1965 were not proportional. The larger the deviations from proportionality (or equivalently, the larger the discrepancies between the corresponding 1964 and 1965 fractions), the larger the 1965 assets information will be. For short, the assets information is a measure for the degree of change of the relative position of the individual assets in total assets as a whole. Note that we may have an arbitrary number of assets (not necessarily four as in Table I) and that we always have one single assets information value. Note also that the measure does *not* tell us in which direction an individual asset moves, up or down; that is a different problem. The information expectations (2.2) is a distance measure for two sets of fractions. When applied to assets fractions in two consecutive years, this distance measure tells us "how far we have to travel" from the fractions of the first year to those of the second; it does not tell us the direction to travel.

It was stated above that the information expectation increases when the two sets of fractions differ to a greater extent. To evaluate this in more specific terms, we will expand the information expectation (2.2) according to powers of $p_i - q_i$ under the temporary assumption that the logs are natural logarithms:

$$\begin{aligned} \sum_{i=1}^{n} q_i \log q_i/p_i &= -\sum_{i=1}^{n} q_i \log p_i/q_i \\ &= -\sum_{i=1}^{n} q_i \log \left(1 + \frac{p_i - q_i}{q_i}\right) \\ &= -\sum_{i=1}^{n} q_i \frac{p_i - q_i}{q_i} + \frac{1}{2} \sum_{i=1}^{n} q_i \left(\frac{p_i - q_i}{q_i}\right)^2 - \ldots \\ &= \frac{1}{2} \sum_{i=1}^{n} \frac{(p_i - q_i)^2}{q_i} - \ldots \end{aligned} \quad (3.2)$$

[Note that the expansion converges only if $p_i$ and $q_i$, $i = 1, \ldots, n$ are sufficiently close to each other.] The conclusion is that the information expectation $I(q{:}p)$ is in first approximation equal to a weighted sum of squares of the differences between corresponding prior and posterior probabilities, with the weights inversely proportional to the latter probabilities. The value ½ on the last line of (3.2) before the summation sign is applicable only when we use natural logs; when logarithms to the base 2 are used, the coefficient before the summation sign becomes $\frac{1}{2} \log_2 e \approx .721$. It is quickly apparent that the value obtained in (3.1) implies very small differences between corresponding 1964 and 1965 assets shares.

Note that the weighting scheme on the last line of (3.2) implies that the squared differences $(p_i - q_i)^2$ of small items ($p_i$ and $q_i$ close to zero) are weighted heavily. Note also, however, that the opposite holds when we formulate the differences in relative terms, $(p_i - q_i)/q_i$:

$$\sum_{i=1}^{n} \frac{(p_i - q_i)^2}{q_i} = \sum_{i=1}^{n} q_i \left( \frac{p_i - q_i}{q_i} \right)^2 .$$

Thus, the weights of the squared relative changes are small for those items which are small themselves.

The above deals exclusively with the assets side of the balance sheet. We can proceed in an analogous way for the other side by interpreting the 1964 liabilities fractions as prior probabilities and those of 1965 as posterior probabilities. This leads to the 1965 *liabilities information*, which is computed straightforwardly from the liabilities side of Table 1:

$$\frac{2610}{7596} \log \frac{2610/7596}{2062/6459} + \ldots + \frac{4490}{7596} \log \frac{4490/7596}{4011/6459} = 2730 \times 10^{-6} \text{ bits.} \qquad (3.3)$$

On comparing this result with (3.1) we conclude that the behavior of the separate liability items from 1964 to 1965 was not nearly as close to proportionality as that of the assets.

## 4. Disaggregation of the Assets and Liabilities Information

The computation of the 1965 liabilities information is based on all items on the liabilities side of the balance sheet including stockholders' equity. Since this last item has a character somewhat different from the liabilities in the narrow sense, it may be considered attractive to compute the 1965 liabilities information for the latter liabilities only. This raises the question of what can be said about the relationship between these two information values. The present section is devoted to problems of this kind.

We return to Section 2 and assume that events are combined to groups of events. For example, $E_1$ and $E_2$ are combined to a pair of events, $(E_1, E_2)$, for which the prior and posterior probabilities are obviously $p_1 + p_2$ and $q_1 + q_2$, respectively. More generally, let there be $G$ such combinations, to be denoted by $S_1, \ldots, S_G$, with the following prior and posterior probabilities:

$$P_g = \sum_{i \in S_g} p_i \qquad Q_g = \sum_{i \in S_g} q_i, \qquad g = 1, \cdots, G. \tag{4.1}$$

If we confine ourselves to the $S$'s rather than the $E$'s, the information expectation (2.2) becomes

$$I_0(q:p) = \sum_{g=1}^{G} Q_g \log Q_g / P_g\,, \tag{4.2}$$

and the obvious question is: What can be said about the relationship between the "macroscopic" information expectation (4.2) and its "microscopic" analogue (2.2)? For this purpose we introduce the conditional probabilities $p_i/P_g$ (prior) and $q_i/Q_g$ (posterior), $i \in S_g$, $g = 1, \ldots, G$. They are, respectively, the prior probability that $E_i$ will occur, given that it is known that one of the events of $S_g$ will occur ($E_i$ being part of $S_g$), and the analogous conditional posterior probability. Then

$$I_g(q:p) = \sum_{i \in S_g} \frac{q_i}{Q_g} \log \frac{q_i/Q_g}{p_i/P_g} \qquad i \in S_g \tag{4.3}$$

is the expected information of the message which transforms the conditional prior probabilities $p_i/P_g$ to the conditional posterior probabilities $q_i/Q_g$ ($i \in S_g$). Thus, (4.3) is confined to the $E$'s which fall under $S_g$, (4.2) refers solely to the $S$'s and is not concerned with the $E$'s at all, and (2.2) considers all $E$'s.

Consider now a weighted average of the $G$ conditional information expectations (4.3) with weights equal to the corresponding posterior probabilities $Q_g$:

$$\begin{aligned}
\sum_{g=1}^{G} Q_g\, I_g(q:p) &= \sum_{g=1}^{G} \sum_{i \in S_g} q_i \log \frac{q_i/Q_g}{p_i/P_g}\,, \\
&= \sum_{g=1}^{G} \sum_{i \in S_g} q_i \log q_i/p_i - \sum_{g=1}^{G} \sum_{i \in S_g} q_i \log Q_g/P_g\,, \\
&= \sum_{i=1}^{n} q_i \log q_i/p_i - \sum_{g=1}^{G} Q_g \log Q_g/P_g,
\end{aligned}$$

or equivalently:

$$I(q:p) = I_0(q:p) + \sum_{g=1}^{G} Q_g I_g(q:p) . \tag{4.4}$$

In words: The microscopic information expectation (2.2) is equal to the sum of the macroscopic information expectation (4.2) and a weighted average of the $G$ conditional information expectations (4.3), the weights being equal to the posterior probabilities $Q_1, \ldots, Q_G$.

We shall apply this decomposition to assets and liabilities information and take Table II as our starting point, which is a disaggregated version of Table I. It contains 11 assets as a whole, 5 of which fall under current assets, 2 under investments and non-current receivables, 3 under property, plant and equipment, while taxes and other expenses allocable to future years are not disaggregated. Similarly, the liabilities side contains now 13 items rather than 4.

Considering the assets side first, we define:

$S_1$ Current assets;

$S_2$ Investments and other noncurrent receivables;

$S_3$ Property, plant and equipment;

$S_4$ Taxes and other expenses allocable to future years.

The 1965 information expectation for the items following under current assets is then according to (4.3):

$$I_1(q:p) = \frac{238}{3733} \log \frac{238/3733}{154/3156} + \ldots + \frac{64}{3733} \log \frac{64/3733}{62/3156} = 3788 \times 10^{-6} \text{ bits.} \tag{4.5}$$

For $S_2$, $S_3$ and $S_4$ we obtain in the same way:

$$\begin{aligned} I_2(q:p) &= 3892 \times 10^{-6} \text{ bits,} \\ I_3(q:p) &= 628 \times 10^{-6} \text{ bits,} \\ I_4(q:p) &= 0. \end{aligned} \tag{4.6}$$

The conclusion is that for current assets ($S_1$) and investments and other noncurrent receivables ($S_2$) the behavior of the individual items was about equally close to proportionality; and that for the three items of plant, property and equipment ($S_3$) the proportionality assumption is satisfied more closely than for the components of $S_1$ and $S_2$. The zero value of $I_4(q:p)$ is due to the fact that $S_4$ is not disaggregated.

We proceed to consider the information decomposition (4.4). The left-hand side is found straightforwardly from the assets of Table II:

$$I(q{:}p) = \frac{238}{7596}\log\frac{238/7596}{154/6459} + \ldots + \frac{150}{7596}\log\frac{150/7596}{129/6459} = 2499\times 10^{-6}\text{ bits.} \quad (4.7)$$

The first right-hand term of (4.4), $I_0(q{:}p)$, is in the present application nothing other than the value computed in (3.1) for the original four assets. The decomposition (4.4) is therefore

$$2499 = 33 + \left(\frac{3733}{7596}\,3788 + \frac{693}{7596}\,3892 + \frac{3020}{7596}\,628 + \frac{150}{7596}\,0\right),$$

or in abbreviated form:

$$2499 = 33 + 2466 \qquad (\text{in } 10^{-6}\text{ bits}). \quad (4.8)$$

**TABLE II.** Disaggregated Balance Sheets for 1964 and 1965 ($10^6$ Dollars)

| Assets | 1965 | 1964 | Liabilities | 1965 | 1964 |
|---|---|---|---|---|---|
| *Current Assets* | | | *Current liabilities* | | |
| Cash | 238 | 154 | Accounts payable and accrued liabilities | 1772 | 1432 |
| Marketable securities | 900 | 740 | | | |
| Receivables | 862 | 756 | U.S. income taxes | 337 | 270 |
| Inventories | 1669 | 1444 | Foreign income taxes | 102 | 91 |
| Other current assets | 64 | 62 | Long-term debt, payable within one year | 30 | 21 |
| Total current Assets | 3733 | 3156 | | | |
| *Investments and noncurrent receivables* | | | Short-term debt of consolidated subsidiaries | 369 | 248 |
| Investments in subsidiaries | 635 | 548 | Total current liabilities | 2610 | 2062 |
| Other investments and noncurrent receivables | 58 | 38 | *Long-term debt* | 295 | 227 |
| | | | *Other liabilities and reserves* | | |
| Total investments and noncurrent receivables | 693 | 586 | Supplemental compensation reserve | 88 | 73 |
| *Property, plant and equipment* | | | Deferred investment credit | 37 | 22 |
| Property and plant less depreciation | 1070 | 922 | Reserve for foreign operations | 52 | 49 |
| Equipment less depreciation | 1504 | 1310 | Other | 24 | 15 |
| Special tools | 446 | 356 | Total other liabilities and reserves | 201 | 159 |
| Total property, plant and equipment | 3020 | 2588 | | | |
| | | | *Stockholders' equity* | | |
| *Taxes and other expenses allocable to future years* | 150 | 129 | Capital stock at par value | 278 | 277 |
| | | | Capital account in excess of par value | 331 | 322 |
| Total assets | 7596 | 6459 | | | |
| | | | Earnings retained for use in business | 3881 | 3412 |
| | | | Total stockbrokers' equity | 4490 | 4011 |
| | | | Total liabilities (including shareholders' equity) | 7596 | 6459 |

This result shows that the behavior of the four assets groups is much closer to proportionality than that of the individual assets within the groups. Note that the expression "the behavior of the individual assets within the groups" is to be interpreted in the sense of an average over the four groups; witness the zero value of $I_4(q{:}p)$.

We now proceed to the liabilities side to answer the question raised in the beginning of this section. If we confine ourselves to the liabilities of Table I in the narrow sense, we obtain for the 1965 liabilities information

$$\frac{2610}{7596-4490}\log\frac{2610/(7596-4490)}{2062/(6459-4011)}+\frac{295}{7596-4490}\log\frac{295/(7596-4490}{227/(6459-4011)} \qquad (4.9)$$
$$+\frac{201}{7596-4490}\log\frac{201/(7596-4490)}{159/(6459-4011)}=43\times10^{-6}\text{ bits.}$$

The relationship between this figure and that of (3.3) is easily established on the basis of the information decomposition (4.4). Define:

$S'_1$ Liabilities;
$S'_2$ Stockholders' equity.

Then the 1965 information which refers to these two categories only is

$$\frac{7596-4490}{7596}\log\frac{(7596-4490)/7596}{(6459-4011)/6459} \qquad (4.10)$$
$$+\frac{4490}{7596}\log\frac{4490/7596}{4011/6459}=2713\times10^{-6}\text{ bits.}$$

This is $I_0(q{:}p)$ under the present interpretation and $I(q{:}p)$ is now the value given in (3.3). Hence the information decomposition (4.4) takes the following numerical form:

$$2730=2713+\frac{7596-4490}{7596}43 \qquad (\text{in } 10^{-6}\text{ bits.}) \qquad (4.11)$$

The second right-hand term is the ratio of total liabilities to total liabilities plus stockholders' equity in 1965, multiplied by the value of (4.9). [Note that this is the only nonzero component of the weighted average in the right-hand side of (4.4), because stockholders' equity is considered here as one item.] We conclude from (4.11) that in this case the between-group term is much larger than the within-group term in contrast to (4.8) of the assets information decomposition. An inspection of Table I shows that this is due to the relatively small increase of stockholders' equity in comparison with that of the three liabilities in the narrow sense.

It goes without saying that additional decompositions are possible. For example, we may take Table II and its 10 liability items (in the narrow sense) as a starting point; we then compute $I(q{:}p)$ for these. Now current items, the long-term debt, and other liabilities and reserves are the three macroscopic liability items, so that the value of (4.9) is $I_0(q{:}p)$ under the present interpretation. The difference between $I(q{:}p)$ and $I_0(q{:}p)$ is then a weighted average of the three 1965 information values within the three liability groups. Similarly, one can compute the 1965 information for the three items of stockholders' equity. Such summarizing measures are particularly useful when the number of categories ($n$ or $G$) is large, because a simple inspection of the amounts in dollars is then no longer sufficient to obtain an adequate picture. Also, further subdivisions can be handled straightforwardly. For example, take marketable securities (one of the current assets). One may divide these securities into groups and analyze the development of the relative size of these groups. The decomposition (4.4) is applicable to this case also. However, even though it is true that the advantage of summarizing measures is greatest in complicated situations, we shall nevertheless continue presenting simple examples in order not to overburden the exposition.

## 5. Sales Information and Costs and Expenses Information

One can proceed in a fully analogous way for the two sides of the income statement. Thus, there is a 1965 cost and expense information as well as a 1965 sales information, the first being based on a breakdown of total costs and expenses per year and the second on a breakdown of total sales per year. The only difference is that total costs and expenses are not equal to total sales except for the case of zero net profits, whereas the equality of the two totals of the balance sheet do add up to the same number. It is possible to impose equality of the two totals of the income statement by adding net profits to costs and expenses, but this is not really attractive in view of the possibility of negative net profits, which cannot be handled by the probabilities of information theory. Of course, we have the same situation for total assets and liabilities when the stockholders' equity is deleted from the latter. Both this equity and net profits are actually residual items.[3]

An interesting case for consideration is that of sales distinguished according to two criteria, say area and kind of products. For example, let the sales of our company in 1964 and 1965 be 9671 and 11537, respectively, in millions of dollars per year, and let the breakdown by cars and other vehicles and by three regions of the United States and the rest of the world be as shown in Table III.

If we divide the 1964 figures by their total (9671), we obtain a rectangular array of numbers of the following form:

[3] Given this residual nature, stockholders' equity can be negative too. However, such near-bankruptcy situations are much less frequent than those of negative net profits in any given year.

$$\begin{array}{cccc|c} p_{11} & p_{12} & \cdots & p_{1n} & p_{1.} \\ p_{21} & p_{22} & \cdots & p_{2n} & p_{2.} \\ \vdots & \vdots & & \vdots & \vdots \\ p_{m1} & p_{m2} & \cdots & p_{mn} & p_{m.} \\ \hline p_{.1} & p_{.2} & \cdots & p_{.n} & 1 \end{array} \tag{5.1}$$

**TABLE III.** Sales in 1964 and 1965 ($10^6$ Dollars per Year)

| Region | Cars | Other vehicles | Total | Cars | Other vehicles | Total |
|---|---|---|---|---|---|---|
| | | 1965 | | | 1964 | |
| East | 3511 | 708 | 4219 | 3050 | 614 | 3664 |
| Center | 2516 | 671 | 3187 | 1850 | 550 | 2400 |
| West | 2023 | 535 | 2558 | 1790 | 402 | 2192 |
| Foreign countries | 977 | 596 | 1573 | 813 | 602 | 1415 |
| Total | 9027 | 2510 | 11537 | 7503 | 2168 | 9671 |

Thus, in our case $p_{11} = 3050/9671 \approx .315$, and so on, and $m = 4$ (the number of regions) and $n = 2$ (the number of products). For 1965 we have an array similar to (5.1), to be denoted by $q$'s instead of $p$'s. Consider then first the 1965 sales information by regions only:

$$\begin{aligned} I_R(q:p) &= \sum_{i=1}^{4} q_{i.} \log q_{i.}/p_{i.} \\ &= \frac{4219}{11537} \log \frac{4219/11537}{3664/9671} + \ldots + \frac{1573}{11537} \log \frac{1573/11537}{1415/9671} \\ &= 3123 \times 10^{-6} \text{ bits.} \end{aligned} \tag{5.2}$$

and the 1965 sales information by both regions and products:

$$I_{RP}(q:p) = \sum_{i=1}^{4} \sum_{j=1}^{2} q_{ij} \log q_{ij} / p_{ij}$$

$$= \frac{3511}{11537} \log \frac{3511/11537}{3050/9671} + \ldots + \frac{596}{11537} \log \frac{596/11537}{602/9671} \tag{5.3}$$

$$= 5089 \times 10^{-6} \quad \text{bits.}$$

We conclude that the latter information value exceeds the former. Consider their difference more explicitly:

$$I_{RP}(q:p) - I_R(q:p) = \sum_{i=1}^{4} \sum_{j=1}^{2} q_{ij} \, [\log q_{ij}/p_{ij} - \log q_{i.}/p_{i.}]$$
$$= \sum_{i=1}^{4} q_{i.} \sum_{j=1}^{2} q_{ij}/q_{i.} \log (q_{ij}/q_{i.})/(p_{ij}/p_{i.}) \,. \tag{5.4}$$

Now $p_{ij}/p_{i\cdot}$ for $j = 1$ represents the sales of cars in 1964 in the $i^{\text{th}}$ region measured as a fraction of total sales in that region in that year. Similarly, $p_{ij}/p_{i\cdot}$ for $j = 2$ has the same interpretation except that it refers to other vehicles, and $q_{ij}/q_{i\cdot}$ is also similar except that it deals with the 1965 data. Therefore, the expression

$$\sum_{j=1}^{2} q_{ij}/q_{i.} \log (q_{ij}/q_{i.})/(p_{ij}/p_{i.}) \,, \qquad i = 1, \ldots, 4 \,, \tag{5.5}$$

is the 1965 sales information by products of the $i^{\text{th}}$ region. We conclude from (5.4) that the *excess of the 1965 sales information by regions and products over the 1965 information by regions only is equal to a weighted average of the 1965 sales information values by products of the individual regions*, the weights being equal to the regions' shares of total sales ($q_{i\cdot}$). In our case the four successive values of (5.5) are

0 1445 3087 6465 (in $10^{-6}$ bits)

so that the decomposition (5.4) takes the following numerical form

$$5089 - 3123 = \frac{4219}{11537} 0 + \frac{3187}{11537} 1445 + \frac{2558}{11537} 2558 + \frac{1573}{11537} 6465 \,. \tag{5.6}$$

It should be intuitively obvious that a similar decomposition is obtained when we interchange the roles of regions and products. This does not affect $I_{RP}(q{:}p)$, but instead of $I_R(q{:}p)$ we obtain

$$\begin{aligned} IP(q{:}p) &= \sum_{j=1}^{2} q_{.j} \log q_{.j}/p_{.j} \\ &= \frac{9027}{11537}\log\frac{9027/11537}{7503/9671} + \frac{2510}{11537}\log\frac{2510/11537}{2168/9671} = 183\times10^{-6} \text{ bits} \end{aligned} \tag{5.7}$$

which is the 1965 sales information by products. The difference between this information value and $I_{RP}(q{:}p)$ is

$$\begin{aligned} I_{RP}(q{:}p) - I_p(q{:}p) &= \sum_{i=1}^{4}\sum_{j=1}^{2} q_{ij}\,[\,\log q_{ij}/p_{ij} - \log q_{.j}/p_{.j}\,] \\ &= \sum_{j=1}^{2} q_{.j}\sum_{i=1}^{4} q_{ij}/q_{.j}\log\,(q_{ij}/q_{.j})/(p_{ij}/p_{.j})\,. \end{aligned} \tag{5.8}$$

The expression on the second line is a weighted average (with weights $q_{.j}$, the products' shares of total sales) of the 1965 information values by regions of the two products.

## 6. Measuring the Degree of Dependence of Double-Entry Sales Statements

The exposition until this point has dealt exclusively with changes in a number of items from one year to the next. In this section we will be concerned with data of one year only.

The problem to be considered can be illustrated with the data of Table III. We observe that in 1964 the sales of cars were a fraction 7503/9671 ≈ .776 of total sales. If we confine ourselves to sales abroad, however, this fraction is only 813/1415 ≈ .575. If such fractions were the same for every region, the distribution of sales over regions and products would be characterized by (stochastic) independence. For the data of Table III this is evidently not the case, and it may be considered interesting to have a quantitative measure for the degree of dependence. The objective of this section is to formulate and analyze such a measure.

Consider the bivariate probability array (5.1) and in particular the expression

$$\log p_{ij}/p_{i.}p_{.j}\,, \qquad i = 1,\ldots,m, \qquad j = 1,\ldots,n\,. \tag{6.1}$$

In communication theory the first index ($i$) frequently refers to the message sent and the second ($j$) to the message received. In that context the expression (6.1) is known as the mutual information of the $i^{\text{th}}$ message sent and the $j^{\text{th}}$ message received. Note that the mutual information vanishes in the case of stochastic independence ($p_{ij} = p_{i.}p_{.j}$), that it is positive when the $j^{\text{th}}$ message is received more frequently after the $i^{\text{th}}$ is sent than the independence pattern implies ($p_{ij} > p_{i.}p_{.j}$), and that it is negative in the opposite case. If we weight the mutual information values by the corresponding probabilities $p_{ij}$, we obtain

$$I_{RP} = \sum_{i=1}^{m} \sum_{j=1}^{n} p_{ij} \log p_{ij} / p_{i.} p_{.j} \tag{6.2}$$

which is known as the *expected mutual information* of the messages sent and received. In the sales case we interpret $I_{RP}$ as the expected mutual information of regions and products, as the subscripts $R$ and $P$ indicate.

It is seen immediately that $I_{RP}$ can be regarded as the expected information of a message corresponding to $p_{i.}p_{.j}$ as prior probabilities and $p_{ij}$ as posterior probabilities [see (2.2)]. Therefore, $I_{RP}$ is nonnegative and it is zero if and only if the prior and posterior probabilities are all pairwise equal: $p_{ij} = p_{i.}p_{.j}$ for all values of the subscripts. This means that $I_{RP} = 0$ in the case of independence and $I_{RP} > 0$ as soon as there is no independence.

The role of $I_{RP}$ as a measure of the degree of dependence can be illustrated further when we consider the entropy concept (2.1) and apply it to the bivariate distribution and the two marginal distributions. The 1964 entropy of sales by regions and products jointly is

$$H(R,P) = \sum_{i=1}^{m} \sum_{j=1}^{n} p_{ij} \log 1/p_{ij} \tag{6.3}$$

and the entropies by regions only and by products only are

$$H(R) = \sum_{i=1}^{m} p_{i.} \log 1/p_{i.}, \qquad H(P) = \sum_{j=1}^{n} p_{.j} \log 1/p_{.j} \tag{6.4}$$

Consider then the excess of the sum of the two marginal entropies over the bivariate entropy:

$$
\begin{aligned}
H(R)+H(P)-H(R,P) &= \sum_{i=1}^{m}\sum_{j=1}^{n} p_{ij}[\log 1/p_{i.} + \log 1/p_{.j} - \log 1/p_{ij}] \\
&= \sum_{i=1}^{m}\sum_{j=1}^{n} p_{ij}\log p_{ij}/p_{i.}p_{.j} \qquad (6.5)\\
&= I_{RP}
\end{aligned}
$$

We conclude that the entropy by regions plus the entropy by products is equal to the entropy by both regions and products if and only if $I_{RP} = 0$, i.e., if and only if the distribution of sales by regions and products is characterized by independence. In all other cases the joint entropy is *less* than the sum of the two marginal entropies and the difference is equal to the expected mutual information. Intuitively, this result is not difficult to understand. For entropy is a measure of uncertainty and in this case there is uncertainty of two kinds: What is sold and where is it sold? If "what" and "where" are independent, the joint uncertainty as measured by $H(R,P)$ is equal to the sum of the two separate uncertainties (because entropy is an additive concept, see the second paragraph of section 2). If "what" and "where" are dependent, the joint uncertainty is reduced relative to the separate uncertainties just because of this dependence, since a definite message on "what" partially removes the uncertainty as to "where" (and vice versa).

The reduction just mentioned can be shown more explicitly when we consider entropies of conditonal distributions. Take the $i^{\text{th}}$ region, for which the sales distribution over products is determined by the proportions $p_{i1}/p_{i.}, \ldots, p_{in}/p_{i.}$ ($n = 2$ in the case of Table III). The entropy of this distribution is

$$
H_{R_i}(P) = \sum_{j=1}^{n} p_{ij}/p_{i.} \log p_{i.}/p_{ij}, \qquad i = 1, \ldots, m, \qquad (6.6)
$$

where the subscript $R_i$ on the left indicates that this is the conditional sales entropy by products, the condition being that sales take place in the $i^{\text{th}}$ region. Next we take a weighted average of these conditional entropies with weights equal to the regional sales shares:

$$
\begin{aligned}
H_R(P) &= \sum_{i=1}^{m} P_{i.} H_{R_i}(P) \\
&= \sum_{i=1}^{m}\sum_{j=1}^{n} p_{ij}\log p_{i.}/p_{ij}\,. \qquad (6.7)
\end{aligned}
$$

This is the *average conditional sales entropy by products, given the regions.* It is equal to the excess of the two-dimensional entropy $H(R,P)$ over the one-dimensional marginal entropy of the condition $(R)$:

$$H_R(P) = H(R,P) - H(R) \tag{6.8}$$

which is verified as follows:

$$\begin{aligned} H(R,P) - H(R) &= \sum_{i=1}^{m}\sum_{j=1}^{n} p_{ij}[\log 1/p_{ij} - \log 1/p_{i.}] \\ &= \sum_{i=1}^{m}\sum_{j=1}^{n} p_{ij}\log p_{i.}/p_{ij} \qquad \text{[see (6.7)].} \\ &= H_R(P) \, , \end{aligned}$$

Two things ought to be noted. *First,* since $H_R(P)$ is a weighted average with non-negative weights of the nonnegative entropies (6.6), it is nonnegative itself. Hence (6.8) implies that the joint entropy cannot be smaller than the marginal entropy $H(R)$. The latter two entropies are equal if and only if $H_R(P) = 0$, *i.e.*, if and only if each of the conditional entropies (6.6) are zero for which $p_{i.} > 0$, which in the sales case requires that in each of the four regions either only cars be sold or only other vehicles but not both. This condition is obviously not fulfilled by the data of Table III, so that $H_R(P) > 0$. *Second,* the excess of the marginal entropy $H(P)$ by products over the average conditional entropy $H_R(P)$ by products given the regions is equal to the expected mutual information $I_{RP}$:

$$\begin{aligned} H(P) - H_R(P) &= \sum_{i=1}^{m}\sum_{j=1}^{n} p_{ij}[\log 1/p_{.j} - \log p_{i.}/p_{ij}] \\ &= \sum_{i=1}^{m}\sum_{j=1}^{n} p_{ij}\log p_{ij}/p_{i.}p_{.j} \qquad \text{[see (6.2)]} \\ &= I_{RP} \, , \end{aligned}$$

The left-hand side stands for the average reduction of uncertainty as to the kind of products sold (cars or other vehicles) when the region in which the sales take place is known. The equation implies that this is equal to the expected mutual information and hence always positive except when "what" and "where" are independent, in which case there is a zero average reduction of uncertainty.

**TABLE IV.** Sales Entropy by Regions and Products in 1964 and 1965 (Bits)

| Symbol | Brief description | 1965 | 1964 |
|---|---|---|---|
| $H(R,P)$ | Joint entropy | 2.6556 | 2.6601 |
| $H(R)$ | Entropy by regions | 1.9172 | 1.9205 |
| $H(P)$ | Entropy by products | .7557 | .7677 |
| $I_{RP}$ | Expected mutual information | .0173 | .0282 |
| $H_P(R)$ | Conditional entropy by regions | 1.8999 | 1.8924 |
| $H_R(P)$ | Conditional entropy by products | .7384 | .7396 |

It will be obvious that one can interchange the roles of regions and products. Consider

$$H_{P_j}(R) = \sum_{i=1}^{m} p_{ij}/p_{.j} \log p_{.j}/p_{ij}, \qquad j = 1, \ldots, n, \tag{6.10}$$

which is the conditional sales entropy by regions of the $j^{\text{th}}$ product ($j$ = 1, cars; $j$ = 2, other vehicles). The average conditional sales entropy by regions, given the products, is

$$\begin{aligned} H_P(R) &= \sum_{j=1}^{n} p_{.j} H_{P_j}(R) \\ &= \sum_{i=1}^{m} \sum_{j=1}^{n} p_{ij} \log p_{.j}/p_{ij} \end{aligned} \tag{6.11}$$

which satisfies

$$H_P(R) = H(R,P) - H(P) = H(R) - I_{RP} \tag{6.12}$$

in accordance with (6.8) and (6.9) when $P$ and $R$ are interchanged. For the interpretation see the previous paragraph.

It was announced at the beginning of this section that we would consider data of one year only, not changes from year to year as in the previous section. In fact, we are considering here only the distribution of sales over regions and products in any given period. On the other hand, one will frequently be interested in the development over time of such one-period measures. For the figures of Table III they are shown in Table IV for 1964 and 1965. The entropy by regions is close to the maximum value of 2 bits (for $4 = 2^2$ regions) and the entropy by products is much smaller relative to its maximum (1 bit for 2 products); this reflects the domination of cars over other vehicles. The joint entropy is close to the sum of these marginal entropies, witness the small (and declining) value of the expected mutual information. The conclusion is that sales by regions and products are close to independence and that they moved even closer to independence in 1965. Consequently, the average conditional entropies are not much below the corresponding marginal entropies.

## 7. A Bivariate Interpretation of the Balance Sheet; The Information Balance Sheet

We return to annual changes in the items of the balance sheet in order to apply some of the bivariate ideas discussed in the last two sections. Consider then the balance sheets of Table I and note that current assets on the left and current liabilities on the right are similar to the extent that both are concerned with current items. Similarly, property, plant, and equipment on the left and stockholders' equity on the right are comparable in that both are concerned with fixed items.[4] Finally, let us make the simplifying assumption that all other items are medium-term. This applies on the left to investments and noncurrent receivables as well as taxes and other expenses on the right. Clearly, in doing so we apply similar labels to assets and liabilities, so that the two balance sheets can be written in the form of Table V.

**TABLE V.** Bivariate Balance Sheets for 1964 and 1965 ($10^6$ Dollars)

| Time Horizon | Assets | Liabilities | Total | Assets | Liabilities | Total |
|---|---|---|---|---|---|---|
| | 1965 | | | 1964 | | |
| Current | 3733 | 2610 | 6343 | 3156 | 2062 | 5218 |
| Medium-term | 843 | 496 | 1339 | 715 | 386 | 1101 |
| Fixed | 3020 | 4490 | 7510 | 2588 | 4011 | 6599 |
| Total | 7596 | 7596 | 15192 | 6459 | 6459 | 12918 |

A comparison of this table with Table III shows that they have the same general format, the major difference being that the column sums of Table V are always equal. It is therefore interesting to apply the approach of section 5 to the balance sheets in the bivariate form of Table V and see to what extent this difference leads to interesting special results. For this purpose we divide the 1964 figures by 12918 and those of 1965 by 15192 and we denote the resulting ratios by $p_{ij}$ and $q_{ij}$, respectively. The index $i$ takes the values 1 (current) and 2 (medium-term) and 3 (fixed); the index $j$ takes only two values, 1 (assets) and 2 (liabilities). For the marginal probabilities we have

$$p_{.j} = q_{.j} = \frac{1}{2} \quad for \quad j = 1 \text{ and } 2 \tag{7.1}$$

[4] Note that in this and in the next sections stockholders' equity is regarded as part of total liabilities.

in view of the equality of total assets and total liabilities. The row totals $p_{1.}, q_{1.}$ (total current items), $p_{2.}, q_{2.}$ (total medium-term items) and $p_{3.}, q_{3.}$ (total fixed items) are not subject to any restrictions of the type (7.1).

Consider then the 1965 information of the bivariate type:

$$I(q:p) = \sum_{i=1}^{3} \sum_{j=1}^{2} q_{ij} \log q_{ij} / p_{ij}$$

$$= \frac{3733}{15192} \log \frac{3733/15192}{3156/12918} + \ldots + \frac{4490}{15192} \log \frac{4490/15192}{4011/12918} \tag{7.2}$$

$$= 1376 \times 10^{-6} \text{ bits.}$$

This will be called the 1965 *balance sheet information*, because it is based on all items of the balance sheet simultaneously, both assets and liabilities. It is an aggregative measure for the changes in the relative positions of all assets and liabilities jointly. Clearly, this $I(q:p)$ has the same mathematical form as $I_{RP}(q:p)$ of (5.3).

Next, consider the following decomposition:

$$I(q:p) = \sum_{j=1}^{2} q_{.j} \sum_{i=1}^{3} \frac{q_{ij}}{q_{.j}} \left[ \log \frac{q_{ij}/q_{.j}}{p_{ij}/p_{.j}} + \log \frac{q_{.j}}{p_{.j}} \right]$$

$$= \sum_{j=1}^{2} q_{.j} \sum_{i=1}^{3} \frac{q_{ij}}{q_{.j}} \log \frac{q_{ij}/q_{.j}}{p_{ij}/p_{.j}} + \sum_{j=1}^{2} q_{.j} \log \frac{q_{.j}}{p_{.j}} .$$

The last term on the second line vanishes in view of (7.1). The first term can be written as

$$\frac{1}{2} \sum_{i=1}^{3} (2q_{i1}) \log 2q_{i1} / 2p_{i1} + \frac{1}{2} \sum_{i=1}^{3} (2q_{i2}) \log 2q_{i2} / 2p_{i2} .$$

This is simply one-half of the 1965 assets information plus one-half of the 1965 liabilities information (see section 3), because $2q_{i1} = q_{i1}/\frac{1}{2} = q_{i1}/q_{i.}$ is the 1965 value of the $i^{\text{th}}$ asset measured as a fraction of total assets, $2q_{i2}$ is the 1965 value of the $i^{\text{th}}$ liability measured as a fraction of total liabilities (including stockholders' equity and similarly for $2p_{i1}$ and $2p_{i2}$ for 1964. We thus have:

$$I(q:p) = (I_A(q:p) + I_L(q:p))/2 . \tag{7.3}$$

In words: *The balance sheet information is equal to the arithmetic mean of the assets information $I_A(q{:}p)$ and the liabilities information $I_L(q{:}p)$.* For the latter two information values we obtain on the basis of Table V:

$$\begin{aligned} I_A(q{:}p) &= \sum_{i=1}^{3} (2q_{i1}) \log 2q_{i1}/2p_{i1} = 30 \times 10^{-6} \text{ bits} \\ I_L(q{:}p) &= \sum_{i=1}^{3} (2q_{i2}) \log 2q_{i2}/2p_{i2} = 2722 \times 10^{-6} \text{ bits}, \end{aligned} \tag{7.4}$$

the average of which is indeed equal to the value of (7.2). Note that $I_A(q{:}p)$ is smaller than the value of (3.1) and $I_L(q{:}p)$ smaller than that of (3.3). It is easily verified that this is in accordance with the aggregation analysis of section 4, since two assets items and two liability items of Table I are combined to one item each in Table V. This reduces the information expectation by a nonnegative amount [the within-group term of the decomposition (4.4)].

We have the following alternative decomposition of the balance sheet information:

$$\begin{aligned} I(q{:}p) &= \sum_{i=1}^{3} q_{i.} \sum_{j=1}^{2} \frac{q_{ij}}{q_{i.}} \left[ \log \frac{q_{ij}/q_{i.}}{p_{ij}/p_{i.}} + \log \frac{q_{i.}}{p_{i.}} \right] \\ &= \sum_{i=1}^{3} q_{i.} \left[ \sum_{j=1}^{2} \frac{q_{ij}}{q_{i.}} \log \frac{q_{ij}/q_{i.}}{p_{ij}/p_{i.}} \right] + \sum_{i=1}^{3} q_{i.} \log \frac{q_{i.}}{p_{i.}} . \end{aligned} \tag{7.5}$$

First, consider the last term on the second line:

$$I_T(q{:}p) = \sum_{i=1}^{3} q_{i.} \log q_{i.}/p_{i.} . \tag{7.6}$$

This is the expected information associated with $p_{1.}$, $p_{2.}$ and $p_{3.}$ as prior probabilities and $q_{1.}$,$q_{2.}$ and $q_{3.}$ as posterior probabilities. Evidently, $I_T(q{:}p)$ is concerned with changes in the relative positions of all current items (assets and liabilities combined), all medium-term items, and all fixed items. As an example, suppose $p_{1.} < q_{1.}$, $p_{2.} = q_{2.}$, $p_{3.} > q_{3.}$ ; then the relative position of fixed items decreased in favor of current items, medium-term items remaining at the same level, so that the company's assets and liabilities have become more "current" as a whole. The information expectation (7.6) measures this kind of change. We shall refer to it as the 1965 *time horizon information.* Note again that it refers to assets and liabilities jointly.

The first term on the second line of (7.5) does make a distinction between assets and liabilities. Consider the expression in square brackets for $i = 1$:

$$\frac{q_{11}}{q_{1.}} \log \frac{q_{11}/q_{1.}}{p_{11}/p_{1.}} + \frac{q_{12}}{q_{1.}} \log \frac{q_{12}/q_{1.}}{p_{12}/p_{1.}} \,. \tag{7.7}$$

The ratio $q_{11}/q_{1.}$ is the amount of current assets expressed as a fraction of current items plus current liabilities; similarly, $q_{12}/q_{1.}$ is current liabilities expressed in the same way and $p_{11}/p_{1.}$ and $p_{12}/p_{1.}$ are analogous ratios for the earlier year. The information expectation (7.7) is zero if and only if $p_{11}/p_{1.} = q_{11}/q_{1.}$ and $p_{12}/p_{1.} = q_{12}/q_{1.}$, which means that the ratio of current assets to current liabilities remains unchanged during the two consecutive years. We have a positive expectation as soon as this ratio changes. Therefore, we shall call the expression (7.7) the 1965 *current items information.* In the same way we shall refer to the expression in square brackets on the second line of (7.5) for $i = 2$ as the 1965 *medium-term items information* and for $i = 3$ as the 1965 *fixed items information.* Thus, the decomposition (7.5) implies that *the balance sheet information is equal to the time horizon information plus a weighted average of the current items, medium-term items, and fixed items information*, the weights being equal to the items' shares of the 1965 balance sheet.

The conclusion is that there are two different decompositions of the balance sheet information, (7.3) and (7.5). The latter will be called the *time horizon decomposition*, the former the *assets and liabilities decomposition.* A convenient presentation is in the form of the *information balance sheet* shown in Table VI. The assets and liabilities side was discussed in section 3, so it need not be considered here. The time horizon information is in this example larger than but of the same order of magnitude as the weighted average on the second line (7.5), which means that on the average the deviations from a proportional development between and within the current, medium-term and fixed groups are of comparable size. However, there are sizable differences between these three groups, since the ratio of medium-term assets to medium-term liabilities gives rise to a considerably larger information value than the corresponding ratio of the fixed items.

**TABLE VI.** Information Balance Sheet, 1965-64 ($10^{-6}$ Bits)

| Time horizon decomposition | | Assets and liabilities decomposition | |
|---|---|---|---|
| $I_1$ Current items information | 799 | $I_A$ Assets information | 30 |
| $I_2$ Medium-term items information | 1236 | $I_L$ Liabilities information | 2722 |
| $I_3$ Fixed items information | 299 | Arithmetic Mean | 1376 |
| Weighted mean | 590 | Balance sheet information | 1376 |
| $I_T$ Time horizon information | 786 | | |
| Balance sheet information | 1376 | | |

## 8. Intercompany Comparisons

Our information measures with the exception of those of section 6 deal with changes from one year to the next. Basically, they are all of the form

$$\sum_{i} q_i \log q_i / p_i \tag{8.1}$$

where the $q$'s are this year's and the $p$'s are last year's fractions. Note that (8.1) is symmetric in the two years; if we interchange the $p$'s and $q$'s we obtain a different measure. This is not serious for intertemporal comparisons, because time moves in a unilateral manner and any questions on a behavior over time are therefore inherently symmetric. This is not true, however, for intercompany comparisons. If we compare the assets of company $A$ with those of company $B$ and use (8.1) for this purpose with the $p$'s interpreted as the assets fractions of $A$ and the $q$'s as those of $B$, we obtain a result which is not invariant against interchanging the roles of the two companies. This is clearly unsatisfactory.

It is possible, however, to use informational measures for a comparison of all companies of the same industry in any given year. The objective of this section is to present such a cross-section extension for the analysis of Section 7. Let the industry consist of $N$ industries; see Table VII for a numerical example ($N = 3$). Write $q_{ij}$ for any asset or liability of the $c^{\text{th}}$ company measured as a fraction of total assets plus total liabilities of that company. Specifically, $q_{i1c}$ stands for the $i^{\text{th}}$ asset and $q_{i2c}$ for the $i^{\text{th}}$ liability, measured in the way indicated. Hence $q_{ijc}$ is similar to $q_{ij}$ of Section 7 except that the year 1965 is now irrelevant but that the company index $c$ is relevant. Next, define

**TABLE VII.** Bivariate Balance Sheets of Three Companies

| Time horizon | Assets | Liabilities | Total |
|---|---|---|---|
| | | *Company 1* | |
| Current | 3733 | 2610 | 6343 |
| Medium-term | 843 | 496 | 1339 |
| Fixed | 3020 | 4490 | 7510 |
| Total | 7596 | 7596 | 15192 |
| | | *Company 2* | |
| Current | 5510 | 4520 | 10030 |
| Medium-term | 1503 | 1433 | 2936 |
| Fixed | 4080 | 5140 | 9220 |
| Total | 11093 | 11093 | 22186 |
| | | *Company 3* | |
| Current | 2020 | 1070 | 3090 |
| Medium-term | 518 | 604 | 1122 |
| Fixed | 2540 | 3404 | 5944 |
| Total | 5078 | 5078 | 10156 |
| | | *Industry* | |
| Current | 11263 | 8200 | 19463 |
| Medium-term | 2864 | 2533 | 5397 |
| Fixed | 9640 | 13034 | 22674 |
| Total | 23767 | 23767 | 47534 |

$$w_c = \text{total assets of } c^{th} \text{ company / total assets of industry} \qquad (8.2)$$
$$= \text{total liabilities of } c^{th} \text{ company / total liabilities of industry} .$$

Obviously, $w_1, \cdots, w_N$ are nonnegative fractions adding up to unity. We also define

$$p_{ij} = \sum_{c=1}^{N} w_c q_{ijc} , \qquad i = 1, 2, 3; \quad j = 1, 2, \qquad (8.3)$$

which is the $i^{\text{th}}$ asset ($j$ = 1) or the $i^{\text{th}}$ liability ($j$ = 2) of the industry measured as a fraction of total assets plus total liabilities of the industry. Take *e.g.* $j = 1$:

$$\sum_{c=1}^{N} w_c q_{i1c}$$
$$= \sum_{c=1}^{N} \text{total assets of c}^{\text{th}} \text{ company/total assets of industry}$$
$$\times \, i^{th} \text{ asset of } c^{th} \text{ company/2 (total assets of } c^{th} \text{ company)}$$
$$= \sum_{c=1}^{N} (i^{th} \text{ asset of } c^{th} \text{ company})/2 \text{ (total assets of industry)} = p_{i1} .$$

We shall now regard the industry's $p_{ij}$ as a prior probability and the company's $q_{ijc}$ (for an arbitrary company) as the corresponding posterior probability. The expected information of this message is

$$\sum_{i=1}^{3} \sum_{j=1}^{2} q_{ijc} \log q_{ijc}/p_{ij} , \qquad c = 1, \ldots, N . \qquad (8.4)$$

This expression vanishes when the balance sheet of the $c^{\text{th}}$ company is identical with that of the industry as a whole except for a scale factor, and it is positive otherwise. Obviously, the information values (8.4) will generally vary from company to company. We obtain a measure for all companies of the industry jointly by taking a weighted average with the $w$'s as weights:

$$I(q:p) = \sum_{c=1}^{N} w_c \sum_{i=1}^{3} \sum_{j=1}^{2} q_{ijc} \log q_{ijc}/p_{ij} . \qquad (8.5)$$

This is the *industry-wide balance sheet information.* It measures the extent to which the relative positions of the balance sheet items of the individual companies differ from those of the industry as a whole, or equivalently, the extent to which these relative positions differ among companies.

We proceed to consider the decompositions of the information value (8.5) and note that $2q_{i1c}$ and $2p_{i1}$ are the $i^{\text{th}}$ assets measured as a fraction of total assets for the $c^{\text{th}}$ company and for the industry, respectively. Hence

$$\sum_{i=1}^{3} (2q_{i1c}) \log q_{i1c}/p_{i1}$$

is the assets information when we use the industry assets fractions as prior probabilities and those of the $c^{\text{th}}$ company as posterior probabilities. Their weighted average:

$$I_A(q:p) = 2\sum_{c=1}^{N} w_c \sum_{i=1}^{3} q_{i1c} \log q_{i1c}/p_{i1} \tag{8.6}$$

is the *industry-wide assets information*, which measures the extent to which the assets structures of the individual companies differ from each other. It is verified straightforwardly that

$$I_L(q:p) = 2\sum_{c=1}^{N} w_c \sum_{i=1}^{3} q_{i2c} \log q_{i2c}/p_{i2} \tag{8.7}$$

can in the same way be regarded as the *industry-wide liabilities information*, and that

$$I(q:p) = (I_A(q:p) + I_L(q:p))/2 \tag{8.8}$$

is true for the definitions (8.5), (8.6), and (8.7), which is the same result as (7.3) for intertemporal comparisons of balance sheets of the same company.

To consider the time horizon decomposition we introduce

$$p_{i.} = \sum_{j=1}^{2} p_{ij}, \qquad q_{i.c} = \sum_{j=1}^{2} q_{ijc}, \qquad i = 1, 2, 3;\ c = 1, \ldots, N, \tag{8.9}$$

which are, for $i$ = 1, the fractions of current items (assets plus liabilities) of the industry and the $c^{\text{th}}$ company,, respectively; the interpretation for $i$ = 2 (medium-term) and $i$ = 3 (fixed) is analogous. The decomposition of (8.4) corresponding to (7.5) is then as follows:

$$\sum_{i=1}^{3}\sum_{j=1}^{2} q_{ijc}\log q_{ijc}/p_{ij} = \sum_{i=1}^{3} q_{i.c}\sum_{j=1}^{2}\frac{q_{ijc}}{q_{i.c}}\left[\log\frac{q_{ijc}/q_{i.c}}{p_{ij}/p_{i.}} + \log\frac{q_{i.c}}{p_{i.}}\right] \tag{8.10}$$

$$= \sum_{i=1}^{3} q_{i.c}\left[\sum_{j=1}^{2} q_{ijc}/q_{i.c}\log\frac{q_{ijc}/q_{i.c}}{p_{ij}/p_{i.}}\right] + \sum_{i=1}^{3} q_{i.c}\log q_{i.c}/p_{i.}\ .$$

When we take a weighted average with the $w$'s as weights, the second term on the last line becomes

$$I_T(q{:}p) = \sum_{c=1}^{N} w_c \sum_{i=1}^{3} q_{i.c}\log q_{i.c}/p_{i.} \tag{8.11}$$

which is the *industry-wide time horizon information*. It measures the extent to which the relative positions of current, medium-term and fixed items vary among the companies of the industry.

The weighted average of the first term of the last line of (8.10) is written as follows:

$$\sum_{c=1}^{N} w_c \sum_{i=1}^{3} q_{i.c}\left[\sum_{j=1}^{2}\frac{q_{ijc}}{q_{i.c}}\log\frac{q_{ijc}/q_{i.c}}{p_{ij}/p_{i.}}\right]$$

$$= \sum_{i=1}^{3} p_{i.}\left[\sum_{c=1}^{N}\frac{w_c q_{i.c}}{p_{i.}}\sum_{j=1}^{2}\frac{q_{ijc}}{q_{i.c}}\log\frac{q_{ijc}/q_{i.c}}{p_{ij}/p_{i.}}\right] \tag{8.12}$$

$$= \sum_{i=1}^{3} p_{i.} I_i(q{:}p)$$

where

$$I_i(q{:}p) = \sum_{c=1}^{N}\frac{w_c q_{i.c}}{p_{i.}}\sum_{j=1}^{2}\frac{q_{ijc}}{q_{i.c}}\log\frac{q_{ijc}/q_{i.c}}{p_{ij}/p_{i.}}\ . \tag{8.13}$$

Note that $I_i(q{:}p)$ is a weighted average of $N$ information expectations corresponding to the prior probabilities $p_{i1}/p_{i.}$ and $p_{i2}/p_{i.}$ and the posterior probabilities $q_{i1c}/q_{i.c}$ and $q_{i2c}/q_{i.c}$. The weights are of the form $w_c q_{i.c}/p_{i.}$, which measures company $c$'s share of total current items ($i = 1$), total medium-term items ($i = 2$), or total fixed items ($i = 3$); it follows from (8.3) and (8.9) that these weights add up to unity. It will be obvious that the expressions $I_i(q{:}p)$ measure the differences between the companies' ratios of current assets to current liabilities ($i$ = 1), of medium-term assets to medium-term liabilities ($i$ = 2), and of fixed assets to fixed liabilities ($i$ = 3), and that weighting takes place in accordance with the company's size as far as the relevant item ($i$) is concerned. We shall therefore call $I_1(q{:}p)$ the *industry-wide current items information* and use an analogous terminology for $I_2(q{:}p)$ and $I_3(q{:}p)$.

On combining (8.10) - (8.12) we thus have the following time horizon decomposition:

$$I(q{:}p) = \sum_{i=1}^{3} p_{i.} I_i(q{:}p) + I_T(q{:}p) \tag{8.14}$$

which is completely analogous to (7.5) except that the weights $p_{i.}$ in (8.14) are prior probabilities, whereas the weights $q_{i.}$ before the square brackets in (7.5) are posterior probabilities. [It will be obvious that we cannot use the posterior $q_{i.c}$ as weights in the present decomposition because of their dependence on the index $c$ of the individual company.] Apart from this exception we have an *industry-wide information balance sheet* comparable to Table VI for intertemporal comparisons. The information balance sheet corresponding to Table VII is given in Table VIII, the interpretation of which is straightforward. Note that the information values of Table VIII (in $10^{-4}$ bits) are larger than those of Table VI. One should expect that this is normally the case, since the structure of balance sheets of different companies usually differs more than that of successive balance sheets of the same company.

We conclude this section by noting that the intercompany analysis can also be formulated in terms of three-variate information concepts. For this purpose we express the assets and liabilities of each company as fractions of total assets plus total liabilities of the industry:

$$\begin{aligned} r_{i1c} &= i^{th} \text{ asset of } c^{th} \text{ company} / 2\,(\text{total assets of industry})\,, \\ r_{i2c} &= i^{th} \text{ liability of } c^{th} \text{ company} / 2\,(\text{total liabilities of industry})\,. \end{aligned} \tag{8.15}$$

**TABLE VIII.** Industry-Wide Information Balance Sheet ($10^{-4}$ Bits)

| Time horizon decomposition | | Assets and liabilities decomposition | |
|---|---|---|---|
| $I_1$ Current items information | 41.0 | $I_A$ Assets information | 81.7 |
| $I_2$ Medium-term items information | 105.6 | $I_L$ Liabilities information | 283.1 |
| $I_3$ Fixed items information | 8.9 | | |
| Weighted mean | 33.0 | Arithmetic mean | 182.4 |
| $I_T$ Time horizon information | 149.4 | | |
| Balance sheet information | 182.4 | Balance sheet information | 182.4 |

The sum of $r_{ijc}$ over $i$, $j$, and $c$ is equal to unity, so that the $r$'s can be regarded as probabilities of a three-variate distribution. When indicating by dots as subscripts summation over the corresponding index, we have

$$\begin{aligned} r_{.1.} &= r_{.2.} = \frac{1}{2} \\ r_{..c} &= 2r_{.1c} = 2r_{.2c} = w_c \\ r_{ij.} &= p_{ij} \\ r_{ijc}/r_{..c} &= q_{ijc} \,. \end{aligned} \tag{8.16}$$

The industry-wide balance sheet information (8.5) can then be expressed in the $r$'s as follows:

$$\begin{aligned} I(q:p) &= \sum_{c=1}^{N} r_{..c} \sum_{i=1}^{3} \sum_{j=1}^{2} (r_{ijc}/r_{..c}) \log (r_{ijc}/r_{..c})/r_{ij.} \\ &= \sum_{c=1}^{N} \sum_{i=1}^{3} \sum_{j=1}^{2} r_{ijc} \log 1/r_{ij.} - \sum_{c=1}^{N} \sum_{i=1}^{3} \sum_{j=1}^{2} r_{ijc} \log r_{..c}/r_{ijc} \\ &= H(I,J) - H_C(I,J) \end{aligned} \tag{8.17}$$

where $H(I,J)$ is the marginal entropy of the companies' balance sheet items (joint over the items $i$ and the assets and liabilities $j$) and $H_C(I,J)$ is the average conditional entropy of these balance sheet items, given the separate companies:

$$\begin{aligned} H(I,J) &= \sum_{i=1}^{3} \sum_{j=1}^{2} r_{ij.} \log 1/r_{ij.} \\ H_C(I,J) &= \sum_{c=1}^{N} \sum_{i=1}^{3} \sum_{j=1}^{2} r_{ijc} \log r_{..c}/r_{ijc} \,. \end{aligned} \tag{8.18}$$

These concepts are completely analogous to $H(P)$ of (6.4) and $H_R(P)$ of (6.7). It is verified straightforwardly [see (6.9)] that the excess of the marginal $H(I,J)$ over the conditional $H_C(I,J)$ and hence the industry-wide balance sheet information given in (8.17) are always positive except when the balance sheets of all companies are identical but for scale factors. The corresponding three-dimensional interpretation for the components of the balance sheet information is left to the reader.

## 9. Concluding Remarks

Whenever we have a number of items which add up to some total, information theory concepts may be used to measure the size of their shares, the change in size, as well as their size in relation to other decompositions. The mere fact that these concepts were originally developed for communication engineering and formulated in probabilistic terms should not be regarded as an indication that such concepts cannot be used in areas where a probabilistic interpretation is less obvious. To the contrary, probability theory in the sense of the discipline of decision-making under uncertainty is actually part of the wider field of the allocation of some total to various ends, and the allocation of industry assets to companies and of company assets to various types of assets also fall under this general heading.

The application of information theory concepts to financial statements is certainly not exhausted by the examples given in this article. It should be noted, however, that the nonnegativity constraint on the shares is a real constraint, since negative items do occur in financial statements (i.e., inventory changes). The only way to handle them is by aggregation with positive items such that the sum is positive.

## References

Hartley, R.V.L.: 1928, "Transmission of Information," *Bell System Technical Journal*, **7**, 535-563.

Shannon, C.E.: 1948, "A Mathematical Theory of Communication," *Bell System Technical Journal*, **27**, 379-423, 623-656.

Theil, H.: 1967, *Economics and Information Theory*, Rand McNally and Co. and North-Holland Publishing Company, Chicago and Amsterdam.

Theil, H. and A.J. Finizza: 1967, "An Informational Approach to the Measurement of Racial Segregation of Schools," Report 6712 of the Center for Mathematical Studies in Business and Economics, The University of Chicago.

# SECTION 4.6: APPLICATIONS IN SOCIAL SCIENCES

CHAPTER 60

# THE DESIRED POLITICAL ENTROPY*

HENRI THEIL
*University of Chicago*
*Chicago, Illinois, U.S.A.*

## 1. Introduction

In an article published in the December 30, 1967 issue of the Dutch weekly magazine *Vrij Nederland*, Mr. Frans Grosfeld suggested the following modification of the procedure of parliamentary representation of political parties. Instead of the conventional method of allocating to each party a number of representatives proportional to the number of votes cast for the party, he proposed to allocate a number of representatives which is proportional to the square of the number of votes. Thus, when there are $n$ parties and when $p_1, ..., p_n$ are the proportions of the total number of votes obtained by these parties, the idea is to allocate a fraction $q_i$ of the representatives to the $i$th party determined by

$$q_i = p_i^2 / \sum_{j=1}^{n} p_j^2 \qquad i = 1,...,n \tag{1.1}$$

Mr. Grosfeld made this suggestion for the Dutch political system, because in his view $n$ is so large and even the largest $p_i$ belongs to a minority party, so that on many occasions several months of negotiations were necessary to obtain a coalition cabinet of one form or another. By squaring the $p_i$'s one obtains much larger relative differences between the larger and the smaller parties, and one party or a pair of politically related parties then has a much better chance of obtaining a parliamentary majority. Also, the system (1.1) provides an incentive for parties to merge, which contributes to a reduction of the degree to which the country is politically divided. This system should be contrasted with another system which is applied on a rather large scale, viz., that of declining any seat to those parties whose $p_i$ is less than a pre-assigned fraction θ (for example, θ = .03). The fractions in the parliament are then:

$$q_i = \begin{cases} 0 & \text{if } p_i < \theta \\ p_i/(1 - A) & \text{if } p_i \geq \theta \end{cases} \tag{1.2}$$

* This article first appeared in the *American Political Science Review* **63** (1969) 521-525. Reprinted with the permission of the American Political Science Association.

where $A = \Sigma p_j$, the summation being extended over those values of the subscript $j$ for which $p_j < \theta$.[1] The cut-off system (1.2) also discriminates against small parties, but the system (1.1) proceeds in a more continuous manner.

It is interesting in this connection that the International Federation of Operational Research Societies (IFORS) faces a similar problem but in precisely the opposite direction. The problem is that the national member societies are of very unequal size, so that IFORS could be dominated more or less permanently by the societies of one or two countries if proportional representation based on national membership were applied. To prevent this, a rule has been adopted which gives each member society a number of votes proportional to the square root of the number of members:

$$q_i = p_i^{\frac{1}{2}} / \sum_{j=1}^{n} p_j^{\frac{1}{2}} \qquad i = 1,\dots,n \tag{1.3}$$

where $n$ is the number of member societies, $p_i$ the $i$th society's share of total membership, and $q_i$ its share in the IFORS voting procedure. Thus, if the $i$th society has four times as many members as the $j$th, the number of its votes is only twice as large.

The system of ratios squared (1.1) and the square-root system (1.3) are both special cases of

$$q_i = p_i^{\alpha} / \sum_{j=1}^{n} p_j^{\alpha} \qquad i = 1,\dots,n \ . \tag{1.4}$$

A specification $\alpha > 1$ serves to raise the size of the larger groups and to reduce that of the smaller groups, whereas $\alpha < 1$ has the opposite effect. The latter variant is sometimes used to protect geographical minorities. The IFORS case is one example; the U.S. Senate is another, since it gives equal representation to all 50 states independent of their population. Thus, if $p_i$ stands for the number of voters of the $i$th state measured as a fraction of the national total and $q_i$ for the proportion of Senators allocated to this state (1/50), (1.4) applies to this case when we specify $\alpha = 0$.

There are thus several examples of the representation system (1.4): $\alpha = 0$ (U.S. Senate), $\alpha = \frac{1}{2}$ (IFORS), $\alpha = 1$ (proportional representation), and $\alpha = 2$ (Mr. Grosfeld's

[1] Since the number of representatives allocated to each party must be a nonnegative integer, the actual $q_i$'s will be slightly different from those defined in (1.1) and (1.2). This feature will be disregarded in the present note, but it should be stressed that the criterion used in Section 2 — the minimization of the information expectation defined in eq. (2.4) — can be used to handle this problem. The approach is then to minimize the information expectation subject to the constraint that each $q_i$ be a nonnegative multiple of $1/N$, where $N$ is the total number of parliamentary seats.

proposal).[2] This makes the system (1.4) interesting by itself, but it is clear that this particular one-parameter family is only one choice out of many. In this note I shall show that the family of representation systems (1.4) has certain optimal properties. In Section 2 I shall derive this family by means of a constrained optimization technique based on some elementary concepts from information theory. In Section 3 I will derive the same family from some simple axioms, after which some concluding remarks follow in Section 4.

## 2. An Informational Approach

There can be no doubt that the representation system $q_i = p_i$ is the simplest and most straightforward, and the reason for choosing a different system is basically the same in all cases discussed above: One is dissatisfied with the degree to which the total representation is divided into parts, and the "dividedness" is either regarded as too large, in which case one would like to reduce it (by choosing $\alpha > 1$ in the system (1.4)), or it is regarded as too small. Therefore, what is needed in the first place is a measure which describes the degree to which the total is subdivided. A natural and well-known measure, based on concepts from information theory, is the *entropy*.[3] For the fractions $p_1, ..., p_n$ the entropy is defined as

$$H_p = -\sum_{i=1}^{n} p_i \log p_i \tag{2.1}$$

which is nonnegative and which vanishes if and only if $p_i = 1$ for some $i$ (and hence $p_j = 0$ for $j \neq i$). The maximum is log $n$, which is attained when the $p_i$'s are all equal to $1/n$. Thus, the entropy takes the smallest value when the scene is dominated completely by one group (which amounts to a minimum of "dividedness") and the largest value when all groups are of equal size; and this maximum, log $n$, increases in turn when the number of groups ($n$) increases. We shall exclude the possibility that $H_p$ is equal to either limit:

$$0 < H_p < \log n \,. \tag{2.2}$$

If $H_p = 0$, then some $p_i$ is equal to one and all others are zero. Clearly, there exists no non-arbitrary way of assigning parliament seats to parties which did not receive any vote

---

[2] Plus the case $\alpha = \infty$ (i.e., allocating all seats to the ruling party), a procedure used in some of the democratically less advanced countries.

[3] For a brief introduction to the informational concepts used in this section, see. e.g. Chapters 1 and 2 of the author's *Economics and Information Theory* (Chicago: Rand McNally and Company, and Amsterdam: North-Holland Publishing Company, 1967). The idea of using the entropy for this particular purpose is due to Mr. B.M.S. van Praag of the Econometric Institute in Rotterdam.

at all. If $H_p = \log n$, all $n$ parties received the same number of votes, and there exists no reasonable way of allocating parliament seats to these parties on another than equal basis.

But if $H_p$ satisfies the constraint (2.2), as is normally the case, one can conceive of a set of parliamentary fractions $q_1, ..., q_n$ whose entropy

$$H_q = -\sum_{i=1}^{n} q_i \log q_i \tag{2.3}$$

differs from $H_p$. Obviously, if we fix $H_q$ at a pre-assigned level, we still have freedom as to the choice of $q_1, ..., q_n$ when $n \geq 2$,[4] and we would like to choose the $q$'s as closely to the corresponding $p$'s as is possible. Given that the informational concepts $H_p$ and $H_q$ are used to measure "dividedness," a natural way of specifying "as close as possible" is the following. Consider $p_1, ..., p_n$ as the prior probabilities of $n$ events and imagine that a message arrives which indicates that the odds in favor of these events have changed to the extent that the new (posterior) probabilities are $q_1, ..., q_n$. The expected information of this message is defined in information theory as

$$I(q:p) = \sum_{i=1}^{n} q_i \log \frac{q_i}{p_i} \tag{2.4}$$

where $p$ and $q$ on the left stand for $q_1, ..., q_n$ and $p_1, ..., p_n$, respectively. The information expectation is never negative. It vanishes if and only if $p_i = q_i$ for each $i$, and it takes larger and larger values when the $p$'s and $q$'s are pairwise more different.[5]

The information expectation (2.4) is a measure of the degree to which we are surprised when we are informed that the prior probabilities $p_1, ..., p_n$ are replaced by the posterior probabilities $q_1, ..., q_n$. Interpret now the $p_i$'s again as the proportions of the votes cast for the various parties and the $q_i$'s as the corresponding proportions of

[4] Even for $n = 2$ the entropy does not determine the $q$'s uniquely, because $(\theta, 1-\theta)$ and $(1-\theta, \theta)$ have the same entropy for any $\theta$ in the interval (0,1). It is obvious, however, that the present discussion loses much of its interest when $n = 2$ instead of $n > 2$.

[5] This becomes particularly clear when $I(q:p)$ is expanded according to powers of $(q_i - p_i)/p_i$. If we use natural logarithms (which is done throughout this paper) and disregard third and higher powers, the result is

$$I(q:p) \approx \frac{1}{2} \sum_{i=1}^{n} \frac{(q_i - p_i)^2}{p_i}$$

provided that the $p$'s and $q$'s are pairwise sufficiently close to each other (so that the expansions converge). The right-hand side of this approximation is proportional to a chi-square with the $p$'s as theoretical probabilities and the $q$'s as observed frequencies.

parliamentary seats.[6] Obviously, the electorate ought to be surprised as little as possible. Consider then:

Theorem 1. *Let $p_1, ..., p_n$ be the proportions of the total number of votes cast for the n parties and suppose that (2.2) is satisfied. Then the parliamentary representation $q_1, ..., q_n$ which minimizes the information expectation (2.4) subject to the entropy constraint (2.3) is given by eq. (1.4), where $\alpha$ is the solution of eq. (2.11) below. This solution exists and is unique for any pre-assigned value of the entropy $H_q$ in the interval (0,* log *n) if exactly one party has the largest number of votes.*

The remainder of this section is concerned with the proof of this theorem. We note first that under condition (2.3) the information expectation (2.4) can be written as

$$I(q{:}p) = -H_q - \sum_{i=1}^{n} q_i \log p_i \tag{2.5}$$

so that we should minimize $-\Sigma\, q_i \log p_i$ subject to the constraints (2.3) and $\Sigma\, q_i = 1$. So we form the Lagrangian expression:

$$\begin{aligned} &- \sum_{i=1}^{n} q_i \log p_i - \lambda\left( - \sum_{i=1}^{n} q_i \log q_i - H_q \right) \\ &- \mu\left( \sum_{i=1}^{n} q_i - 1 \right) \end{aligned} \tag{2.6}$$

where $\lambda$ and $\mu$ are Lagrangian multipliers. We differentiate with respect to $q_i$ and equate the result to zero:

$$-\log p_i + \lambda(1 + \log q_i) - \mu = 0 \qquad i = 1,...,n\ . \tag{2.7}$$

If $\lambda = 0$, this amounts to $\log p_i = -\mu$, which implies that all $p_i$'s must be equal to $1/n$ and hence $H_p = \log n$. This, however, is excluded by (2.2). So $\lambda \neq 0$ and hence:

$$\log q_i = -1 + \frac{\mu}{\lambda} + \frac{1}{\lambda} \log p_i \qquad i = 1,...,n \tag{2.8}$$

or equivalently:

[6] To make the discussion more concrete, we will talk about parties and parliamentary seats rather than about both these and the geographic representations such as those of IFORS and the U.S. Senate.

$$q_i = \frac{p_i^{1/\lambda}}{C} \quad \text{where } C = e^{1-\mu/\lambda} . \tag{2.9}$$

We now write $\alpha = 1/\lambda$, so that $q_i = p_i^\alpha/C$ in accordance with (1.4), and $C$ obviously satisfies

$$C = \sum_{i=1}^{n} p_i^\alpha \tag{2.10}$$

in view of the sum constraint $\Sigma\, q_i = 1$.

Next substitute $p_i^\alpha/C$ for $q_i$ in the entropy constraint (2.3):

$$H_q = -\sum_{i=1}^{n} (p_i^\alpha/C)\log(p_i^\alpha/C)$$

$$= \frac{-\sum_{i=1}^{n} p_i^\alpha \log p_i^\alpha + \left(\sum_{i=1}^{n} p_i^\alpha\right)\log\sum_{i=1}^{n} p_i^\alpha}{\sum_{i=1}^{n} p_i^\alpha}$$

or

$$H_q = \log\sum_{i=1}^{n} p_i^\alpha - \frac{\alpha\sum_{i=1}^{n} p_i^\alpha \log p_i}{\sum_{i=1}^{n} p_i^\alpha} . \tag{2.11}$$

For given $H_q, p_1, \ldots, p_n$ this is a nonlinear equation in $\alpha$. The right-hand side is equal to $\log n$ for $\alpha = 0$ and to zero in the limit for $\alpha$ increasing indefinitely, provided that one party has the largest $p_i$.[7] To prove that (2.11) gives a unique solution for any $H_q$ between

[7] Write $p_1$ for the largest $p_i$, then $q_1$ converges to 1 as $\alpha \to \infty$, so that $H_q = 0$ in the limit. If $p_1 = p_2$ and if all other $p_i$'s are smaller, then $q_1 = q_2 = \frac{1}{2}$ in the limit and hence $H_q > 0$ even when $\alpha = \infty$. In the case of a $k$-fold multiple maximum, $p_1 = \ldots = p_k > p_{k+1} \geq \ldots \geq p_n$, the interval for $H_q$ mentioned in Theorem 1 should be confined to $(\log k, \log n)$.

these limits it is sufficient to show that the right-hand side is a monotonically decreasing function of α. So we consider its derivative with respect to α, which turns out to be:

$$-\frac{\alpha\sum_{i=1}^{n} p_i^{\alpha}(\log p_i)^2}{\sum_{i=1}^{n} p_i^{\alpha}} + \frac{\alpha\left(\sum_{i=1}^{n} p_i^{\alpha}\log p_i\right)^2}{\left(\sum_{i=1}^{n} p_i^{\alpha}\right)^2} \tag{2.12}$$

$$= -\alpha\sum_{i=1}^{n} q_i\left(\log p_i - \sum_{j=1}^{n} q_j \log p_j\right)^2 .$$

The expression on the second line is a multiple -α of the weighted variance of $\log p_1, ..., \log p_n$ with $q_1, ..., q_n$ as weights.[8] The derivative is therefore negative for all positive α except when the variance vanishes, and this variance vanishes only if $p_i = 1$ and hence $q_i = 1$ for some $i$ ($H_p = 0$) or if $p_i = 1/n$ for each $i$ ($H_p = \log n$).

## 3. An Axiomatic Approach

In the system of proportional representation the number of parliamentary seats allocated to each party, measured as a fraction of the total number of seats, is determined uniquely by the number of party votes relative to the total number of votes. In fact, the rule is simply $q_i = p_i$, $i = 1, ..., n$. Other systems such as (1.4) do not have this property, but a weaker variant, which may be called the condition of *weak proportionality*, certainly seems reasonable. Consider any two parties $i$ and $j$; then the number of parliamentary seats allocated to $i$ relative to the number of seats allocated to $j$ should be determined uniquely by the ratio of the number of votes cast for $i$ to that cast for $j$, and the underlying relationship should be the same for all pairs $(i,j)$ and it should be nondecreasing. This means:

---

[8] By substituting $\log q_i$ for $\alpha \log p_i - \log C$ in the second line of (2.12) we obtain a result that can be written as follows

$$\frac{\partial H_q}{\partial(\log\alpha)} = -\sum_{i=1}^{n} q_i(-\log q_i - H_q)^2 \qquad \alpha > 0$$

which means that a small relative increase in α reduces the entropy $H_q$ by $k$ times this increase, where $k$ is the variance of the distribution whose values are $-\log q_1, ..., -\log q_n$ and whose probabilities are $q_1, ..., q_n$. Obviously, the mean of this distribution is the entropy $H_q$.

$$\frac{q_i}{q_j} = f\left(\frac{p_i}{p_j}\right) \quad i,j = 1,...,n \tag{3.1}$$

where $f(\ )$ is a nondecreasing function which takes positive values for all positive values of the argument.

Consider then any triple of parties, $(i,j,k)$. We obviously have

$$\frac{p_i}{p_k} = \frac{p_i}{p_j}\frac{p_j}{p_k} \qquad \frac{q_i}{q_k} = \frac{q_i}{q_j}\frac{q_j}{q_k} \tag{3.2}$$

which means $f(p_i/p_k) = f(p_i/p_j)f(p_j/p_k)$. Since this equation holds for any positive values of the arguments, we may write it as

$$f(x)f(y) \equiv f(xy) \quad x,y > 0 \tag{3.3}$$

Write $\xi = \log x$ and $\eta = \log y$, so that

$$\log f(x) \equiv \log f(e^{\xi}) \equiv \phi(\xi) \quad \text{say} . \tag{3.4}$$

Taking logarithms on both sides of (3.3) we obtain

$$\phi(\xi) + \phi(\eta) \equiv \phi(\xi + \eta) \quad -\infty < \xi, \quad \eta < \infty \tag{3.5}$$

from which it follows immediately that, if $f(\ )$ and hence $\phi(\ )$ are continuous functions, $\phi(\xi)$ must be of the form $\alpha\xi$ for some constant $\alpha$.[9]
Hence

$$f(x) \equiv e^{\phi(\xi)} \equiv (e^{\xi})^{\alpha} \equiv x^{\alpha} \tag{3.6}$$

so that we obtain:

---

[9] For details, see e.g. *Economics and Information Theory* (quoted in footnote 3), p. 7, or B.O. Koopman and G.E. Kimball, "Information Theory," Chapter 9 of *Notes on Operations Research 1959*, assembled by the Operations Research Center, Massachusetts Institute of Technology (Cambridge, Mass.: The Technology Press, M.I.T., 1959).

$$\frac{q_i}{q_j} = \left(\frac{p_i}{p_j}\right)^{\alpha} \qquad i,j = 1,...,n \; . \tag{3.7}$$

This condition determines the ratios of all $q$'s. Since they add up to one, they are thus individually determined and it is immediately obvious that they are of the form (1.4). The condition that $f(\;)$ be nondecreasing implies $\alpha \geq 0$. We have thus proved:

Theorem 2. *Let $p_1$, ..., $p_n$ be the proportions of the total number of votes cast for the n parties and $q_1$, ..., $q_n$ the corresponding parliamentary representation. If weak proportionality is imposed in the sense of (3.1) where $f(\;)$ is a continuous nondecreasing function satisfying $f(x) > 0$ for any $x > 0$, then the q's are determined by the p's as described in eq. (1.4) for some $\alpha \geq 0$.*

## 4. Concluding Remarks

The results obtained in the two previous sections indicate that, if one is dissatisfied with proportional representation, there are rather cogent reasons for choosing a member of the family (1.4). The next problem is then the specification of the parameter $\alpha$. In Mr. Grosfeld's proposal the value 2 is chosen a priori, but it may be argued that the voters should have a say in the matter. In fact, a plea can be made for the idea that the citizens of a country should have the right to vote on the degree to which they will be politically divided in their own Parliament. This would give the voting procedure a two-dimensional character: Each citizen votes for the party of his preference, thus raising the corresponding $p_i$ at the expense of all other $p$'s, and he also votes for a particular numerical value of the parliamentary entropy[10], thus indicating how in his view $p_1$, ..., $p_n$ should be transformed to the parliamentary fractions $q_1$, ..., $q_n$. In theory, there will be as many different desired entropy values as there are voters; an obvious choice is to substitute the median for $H_q$ in the entropy constraint (2.3). One may also argue that the voters collectively decide on the fractions $p_1$, ..., $p_n$ and that, therefore, $H_q$ is the implied desired entropy, which is normally different from the median of the "directly" desired entropies. This conflict can be resolved by substituting for $H_q$ in (2.3) the average of $H_p$ and the median desired entropy. Clearly, there are many possibilities.

It is also important to reflect on the degree of association between the two components of each citizen's vote. A priori, one may be inclined to speculate that, if a person votes for a large party, there is a large chance that he will vote for a small entropy. Specifically, let us arrange the parties according to decreasing size:

[10] This will of course require the teaching of logarithms at an early stage. Mathematics teachers should regard it as a challenge to teach a subject with immediate political science applications.

$$p_1 \geq p_2 \geq \dots \geq p_n \tag{4.1}$$

and let us write $\pi_i$ for the probability that the person votes for an entropy $< H_p$, given that his vote goes to the $i$th party. The above speculation in more specific form is then:

$$\pi_1 \geq \pi_2 \geq \dots \geq \pi_n \tag{4.2}$$

The proportion of votes for an entropy $< H_p$ is then $\pi_1 p_1 + \dots + \pi_n p_n$, which may be quite high because the $p$'s and $\pi$'s are positively correlated according to (4.1) and (4.2). Thus, the presumption indicates that there will normally be a tendency for the median desired entropy to be on the low side, which favors the largest party.

The underlying assumptions are questionable, however. First, there are many situations in which it is far from certain which party will be the largest. If $i$ and $j$ are the leading contenders, and if a voter favoring $i$ tries to help this party by voting for a small entropy, his efforts will be in favor of $j$ rather than $i$ if $p_j$ turns out to be larger than $p_i$. Second, even if a voter prefers a party which in his view will definitely be the largest, he may nevertheless be in favor of a fairly large parliamentary entropy when he is violently against the second-largest party and when he wants a coalition cabinet of his preferred party with one or two smaller parties. Voting for the parliamentary entropy requires that the citizen considers the political structure as a whole. This is an appeal to his intelligence, which has its merits in and by itself.

## CHAPTER 61

# A NOTE ON THE MEASUREMENT OF RACIAL INTEGRATION OF SCHOOLS BY MEANS OF INFORMATIONAL CONCEPTS*[1]

HENRI THEIL
*University of Chicago*
*Chicago, Illinois, U.S.A.*

ANTHONY J. FINIZZA
*University of Chicago*
*Chicago, Illinois, U.S.A.*

This note is concerned with the measurement of racial integration of schools in a way that permits a simple aggregation of the measure to sets of schools such as school districts. [The procedure can be applied to institutions other than schools, but we prefer a more specific terminology.] There are several standard procedures for measuring integration, but the dissimilarity index appears to be more popular than any other index.[2] This index is based on a comparison of the number of white students in each school, measured as a fraction of the total number of white students in the city, and the analogous nonwhite proportion of the same school. The index is defined as one-half of the sum over all schools of the absolute differences of these proportions. The value of the index is zero when the racial compositions of all schools are identical and it takes larger and larger positive values (up to a maximum of 1) when the racial compositions are more different; also, it has a simple interpretation in terms of minimum shifts which are needed in order to obtain identical racial compositions in all schools. However, the use of absolute differences makes the dissimilarity index less suitable when one wants to aggregate schools to school districts.[3] The objective of this note is to show that there are some simple measures derived from information theory which are superior in this respect, and to illustrate their use by means of data on the elementary schools of the Chicago public school system for the years 1963-1969.

* This article first appeared in *The Journal of Mathematical Sociology* **1** (1971) 187-194. Reprinted with permission. 

[1] The authors wish to thank the Chicago Board of Education and the Chicago Urban League for providing the data which are used in this article. The staffs of several school districts were helpful in correcting a number of errors in the data. The research reported in this article was supported in part by the National Science Foundation under grant GS-2607.

[2] The most well-known article in this area is that by O.D. Duncan and B. Duncan, 'A Methodological Analysis of Segregation Indexes,' *American Sociological Review*, Vol. 20 (1955), pp. 210-217; this article contains several references to the earlier literature in this field.

[3] Basically, the point is that a racial comparison of all schools in the city requires a comparison of their white-nonwhite ratios with that of the city as a whole, whereas an analysis of schools within each district followed by an analysis of the district racial compositions requires a comparison of the white-nonwhite ratios of the schools with that of the district to which they belong. It is this analysis of within-district and between-districts racial differences that is seriously hampered by the use of absolute differences. The same objection applies to the Gini index of concentration.

**Racial Entropy**

Write $n$ for the total number of schools in the city and $w_i$ for the number of white students of the $i$th school, measured as a fraction of the total number of students of that school. Hence 1-$w_i$ is the nonwhite proportion of the school's student body. The entropy of a distribution with proportions $w_i$ and 1-$w_i$ is defined as

$$E_i = w_i \log \frac{1}{w_i} + (1 - w_i) \log \frac{1}{1 - w_i} \tag{1}$$

We shall refer to $E_i$ as the racial entropy of the student body of the $i$th school. It takes the zero value — the minimum — when all students are of one race ($w_i$ = 0 or 1); otherwise it is positive, and the maximum is log 2, which is reached for a fifty-fifty racial composition. This maximum is equal to 1 when we choose 2 as the base of the logarithm, in which case the entropy is said to be measured in binary digits or, for short, bits. The racial entropy is thus a number between 0 and 1, and it should also be noted that it is completely symmetric in $w_i$ and 1-$w_i$.

Write $p_i$ for the total number of students in the $i$th school, expressed as a fraction of all students in the city, so that $p_1 + ... + p_n = 1$. Imagine that the city is divided into $G$ districts, $D_1, ..., D_G$, and write $P_g$ for the total number of students in $D_g$ (also expressed as a fraction of the city total):

$$P_g = \sum_{i \in D_g} p_i \qquad g = 1,..., G \tag{2}$$

Then the average racial entropy of the schools in $D_g$ is

$$\bar{E}_g = \sum_{i \in D_g} \frac{p_i}{P_g} E_i = \sum_{i \in D_g} \frac{p_i}{P_g} \left[ w_i \log \frac{1}{w_i} + (1 - w_i) \log \frac{1}{1 - w_i} \right] \tag{3}$$

where 'average' is to be interpreted as a weighted average with weights proportional to the numbers of students in the schools. The average racial entropy of all $n$ schools in the city is

$$\bar{E} = \sum_{i=1}^{n} p_i E_i = \sum_{i=1}^{n} p_i \left[ w_i \log \frac{1}{w_i} + (1 - w_i) \log \frac{1}{1 - w_i} \right]. \tag{4}$$

Note that these measures are aggregation-consistent in the sense that the city average $\bar{E}$ coincides with the weighted average of the district averages $\bar{E}_1, \ldots, \bar{E}_G$ with weights proportional to the number of students in the relevant districts:

$$\sum_{g=1}^{G} P_g \bar{E}_g = \sum_{g=1}^{G} P_g \sum_{i \in D_g} \frac{p_i}{P_g} E_i = \sum_{i=1}^{n} p_i E_i = \bar{E}$$

Table 1 contains some summary statistics for the elementary schools of the Chicago public school system in the years 1963-1969.[4] Each row refers to one of the 27 school districts. Column (2) contains the number of schools in each district in 1969, column (3) the percentage of students in that year ($100P_g$ in 1969), and column (4) the percentage of white students in the district in 1969. The average racial entropy of the schools in each district in the years 1963-1969 is given in columns (5) to (11); it is expressed as a percentage of one bit and can thus vary from 0 to 100. The results indicate that none of the values exceed one-half of the upper limit. In fact, the city average ( $\bar{E}$ ) is only about one-seventh of this limit; it decreased slightly from 1963 until the middle of the seven-year period, and it increased slightly thereafter.

## An Informational Measure of Segregation

The use of the racial entropy permits the analyst to verify systematically the extent to which the student body of a school (or any other set of people) is 'racially divided.'[5] However, it is not the case that the entropy is a good measure for 'segregation.' If 50 per cent of the students of a school district is nonwhite, each school of this district can have a one bit racial entropy (which requires a 50-50 racial composition of each school), but this is evidently not possible when 20 or 80 per cent of the district is nonwhite. Some schools can still be 50-50 in the latter two cases, but evidently not all, so that the average racial entropy of all schools of such a district must have an upper limit of less than one bit. Intuitively, one would expect that this upper limit has something to do with the racial entropy of the student body of the district as a whole, and this is indeed correct.

---

[4] The statement on race was made by teachers or principals in the autumn of each year. The classification varied over the years; in the first four years the groups were Caucasian, Negroid, and Other; in the last years a Puerto Rican category was formed from the Other category. To obtain comparability the authors decided to combine the Puerto Rican and Other groups with the whites ('Caucasians'), so that the white-nonwhite distinction actually amounts to not-Negro versus Negro.

[5] The measure can be easily extended to more races than two. If their proportions are $q_1, \ldots, q_N$, the associated entropy is equal to $\Sigma_j q_j \log (1/q_j)$, which takes the maximum value when all $q$'s are equal to $1/N$. In fact, it can be shown that if one accepts certain axioms (the crucial one requiring additivity), the *only* measure of 'dividedness' which satisfies these is the entropy.

**TABLE 1.** Entropy Measures for the Racial Composition of the Public School Districts of Chicago

| District | Data for 1969 Number of Schools | $100P_g$ | $100W_g$ | $100\bar{E}_g$ 1963 | 1964 | 1965 | 1966 | 1967 | 1968 | 1969 | $100E_{(g)}$ 1963 | 1964 | 1965 | 1966 | 1967 | 1968 | 1969 | $100\bar{I}_g$ 1963 | 1964 | 1965 | 1966 | 1967 | 1968 | 1969 |
|---|---|---|---|---|---|---|---|---|---|---|---|---|---|---|---|---|---|---|---|---|---|---|---|---|
| (1) | (2) | (3) | (4) | (5) | (6) | (7) | (8) | (9) | (10) | (11) | (12) | (13) | (14) | (15) | (16) | (17) | (18) | (19) | (20) | (21) | (22) | (23) | (24) | (25) |
| 1 | 27 | 3.40 | 99.9 | .1 | .2 | .6 | .8 | .6 | .9 | 1.0 | .1 | .3 | .9 | 1.0 | .8 | 1.1 | 1.2 | .0 | .1 | .3 | .2 | .2 | .2 | .2 |
| 2 | 11 | 1.73 | 99.7 | .3 | .3 | .1 | .1 | .5 | 1.3 | 2.5 | .3 | .3 | .2 | .2 | .6 | 1.6 | 2.9 | .1 | .1 | .0 | .0 | .1 | .2 | .4 |
| 3 | 17 | 3.89 | 99.7 | .6 | 2.4 | 2.7 | 2.5 | 2.0 | 3.2 | 2.6 | .8 | 3.0 | 3.4 | 3.1 | 2.5 | 3.9 | 3.0 | .1 | .7 | .7 | .6 | .5 | .7 | .4 |
| 4 | 23 | 4.30 | 64.3 | 6.7 | 8.8 | 14.0 | 20.7 | 19.7 | 35.5 | 35.5 | 10.7 | 15.9 | 22.9 | 46.9 | 68.2 | 82.8 | 94.0 | 4.0 | 7.1 | 8.9 | 26.2 | 48.5 | 47.2 | 58.5 |
| 5 | 25 | 4.83 | 99.8 | .1 | .1 | .0 | .2 | .3 | .3 | 1.5 | .2 | .1 | .0 | .3 | .4 | .4 | 1.8 | .0 | .0 | .0 | .1 | .1 | .1 | .3 |
| 6 | 25 | 5.32 | 94.0 | 17.8 | 18.6 | 18.4 | 19.1 | 20.9 | 22.7 | 25.1 | 24.0 | 24.8 | 25.0 | 24.6 | 26.8 | 29.6 | 32.6 | 6.1 | 6.2 | 6.6 | 5.5 | 5.9 | 6.9 | 7.5 |
| 7 | 20 | 3.84 | 43.1 | 32.7 | 32.0 | 29.7 | 30.0 | 29.7 | 27.1 | 28.2 | 99.9 | 99.9 | 100.0 | 100.0 | 99.9 | 99.4 | 98.6 | 67.2 | 67.9 | 70.2 | 70.0 | 70.1 | 72.3 | 70.4 |
| 8 | 18 | 4.48 | 1.7 | 28.5 | 23.6 | 17.7 | 12.8 | 11.6 | 9.6 | 7.9 | 42.7 | 33.6 | 22.9 | 16.3 | 15.3 | 13.4 | 12.3 | 14.3 | 10.0 | 5.1 | 3.5 | 3.8 | 3.8 | 4.4 |
| 9 | 25 | 4.27 | 10.6 | 26.9 | 26.1 | 23.6 | 20.2 | 17.8 | 16.7 | 14.6 | 68.4 | 63.1 | 58.5 | 53.9 | 53.3 | 48.9 | 48.8 | 41.5 | 37.0 | 35.0 | 33.7 | 35.5 | 32.2 | 34.2 |
| 10 | 16 | 4.31 | 19.2 | 10.7 | 7.0 | 6.2 | 7.1 | 7.3 | 8.1 | 8.9 | 53.9 | 55.8 | 55.4 | 57.7 | 61.2 | 65.8 | 70.5 | 43.2 | 48.8 | 49.2 | 50.6 | 53.8 | 57.7 | 61.6 |
| 11 | 19 | 3.61 | 4.3 | 13.3 | 9.9 | 10.0 | 8.4 | 9.5 | 9.5 | 11.2 | 25.7 | 23.6 | 24.6 | 20.9 | 21.9 | 22.7 | 25.6 | 12.4 | 13.7 | 14.6 | 12.5 | 12.4 | 13.3 | 14.4 |
| 12 | 26 | 3.44 | 91.6 | 12.7 | 12.4 | 12.1 | 11.6 | 10.3 | 10.4 | 9.1 | 39.7 | 39.1 | 39.6 | 38.3 | 39.7 | 39.6 | 41.8 | 27.1 | 26.7 | 27.5 | 26.7 | 29.4 | 29.3 | 32.6 |
| 13 | 18 | 4.19 | .0 | .3 | .5 | .5 | .2 | .2 | .3 | .3 | .4 | .6 | .7 | .2 | .3 | .4 | .4 | .1 | .1 | .1 | .1 | .1 | .1 | .1 |
| 14 | 17 | 2.84 | 9.4 | 30.2 | 28.4 | 24.9 | 22.6 | 20.8 | 21.6 | 20.9 | 53.8 | 52.1 | 50.0 | 49.0 | 46.6 | 47.1 | 45.1 | 23.6 | 23.7 | 25.1 | 26.4 | 25.8 | 25.5 | 24.2 |
| 15 | 24 | 4.03 | 73.2 | 20.8 | 18.5 | 14.2 | 13.1 | 13.7 | 15.2 | 25.8 | 63.8 | 71.3 | 75.4 | 78.9 | 77.5 | 78.0 | 83.8 | 43.0 | 52.9 | 61.2 | 65.8 | 63.8 | 62.8 | 58.0 |
| 16 | 23 | 5.06 | 6.4 | 30.6 | 28.1 | 28.1 | 24.6 | 21.8 | 20.5 | 14.5 | 93.5 | 85.9 | 77.3 | 66.2 | 55.9 | 43.0 | 34.4 | 62.9 | 57.8 | 49.2 | 41.6 | 34.1 | 22.5 | 19.9 |
| 17 | 20 | 3.12 | 74.9 | 14.1 | 18.3 | 20.6 | 24.1 | 25.8 | 30.0 | 36.4 | 35.3 | 38.0 | 41.6 | 48.9 | 58.1 | 68.4 | 81.2 | 21.1 | 19.7 | 21.0 | 24.8 | 32.3 | 38.3 | 44.9 |
| 18 | 35 | 5.55 | 45.0 | 6.7 | 7.2 | 11.4 | 16.1 | 20.4 | 22.6 | 22.6 | 93.2 | 96.3 | 97.5 | 98.3 | 99.4 | 100.0 | 99.3 | 86.5 | 89.1 | 86.1 | 82.2 | 78.9 | 77.4 | 76.7 |
| 19 | 20 | 4.34 | 44.2 | 10.6 | 11.1 | 11.1 | 11.0 | 12.1 | 11.9 | 11.6 | 95.3 | 95.7 | 96.1 | 96.3 | 97.1 | 97.8 | 99.0 | 84.7 | 84.6 | 85.0 | 85.4 | 85.0 | 85.9 | 87.4 |
| 20 | 15 | 3.96 | .1 | 4.0 | 5.4 | 3.8 | 2.9 | 2.5 | 1.8 | .9 | 4.1 | 6.1 | 4.2 | 3.0 | 2.8 | 2.1 | 1.1 | .1 | .7 | .3 | .1 | .2 | .2 | .1 |
| 21 | 13 | 3.05 | .3 | 2.6 | 1.7 | 1.6 | 1.4 | 1.9 | 1.5 | 2.1 | 2.8 | 1.9 | 1.8 | 1.5 | 2.2 | 1.7 | 2.7 | .2 | .2 | .2 | .1 | .3 | .2 | .6 |
| 22 | 9 | 1.98 | 23.1 | 37.7 | 46.8 | 46.6 | 44.2 | 48.2 | 48.8 | 42.5 | 79.2 | 95.3 | 99.6 | 99.7 | 98.0 | 91.1 | 77.8 | 41.6 | 48.5 | 53.0 | 55.5 | 49.9 | 42.3 | 35.4 |
| 23 | 16 | 2.64 | .1 | 1.6 | 1.2 | 1.5 | .9 | 1.0 | 1.0 | .7 | 1.8 | 1.4 | 1.8 | 1.1 | 1.3 | 1.2 | .9 | .2 | .2 | .3 | .2 | .3 | .2 | .2 |
| 24 | 16 | 2.57 | 96.7 | 3.3 | 3.7 | 5.1 | 7.7 | 8.1 | 12.5 | 17.6 | 4.0 | 4.7 | 6.3 | 9.2 | 10.1 | 14.5 | 20.9 | .7 | 1.0 | 1.2 | 1.5 | 2.0 | 2.0 | 3.3 |
| 25 | 16 | 3.87 | 32.9 | 22.9 | 27.4 | 26.2 | 24.3 | 23.0 | 24.7 | 20.1 | 100.0 | 99.0 | 97.5 | 96.5 | 95.4 | 93.8 | 91.4 | 77.1 | 71.6 | 71.3 | 72.1 | 72.4 | 69.1 | 71.3 |
| 26 | 13 | 3.03 | 58.4 | 15.2 | 15.9 | 18.9 | 20.9 | 23.5 | 23.3 | 18.1 | 88.2 | 87.0 | 86.5 | 88.0 | 90.9 | 96.3 | 98.0 | 73.0 | 71.1 | 67.6 | 67.1 | 67.4 | 73.0 | 79.9 |
| 27 | 11 | 2.33 | .7 | 22.7 | 20.8 | 16.3 | 12.2 | 9.6 | 7.9 | 5.8 | 35.3 | 28.3 | 22.0 | 15.3 | 11.7 | 9.0 | 6.3 | 12.6 | 7.5 | 5.8 | 3.1 | 2.0 | 1.1 | .5 |
| City average | 518† | 100† | 44.2 | 14.0 | 13.7 | 13.2 | 12.9 | 13.1 | 14.1 | 14.4 | 42.7 | 42.7 | 42.2 | 42.3 | 43.1 | 44.0 | 45.5 | 28.8 | 29.0 | 29.0 | 29.3 | 30.0 | 29.9 | 31.1 |

†City total

Write $W_g$ for the proportion of the white students in district $D_g$:

$$W_g = \sum_{i \in D_g} \frac{p_i}{P_g} w_i \qquad g = 1,...,G \tag{5}$$

so that the racial entropy of this district is

$$E_{(g)} = W_g \log \frac{1}{W_g} + (1 - W_g) \log \frac{1}{1 - W_g} . \tag{6}$$

Suppose for a moment that the racial composition of each school of $D_g$ is identical with that of the district: $w_i = W_g$ for each $i \in D_g$. In that case it can hardly be argued that there is segregation at the level of the schools; if there is then a low level of racial entropy in these schools, it is merely a matter of the racial composition of the district. On the other hand, it is also possible that some schools of $D_g$ are 100 per cent white and all others are 100 per cent nonwhite. This is the other extreme, because it implies a zero racial entropy for each school and hence a zero average racial entropy of the schools of $D_g$.

These considerations suggest that it is worthwhile to compare, for each $i \in D_g$, the school's racial composition ($w_i$, 1-$w_i$) with that of the district, ($W_g$, 1-$W_g$). Consider:

$$I_i = w_i \log \frac{w_i}{W_g} + (1 - w_i) \log \frac{1 - w_i}{1 - W_g} \qquad i \in D_g \tag{7}$$

which is known in information theory as the expected information of the message that transforms the proportions ($W_g$, 1-$W_g$) to a second set of proportions ($w_i$, 1-$w_i$). The value of this information expectation is zero when the two sets of proportions are identical; it takes larger and larger positive values when the two sets are more different. For $w_i = 1$ the value of (7) is $\log(1/W_g)$ and for $w_i = 0$ it is $\log[1/(1-W_g)]$. Thus, when a district is predominantly nonwhite ($W_g$ small), the presence of an all-white school implies a large value of $I_i$. This is intuitively reasonable for a measure of segregation.

Consider the weighted average of the information expectations (7) over all schools in $D_g$ with weights proportional to their student bodies:

$$\begin{aligned}\bar{I}_g &= \sum_{i\in D_g} \frac{p_i}{P_g}\left[w_i \log \frac{w_i}{W_g} + (1-w_i)\log \frac{1-w_i}{1-W_g}\right] \\ &= \left[\sum_{i\in D_g} \frac{p_i}{P_g} w_i\right] \log \frac{1}{W_g} + \left[\sum_{i\in D_g} \frac{p_i}{P_g}(1-w_i)\right] \log \frac{1}{1-W_g} \\ &\quad - \sum_{i\in D_g} \frac{p_i}{P_g}\left[w_i \log \frac{1}{w_i} + (1-w_i)\log \frac{1}{1-w_i}\right] \\ &= W_g \log \frac{1}{W_g} + (1-W_g)\log \frac{1}{1-W_g} - \bar{E}_g = E_{(g)} - \bar{E}_g\end{aligned}$$

where use is made of (6) in the last step. We can write this result as

$$\bar{E}_g = E_{(g)} - \bar{I}_g \qquad g = 1,...,G \tag{8}$$

which means that the average racial entropy of the schools in any district cannot be larger than the racial entropy of the district. The difference between these two entropies is the average $\bar{I}_g$ of the information expectations (7) for all $i \in D_g$, each of which is a measure for the extent to which the district racial composition differs from that of one of its schools. This $\bar{I}_g$ is a measure of segregation; it indicates by how much the average racial entropy of the schools in $D_g$ is depressed below the maximum that is permitted by the racial composition of $D_g$.

Columns (12) to (18) of Table 1 contain the district racial entropies and columns (19) to (25) give the $\bar{I}_g$'s. It appears that about one-half of the 27 districts had a racial entropy exceeding $\frac{1}{2}$ bit in at least one of the seven years. [Recall that none of them ever had an average racial entropy of its schools which is so large.] The city average of the district racial entropies, obtained by weighting $E_{(1)}, ..., E_{(27)}$ by $P_1, ..., P_{27}$, varied between .42 and .46 bit. This average decreased slightly from 1963 until the middle of the seven-year period and it increased thereafter; this development is similar to that of the city average of the racial entropies of the schools. The $\bar{I}_g$'s are substantial for several districts, particularly those that have large $E_{(g)}$'s. The city average of the $\bar{I}_g$'s (also obtained by weighting with the $P_g$'s) increased gradually from less than .29 bit in 1963 to more than .31 bit in 1969. Clearly, insofar as there is any evidence of change, it is in the direction of more segregation.

**Comparisons on a Relative Basis**

Although the objective of this note is merely to introduce and illustrate informational concepts for racial decompositions, it is worthwhile to add that data of this kind can be used as raw material for further analysis. One such attempt is made in Table 2, which contains $\bar{I}_g$ as a percentage of the corresponding $E_{(g)}$ for each district and each year. This amounts to the relative reduction of the average racial entropy of the schools below the entropy of their district. The figures evidently vary widely from one district to the other, but they do exhibit regularity as is shown in the last three lines. In each year, the 27 districts are divided into three groups consisting of nine districts each, one with the smallest racial entropies $E_{(g)}$, one with the largest, and one with 'medium' entropies. The figures for each year are the median ratios $\bar{I}_g/E_{(g)}$ in percentage form.

They show that on the average (in the median sense) the reduction of the average racial entropies of the schools below that of their districts is about 20 per cent for districts with low racial entropies, about 70 per cent for those with large racial entropies, and about 50 per cent for 'medium' districts. This indicates a higher degree of segregation in those districts in which the racial entropy could have been very high.

Do we find the same phenomenon for individual districts on a time series basis? Unfortunately, the time series are too short to provide a conclusive answer. Two-thirds of the districts have an $E_{(g)}$ in 1969 which differs from that of 1963 by less than .1 bit, and it should cause no surprise that the change in $\bar{I}_g/E_{(g)}$ from 1963 to 1969 was equally often positive as negative for this group. There are two outstanding cases that are in agreement with our presumption (District 4 with $E_{(4)}$ increasing from .11 to .94 bit and $\bar{I}_4/E_{(4)}$ increasing from .37 to .62, and District 27 with $E_{(27)}$ decreasing from .35 to .06 bit and $I_{27}/E_{(27)}$ decreasing from .36 to .08), but the available evidence is not impressive. It is possible that $\bar{I}_g/E_{(g)}$ reacts to changes in $E_{(g)}$ after some time lag, and a larger number of observations is needed to find this out.

**TABLE 2.** Relative Segregation Measures: 100 $I_g/E_{(g)}$

| District | 1963 | 1964 | 1965 | 1966 | 1967 | 1968 | 1969 |
|---|---|---|---|---|---|---|---|
| 1 | 26 | 22 | 34 | 24 | 21 | 20 | 16 |
| 2 | 24 | 24 | 21 | 22 | 17 | 15 | 13 |
| 3 | 17 | 22 | 21 | 20 | 19 | 17 | 14 |
| 4 | 37 | 45 | 39 | 56 | 71 | 57 | 62 |
| 5 | 23 | 34 | * | 29 | 27 | 26 | 18 |
| 6 | 26 | 25 | 26 | 22 | 22 | 23 | 23 |
| 7 | 67 | 68 | 70 | 70 | 70 | 73 | 71 |
| 8 | 33 | 30 | 22 | 22 | 24 | 29 | 36 |
| 9 | 61 | 59 | 60 | 63 | 67 | 66 | 70 |
| 10 | 80 | 88 | 89 | 88 | 88 | 88 | 87 |
| 11 | 48 | 58 | 59 | 60 | 57 | 58 | 56 |
| 12 | 68 | 68 | 69 | 70 | 74 | 74 | 78 |
| 13 | 16 | 15 | 20 | 28 | 23 | 26 | 24 |
| 14 | 44 | 46 | 50 | 54 | 55 | 54 | 54 |
| 15 | 67 | 74 | 81 | 83 | 82 | 81 | 69 |
| 16 | 67 | 67 | 64 | 63 | 61 | 52 | 58 |
| 17 | 60 | 52 | 50 | 51 | 56 | 56 | 55 |
| 18 | 93 | 92 | 88 | 84 | 79 | 77 | 77 |
| 19 | 89 | 88 | 88 | 89 | 87 | 88 | 88 |
| 20 | 3 | 11 | 8 | 4 | 8 | 11 | 13 |
| 21 | 8 | 8 | 9 | 8 | 13 | 11 | 23 |
| 22 | 52 | 51 | 53 | 56 | 51 | 46 | 45 |
| 23 | 12 | 16 | 18 | 17 | 24 | 19 | 19 |
| 24 | 18 | 21 | 20 | 16 | 20 | 14 | 16 |
| 25 | 77 | 72 | 73 | 75 | 76 | 74 | 78 |
| 26 | 83 | 82 | 78 | 76 | 74 | 76 | 82 |
| 27 | 36 | 27 | 26 | 20 | 17 | 12 | 8 |
| Districts with: | | | *Medians* | | | | |
| small $E_{(g)}$ | 17 | 21 | 20 | 20 | 20 | 17 | 16 |
| medium $E_{(g)}$ | 44 | 46 | 50 | 54 | 56 | 54 | 56 |
| large $E_{(g)}$ | 67 | 72 | 73 | 76 | 76 | 74 | 71 |

* Of the form 0/0.

# INDEX

## Advanced Studies in Theoretical and Applied Econometrics

1. J.H.P. Paelinck (ed.): *Qualitative and Quantitative Mathematical Economics.* 1982 ISBN 90-247-2623-9
2. J.P. Ancot (ed.): *Analysing the Structure of Econometric Models.* 1984 ISBN 90-247-2894-0
3. A.J. Hughes Hallet (ed.): *Applied Decision Analysis and Economic Behaviour.* 1984 ISBN 90-247-2968-8
4. J.K. Sengupta: *Information and Efficiency in Economic Decision.* 1985 ISBN 90-247-3072-4
5. P. Artus and O. Guvenen (eds.), in collaboration with F. Gagey: *International Macroeconomic Modelling for Policy Decisions.* 1986 ISBN 90-247-3201-8
6. M.J. Vilares: *Structural Change in Macroeconomic Models.* Theory and Estimation. 1986 ISBN 90-247-3277-8
7. C. Carraro and D. Sartore (eds.): *Development of Control Theory for Economic Analysis.* 1987 ISBN 90-247-3345-6
8. D.P. Broer: *Neoclassical Theory and Empirical Models of Aggregate Firm Behaviour.* 1987 ISBN 90-247-3412-6
9. A. Italianer: *Theory and Practice of International Trade Linkage Models.* 1986 ISBN 90-247-3407-X
10. D.A. Kendrick: *Feedback.* A New Framework for Macroeconomic Policy. 1988 ISBN 90-247-3593-9; Pb: 90-247-3650-1
11. J.K. Sengupta and G.K. Kadekodi (eds.): *Econometrics of Planning and Efficiency.* 1988 ISBN 90-247-3602-1
12. D.A. Griffith: *Advanced Spatial Statistics.* Special Topics in the Exploration of Quantitative Spatial Data Series. 1988 ISBN 90-247-3627-7
13. O. Guvenen (ed.): *International Commodity Market Models and Policy Analysis.* 1988 ISBN 90-247-3768-0
14. G. Arbia: *Spatial Data Configuration in Statistical Analysis of Regional Economic and Related Problems.* 1989 ISBN 0-7923-0284-2
15. B. Raj (ed.): *Advances in Econometrics and Modelling.* 1989 ISBN 0-7923-0299-0
16. A. Aznar Grasa: *Econometric Model Selection.* A New Approach. 1989 ISBN 0-7923-0321-0
17. L.R. Klein and J. Marquez (eds.): *Economics in Theory and Practice.* An Eclectic Approach. Essays in Honor of F. G. Adams. 1989 ISBN 0-7923-0410-1
18. D.A. Kendrick: *Models for Analyzing Comparative Advantage.* 1990 ISBN 0-7923-0528-0
19. P. Artus and Y. Barroux (eds.): *Monetary Policy.* A Theoretical and Econometric Approach. 1990 ISBN 0-7923-0626-0

## Advanced Studies in Theoretical and Applied Econometrics

20. G. Duru and J.H.P. Paelinck (eds.): *Econometrics of Health Care.* 1990
ISBN 0-7923-0766-6
21. L. Phlips (ed.): *Commodity, Futures and Financial Markets.* 1991
ISBN 0-7923-1043-8
22. H.M. Amman, D.A. Belsley and L.F. Pau (eds.): *Computational Economics and Econometrics.* 1992 ISBN 0-7923-1287-2
23. B. Raj and J. Koerts (eds.): *Henri Theil's Contributions to Economics and Econometrics.* Vol. I: Econometric Theory and Methodology. 1992
ISBN 0-7923-1548-0; Set ISBN 0-7923-1666-5
24. B. Raj and J. Koerts (eds.): *Henri Theil's Contributions to Economics and Econometrics.* Vol. II: Consumer Demand Analysis and Information Theory. 1992
ISBN 0-7923-1664-9; Set ISBN 0-7923-1666-5
25. B. Raj and J. Koerts (eds.): *Henri Theil's Contributions to Economics and Econometrics.* Vol. III: Economic Policy and Forecasts, and Management Science. 1992 ISBN 0-7923-1665-7; Set ISBN 0-7923-1666-5

**Kluwer Academic Publishers – Dordrecht / Boston / London**

MIX
Papier aus verantwortungsvollen Quellen
Paper from responsible sources
FSC® C105338

If you have any concerns about our products,
you can contact us on
**ProductSafety@springernature.com**

In case Publisher is established outside the EU,
the EU authorized representative is:
**Springer Nature Customer Service Center GmbH**
**Europaplatz 3, 69115 Heidelberg, Germany**

Printed by Libri Plureos GmbH
in Hamburg, Germany